A Day of Blood

The 1898 Wilmington Race Riot

A ca. 1900 image of Wilmington looking east from the corner of Fourth and Market streets. The Wilmington Light Infantry Armory (*left, center*) served as a focal point of demonstrations and planning sessions in the weeks leading up to November 10, 1898. Also pictured are the First Baptist Church (*center*), the Temple of Israel synagogue (*right*), and the spire of St. Paul's Evangelical Lutheran Church, seen in the distance. Image courtesy of the State Archives, North Carolina Office of Archives and History, Raleigh.

A Day of Blood

The 1898 Wilmington Race Riot

By

LeRae S. Umfleet

For Leslie —

LeRae Umfleet

North Carolina Office of Archives and History
Raleigh
2009

In association with the African American Heritage Commission
Raleigh

NORTH CAROLINA DEPARTMENT OF CULTURAL RESOURCES

Linda A. Carlisle
Secretary

OFFICE OF ARCHIVES AND HISTORY

Jeffrey J. Crow
Deputy Secretary

DIVISION OF HISTORICAL RESOURCES

David L. S. Brook
Director

HISTORICAL PUBLICATIONS SECTION

Donna E. Kelly
Administrator

Front cover: Disturbing images are evocative of the 1898 Wilmington Race Riot.

Inflammatory cartoons by Norman E. Jennett were published in Raleigh's *News and Observer* during the fall of 1898 as the Democratic Party waged a white-supremacy campaign and warned of black domination in local politics and the Republican Party. Top cartoon: "A Warning. Get Back! We Will Not Stand It." *News and Observer*, August 30, 1898. Bottom cartoon: "A Serious Question—How Long Will This Last?" *News and Observer*, August 13, 1898. Both images courtesy of the State Library of North Carolina.

The destruction of the office and press of A. L. Manly's *Daily Record* marked the beginning of the violence in Wilmington on November 10, 1898. Negative image of building remains and excerpted positive image of onlookers, courtesy of the New Hanover County Public Library. Image of armed men in front of the burned *Daily Record* office, courtesy of the State Archives, North Carolina Office of Archives and History.

Headlines and background newsprint are from the *News and Observer*'s November 11, 1898, front-page report on the riot. Image courtesy of the State Library of North Carolina.

Printed by Four Colour Print Group, Louisville, Kentucky

Some time, we are told, when the cycle of years has rolled around, there is to be another golden age, when all men will dwell together in love and harmony, and when peace and righteousness shall prevail for a thousand years. God speed the day, and let not the shining thread of hope become so enmeshed in the web of circumstance that we lose sight of it; but give us here and there, and now and then, some little foretaste of this golden age, that we may the more patiently and hopefully await its coming!

—Charles Waddell Chesnutt
The Wife of his Youth and Other Stories of the Color Line (1899)

Chesnutt, former North Carolina resident, wrote *The Marrow of Tradition* (1901), based on the Wilmington events of 1898.

Contents

Contents

Contents

Maps and Illustrations

Maps and Illustrations

Maps and Illustrations

Foreword

In 2000 the North Carolina General Assembly established the 1898 Wilmington Race Riot Commission (WRRC) to develop an accurate account of the racial violence surrounding November 10, 1898. One of the charges to the commission was to assess the long-term economic impact of the riot on African Americans in Wilmington.

Similar commissions in Florida and Oklahoma served as models for the WRRC. Those commissions studied riots in Rosewood (1923) and Tulsa (1921) and made recommendations to their respective state legislatures. Florida released its report in 1993 and Oklahoma in 2001.

Under the 2000 legislation, the North Carolina Department of Cultural Resources, Office of Archives and History, provided administrative support for the WRRC's work. In addition, the department conducted critical research to compile the commission's final report. Michael Hill, supervisor of the Research Branch, served as secretary to the commission and initiated the research. In 2003 Hill assigned LeRae Umfleet, then a researcher in the branch, the responsibility for preparing a history of the event. She spent three years examining primary and secondary sources to document the 1898 Wilmington Race Riot and to evaluate its consequences.

The draft report was released on December 15, 2005, at Thalian Hall in Wilmington. It was also posted on the Archives and History Web site. The report contained more than 600 pages of narrative, footnotes, maps, pictures, and charts. Not only did the report detail the course of events before and after the riot, but it also measured the economic impact on Wilmington's large and prospering African American community. The research, moreover, demonstrated the shift in the city's demographics as many blacks fled or were forced out of town. The WRRC submitted the final report with a number of findings and recommendations to the North Carolina General Assembly on May 31, 2006.

That report has been revised and edited for publication as *A Day of Blood: The 1898 Wilmington Race Riot*. The African American Heritage Commission (AAHC) is pleased to sponsor publication of this important study. The North Carolina General Assembly established the commission in 2008. The AAHC recognizes the signal work accomplished by the WRRC. Among the Wilmington commission's recommendations was the dissemination of educational information about the events of 1898 through publications, media, and the Worldwide Web. The AAHC's powers and duties include the promotion of "public awareness of historic buildings, sites, structures, artwork, and culture associated with North Carolina's African-American heritage through special programs, exhibits, and publications." Publication of this book provides a lasting record of the racial violence in Wilmington that changed North Carolina's history and the arc of its politics, economy, and society for decades to come.

Interpreting African American history can be painful at times. When a reporter asked Lottie Clinton, a member of the WRRC, why it was important to remember the disturbing events of 1898, she replied: "Simply tell the truth. Is there anything else?"

Dr. Jean G. Spaulding, *Chair*
African American
Heritage Commission

August 2009

Acknowledgments

This long-term project has had the assistance of many helpful and supportive people over the years. Proper acknowledgment of all who contributed to the project will be difficult, but I will make a humble attempt. Thanks to members of the Wilmington Race Riot Commission who volunteered their time to assist with research and read drafts of the report—Lottie Clinton, Kenneth Davis, Ruth Haas, John Haley, Irv Joyner, Helyn Lofton, Harper Peterson, Alfred Thomas, and Representative Thomas Wright— for they led the way. Special thanks should go to Beverly Tetterton of the New Hanover County Public Library for her depth of knowledge about Wilmington history and willingness to answer my incessant questions; without Beverly's help in locating resources, particularly those of the late Bill Reaves, the work would be less complete. The staff of the Research Branch, the Office of Archives and History, and the State Library of North Carolina deserve compliment for their understanding and helpfulness in facilitating this project—Mary Ajiboye, Katherine Beery, Debbi Blake, Dr. David Brook, Claudia Brown, Chandrea Burch, Matt Burton, Steve Case, Steve Claggett, Lisa Coombes, Dr. Jeffrey Crow, Kim Cumber, Dennis Daniels, Judy Easley, Chris Graham, Sion H. Harrington III, Joy Heitman, Fay Henderson, Michael Hill, Josh Howard, Earl Ijames, Cynthia Jones, Hilary Kanupp, Lisa Keenum, Donna Kelly, Dick Lankford, Steve Massengill, Gwen Mays, Vivian McDuffie, Cheryl McLean, Chris Meekins, Mark Moore, Bonnie Spiers, Joyce Throckmorton, Kay Tillotson, Pam Toms, Susan Trimble, Ron Vestal, Tom Vincent, Ansley Wegner, Alan Westmoreland, and Jo Ann Williford, among others. A special thanks to my editors, Denise Craig and Robert Topkins, as well.

Outside of state government, special thanks for assistance, brainstorms, technical support, and editing skills, among a host of other helpful work, goes to Robert Adams, Larry Alford, Beverly Ayscue, Rev. Hudson Barksdale, Catherine Bishir, Tim Bottoms, Mark Bradley, Rev. Joseph Brown, Rev. John D. Burton, David Cecelski, Kent Chatfield, Sue Cody, Gwendolyn Cottman, Dr. William Darity, Janet Davidson, Chris Fonvielle, the late John Hope Franklin, Tod Hamilton, Elizabeth Hines, Rudolph Knight, Adolph H. Lewis, Hugh MacRae, Steve McAllister, Melton McLaurin, Janet Metzger, Sarah Nerney, Haywood Newkirk, Rev. Artie L. Odom Jr., Donna Pope, Anne Russell, Janet Seapker, Walker Taylor III, Mary Alice Jervay Thatch, Bernard Thuersam, Ed Turberg, Alan Watson, Harry Watson, Heather Williams, Bob Wooley, Jim Wrenn, and the North Carolina Collection staff: Bob Anthony, Chrystabelle Brown, Cynthia J. Brown, Grace Byrd, Inez Campbell, Katherine Ennett, Nicholas Graham, Eli Naeher, Bertha Todd, Theresa Moore Walker, and interns Erica Hink and James Vincent Lowery.

I would like to give a special thank you to my loving and supportive family who understood all those days and nights when Mommy was away in Wilmington—my husband Chris and sons Alex and Fletcher Umfleet.

—LeRae Umfleet
May 31, 2009

The North Carolina Office of Archives and History gratefully acknowledges the financial support of the African American Heritage Commission in making this publication possible.

Over the years, scores of authors have written about the 1898 Wilmington Race Riot, but the state of North Carolina has never formally investigated the insurrection. On the heels of Florida's inquiry into the 1923 Rosewood Massacre, Oklahoma's scrutiny of the 1921 Tulsa Race Riot, and the centennial of the port city's tragic event of 1898, the General Assembly in 2000 enacted legislation calling for the creation of a commission to examine the riot and to develop a historical record. The law also called on the commission to delve into the "economic impact of the riot on African-Americans in this State." The commission built upon earlier work done to commemorate the centennial anniversary in 1998, when local residents of both races participated in a variety of programs that brought renewed interest to the subject. Staff members of the North Carolina Department of Cultural Resources (DCR) provided research and administrative assistance. This book grew out of the research report created for the commission.

In recent decades, authors of books, articles, theses, and dissertations have studied causes of the Wilmington riot and the subsequent event itself, but few have sought to determine what the riot did to the city of Wilmington. This work examines the African American community in Wilmington within the framework of an overall story of the city's growth from the 1860s to the first decades of the twentieth century. Its chapters follow a chronological format that commences with the Civil War and Reconstruction and ends with an analysis of the destructive and negative influence both of the riot and the Democratic Party's white-supremacy campaign of 1898 on African Americans in New Hanover County.

For the purposes of this book, analysis and discussion of African American life in twentieth-century Wilmington ends just before the advent of World War I. Simply put, beginning with the First World War, the port city began to undergo a series of economic changes similar to those occurring in the rest of the state and nation that affected all citizens, regardless of race. Wartime building booms interspersed with depression and economic lulls combined with the advent of the modern civil rights movement to create new dynamics in race relations. A singular event, still remembered by many residents, was the so-called "Wilmington 10" incident of February 1971. Mindful of their past, participants in and witnesses to that episode drew connections to the 1898 riot and saw the violence of 1971 as distinctly related to unresolved conflicts of 1898.

In researching the causes and effects of the violence, the author employed a wide variety of sources. Primary source materials, some used extensively by previous historians and others uncovered in the research process, were consulted wherever possible. Most of the work involved in searching for primary source materials such as letters, diaries, contemporary newspaper articles, and oral history interviews focused on learning more about the African American community, the specific events of the campaign and violence of 1898, and the lasting effects of the violence.

Secondary source materials, in addition to providing insight into the overall history of the state and nation, were used to supplement the history of Wilmington during Reconstruction and the years leading up to the 1890s. Controversial sources were cited in the document where appropriate. Most modern historians acknowledge that early histories of Reconstruction such as those written by students under the influence of Prof. William A. Dunning of Columbia University—what has become known as the "Dunning School"—generated a great deal of literature after the turn of the twentieth century on the history of the South and Reconstruction. Those histories reflected their belief systems on race grounded in the concepts of second-class status for African Americans and the inherent supremacy of the white race. Thus, when leading North Carolina scholars such as J. G. de Roulhac Hamilton, R. D. W. Connor, and Samuel A. Ashe wrote state histories, the narratives were laced with presuppositions about the "rights" of white citizens, the supposed failures of Reconstruction, and the drawbacks of universal suffrage.

Many local historians have repeated the narrative developed by participants in, witnesses to, and beneficiaries of the 1898 campaign—men such as Alfred Moore Waddell, James Sprunt, and William Lord de Rosset. Those men repeated the story of the riot and its causes as a response of white citizens to a corrupt municipal government unable to reduce crime or facilitate economic improvements for residents. A counter-narrative that contradicted that story was less widely circulated and not widely accepted by readership. Examples include Charles W. Chesnutt's *The Marrow of Tradition* (Boston: Houghton, Mifflin, 1901) and David Bryant Fulton's *Hanover; or The Persecution of the Lowly, a Story of the Wilmington Massacre* (N.p.: M. C. L. Hill, 1901). Not until the publication of *The Negro in Fusion Politics* (1951), by African American scholar Helen G. Edmonds, did the counter-narrative receive scholarly attention. Leading citizens of Wilmington vilified Edmonds at the time her work was published, and not until later publications, specifically *We Have Taken a City*, by H. Leon Prather (1984), did the counter-narrative receive legitimacy equal to that accorded the nearly 100-year-old story perpetuated by Waddell and his contemporaries. Subsequent study has focused on various aspects of the riot, its causes and its participants, and has incorporated both the "necessary evil" narrative of white leaders and the African American perspective. This book seeks to bridge the gap between what the white leaders said and did before and after November 1898 and the realities of the status, lives, and contributions of members of Wilmington's African American community. Although white leaders attempted to justify their actions in every word and deed after that date, the truth of what happened has remained obscured by their clouded narratives.

One of the most helpful white narratives of the event was written by Harry Hayden, a Wilmington newspaperman. Hayden, having been only a child at the time of the riot, interviewed participants in and witnesses to the event. His work is infused with the narrative developed by the white leadership, specifically the perceived necessity of their actions, but contains details of conspiracy, murder, and intrigue not found in other contemporary sources. Corroboration of portions of Hayden's work has been possible, and the documents have been treated as resting somewhere between primary and secondary source materials. A personal copy of Hayden's narrative that originally belonged to J. Allan Taylor, a member of the "Secret Nine," the influential body of white businessmen who led the campaign that resulted in the violence and overthrow of municipal government, is located in the North Carolina Collection at the University of North Carolina at Chapel Hill. Taylor scribbled commentary in the margins of the booklet; his most revealing notation was "masterful duplicity."

Taylor's pithy inscription referred to the ability of white leadership in Wilmington to develop long-range plans for instigating violence, to implement a strategy to quell that violence, and to call the affair a riot, implying a sudden break in peacefulness rather than what it actually was—a planned insurrection. The ultimate goal for Taylor and other leaders was the resurgence of white rule of the city and state for a handful of men through whatever means necessary. Many people familiar with the history of the city and the events of November 10, 1898, will hasten to declare that the coup d'etat—the overthrow of democratically elected officials—on the afternoon of November 10 is just as important to understand as are the murders and banishment campaign. The change in government on that day completely terminated black participation in city and county government until the advent of the civil rights era. Moreover, the 1898 political campaign, capped as it was by violence in Wilmington, proved to be a catalyst for the state: Jim Crow legislation and the subjugation of African Americans was the result throughout North Carolina. Because Wilmington rioters were able to murder blacks in daylight and overthrow a legitimately elected Republican government without penalty or federal intervention, everyone in the state, regardless of race, knew that the white-supremacy campaign was triumphant on all fronts.

The impact of the riot—the economic, cultural, and physical changes to the Wilmington landscape—is difficult to document. Some changes took place immediately, and others developed over time. Black entrepreneurship and employment were dramatically curtailed, cultural institutions were diminished, and educational opportunities were restricted. The destruction of Alexander Manly s newspaper office silenced the black press in the city until the appearance of the *Cape Fear Journal* in 1927.

The riot was not an isolated, spontaneous incident but was the result of a series of events that were directed and planned by upper-class white businessmen in order to regain control of government. What happened in Wilmington should not be viewed as existing in a vacuum, in that it was part of a larger campaign to take over state government in 1898. Indeed, Democratic Party strategists thrust the city into the spotlight as an example of Republican corruption and bad government because of the participation of African Americans in local politics. There is no clear answer to the question of how many people died as a result of the violence. Extant records and physical evidence cannot completely supply a solution. No evidence was found to prove that whites seized black property or forced blacks to sell at deflated prices immediately after the riot, and unethical behavior by some whites in the years after the riot did not translate into citywide property transitions. The violence and campaign did, however, affect all aspects of African American life—churches, cultural celebrations such as Emancipation Day and Jonkonnu, business development, and schools.

This 1873 stereo view of Wilmington was taken by Rufus Morgan. It faces northeast from Orange and S. Fourth streets. The spire on the left is that of the First Baptist Church and the one to the right belongs to St. Paul's Evangelical Lutheran Church. The image may have been taken from the First Presbyterian Church Manse. Image courtesy of the State Archives.

Chapter 1

Into Reconstruction and Out Again

Wilmington, initially known as Newton, was one of the earliest towns settled in southeastern North Carolina. It was incorporated in 1739 on the banks of the Cape Fear River.[1] During the antebellum years, Wilmington emerged as North Carolina's largest city.[2] Surrounded by vast acres of timber and rice plantations, Wilmington boasted an economy fed by naval stores and agricultural interests. The city dominated New Hanover County, with most of the county's residents living or working in Wilmington. As a result of enterprising railroad construction and the booming turpentine industry, Wilmington was the state's largest and most active port.[3] Wilmington's importance in the state and region was unmistakable, and, as a result, its interests were in the mainstream and forefront of state social and political affairs.[4]

Wilmington at the End of the Civil War

During the Civil War, Wilmington was a vital link in the Confederacy's supply line. The port, under the powerful guns of nearby Fort Fisher, remained open to blockade-running traffic for all but the last weeks of the conflict. The fort fell to Union forces in January 1865 after an immense bombardment campaign. The city soon fell as Union forces marched into town on February 22, 1865, leading to a long period of occupation marked by social and economic upheaval.[5]

The occupation of the city was carried out in a relatively smooth transition. The Federal commander, Gen. John Schofield, promised that the military would not interfere in local affairs as long as citizens respected United States rule. Locals gave Union troops mixed receptions. Some upper-class planters fled the city, seeking protection farther inland, while other Confederate sympathizers watched the occupation from

behind closed doors. Some residents, white and black, welcomed the troops. One observer noted that the "aristocrats" for the most part were quiet as the troops marched in, whereas the "commoners" were excited to see the Federal forces. African American residents saw the soldiers as harbingers of good fortune and freedom and eagerly cheered the incoming forces, which included approximately 4,000 African American troops.[6] A reporter described black troops marching proudly past jubilant spectators who danced in the street and exclaimed that their salvation had arrived. "The march of the Union army through Wilmington," one member of the U.S. Colored Troops wrote, "will live forever in the memory of the colored people."[7]

Once Wilmington fell to Union occupation in 1865, newly freed blacks made their way into the city. A northern journalist wrote that the "native Negroes of Wilmington . . . are doing well. They are of a much higher order of intelligence than those from the country; are generally in comfortable circumstances, and already find time to look into politics. They have a Union League formed among themselves, the object of which is to stimulate industry and education, and to secure combined effort for suffrage, without which they will soon be practically enslaved again."[8] Many of Wilmington's native freedmen remained and became important in the city's economic, cultural, and political development. The leading African American–owned businesses were those of artisans who had been free blacks or slaves in the city before the war. These men had knowledge of financial matters, working relationships with many of the most powerful whites, and a desire to improve their lot for future generations.[9]

The Civil War ended a few months after the fall of Wilmington with the surrender of the Confederacy in April 1865. North Carolina was left in upheaval as former soldiers returned to war-damaged homes, some still occupied by Federal troops. White men and women from all economic backgrounds faced rebuilding their homes and farms, and plantation owners encountered a shortage of available labor formerly performed by slaves.[10] For the newly freed African American population, emancipation brought a life of hope mixed with uncertainty. Most owned no land, and many were displaced from family and homes they knew before the war. Thousands migrated to other parts of the state to find work and stability in their freedom. Many whites sought to preserve the prewar norms of white leadership and black subservience. Others believed that only through the intervention of Federal authorities—a process that has become known as Reconstruction—would safety and equality for freed slaves be assured.[11]

Wilmington's Post-Civil War Social and Class Structure

In 1860 many distinct types of people lived and worked in Wilmington within a time-honored system of social hierarchy and wealth. The individual groups survived the ravages of the war, albeit with slightly redefined positions within Wilmington's civic and social life. By the late antebellum period, the largest and most prosperous plantations were owned by men who had inherited their property and wealth from long lines of Cape Fear planters. These men and women also inherited an intricate philosophy of life—a world view that placed them at the top of the socioeconomic pyramid.[12] This "stable, hereditary, cultivated gentry" was involved closely with politics and the social life of the state.[13] At the top of the pyramid were the traditional elite, whose living was based on plantation slavery and inherited status. These people, in the forefront of Wilmington society, maintained their connections to inland planta-tions and often intermarried. As a result, by the time the first shots were fired at Fort Sumter, these men and women were closely connected and supportive of each other.[14] Within the gentry

class were planters, men who owned 20 or more slaves. Few of New Hanover County's slave-holders fell into that category. Of the 938 slaveholders in the county in 1860, only 145 (16 percent) owned 25 or more slaves, whereas 593 (63 percent) owned fewer than 10 slaves. New Hanover's 1860 slave population of 7,103 was the tenth largest in a state in which an average of about 3,800 slaves resided in each county.[15]

Wilmington Society, 1860

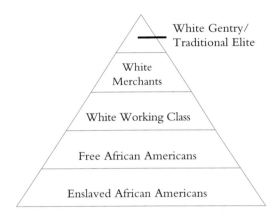

Next on the socioeconomic scale were the merchants and businessmen of the city. Before the Civil War, some of Wilmington's white businessmen were more financially secure than were members of the traditional planter class.[16] Some of the wealthiest merchants were recent immigrants to the city from New England or abroad.[17] In addition to the successful businesses that served the needs of the Wilmington area, a wholesale trade prospered because goods arriving on ships could quickly be delivered inland by rail or inland shipping lines. Commission merchants thrived as they traded with interests in other markets nationally and internationally to sell naval stores, cotton, and rice on behalf of planters.[18] The merchants owned property in town and in the countryside, and many owned slaves to work for them. Although some of the merchants were as wealthy as the traditional aristocracy, the two groups were often at odds socially, politically, and economically.[19] Some of the leading businessmen were immigrants who worked in retail trades. Wilmington historians have noted that these successful immigrant businessmen were mostly of German descent and that their success was largely attributable to their ability to adapt to changes in the economy.[20] Because of a steady influx of foreigners into Wilmington, the percentage of immigrants among the city's population was the highest in the state throughout the nineteenth century. Many of the immigrants who arrived in Wilmington formed their own social frameworks for sharing and maintaining their European cultural roots.[21]

In descending order, the next class to be found in the city was the white working class. This level of white society was multifaceted but shared the common bond of being excluded from the highest levels of society because its members lacked wealth or status. Some working-class whites in Wilmington were able to earn a comfortable living for their families, whereas others lived at the poverty level. Before the war, white laborers competed with African Americans, both slave and free.[22] Because of limited options in town, men supplemented their incomes through rural hunting, fishing, and tapping pine trees to send tar, pitch, and turpentine into the city for shipment. The working class formed the largest group of whites in Wilmington, and the category included all types of workers, from skilled artisans to unskilled day laborers. These men reflected the generally prevailing view of the South in that they harbored contempt toward blacks, slave and free, largely because of the economics of the labor system in which they lived.[23] A northern journalist declared in September 1865 that white North Carolinians, regardless of class or political slant, "unaffectedly and heartily do despise the negro."[24] Upper-class elites observed that some whites refused to work as carpenters and masons, professions traditionally dominated by enslaved and free black artisans in Wilmington, because they believed the work to be beneath them.[25]

The very nature of the slave-labor system meant less demand for paid labor from working whites.[26] Further exacerbating the plight of poor whites was their inability to participate in government; few were literate and able to spare the time to run for political office. In Wilmington the margin of wealth between upper-class and lower-class whites was wide. Evidence of that disparity was the contrast between the simple immigrant dwellings on the outskirts of town and the more substantial residences within the town. Although the economic situation of Wilmington's poor whites was tenuous, those working in wage-earning jobs earned slightly more annually than did their counterparts in other areas of the state.[27] Of the white population in the city, only a small fraction was employed in wage-earning jobs, while others worked in trades, shipping, retail, or railroad-related pursuits.[28]

Economic insecurity and a marginalized position within government placed white workers at odds with the next class of Wilmington occupants—free blacks—both before and after the Civil War.[29] Just before the Civil War, New Hanover County's free black population ranked as the fourteenth largest in the state, with 573 (85 percent) of the county's 672 free blacks living in Wilmington.[30] Many of the free blacks were employed as carpenters, masons, or laundresses.[31] Free black families flourished in the decades before the Civil War, amassing small savings, buying property, and establishing a network of connections within the white community that would transcend slavery and politics well into the twentieth century. The process by which slaves became free was a tangled web. Freedom could be purchased from or granted by an owner, but both paths were fraught with danger.[32] Once free, men and women worked to purchase and free other family members, as well as to establish a financial foothold for future generations. Men such as Alfred and Anthony Howe and Elvin Artis are examples of free blacks living and working in Wilmington who forged a life for their families in an otherwise hostile environment. Another man, James D. Sampson, was freed by his white planter father. Sampson worked in Wilmington as a carpenter and, according to the 1860 census, was the wealthiest freedman in the city, owning real estate valued at $26,000, personal property valued at $10,000, and twenty-five slaves. Sampson's children were educated in northern cities, and

3

one of his sons returned to Wilmington to work with the Freedmen's Bureau after the Civil War.[33]

The last group of Wilmington residents, the bottom rung on the socioeconomic ladder, was the enslaved population (known after the war as freedmen). In 1860 there were 7,103 slaves in New Hanover, with 3,777 (53 percent) living inside the city.[34] Many urban slaves, such as the nine men, women, and children who worked for the Bellamy family, were associated with households or were employed by their masters as artisans or in shipping operations.[35] Slaveholders in Wilmington with the largest concentrations of ownership were the railroad companies, followed by those who owned steam mills or turpentine distilleries.[36] A large number of slaves worked in maritime trades as pilots or boatmen, ferrying people and supplies up and down the Cape Fear River.[37]

Wilmington's artisan slaves, able to learn a valuable trade and gain experience in business dealings and handling money, occupied a unique position among the slave work force. Some, such as brick mason Abraham Galloway, managed to broker their own lives because they were able to hire themselves out and keep the profits of their work so long as they paid their masters for the privilege. After slavery was abolished, such skills enabled artisans to establish financial footholds more easily than did less-skilled freedmen.[38]

Wilmington's slaves lived and worked in an intricate network of secrecy. They operated a hidden economy, trading goods, either stolen or personally made, in order to accumulate money to buy their freedom or to assist in an escape attempt. Wilmington was a destination point for escaped slaves hoping for assistance in their northward flight through the city's underground abolitionist network. Many of the white merchants and sailors who assisted these fugitive slaves were relatively recent arrivals in Wilmington from northern ports who had relocated to Wilmington largely to take advantage of booms in the naval-stores and cotton industries; their arrival in the city contributed significantly to its growth.

After the Civil War, Wilmington society underwent a series of changes that resulted in an

"Fugitive slaves escaping to the protection of our army at Wilmington—scene on the Cape Fear River." *Frank Leslie's Illustrated Newspaper*, June 17, 1865. Image courtesy of the North Carolina Collection, Wilson Library, University of North Carolina at Chapel Hill, Chapel Hill.

uneasy merger of the primary interests of the former planter gentry and the successful merchants. Working-class whites such as artisans, clerks, and railroad employees occupied the upper levels of their category, while a goodly number of whites who labored in mills and in transient jobs made up the lower levels. Immediately following emancipation, African Americans separated into two basic categories related to their prewar status as either slaves or free blacks and also in accordance with their prewar occupations: artisans such as builders and tradesmen were more secure than those who had previously worked only as unskilled laborers on plantations.[39]

Despite emancipation, Wilmington's gentry emerged from the Civil War with its social framework largely intact—although its financial foothold was slippery: a declining demand for agricultural products, the collapse of the credit system upon which it relied, a loss of property resulting from seizures by Federal forces, and the prospect of having to pay a work force all contributed to the financial insecurity.[40] In 1868, one year after Congress had enacted a national bankruptcy act, sixty-five people in Wilmington declared their inability to pay their debts. The common explanations were that some debts were contracted by people who employed slaves as collateral or that property values had depreciated and thus affected debtors' abilities to pay. Many of Wilmington's gentry looked to professions in law and medicine to supplement their traditional agricultural incomes. As Reconstruction continued into the 1870s, however, the old gentry class (also known as "bloods" in Wilmington slang), once comprised solely of planters, slowly evolved as its members developed more associations with the merchant class, whose wealth derived more from business interests and less from agriculture. Thus, despite lingering cultural differences, the interests of the native gentry and the wealthy business class combined and grew together, resulting in a powerful conservative political element that ran city affairs for many years thereafter.[41]

Wilmington Society, 1870

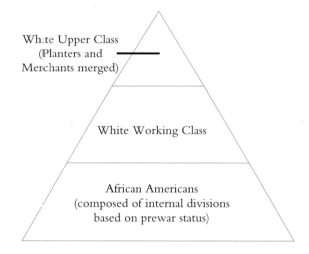

During the Civil War, the merchant class had prospered in Wilmington, boosted by an influx of goods running through the Union blockade and into the port. Most of the cargo ferried into Wilmington was bound northward on the Wilmington and Weldon Railroad line to supply Robert E. Lee's Confederate army. Other supplies arrived for the starving consumer market. Spurred by a large flood of shipping interests eager to make their way in the South, the merchant/business class thrived.[42] The boom continued after the war, and the gradual addition

Shipping interests in Wilmington bolstered the growth of the city's merchant/business class. An 1870s view of Wilmington's wharf. Image courtesy of the North Carolina Collection.

of railroad and shipping interests in the city bolstered the growth of the city's merchant/business class.[43] As a result of rapid growth in the railroad industry during the postwar period, the Seaboard Air Line, the Atlantic Coast Line, the Carolina Central Railroad, and the Wilmington and Weldon Railroad constructed rail lines that terminated at Wilmington's port; moreover, the Seaboard Air Line and the Atlantic Coast Line constructed major offices and repair facilities in Wilmington.[44] Manufacturing in the city prospered with the development of factories for processing the surrounding region's abundant natural resources of rice, cotton, grains, and wood products, including lumber and naval stores.[45]

In the postwar years, the white working population grew at a rate consistent with that of the merchant class, mostly because of an influx of new residents from the surrounding countryside, the North, and overseas, all seeking employment. Wilmington employers encouraged migration to the city through the Southern Immigration Society. To entice immigrants, that organization opened an agency in Wilmington during 1867 and 1868, helped establish wages of immigrants,

5

and extended credit to assist with relocation. One employer, F. W. Foster and Company, opened an office in Wilmington in 1865 and brought thirty-seven German laborers to the city.[46] In light of Wilmington's postwar prosperity, the city's white wage earners brought home much more money in 1870 than they did in 1860—even though there was more competition from new residents of the city. Nevertheless, by 1870 only about 15 percent of Wilmington's wage earners were employed in well-paying manufacturing jobs.[47] Just as laboring whites had competed with free blacks before the war, similar competition remained after occupation ended. In prosperous postwar Wilmington, poor white workers were in a difficult position in that they were forced to compete with a large free black population that included a considerable number of skilled workers. A distinct area within Wilmington developed to accommodate the poor whites and immigrants. Those who inhabited the section in the southern part of town called it "Dry Pond" because of its low-lying ground. Modest residences characterized the area, and upper-class residents regarded it as a less-than-desirable place to be.[48]

With the demise of Reconstruction after the mid-1870s, unskilled white laborers prospered along with the city. One important factor in their success was the Wilmington Cotton Mill. That facility, opened in 1874 in the southern end of town, employed most of the workers in that section.[49] Consistent with a statewide trend, wages for working-class residents of Wilmington dropped substantially by 1880, reflecting changes in the county's size and a diminution in the importance of naval stores; nevertheless, the city's average wage remained well above that of the state.[50]

Members of the various groups that formed Wilmington's social structure after the Civil War—upper-class whites, working-class whites, free blacks, and freed slaves—resided and worked in Wilmington in a radically changed environment in which former slaves had been granted freedom and promised equality. For the most part, these men, women, and children sought to respond to the challenges presented by the sudden social upheaval and to create a new city. The

Manufacturing and various other businesses prospered after the Civil War. An 1870s view of Wilmington's business district. Image courtesy of the North Carolina Collection.

reality of Wilmington after the war, however, was fraught with conflict between the races, often muted, as African Americans asserted themselves in their new roles and whites became increasingly fearful of losing not only their status but also their control of virtually every aspect of life in the port city.[51] Reconstruction, a long, drawn-out process, did not alleviate the troubles connected with rebuilding after the war, as many hoped, but instead drew sharper definitions of many underlying problems facing Wilmington and the South.[52]

Reconstruction in North Carolina

Reconstruction in North Carolina effectively began when Confederate general Joseph E. Johnston surrendered his army to Union general William T. Sherman in April 1865. While preparing to depart the state after accepting Johnston's surrender, Sherman placed Gen. John Schofield in charge of the state to maintain law and order and provide for improved conditions for freed slaves. Andrew Johnson, who had become president on April 14, 1865, following Lincoln's death, chose to implement a plan that sought the timely readmission of the former Confederate states into the Union through a series of moderate programs aimed at mending the breach between southern and northern states. Johnson's first act was to pardon former Confederate soldiers, with the exception of primary Confederate political and military leaders. He then established a provisional government in each southern state. In the case of North Carolina, Johnson appointed William W. Holden as governor. Although Holden had been a states' rights activist before the war, he openly criticized the Confederate government, and, for that criticism, it is believed, Republicans rewarded him with Johnson's appointment.[53] Holden's first priority as governor was to call a convention to create a new state constitution with the assistance of the military authorities so that the state could rejoin the Union as quickly as possible. Voters who were eligible to vote prior to the war and who had received a pardon were allowed to elect delegates to the convention. The regulations concerning voter eligibility effectively blocked African Americans from representation at the convention.[54]

As white men secured pardons and prepared for the constitutional convention, some of North Carolina's first African American leaders, drawn principally from former slaves who had escaped northward before the war, called for a "Freedmen's Convention." That conclave, which met in Raleigh in September 1865, drew approximately 120 men from forty counties. Far from a homogeneous group, the representatives came from various backgrounds. Some, such as Wilmington's John P. Sampson, were well educated and financially secure, whereas others were poor and illiterate. United by a common cause—the overall betterment of their race—the men convened to discuss ways to achieve, as stated by convention president James Walker Hood, 'equal rights before the law." Most of the resolutions the convention adopted focused on legal provisions designed to safeguard the rights of blacks in courts, labor contracts, and education and, to a lesser degree, suffrage rights. The resolutions were couched in deferential language designed not to intimidate. The white men engaged in writing a new state constitution completely disregarded them. The end result of

the Freedmen's Convention was the creation of a statewide organizational network of black leaders who would lay the groundwork for future political struggles.[55]

After much debate, Holden and the convention eventually accomplished their tasks and called for an election to be held in November 1865. In the statewide balloting, Jonathan Worth defeated Holden for the governor's office, but Holden's supporters won a majority in the legislature.[56] Most significantly, the convention rejected the proposed new state constitution.[57] The North Carolina General Assembly elected pro-Union men from the Democratic Party to serve as representatives in Washington, D.C. In Washington, however, Radical Republicans controlled Congress and, contrary to President Johnson's wishes, sought to prevent southern states, and Democrats (by then known as Conservatives), from rejoining the Union until more stringent conditions—namely, additional legal protection and suffrage rights for freed blacks—were met. As a result, they refused to recognize

7

John P. Sampson was born free in Wilmington in 1837. After the Civil War he organized or led numerous meetings demanding universal suffrage, including the Freedmen's Convention. During Reconstruction he ran unsuccessfully for Congress. Image from I. Garland Penn, *The Afro-American Press and Its Editors* (Springfield, Mass.: Wiley & Co., Publishers, 1891), 89.

Chronology of Reconstruction

1863   Abraham Lincoln's Proclamation of Amnesty and Reconstruction. Declares that states could be readmitted to the Union provided that 10 percent of the 1860 electorate in each take an oath of loyalty to the Union and that the state agree to recognize emancipation of former slaves. Congress refuses to recognize the plan.

1864   Congress enacts into law the Wade-Davis Bill, which is more restrictive than Lincoln's plan. Lincoln vetoes the bill.

1865

    MARCH 3   Congress establishes the Bureau of Refugees, Freedmen and Abandoned Lands (the Freedmen's Bureau) and charters the Freedman's Savings and Trust Company.

    APRIL   Lincoln is assassinated, and Andrew Johnson becomes president.

    SUMMER   Johnson organizes provisional governments and calls on them to amend constitutions, abolish slavery, nullify secession, repudiate war debt, and enfranchise blacks voluntarily.

    DECEMBER   Johnson announces that the Union has been "restored." Congress refuses to endorse Johnson's plan of Reconstruction. Radical Republicans are angered by southern attempts to legislate second-class-citizen status for blacks through harsh "Black Codes," which effectively reestablish slavery. The Thirteenth Amendment to the Constitution, abolishing slavery, is proclaimed in effect following ratification by twenty-seven states.

1866

    MARCH   Congress enacts the Civil Rights Act, which grants equal rights to all persons born in the United States and affirms freedmen's rights to make contracts; sue; offer evidence; and buy, lease, and convey personal and real property. The legislation fails to address any state statutes on segregation, however, and lacks provisions to enforce full public accommodations, thus legitimizing the doctrine of "separate but equal" public facilities. Johnson vetoes the bill on the grounds that it was passed in the absence of southern congressmen and was thus a violation of states' rights and unconstitutional.

    JUNE   To address doubts concerning the constitutionality of the Civil Rights Act, Congress enacts the Fourteenth Amendment, which grants rights of citizenship. Ratification of the amendment is eventually made a condition for southern states to be readmitted to the Union. Congress likewise enacts the Southern Homestead Act, which grants to freedmen 44 million acres of land (80 acres per family), mostly plots of poor soil quality.

    FALL   Congressional elections. Republicans win an overwhelming victory with a 43-11 majority in the Senate and a 143-49 majority in the House. With the ability to override a presidential veto, Radical Republicans gain the ability to control Reconstruction.

1867   Congressional Reconstruction. Radical Republicans, facing strong resistance in the South, are determined to crush the old southern ruling class. The Reconstruction Acts did not go as far as Radicals wanted. Johnson resists the Reconstruction Acts by appointing governors who refuse to comply fully.

---

the newly elected delegates from the South. That action by the Radical Republicans effectively removed the Reconstruction process from the president's hands and deprived North Carolina of representation in Congress for approximately two years.[58]

Reconstruction in North Carolina lasted until 1877, and the previous twelve years had been full of strife as Congress, military leaders, and elected officials struggled to implement new laws designed to guarantee freedom and equality for African Americans. The passage of the Thirteenth Amendment forever freed from slavery about 350,000 African Americans in the state.[59] Questions then arose as to the legal status of freed slaves. Based on conclusions reached by a commission Governor Holden had organized on the subject of the "negro question," the General Assembly in 1866 established a "Black Code" to provide a basic legal standing for African Americans, including recognition of their marriages and protection of their rights in

Chronology of Reconstruction

1867 (continued)

MARCH 2	First Reconstruction Act. This legislation divides the South into five military districts and declares existing state governments provisional only. It requires governors of those states to call constitutional conventions and to recognize full manhood suffrage in electing delegates to those conventions. Further, it declares blacks eligible to register to vote. Finally, it requires the states to ratify the new state constitutions and the Fourteenth Amendment before its elected representatives to Congress can be readmitted.
MARCH 23, 1867– MARCH 1868	Supplementary Reconstruction Acts. This legislation closes loopholes in the First Reconstruction Act and employs the authority of military governors to enforce voter-registration procedures.
1867–1868	Military Reconstruction. Federal troops occupy southern states, and military commanders replace President Johnson's provisional governments. A small group of southern Unionists forms the core of the southern Republican Party, and blacks join en masse. The black-white coalition includes freedmen, southern loyalists (known as "scalawags"), and northern Republicans in the South (known as "carpetbaggers").
1868	Impeachment of Andrew Johnson. Radical Republicans in Congress, convinced that Johnson has failed to enforce Reconstruction Acts, attempt to remove him from office but fall short of the two-thirds vote by the Senate required for a conviction. Popular opinion begins to turn against the Radical Republicans, who seem willing to subvert the Constitution to accomplish what they want.
1869	Congress passes the Fifteenth Amendment to force southern states to grant blacks the right to vote.
1870–1871	To help enforce the Fifteenth Amendment, Congress passes the Ku Klux Klan Act, which authorizes the president to use military force to quell insurrections.
1875 (SUMMER)	Congress passes the Civil Rights Act of 1875, which guarantees equal rights to blacks in public accommodations and for jury duty.
1876–1877	Many citizens, north and south, become tired of Reconstruction. The winter of 1876–1877 is one of sectional strife. The 1876 election is marked by fraud, and from election day, November 2, until inauguration day, March 4, 1877, no one knows for sure who will become president. The Hayes-Tilden Compromise of 1877 ends the conflict over the presidential election and marks the end of Reconstruction. Republican Rutherford B. Hayes is declared president in exchange for an end to Military Reconstruction (in essence, the removal of Federal troops from southern states), inclusion of a southerner in the cabinet, and funding for internal improvements in the South.

9

business contracts and in court. The Black Code, as with similar legal measures enacted by other southern states, did not, however, afford full protection to the interests of black men, in that it lacked a provision guaranteeing the rights to vote and to testify in court.[60] The code, revised several times, resulted in a loosely worded rule book for segregating and limiting blacks in virtually all aspects of their lives.

One of the first congressional actions to provide for the needs of newly freed slaves was the creation in 1865 of the Freedmen's Bureau to ease the transition from slavery to citizenship. The agency was created as part of the War Department, and its job was to assist emancipated southern blacks and manage abandoned southern lands. The bureau established itself in North Carolina in July 1865 and remained until the end of 1868. It assisted with immediate needs of food and housing and also provided health care and educational benefits. In its advocacy for African Americans, the bureau helped in negotiating labor contracts between blacks and whites, provided loans for land purchases, formed military courts to hear complaints, established banks to serve blacks and enable them to learn financial responsibility, and trained blacks to work among themselves as teachers, nurses, and other professionals.

Much of the agency's work was conducted by concerned northerners, both male and female, who traveled to southern states to work for little pay in sometimes hostile environments, and by occupying soldiers, who distributed food and clothing.[61] Assisting the bureau were many benevolent organizations such as the American Missionary Association, which helped primarily with educational advancement. Contemporary whites saw the Freedmen's Bureau schools as center of political organization, inasmuch as bureau agents encouraged membership in the Union League and those organizations held meetings in the bureau schoolhouses. As a result, many such schools were destroyed by fire to prevent their use as meeting places for political activity. An early historian of Reconstruction suggested that, on balance, the bureau, by engaging in such activity, created problems for the freed slaves by provoking white hostility.[62]

During Jonathan Worth's two terms as governor (1865–1868), Holden was positioning himself to run for that office by helping fuel the growth of the fledgling statewide Republican Party, which emerged as a formidable force as Congress took control of Reconstruction. During his tenure, Worth took steps to return North Carolina to the Union despite opposition from Radical Republicans in Congress, who sought to remove Reconstruction from the White House and place it in their own hands. Efforts by the Radicals to employ harsh methods to reconstruct the South were realized when in March 1867 Congress enacted a series of laws that effectively bypassed the president's authority and reorganized "un-reconstructed" southern states into five military districts. Furthermore, Radicals in Congress returned the existing state governments to provisional status, making them subject to changes by the federal government. Finally, the Radical Republicans in charge of Congressional

Reconstruction imposed still another barrier to readmission to the Union: a requirement that the former Confederate states draft new constitutions wholly in compliance with the federal Constitution. Moreover, they insisted that, with minor exceptions, delegates to conventions charged with creating new state constitutions be elected by all resident male citizens over the age of twenty-one, regardless of race or previous condition.[63]

White North Carolinians viewed the congressional Reconstruction Acts with skepticism but, seeing no recourse, resigned themselves to compliance. In 1866 North Carolina, along with South Carolina, found itself in the Second Military District, under the military command of Maj. Gen. Daniel Sickles, a New York attorney who had defended the rights of southern states to secede before the war.[64] Because of Sickles's sympathetic views, coupled with his efforts at odds with congressional plans, he was replaced in August 1867 by Gen. E. R. S. Canby. Canby employed the Reconstruction Acts liberally and with forcefulness, effectively attenuating the governor's office and the legislature to symbolic posts with no real power over the state's affairs. The end result of Canby's strident management of statewide and local affairs was to stir racial strife and create tensions within the Democratic Party.[65] In the meantime, William W. Holden, who had not abandoned his aspirations to serve as governor, began to work toward that end. He organized groups of men dissatisfied with Worth's actions as governor, particularly what seemed to many as Worth's efforts to stall North Carolina's readmission to the Union. In the spring of 1867, Holden, emboldened by the success of these activities, spurred the formation of the Republican Party in North Carolina. Sustained by the national Republican Party and the Union League, Holden openly supported the military commanders and Radical Reconstruction imposed by Congress.[66]

When in November 1867 Canby called for a new constitutional convention, Congress had disfranchised approximately 10 percent of whites in the South because of previous Confederate service, and other whites, disgusted with

Reconstruction practices, failed to register to vote for delegates to the new convention.[67] Blacks, eager to exercise their new voting rights, registered in great numbers, and the resulting convention delegation consisted of 107 Republicans, fifteen of whom were black, including Abraham Galloway of New Hanover County, James H. Harris of Wake County, and James W. Hood of Cumberland County.[68] Also elected to serve in the delegation were a handful of relocated northerners, most notably Albion W. Tourgée, who worked themselves into prominent positions as committee chairmen within the conventions.[69] The new constitution, completed by March 1868, was highly criticized by the newspapers, but most of its provisions remained in place, despite periodic revisions by subsequent legislatures. The 1868 constitution affected all levels of state and local government and included provisions for universal manhood suffrage; in general, it made the state more democratic in voting and officeholding. Critics of the new constitution, notably the former ruling elite, most of whom remained disfranchised because of their former Confederate war service, feared that the ability of blacks to vote and hold office would result in their political subjugation to the poorer classes of both races.[70]

The new constitution was placed before voters for ratification in April 1868—at the same time that a new election for state and county officials was held. The resulting pre-election debates were bitterly fought, with both the Union League and the Ku Klux Klan, organizations imported to the state as a result of Reconstruction, bringing their agendas to bear. Whereas the Union League employed methods to ensure that blacks would remain loyal to the Republican Party, the Klan established itself in North Carolina by 1868 as a tool for the Democratic Party. Although it may have been in place prior to the 1868 election, the Klan's first organized public appearances in North Carolina occurred during the contest, when members sought to prevent blacks from voting or having a role in government.[71] Despite the Klan's efforts to intimidate black and poor white voters, Republicans carried a majority of counties, the constitution was ratified, and Holden was

Abraham Galloway escaped from slavery in 1857 and became a Union spy. During Reconstruction he led a black militia that fought the KKK in Wilmington. In 1868 he was one of the first black men elected to the North Carolina General Assembly. Image from William Still, *The Underground Rail Road* (Philadelphia, Pa.: Porter and Coates, 1872), 150.

11

elected governor.[72] The new General Assembly, thoroughly dominated by the Republicans, promptly ratified the Fourteenth Amendment and elected two Republicans to the United States Senate. Congress seated the newly elected Republican representatives and senators from North Carolina in July 1868, thus allowing the state to re-enter the Union.[73] Despite the state's reinstatement to the Union, occupying federal troops remained, although overt military interference with government ceased. The new Republican government lasted for only two years, because while it was in power it provided enough fodder for the Democratic Party's propaganda machine to ensure defeat in the ensuing election.[74]

The new Republican legislature and governor faced the problems posed by the state's ragged economy and mutilated infrastructure, which still suffered from the ravages of the Civil War and federal occupation. The legislature sought to repair the economy by issuing a large volume of railroad bonds, which drove the state deeper into debt instead of remedying the situation. Corruption and fraudulent activities were rampant in Raleigh. Numerous legislators engaged in unethical practices, and some became rich as a result of their positions in government. Conservative Democratic newspaper editors picked up stories of fraud and bribery, calling the new government oppressive, brutal, and corrupt. Foremost among their targets were carpetbaggers and African Americans in the legislature.[75]

Another problem for the Republican administration was the Ku Klux Klan. The Klan, first seen in the state during the 1868 election, became more organized and sought to reverse the power and influence of the Union League on African American voters. One of the state's first manifestations of the Klan occurred in Wilmington in March 1868, when Col. Roger Moore led Klan members on periodic organized "rides" of mounted men dressed as apparitions through black sections of the city to intimidate the residents. In his capacity as editor of the *Wilmington Journal*, Klan leader and Wilmington native William L. Saunders publicized the actions of the Klan. Because local Wilmington blacks organized their own armed patrols to combat the intimidation, Moore's ploy failed, and after four nights of activity just prior to the election, Republicans carried the city.[76]

With minor exceptions, the Ku Klux Klan never grew into a powerful force in Wilmington because of the large, well-organized black population there. As a result, the Klan's intimidation techniques failed to facilitate a Democratic victory there in the election of 1868, and after the election Klan activity in the city subsided. A large Republican majority in Wilmington that was organized and able to resist Klan intimidation enabled residents of the port city to experience relative political calm while others in the state were witnessing violent Klan action. Both political parties were able to host public debate and organize nonviolent demonstrations in the city.[77]

Whereas the Klan diminished in strength in Wilmington, it grew in intensity in parts of the

This costume was worn by Klansmen in North Carolina during the 1870s. Image courtesy of the State Archives.

state with rural black populations. The continuous pressure exerted by Klan organizations in Piedmont counties throughout Holden's tenure as governor aggravated his efforts to reinstate peace and bring the Republican Party together. Forced into action as the 1870 election neared, Holden called out troops, providing Klan members and Democratic papers with a campaign issue—military occupation and abuses of civil liberties by the governor. Through an effective use of newspapers throughout the state, and despite Holden's efforts to stop Klan violence, the Democratic Party was able to regain control of the legislature and effect changes to the state through legal avenues.[78]

Conservatives in Wilmington stepped up efforts to curtail both black and white Republican participation in government and politics. One argument that gained popularity during the 1868 campaign, recalled in later elections, focused on property ownership and taxes. Business-minded political pundits pointed out that of the 3,500 voters in the city, 2,000 were employed by Conservatives. Therefore, they argued, taxpayers and those with business interests should dictate the city's future. Conservatives overtly threatened the livelihood of black office seekers by identifying them and their businesses so as to encourage consumers to shop elsewhere and employers to hire like-minded, i.e., Conservative, employees.[79] Hampered by Conservative activity and internal strife, the New Hanover County Republican Party had trouble maintaining its organizational control. Key to the party's internal strife was its inability to reconcile the agendas of its white and black members.[80]

The North Carolina General Assembly, dominated by the Democratic Party, met in November 1870 and determined that Holden's efforts to rein in the Klan constituted enough of a miscarriage of justice and an inappropriate use of his office that it sought to impeach him. Klan members figured prominently in the new legislature, with some boasting of their membership in the organization to fellow legislators. Holden's impeachment trial lasted until March 22, 1871, when he was convicted on six out of eight charges. Lt. Gov. Tod R. Caldwell, who succeeded Holden, was powerless to curtail the actions of the new legislature as it reversed Holden's actions on almost every front.[81]

After the Democrats regained control of state government, the Klan was no longer needed as a political tool. Nonetheless, Klan violence escalated in western sections of the state, and, as a consequence, Republicans successfully lobbied the federal government for assistance. The ensuing investigations by a congressional committee resulted in the passage of several laws, most specifically the Ku Klux Klan Act, which defined traditional Klan actions and assigned penalties

for them. The act also authorized the federal government to declare Klan-affected areas in rebellion in order to employ federal forces to restore order. Following passage of the act, federal troops were sent into the state, resulting in hundreds of arrests and as many as 1,400 indictments. The trials that followed effectively employed sworn testimony and confessions to turn Klan members against each other. The secret organization disappeared in North Carolina by late 1872 and did not become a major factor in state politics again until the 1920s.[82]

The presence of Federal forces reinforced the position of the Republican Party somewhat, enabling Caldwell to win the 1872 gubernatorial election over his Democratic challenger. But even though a Republican was elected governor, Conservative Democrats still maintained control of the General Assembly. They made changes to the state constitution in 1873 and 1875, effectively developing a mechanism through which the Democratic Party, by removing the ability of local blacks and Republicans to hold county offices, could control as much of state and local government as possible from Raleigh. The Democrats' changes to the constitution also drew sharper lines between the races, instituting stipulations that whites and blacks could not attend school together or intermarry.[83]

Conservatives employed a variety of methods to minimize the impact of Republican dominance in the Cape Fear region. First they lopped off the northern two-thirds of New Hanover County to create Pender County. Another effort involved redrafting Wilmington's municipal charter to guarantee Conservatives in the city a majority in city government.[84] Both the Democratic and Republican parties used newspapers as mouthpieces, but in 1875 the Democratic Party embarked upon a more effective use of the papers to achieve electoral victory. The *Wilmington Journal* under editor William L. Saunders emerged as a leading Democratic organ for the state at that time.[85]

The Democrats "redeemed" the state as they secured the governor's office in 1876 with the reelection of wartime governor Zebulon B. Vance. That year is regarded as a watershed for

13

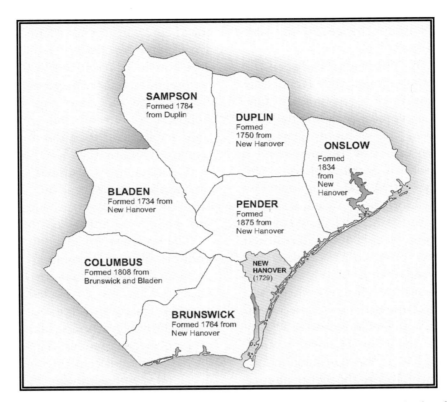

In an effort to weaken Republican dominance in the Cape Fear region, Conservatives strategized to form a new county (Pender) out of the northern two-thirds of New Hanover County in 1875. Map prepared by Mark A. Moore.

the Democratic Party in that it marked the end of Republican control of state politics.[86] Staunchly Democratic historians such as R. D. W. Connor and Samuel A. Ashe described party victories in 1876 as sweeping triumphs.[87] Another early-twentieth-century historian, J. G. de Roulhac Hamilton, remarked that if not for the "crime" of Reconstruction, control of North Carolina politics would have remained in the hands of the Republican Party.[88]

The Legacy of Reconstruction

Reconstruction effectively ended in North Carolina in 1877 as the newly elected Democrats took control of all aspects of state and local governments.[89] The Reconstruction era had seen advancements in education, transportation, industry, and agriculture and had enabled North Carolina's population to develop beyond prewar standards. Growth was uneven among the various groups, however. Farmers suffered from high taxes, a lack of capital, and the rise of sharecropping as

an alternative to slave labor. Sharecropping enabled large plantation owners to retain ownership of their land but relegated tenants, both white and black, into a quagmire of poverty that could not be easily overcome. Industry prospered, however, through the growth of tobacco and textile products created in mills, paving the way for future growth in the 1880s. Fueling the growth of the state into the 1880s was the development of railroads, which connected most parts of the state's backcountry with the coast and other states, encouraging trade and transportation.[90]

Both blacks and whites made gains during Reconstruction. Provisions of the 1868 constitution and a series of Republican-sponsored laws enacted after that date sought to revive public education, but progress was slow, and by the end of Reconstruction most children still did not have a basic education. The Freedmen's Bureau, the American Missionary Association, and private donors sought to establish schools for freed blacks. They were successful in creating a number of schools and colleges designed specifically to allow African Americans to obtain a quality education; Shaw University in Raleigh and Gregory Normal Institute in Wilmington are but two examples.[91]

As white Democrats legislated Reconstruction-era reforms into ineffectiveness, black leaders responded to the setbacks on all fronts by organizing themselves to combat inequalities in education and business. One of the most successful challenges to Democratic efforts to minimize black interests was connected with education. Wilmington's white Republican leaders encouraged local blacks to fight for their rights through consistent protests and actions directed against Conservative Democrats in the legislature. Black leaders were successful in forcing the State Board of Education to use unbiased textbooks, but their most significant achievement was an organized campaign to suppress the so-called Dortch Act. That legislation, proposed in 1883 and named for its sponsor, state senator William T. Dortch of Wayne County, would have authorized appropriation of tax dollars to schools based on racial division: taxes collected from blacks would support black schools and vice-versa. The proposal threatened the poorer black schools with severe underfunding. Because of a consistent lobbying campaign by black leaders, the Dortch Act was never fully implemented and was

annulled by the state supreme court in 1886. Nonetheless, Conservatives were quick to remind blacks that the essential principles of the Dortch Act could re-emerge in other legislation.[92]

Reconstruction in Wilmington

Wilmington's experiences during the era of Reconstruction reflected its position as the state's primary port and largest city. Soon after the city fell, occupying Union forces began to work to restore the city's infrastructure and economic base. Before citizens could rebuild their city, they had to accommodate the demands of the occupying forces, which seized provisions for distribution to refugees and released prisoners and commandeered homes and churches for troop housing and hospitals. Military authorities made many attempts to improve the city's economy in the face of severe shortages. On February 27, 1865, General Schofield issued an order that allowed people who came forward voluntarily to swear an oath of allegiance to the United States and regain citizenship status. Those whose citizenship was thus restored were allowed to participate in commerce again, and the military sought to employ local labor in carrying out building projects. Many businessmen felt immense pressure to take the oath simply to maintain their businesses and keep them financially afloat.

15

Gregory Normal Institute, founded in 1866 by the American Missionary Association, allowed African Americans the opportunity to obtain a quality education. This ca. 1910 image is from W. N. Hartshorn and George W. Penniman, eds., *An Era of Progress and Promise, 1863-1910; The Religious, Moral, and Educational Development of the American Negro since his Emancipation* (Boston: Priscilla Publishing Company, 1910), 160.

Joseph R. Hawley (1826–1905) was born near Laurinburg, where his Connecticut-born father pastored a Baptist church. During the Civil War he rose to the rank of brigadier general of Union volunteers in 1864. After the capture of Wilmington the following year, Hawley assumed command of the forces in southeastern North Carolina. Image from Prints and Photographs Division, Library of Congress, Washington, D.C.

Moreover, Union soldiers represented practically the only group in the city with any purchasing power. To accommodate soldiers' needs, the military allowed certain merchants to import goods into the port through the Union naval blockade and purchased privately owned products such as cotton from locals.[93]

As Wilmington slowly began to recover from the physical and economic effects of war and occupation, its citizens sought to protect themselves politically. Radical Reconstruction under the auspices of Congress did not begin in earnest nationwide until 1867, but because the commander of the local occupying authority, Brig. Gen. Joseph R. Hawley (a native of North Carolina), was a staunch Radical Republican, the city's former Confederates faced a strong hand early in Reconstruction, while its downtrodden poor whites and blacks received a hand up.[94]

In March 1865, attempting to determine Wilmington's best path under occupation, incumbent mayor John Dawson called a "Grand Rally of the People" at City Hall/Thalian Hall, which about one thousand of the city's residents attended. Federal soldiers were barred from the pro-Union rally, which was promoted as a meeting of the city's citizens to plan for its future. Amid waving American flags and pro-Union speeches, Mayor Dawson called for those in attendance to "live for the future, resolving that henceforth it shall be our aim and object to secure peace, promote prosperity and add to the glory and grandeur of our common country."[95] A committee was appointed to draw up eight resolutions asserting that the people of the city were citizens of the United States and appealing for the cessation of hostilities nationwide; those in attendance signed the documents. Copies of the resolutions and signatures were sent to President Lincoln and Governor Vance. Pro-Confederate newspaper editors and others throughout North Carolina ridiculed the resolutions and accused the city of selling out to ease its suffering, even as men were still dying on the battlefield.[96]

Despite the presence of an active Radical Republican element in Wilmington before the end of the war, Conservative elements in the city reclaimed control there during Presidential Reconstruction. Presidential Reconstruction essentially began in the city on June 20, 1865, when Gen. John W. Ames, a moderate, replaced Brig. Gen. Joseph R. Hawley as commander of occupying Union forces. Ames reversed many of Hawley's Radical orders. One aspect of Hawley's tenure that had been especially onerous to Wilmington's Conservatives was his deployment of African American troops in the city. The presence of black troops instilled fear in white residents, who were worried that the soldiers would incite rioting among the city's freedmen. For the most part, the soldiers did not instigate disturbances but instead provided a sense of security for freedmen who sought to exercise their newfound freedoms. Fears of black violence were largely unfounded, although instances of black soldiers using their military influence and power over whites could be found during Presidential Reconstruction.[97]

Three civil disturbances erupted in Wilmington during Presidential Reconstruction. The first took place in August 1865 when a black mob forced the resignation of Mayor Dawson and the Conservative municipal government, including the police force staffed by Confederate veterans. The uprising was short-lived, because General Ames and the occupying Union army reinstated the Conservative government the following day. The city's police force, aided by eight groups of newly organized white militia units, then sought to disarm the city's blacks. The number of black soldiers in the city began to decline during Ames's administration, and most of them were mustered out of service by the end of September 1866. The second and third disturbances occurred in February 1866 and June 1868 respectively and were a result of mobs attempting to free prisoners in the city jail. A similar instance of white fear of a black uprising played out in the summer of 1866 when white leaders refused to allow blacks to run for city offices, arguing that the privilege of officeholding should be connected to voter eligibility—which, of course, blacks did not possess at that time.[98]

By the spring of 1868, Wilmington's economy, stimulated by increased sales of tar, turpentine, and cotton and renewed railroad commerce, had begun to recover. Congressional Reconstruction, which began in July 1868 and lasted until August 1870, diminished Conservative control of the city's government. During that period, most Republican activity sought to gain political equality for blacks and resulted in the creation of several black Republican militia units charged with enforcing Republican agendas and maintaining peace.[99]

Although Wilmington was a stronghold of Republican activity, it followed the state as Conservatives regained control of political affairs in 1870.[100] Military occupation of the city by Union troops began to wind down, and the number of Republican militia units there began to diminish.[101] Facilitating the Conservatives' return to power was a split in the New Hanover Republican Party: white northerners who sought the election of a black man whom they could control faced off against native Republicans and black businessmen who desired a white candidate. Historians attribute the Republican Party's

loss of influence in New Hanover County at this time to a shift away from its power base in the local black population once the party had gained control in 1868, as well as its failure to seek an end to factional disputes within its ranks.

The era of Reconstruction had been relatively tranquil in Wilmington. The city experienced less crime and civil disorder when Republicans, with a large, supportive black voter majority, were in control of its affairs than when Conservatives emerged to lead a fragile and often contested municipal government.[102] Moreover, during Reconstruction a powerful resident military force was readily available to further the interests of the Republican Party and contest any action by white militia and Ku Klux Klan groups.[103]

The end result of Reconstruction was that by 1877, after years of political strife and social upheaval following the Civil War and the granting of freedom for thousands of slaves, North Carolina's ruling political elite "redeemed" the state—that is, returned it to their control. Despite initial disfranchisement of former Confederates, whites were able to regain power through Klan violence and political machinations and by employing newspapers and propaganda, all designed to diminish the abilities of blacks to participate in local and state government. Indeed, a reinvigorated Democratic Party emerged from Reconstruction wholly solidified behind the concept of white hegemony in government and political affairs and readily able to portray the opposition Republicans as a party dominated by northern carpetbaggers and illiterate former slaves.

Post-Reconstruction Wilmington

By the 1880s most of Wilmington's residents were eager to put the travails of Reconstruction behind them and move into the remaining decades of the nineteenth century as citizens of a region in which abundant resources such as naval stores and cotton, combined with a tradition of mercantilism, had begun to give rise to industrialization and capitalism. A handful of white businessmen, comfortably in charge of the city's affairs as a result of gerrymandered voting districts and Democratic control of local and state

17

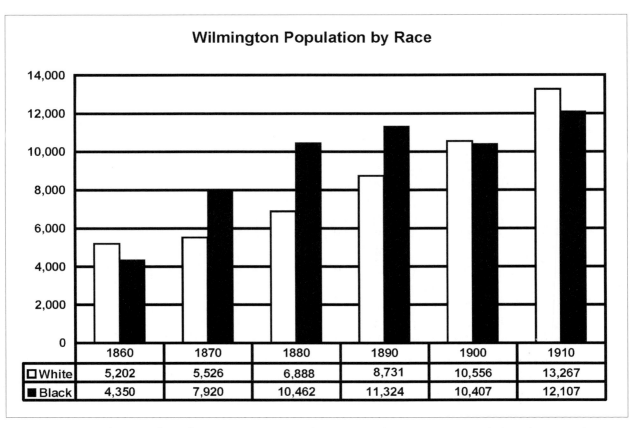

Wilmington Population by Race

	1860	1870	1880	1890	1900	1910
☐ White	5,202	5,526	6,888	8,731	10,556	13,267
■ Black	4,350	7,920	10,462	11,324	10,407	12,107

18

Between 1870 and 1890, the African American population in Wilmington surpassed the white population in number. From "U.S. Census Bureau," http://www.census.gov/prod/www/abs/decennial/index.htm.

government, developed immense fortunes, providing employment and income for working-class whites and blacks.[104] Although control of the city's political affairs was firmly in the hands of Democratic elements, Republicans and blacks still constituted the majority of the city's population, forcing Democrats to accommodate their interests. During the 1870s and 1880s, there emerged a few financially secure black businessmen and entrepreneurs who rivaled many whites in wealth. For their mutual protection from legalized racial discrimination and against latent threats to their security, they created and joined support organizations such as the Masons and Odd Fellows.[105]

The African American population of Wilmington prospered during the 1880s and developed into a complex society. Despite a brief period of extensive out-migration by southern blacks in 1879 and 1880, principally to Kansas, a number of skilled blacks continued to reside in Wilmington. The city's black residents began to

perceive that economic conditions in the city were much better than those found by the black migrants who traveled westward.[106] Regular celebrations of Emancipation Day and Memorial Day, featuring parades and speeches by both blacks and whites, became commonplace.[107] Like other cultural groups in the city, African Americans developed literary societies, built libraries, established benevolent organizations to provide relief for the needy, and formed baseball leagues.[108] In addition to creating new cultural organizations and activities, Wilmington blacks maintained a few traditions developed under slavery, most notably Jonkonnu, a Christmastime tradition with African roots.[109] Central to the development of black cultural and civic life in Wilmington was the church. Several white churches in the city welcomed black worshipers before the Civil War, but afterward most blacks formed their own churches. Some of those new houses of worship were created with the assistance of outsiders from the Freedmen's Bureau, the

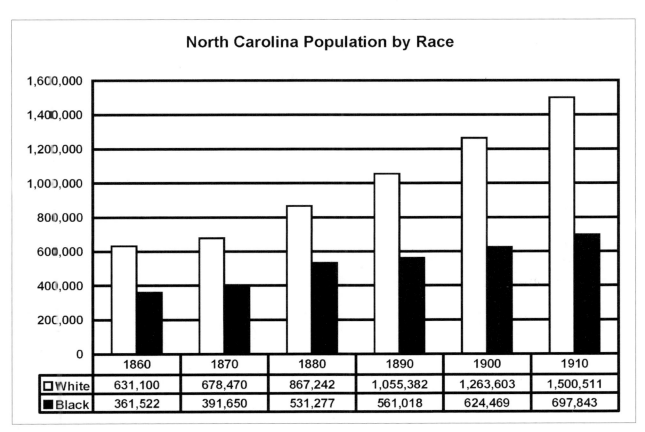

North Carolina Population by Race

	1860	1870	1880	1890	1900	1910
☐White	631,100	678,470	867,242	1,055,382	1,263,603	1,500,511
■Black	361,522	391,650	531,277	561,018	624,469	697,843

North Carolina's population remained proportionately similar (averaging 66% white, 34% black) between 1860 and 1910. From "U.S. Census Bureau," http://www.census.gov/prod/www/abs/decennial/index.htm.

19

American Missionary Association, and other missionary organizations. Two black churches—St. Stephen's AME and St. Luke's AME—boasted large congregations and were highly instrumental in educational and political affairs. Church attendance tended to reflect a social stratification within the city's black population: many of the wealthier blacks attended St. Mark's Episcopal Church or Chestnut Street Presbyterian Church.

Educational development for Wilmington's African American population began in earnest with the arrival of teachers from the Freedmen's Bureau and the American Missionary Association. Those educators brought with them much-needed funding from northern philanthropists. By 1868 the Freedmen's Bureau had established six schools in the city. One of the largest such institutions, established in 1867, became known as the Peabody School—named for its benefactor, George Peabody. Another, known as Williston School, began as a Freedmen's Bureau facility in 1865 and later received funding from the

American Missionary Association. Another AMA school, later known as Gregory Normal Institute, began about 1866 and expanded to provide training for future teachers and leaders, producing alumni who became community leaders in Wilmington and elsewhere.[110]

In community and civic affairs, the African American community fostered the overall development of Wilmington. Especially important to both blacks and whites was the development of fire companies. Such organizations, initially comprised of volunteers, emerged as useful social organizations as well. All-black fire companies were found in several parts of the city, and their equipment, efficiency, and camaraderie were sources of pride in their communities. The Cape Fear Steam Fire Engine Company No. 3, organized in 1871, was one of the earliest. At least thirteen other black fire companies served the city over the last half of the nineteenth century.[111]

African Americans likewise participated in Wilmington politics, chiefly as members and

Williston School was founded in 1865 by the Freedmen's Bureau. Image from William M. Reaves, *"Strength through Struggle": The Chronological and Historical Record of the African-American Community in Wilmington, 1865-1950.* Edited by Beverly Tetterton (Wilmington: New Hanover County Public Library, 1998), 152.

leaders of the Republican Party, their principal vehicle for seeking a voice in government. In 1868 there were 3,968 registered Republicans in New Hanover, and black nominees were elected to office in the 1860s and 1870s. By the time Democrats recaptured control of the state in 1876, dissension in the county Republican Party resulted in fewer blacks securing office. Indeed, dissent reached a critical point by 1888, when the "Independent Faction of the Republican Party" established itself and nominated its own slate of candidates. The situation continued into the 1890s and contributed to the eventual downfall of the Republican Party by the turn of the twentieth century.[112] Despite discord, black officeholding in the city's government was not unusual, particularly for the wards populated by high concentrations of African American voters.

Wilmington's African American population saw some gains in political officeholding, but the realm in which they made the greatest advance was business. Although some black residents of the city emigrated to other parts of the country and a few returned to Africa, most stayed and prospered, creating a viable entrepreneurial center. The 1866 city directory lists numerous black businessmen already in Wilmington, among them shoemakers, carpenters, painters, masons, butchers, teachers, blacksmiths, barbers, wheelwrights, mechanics, and grocers. Those early businessmen, many of whom had pursued their trades in the city as slaves before the war, laid the foundation for subsequent development so that by the 1890s African Americans were wealthy enough to establish corporations and building and loan institutions. Working alongside members of the rising black middle class were laborers, who constituted the majority of black workers in the 1880s. As early as 1865, black workers were organized enough to stage a stevedore strike. Unions were formed within various trades in the 1870s and 1880s, creating a visible presence and a strong voice to advocate for workers' rights. Wilmington's various labor unions, particularly active in the 1880s, were successful in influencing employers to limit their employees' work periods and increase compensation.[113]

The political successes achieved by the Democratic Party in the 1880s set the stage for upheaval in the 1890s. In the first half of the new decade, a powerful combination of whites and blacks would temporarily challenge the Democratic Party's basic underpinnings—racial issues instead of reforms—and achieve temporary political hegemony. Throughout the new decade, Wilmington's population grew in size and wealth as businessmen and laborers enjoyed economic growth. The city's communities, white and black, were growing and creating opportunities for wealth and prosperity—and eventual conflict, as both groups vied for political control of the city and state.

Chapter 2

Forces of Change: Fusion Politics and Wilmington's African Americans

The last decade of the nineteenth century dawned with a bright outlook for Wilmington's population. The city's residents, white and black, were experiencing a high degree of prosperity and a vibrant social life—a promotional booklet praised the city's "growing wealth and prosperity which abound on every hand." The prosperity reached into the African American community as it celebrated success in a variety of ways. St. Stephen's AME Church, one of the city's largest African American houses of worship, with a congregation of 1,700, commemorated the centennial of the African Methodist Episcopal Church of the United States in its new sanctuary.[1]

A few blocks away, another large black congregation attended church at Mt. Zion AME Church. There, in 1888, the congregation heard politically outspoken Rev. Isaiah Aldridge condemn future governor Daniel L. Russell for comments that Aldridge deemed an "assault upon an innocent people." The clergyman declared that he would not vote for or support candidates who "endorsed what Judge Russell had said about the 'savage negroes.' "[2] After delivering his sermon, Aldridge informed the editor of a Wilmington newspaper that he held his political views independent of the larger Republican Party in the city. Aldridge declared his support for the "honest" Republican ticket, despite a warning from "the Bosses" that he should "keep quiet" and vote as expected or he would be fired.[3] This window on Wilmington's African American community delineates the overlap among church, civic, economic, and political life in the city. Not only was the politically charged church sermon well attended, but it was also publicized in local white newspapers, providing clues as to the political culture of the city and the racial discord simmering beneath the surface.

Daniel L. Russell (1845–1908) was elected to two terms in the state House. During Reconstruction he sided with the Republicans and won election as a superior court judge. An ardent critic of the Democrats, he served as a congressman (1879–1880) and governor of the state (1897–1901). Image courtesy of the State Archives.

The Birth of Fusion

By the end of the 1880s, Daniel Russell and other politicians saw potential for a break in the Democratic Party because of the growth of the new Populist Party. Throughout the nation, farmers had grown disenchanted with Democratic legislators, whom they saw as favoring big business and shortchanging agricultural interests. As a result, farmers created and joined political organizations aimed at improving their plight.

By 1889 Leonidas L. Polk had developed the Farmers' Alliance in North Carolina as a political base with members drawn from throughout the state. Membership in the Alliance was limited to whites only. Initially, members of the Alliance sought to work through the two existing political parties without creating a third. The result was that the 1890 Democratic election ticket was dominated by farmers and Alliance members.

Because of the rapidly growing political power of the Farmers' Alliance, Democratic leaders saw political advantages in incorporating many of the organization's goals into the party's platform. Although many Democrats sought to add the farmers' suggestions to its agenda of proposed reforms, none were ever fully addressed. As a result, a split developed within the Alliance, ending its effectiveness as an organization. The more radical members left the Democratic Party and by 1892 had formed the Populist Party. Populists held that the Democratic Party's reforms were insufficient and that control of the state's affairs needed to be removed from the hands of bankers, big business, and attorneys.[4]

When Polk died in 1892, leadership of the Populist Party fell to Marion Butler of Sampson County, who maneuvered the new party through that year's elections. Democrats and Republicans garnered more votes than the new third party; with Democrats winning a majority on a traditional platform that sought to remind voters of the dangers of returning to Reconstruction-era policies should Republicans gain office. Despite an overall loss in 1892, Populists were able to elect fourteen members to the General Assembly. Republicans were heartened by the Populist Party's successes. Some Republicans, such as Daniel Russell, saw the emergence of a new party with a platform based in real issues as a boon to state politics, inasmuch as party lines might then be drawn on "issues other than race and color."[5]

A review of the 1892 election results made clear to Russell and Butler that the Democratic Party was less than cohesive and that the number of black votes cast was the lowest recorded since Reconstruction. By the 1894 election, some sort of combination between the Populists and Republicans, designed to capitalize on the political

Marion Butler (1863–1938) led the Populist Party in support of agrarian reform. He worked with Daniel Russell to form a partnership with Republicans, known as Fusion, to win seats in Congress and the legislature during the 1894 election. Image courtesy of the State Archives.

situation as suggested by the 1892 election results, was an increasingly popular objective. If the Populists could draw more farmers from the Democratic Party and the Republicans could reenergize black voters, together they might be able to defeat the Democrats. The two minority parties, heartened by that theory, received further encouragement when the 1893 Democratic legislature failed to address business- and agriculture-related issues vital to Populist and Republican goals. By the election season of 1894, there emerged a new strategy through which the two groups, Populist and Republican, would work together in pursuit of a common cause. "Fusion," as the merger came to be called, was unique in national politics, and neither the national Republican Party nor the national Populist Party embraced it; further complicating the merger was the fact that not all members of the two parties within North Carolina endorsed it.[6]

Before fusion of the two parties could be achieved, differences between them on a variety of issues had to be addressed. Leadership within each party acknowledged that the only way to achieve victory was to set aside those differences, particularly the ones pertaining to racial matters. The two organizations offered platforms similar to each other in the realms of election reform, increased local governmental authority, and additional support for public schools—a situation conducive to a smooth merger. Fusionists, those most eager for a combination, viewed the 1894 election—a midterm affair in which neither a president nor a governor would be elected—as pivotal in its potential to fill the General Assembly with Populists and Republicans, who would, in return, appoint like-minded men to the United States Senate.[7]

Early Fusion in Wilmington

Just as statewide elections of earlier decades had caused problems in Wilmington and New Hanover County, the 1894 contest spurred even further troubles there. The Democratic Party was split into factions—Reformers and Regulars—that failed to reconcile differences. State Democratic Party leaders were brought in to mediate, albeit unsuccessfully. The Republican Party, harboring internal dissent among its African American members, as evidenced by Rev. Isaiah Aldridge's sermon, pulled itself together to win local election victories in 1894. In that year, Daniel Russell was the Republican leader in New Hanover County; the methods he employed were less than clear at the time.

Russell and his supporters resorted to a series of steps to achieve a Republican victory using tactics not seen before within that party. First, the nomination of candidates was left to a committee instead of a convention, thereby limiting factionalism on a large scale.[8] Once the committee chose its candidates, the Republicans waited until the last minute to make its nominations known. Because the Republicans wanted to avoid the race issue, they put forward only one African American as a candidate. Among the most inventive of their strategies was the nomination of only one candidate for the state House of Representatives, even though two positions were available in the Wilmington

election district. The Democratic ticket for the state House seats included two candidates from opposite factions within the party. The Republican nominating committee knew that factional hostilities among the Democrats were likely to develop further rifts in the party over those two seats. In order to aid and abet that possibility, the Republicans offered to support the Regular Democratic candidates for office, and, in return, the Regulars agreed to discontinue the practice of challenging voter eligibility in Wilmington's traditionally black Republican First and Fifth wards. The result was that a large number of black voters returned to the polls, enabling Russell's candidates to win the election—largely because he had instructed black voters on which contestants to favor. In another important outcome of the 1894 election, Russell demonstrated his ability to manage and achieve victories for the Republican Party.

The 1894 election in New Hanover County showed that when the Republicans were well organized, they could defeat the Democrats. In New Hanover County, Republican candidates were elected to every position for which the party put forward contestants. Leader Russell claimed that the victory was "the most extraordinary political achievement of the period." Three positions—clerk of Superior Court, register of deeds, and one member of the state House of Representatives—went uncontested by the Republicans and by default went to Democrats.[9]

Number of Seats Elected to the 1894 North Carolina General Assembly		
	House	Senate
Populists	36	24
Republicans	38	18
Democrats	46	8

SOURCE: Helen G. Edmonds, *The Negro and Fusion Politics in North Carolina, 1894-1901* (Chapel Hill: University of North Carolina Press, 1951), 37.

23

Throughout North Carolina, the combination of Republicans and Populists proved that it was possible to defeat Democrats. The editor of the *Wilmington Messenger*, T. B. Kingsbury, editorialized that the goal of the next election should be decided upon the question of white government. He attributed the defeat to internal dissent, which had led many Democrats to stay away from the polls, and acknowledged that Fusionists not only were well organized but also had been able to act in secrecy. The Fusionists erased a Democratic majority in the General Assembly and captured upper-level positions in the state senate, the state supreme court, and other statewide seats. Furthermore, the Fusionists, who now controlled the legislature, immediately began fulfilling their campaign promises by implementing changes to various state governmental practices that the Democrats had put into effect after the end of Reconstruction.[10]

Fusion Reforms

Most of the changes wrought by the Fusion legislature in 1895 involved reforming election laws, restructuring the form and powers of county governments, and redrawing the state's electoral districts. Many of the newly enacted election laws were designed to favor blacks and Populists and protect their suffrage rights on election days. Some of the new rules forbade employers from firing or threatening employees over political issues, mandated the use of different-colored ballots for candidates of different parties, and discouraged all types of coercion before and during election days. Additional measures increased the powers of county commissioners and reduced those of justices of the peace. The Fusionists viewed their reforms as beneficial to all concerned, but the Democrats, whose power the reforms substantially limited, saw within the measures a potentially useful tool for future elections—officeholding by African Americans. Because popular elections would henceforth be more open to participation by black voters, the Democrats understood that more blacks would likely be elected; and they decided that that issue was the one they needed to divide the Fusionist Party in future elections.[11]

The Fusionists made sweeping changes in state government, and their measures aimed at reforming local and county government markedly affected Wilmington and New Hanover County. As North Carolina's largest city, Wilmington, with its large urban black population, became a battleground between Democrats and Fusionists. By drawing gerrymandered election districts and establishing in 1877 a board of audit and finance to act as a check on the city's board of aldermen, Democrats had created a system of government in the city that minimized the voice of black Republicans. Under Fusion control, the General Assembly sought to reverse the Democrats' stringent control of Wilmington; one strategy it employed was to amend the city's charter once again.[12] Wilmington Republicans drew up the proposed changes, which included the creation of a Wilmington Police Board, to be appointed by the General Assembly, with responsibility for the appointment and management of the city's police chief, fire chief, city clerk, treasurer, attorney, physician, harbor master, policemen, and service workers. The legislature appointed three white Republicans—William H. Chadbourn, Frederick Rice, and Silas P. Wright—as well as Populist John R. Melton and black Republican John E. Taylor to staff the first board. With its overarching powers of appointment and oversight, the new police board rendered virtually powerless the city's existing—and Democratic—board of audit and finance and board of aldermen.[13]

Local Democrats, still splintered by factionalism, were ineffectual in their response. Meanwhile, the new Wilmington Police Board, manipulated by Russell from behind the scenes, moved to alter city government and reward Democrats who aided in the Fusionist power grab. At the first meeting, the board financially rewarded some of its members. Rice and Melton immediately submitted their resignations to the board and were subsequently elected to two of the highest-paying patronage positions in city government. Rice succeeded a Democrat as city clerk and treasurer, and Melton became the chief of police. In an effort to garner bipartisan support and to forestall efforts by the Democrats to bring the race issue into the 1896 election campaign, the police board was careful to appoint to city positions a goodly number of Democrats, as well as a few blacks. Seeking to improve its image even further, the body established pay scales for employees that were substantially lower than those paid by the previous Democratic board. The combination of tight fiscal management and nonpartisan appointments weakened somewhat the appeal of the Democratic Party and disappointed African American voters.[14]

Not only in Wilmington but also across the state, black voters criticized the Fusionists for what was perceived as discrimination in patronage appointments. A Wilmington paper published an article by a black laborer who wanted more representation by his race in the police and street work forces. Overall, blacks viewed Fusion with skepticism and entertained thoughts of joining forces with Reform Democrats. Because of a potential schism within the normally solid Republican Party, Russell sought to remedy the situation before the 1896 election—in which he hoped to compete for the governor's office. Many blacks felt that Russell's actions were more for public display than to effect major increases in black patronage. As a result, despite Russell's efforts, friction between white and black Republicans continued.[15]

With an eye toward preparations for the 1896 elections, Russell counseled Fusionists that if they stumbled after winning in 1894 and did not act responsibly, the party would see "repudiation by the white people" and "restoration of the Democratic party to power in the state." He offered the opinion that whites "will not submit to negro rule, or anything that looks like it." In order to placate African American voters, Russell clarified that point by indicating that he did not mean "that the colored man shall not hold offices, but we do say that the office holding must be confined to those who are fit for it and who are friendly to the whites, and to such limits as to show that our local affairs will not be controlled by the colored vote."[16]

Leading the Democratic opposition to Russell and other Fusionists was the state's major Democratic newspaper, the Raleigh *News and Observer*. In June 1894, during the campaign

Josephus Daniels (1862–1948). As editor of the *News and Observer*, he strategized with other Democrats to discredit Republicans during the 1896 gubernatorial campaign. Image courtesy of the State Archives.

season leading up to the disastrous defeat of the Democrats by Fusionists, Josephus Daniels of Raleigh and Washington, D.C., and wealthy Democrat Julian S. Carr of Durham devised a plan for Daniels to acquire the *News and Observer* with Carr's financial backing in order to make the paper a tool of the Democratic Party. By 1895 Daniels had returned to Raleigh from Washington, where he had been appointed to a federal government post by President Grover Cleveland. Once back in North Carolina, Daniels employed his paper to provide a voice for the Democratic Party, attacking Republicans, blacks, Populists, and even Democrats he viewed as threats to the party. When Daniels assumed control of the paper, it was financially unstable, but with Carr's assistance and Daniels's personable style, it grew from a struggling local journal to a statewide success.[17]

Fusion Revisited in 1896

Each interested political group in North Carolina laid its groundwork for the 1896 election slowly, holding its own convention and focusing not only on the local and state elections but also the national presidential contest. Throughout the nation, Populists and Democrats differed on standards for coining gold and silver to offset economic problems. Within North Carolina, Populists held the balance of power, and the political party—Republican or Democratic—lucky enough to forge a relationship with the Populists would be victorious in November. Republicans met in Raleigh in May 1896 to plan their strategy and seek methods to woo the Populists. Despite internal dissent, the convention managed to nominate Daniel Russell as its candidate for governor, despite competition from Oliver H. Dockery, the favorite of African American voters. Russell's platform touted the successes of the 1895 legislature and reminded black voters that if Democrats regained power, disfranchisement was certain. The Democrats, who held their convention in June, were still disorganized in the wake of their 1894 defeat; the party's platform was basically a retelling of its past record and featured no new promises for change in its philosophy or goals. Populists held their convention in August and adopted a standard platform and nominated their own set of candidates without acknowledging Fusion as an option.[18]

The 1896 election posed a multitude of problems for the voters of New Hanover County. Although there were clearly three distinct political parties, factions within those parties sought to merge their interests with those of others, creating a jumble of Fusionist possibilities among white Republicans, white Populists, black Republicans, Regular Democrats, and Reform Democrats. With his political skills and brusque personality, well known throughout the county, Daniel Russell maintained a tenuous position as a candidate. Black Republicans viewed his candidacy and Fusionists with skepticism, since some believed that the Republicans could win without the help of former Democrats, who had pushed for white supremacy in the past. Others questioned Russell's commitment to the concerns of African Americans. Still other factions questioned the actions of the police board, citing the changes it had instituted as an example of whites using the black vote to get elected and then turning their backs on the needs of the black community.[19]

Preparations for the election had commenced months earlier when New Hanover County voters

had worked to select candidates and adopt a platform. Black Republicans sponsored numerous meetings to debate the issues, including anti-Russell rallies in which he was portrayed as "against the citizenship of the negro." In the end, the county Republican Party sent forty-five black and nine white pro-Russell delegates to the statewide party convention. In protest, those opposed to Russell held a secondary party convention in the county that adopted anti-Russell resolutions and objected to the Russell delegation. In his Wilmington *Sentinel*, local black editor Armond Scott published anti-Russell articles in which he declared that "the negro race has not an enemy greater than this man [Russell]."[20]

Once candidates and platforms were in place, all parties began to campaign in earnest. Although both Republicans and Democrats courted the Populists, the Populists managed to negotiate a complicated path between both organizations, cooperating with both parties at various levels. The Populists cast their lot with Democrats behind William Jennings Bryan for president, with Republicans for congressional and county candidates, and, in two counties, local races on the state ticket with Democrats. In his newspaper, the *Caucasian*, Marion Butler wrote that the Populists had "undertaken a delicate yet Herculean task and while we want a genuine free silver man as president of the United States, we wish to defeat as disastrously as possible the Democratic organization in this State." In response, Democrats relied heavily upon race issues when attacking the Republicans and Populists instead of approaching the issues of reform advanced by Fusionists.[21]

In Wilmington and New Hanover County, the political parties remained fractured. Although anti-Russell black Republicans had put aside their dislike for the Republican and backed his election, some anti-Russell sentiment could still be found in African American newspapers and meetings. Racist rhetoric in local white newspapers disparaged Republicans, Populists, and the 1895 legislature for imposing black officeholders on the city and county. According to black editor Armond Scott, the end result of the campaign in Wilmington was a "sullen and resentful"

REPUBLICANS
STATE CONVENTION
RALEIGH, N. C., JULY 2.
The VOICE of the People!
The People shall be Heard!

ARE YOU A REPUBLICAN

If so, attend the people's Mass Meeting to be held in

METROPOLITAN HALL, THURSDAY, JULY 2, 1896,

For the purpose of devising some plan to unify the Republican Party and denounce the fraudulent nomination of Daniel L. Russell for Governor of North Carolina.

OUR REASONS.

1. Because he bolted the party in 1888
2. Because he refused to allow his name on the Republican ticket in 1892, and gave as his reason that he was nominated by poor white rascals and a howling pack of negroes.
3. He said he preferred turning the state over to Democracy rather than allow poor white rascals and negroes to control
4. Because he declares in favor of a qualified suffrage If you are a non-property holder he says you may vote for HIM to get in, but he will use his power to disfranchise you in return.
5. Because he insults an important element in the Republican party by saying that negroes are largely savages; that all negroes follow rascals and steal six days in the week and go to church on Sundays and pray it off.
   Negroes, will you acknowledge yourselves to be savages by voting for D. L. Russell? The voice of the people answers NO! White men, can you allow the Republican party to be defeated and go down in disgrace on account of such a man? The people say NO.

REDUCED RATES ON ALL RAILROADS.

This is one of the broadsides circulated prior to the convention of anti-Russell black Republicans held in Raleigh on July 2, 1896. From *Leslie's Weekly Illustrated*, [1896].

relationship between whites and blacks. After the ballots were counted, Fusionists won the election in the city, county, and state. Only one Democrat was elected to a magistrate position, and four blacks were elected to various minor posts.[22]

Complete Fusion Victory

In 1896 the Republicans and Populists were again successful in mounting a fusion of their parties to defeat Democrats. Russell was elected the state's first Republican governor since Reconstruction. As a result of the new election laws put in place by the 1895 General Assembly, more voters turned out in predominantly African American counties. Although still a factor in the election, the Populist Party suffered losses in

overall numbers of voters in 1896 as compared to the numbers that turned out in 1894. The primary reason for the decline was Populists returning to either the Republican or Democratic Party instead of maintaining loyalty to the third party. The General Assembly elected in 1896 consisted of 72 Republicans, 64 Populists, 33 Democrats, and 1 Silverite. Among its members were African Americans Richard Elliott of Chowan County, W. Lee Person of Edgecombe County, William H. Crews of Granville County, John T. Howe of New Hanover County, Edward R. Rawls of Northampton County, W. B. Henderson and Moses C. Peace of Vance County, and James H. Young of Wake County.[23]

In his inaugural address and first actions as governor, Russell indicated to North Carolinians

Jeter C. Pritchard (1857–1921) was elected to the U.S. Senate in 1895 to fill the term of Zebulon B. Vance. He later served on the federal court. Image from Samuel A. Ashe et al., *Biographical History of North Carolina from Colonial Times to the Present*, Vol. 1 (Greensboro, N.C.: Charles L. Van Noppen, 1905), 413.

28

that he intended to follow the policies put in place by the previous legislature. He would seek to revamp local governments through the involvement of the state in municipal affairs. Furthermore, he expressed his determination to involve the state in the control of the North Carolina Railroad. Before leaving office, Russell's predecessor, Elias Carr, had endorsed a plan to lease the use, care, and profit of the railroad to the Southern Railway. Russell, in his inaugural address, made it clear that he would not allow the lease unless the state received adequate compensation. The railroad issue proved to be troublesome for Russell's administration and plagued him for most of his term. Russell viewed the matter, along with other reforms, as a means to combat big business.[24] As soon as the second Fusionist legislature convened in 1897, Russell's divisive appointment of Populist Jeter Pritchard to the United States Senate broke the tenuous bonds of cooperation. Partisanship began to affect all activity. Once again, the Fusionists sought to make changes to election laws and local governments so as to hamper efforts by Democrats to challenge voter eligibility and the outcomes of elections.[25]

Fusion Focus on Wilmington

The legislature turned its attention to managing the state's municipalities, among them Wilmington. Although black Republicans had a voter majority in the city, the gerrymandered wards provided a block to their collective voting power. The Fusionists desired to provide more voice to Wilmington Republicans but at the same time sought to limit black voter strength in order to prevent a black majority on the board of aldermen. They also hoped that restricting black voting power would deprive Democrats of a potential campaign issue. For the Fusionists, the solution lay in amending Wilmington's charter to provide for a board of alderman composed of some members elected by the people and some appointed by the governor. It was their hope that granting Republican governor Russell the ability to place aldermen on the board would counterbalance fears whites had about black rule and the notion that blacks would elect men to office who were "propertyless and ignorant." The city charter, as amended by the Fusionists, stipulated that the voters would elect one alderman from each ward and that the governor would appoint an additional five aldermen; the document did not alter the city's ward boundaries. Once the newly constituted board reflected the Fusionists' tinkering, the General Assembly abolished the Wilmington Police Board—which was no longer needed to limit the authority of the aldermen—in favor of the board of audit and finance.[26] Other Fusionist measures affected Wilmington. To many who resided there, the party's banking, tax, and railroad reforms all appeared aimed at limiting the prosperity of the city's white leaders and their ability to manage the city's affairs for their own benefit.[27]

Because the Democrats in Wilmington had a record of maintaining their members in political office by failing to hold elections regularly, the Republican-dominated General Assembly sought to make municipal elections in the city more egalitarian. The changes the legislature made to Wilmington's charter mandated that municipal elections be held every two years. In March 1897 such a contest was held in Wilmington for the first time in four years.[28] Factions abounded in the city.

For example, the Democratic Party was still split between the old-line Regulars, comfortable with the status quo, and the Reformers, who were tired of seeing the same people in office, particularly those who benefited financially from their posts. The old-line Democrats sought to solidify their party by pulling members together against what they characterized as interference in the everyday rights of citizens by the Republican legislature. Moreover, Wilmington's Democrats planned a legal challenge of the legislature's changes to the city charter affecting elections. During the pre-election confusion, Democrats and Republicans from each of the city wards traveled to Raleigh to appeal to Governor Russell to appoint members from their respective parties to the new board of aldermen.

Russell's appointees to the board would be crucial to the body's political makeup. Rumors circulated that the governor initially planned to appoint Democrats, but, after discovering that the Democrats planned to challenge the new city charter, he decided to fill the positions with Republicans. Russell's final appointments were D. J. Benson, Andrew J. Hewlett, Benjamin F. Keith, John G. Norwood, and Silas P. Wright. Norwood was the only black appointee, and all were Republicans, with the exception of Keith, a disgruntled Democrat who was a member of the Silver Party. For the board of audit and finance, Russell appointed James H. Chadbourn Jr., H. A. DeCove, Henry C. McQueen, John H. Webber, and C. W. Yates. Of those men, Webber was the only black member, Yates and McQueen were Democrats, and the remainder were Republicans.[29]

The March 1897 election of city officials took place without any problems. At the end of the day, two black Republicans—Elijah Green and Andrew J. Walker—were elected to the board of aldermen, as were three Democrats: Owen Fennell, William E. Springer, and Walter E. Yopp. The new board of aldermen was made up of 6 Republicans, 3 Democrats, and 1 member of the Silver Party. On the evening after the polls closed, both the Republicans and the Democrats held caucus meetings to decide their next steps. The Republicans concentrated on who to elect as

mayor; the Democrats on how to regain lost power. The new aldermen were to be sworn in the following day, but the Democrats, who controlled the old board, planned to refuse to vacate their seats, on the grounds that the election was not valid. The Republicans sought to thwart that action by arriving at the meeting early in the day. On the morning of the swearing-in, however, three of the new aldermen, all Democrats, failed to appear. The Republicans, assuming that a quorum was in place, went on with the meeting as the new board members presented their credentials and were sworn in. The new board thereupon elected Silas P. Wright mayor and H. C. Twining to fill Wright's vacancy on the board. It then appointed Populist John Melton chief of police, as well as other members of the police force. After agreeing to wait until its first scheduled day of business in April to make additional appointments, the body adjourned for the day.[30]

But the Democrats had another plan. They had persuaded the three recently elected members of their party not to be part of the new board. Then the old board and Mayor William N. Harriss met in city hall to announce that the election had taken place under altered provisions to the city charter that they deemed unconstitutional and was thus invalid, and therefore it was their duty to retain their legitimately held seats. On the same day, the three newly elected Democrats met with the five Democratic runners-up from the recent contest and declared that those men, following the established pattern that had been in effect since the early 1890s—that is, two men from each ward—had been duly elected. The Democrats likewise organized themselves as the Wilmington Board of Aldermen, presented their election credentials, were sworn in, and elected a mayor from among their ranks. Consequently, on March 26, 1897, Wilmington had three sets of men claiming the authority to run city government.[31]

On March 29 Mayor Wright and his aldermen met to make appointments to remaining city government posts, instructing Chief of Police Melton not to let anyone into the room unless they had specific business with the board. Wright and

29

his colleagues soon completed the process, appointing only Republicans and those relatively new to public office. The Democrats, realizing that the Republicans, once entrenched in city government, could establish a dynasty much like that enjoyed by the Democrats since the end of Reconstruction, now viewed their legal challenge as their only hope of emerging victorious from the debacle. Their objective was to prove that the changes to the city charter made in 1897 were unconstitutional and that the resulting 1897 election was void.[32]

A session of New Hanover County Superior Court convened on April 14, 1897, to hear the Democrats' case. Following three days of testimony, the court found that the 1897 changes to Wilmington's city charter were unconstitutional and that Mayor Harriss and the old board of aldermen represented the legally constituted government for the city until successors were chosen under different election rules. Silas Wright and others filed an appeal to the state supreme court, which heard the case during its September term and ruled that the 1897 election was indeed valid, in that the election laws not only had been altered by the legislature, a duly elected body that existed to represent the people, but also were consistent with the state constitution, itself created by duly elected individuals. The Democrats, roundly chastened by the court finding, were left with no option but to look to the 1898 elections to stem the tide of Republican rule.[33]

Wilmington's African Americans and Fusion

As the political climate swayed in the Fusion breeze, Wilmington's African American community, continuing to build upon a foundation established after the Civil War, created a complex society characterized by clubs and organizations, as well as an entrepreneurial spirit unlike that found in other North Carolina towns.[34] Despite an exodus movement to the states of Mississippi and Arkansas led by African American George Price Jr. in 1889 and 1890, the city continued to include a number of skilled artisans. Wilmington's black residents began to realize that economic conditions

in the city were much better than those encountered by those who traveled westward.[35] Beyond the basic ability to endure, the African American community provided entrepreneurs with a base of capital from which to draw for new ventures, and Wilmington was regarded as a "relatively attractive business environment."[36] New businesses were able to prosper, and black ownership of businesses increased in sustainability in the span of a quarter-century. Many different types of black enterprises operated in the city by 1895. By 1897, Wilmington boasted twenty-four commercially rated black businesses. A number of North Carolina towns were developing a black business class during the period, but the climate that emerged in Wilmington moved beyond the norm of the other cities by the 1890s.[37]

Furthermore, black businesses prospered in direct competition with white enterprises, with several black entrepreneurs opening businesses in fields such as medicine and legal practice, professions typically dominated by whites. Some workers, particularly in education and the ministry, saw no competition from whites. Wilmington became a destination for African American laborers seeking to benefit from the city's growth potential. White employers in surrounding rural sections of the state lamented the loss, complaining that the only black workers left to hire were "rough farm laborers," because the "well trained" workers had moved to the cities.[38] Beyond being a place for those in the lower classes to move up within the black community, Wilmington offered upper-class blacks a chance to collectively further their economic and social standing. Congressman George H. White opened an office in the city, as did new attorneys such as William E. Henderson, who located to Wilmington from Salisbury.[39]

Although a majority of Wilmington's African American workers was employed in unskilled labor positions, growing numbers of them were entering white-collar positions, both at upper and managerial levels.[40] As in most of North Carolina's cities during the last decades of the nineteenth century, African American professionals in Wilmington on average made up less than 5 percent of the black work force. Some black businessmen, such as baker Lorenzo Kennedy, worked for themselves. Although Kennedy's establishment was worth less than $500 in 1893, he was a respected businessman, as suggested by his high credit rating. The most prosperous black-owned businesses in 1893 were those of builder John G. Norwood and undertaker Thomas Rivera, followed by carriage maker James A. Lowery. Although most of the black businesses that existed in Wilmington in 1893 were small, valued at less than $500, and stigmatized by a poor credit rating, the city's reputation as a place for blacks to better themselves financially continued to attract African Americans in search of a better future.[41] One of the more ambitious projects of black business leaders was the incorporation of the Wilmington Livery Stable Company in 1897, led by some of the city's successful businessmen such as John Hargrave, Frederick Sadgwar Sr., Elijah Green, and William Moore.[42]

One trade invaluable in the city's economic life was that of stevedore. Stevedores worked on the docks loading and unloading ships, and African Americans dominated the trade during and after the time that they were enslaved. During the 1890s stevedores began to organize themselves under a "boss." Moreover, they were required to register with the city and pay a fee for the right to ply their trade. Many of the "boss" stevedores, such as Cato Waddell and Thomas Newkirk, who managed the firm of Waddell and Newkirk, were black, but several white firms such as E. G. Parmele

Frederick Sadgwar Sr. worked as a very successful African American building contractor in Wilmington. He served on the short-lived Wilmington Livery Stable Company's board of directors in 1897. Image from Reaves, *"Strength through Struggle,"* 456.

and Company paid black laborers to work their docks and ships.[43]

As part of their effort to better themselves financially, many African Americans in Wilmington sought ways to secure home ownership and economic independence. In the wake of early failures by the Freedman's Bank, blacks were reluctant to patronize banking institutions. In 1889, however, a group of African American leaders banded together to form the Peoples Perpetual Building and Loan Association for the specific purpose of enabling its shareholders to purchase their own homes. Between 1889 and 1898, the organization provided its shareholders with more than seventy loans, most of which were canceled or paid in full.[44] Home ownership was a source of pride. In 1898 a resident noted that Wilmington's black home ownership rates were higher than in other parts of the country and explained that the houses "may be humble, but they have worked for them, paid for them and own them."[45]

Because home ownership was a tool to advance economic and social freedom, black leaders worked to assist others in the attainment of property. The American Union Association (AUA), formed in 1897, pursued the "acquisition of real estate and distributing the same to the poor class of colored people of the city of Wilmington, N.C. and to aid in securing homes for the destitute, the orphan, and the widow."[46] The New Hanover County deed index reveals that the AUA acquired two entire blocks in 1897 and 1899 and then subdivided them, registering 45 deeds for men and women to reside within those blocks between 1897 and 1919.[47] Throughout North Carolina in 1890, about 14 percent of the black population owned their own homes, as compared to approximately 35 percent of the white population. In Wilmington, of the black population that owned property, only 10 percent had property valued under $100. The upper class of black property holders, those whose property was valued above $1,000, represented only 4 percent of the population. The largest property-owning value bracket, 77 percent of the group under examination, encompassed those who owned property valued between $100 and $500.[48]

31

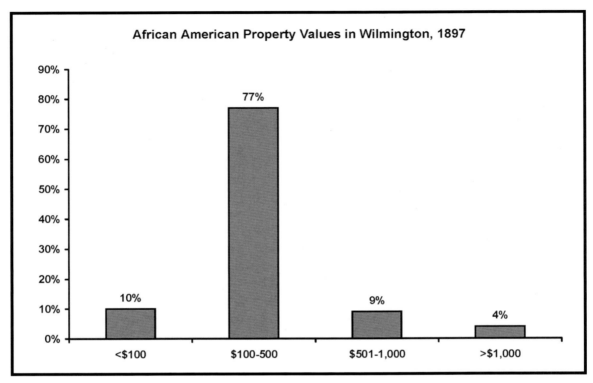

SOURCE: New Hanover County Tax Records, 1779–1909, State Archives.

32

Along with its interest in achieving financial independence, Wilmington's African American community demonstrated a strong commitment to education. The first schools for black children were opened by northern benevolent societies and the Freedmen's Bureau near the end of the Civil War. Following that lead, the African American community slowly began to manage its own educational system. Black leaders served on the county school board, trained and hired local black school teachers and administrators, and created local support organizations to oversee the education of Wilmington's first and second generations of children, who had never known slavery. The Freedmen's Bureau initially supported the Peabody School, but once that agency departed the state, a local support group known as the Wilmington Colored Educational Institute began to assist in funding it.[49] Other schools, such as Williston and Gregory Normal Institute, shared similar beginnings and subsequently received comparable support from the city's blacks. Wilmington's black teachers included some of the city's elite, with the

wives and daughters of the city's most prominent politicians and businessmen working to educate the black children.[50] Still, despite widespread community support for the schools, black teachers were consistently paid less than their white counterparts, and facilities were often underfunded.[51]

Over time, the African American community developed a distinctive social hierarchy. Lura Beam, a northern white educator who taught in Wilmington after the turn of the twentieth century, explained for her readers the difficult complexities of black social classifications. Although Beam was writing ten years after the 1898 incident, her account likely parallels the situation of the 1890s. She explained that the upper class was the financial equivalent of the white middle class. Borrowing from W. E. B. DuBois's widely known phrase, she termed these men and women—many of whom were mulatto and could trace their station to inherited wealth from white relatives—the "talented tenth." Most of the black elite were community leaders who owned homes and sent their children to college.

Mary Washington Howe was the daughter of Alfred Howe, a well-respected freedman in Wilmington. She was educated in the North and became principal of Williston School. Image from Reaves, *"Strength through Struggle,"* 153.

John C. Dancy (1857–1920) was born to free black parents. He was well respected by whites, serving as collector of customs in Wilmington and working actively with the Republican Party between 1880 and 1890. Image from W. H. Quick, *Negro Stars in All Ages of the World* (Richmond: S. B. Adkins and Co., Printers, second edition, 1898), 173.

Beam conceded that some of these people were "too white" and could not easily merge with darker-skinned blacks from other classes, and that for these upper-class blacks, "passing" as white was also considered a form of racial "treason." In descending order, Beam defined the next group of blacks in Wilmington as middle class and few in number. These people owned homes on the fringes of the city. The lowest level of black society, according to Beam, was occupied by poor, dark-skinned laborers who rented substandard housing and who had moved into the city from the countryside. She recalled that that class was "anonymous" and was in constant motion, frequently changing jobs.[52]

Besides seeing advances in their financial status, Wilmington's blacks benefited from their support of Republican politics. Patronage and equitable hiring practices among city and county leaders resulted in more African Americans holding public and visible offices in the city and county.[53] Especially notable was John C. Dancy, whom President Benjamin Harrison nominated and the United States Senate confirmed for the post of collector of customs for the port of Wilmington in 1891. Dancy was paid approximately four thousand dollars a year, more than most top state officials.[54] Many whites viewed the advances achieved by the

black community as a threat to their security. For example, Wilmington author Harry Hayden cited the lament of white workers in 1898 who claimed that employers had given blacks priority in hiring. Writing in 1936, Hayden expressed the opinion that most of Wilmington's artisans were black and that the city was "becoming a Mecca for Negroes and a City of Lost Opportunities for the working class whites." He explained that most of the bricklayers, carpenters, and mechanics were black, a trend that can be traced back to the 1860s, when such jobs were the only ones available to the black worker. In response to this perceived threat to working-class whites, the Democratic Party began developing discriminatory economic platforms and urging white employers to hire only white workers.[55]

33

Plans Are Laid to Force the End of Fusion

Responding to challenges confronting the Democratic Party, the perceived threat to white people posed by advances in African American prosperity and political participation, and an economic downturn in 1897 resulting from lingering effects from the Panic of 1893, many prominent white leaders in Wilmington began to meet in private during the six to twelve months preceding the 1898 election. The men were convinced that if they did not regain control of the city's political machine, they could not prosper. Whoever controlled the city government also controlled its purse, taxation policy, and internal improvements agenda. Moreover, in their eyes, the absence of such control made it difficult to persuade prominent white businesses to relocate to the port city. The promise of attracting major investors and outside business enterprises to Wilmington in the wake of a Democratic victory served as a tangible incentive for white business leaders to take political matters into their own hands. For those men, political victory meant renewed economic stability and prosperity—factors they saw as lacking under Fusion rule.[56]

Most of the men who met together were members of established organizations such as the Wilmington Chamber of Commerce or the Wilmington Merchants Association.[57] But it was not merely members of traditional commercial organizations that assembled. Throwing their support firmly behind the Democratic Party were men who facilitated the development of radical secret organizations dedicated to white supremacy, repressive political campaign tactics, voter intimidation, and outright violence. The efforts put forth by those men in advance of the election of 1898 significantly altered the political landscape in Wilmington, in North Carolina, and throughout the South for decades to come.

34

Chapter 3

Practical Politics

The whole aim of practical politics is to keep the populace alarmed (and hence clamorous to be led to safety) by menacing it with an endless series of hobgoblins, all of them imaginary.

—H. L. Mencken
In Defense of Women (1918)

In preparation for the 1898 elections, political parties began to develop platforms and select candidates. As the election season began in full swing, North Carolinians increasingly divided their attention between national patriotism called forth as a result of the Spanish-American War and the brewing political contest in the state.[1] On April 14, 1898, the United States declared war on Spain.[2] Politicians had impressed upon President William McKinley the potential financial rewards of embarking upon war with the clearly outranked European foe. By the first of May, American warships had engaged the Spanish in naval battle. Two months later, following an American victory at the Battle of San Juan Hill and the destruction of the Spanish fleet, the Spanish pressed for peace.

As a result of a call to arms issued both by the president and Gov. Daniel L. Russell, 106 Wilmington men had enlisted in Company K, Second Regiment North Carolina Volunteer Infantry, also known as the active component of the Wilmington Light Infantry (WLI); another contingent signed on as members of the crew of the USS *Nantucket*, a thirty-five-year-old naval vessel that served with the North Carolina Naval Militia (also known as the naval reserves) after 1895 and provided coastal defense services at Port Royal, South Carolina, during the Spanish-American War. Both Company K and the *Nantucket* crew departed the state to join the war effort, but neither saw action. The *Nantucket* remained in port in South Carolina, and Company K drilled and marched in Raleigh and Georgia.

The men returned home on furlough by the fall. After Governor Russell in April 1898 authorized the creation of a black battalion to participate in the war, a large number of African Americans from North Carolina enlisted for service. Russell appointed Maj. James H. Young commander of the battalion, which in July was mustered into service as the Third Regiment North Carolina Volunteer Infantry. Unlike the Second Regiment, the Third remained in camp and service until it was mustered out in February 1899.[3]

James H. Young (1859–1921) edited the *Signal* (Raleigh) before being elected as a Republican to the General Assembly in 1894 and 1896. Photograph as commander of a black battalion during the Spanish–American War from Josephus Daniels, *Editor in Politics* (Chapel Hill: University of North Carolina Press, 1941), facing 314.

In the wake of the 1896 elections, the Democratic machine had become increasingly organized, and the Populists and Republicans failed to mount a successful offensive. Beginning in 1897, irreparable schisms developed not only between Fusionists and Republicans but also within the respective parties, severely limiting their ability to counter increasingly aggressive Democratic Party tactics. Likewise contributing to the Fusionists' inability to resist the Democratic onslaught was the subtle abandonment by the federal government of its previously firm commitment to the protection of civil and political rights of black citizens.[4]

During Daniel Russell's governorship, splits between and within the Populist and Republican parties widened, despite attempts by Russell and Senator Marion Butler to effect a reconciliation.[5] As the incumbent party, with its leader as governor, the Republicans should have been confident in their reelection possibilities; but the party was fractured, and Russell, widely regarded as a "maverick"—neither a complete Republican nor a complete Populist—garnered little support. Moreover, many Republicans, particularly African Americans, disliked Russell's appointment of Populists to prominent positions. At the beginning of the 1898 election campaign season, Russell feared that he could not control an outright Republican convention as he had in the past and that an uncontrolled convention would abandon him. Russell's fears were realized when the party held its convention in July and failed to invite him to speak or even participate in the proceedings. Instead, the Republicans attempted to woo the Populists in hopes of achieving another Fusion victory. In the face of mounting Democratic Party strength, the two parties managed to hammer out a weak combination late in the campaign, long after the Democrats had embarked upon their campaign of white supremacy.[6]

The Populists were the first to hold their convention, assembling in Raleigh in May 1898. At that conclave, delegates debated the pros and cons of cooperating with both the Republicans and the Democrats, but in the end the party chose to write its own platform and began to chart its own course, waiting, as it had in the past, to court and be courted by the other two parties. Dr. Cyrus P. Thompson and Marion Butler led the Populists during the campaign and repeatedly attempted to point out that the Democrats failed to address the real issues facing North Carolina. Moreover, the Populists, employing a special supplement in the Raleigh *Progressive Farmer* late in the campaign, sought to make the case that the Democratic Party's campaign issues were contrived to support the agenda of a few "Democratic bosses."[7]

Following the Populist gathering by only weeks, the Democratic convention likewise assembled in Raleigh. Newly elected state party leader Furnifold M. Simmons presided, and influential public men such as Charles B. Aycock, Claude Kitchin, Locke Craig, Cameron Morrison, George Rountree, Francis D. Winston, Josephus Daniels, and Wilmington native Alfred Moore Waddell attended. The convention soundly rejected a proposal to form a combination with the Populist Party, and instead adopted a platform that reviled the actions of the two previous Fusion legislatures as evidence of "Negro Domination" and promised "rule by the white men of the State."[8]

Development of the Democratic "Machine"

Beginning with the 1898 campaign, Furnifold Simmons led an evolution of the Democratic Party into a tough, well-organized competitor for political offices. Simmons, a New Bern attorney, had long been involved in state and national politics. He had served as chairman of the North Carolina Democratic Party during the successful 1892 campaign but resigned before the 1894 contest and the subsequent Democratic defeats in 1894 and 1896.[9] Simmons applied his organizational skills to rally supporters and press others into the Democratic fold. He carefully orchestrated the campaign, opening discussions through printed media and a few speeches in late summer, followed by fall speechmaking spectacles with parades and feasts in the last five weeks of the campaign. His approach was to employ newspapers, political rallies, and coercion to win votes. In the *Democratic Party Handbook* for the 1898 campaign and other publications, Simmons focused on a singular topic—incompetent government by the Republican Party—and developed themes pertinent to that topic, many related to the overarching concept of white man's rule. He characterized whites who voted for Russell and Fusion as men

Right: Furnifold M. Simmons (1854–1940) chaired the Democratic Party in 1898. He organized men and women from all walks of life to support the white supremacy campaign. Image courtesy of the North Carolina Collection.

Below: The *Democratic Party Handbook* for the 1898 campaign, prepared by the State Democratic Executive Committee of North Carolina, presented the issues of the campaign to the people in order to "restore good government to our beloved state." It recounted numerous alleged scandals and problems with Republican rule when compared to Democratic rule. Image courtesy of the State Library of North Carolina.

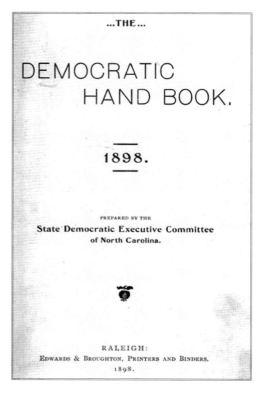

...THE...

DEMOCRATIC HAND BOOK.

1898.

PREPARED BY THE

State Democratic Executive Committee of North Carolina.

RALEIGH:
EDWARDS & BROUGHTON, PRINTERS AND BINDERS.
1898.

that unscrupulous and incompetent men of both races had been allowed to rule state and local governments during Russell's administration.[11]

Advancing the argument, the *Handbook* declared that because white men could manage government better than African Americans, who had demonstrated through Republican rule their inability to manage themselves and others, "this is a white man's country and white men must control and govern it."[12]

Employing such themes, Simmons created a powerful anti-Republican, anti-black position for the Democratic Party. As embodied in previous platforms, the 1898 strategy focused on accomplishments by Democrats when in power and warned against the pitfalls of black officeholding; but the 1898 campaign also broke new ground in planning and preparation for the November elections. Simmons made effective uses of manpower through better party organization and control of county Democratic Party committees. County committee chairmen received from the state headquarters weekly correspondence, as well as quantities of circulars and posters—some two million documents circulated throughout North Carolina during the campaign. As in the successful 1892 campaign, Simmons, employing claims of corruption by "Republican-Negro rule," united various entities that traditionally supported the Democratic Party.[13]

who had been led astray and simply needed to be brought back to the Democratic ranks.[10] The *Handbook* characterized the Republicans as the party of scandal and poor results, leading to debt, ineffectual government, and abuses by officials. More significantly, it asserted that the Republican Party was dominated by blacks who compelled white Republicans to accede to their wishes in order to advance to political office. The end result of that relationship, according to Democrats, was

To fund the campaign, Simmons quietly called on businessmen throughout the state and promised that the Democrats would not raise business taxes if his candidates were elected. Editor Josephus Daniels, a hearty supporter of the Democratic Party's white supremacy platform, recalled that Simmons was "a genius in putting everybody to work—men who could write, men who could speak, and men who could ride—the last by no means the least important." For Simmons, victory was to be achieved with the solid backing of newspapers, the frequent appearance throughout North Carolina of skilled traveling campaign speakers, and the implicit participation of violent bands of men united behind a singular argument—white supremacy.[14]

Wilmington's status as the state's largest city, governed by Populists and Republicans supported by a large black voting majority, made it a perfect test case for Simmons's propaganda program, which singled out the city with claims that it was under "negro domination." The staunchly Democratic Raleigh *News and Observer* and the *Charlotte Observer*, seeking to point out the evils of non-Democratic political leadership, reprinted and expounded upon articles about local leaders that originally appeared in Wilmington's Democratic newspapers. To fuel the argument for the redemption of Wilmington, the *News and Observer* regularly dispatched a correspondent to the city to generate more evidence of the need for white supremacy. Some residents of Wilmington took pride in the fact that the Democratic Party's star speechmaker, Charles B. Aycock, proclaimed that the city was "the center of the white supremacy movement." After listening to speeches at a party rally in Goldsboro in October, Josephus Daniels observed that "the cause of Wilmington became the cause of all."[15]

Men Who Could Write

One of the most visible elements of the 1898 Democratic campaign was the use of newspapers. Simmons enlisted the help of Josephus Daniels, editor of the *News and Observer*, to be the "militant voice of White Supremacy."[16] Daniels, a longtime Democrat, was well connected to others in the

Charles B. Aycock (1859–1912) was one of the leading Democratic spokesmen during the 1898 campaign. He believed that only a Democratic administration could restore white supremacy and peace. Image courtesy of the State Archives.

state's ruling elite and in 1894 had collaborated with wealthy Durham industrialist Julian S. Carr to purchase the *News and Observer* and employ it as a tool on behalf of the Democratic Party in its fight against Fusion. Using the *News and Observer* first as a barometer of public opinion and then as a weapon, Daniels and Simmons worked together in 1898 to develop a powerful argument against Fusion and in favor of white supremacy. The paper slowly introduced the racial issue to its readers, fed stories to other papers, and worked the reading public into a frightened and tense frenzy.

Especially powerful were the *News and Observer*'s editorial cartoons. Daniels had hired cartoonist Norman E. Jennett to draw occasional political cartoons for the paper during the 1896 election season; by 1898 Jennett's cartoons were ever present. Both Daniels and Simmons considered them to be "one of the greatest factors in winning victories."[17] Daniels asserted that he used "every act and argument that we thought would serve to influence the white people" and credited his paper with headlines that "sealed the doom of Fusion." Later in life, Daniels admitted that the paper was occasionally excessive in its bias

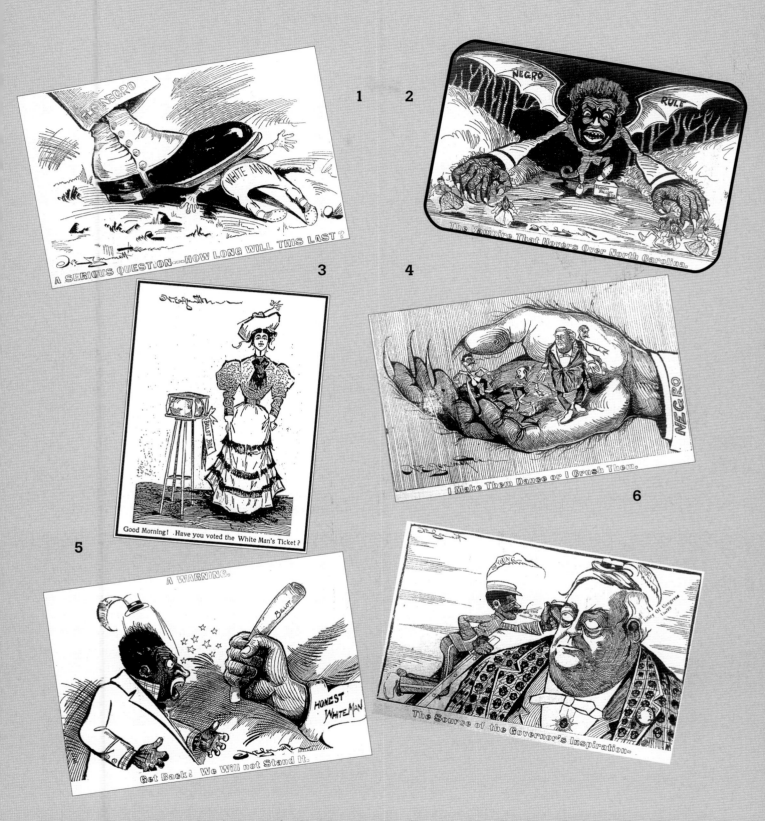

Norman Jennett drew political cartoons for the Democratic Party's mouthpiece—the *News and Observer*. They were a significant factor in influencing the 1898 elections. The cartoons appeared between August and November 1898. **1.** "A Serious Question—How Long Will This Last?" August 13, 1898. **2.** "The Vampire That Hovers Over North Carolina," September 27, 1898. **3.** "Good Morning! Have you voted the White Man's Ticket?" November 8, 1898. **4.** "I Make Them Dance or I Crush Them," October 12, 1898. **5.** "A Warning. Get Back! We Will not Stand It," August 30, 1898. **6.** "The Source of the Governor's Inspiration," September 30, 1898. Images courtesy of the State Library of North Carolina.

toward Democrats and that stories were not fully researched before publication and probably could not be "sustained in a court of justice." He bragged that, because of the print campaign, "people on every side were at such a key of fighting and hate that the Democrats would believe almost any piece of rascality and the Fusionists got into the habit of denying everything." By the end of the campaign, the *News and Observer* was a powerful force in campaign rhetoric, and portions of its articles were published nationwide.[18]

Other editors held up the white supremacy banner and did all within their power to publicize the actions of Republicans and Democrats as part of the larger campaign. One vocal reporter, in some respects a tool of Daniels, was H. E. C. Bryant of the *Charlotte Observer*, who signed his articles "Red Buck." Bryant traveled the state to document the activities of the Democrats and to point out what he perceived as the pitfalls of Fusion government. His work included much investigative work in Wilmington. In an effort to inflame white sentiment against "negro domination," he published an article about Wilmington that named black Fusionist officeholders in the city.[19]

Although the print campaign was successful, Furnifold Simmons was not satisfied with merely circulating newspapers only to paying customers. As a method to entice newspapermen and advance the campaign, Simmons solicited funds from within the Democratic Party to pay for subscriptions for those who otherwise would not have had access to papers such as the *News and Observer* or the *Wilmington Messenger*. Supported financially by men such as Julian S. Carr, Simmons and his committee paid for 25,000 weekly papers to be sent directly to selected voters until the elections. The project was seen as a success, and more names were added to the subscription list. By the time of the election, the number of papers circulated through the use of Democratic Party funds reached 40,000. Moreover, Simmons and his colleagues paid newspaper printers to create 50,000 four-page supplements to regular editions that were sent out with weeklies during the last two months of the campaign. At the conclusion of the contest, Simmons explained that he sought to

reach the large number of voters who were "not immovably wedded to any party, but who love their State and will vote right if they are made to see what is to the best interest of the people and themselves." Simmons observed that many voters rarely read papers or attended speeches and that "if these good people could be reached and given the facts and thus brought to understand the horrible conditions of misrule, corruption and extravagance under the Fusionists they would certainly cast their votes to discontinue in power this unholy combination."[20]

Men Who Could Speak

Another of Simmons's tools was his de facto speaker's bureau. Popular orators such as Charles B. Aycock, Robert B. Glenn, and Henry G. Connor traveled the state at Simmons's behest to boost the white supremacy platform. Simmons planned for most of the speechmaking to take place in the fall, aiming for early speeches to "keep up a running fire, and not enough to tire the people." During the closing weeks of the campaign, he dispatched speakers whose rhetoric was peppered with local tales of the evils of Fusion rule and "negro domination" in every available town hall and commons. Particularly adept with rhetoric was Alfred Moore Waddell, who spoke to rallies late in the campaign and pointed out numerous instances of the injustices heaped upon his hometown of Wilmington as a result of Fusion government.[21]

Charles Aycock, a veteran speaker from earlier campaigns, traveled the state on behalf of the Democratic Party as its "voice." In May 1898, just before the Democratic State Convention assembled, he "sounded the keynote of the 'white supremacy' campaign" in Laurinburg.[22] Because of his dedication to the Democratic Party, combined with his proven record of approval by the state's voters, Aycock was rewarded in 1900 with the governor's office. Another well-known speaker, one who exercised a measure of oratorical restraint in regard to race during the 1898 campaign, was Henry G. Connor. Connor's correspondence and speeches repeatedly indicated that he was "willing to go a very long way to remove the negro from the politics of the state" as he was "managing a campaign of which I shall never be ashamed." Although certainly on the side of white supremacy, Connor voiced the concerns of conservative Democrats when he expressed the hope "that the present conditions may pass away without violence or bloodshed and that our whole people may be wiser and understand each other better." He believed that once the Democrats regained power over the state, they should earnestly seek to improve the lives and education of blacks.[23]

Men Who Could Ride

The newspapers and the speaker's circuit facilitated Simmons's goal of reaching all types of people in the state. Illiterate or working-class people without subscriptions to papers responded well to speechmaking. Businessmen, clerks, and others with access to newspapers were given ample opportunity to read about the campaign's issues, Republican corruption, and the moral duty of white men to vote for the Democratic ticket. The last component of the three-part campaign strategy was Simmons's appeal to groups of white men who could "ride"—that is, be available often and in large numbers to serve as the eyes and ears of the Democratic Party throughout the state and to aid in encouraging white voters to associate themselves with the party. Ostensibly, these men would assist in Simmons's plan to bring Populists back to the Democratic fold through "practicable and honorable means." To establish the first (and most organized) of the proposed collaborative groups, Simmons enlisted the aid of legislator Francis Winston of Bertie County to establish White Government Union (WGU) clubs. The Democratic Party headquarters in Raleigh planned to deploy WGU groups in such eastern North Carolina counties with black voting majorities as New Hanover, Craven, and Pitt. The WGU clubs achieved immediate popularity, and soon there were more than eight hundred of them throughout the state.[24]

The WGU placed emphasis on individuals and their ability to make a difference in local politics. The Democratic Party created and managed the associations and assigned their members to work in multiple capacities: to guarantee full participation

Buttons like this were worn by members of the White Government Union clubs, tools of the Democratic Party used to ensure white voter registration and participation. Image courtesy of the Cape Fear Museum of History and Science, Wilmington.

by all white voters in the Democratic Party; to report to local and state party chairmen concerning "doubtful and floating" voters, who would be targeted for "efforts of the union to win the votes of such voters for the party"; and to attend polls all day on election day. The WGU was a well-oiled machine that featured committees in charge of registration, campaign literature, speakers, and challenges and polls. The first three committees existed to ensure that all white men registered to vote, received campaign literature, and had access to speeches; the fourth was designed to challenge illegal voter registration, deflect challenges against Democratic registrants, and attend polls on election day to ensure that all white men voted for the Democratic Party.[25]

The WGU movement began in earnest in August and gained momentum as the election drew near. Other organizations created for similar purposes were formed in much the same manner as the WGU. One such group was the Young Men's Democratic Club of Wilmington. Another, more visible and violent, was the "Red Shirt," or "Rough Rider," organization. The Red Shirts, unknown in North Carolina before the 1898 campaign, had originated and grown into a powerful white supremacy force in South Carolina under Allianceman and former governor Benjamin R. Tillman and former Confederate cavalryman and Democratic leader Wade Hampton. The first appearance of Red Shirts in North Carolina occurred in October 1898 at a Democratic campaign rally in Fayetteville, where Tillman attended a parade that featured thousands of spectators and two hundred Red Shirts. Also participating in the rally and parade were many

Above: Armed Red Shirts in Laurinburg on election day, 1898. Image courtesy of the State Archives.

Below: This red shirt belonged to Charles B. Aycock. It is unclear if he wore the shirt or if it was given to him in 1898 or 1900. Image courtesy of the North Carolina Museum of History, Raleigh.

WGU clubs and their guests, including delegations from Wilmington and other towns.[26]

With but a short-lived presence in North Carolina politics, the Red Shirts were characterized by their distinctive red outfits, unconcealed weaponry, and blatant public displays of white-supremacy propaganda. Although all levels of society—from wealthy businessmen to working-class farmers and laborers—participated in the Red Shirt brigade, the loudest and most visible members were considered hoodlums, making the Red Shirts effectively a terrorist arm of the Democratic Party. According to a contemporary, their unifying insignia, the red shirt, was of varying style and material, made of "calico, flannel or silk, according to the taste of the owner and the enthusiasm of his womankind."[27]

Red Shirt and Rough Rider brigades, brandishing rifles and pistols, typically paraded or rode horses in plain view within black communities. The actions of these men were well known among African Americans, who either hid in their homes or departed, leaving behind neighborhoods that appeared to be vacant. Josephus Daniels believed that Red Shirt activity was successful because, unlike speechmaking and other measures, it kept black voters from attempting to participate in the political process.

Throughout southeastern North Carolina, the Red Shirts rode day and night to intimidate black voters and bully white Populists and Republicans into voting for the Democratic Party.[28] Although the organizational structure of the Red Shirts is unclear, the brigades were carefully orchestrated displays of Democratic militancy, employed at intervals both to stir up white sentiments and to oppress black or Republican voters. The Red Shirt movement likely grew out of, or was managed by, the WGU clubs created by the Democratic Party. Red Shirt rallies coincided with WGU activities and featured many of the same speakers who stumped throughout the state on behalf of Democrats.[29]

Thus, Simmons rallied together men who could speak, write, and ride to support the white supremacy campaign in a well-organized statewide effort. Daniels summed up the campaign when he observed that "every white man who could talk was on the stump; every white man who could write was writing, and every white man who could ride and could influence a vote was enthusiastically at work."[30] Simmons and his committee took still more steps, including employing the influence of women and members of the clergy, to convince white male voters that duty and responsibility obligated them to cast a Democratic vote. Simmons later wrote that although he disliked "politics in the pulpit," he felt that the use of the clergy was an important tool in a campaign that threatened the "very foundations of our social order and morality." Simmons also understood the usefulness of women in campaigning and included them at every opportunity. The WGU even recruited women members. As visual reminders of the responsibility of white men to protect them, women were invited to attend and even speak at political rallies—uncommon occurrences in North Carolina politics up to that point. Other women participated in parades, fashioned banners for the cause, and cooked quantities of food for rallies.[31]

Republican Reaction

Once the Republicans and Populists realized the futility of working separately against the

Unidentified Wilmington woman. At the top of the photo is written "1898 Riotess." This image of a woman in a pure white dress, armed with a pistol and a rifle, could have been a powerful image used as propaganda. Image courtesy of the Southern Historical Collection, Wilson Library, University of North Carolina at Chapel Hill, Chapel Hill.

43

Democrats, they fused their parties into a weak coalition late in the election season but were ineffective in combating the well-organized Simmons machine. As they watched the Democrats gain momentum, Republican and Populist leaders failed to organize themselves, scheduling few speeches and lacking a cohesive, clearly defined print campaign. Russell warned his compatriots that they were in a "fight for our lives" because a "Democratic Legislature here means an orgy of deviltry the like of which has not been seen."[32] Butler and other Populists reacted to the Democratic campaign by pointing out that Democratic Party speakers did nothing but "howl 'nigger' from one end of the State to the other, hoping under the cover of the negro cry, to get men elected to the legislature" who would place corporate interests ahead of the needs of the average citizen.[33]

African American Republicans likewise feared the outcome of the campaign. Early in the campaign season, black leader James H. Young cautioned that if the Democrats returned to power, blacks would be disfranchised.[34]

In response to the Democratic rhetoric, black Republican congressman George H. White and representatives of the Populists met with President McKinley periodically to warn him about the "unholy war that Democrats are making on the color line" and to ask for assistance. Democratic partisans knew about the visits to Washington and publicized them in the newspapers. One rumor circulated that North Carolina senator Jeter Pritchard had visited with the president and had requested that federal troops be dispatched to the state to ensure a fair election. Pritchard replied that he had not requested troops but had instead alerted the president to the situation in the state and had recommended to him that Governor Russell exhaust his resources before federal troops be sent. Another news item had it that Senator Pritchard had written to U.S. Attorney General John W. Griggs, asking for assistance in the form of troops—evoking the specter of Reconstruction. It was reported that the president's cabinet discussed the idea and decided that no troops would be sent unless Governor Russell requested them or mail delivery was disrupted. The editor of the Wilmington *Morning Star* pronounced that "Federal troops cannot legally be ordered to any State to preserve the peace until both civil and military powers of the State have been exhausted." President McKinley reportedly handed the matter over to his attorney general for consideration. In an interview, Griggs was quoted as saying that "if necessary to preserve order, troops will overrun the State."[35]

In addition to their political troubles, the state's leading Republicans and Populists faced threats to their personal safety. Populist senator Marion Butler was pelted with rotten eggs while giving speeches, and both Governor Russell and Butler were threatened with personal violence. More than most politicians, Russell was the target of Red Shirt hatred. As a result of his treatment, he resorted to using armed bodyguards to protect himself, even in the Governor's Mansion. A culminating event occurred while Russell was returning to Raleigh following a trip to Wilmington on election day to cast his ballot. In Hamlet and Maxton, Red Shirts halted the governor's train and boarded it. Russell's life was saved only because railroad officials were warned of the impending threat and helped move the governor into a baggage car at the rear of the train.[36]

George H. White (1852–1918) was a Republican congressman in 1898 who feared the ramifications for African Americans if Democrats won the election. Image from Photographs and Graphic Works, National Archives and Records Administration, College Park, Md.

Wilmington's Democrats Organize

In April 1898, Col. Thomas W. Strange was selected to serve as chairman of the New Hanover County Democratic campaign committee and worked closely with others in developing aspects of the white-supremacy campaign in the city.[37] Although Furnifold Simmons attempted to control his county committees tightly, Democrats in Wilmington turned the statewide campaign to their benefit and altered components of Simmons's scheme to fit their needs. As a result, Simmons sought to rein in Wilmington's leaders, for fear that they might make "some deal that they [the Democratic Party State Executive Committee] would not approve of." In response, local Democratic Party leader George Rountree informed Simmons that he might "go to H - - - , as we were going to run the campaign to suit ourselves down here."[38] Following the statewide pattern other organizations such as the WGU clubs and Red Shirts emerged in Wilmington. Clandestine groups likewise began to script plans to assist in a Democratic victory. The local Democratic Party, seeking to orchestrate a tightly woven white-supremacy, anti-Republican campaign, carefully monitored the activities of the various groups.[39]

Essential to the rhetoric of the white-supremacy campaign in Wilmington and New Hanover County was the statewide refrain of bad incumbent government. Local Democrats, seeking to link their Republican counterparts to the sinking ship of Fusion, refused to cooperate with Populists who sought to create a Democratic-Populist fusion. Rather, the Democrats identified and discredited the actions, businesses, and character of leading local Populists and Republicans. They targeted chiefly the "Big Four"— mayor and physician Silas P. Wright, northern politician George Z. French, business leader William H. Chadbourn, and northern businessman Flavel W. Foster. They accused those men of rallying black voters behind candidates in order to achieve political victory at any cost. Democrats raised the specter of "negro domination" to mean not only a black voting majority in the city or black officeholding, but also the capability of blacks to dictate the choice of candidates and platforms because of their voting strength.[40]

Local Democrats also targeted wealthy Wilmington businessman and Populist Benjamin F. Keith and a host of other Populists and Republicans, regardless of their race. Keith held fast to his principles throughout the 1898 campaign, refusing multiple attempts to threaten him into joining the Red Shirts. As the 1898 election drew near, Keith wrote his Populist compatriot Marion Butler to explain that "they have not killed or run me out of town yet although they hate me with all the hatred that corporation influence can aspire. I trust that things will turn out all ok." After threats failed to intimidate Keith, a mob forced its way into his yard at night, where Keith, his wife, and his eleven-year-old son, all well armed and ready to open fire, stood their ground. When physical intimidation failed, the Democrats and Red Shirts targeted Keith's business, forcing it into ruin by intimidating its customers and traveling agents alike.[41]

As the campaign progressed, the Democrats, both in their speechmaking and in printed campaign literature, expanded their list of special targets from four to six. The two men added to the list were Chief of Police John R. Melton and white attorney Caleb B. Lockey. Handbills and posters titled "Remember the Six" began circulating throughout the city, and the targeted men knew they were marked for death. One Wilmington observer remarked that the "Big Six" were to be shot because they worked "for the interest of the Republican Party."[42]

One of the Big Six, Republican William H. Chadbourn, was postmaster of Wilmington and a member of a wealthy family that operated Chadbourn Lumber Company and employed white and black workers in seasonal jobs. In response to the charge by Democrats that Wilmington suffered from "negro domination," Chadbourn, in a September 1898 letter to Republican senator Jeter Pritchard, denied the charge and observed that the Democrats' principal goal was to regain control of political offices in the city. The local press managed to obtain the letter, and such pro-Democratic newspapers as the *Wilmington Messenger*, the Wilmington *Morning Star*, and the

45

Raleigh *News and Observer* published it. Ensuing pressure from Democrats compelled Chadbourn to retract his statement and, in another letter, to declare himself "for white supremacy."[43] Following Chadbourn's change of heart, apparently rendering him "immune from the slaughter," the newspapers began referring to the "Big Five" instead of the "Big Six."[44] George Rountree and other Democrats thereupon turned their attention to Flavel Foster, one of the original "Big Four," and during an hours-long, late-night visit compelled him to sign a statement that allegedly discouraged the Republicans from competing in the coming election.[45]

The Democrats began intimidating other Wilmington Republicans and Populists as well. James S. Worth, a Wilmington Democrat and businessman, wrote his wife the week before the election to give her details on the city's affairs since she left town. Worth indicated that he had spoken to several different Fusionists in the city and reported on their replies. In a virtual laundry list of Democratic Party targets, written in language reflective of the larger campaign, Worth informed his wife that George Lutterloh, a white man, had changed his mind and had promised not to vote; that African American Junius Murray and "his whole gang" did not register; and that African American Jim Howe had promised not to vote, that his father and brother felt the same way, and that Howe claimed to be able to locate at least another 150 men "only too glad . . . not to vote." Worth went on to explain that George Z. French planned to go to Maine after voting, just as "Foster, Rice and the others were to leave on short notice." Worth concluded his thoughts on the campaign by declaring that "the small fry leaders such as Lockey and his gang were told that no 'monkeying' would be taken from such 'small potatoes' and that if he undertook to help the niggers or if he failed to support in every way Russell's pledge, that no second notice would be sent to him." Worth added that Lockey "came down at once like the cur that he is." At about the same time, Democrat A. J. Costin wrote Douglas Cronly that "all the gentlemen that you requested me to call on have signed the paper—Mr. Parsley,

declined to sign at first, but afterwards did so—making a promise."[46]

Increasingly throughout the campaign, speeches by Democratic politicians and articles in Democratic newspapers targeted and vilified white men perceived as leaders of the Republican Party. The recollections of James H. Cowan, editor of the Wilmington *Evening Dispatch*, reflect the criticism and hatred showered upon the men. Cowan claimed that the "lily white" leaders of the Republican Party were "scum and trash, remnants of the carpet bag regime . . . interested only in their own nefarious plans and objectives" and "used the negroes votes for their own purposes."[47] Republican leaders received numerous letters and circulars that displayed "crossbones" and notification that "if there was any trouble with the negroes," the leaders would be killed.[48] As the campaign drew to a close, statewide Republican and Populist leaders such as Governor Russell and Senator Butler scheduled a rally in Wilmington for October 29 but canceled it after Democrats warned them that if they came to speak there would be bloodshed. Republican congressional candidate Oliver Dockery went to the city anyway but did not speak because of the hostile climate.[49]

Although Furnifold Simmons appeared to have the state Democratic machine under his control, the party's leaders in Wilmington most likely worked independently of Simmons but still employed his tactics and connections to their benefit. According to Thomas Clawson, editor of the *Wilmington Messenger,* "for a period of six to twelve months prior to November 10, 1898, the white citizens of Wilmington prepared quietly but effectively for the day when action would be necessary."[50] How effective and well organized that allegedly independent movement was is debatable, since many of the overt actions attributed to the groups are reported in newspapers and accounts and reflect the overarching themes and characteristics of the statewide campaign. There is no doubt that leading white men in Wilmington, determined to win the election, worked together to lend a distinctive cast to the Democratic campaign in the city, but it must be remembered that various members of

These degenerate sons of the white race who control the republican machine in this county, or those whose positions made them influential in putting negro rule on the whites, will suffer the penalty of their responsibility for any disturbance consequent on the determination of the white men of this county to carry the election at any cost.

"Remember the 6" handbills were distributed during the 1898 campaign to emphasize how badly the incumbent Republican government operated, according to Democrats. Six men were targeted: mayor and physician Silas P. Wright, northern politician George Z. French, business leader William H. Chadbourn, northern businessman Flavel W. Foster, Chief of Police John Melton, and white attorney Caleb B. Lockey. Image courtesy of the North Carolina Collection.

47

those "secret" groups were also well-known and visible leaders of the county Democratic Party. In his history of the Wilmington Light Infantry and also in his *Story of the Wilmington Rebellion*, local chronicler Harry Hayden told of two shadowy groups of white leaders known as the "Secret Nine" and "Group Six" and their respective activities designed to return the city to Democratic Party control.[51] Hayden, relying upon the recollections of those who claimed to have participated in or observed the activities of the Secret Nine, further described the organization as a group of men who met first at the home of Hugh MacRae and then regularly at the home of Walter L. Parsley. The actual nine were Hardy L. Fennell, William Gilchrist, William A. Johnson, Edward S. Lathrop, Hugh MacRae, Pierre B. Manning, Walter L. Parsley, L. B. Sasser, and J. Allan Taylor. At their meetings, the men developed a citywide campaign that dovetailed with Furnifold Simmons's statewide white supremacy movement. In addition to their plans to provide special protection for the city's white women and children in the event of unrest, they understood

that they were also planning a "revolt" to overthrow city government.

Even as the Secret Nine planned their activities, "Group Six," a disparate group of men, met at the home of another prominent Wilmington leader, William L. Smith. The other members of Group Six were John Beery, Henry G. Fennell, Thomas D. Meares, William F. Robertson, and Col. Walker Taylor. The two organizations shared multiple business and family connections. For example, the Taylor and Fennell families had members in both organizations. Col. Walker Taylor was a member of the Democratic Party County Campaign Committee and leader of the state's regional State Guard unit. Moreover, both groups worked with Democratic Party leaders to fuel the campaign, particularly in organizing Wilmington's citizens into proactive units ready for whatever unrest might result from their plans. Once the campaign was in full swing, certain activities of the Secret Nine and Group Six apparently became merged with those of the official Democratic Party, the WGU clubs, and the Red Shirts.[52]

The county Democratic Committee made itself compatible with the WGU groups and the Red Shirts. Spokes of the Democratic wheel included the Wilmington Chamber of Commerce, churches, the Wilmington Light Infantry, the Wilmington Merchants Association, and a host of other civic and fraternal organizations.[53] Pulling these disparate organizations together was a handful of closely connected men who shared similar backgrounds, political desires, and social savvy and who were able to motivate others to write, speak, and ride. Wilmington's newspapers joined in the fight. Employing themes of black "insolence," ineffective city government, corrupt and unqualified police and judges, and dangers to the purity of white women and girls represented by black "brutes," the papers published and reprinted glaring examples of black misconduct.[54]

As the campaign progressed, Wilmington editors increasingly filled their columns with instances of violence directed by blacks against whites and ineffective responses to that violence by city government. Front-page coverage of national news and politics declined, and headlines such as "White Supremacy," "Russell's Deviltry," "Republican White Elephant," and "The Negroized East" became standard fare.[55] Although the papers had routinely reported criminal cases and arrests of blacks before the election campaign, those normally trivial topics gained importance in the pages of the *Wilmington Messenger*, the *Evening Dispatch*, and the *Morning Star*, providing printed fuel for the white supremacy firestorm. After reading the papers, many Wilmington residents were on edge and ready for the impending doom those journals heralded. Following the lead of Josephus Daniels in Raleigh, Wilmington papers invited correspondents from throughout the state and nation to visit their city. Whenever those reporters visited, they were treated as royalty, enjoying unfettered access to white leaders and their homes and participating in all aspects of the campaign—even being escorted through town in Red Shirt parades.[56]

Again, falling in line with Simmons's example, Wilmington Democrats brought a host of speakers to the city throughout the campaign. Those orators addressed large crowds at rallies and at spots such as Thalian Hall and also spoke to smaller groups as they stood outside Democratic Party headquarters, in the homes of prominent men, and at club meetings. Local Wilmington leaders joined out-of-town speechmakers in making their case for the Democratic cause. In October, for example, J. Allan Taylor of the Secret Nine read a prepared statement to the Wilmington Chamber of Commerce that was later published in the newspapers.[57] Attorney and Democratic Party leader George Rountree met with a chapter of the WGU and planned to "inflame the white men's sentiment." Rountree subsequently discovered, however, that his prepared speech was unnecessary because the men were "already willing to kill all of the office holders and all the negroes."[58] As evidenced by Rountree's experience, the speeches and the print campaign represented a valuable, effective tool to inflame the city's residents.

Alfred Moore Waddell

While not the most prolific of the speakers for Simmons's early campaign, Wilmington resident Alfred Moore Waddell proved the most incendiary of performers. Waddell, an aging member of Wilmington's upper class and a political conservative, had served in the U.S. House of Representatives from 1871 to 1879 and by the end of the 1898 campaign had worked himself into a position of prominence as a champion of oppressed whites in New Hanover and a symbol of redemption for the county's inflamed white voters.[59] Waddell emerged as the fieriest of speechmakers on behalf of white supremacy after an oration he delivered in Wilmington on October 24, 1898. Attending the speech was a wide array of Wilmington residents, including a large number of Red Shirts and the wives of leading businessmen. Waddell was situated on the stage alongside "sixty of Wilmington's most prominent citizens." Waddell opened calmly, explaining that if the election season were an ordinary one, he wouldn't be offering a speech, but, since he could no longer "remain silent as I have done for some years," felt compelled to speak. As was the case with many speeches of the period, Waddell's oration was published in the

Left: Alfred Moore Waddell (1834–1912) was a provocative speaker on behalf of the Democratic Party in the 1898 campaign. He fervently opposed "negro domination" and what he perceived as bad Fusion government. Image courtesy of the Cape Fear Museum.

Below: Excerpt from Waddell's October 24, 1898, speech at Thalian Hall. The address was printed in its entirety in the *Wilmington Messenger*, October 25, 1898.

We are the sons of the men who won the first victory of the Revolution at Moore's Creek Bridge . . . who stained with bleeding feet the snows of Valley Forge . . . and only left the service of their country when its independent sovereignty was secured. We are the brothers of men who wrote with their swords from Bethel to Bentonville the most heroic chapter in American annals and we ourselves are men who, inspired by these memories intend to preserve at the cost of our lives if necessary the heritage that is ours. We maintained it against overwhelming armies of men of our own race, shall we surrender it to a ragged rabble of negroes led by a handful of white cowards who at the first sound of conflict will seek to hide themselves from the righteous vengeance which they shall not escape? No! A thousand times no! Let them understand once and for all that we will have no more of the intolerable conditions under which we live. We are resolved to change them, if we have to choke the current of the Cape Fear with carcasses. The time for smooth words has gone by, the extremest limit of forbearance has been reached. Negro domination shall henceforth be only a shameful memory to us and an everlasting warning to those who shall ever again seek to revive it. To this declaration we are irrevocably committed and true men everywhere will hail it with a hearty Amen!

Thalian Hall hosted large crowds who heard various orators for the Democratic cause, including Alfred Waddell. This ca. 1903 image is courtesy of the New Hanover County Public Library.

newspapers.[60] Waddell's words clearly reflect a certain inflammatory mindset in regard to the campaign and race relations in general.

Waddell contended that it was "best and wisest for both races" that white people who worked to make the United States the "grandest country on the globe . . . should alone govern it as a whole in all its parts." He suggested that blacks had been misled by people who professed to be their friends and maintained that "the mass of them are ignorant and . . . have been played upon and preyed upon by vicious leaders of their own race and by mean white men who make this agitation a source of profit." Waddell continued to make racist assumptions and draw racist conclusions about African Americans: he claimed that if they were allowed to rule the South, "in less than a hundred years" they would return to "savagery"; and he asserted that "the greatest crime that has ever been perpetrated against modern civilization was the investment of the negro with the right of suffrage."[61]

Moving from his analysis of the black race, Waddell claimed that "the salvation of society depends on the outcome of this election." He then declared emphatically that the present situation was attributable to the actions of Governor Russell: "I do not hesitate to say thus publicly that if a race conflict occurs in North Carolina the very first men that ought to be held to account are the white leaders of the negroes who will be chiefly responsible for it and the work ought to begin at the top of the list. I scorn to leave any doubt as to whom I mean by this phrase—I mean the governor of this state, who is the engineer of all the deviltry and meanness." Waddell expressed the hope that violence was not to be the duty of white men but proclaimed that if violence were necessary, "I trust that it will be rigidly and fearlessly performed."

On the topic of "negro domination," Waddell contended that blacks constituted a voting block that could determine the outcome of elections. To that point, he asked the crowd, "who 'dominates' any corporation or businesses, its agents appointed to carry it on or the owners who select them?" Waddell concluded that his "heart leaps out to the man who, in this crisis, talks and acts" like an

This I do not believe for a moment that they will submit any longer it is time for the oft quoted shotgun to play a part, and an active one, in the elections. More especially if that infamous malignant blot upon the state our chief executive Russell gets his Yankee bayonets. I do most earnestly trust if it comes to blows that he will chamber the first ball fired in that mass of valvular tissue which does duty for a heart in the gubernatorial carcass. I never thought to be ashamed of the manhood of North Carolina but I am ashamed now. We applaud to the echo your determination that our old historic river should be choked with the bodies of our enemies, white and black, but what this state shall be redeemed. It has reached the point where blood letting is needed for the health of the commonwealth and when [it] commences <u>let it be thorough!</u>

Solomon says "there is a time to kill." That time seems to have come so get to work and don't stop short of a complete clearing of the decks. If you have to start make a finish once for all and then we will talk about calling a convention to alter the constitution sufficiently to disfranchise now and forever all the negroes white and black. You go forward to your work bloody tho' it may be, with the heart felt approval of many good women in the State. We say AMEN to it as did our great grandmothers in '76 and our mothers in '61.

Rebecca Cameron to Alfred Moore Waddell, October 26, 1898

SOURCE: Alfred Moore Waddell Papers, Southern Historical Collection.

51

"Anglo-Saxon who . . . feels that he is the sovereign and the master on the soil . . . and dares all who question it to put it to the test." The final point of Waddell's speech stirred patriotic sentiment in his audience and included lines destined to be cited frequently in subsequent days and years— that whites would "choke the current of the Cape Fear with [black] carcasses" in order to win the election. After the speech, Waddell received hearty applause, and the paper claimed that the speech "electrified his hearers," as it was "the most remarkable delivery ever heard in a campaign here in the memory of this generation." The writer's closing assertion that the speech "will ring for all time" proved prophetic.

As a result of Waddell's speech at Thalian Hall, his popularity as a powerful speaker able to move his audience remained high throughout the remainder of the campaign. He received requests to deliver speeches almost daily. At a large campaign rally in Goldsboro on October 28, Waddell thrust Wilmington into the spotlight as he detailed the "outrages" in the city since it had come under Fusion rule. His Goldsboro speech included another incarnation of his infamous observation that Democrats would win the election if they had to clog the Cape Fear River with "carcasses."[62] After Waddell's first October speech appeared in the newspapers, he received fulsome praise from his cousin Rebecca Cameron of Hillsborough. Cameron opened her letter by informing Waddell that women were "amazed, confounded, and bitterly ashamed of the acquiescence and quiescence of the men of North Carolina at the existing conditions; and more than once have we asked wonderingly: where are the white men and the shotguns!" She continued with a full letter supporting his speech, then concluded her diatribe by informing Waddell that the ladies "are aflame with anger here. I wish you could see Anna, she is fairly rampant and blood thirsty. These blond women are terrible when their fighting blood is up." She added as a last thought, "I hope it will not come to the last resort but when it does, let it be Winchesters and buckshot at close range."[63]

Waddell claimed that he did not seek prominence but was instead "begged to make a speech and did so, and that started the fire and from that time until now I have acted entirely upon the request of the people."[64] As part of the speechmaking campaign, Democratic Party leaders recruited Waddell in the late stages of the campaign; but after Waddell's speeches had intimated at violence, Democratic Party leaders decided that the "temper of the community was hot enough and needed quieting down rather than heating up."[65] As the campaign approached its conclusion, behind-the-scenes Democratic leaders apparently sought to temper other examples of Democratic campaign rhetoric, but many voters regarded well-received, highly motivational speakers such as Waddell as leaders of the party.

In Wilmington the combined impact of the print campaign and the inflammatory speeches moved beyond the standard "white men must rule" rhetoric, and another useful tool in the white supremacy arsenal—fear—emerged. Benjamin Keith observed that the papers had readers "believing everything that was printed, as well as news that was circulated and peddled on the streets." Keith saw that the "frenzied excitement went on until every one but those who were behind the plot, with a few exceptions, were led to believe that the negroes were going to rise up and kill all the whites."[66] A news correspondent explained that whites were fearful of an uprising because blacks had received "from their churches and from their lodges . . . reports of incendiary speeches, of impassioned appeals to the blacks to use the bullet that had no respect for color, and the kerosene and torch that would play havoc with the white man's cotton in bale and warehouse." The correspondent who made that observation further explained that the fear of a black uprising was an "ostensible ground for the general display of arms," and even if the blacks were acquiescent, the whites still would have armed themselves as a tool to demonstrate their determination to win the

52

election.[67] Much later in his life, editor Josephus Daniels acknowledged that he helped to fuel a "reign of terror" by printing sometimes unsubstantiated stories written so as to instill fear and anger in readers.[68]

Because many white men feared that they could not protect their families in the event of trouble, some white women left Wilmington before the election. By November 3, for instance, James S. Worth had sent his wife and children out of the city; and by November 5, Richard and Louis Meares had escorted their mother to South Carolina.[69] In her account of the riot, Wilmington resident Jane Cronly recorded that on the evening of the election, her family heard a rumor that the blacks, "disappointed in having been cheated out of the election, might set fire to somebody's property." She noted that "this fear was probably the outcome of anxiety on the part of those people, who having abused and maltreated the negroes were fearful of their just vengeance" and that the warning was false.[70] On the other hand, Mary Parsley of Wilmington wrote to her sister Sallie in New York and apologized for a disorganized letter because her "head is so full of the scary times I don't know what to do." In a later missive to Sallie, her mother described election day in Wilmington as one of "intense uneasiness . . . no one can realize the torture or suspense until experienced."[71]

Other residents of Wilmington were not so susceptible to the fear-inducing propaganda that accompanied the election contest. Mill employee Robert Mason wrote his cousin on election day that all was quiet and that the situation was exaggerated by the newspapers and "in the excited minds of some of the extremists." He expressed his hope that the "conservative elements will keep things down." In response to fears among his workers that a riot was imminent, Mason claimed that it was "idiotic" to close the mill since he thought that to do so would acknowledge a threat that he perceived did not exist.[72] That view, reflected by upper-class businessmen, held that the threat of violence was sufficient to prevent the occurrence of actual violence. Louis Meares, a member of that class, wrote that he had "great confidence in the ability of our people to suppress the indiscretion of a certain class of whites who are inclined to urge a conflict and so to smooth over the pending trouble."[73]

The White Government Union emerged as a primary outlet for the dissemination of information and the organization of the citizenry in Wilmington. Attorney William B. McKoy and other leaders organized WGU meetings throughout the city, and by mid-August Wilmington had a WGU in every ward, its members proudly displaying their large "White Government Union" campaign buttons. WGU meetings occurred at regular intervals, and the newspapers advertised meeting times and places for each ward and precinct. Most of the meetings took place in prominent locations such as the office of congressional candidate John D. Bellamy Jr., the office of attorney William B. McKoy, Democratic headquarters in the old National Bank Building, or the Seaboard Air Line Railroad building. Membership was open to anyone who desired "decent government," even women, who could participate in meetings but had no vote in union decisions. The night before the election, Wilmington's WGU, with all its individual clubs in attendance, met at the courthouse under the chairmanship of Democratic campaign committeeman Frank Stedman. Following speeches by Waddell and Bellamy, the group named more than 150 men to attend polls in their wards and precincts all day during the election, asked businesses that employed voters who planned to vote Democratic to close, and appointed an additional group of more than eighty men to represent the interests of Democratic candidates during ballot counting.[74]

The relationship between the WGU and the Red Shirt/Rough Rider phenomenon was much more evident in Wilmington than in other areas of North Carolina. Mike Dowling, admitted leader of Red Shirt/Rough Rider activity and member of a WGU chapter, declared that the organization sought to win the election "at all hazards and by any means necessary." Its methods included the use of intimidation—WGU club members would "announce on all occasions that they would succeed if they had to shoot every negro in the city." To facilitate their goal, all members were

Mike Dowling (ca. 1874–1916) served as captain of the Red Shirts, as a member of the WGU, and as chair of the White Laborers' Union. This ca. 1890 photograph is provided courtesy of Dowling's grandson, Michael Edward Dowling, of Wilmington.

armed and paraded the streets day and night. Dowling even reported that the county Democratic Party had provided the red shirts he and his men wore. Dowling, captain of the Rough Riders, plied his men with whiskey during parades to "fire them up, and make them fiercer and more terrorizing in their conduct." Even after Mayor Silas Wright ordered the closure of saloons, Dowling claimed that Democratic congressional candidate John D. Bellamy Jr. "distributed the whiskey from his office."[75]

With the increase in Red Shirt activity toward the end of the election campaign, the contest in Wilmington again mirrored the statewide campaign. According to several of Wilmington's Populists and Republicans, the Red Shirts provided a frightful, dangerous inducement to remain quiet and at home in the weeks prior to the election.[76] In Wilmington a large Red Shirt rally led by Chief Marshal Roger Moore and his aides took place on November 3; participants attired in their regalia marched or rode horses throughout town. The parade began downtown and, following a procession through traditionally black neighborhoods, most notably Brooklyn, ended at Hilton Park, where there were a number of speakers and a large picnic.[77] Although contemporary newspaper accounts pointed to the peaceful conduct of the rally, just one day later the Rough Riders got out of hand. "Condemned by all true and good citizens," the Rough Riders spilled into South Front Street and jeopardized all of the careful advanced planning carried out by the Democrats as they attacked "inoffensive persons" and "ran amuck" on the streets. The following day, November 5, one newspaper reprimanded the men and explained that "in their wild rowdyism, they represented nothing but themselves" and nearly "invited riot."[78] Chief of Police John Melton received a report from two black men who had been assaulted with a sword by the Rough Riders and Red Shirts. The men "showed marks of violence on their persons" from the attacks and were later confined at home, unable to swear out warrants against their attackers.[79]

As in the statewide Democratic campaign, participants in the Red Shirts were drawn from various levels of society. Nonetheless, the makeup of the Red Shirt/Rough Rider brigades in Wilmington is somewhat difficult to ascertain. As evidenced by their leader, Mike Dowling, some of the Red Shirts were either Irish immigrants or considered to be so.[80] Historian Sheila Smith McKoy observed that for some of Wilmington's Irish residents, "attaining whiteness—the process of replacing an ethnic identity for a racial identity—was integral to their participation in the white riot." Moreover, McKoy contended that "the Irish embraced white supremacy in order to make their whiteness visible" in a world in which the economic and social plight of poor whites was often invisible to the greater Democratic Party machine.[81] Other rhetoric tied the Red Shirts to Scottish roots. During a speech he delivered at a rally, lawyer William B. McKoy explained that the concept of the red shirt as a sign of battle originated in Scotland, where widowed Highlanders used their husbands' bloody shirts as banners to

demonstrate their plight to the king. Although McKoy's explanation of the use of the red shirt appears to be weak, it nevertheless found some appeal in an area of strong Scots heritage that placed emphasis on concepts of homeland, protection of women, and honor.[82]

Non-Democrats in Wilmington watched the activities of the Red Shirts with trepidation. W. J. Harris, a white "borned and bred Republican" appointed inspector of weights and measures by the Fusionists, observed that the "hatching of the Red Shirts" was effective since he "was right smartly intimidated" at election time. He explained that "Populists voted the white supremacy ticket through fear," even as he and others felt that the Democrats' talk of guns and force was a bluff. Harris considered the Red Shirts to be a gang and sometimes called them a "militia," with their strength centered in the poor white area of Dry Pond. Before the election, he witnessed their violence against blacks on Front Street after they had been drinking "fighting whiskey," and, as a result, he tried to stay out of the Red Shirts' path. But, Harris explained, because he had held political office and was seen as a minor leader within the Republican Party, "the night of the election they come and give me a salute of about thirty-six guns but I didn't let them know I was there." The following day, one of Harris's friends was surprised to see him alive, and the Red Shirts visited him again the next night. Harris overheard two Red Shirts complaining that northern reporters had left the city the day after the election because there had been no riot. Harris heard the Red Shirts say that the riot would occur the following day, attesting to the planned nature of the impending riot and coup. Harris concluded his explanation of the organization by saying that although the sheriff tried to arrest rowdy Red Shirts, they would be released on bail and back to their tricks within a day—"about as well to arrest the Cape Fear River as to do anything with that gang."[83]

During the 1898 campaign the Red Shirts succeeded in frightening many in the African American community. Black Wilmington resident Nada Cotton recalled that the "Red Shirt campaign was started to intimidate the negro and keep him from the polls." She remembered that the Red Shirts paraded in the streets and that "every able-bodied white was armed." An outside correspondent noted that a "great mass" of blacks were "in a state of terror amounting almost to distress." Wilmington resident Jane Cronly observed that despite "all the abuse which has been vented upon them for months they have gone quietly on and have been almost obsequiously polite as if to ward off the persecution they seemed involuntarily to have felt to be in the air." She continued: "in spite of all the goading and persecuting that has been done all summer the negroes have done nothing that could call vengeance on their heads." On the night of the election, Michael Cronly's block commander called him out in the "cold and damp for three hours" to defend the block against a threat of fire. Cronly remarked that they all acknowledged that it was "perfect farce . . . to be out there in the damp and cold, watching for poor cowed disarmed negroes frightened to death by the threats that had been made against them and too glad to huddle in their homes and keep quiet."[84]

Other Wilmington residents circulated a few unsubstantiated rumors that the blacks were organized in efforts to band together against the intimidation. On November 7 James Worth informed his wife, whom he had sent out of town before the election, that he "wouldn't be greatly surprised if there should be some kind of conflict with the blacks tonight." He explained that "the last two nights they were to avenge the 'red shirt' wrong of a few nights ago." He added that "it has not as yet amounted to much except a few brickbats thrown, flourishing of a few guns and pistols and lots of talk."[85] The Wilmington newspapers recounted almost daily incidents of black crime and characterized it as yet another means of retaliation against whites. Whether true or contrived by the papers, these accounts spread throughout the state and further united Wilmington whites in their resolve to deal forcefully with blacks.[86]

Democrats also used economic pressures against their targets. The city's leading businessmen contended that "the substitution of white for negro labor" would solve many of the city's problems. These men needed the political contest to be over so they could return to business. As previously mentioned, Wilmington's unsettled political situation appeared to be limiting the city's ability to attract outside capital and new enterprises, a condition city leaders viewed as "detrimental to every business interest."[87] At the beginning of October the chamber of commerce met and adopted resolutions requiring members to "exert . . . utmost influence and personal effort to effect results which will restore order" and protect property and lives. The Wilmington Merchants Association met on October 7 and developed a plan to establish a "permanent labor bureau for the purpose of procuring white labor for employers." The group agreed to meet weekly and promised that its mission to hire more white men would not falter after the election.[88] For their part, the city's white laborers pressured leaders to acknowledge their economic plight, and at the end of October about thirty-five laborers organized a "White Laborers' Union" to ensure that their needs would be addressed once the Democrats regained power. Members elected as chairman Red Shirt leader Mike Dowling and stated that their purpose in organizing the body was "replacing negro labor with white labor and with this object in view to co-operate with the Wilmington Labor Bureau recently organized as a result of the meeting of the business men and tax payers of Wilmington."[89]

Vigilance Committees and Paramilitary Organizations

Another component of the Wilmington campaign, apparently unique to the city, was the development of a "Vigilance Committee" under the umbrella of the militia-like organization led by Col. Roger Moore. The Vigilance Committee, whose creation is attributed to the Secret Nine, was also known as the "citizens' patrol"; it attempted to gain control over the Red Shirts and WGU chapters. By the time the election actually occurred, any lines that had previously separated the various organizations had virtually vanished. Some of the highest-ranking leaders of the Democratic Party in New Hanover County lost oversight and control of the Vigilance Committee because, as George Rountree admitted, they were "busy in other activities."[90] Even though Alfred Moore Waddell was a spokesman for the Democrats, his proclamation in late October that "we are going to protect our firesides and our loved ones or we will die in the attempt" found wide acceptance among members of the Vigilance Committee.[91]

In order to protect homes, women, and children, white leaders divided the city into five sections along ward lines. In typical military chain-of-command fashion, one man was chosen to serve as ward captain in each of the five wards. (Harry Hayden indicated that two members of the Secret Nine—Edward S. Lathrop and Pierre B. Manning—served as contacts to enable the ward captains to communicate with leaders of other organizations.) Moreover, each ward captain selected a lieutenant to command individual blocks. Lieutenants reported daily to the ward captain the number of armed men they represented and the numbers of women, children, and invalids that would need protection. The block captains then ordered their lieutenants to organize the men of each block for regular patrols. An outsider commented that the city "might have been preparing for a siege instead of an election" because men of all backgrounds had "brushed aside the great principles that divide parties and individuals and stood together as one man." One method of identification used by the citizens' patrol was a white handkerchief tied to the left arm.[92]

Democratic leader Thomas W. Strange said that the city was "like an armed camp" because of nightly street patrols.[93] A reporter for the *Richmond Times* visited Wilmington just before the election and attended a meeting at the home of "a leading citizen," who was involved in a conference with ward captains. The reporter explained that the men, some of whom were Confederate veterans, had "every detail arranged" and were not "hot-headed boys" but were instead "the most prominent men in the city who have resolved that there shall be no further negro rule." The reporter took pains to point out the differences between the organized businessmen and the rowdy Red Shirts, even as he recognized that the Red Shirts were the "outward and visible sign of the determination here to prevent the negroes from voting."[94]

A crucial figure in preparing Wilmington for the potential of violence on election day was Col. Roger Moore. Moore, a former Confederate cavalry officer, was a member of the city's aristocratic elite. His family, early settlers of the Cape Fear region, was politically and economically prominent across several generations. In 1868 Moore had organized the first Ku Klux Klan efforts in Wilmington. Because of his military background and participation in the Klan, Moore was selected at the age of sixty to command the citizen paramilitary units. Moore developed the organizational framework in which Wilmington whites found themselves on November 10, 1898—paramilitary patrols manned by armed, exhausted, tense men, unfamiliar with near-battle conditions, engaged in street fighting on a large scale.[95]

Because of his experience as a Confederate cavalry officer and his Ku Klux Klan participation, Roger Moore (1839–1900) was chosen to lead a militia-like organization in November 1898. Image from William Lord deRosset, *Pictorial and Historical New Hanover County and Wilmngton, North Carolina, 1723-1938* (Wilmington: The Author, 1938), [31].

An unidentified member of the Wilmington Light Infantry, which had been formed in 1853 and served as a volunteer militia group after the Civil War. Image courtesy of the Cape Fear Museum.

57

The Wilmington Light Infantry

The Wilmington Light Infantry (WLI) boasted a long history of militia service to North Carolina, having been formed in 1853. Members of the WLI fought in the Civil War after being mustered into service by the North Carolina General Assembly on May 10, 1861. After the Civil War, members returned to Wilmington and maintained the volunteer militia group as part of the State Guard, an active statewide militia force of nineteen armed companies created in North Carolina in 1877 and placed under the command of the adjutant general of North Carolina. In 1892, as veteran members of the WLI advanced in age, they organized a Veteran Corps and a Reserve Corps. The Veteran Corps was comprised of men who were members prior to April 15, 1861; the Reserve Corps was made up of members who had been active members in good standing for five years. The members of both organizations, leading by example, assisted those who served as active members of the WLI, "inspiring them with that 'esprit de corps' so essential to the welfare of a military organization."[96] The men of the Reserve Corps also provided behind-the-scenes management within the WLI, connecting it with other facets of the white-supremacy movement.

Members of the WLI came from throughout the city and represented a cross section of upper- and middle-class families. Sons of prominent white Wilmington businessmen served in the WLI as they worked themselves up through the ranks of Wilmington businesses as clerks, accountants, and bookkeepers. Candidates for membership were required to apply by letter, and their applications were then voted on by other members; five negative votes meant rejection. Once a member, the initiate was required to participate in drills and meetings. Prompt payment of dues and expenses related to membership was expected. Even more important, the corps required members to uphold strict guidelines for conduct and public appearances while in uniform.[97]

The leadership of the WLI took pains to separate the renowned infantry company from the citizens' patrol, even though Col. Walker Taylor, commander of the WLI, was a prominent member of the Democratic Party's county committee and clandestine organizations. (Other members of the WLI were also members of the WGU.) In the literature generated by participants and witnesses to the violence, a distinction is drawn between the WLI, the citizens' patrol, and the official state militia. Their accounts make it clear that they understood that the WLI and the state militia had a specific governmental role—that of keeping the peace—and that the citizens' patrols were extralegal operations. As part of its role as a component of the North Carolina State Guard, the WLI took special measures to safeguard the peace in the city. WLI member John V. B. Metts wrote on November 9 that the past week had been exceptionally busy. On the Saturday night before the election, his captain had instructed him to "order the company up," because there were reports of blacks forming mobs in the northern and southern sections of the city. The reports proved false but nonetheless demonstrate the WLI's readiness.[98] In addition, there were in the city furloughed members of Company K, Second Regiment North Carolina Volunteer Infantry, and the North Carolina Naval Militia—men still in federal service for the Spanish-American War effort.[99]

Amid heated rhetoric designed to instill fears of attempts by blacks to retaliate against white leaders, the men and women of Wilmington prepared for whatever violence might transpire—and all expected some sort of outbreak. A reporter commented that "the whites, or some of them, would welcome a little 'unpleasantness,' " since they were "prepared for it." The newsman provided a metaphor for the impending conflict as he declared that "it requires an electric storm to purify the atmosphere."[100] Many Wilmington whites were on edge; the city had been worked into a fever over repeated reports, true and contrived, of violence by blacks against whites.

Mrs. Edward Wootten, a Wilmington resident, wrote her son on November 8 that their block captain had told her husband that he should be ready on a moment's notice. She had her husband buy extra bread so that they would have something to eat if violence broke out. The "safe place" for her block was a nearby church, but she decided that if the Presbyterian church bell sounded the alarm, she would stay at her home because each block was guarded by groups of four to eight men at each corner. She lamented the fact that she had no gun, because they were all in the hands of her male family members, but did note that the "hatchets were handy." She prepared coffee for the men guarding her block and assured them that she would prepare more if "trouble came." She did not believe "the negroes will dare start so terrible a thing but if they are drinking they may do more than if sober and it would take a small match to set all on fire." Considering herself a strong woman, she felt "truly sorry for timid women and the little children." Her letter ended the next morning with a short statement from her husband: "All quiet—we lay by our arms all night for riot—all quiet."[101]

Adding to the fever pitch was an interest in weaponry. Wilmington's newspapers had editorialized several times during the election campaign that the city needed to purchase a rapid-fire gun for purposes of general protection, and various articles proclaimed that "guns were still coming to North Carolina" in advance of the election. Adding to the fear of riot the newspapers instilled in their readers, Wilmington's editors simultaneously reported that everyone in the city, black and white, was armed. The city's white businessmen acted, and "at the cost of $1,200" they "purchased, equipped, and manned a rapid-fire gun," asserting that "complete preparation would best assure protection."[102] Once the weapon arrived in the city, a newly recruited gun squad placed it aboard a vessel and on November 1, 1898, assembled a group of black community leaders to witness a demonstration of the weapon's capabilities.[103]

African Americans in Wilmington sought to arm themselves, given the atmosphere surrounding the 1898 campaign. An attempt to order rifles from the Winchester Repeating Arms Company was thwarted. This 1898 magazine advertisement boasts of "guns for all kinds of shooting." Image from Google Books.

Chief of Police Melton estimated that there were between 2,000 and 3,000 guns in the city by the election. Reports of accidental shootings were scattered throughout the papers. On the day of the election, two articles in the *Morning Star* reported that a white man accidentally shot a compatriot while "inspecting" a pistol on the street and that in the Brooklyn neighborhood a black man had wounded a white "guard" with an "old fashioned rifle or shotgun loaded with buck." The day before, the *Messenger* claimed that Norfolk merchants were shipping guns to North Carolina in record numbers over the past thirty days. The paper expressed the belief that "there will be no guns or pistols publicly displayed at the voting places . . . but the bushes will be full of them." A reporter visiting the city estimated that there were "enough small arms imported in[to] the state in the last sixty days to equip an entire division of the United States army." He noted that whites were armed with Winchesters and that blacks were equipped with "old army muskets, shotguns, or pistols."

Waddell's pre-election-night speech summed up the mood of the Democrats: "You are Anglo-Saxons. You are armed and prepared, and you will do your duty. Be ready at a moment's notice. Go to the polls tomorrow, and if you find the Negro out voting, tell him to leave the polls and if he refuses kill, shoot him down in his tracks. We shall win tomorrow if we have to do it with guns."[104]

In such an atmosphere, African Americans likewise sought to arm themselves, but whites soon identified such efforts. One such attempt was widely publicized in local and state papers. According to Democratic newspapers, African Americans William Lee and M. H. McAllister tried to order rifles from the Winchester Repeating Arms Company. The company referred the request to its North Carolina agent, Odell Hardware Company of Greensboro. Odell's manager, Charles H. Ireland, suspicious of the order, contacted Wilmington merchants William E. Worth and Nathaniel Jacobi. After learning that Lee and McAllister were black, Odell refused to fill the order and forwarded the request to the Raleigh *News and Observer*, which then investigated the matter. Editor Josephus Daniels discussed the issue with prominent Wilmington attorney and Democrat Iredell Meares, who said that William Lee was actually John William Lee, chairman of the New Hanover County Republican Executive Committee. Daniels thereupon published a story about the matter. Local Republicans denounced the story as published in the *News and Observer* and other papers, particularly since the county Republican chairman's full name was actually John *Wesley* Lee, and he claimed no knowledge of the order.[105]

Rumors circulated throughout the state that outsiders were attempting to help local African Americans defend themselves against heavily armed whites. One story receiving particular attention was that black congressman George H. White of Tarboro sought to employ his wife to purchase guns to arm blacks. In an article published the week before the election, the Wilmington *Evening Dispatch* declared that not only was a Wilmington black leader in Norfolk and Baltimore purchasing guns and ammunition but that other black leaders such as Congressman White were also assisting the effort. The paper quoted the *News and Observer*'s assertion that whites in Tarboro had discovered that the congressman's wife received an "express package containing rifles, name of shipper withheld." The paper concluded the article with a simple but chilling statement: "[W]hite people are ready and prepared for any emergency."[106] Such intimations that blacks were arming themselves motivated leading Wilmington white leaders to hire two detectives, one of each race, to determine the number of weapons stockpiled in the black community. The detectives informed the men that the blacks "were doing practically nothing." Additionally, the white men of Group Six hired two black Pinkerton agents to investigate.

Those detectives informed Col. Walker Taylor of Group Six that certain blacks were contemplating arson instead of arming themselves.[107]

After the election, many of the city's merchants were called to testify in a court case challenging the validity of John Bellamy's victory over Oliver Dockery in November. Attorneys in the case requested specifics on the number of guns sold in the days and weeks leading up to the election. Two merchants, Joseph Jacobi and William E. Springer, were evasive in their answers and provided little information as to the number of guns they sold. Three other merchants, however, provided a glimpse into the total sales of weapons in the city. Charles D. Foard testified that he sold 25 to 30 guns and pistols between November 1 and 10; Owen F. Love, a member of the Second Ward WGU chapter, declared that he did not believe the WGU would tolerate violence but nevertheless sold about 59 guns. J. W. Murchison reported sales of about 200 pistols, 40 to 50 shotguns, and 125 repeating rifles. Under cross-examination, Murchison revealed that his sales for 1898 were similar to those in other election years. Responses to the line of questioning suggest that gun sales increased in election years and that the merchants sold weapons only to white people.[108]

The election campaign of 1898 represented both the beginning of the end for the Republican Party and the promise of full control over state politics by 1900 for the Democrats. The use both of overt and clandestine violence and intimidation proved a successful model for the Democratic Party in its efforts to disassemble the fragile framework of cooperation that existed between white and black Republicans and Populists. In Wilmington, Democratic victory at the ballot box, whether honestly or fraudulently obtained, was a reality. Less clear was how the hysteria and fear produced by the campaign would dissipate.

Chapter 4

Eve of Destruction

The goal for Democrats was a complete sweep on election day, November 8, 1898. The party's strategy was to resort to intimidation and scare tactics to keep black Republicans away from the polls and white Fusionists at bay. Toward the end of the campaign, leading Republicans saw clearly that the game was lost and that they should seek to prevent outright bloodshed in the name of politics. The final days of the campaign were hectic, with politicians making last-minute deals and the press relishing the fracas.

A Unifying Issue

Discussion of the 1898 white-supremacy campaign could not be complete without examining the role of African American newspaper

Alexander Manly was the African American newspaper editor of the *Daily Record*. His August 18, 1898, editorial, in response to a white-supremacist article, led to racial unrest in Wilmington. Image from *The Literary Digest* 17 (December 3, 1898): 652.

editor Alexander Manly in the political circus. An editorial published in the *Daily Record*, Manly's Wilmington newspaper, provided another weapon in the Democrats' white-supremacy arsenal by challenging accepted beliefs in the realm of interracial relationships. Alexander Manly, born in 1866, a descendant of Gov. Charles Manly, and a native of Wake County, relocated to Wilmington after receiving an education at Hampton Institute. He was soon joined in business by several of his brothers, who assisted him in establishing the city's leading black newspaper, the *Record*. Manly acquired a used printing press from Thomas Clawson, editor of the *Wilmington Messenger*, and successfully operated the paper for a number of years prior to the 1898 campaign. In addition to his publishing operations, Manly became involved in city politics and social life, teaching Sunday school at the Chestnut Street Presbyterian Church and serving as deputy register of deeds. Manly's journal was considered "a very creditable colored paper" and received white support through subscriptions and advertising. Because the paper attained wide readership throughout the state, Manly in 1897 expanded its frequency of publication from weekly to daily. Although the white community helped to support the *Daily Record* through advertising, Manly employed his journal as a progressive voice for the improvement of conditions in Wilmington's African American community. The paper advocated internal improvements, and its editorials managed to raise the ire of some whites.[1]

The editorial that proved to be the undoing of the *Daily Record* appeared in August 1898 as a response to a speech by Rebecca L. Felton of Georgia.[2] Felton had developed a reputation in her home state as an outspoken advocate of lynching African American males accused of raping white women, and her speeches reflected her racist and stereotypical attitudes. Much analysis has been

Mrs. Felton Speaks

She Makes a Sensational Speech Before Agricultural Society

Believes Lynching Should Prevail as Long as Defenseless Woman is Not Better Protected.

[J. A. Holman, Special to *Atlanta Journal*]

South Bend Hotel, Tybee, GA., August 12 [1897] The feature of the session yesterday afternoon was the address by Mrs. W. H. Felton, of Bartow County, in which she discussed at length the public questions of interest in Georgia at this time, and dwelt with particular emphasis on the lynching problem. She reiterated her plea for co-education at the State University. Mrs. Felton spoke of the necessity for the better education of farmers' daughters as a protection from the assaulter, and declared that instead of so much money being expended for foreign missions it might be used to even better advantage in educating the heathen at home, even in Georgia.

I hear much of the millions sent abroad to Japan, China, India, Brazil and Mexico, but I feel that the heathen at home are so close at hand and need so much that I must make a strong effort to stop lynching, by keeping closer watch over the poor white girls on the secluded farms; and if these poor maidens are destroyed in a land that their fathers died to save from the invader's foot, I say the shame lies with the survivors who fail to be protectors for the children of their dead comrades.

I do not discount foreign missions. I simply say the heathens are destroyed in sight of your opulence and magnificence and when your temples of justice are put to shame by the lynchers' rope. If your courthouses are shams and frauds and the law's delay is the villain's bulwark, then I say let judgment begin at the house of God and redeem this country from the cloud of shame that rests upon it.

When there is not enough religion in the pulpit to organize a crusade against sin; nor justice in the courthouse to promptly punish crime; nor manhood enough in the nation to put a sheltering arm about innocence and virtue — if it needs lynching to protect woman's dearest possession from the ravening human beasts — then I say lynch; a thousand times a week if necessary.

The poor girl would choose any death in preference to such ignominy and outrage, and a quick death is mercy to the rapist compared to the suffering of innocence and modesty in a land of bibles and churches, where violence is becoming omnipotent except with the rich and powerful before the law.

The crying need of women on the farms is security in their lives and in their homes. Strong, able-bodied men have told me they stopped farming and moved to town because their women folks were scared to death if left alone.

I say it is a disgrace in a free country when such things are a public reproach and the best part of God's creation are trembling and crying for protection in their own homes. And I say, with due respect to all who listen to me, that so long as your politics takes the colored man into your embraces on election day to control the vote; and so long as the politicians use liquor to befuddle his understanding and make him think he is a man and brother when they propose to defeat the opposition by honey-snuggling him at the polls, and so long as he is made familiar with their dirty tricks in politics, so long will lynchings prevail, because the causes of it grow and increase.

[Mrs. Felton is one of the most distinguished women of Georgia, intellectually and socially. She is the wife of Dr. W. H. Felton, a former Representative in Congress, and takes a prominent part in everything pertaining to the advancement and protection of her sex. Editor *Star*]

Reprinted in the *Morning Star* (Wilmington), August 18, 26, 1898.

Alex Manly's Editorial

A Mrs. Felton from Georgia, made a speech before the Agricultural Society at Tybee Ga, in which she advocates lynching as an extreme measure. This woman makes a strong plea for womanhood and if the alleged crimes of rape were half so frequent as is oft times reported, her plea would be worthy of consideration.

Mrs. Felton like many other so-called Christians loses sight of the basic principle of the religion of Christ in her plea for one class of religion as against another. If a missionary spirit is essential for the uplifting of the poor white girls, why is it? The morals of the poor white people are on a par with their colored neighbors of like conditions and if one doubts the statement let him visit among them. The whole lump needs to be leavened by those who profess so much religion and showing them that the preservation of virtue is an essential for the life of any people.

Mrs. Felton begins well for she admits that education will better protect the girls on the farm from the assaulter. This we admit and it should not be confined to the white any more than to the colored girls. The papers are filled often with reports of rapes of white women, and the subsequent lynching of the alleged rapist. The editors pour forth volumes of aspersions against all Negroes because of the few who may be guilty. If the papers and speakers of the other race would condemn the commission of crime because it is crime and not try to make it appear that the Negroes were the only criminals, they would find their strongest allies in the intelligent Negroes themselves; and together the whites and blacks would root the evil out of both races.

We suggest that the whites guard their women more closely, as Mrs. Felton says, thus giving no opportunity for the human fiend be he white or black. You leave your goods out of doors and then complain because they are taken away. Poor white men are careless in the matter of protecting their women, especially on the farms. They are careless of their conduct toward them, and our experience among poor white people in the country teaches us that the women of that race are not any more particular in the matter of clandestine meetings with colored men than are the white men with colored women. Meetings of this kind go on for some time until the womans infatuation or the mans boldness bring attention to them and the man is lynched for rape. Every Negro lynched is called a "big, burly, black brute," when in fact many of those who have thus been dealt with had white men for their fathers, and were not only not "black" and "burly" but were sufficiently attractive for white girls of culture and refinement to fall in love with them as is very well known to all.

Mrs. Felton must begin at the fountain head if she wishes to purify the stream.

Teach your men purity. Let virtue be something more than an excuse for them to intimidate and torture a helpless people. Tell your men that it is no worse for a black man to be intimate with a white woman, than for a white man to be intimate with a colored woman.

You set yourselves down as a lot of carping hypocrites in that you cry aloud for the virtue of your women while you seek to destroy the morality of ours.

Don't think ever that your women will remain pure while you are debauching ours. You sow the seed—the harvest will come in due time.

Daily Record (Wilmington), August 18, 1898

done on Felton's arguments in support of lynching, but her core beliefs about interracial relationships were the basis for her argument. Felton rejected mulattoes and the relationships that generated mixed-race children as base and degenerate and reprimanded whites who countenanced black-white unions. Her proposed method of dealing with white women who participated in biracial relationships was to exterminate black men who attracted those women and to humiliate white women who dallied with black men. Her reprimands developed over time into a diatribe that advocated violence against all black men. The specific speech of Felton's that generated reaction in Manly's paper cautioned white men to better protect and oversee white women on isolated farms so as to prevent them from being harmed by interaction with black men; Felton had delivered it more than a year earlier.[3]

Manly's editorial response agreed with Felton on many points but diverged by declaring that white women of poorer classes "are not any more particular in the matter of clandestine meetings with colored men than the white men with colored women." Manly pursued Felton's argument further, and his own well-known mulatto genealogy made his words even more pointed: "[E]very Negro lynched is called a 'big, burly, black brute' when in fact many of those who have thus been dealt with had white men for their fathers, and were not only not 'black' and 'burly' but were sufficiently attractive for white girls of culture and refinement to fall in love with them as is very well known to all." Manly ended his editorial by appealing to whites to "teach your men purity" because he saw that it was "no worse for a black man to be intimate with a white woman, than for a white man to be intimate with a colored woman."[4]

Manly's editorial appeared on August 18, but it was not until weeks later that Democratic Party officials began to make political hay out of its content. Col. Walker Taylor later recalled for members of the Wilmington Light Infantry that "when that article appeared, it required the best efforts we could put forth" to prevent whites from lynching Manly. Taylor went on to explain that white leaders did not immediately make an issue of

the article, thus keeping white anger in check. The *Morning Star*, for example, asked its readers to "be brave, but be prudent" because "self-control is one of the highest attributes of courageous manhood." "[Furnifold] Simmons, who was here at the time," Taylor recalled, "told us that the article would make it an easy victory for us" in November. Simmons also urged Wilmington's Democratic Party leaders to "try and prevent any riot until after the election."[5]

Although Democrats sought to limit any response to the article, there was an immediate reaction among both the black and white reading public. Rumors circulated that Manly would be lynched, and it was reported that he had received written threats to leave Wilmington. In response, groups of black men armed themselves to protect him and the *Daily Record* office at its downtown location at the corner of Water and Princess streets. Wilmington police were able to disperse the crowd, but a few officers remained on guard duty for the night. Wilmington's ministerial union and other black organizations defended Manly's right to publish on behalf of his race.[6] Moreover, toward the end of the campaign, Wilmington's African American women, through an article in the *Daily Record*, explained that they supported Manly because his was the "one medium that has stood up for our rights when others have forsaken us." In an opposite reaction to Manly's editorial, white advertisers pulled their ads from the paper, greatly curtailing its income. Further, the owner of the building in which the *Daily Record* press office was located informed Manly that he had to vacate the building. Within days of the disturbance at the *Daily Record*'s downtown office, Manly moved his press to Love and Charity Hall (also known as Ruth Hall or Free Love Hall) on South Seventh Street, prompting Wilmington's ministerial union to encourage pastors to "endeavor to sustain the paper by swelling its subscription list."[7]

Although Manly's editorial received early support from segments of the black community, other African Americans, who understood the awkward position in which it had placed them, criticized it. It was clear to those blacks that to support Manly would lead to certain trouble with Democrats. The Republican Executive Committee,

64

This masthead for the *Daily Record* is dated August 18, 1898, the day Manly's editorial appeared. Only a few issues of the paper are extant. Image courtesy of the North Carolina Collection.

which included twelve black leaders, met at the end of August, criticized the article, and refuted Democratic Party claims that Manly or the *Daily Record* represented the Republican Party. Black leaders from as far away as Raleigh condemned the article, while others remained silent on the issue. Local Fusionists such as Populist Benjamin Keith likewise discounted the article, claiming that it was "the product of a gross slanderer who is no better than a brute." In light of increasing animosity toward Manly, John Wesley Yarborough, a black leader in Wilmington, cautioned that support of Manly might reduce donations by whites to black churches.[8]

Wilmington newspapers picked up the editorial and ran portions of it as an example of a "Horrid Slander" against the virtuous white women of Wilmington and North Carolina. The papers reprinted similar comments about the article on a daily basis, and each issue featured multiple references to the "vile" and "villainous" editor of the *Daily Record*. The Raleigh *News and Observer*, North Carolina's leading Democratic paper, adding to the firestorm, reprinted the article and accompanied it with anti-Manly editorials and cartoons. Because Manly's editorial pointed more to rural women than to those in cities, North Carolina Democrats saw in it an opportunity to draw into the campaign rural men who would otherwise be indifferent to political events unfolding in a city. As a result of so much attention being paid to the article and to race relations in general, reporters from throughout the nation flocked to Wilmington to report on the controversy.[9]

Democrats made effective use of the article, with its implications of miscegenation and threats to white men's control over white women, black women, and black men. Because the editorial became such an easily identifiable touchstone for the campaign, many cited it as justification for the violence that followed the election. Other Democrats joined in attacks on Manly. Near the end of October, Senator Ben Tillman of South Carolina, who had helped to organize Red Shirt activities, spoke at a rally in Fayetteville. "Why didn't you kill that nigger editor who wrote that?" Tillman asked. "Send him to South Carolina and let him publish any such offensive stuff, and he would be killed." At a rally in Charlotte just before the election, Tillman continued his rant: "In South Carolina no negro editor could slander the white women of the State as that Wilmington negro did. That negro ought now to be food for catfish in the bottom of the Cape Fear River instead of going around above ground."[10]

Response by Wilmington's Non-Democrats and African Americans

The Democratic Party thoroughly intimidated white residents of Wilmington who were not openly supportive. Gov. Daniel L. Russell and leading Fusionist politicians were in fear for their lives, and rank-and-file Fusionists gave in to pressure to rejoin the Democratic Party. Although local Democratic newspapers took satisfaction in successfully disarming Fusionists, they did not relent in their attacks and continued to print inflammatory articles.

With its every move monitored in the papers, the Wilmington Board of Aldermen attempted to meet and carry on its business in the best interest of the city. The board voted to close bars and saloons on the days surrounding the November 8 election—from midday Saturday, November 5, until early morning on Thursday, November 10. Board members hoped that men of all races would be less hotheaded if they were deprived of alcohol and a public place to consume it. The board also authorized the hiring of an additional one hundred special policemen for election day. The board acted to close bars because many accounts of pre-election violence included explanations that the participants were drunk when tempers flared. For example, on October 12, following a White Government Union (WGU) meeting, an armed group of white men adjourned to a bar. Freshly renewed with white-supremacy rhetoric and alcohol, they left a saloon at Sixth and Castle streets and encountered a group of blacks. A fight broke out between two men and escalated to a point at which the white men began firing into the crowd of black men, who quickly retreated.[11]

Members of Wilmington's African American community watched the growing hostility toward their race with trepidation while continuing to make a place for themselves in the city. In September some of the city's black leaders attempted to preempt the campaign when they requested that Sheriff George Z. French dismiss four of his black deputies as "incompetent." Instead of removing fodder for the Democratic press, these men provided yet another headline, in which their request was labeled a "Political Dodge" that "will not deceive Democrats." One Wilmington newspaper claimed that the request was more a ploy dictated by Russell than a measure motivated by the city's African American leaders. The paper declared that the requested dismissals demonstrated Republican "weakness" that would "only serve to make the Democrats more aggressive in their fight for freedom."[12]

Some of Wilmington's blacks unintentionally aided the Democratic Party press. The prime example was Manly, but others, such as Carter Peamon and Frank Thompson, reacting to Democratic prodding, provided fodder for the Democratic press as it preached the dangers of "negro domination." During pre-election voter registration in October, Republican leader Carter Peamon, resisting threats, registered to vote in the

White voter registration officials tried to intimidate Willis Stevens (Drake) out of registering. He had been a candidate for mayor and was supposedly insane. To play up fears of Negro rule and potential violence, this card was probably used as propaganda. The photograph was more than likely staged, since his hat says "Mayor" and the gun still has a price tag on it. Image courtesy of the Bonitz Collection, Southern Historical Collection.

First Ward. In response to Peamon's action, a white man named S. Hill Terry at some point confronted Peamon, who, as he seized a knife from Terry's hands, said that he would like to "slap the jaws of every white man."[13]

In another incident, Frank Thompson was arrested and accused of being the leader of efforts to "incite a riot" in Brooklyn on the Saturday before the election. Thompson, an employee of the Champion Cotton Compress, and other blacks were gathered on the street in Brooklyn near the intersection of Fourth and Nixon streets around eleven o'clock at night on the Saturday before the election. A Red Shirt who lived in the neighborhood stepped off the streetcar at the intersection and was immediately confronted by the black men who, according to the paper, moved toward the white man "as though to make an attack." As the Red Shirt unwrapped his concealed Winchester, the black men pelted him with rocks, and Thompson apparently brandished pistols. Some of the rocks hit the streetcar behind the man. It was reported that the black men declared "they would stop the cars from running." The police arrested Thompson and, joined by "influential" and "peaceful" African Americans, dispersed the crowd. Later that night, according to an article in a local newspaper, "prominent citizens" investigated the incident and found that blacks had "boasted that their children all had matches and bottles of kerosene, knew how to use them and would run some women out of their homes before morning." True or not, the article served as another Democratic tool to intensify fear and anger in Wilmington. Other local papers confused the specifics of the event, such as the number of black men at the intersection, what Thompson actually did, and the chronology of the activity that night. Despite the many questions surrounding Thompson's true actions, he was charged with assault with a deadly weapon against the streetcar conductor. Another Wilmington newspaper commented that it looked as if "citizens of Brooklyn would need their new Winchesters."[14]

Since emancipation, African Americans had harbored a strong desire to vote; however, during the white-supremacy campaign, exercising the right of suffrage had become dangerous. An African American newspaper in Kinston reportedly encouraged every black voter to go to the polls on election day and "stick to the Republican Party because it had freed him."[15] A white woman in Wilmington echoed that sentiment when she suggested that the average black held "a most exalted opinion of the value of his vote" because he "imagines the whole constitution will fall to pieces if his vote fails it." Despite threats that they would be fired if they registered to vote, blacks called the Democrats' bluff and registered to vote in the November elections. Many found themselves discharged from their jobs for exercising their right of suffrage.[16]

Robert Mason, a manager for the North Carolina Cotton Oil Company, noted that several of his black employees had voted but that most did not. He said, "[A] great many people have made a mistake in discharging old and faithful servants because I think sooner or later they will have to take them back, although, of course, such an idea is hooted at now." Mason believed that blacks were the "least troublesome labor we can handle" and observed that "their natural disposition when unmolested by mean white people is to know their places and keep in them."[17] Chief of Police John R. Melton later testified that Wilmington's blacks were "scared" and that a "great many" of them came to him to tell him they were not going to register or vote because "they thought more of their lives than they did of their votes or politics." Despite intimidation and promises of blacks not to vote, Democrats were still wary, because after the final registration tallies were in, 2,965 blacks and 2,918 whites had registered to vote.[18]

African American women likewise took part in the political process. In late October an article from "an organization of colored ladies" appeared in Manly's *Daily Record*. The article urged black men to register and vote in the election despite white threats of being fired for voting. As could be predicted, Democrats pointed to the activism of black women as yet another area in which white men had lost control under Fusion.[19] After reprinting the article, the *Messenger* reprimanded the women with these words: "[T]he colored women of this country should be most interested in . . . the education and moral uplifting of their race and less politics."[20]

Final Maneuvers

Amid armed threats and heated rhetoric, the Republicans and Populists tried to find ways to assuage Democrats. At the center of such efforts was Gov. Daniel Russell, and both Republicans and Democrats looked to him to alleviate tensions in the city. Late in October, Wilmington Democrats acknowledged that the city's Republicans would likely win any contest in which they were allowed to put African American candidates on the ballot. Therefore, the Democrats moved to

Whereas, since it has become apparent that there is a disposition to intimidate the voting element of our race by discharging them from various places of employment in the event that they register to vote, and whereas it has come to the notice of us, the colored ladies—the laboring class—that certain of our men have refused to register because of the intimidation mentioned above, we have therefore resolved that every negro who refuses to register his name next Saturday that he may vote, we shall make it our business to deal with him in a way that will not be pleasant. He shall be branded a white livered coward who would sell his liberty and the liberty of our whole race to the demons who are even now seeking to take away the most sacred rights vouchsafed to any people. We are further resolved that we teach our daughters to recognize only those young men who have the courage and manhood to stand up for the liberty which under God he now has, be he ever so poor. We are farther resolved to lend our assistance in every way to perpetuate the liberties which we now enjoy, regardless of the insults and threats thrown out at us by those who seek to crush us. We have resolved to teach our children to love the party of manhood's rights and liberties, trusting in God to restore order out of the present confusion. Be is resolved further that we have these resolutions published in our Daily Record, the one medium that has stood up for our rights when others have forsaken us. Respectfully submitted, An Organization of Colored Ladies.

Wilmington Messenger, October 21, 1898

68

prevent the Republicans from mounting a slate. After capitulating to the Democrats in October, prominent Republicans William H. Chadbourn and Flavel Foster urged members of their party not to put forth a ticket in the race for county offices, which would effectively enable the Democrats to gain control of county government through election.[21]

Still, local Democratic Party leader George Rountree claimed that the Republicans, under the leadership of George Z. French, planned to place nominees on the ballot despite threats of violence. Believing that intervention by Governor Russell would alleviate the problem, he encouraged merchants E. K. Bryan, James Sprunt, and James H. Chadbourn Jr. to visit Russell at the Executive Mansion in Raleigh. Sprunt, as representative of the businessmen, wrote to Russell on October 24 and explained that things were out of control in

the city and entreated Russell to do what he could to prevent violence.[22] Russell, who before meeting with Bryant, Sprunt, and Chadbourn had attempted to promote white businessmen as Republican candidates, came to a compromise with Sprunt: the Democrats removed some of their candidates and replaced them with others less offensive to the Republican Party, and the Republicans removed from the contest their entire slate of candidates.[23] Russell then summoned George French to Raleigh to explain the compromise.[24] French returned to Wilmington just before the October 29 Republican convention, at which county Republicans reluctantly complied.[25] The last African American candidate, incumbent register of deeds Charles Norwood, announced on November 3 that he would not run for reelection. Norwood stated in the paper that because "it was evident to him that a race war was being stirred up," he wanted to "take no part in any such proceedings" and "thought it advisable to withdraw."[26]

The compromise was tenuous at best, and Wilmington Republicans were unhappy with Democratic Party machinations.[27] Flavel Foster, already quieted by a visit from the Democrats earlier in the month, wrote Sprunt that he was sorry to see that the businessmen did not select legislative candidates favorable to the Republicans but instead "practically turned it over to the political machine[,] which [he believed had] a majority in [Sprunt's] joint committee" (i.e., the Democratic Party Campaign Committee and the Merchants Association). Foster declared that he was "the first and strongest advocate of . . . putting out no ticket in consideration of the business interest of the city, and the elimination of any possible race conflict," and "in consideration of the Governor's generous proposition I trust that you, as the representative of the businessmen will see that no one is nominated who is as politically offensive to the Governor as the regular nominees were." Foster concluded, "[T]his is only a reasonable request in consideration of what we are giving up."[28]

Reinforcing the tensions, the Democrats did not completely comply with the compromise, and additional discussion between Russell and Sprunt focused on the militant nature of the city's armed whites. In a telegram to Sprunt four days before the election, Russell declared: "Am astonished to hear that merchants refuse to aid in preserving order if appeal is made to Republicans to vote. . . . You know the agreement. I appeal to you and all conservative men to enforce it." Sprunt, ignoring the increasing numbers of guns on the streets, replied that he "conferred with several leaders and businessmen and so far as we are aware there has been no agreement understanding or effort looking towards the use of any force or other disorderly methods of obstructing voters." Sprunt closed the telegram with a promise to call his committee and send further communication the following day. The next morning Sprunt wired Russell again that the "Merchants and Campaign Committee will carry out agreement in good faith"—although he also indicated that other groups beyond his control were operating in the city.[29]

At the end of October, Governor Russell issued a proclamation in response to the heightened sense of militancy. The proclamation acknowledged "lawlessness in certain counties in this state" and declared that those counties "have been actually invaded by certain armed and lawless men from another state" and that "citizens have been taken from their homes at night and whipped." Moreover, Russell declared that he knew that "in several counties peaceful citizens have been intimidated and terrorized by threats of violence to their persons and their property, until they are afraid to register themselves preparatory to exercising that highest duty of freemen—the casting of one free vote at a ballot box for men of their own choice." Russell cautioned "ill disposed persons" to "immediately desist from all unlawful

James Sprunt (1846–1924) was a well-respected merchant in Wilmington who led a joint committee of the Democratic Party Campaign Committee and the Merchants Association in formulating a compromise regarding the slate of candidates. He was a moderate Democrat trying to avoid conflict between the races. Image from deRosset, *Pictorial and Historical New Hanover County and Wilmington*, [7].

practices and all turbulent conduct," even as he counseled "good and law abiding citizens not to allow themselves to become excited by any appeals that may be made to their passions and prejudices . . . but to keep cool heads." He commanded judges and officers of the law to bring offenders to trial and to protect the civil rights of all citizens. Finally, Russell advised that troublemakers from outside the state should leave "upon pain of being arrested and dealt with according to law."[30]

In response to Russell's fears of violence and as a follow-up to correspondence between Russell and New Hanover County's Democratic Party leaders, Rev. Peyton H. Hoge of the First Presbyterian Church penned a letter to the governor on November 5. Hoge reassured Russell that he had been in contact with "several prominent members of the campaign committee and [had] positive assurances from them" that the election would proceed peacefully. He further explained that "if negroes . . . go to the polls and cast their ballots quietly and go home; I have no idea that there will be any disturbance." Hoge provided a bit of insight into the mindset of the white leaders when he assured Russell that "members of our committee feel that their honor is involved in seeing that this agreement is carried out in good faith."[31]

Election Day

The night before the election, both sides readied for what all thought would be a day of violence. The WGU held a joint meeting at the courthouse, where "red hot speeches were made" and it was "clearly evident that white men [would] have the victory, cost what it may."[32] The same day, African American ministers called upon the community to observe a day of fasting and prayer as a means of demonstrating their dedication to preserving the peace.[33] Other, more militant, African Americans met at Ruth Hall; and although their discussions have not been documented, Democratic Party papers claimed that two of the speakers present encouraged listeners to "go to the polls tomorrow and raise h—l."[34] The white leadership, vested in the Secret Nine, apparently became alarmed at this point because the threat of violence was very real and jeopardized plans by the

group to control the overthrow of municipal government after the election as well as the validity of the election itself.[35]

Election day dawned "bright and clear" on November 8, 1898, as a tense city and state prepared to vote.[36] Across North Carolina, voters took to the polls in record numbers with few incidents of violence reported. In Wilmington, white men were armed and prepared for the day with patrols posted on every block. The polls opened at seven o'clock in the morning and closed at sundown, and reports had it that nearly all of the "white votes" had been cast by three o'clock.[37]

Although election day appeared to pass as a normal voting day, residents of Wilmington knew all too well that it was unlike any other the city had experienced. Roving bands of armed men intimidated blacks and Republicans, while others escorted less-energetic Democrats to the polls to cast ballots under the watchful scrutiny of members of the WGU. The day before the election, the WGU posted its members at polls all day to ensure Democratic Party victory. It instructed the men to "never look a [white] voter square in the face, even if they knew that John Smith was voting as Willie James and the latter was dead and buried in Oakdale cemetery for lo many years."[38] As the end of the voting day drew near, men who planned to watch and, if necessary, obstruct the counting of ballots took the place of men who had observed the actual voting. Red Shirt/Rough Rider leader and election officer Mike Dowling explained that a great deal of planning went into disrupting the count. Dowling and others had been taught "how to deposit Republican ballots so they could be replaced."[39] Leaders of the Democratic Party and the Secret Nine, on the other hand, sought to avoid trouble at the polls and during the counting so that the courts could not rule the election invalid.[40] Most of the ballot counting took place without trouble, but in some of the precincts there was difficulty.

Governor Russell's visit to Wilmington to cast his vote generated still more commotion. Russell voted in the city despite threats made against him. To ensure his safety while in town, two prominent Democrats—Col. Walker Taylor and E. W. Sawyer (both related to Russell)—accompanied him.

As mentioned in the previous chapter, during Russell's return trip to Raleigh, Red Shirts twice stopped his train and boarded it; Russell, reduced to hiding out in the train's baggage car, emerged unscathed. While Russell was enduring that humiliation, Red Shirts in Raleigh shouted taunts at his family in the governor's mansion.[41]

Many of Wilmington's armed residents were prepared for retaliation from blacks that never came. On election day the city mobilized, and leaders of the Wilmington Light Infantry ordered the unit to the armory and posted it there until early morning on the ninth to await a possible call-up. During the unit's time at the armory, a group of Wilmington's ladies provided the men with plenty of food. On the night of the election, members of the WLI heard gunshots all night long, and John V. B. Metts, a member of the unit, concluded that if there had been any unrest, it had been "settled without us." Metts was exhausted, having been "kept on the go from the time I reached the armory yesterday [November 8] at three o'clock until this morning at five when I laid on the floor, with an overcoat for a pillow and then I was called each time I'd get asleep."[42]

An incident that occurred in the Fifth Division of Wilmington's predominantly African American First Ward during ballot counting sheds light on the election day tensions.[43] African American drayman Albert Lamb had been a resident of Wilmington for about nine years and was the election judge at a store that served as the division precinct. Likewise working at that precinct—as registrar—was African American carpenter Abram Fulton, a resident of the city for twenty-five years. Both Fulton and Lamb later testified that although the day passed without incident, as they began to count ballots a crowd of between 150 and 200 white men either entered the building or were stationed outside. Lamb explained that the precinct was predominantly Republican, that the men who were at the precinct were "strangers," and that none of the men gathered there were registered to vote at that polling place. Soon after the crowd of whites arrived, a minor scuffle ensued, someone knocked lamps off the tables, and the room went dark. Fulton tried to make his way to

the back of the store to find a way out, and as soon as the lights were relit, Lamb left the precinct before the ballots were fully counted. Fulton could not find a way out and resumed counting ballots once candles were lit. After counting the ballots, Fulton departed as soon as he could, but he did not sign the election returns that night. Lamb explained that he left because he was "scared" and "did not know what would happen." Fulton fully believed that his life was in "imminent danger" when the crowd rushed in to extinguish the lamps. Fulton further testified that only about 20 to 30 whites were registered to vote in the precinct, whereas about 300 Republicans were registered, making it the "strongest Republican precinct" in the city; he knew of no black Democrats residing in the precinct.[44]

Other precinct workers—white grocer Joe Benton and white dairyman George Bates—were on hand at Lamb's precinct during the ballot counting and supported the testimony of Fulton and Lamb.[45] Benton, who had served as judge of the election, later testified that scattered among the crowd were "between nine and twelve policemen" who did not attempt to "prevent the disturbance." Benton also revealed that the room in which the counting took place was small, measuring approximately 16 by 20 feet.[46] Bates, like Fulton a registrar, claimed that the crowd was orderly while the counting was taking place but that when the poll workers came across a set of ballots in the wrong box, members of the crowd objected to the counting method. Bates later testified that while the registrars were still counting the contested box for the election of W. J. Davis, the lamps were extinguished. Once the lamps were relit, Bates noted that Davis "got more votes by nearly two hundred than there were people registered in the precinct." Bates also explained that once light was restored, the white men of the crowd donned white handkerchiefs on their arms and were going through the store with pistols and guns.[47]

Confirming previous testimony, Chief of Police Melton testified that the precinct building, located at the corner of Tenth and Princess streets, was the site of anticipated trouble and that he had

Number of Registered Voters and Number of Votes Cast for State Senator
New Hanover County, November 8, 1898

	# White Registered Voters	# Black Registered Voters	Total # Registered Voters	Votes for Democratic Candidate	Votes for Republican Candidate	Official Vote Total
First Ward						
1st Precinct	192	177	369	195	135	330
2nd Precinct	140	242	382	135	216	351
3rd Precinct	69	337	406	70	302	372
4th Precinct	35	337	372	33	94	127
5th Precinct	30	313	343	456	151	607
Second Ward						
1st Precinct	220	24	244	317	20	237
2nd Precinct	271	25	296	266	26	292
Third Ward						
1st Precinct	321	46	367	322	30	352
2nd Precinct	216	57	273	211	48	259
Fourth Ward						
1st Precinct	256	25	281	250	6	256
2nd Precinct	171	76	247	166	69	235
Fifth Ward						
1st Precinct	215	112	327	213	106	319
2nd Precinct	225	154	379	251	39	290
3rd Precinct	153	170	323	172	135	307
4th Precinct	43	309	352	43	300	343
Other Townships						
Masonboro	94	65	159	83	53	136
Cape Fear	68	184	252	85	146	231
Harnett	178	228	406	150	210	360
Federal Point	21	84	105	10	66	76

Votes in the 5th Precinct of the First Ward and the 2nd Precinct of the Fifth Ward were later disputed because of intimidation, claims of fraudulent ballots, and inaccurate counts.

SOURCE: *Contested Election Case of Oliver H. Dockery vs. John D. Bellamy from the Sixth Congressional District of the State of North Carolina* (Washington, D.C.: Government Printing Office, 1899), 226, and the Wilmington *Morning Star*, November 12, 1898.

posted patrolmen in that vicinity. His men reported to him that when the officers arrived after the crowd of white men assembled, they were "ousted," lamps were extinguished, and the electric lights in the neighborhood were "muffled." The patrolmen reported that once the situation was "straight again" with renewed lighting, it was evident that the ballot box had been stuffed.[48]

The city was tense overnight. Blacks, angered at the preliminary tallies and the intimidation they had endured, milled about in town, possibly engendering a rumor that a mob of blacks was prepared to attack the Fifth Ward Rough Riders. In response, white men moved to protect their families and posted extra sentries in the neighborhood. The rumor was false, but groups of white men remained on the streets, apparently eager for action. White leaders attempted to calm them and asked them to go home and assemble again in the morning for a newly scheduled mass meeting.[49] Throughout the night, Democrats across the state were in constant contact by telephone and telegram as they tallied their votes and assured themselves of victory. On the night of the election, Robert Mason wrote that at 10:50 he had "just telephoned downtown as to results and everything is very encouraging." On that same night John V. B. Metts wrote that the men in charge of city government were "nowhere" to be seen and that every man he met on the street was white, armed with a Winchester, and wearing a white handkerchief on his arm. Although Metts reported no violence, he said that guns were fired in the city all night following the election. Rev. J. Allen Kirk, African American minister of Central Baptist Church, recalled that "there was an army of white citizens mobilized in the old field back of Tenth Street, on Tuesday night, waiting for signals from the sentinels." A woman in New York received from her mother in Wilmington a letter that claimed election victory. The mother wrote that "the white man to-day has gained his point, rule or die." She also reported that blacks were not allowed across the Fourth Street Bridge into town and that the Wilmington Light Infantry was out conducting patrols without their uniforms.[50]

The day after the election, all residents of Wilmington breathed a sigh of relief. Chief of Police Melton noted that the day was fairly quiet.[51] Most white residents who had expected trouble now felt that the tensions would dissipate. Indeed on the day after the election, Wilmington resident Jane Cronly noted that she "heard the colored people going by to their work talking cheerfully together as had not been the case for many days."[52]

November 9: Mass Meeting of White Citizens

Despite indications that calm would prevail, some white leaders in Wilmington were still at work after the election. A notice that appeared in two Wilmington newspapers on the morning of November 9 called for an eleven o'clock meeting of the city's white citizens at the New Hanover County Courthouse. The official leaders of the Democratic Party who were not privy to the machinations of the Secret Nine—men such as George Rountree—may have been taken aback by the newspaper notice.[53] Because early reports from the polls had indicated to Democratic leaders that their campaign had succeeded and that their party had won an overwhelming victory, men such as Rountree were prepared to rest on their laurels. Surprised by the announcement, Rountree attended the meeting and observed that he had "never seen more people in the courthouse" as Alfred Moore Waddell was called to the fore.[54] It was, Rountree later recalled, "a respectable representative assemblage of business men, merchants, lawyers, doctors, divines and mechanics."[55]

Many of the city's business leaders were present. Speakers included newly elected congressman John D. Bellamy, who claimed no prior knowledge of the meeting's purpose.[56] Waddell explained that he did not know what the meeting was about but had been asked to read a statement.[57] The document he read consisted of a series of resolutions that employed very structured language and has come to be called the "White Declaration of Independence." The document asserted the basic notion that the white men of Wilmington would no longer live under the rule

73

Copyright 1905 by the Rotograph Co.

G 12231 Court House, Wilmington, N C

74

A mass meeting of white citizens was scheduled to be held on the morning of November 9, 1898, at the New Hanover County Courthouse. This image, from a 1905 postcard, is courtesy of the State Archives.

of "men of African origin." Its preamble, which drew upon patriotic sentiment similar to that expressed in Waddell's earlier rhetoric, was followed by a series of seven statements that included a variety of arguments used in the white supremacy campaign. The declaration ended with a call for Alexander Manly's removal from the city. Members of the press were called upon to serve as secretaries of the meeting.[58]

After Waddell finished reading the document, the crowd responded with a standing ovation. Former mayor Silas H. Fishblate expressed his desire for additional wording to be added to the resolutions that would require the resignations of the mayor, chief of police, and board of aldermen. George Rountree then stepped forward to move that a committee of five men review the resolutions and proposed amendment and then report back to the assembly with any necessary changes or recommendations. After Rountree's suggestion was approved, he was named a member of the committee along with Iredell Meares, Hugh MacRae, Walker Taylor, and S. H. Fishblate.[59]

The committee reviewed the resolutions and amendment while others called for a speech from Waddell, who advocated peaceful measures, since he felt it unnecessary to "adopt violent measures[,] as the editor of the *Record* would be dealt with." In response, there were shouts to "fumigate the city with the *Record*." Bellamy was likewise called to the podium, and he, too, pressed for a peaceful end to the affair. Another speaker, Pierre B. Manning, urged moderation and claimed that the reason why the "people of Wilmington had not avenged the *Record*'s vile slander long before" was because they "had not had the time" because of the "great work of the campaign." Manning, apparently placing his faith in the new legislature to "make a clean sweep of the City Hall," declared that to adopt Fishblate's additional wording to the resolution would amount to "anarchy."[60]

Members of the committee returned to the podium with their recommendations for changes to the resolution. The committee announced that it had rejected Fishblate's proposal to force the resignations of the entire city government in favor

George Rountree (1855–1942) was a Democratic leader in Wilmington who represented the business interests of the city. He attended the meeting that produced the "White Declaration of Independence." Image from C. Beauregard Poland, *North Carolina's Glorious Victory, 1898. Sketches of Able Democratic Leaders and Statesmen* (Raleigh: [Democratic Executive Committee, 1899], [47].

of pushing for the resignations only of the mayor and chief of police. Fishblate and another businessman, Nathaniel Jacobi, felt that the committee's recommended changes did not "go far enough," and Jacobi replied by offering the opinion that the leaders "should be commanded to resign one by one." In response, Rountree declared that the "matter would be attended to." Following a second reading and assurances that the subject of the entire board of aldermen would be addressed, the men present approved the revisal. The revised amendment read: "It is the sense of this meeting that Mayor S. P. Wright and Chief of Police Jno. R. Melton, having demonstrated their utter incapacity to give the city a decent government and keep order therein, their continuance in office being a constant menace to the peace and welfare of this community, they ought forthwith to resign."[61]

After the amendment had been thoroughly discussed, Waddell was chosen to head a committee of twenty-five men who would "direct the execution of the provisions of the resolutions." Speakers thanked the County Executive Committee of the Democratic Party, which had

"successfully conducted this magnificent campaign," and the newspapers "for the able and effective work done during the great campaign for the overthrow of Republican negro rule." Moreover, G. J. Boney made a motion that thanks be expressed to Furnifold Simmons for his work. The meeting then adjourned, and after 445 men signed the resolutions, Waddell and others selected the men to serve on the so-called Committee of Twenty-five. The following day, the Wilmington newspapers published the resolutions, signatures, and committeemen's names.[62]

Local residents quickly informed their correspondents of the election victory and the citizens' meeting. While the meeting was taking place, John V. B. Metts wrote a young lady in Raleigh that the "businessmen are at present holding a big meeting to take steps to run the mayor and some prominent negroes out of town." He included and underlined the words "Don't mention this," supposedly because the information he shared was restricted to only a few leaders.[63] Like Metts, James Worth shared details of the conclave; he explained to his out-of-town wife that on the morning of November 9 about one thousand men had attended a citizens' meeting and had passed resolutions requiring that the staff of the *Daily Record* leave town within twelve hours and demanding the resignations of Mayor Silas P. Wright and Chief of Police John R. Melton. Worth explained that a committee of twenty-five men was appointed to "carry into effect the resolutions."[64]

After members of the Committee of Twenty-five had assembled on November 9, they moved their meeting to the Merchants Association rooms for a meeting at 3:30 in the afternoon. After discussing methods of implementing the resolutions, the members drew up a list of men they considered leaders and representatives of the African American community. Those men, called the Committee of Colored Citizens (CCC), were attorneys, businessmen, laborers, ministers, and politicians.[65] The Committee of Twenty-five then approved the issuance of a summons to members of the CCC, requesting them to appear before the white leaders at six o'clock that evening to hear the demands of the whites regarding Manly and the

75

"White Declaration of Independence"

Believing that the Constitution of the United States contemplated a government to be carried on by an enlightened people; Believing that its framers did not anticipate the enfranchisement of an ignorant population of African origin, and believing that those men of the State of North Carolina, who joined in forming the Union, did not contemplate for their descendants subjection to an inferior race: —

We, the undersigned citizens of the City of Wilmington and County of New Hanover, do hereby declare that we will no longer be ruled, and will never again be ruled by men of African origin. This condition we have in part endured because we felt that the consequences of the War of Secession were such as to deprive us of the fair consideration of many of our countrymen. We believe that, after more than thirty years, this is no longer the case.

The stand we now pledge ourselves to is forced upon us suddenly by a crisis and our eyes are open to the fact that we must act now or leave our descendants to a fate too gloomy to be borne.

While we recognize the authority of the United States, and will yield to it if exerted, we would not for a moment believe that it is the purpose of more than sixty million of our own race to subject us permanently to a fate to which no Anglo Saxon has ever been forced to submit.

We therefore, believing that we represent unequivocally the sentiment of the White People of the County and City, hereby for ourselves, and as representing them, proclaim:

First
That the time has passed for the intelligent citizens of the community owning 90% of the property and paying taxes in like proportion, to be ruled by negroes.

Second
That we will not tolerate the action of unscrupulous white men in affiliating with the negroes so that by means of their votes they can dominate the intelligent and thrifty element in the community, thus causing business to stagnate and progress to be out of the question.

Third
That the negro has demonstrated by antagonizing our interest in every way, and especially by his ballot, that he is incapable of realizing that his interests are and should be identical with those of the community.

general situation in Wilmington. The summons read: "The following named colored citizens of Wilmington are requested to meet a committee of citizens appointed by authority of the meeting of business men and taxpayers held this morning at 6 o'clock this evening [*sic*] at the Merchants' Rooms, Seaboard Air Line building on Front Street to consider a matter of grave consequence to the negroes of Wilmington."[66]

At the appointed hour, the committees met to discuss the resolutions passed earlier in the day.[67] The black representatives sat across the table from the whites in a rigidly controlled meeting. Waddell "presented the resolutions as an ultimatum" and "firmly explained the purpose of the meeting." Waddell would not entertain discussion, and the black men were told in simple terms that they should "use their influence in carrying out the resolutions." Rev. W. H. Lee indicated that he

Fourth

That the progressive element in any community is the white population and that the giving of nearly all the employment to negro laborers has been against the best interests of this County and City and is a sufficient reason why the City of Wilmington, with its natural advantages has not become a city of at least fifty thousand inhabitants.

Fifth

That we propose in the future to give to white men a large part of the employment heretofore given to negroes because we realize that white families cannot thrive here unless there are more opportunities for the employment of the different members of said families.

Sixth

That the white men expect to live in this community peaceably; to have and provide absolute protection for their families, who shall be safe from insult or injury from all persons, whomsoever. We are prepared to treat the negroes with justice and consideration in all matters which do not involve sacrifices of the interest of the intelligent and progressive portion of the community. But are equally prepared now and immediately to enforce what we know to be our rights.

Seventh

That we have been, in our desire for harmony and peace, blinded both to our best interests and our rights. A climax was reached when the negro paper of this city published an article so vile and slanderous that it would in most communities have resulted in the lynching of the editor. We deprecate lynching and yet there is no punishment, provided by the courts, adequate for this offense. We therefore owe it to the people of this community and of this city, as a protection against such license in the future, that the paper known as the "Record" cease to be published and that its editor be banished from this community.

We demand that he leave this City forever within twenty-four hours after the issuance of this proclamation. Second, that the printing press from which the "Record" has been issued be packed and shipped from the City without delay, that we be notified within twelve hours of the acceptance or rejection of this demand.

If the demand is agreed to, within twelve hours we counsel forbearance on the part of all white men. If the demand is refused or if no answer is given within the time mentioned then the editor, Manly, will be expelled by force.

SOURCE: *Wilmington Messenger*, November 10, 1898

would advise Manly and his family to leave Wilmington, and William E. Henderson stated that he thought that Manly's *Daily Record* could be moved along with the Manlys.[68] There being no further discussion, the Committee of Twenty-five gave the CCC until 7:30 the next morning to provide Waddell a reply "as to whether the resolutions will be complied with without the use of strong measures."[69]

Another tense night of readiness faced both whites and blacks on the ninth. The CCC left the meeting with Waddell and reconvened at David Jacobs's barbershop on Dock Street to draft a reply. The CCC's response was short and accommodating but did not address the municipal issue, and it reminded the whites that they were not in a position to dictate to the rest of the community. After the CCC had drafted its response, it assigned

Armond Scott, a young attorney, the responsibility of delivering it to Waddell's home by the appointed hour. As Scott began to walk toward Waddell's home, however, he encountered large numbers of hostile armed whites in the neighborhood. Scott, along with several members of the CCC, then took the letter to the post office for delivery instead. While Scott was attempting to deliver the letter, other members of the CCC, thinking that Alexander Manly had already departed Wilmington, tried to find Frank Manly, Alexander's brother, to encourage him to leave and take the *Daily Record* with him. Still another member of the CCC met with George Rountree and informed him that "everything was all right," because an appropriate response had been drafted and delivered to Waddell. Moreover, because the contents of the letter were being made public even as the missive was being delivered to Waddell (as CCC members believed), those in the black community felt that peace would prevail.[70]

On November 10, Wilmington's morning papers reported the previous afternoon's meeting between the white and black factions of the city and that a formal reply from the CCC was expected early in the morning. Implicit in the reports was the assumption that Alexander Manly had already departed the city, never to return.[71] In a small news article, the *Wilmington Messenger* announced that the *Daily Record* had suspended publication and that the "outfit of the company will be turned over to creditors and the affairs of the paper will be closed up at once." In addition to speculating about Manly's course of action, the *Messenger* published a rumor that some members of the board of aldermen had decided to resign. Further, the paper predicted that a solution for changing the face of the board would present itself.[72]

Yet another stressful, sleepless night was ahead for many of Wilmington's citizens of both races. White sentries patrolled the town while others planned their next step. A group of whites secretly

Alfred Waddell claimed that he received this letter from the Committee of Colored Citizens, and it was reprinted in the newspapers. However, the letter's authenticity was questioned years later by Armond Scott, who wrote the actual response. Image courtesy of the Alfred Moore Waddell Papers, Southern Historical Collection.

Alexander Manly (*left*) is shown here preparing to leave Wilmington. His companion was either his brother Frank or Robert Strange. Image from Reaves, *"Strength through Struggle,"* 310.

assembled in front of the First Baptist Church and resolved to destroy the printing offices of the *Daily Record* and to lynch Manly if the demands of the White Declaration of Independence were not met. The men decided to station members of the Vigilance Committee established by Col. Roger Moore throughout the town in the event of violence that might arise in case Manly's newspaper office should be destroyed. They also decided that Colonel Moore would lead the march upon the press office if need be.[73]

The mass meeting, complete with the public unveiling of the White Declaration of Independence, combined with the inflamed attitudes of those in attendance, gave the Secret Nine an opportunity to enact its plan to overthrow the city government. Although the state and county were firmly in the hands of Democrats, the municipal government was not slated for replacement through the ballot box until the following spring. Nonetheless, leading white citizens felt that a complete overhaul of city government was necessary, in accordance with the demands of the White Declaration. They felt that there were others better equipped or more entitled to manage the city and who should be returned to power despite their minority status.[74]

On the night of November 9, James Worth wrote his wife to inform her both of the day's events and of the trouble that was widely expected in response to the actions of the Committee of Twenty-five. He expressed the belief that Manly would "of course go dead or alive—but which I am unable to say." Worth anticipated "warm times in the old town" that night, but the night was quiet as the city awaited word from Waddell and the Committee of Colored Citizens.[75]

Leading 1898 Conspirators

The men who were members of these and other groups such as the Vigilance Committee under Roger Moore, the Red Shirts/Rough Riders under Mike Dowling, or the White Government Union clubs all played a role in creating tensions in Wilmington that led to bloodshed on November 10, 1898. Though not complete rosters, it can be noted that many men were members of more than one organization listed.

Wilmington Chamber of Commerce

John L. Cantwell

James H. Chadbourn Jr.

Thomas Clawson

Silas H. Fishblate

Thomas C. James

William R. Kenan

Hugh MacRae

Samuel Northrop

Walter Parsley

George Rountree

Frank Stedman

Thomas Strange

J. Allan Taylor

Walker Taylor

William E. Worth

County Democratic Party Campaign Committee

Edgar Parmele

George Rountree

Frank Stedman

Walker Taylor

The Secret Nine

Hardy Fennell

William Gilchrist

W. A. Johnson

Edward S. Lathrop

Hugh MacRae

Pierre B. Manning

Walter Parsley

L. B. Sasser

J. Allan Taylor

Group Six

John Berry

Henry Fennell

Thomas Meares

William F. Robertson

William L. Smith

Walker Taylor

Chapter 5

November 10: "Hell Jolted Loose"

You cannot think or imagine anything to equal or compare to the policy the Democrats seem to have adopted to carry this section. I look for a lot of innocent men killed here if things continue as they are now.

—Benjamin Keith to Marion Butler,
October 17, 1898, Marion Butler Papers

The events of Thursday, November 10, 1898, were multifaceted. Foremost, planned action to suppress the African American and Republican communities grew into unplanned bloodshed. Anticipating aggressive reprisals from the black community, white leaders had established a framework of pre-election preparations that broke down as violence escalated. The goal of advance planning by the Secret Nine and men such as Col. Roger Moore and Col. Walker Taylor appeared to be additional protection for citizens and control of the election rather than an outright offensive strike into the black community. But the frenzy over white supremacy, incessantly repeated by orators such as Alfred Moore Waddell and Charles B. Aycock, simply could not be quieted—even in the wake of an overwhelming and somewhat anticlimactic election victory.

The fever pitch of white-supremacy rhetoric reached a breaking point in Wilmington on November 10. On that date, the mother of Edward Wootten, a student at Virginia Polytechnic Institute, wrote to her son from Wilmington, telling him that although she feared violence, "we need it and . . . it must come before things are settled."[1] A few days after the riot, the editor of a Wilmington newspaper echoed Mrs. Wootten's sentiments by declaring that "the relations between the races were too strained for it to be avoided," since "matters had reached a point in Wilmington at which a conflict between the races was inevitable."[2] For the leaders of the Democratic

Party, the election and its aftermath brought victory and gratification; for the masses of Wilmington's citizens, violence triumphed over deliberative thought in the wake of the mass meeting on November 9.[3]

After the previous day's efforts to arrange a meeting of the leading black citizens and secure their assistance in calming the city, some of Wilmington's Democratic Party leaders felt it unnecessary to attend the morning meeting on Thursday, November 10, to hear the response of the Committee of Colored Citizens (CCC). White attorney George Rountree had met with one of the leading members of the black community late on the ninth and received assurances that all was well. Rountree was informed that Alexander Manly was planning to leave Wilmington at once and that attorney Armond Scott would deliver an answer to Waddell. Because Rountree and others did not realize that the timely delivery of the response to Waddell had gone amiss, they felt no need to attend an early-morning meeting scheduled to take place at the Wilmington Light Infantry (WLI) Armory on Market Street on the tenth. Those behind-the-scenes leaders failed to see that the strict control they had exercised over the Red Shirts and White Government Union (WGU) clubs had eroded.[4]

According to the plans of the Committee of Twenty-five, Alfred Moore Waddell waited at home until about 8:00 A.M., approximately a half hour longer than the deadline for a reply from the CCC. He then proceeded to walk down Fifth Street to the WLI Armory. Once Waddell arrived, he was met by a crowd of about five hundred men eager to learn the CCC's answer to the White Declaration of Independence. The *Wilmington Messenger* remarked that the assembled crowd was armed and represented a cross section of the town, including a large number of professionals and clergy. Some of the men were exhausted; many

The Wilmington Light Infantry Armory served as the meeting place for the Committee of Twenty-five, as well as the Red Shirts, on the morning of November 10, 1898. Image courtesy of the New Hanover County Public Library.

had been on patrol all night, and others had slept at the armory, a focal point of demonstrations and planning sessions in the days and weeks leading up to November 10.[5]

In addition to Col. Roger Moore's paramilitary organization, groups of actual military units were in the city—the State Guard militia unit of the WLI under Capt. Thomas C. James; active-duty federal troops in Company K, Second Regiment North Carolina Volunteer Infantry, under Capt. Donald MacRae; and federal troops from the North Carolina Naval Militia under Commander George L. Morton. These men awaited the morning of the tenth with a tense readiness. To keep their troops occupied and out of harm's way, the military leaders put them through drills, thus preventing an anxious boredom until the men were needed. Although their role was that of peace-keepers, their leader and post commander,

Col. Walker Taylor, understood the important role the WLI could play in the event of violence. Members of the WLI had participated in previous patrols and activities in the city, but not as a uniformed, organized company. Taylor could not actively engage his men in the city until violence broke out. For that reason, Col. Roger Moore's system of civilian block captains and leaders, a framework based on military protocol, was the front line of organized armed men.[6]

Moore's civilian men knew their place in the ranks and took orders from their leaders, who ultimately reported to him. Once Gov. Daniel Russell called out the official military in the form of the WLI and the State Guard on November 10, however, Moore's men either dispersed or joined WLI peace-keeping forays, even as the Red Shirts and Rough Riders continued to act on their own.[7]

82

The March to the *Daily Record*

Waddell arrived at the armory around 8:15 A.M. and informed the crowd that no response had been received from the CCC. The previously "orderly" crowd became restless and called for someone to step up and lead them to wreck the *Daily Record* office. Waddell, who had been informed of the contents of the letter drafted by the CCC and that it had been mailed instead of hand-delivered, did not share that information with the assembled crowd. Other leaders of the campaign were conspicuously absent, including Col. Roger Moore and Col. Walker Taylor. Moore, as organizational leader of Wilmington's defenses on behalf of armed whites, was at his predetermined station, and others under his command were in their positions throughout the city, posted so as to be ready to respond quickly. Furthermore, Moore had instructed Waddell to inform him by telephone if it became necessary to march on the *Daily Record*. However, because of personality conflicts between the two men, Waddell took matters into his own hands and did not contact Moore to step forward and lead the crowd, even though some men called for Moore's leadership.[8]

Colonel Taylor and Captain James understood the tenuous position of the WLI in the upcoming activities, since the infantry company, as a local North Carolina State Guard unit, was pledged to maintain peace and order. After consulting with Taylor, James refused to allow the WLI to participate officially in the destruction of Manly's press. The WLI could not and would not lead the march to the *Daily Record* office.[9]

Waddell assembled the crowd in military fashion, in columns of four for the length of two city blocks, with himself and other leaders of the Committee of Twenty-five, Red Shirts, and business interests leading the march. Those in the front ranks included Waddell, escorted by Mike Dowling of the Red Shirts, followed by F. H. Fechtig, W. C. Galloway, A. B. Skelding, and Edward S. Lathrop of the Committee of Twenty-five. Also named by witnesses as leaders of the march were John D. Bellamy and former mayor Silas Fishblate.[10]

Once the main body of the crowd had left for the *Daily Record* office, Taylor and James met at the armory and discussed the potential for trouble. Taylor, both a member of the WLI and a leading businessman, felt compelled to control the situation as much as possible and composed a telegram to the governor: "Situation here serious. I hold military awaiting your prompt orders."[11]

Taylor and his men then waited at the armory for a reply while the crowd descended on the press office. John V. B. Metts, a

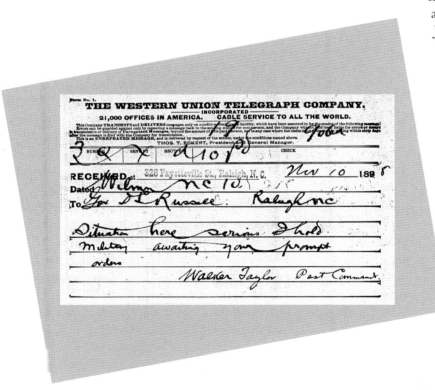

This telegram from Walker Taylor to Governor Russell was sent at 9:00 A.M. in an effort to control the situation. Image from Correspondence, Petitions, Etc., Nov. 1, 1898-Nov. 29, 1898, Daniel L. Russell, Governors' Papers, State Archives.

83

sergeant in the WLI, wrote that he and the other members of the unit were "kept under arms" in the armory until eleven o'clock while the citizens met there and "proceeded to burn the *Record* building."[12] Another member of the WLI, Pvt. James D. Nutt, expressed the men's eagerness for active involvement after Captain James had denied his earlier request to leave the armory and participate and had instead "marched them around the yard [of the armory] about eight times."[13]

Waddell's column of men marched east on Market Street and turned onto Seventh Street. White residents in homes they passed viewed the crowd with mixed emotions, even as husbands and sons joined the march from their porches. William Parsley wrote to his sister-in-law in New York that her mother broke into a "fit of hysterics sufficiently violent to alarm me" when the armed group of men led by Waddell marched by their house but that she soon was calm enough for him to join the procession. Furthermore, his young daughter, Mannie, "distinguished herself" as she joined the procession from the sidewalk for a short distance while walking toward her grandparents' house at 619 Orange Street. Parsley recalled that Mannie enjoyed the walk but that his wife and mother were not so charmed by the girl's activities.[14]

Waddell's march to the press passed through affluent neighborhoods on Market Street, but once the men turned onto Seventh Street and passed Orange Street, the surroundings became distinctly different. That portion of Wilmington was occupied almost entirely by blacks, who watched the procession from within their homes and other concealed locations. Chief of Police John R. Melton observed the procession and recalled that it took about an hour for the 1,000 to 1,500 men to pass. The *Daily Record* occupied a building known as Ruth Hall or Love and Charity Hall, which stood in the heart of a black neighborhood near the corner of Seventh and Nun streets.[15]

Since members of the white paramilitary organization were in what could be assumed to be hostile territory, and given the fact that armed groups of black men had clustered around the *Daily Record* office in August as a defensive measure after threats were first made against Manly and the paper, the white men sent out pickets, or guards, along the streets in the southern section of town. One participant later recalled that his ward captain instructed him to run a patrol on Church Street, and in advance of the riot he subsequently extended his patrols along Castle Street to Seventh Street.[16]

With his perimeter secured by the pickets and guard patrols, Waddell, wielding a Winchester rifle, knocked on the door of Love and Charity Hall. The knock yielded no answer, inasmuch as white reporter Thomas Clawson had previously warned Manly of the dangers to his life and property.[17] The men then forced the door open and poured inside to demolish the equipment and supplies of the *Daily Record*—marking the beginning of overt violence in the city. The men cheered as they entered the building, destroying office furniture and the printing press. Once inside, to the cheers of onlookers unable to join them, they threw into the street such items as a beaver hat, drawings of Manly, and a sign reading "The Record Publishing Co."[18] A fire started in the building, forcing the men inside to leave the structure and return to the street to watch it burn. Later investigation among the ranks of men involved concluded that kerosene lamps hanging inside the building were knocked to the floor, which was saturated with additional kerosene found stored in a closet. The person who actually set the fire was never named, but William Watson and Dan Rowan were identified as the men responsible for spreading the kerosene, which accelerated the fire as it spread quickly throughout the two-story frame building.[19] Waddell and other leaders were displeased that the fire broke out, since they sought only to damage the press office and limit the ability of the black community to produce a newspaper.[20]

Moreover, the building stood perilously close to the prominent St. Luke's AME Church and to private homes. As hot cinders began to ignite fires on the shingles of nearby houses, the alarm was sounded from a firebox at the corner, and men from the neighborhood fire station responded to the call. Whites involved in the destruction of the press assisted with extinguishing the small roof fires

Left: The remains of Love and Charity Hall/*Daily Record* printing office. African American firefighters are visible on the second floor, and spectators observe from the steps of St. Luke's AME Church. Image courtesy of the New Hanover County Public Library.

Below: Armed rioters in front of the destroyed building. This photograph was reproduced in *Collier's Weekly*. Image courtesy of the State Archives.

The charred remnants of the *Daily Record* printing press, courtesy of the New Hanover County Public Library.

on nearby houses.[21] On orders of fire chief Charles Schnibben, W. T. Savage halted the all-black fire crew at Sixth and Castle streets until it was certain that the Love and Charity Hall had been destroyed beyond repair.[22] Once that crew was allowed to approach the scene, it was met by a barrage of shouts and a "fusillade of gun and pistol shots."[23] The whites watched as the firemen fought to douse the flames. Later accounts by observers expressed admiration for the fortitude of the fire fighters, who did their job in spite of harrowing circumstances—taming a raging fire in close proximity to other buildings under the watchful eyes of hundreds of armed, antagonistic men.[24] After the fire was extinguished, some whites paused a moment to pose for photographs, rifles in their hands, in front of the destroyed building.

The black community reacted in a multitude of ways: children at a nearby school ran through the neighborhood in a frightened panic, and an elderly lady stood on the street and "invoked the wrath of Heaven" on the perpetrators as they worked to destroy the *Daily Record* office and building.[25] Although the number of participants swelled to as many as 2,000 at the time the building began to burn, many whites were not a part of the assault but were alerted to the violence by the sounds of gunshots, fire bells, and shouts.[26] After the crowd dispersed, fire crews tore down the remains of the building.

Waddell and the white men present at the fire then re-formed their lines and returned to the armory. There, Waddell counseled the men: "Now you have performed the duty you called on me to lead you to perform. Now let us go quietly to our homes and about our business and obey the law, unless we are forced in self-defense to do otherwise."[27] But Waddell's cautions fell on deaf ears, for there were already roving clusters of armed men in a state of recklessness throughout the city. The white-supremacy monster that Waddell and other members of the Democratic Party had spawned—and previously held in check—now exceeded their control.

Once the *Daily Record* office was destroyed, Wilmington descended into a state of panic. Women and children were ushered inside behind locked doors and windows, and workers of both races rushed to the city's center to ascertain what had happened. With the telephone and telegraph available to the progressive business community, news traveled quickly among the white elites, making it easier for them to organize military and civilian support and to seek medical assistance.[28] Racing across the city to find family members, black men and women spread rumors of murder and fire well in advance of the full-scale conflict.

Because of the frantic nature of the story and the way in which it was reported at the time of the event—often with papers going to press while guns were being fired in the streets—many inaccurate or incomplete accounts were circulated and have survived. Confusion has arisen over the accuracy and truthfulness of contemporary newspaper articles and similar data. Letters and other primary documents penned by eyewitnesses and participants add personal experiences to printed versions of the day's activities, but the inaccurate memories of some who participated in the riot and later recalled the day in order to record the "rebellion" for posterity have added to the many misstatements in the reporting. Therefore, one must piece the day's events together using multiple, often overlapping, information sources.

To comprehend the ensuing riot, it must be understood that groups of four to eight armed white men were patrolling every block throughout the city from the day's first light until nightfall, and they had been conducting similar patrols during the weeks leading up to the election. Because tensions were high after the mass meeting on the ninth, the men and their patrols were even more on edge than before. Exhaustion and fear were prevalent emotions. Still, many black and white workers went about their lives as if nothing had changed. In addition to the patrols, the WLI and the naval militia were well prepared, having at the ready several horse-drawn wagons equipped with machine guns and cannons or designed for troop transport.[29]

"Hell Jolted Loose"

Harry Hayden wrote that "Hell jolted loose" about an hour after the *Daily Record* office was destroyed. The majority of the violence and bloodshed took place in Brooklyn, the traditionally African American neighborhood in the northern section of Wilmington.[30] The first shots between whites and blacks were fired at Fourth and Harnett streets as armed white men returned from the fire to their neighborhoods. The northern part of the city exploded with violent outbreaks at multiple intersections and landmarks during the day. The precise time line of events remains unclear.

Standoff at the Sprunt Cotton Compress

One of the areas in which panic and fear ignited tensions was the Sprunt Cotton Compress, located near the Cape Fear River on Front Street between Walnut and Red Cross streets. James Sprunt, among the city's wealthiest white men and a member of the chamber of commerce, employed hundreds of black men as stevedores who loaded cotton onto ships, as laborers at the large compress, and as equipment operators to process the cotton. The men working at the compress were unaware of the activity on the other side of town until the fire bell rang. Workers' wives fled to the compress to tell their husbands about the *Daily Record* fire and that whites were burning black residences and firing weapons at blacks throughout the city.[31] In short order, several hundred employees gathered in a state of confusion outside the compress, and work stopped as laborers left their posts. The unarmed black workers, according to one newspaper report, were "in a state of bewilderment, wondering what had happened, and what might eventuate."[32] They told Sprunt that they were "hard working . . . and that the whites ought not to stir them up and terrorize them."[33] Seeking to protect his workers, Sprunt encouraged them to stay on his property and away from town in hopes that they would not be involved in violence.[34]

Joining Sprunt in attempting to calm the workers and prevent them from going to their homes were Junius Davis, George Rountree, and Col. Roger Moore. At about the same time, however, a large number of white men, learning of a rumored gathering of black workers at

Sprunt's business and prepared to keep the "mob" under control, approached the cotton compress with guns on their shoulders. Some of the whites confronted Moore and told him that "if he did not give the order to shoot into the negroes on the opposite corner," the mob would do so anyway. Moore responded that he had been placed in "command" by his fellow citizens, and until he was removed from command he would not allow bloodshed and would have the instigators arrested. The men stood down and took their places in the ranks.[35]

Capt. Donald MacRae, recently returned to Wilmington from the Spanish-American War, recalled that while he watched a crowd going in the direction of Sprunt's compress, someone told him to go home and get his gun. MacRae returned to the street armed with a "riot gun and about seventy five pounds of riot cartridges and two pistols and a bowie knife or two" and headed for a group of people gathered near the compress. While standing in the crowd watching Sprunt attempt to calm his employees, MacRae was recognized as a soldier and was asked to lead the group, which wanted to "kill the whole gang of

87

Donald MacRae (1861–1928), a recent veteran of the Spanish-American War, was called upon to lead a gathering of white men who sought to confront black workers at the Sprunt Cotton Compress. Image from deRosset, *Pictorial and Historical New Hanover County and Wilmington*, [89].

negroes."[36] MacRae recalled that he "had very little stomach for it[,] and as very few of the negroes were armed, it was little less than murder that they [the crowd of whites] proposed." He also acknowledged that all the black men were concerned about was their homes.[37]

George Rountree was surprised by the outbreak of violence, having been asleep during the burning of the *Daily Record* office by Waddell's followers. Rountree had awakened to gunshots and rushed to the post office, meeting businessman and postmaster William H. Chadbourn there. The two men immediately began planning steps they might take to mount a political coup. Rountree thereupon returned home, retrieved his Winchester, and walked to the corner with his gun on his shoulder, "feeling very much like a fool," he later recalled. After seeing no action, he returned his gun to his house, went back to the corner near Sprunt's compress, and watched as the black workers began to congregate. As he helped to calm the crowd, one of the black workers asked him what they had done to justify being the target of armed whites eager to shoot; Rountree later acknowledged that he could not supply an answer.[38]

Sprunt and other white business leaders continued to try to calm the blacks and encouraged them to disperse and return to work. They likewise attempted to pacify the whites who wanted to open fire into the crowd of blacks who failed to disperse quickly enough. In an effort to convince his workers that their houses were not in jeopardy, Sprunt dispatched a trusted black man accompanied by a white man out into the black community in Sprunt's personal buggy to ascertain the damage and danger and report his findings to his fellow employees. Once the worker returned and reported that only the *Daily Record* office had been burned, the crowd seemed a bit calmer and began to disperse. Small groups of armed white men then escorted a number of Sprunt's workers to their homes.[39]

The riverfront area in which the Sprunt compress was located was also home to several other employers of blacks, including railroad offices, lumberyards, pitch and turpentine plants, and shipping firms. As African American workers

along the waterfront received news of the disturbance at Sprunt's and the appearance of armed mobs of white men throughout the city, they sought to make their way to their homes but were stopped and turned back by armed white patrols.[40]

Only a short time earlier, Waddell's speech cautioning men to return home peacefully had failed to calm tempers. After burning the *Daily Record* office, some white men boarded the city streetcar trolley and rode it along its route, traveling south on Sixth Street, turning west on Castle Street, and then turning north on Front Street into the northern sections of town. As the streetcar entered black neighborhoods along Castle Street, the men, flushed with excitement from the fire, fired their rifles into the homes and businesses of black residents.[41] By the time the white men who lived in the Brooklyn area had returned home, by foot or streetcar, their excitement was at a fever pitch, and tensions were high.

Eye of the Storm—Fourth and Harnett Streets

The bloodshed began when armed white men confronted black workers from the waterfront industrial yards and black residents of Brooklyn. The precise spot at which the peace was fractured was the corner of Fourth and Harnett streets in Brooklyn, a mixed-race neighborhood on the edge of the predominantly black section of Wilmington. A group of blacks was gathered on the southwest corner of that intersection near Brunjes' Saloon in George Heyer's store when armed whites returned to the neighborhood. A streetcar filled with men who had just been involved in burning the *Daily Record* office likewise entered the area. As the groups exchanged verbal assaults from opposite street corners, whites and blacks alike sought to calm their fellow citizens.[42]

Norman Lindsay encouraged his fellow blacks to go home: "For the sake of your lives, your families, your children, and your country," he cried, "go home and stay there!"[43] In response to Lindsay's plea, the group of blacks moved to the

88

opposite corner at W. A. Walker's grocery store, while the whites took up a position between Heyer's store and St. Matthew's English Lutheran Church. Aaron Lockamy, a newly deputized white police officer, likewise attempted to diffuse the problem by moving back and forth between both groups and urging them to disperse. He recalled that while serving as a special policeman during the aftermath of the election, he was stationed in Brooklyn to ensure that the opening of two bars on Fourth Street would be peaceful. Instructed by police chief John R. Melton not to arrest anyone, Lockamy asked the blacks to disperse and go home for their own safety. They refused but moved as a group a bit farther away from the corner. Aaron Lockamy's inability to disperse the crowd angered the white men at the opposite corner. Lockamy felt that he had done all

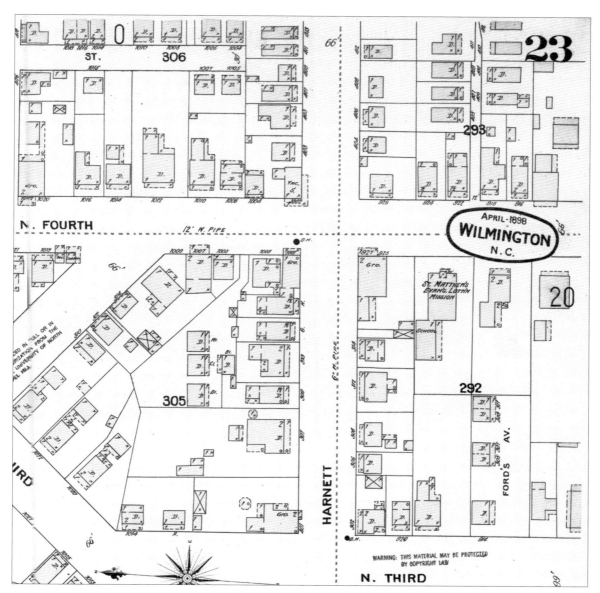

The intersection of Fourth and Harnett streets, taken from the April 1898 Sanborn Fire Insurance map. Reproduced with permission, Sanborn Map Library, LLC.

The W. A. Walker Grocery Store, located on the northeast corner of Fourth and Harnett streets. Two white Xs mark spots where the first two victims fell when a crowd of whites fired shots at blacks there. Image courtesy of the New Hanover County Public Library.

Another view of the intersection, showing more of Harnett Street. Some of the men wounded in the shooting here ran into some of the homes just east of the corner store. Image by Henry Cronenberg, courtesy of the New Hanover County Public Library.

he could in the turf war and went back to his post on Fourth Street, near Brunswick. From that point forward for several hours, gunshots rang throughout the city.[44]

White and black witnesses to the incident at the intersection of Fourth and Harnett streets each claimed that the other side fired the first shots. The newspapers cited an affidavit, probably taken by George Rountree, to counter accounts from black witnesses such as George Henry Davis, a black man wounded at the intersection and interviewed by reporter Thomas Clawson for the *Wilmington*

Messenger. Aaron Lockamy, who had moved back and forth between the clusters of whites and blacks on opposing corners at Fourth and Harnett at least two times, later asserted that the only people on the corner who were armed were whites.[45] Whoever fired a weapon first, once the first shot rang out, whites launched a fusillade of bullets toward the blacks congregated near Walker's store. Several black men fell injured, but most were able to get up and flee the scene. Most accounts agree that three men died instantly at Walker's and that two injured men ran around the

The George Heyer Store, which was occupied by a saloon operated by John H. Brunjes, was located on the southwest corner of Fourth and Harnett streets. Blacks were gathered here when armed whites returned to the neighborhood. Image courtesy of the New Hanover County Public Library.

During the chaos, William May (white) was wounded near his home, located at 307 Harnett Street. This act, presumed to have been committed by a black man, presented a rallying point for the whites who retaliated against any blacks they encountered. Image of Mayo's house courtesy of the New Hanover County Public Library.

corner into a dwelling at 411 Harnett. One of these men, whose surname was Bizzell, died in the house, while the other, George Henry Davis, who apparently lived at the residence, had been wounded in his left thigh and had a bullet lodged between his shoulders. Reporter Clawson found Davis in the house along with another dead black man and three women; all were taken to the hospital on the eleventh. Although Davis eventually recovered, Clawson recalled that after he sent for a white doctor, W. D. MacMillan, and a black doctor, Thomas R. Mask, "it appeared impossible for one so desperately wounded ever to recover."[46]

The rest of the black men fled west on Harnett Street, reportedly firing at whites as they ran. Although it was difficult for black men to purchase weapons in the weeks and months just prior to the election, many already owned firearms for hunting or personal safety. Men identified by newspapers as having been killed at Fourth and Harnett were John Townsend (Townsell?), Charles Lindsay (also known as Silas Brown), William Mouzon, and John L. Gregory. Black men identified as having been wounded at the intersection were Alfred White, William Lindsay, and Sam McFarland. Whites identified as having been present at the scene were S. Hill Terry (armed with a double-barrel shotgun loaded with buckshot), Theodore Curtis, N. B. (Burt) Chadwick (armed with a 16-shot Colt or Remington rifle), Sam Matthews (armed with a .44 caliber navy rifle), and George Piner.[47]

After the first shots were fired, a streetcar from Brooklyn entered the business section in downtown, and the conductor told white men gathered there that blacks had shot into the car. The men thereupon crowded into the car bound for Brooklyn. One of those "first responders" was Capt. Donald MacRae of Company K, fresh from the tense situation at Sprunt's cotton compress. MacRae later recalled that once he arrived in Brooklyn after hearing reports of fighting, he began to establish a skirmish line with other white men in the area. Another man stopped MacRae

because he was still a captain in the U.S. Army, and some of the white leaders viewed his involvement in the riot as inappropriate.[48]

Having feared the worst in the weeks prior to the election, leaders Col. Roger Moore and Col. Walker Taylor had developed a strategy for quelling potential violence by stationing contacts throughout the city and instructing them to notify Moore and Taylor if trouble erupted. The contact in the Fourth Street area near Harnett Street was Bernice Moore, who owned a drugstore at 901 North Fourth Street. J. Allan Taylor of the Secret Nine instructed Moore to sound the "riot alarm" to alert the WLI and the naval militia in the event of violence. As soon as he heard gunshots, Moore telephoned the armory to inform the leaders there that shots were being fired in Brooklyn. Once the riot alarm was sounded, Col. Walker Taylor declared martial law, and the WLI and the naval militia began to make their way into the Brooklyn neighborhood.[49]

Telegram to Col. Walker Taylor directing him to "take command of Captain James Company at Wilmington and preserve the peace" Image from the Daniel L. Russell, Governors' Papers, State Archives.

Just before Roger Moore's call for backup was received at the armory, a telegram from Governor Russell that instructed Colonel Taylor to "take command of Captain James company . . . and preserve the peace" arrived there.[50] Before the telegram arrived, Commander George Morton of the naval militia had sought approval from the city to authorize the military to take charge, but he claimed he could not locate the mayor or a police officer. Instead, Morton's men found Deputy Sheriff George Z. French in his room at the Orton Hotel and requested permission to march the naval militia from his headquarters in Brooklyn into the affected areas. French complied with the request, possibly under duress, and wrote out an order instructing Commander Morton to "use all force at your disposal to quell the existing violation of the peace in this city." Morton then dispatched a telegram to the governor, informing him of his plan of action and also notified Col. Walker Taylor of his intentions. The governor later ordered Morton to place his men under Taylor's authority (although the transfer of command had already taken place by the time the telegram was received). Morton's men, equipped with Lee magazine rifles and a Hotchkiss rapid-firing gun, assembled at the corner of Third and Princess streets.[51]

As soon as the first shots were fired, a "running firefight" erupted on Harnett Street, with scores of men, black and white, running in all directions away from the intersection, some firing at the opposite side as they ran. William Mayo, a white man who lived at 307 Harnett, was seriously wounded by a stray bullet. Mayo's wounding presented a rallying point for the whites, who retaliated by aiming for any blacks who came within sight and firing in unison into a group of black men, killing another five or six of them near the intersection of Harnett and Fourth streets. Mayo was taken to a nearby drugstore for treatment by Dr. John T. Schonwald, who lived close to the scene. Mayo's injury was serious, but receiving quick care, he survived an otherwise life-threatening injury.[52]

In addition, two other white men, Burt Chadwick and George Piner, were injured and treated alongside Mayo. The white men involved in the first scuffle not only desired to avenge Mayo but also sought to identify the individual who shot him, perhaps as a means to stop random shootings. Later in the afternoon, after some simple investigation and finger pointing, it was decided that Daniel Wright, who lived nearby at 810 North Third Street, was the culprit responsible for shooting not only Mayo but also Piner. A manhunt was launched for Wright.[53]

As large groups of white men gathered in the vicinity of Fourth and Harnett streets—milling about, angry, and eager to avenge Mayo's shooting—a "half breed Indian" told J. Allan Taylor that Wright had shot Mayo. Taylor was shown a house in which he was told Wright was hiding and that the suspect could be identified by "a missing thumb on his right hand and the possession of an outmoded rifle with a large bore."[54] Captain MacRae later recalled the incident with the Indian, saying that he felt the man had a grudge against local blacks.[55] Taylor then sent a group of men led by John S. Watters to identify and capture Wright. White eyewitnesses later claimed that once Wright's house was surrounded, the suspect went into the attic and shot into the approaching crowd, wounding Will Terry and George Bland.[56]

Wright's house was set afire, and he tried to escape but was captured while his wife watched from the street. Once in custody, Wright was marched into the street and hit in the head with a length of gas pipe. When he stood back up, someone in the crowd suggested that Wright be hanged from a nearby lamppost. Before a rope could be found, a member of the citizens' patrol drove up and suggested that Wright be given the chance to run for his freedom. Wright was given that opportunity, but after he had run about fifty yards, "at least forty guns of all descriptions turned loose on him." Wright was left in the street for about a half hour, bleeding and severely wounded by about thirteen gunshot wounds, five of which entered through his shoulders and back, before he was picked up and carried to the hospital. Doctors at the hospital observed that they had never seen anyone with as many gunshot wounds live for as long as Wright did. He held onto life until early the next morning, and his body was handed over to undertaker Thomas Rivera for burial following a formal inquest by coroner David Jacobs.[57]

This photograph shows the area on N. Third Street where two black men were killed. Two "X" marks indicated by white boxes are visible. The one on the right may be the spot where Daniel Wright fell with multiple bullet wounds. Image courtesy of the New Hanover County Public Library.

94

Additional shots rang throughout the area as more and more whites and blacks made their way into the Brooklyn neighborhood. Among the white onlookers was attorney George Rountree. Having just mediated the safety of blacks at Sprunt's compress, Rountree went to investigate the rioting so that in case a governmental inquiry took place he would be prepared to answer questions. Rountree is probably the person responsible for filing the sworn affidavit of William McAllister, published repeatedly in local and statewide newspapers, indicating that a black man was responsible for firing the first shots.[58] Rountree recalled that he and several others attempted to "quiet the situation and to prevent any further shooting" but acknowledged that "at this time I had no influence whatever with the rioters" and was pleased that the arrival of the military "quieted the matter down as quickly as possible."[59]

The Wilmington Light Infantry Enters Brooklyn

Once the riot alarm was sounded and the governor authorized military action, Capt. Thomas C. James, upon orders of Col. Walker Taylor, mobilized the waiting forces of the Wilmington Light Infantry (WLI) to march into the Brooklyn neighborhood. The company marched down Market Street to Third, then over to the intersection with Princess, where it stopped in front of James Woolvin's funeral parlor at 105 North Third and waited for the naval militia to join its procession. Once the WLI moved again, it marched down Third to Mulberry and on to Fourth Street to cross into Brooklyn. At the Fourth Street Bridge, Captain James halted the group and announced: "[N]ow boys I want to tell you right now I want you all to load and when I give the command to shoot, I want you to shoot to kill." As James concluded his announcement, a shot was fired at the group, but the infantry company could not determine who had fired.[60]

This photograph depicts the intersection of Third and Harnett streets. According to the caption, a "cross (X) on fence is where white man [presumably William Mayo] was shot." A white box indicates the X mark on the fence. Mayo's home was next to this grocery store, owned and operated by John Doscher. The image is looking up Harnett Street toward the intersection of Fourth and Harnett. Image courtesy of the New Hanover County Public Library.

Pvt. James D. Nutt recalled that by the time his WLI unit had returned to the armory from its march through the Brooklyn area, he still had all of his cartridges, not having fired a shot.[61] Members of the WLI remembered other facets of their marches through town. John V. B. Metts wrote to his "Dear Miss Elizabeth" on November 12, the first day he had been home since the ninth, that as the WLI marched "out in the northern end of town where the negroes had congregated . . . I nearly stepped on negroes laying in the street dead. Oh, it was awful." Metts reported that he and other members of the company had been fired upon but that no one in his "crowd" got hurt. He stated that "we killed a 'few negroes,' " that it was his first experience "under fire," and that "[I was] not near as much excited as I expected to be." He concluded his thoughts on the activities of the WLI during the riot: "I'll tell you things are stirred up and I am glad to say I am still living but we have not killed enough negroes—two or three white men were wounded and we have not gotten enough to make up for it."[62]

Several other groups, namely the Red Shirts and the Rough Riders, who had assembled at Dry Pond, were ready when the signal was given. Once Bernice Moore's call activated the WLI, word spread to those men that fighting was taking place across town, and they quickly made their way to the scene.[63]

By noon violence was widespread in the Brooklyn section of Wilmington. Reports of shootings and fires are found throughout the historical record of the riot. In addition to armed whites moving into action around Brooklyn, black workers found themselves in the midst of a veritable war zone, caught between the Cape Fear River and gunfire. The laborers, still wearing their work coveralls, moved into town to help their friends and neighbors along Harnett Street. A patrol of whites told them to go back and not approach, but, once the black men refused, the whites shot at them as they ran back toward the railroad. One of the black men died on the Carolina Central Railroad tracks.[64]

Several black men were caught in the cross fire, among them Sam Gregory, who was wounded and fell on Fourth Street between Harnett and Swann. An unnamed man was wounded and seen crawling under the house of Mrs. W. H. Strauss on Fourth between Harnett and Swann, where he was later found near death. A patrol picked him up on the eleventh, but he died later at the hospital of his wounds.[65] Another man, Sam McFarland, was shot as a group of laborers came into the area from the waterfront along Harnett Street. McFarland's obituary stated that he was shot on Harnett at the Seaboard tracks as he left his employers, Belden and Howie, on his way home to dinner. He was "among a lot of hands who it was thought were going to Brooklyn to take a hand in the riot."

McFarland was first thought dead but was later picked up and taken to the hospital, where he died.[66] Reporter Clawson recalled that as he was traveling through the city to report the fighting, "gunfire rattled all around us and bullets whistled closely."[67]

Machine Gun Squads

One of the most intimidating components of the Wilmington Light Infantry was the machine gun squad. The squad manned a rapid-firing Colt gun capable of firing 420 .23 caliber bullets per minute. The weapon, purchased by local business interests, was mounted on a two-horse-drawn wagon furnished by Orrell's Livery Stables and

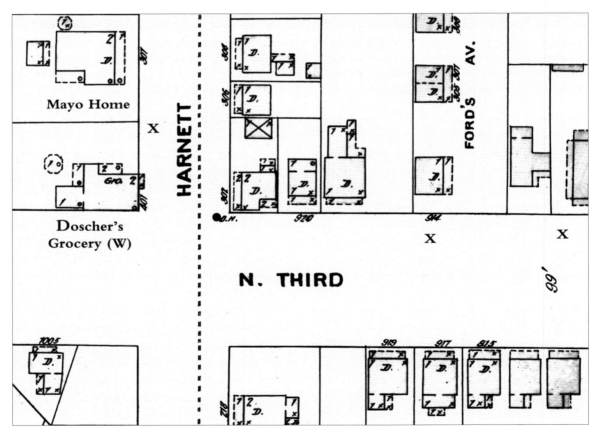

This map includes identifications for William Mayo's house, where he may have been shot, and the locations where two black men were mortally wounded on N. Third Street. Portion adapted from the April 1898 Sanborn Fire Insurance Map for Wilmington. Reproduced with permission, Sanborn Map Library, LLC.

The Wilmington Light Infantry (WLI) machine gun squad. This undated photograph was probably made in the rear yard of the WLI Armory. Image courtesy of the Cape Fear Museum.

driven by Sgt. Pierre Harriss. Reporter Clawson later praised the city's forward-thinking attitude in purchasing the gun as a display of wisdom.[68]

Capt. William Rand Kenan and First Lt. Charles H. White led the WLI gun squad, whose other members were Robert Rankin, John F. Furlong, Edward Furlong, James Williams, John Quelch, and William Whitney. Although the gun was under the command of the WLI, not all of the men in the gun squad were members of the WLI. Members of both organizations believed that showing the gun in the black sections of the city would serve to intimidate into quietude those who saw the weapon. Later recollections suggest that the gun likewise had a calming effect on white rioters, who were beyond the control of the military.[69]

The squad hauled the machine gun through Brooklyn after first crossing the Fourth Street Bridge and into the scene of the first shots. As the gun crew proceeded through town, it was fired upon near the intersection of Sixth and Brunswick, just on the north side of the Sixth Street Bridge. The gunners were armed with rifles, and

A machine gun was used to guard the railroad bridge into town at Hilton Park. It was rumored that blacks from Navassa, just west of Wilmington, were planning to march into town from that direction. Image courtesy of the North Carolina Collection.

George Morton and part of his crew at his home in Brooklyn on the day of the riot. Morton's home, located at 720 N. Fourth Street, became the headquarters for the military presence in Brooklyn. Image courtesy of the New Hanover County Public Library.

98

they returned fire, killing as many as twenty-five black men at that intersection.[70] The gun crew was also engaged in fighting in the vicinity of Manhattan Park. African American attorney William Henderson later claimed that a rapid-fire gun was discharged into a house, killing three blacks inside.[71] The squad returned the gun to the armory, only to send it out again to guard the bridge into town at Hilton Park. The squad was responding to rumors that blacks from the small village of Navassa just west of Wilmington across the Cape Fear River were planning to march into town from that direction.[72]

There were at least two rapid-firing guns in the city. The second weapon, deployed by the naval militia, was a Hotchkiss gun that could fire 80 to 100 shots per minute with a range of five miles. The gun arrived in Wilmington from New York just two days before the riot and proved a formidable weapon. Commander George Morton and his men wheeled the weapon through town, aiming it at crowds to coerce groups into dispersing. The WLI machine gun squad's rapid-fire Colt received more attention in the local media than did the naval militia's Hotchkiss gun, inasmuch as it had been purchased with funds gathered from Wilmington's business community. Journalist Thomas Clawson of the *Messenger*

followed the activity of the WLI's rapid-fire gun especially closely.[73]

Still another group of people, mostly armed white citizens and reporters, made their way into the melee in Brooklyn.[74] Clawson, along with other reporters who were in town to cover the election, ventured into Brooklyn to witness the fighting. In a later account of the conflict, he wrote that he was particularly impressed by the machine gun squad. He attributed leadership of the body to Col. Roger Moore and Capt. William R. Kenan and wrote that the two "heroic figures" led the "spectacular action of the machine gun outfit." Clawson further recalled: "I have yet a vivid mental picture of these two magnificent Wilmingtonians as they grimly stood upright by their machine gun." The gun was mounted on a large horse-drawn truck and was conveyed "at a rapid rate through every section of Brooklyn." Clawson indicated that the men paused with the machine gun for a photograph and then were rushed off to a section of the city where they were needed. Clawson was proud of the squad for their bravery, since they were exposed to sniper fire. Because members of the squad were among the first to arrive on the scene after the fighting began, they had "the situation well in hand when the military companies arrived." Clawson firmly believed that there would have been considerably more blood-shed without the participation of the "flying machine-gun squadron."[75]

The rapid-fire guns were used not only to intimidate black men on the streets but also to force African American churches to comply with particular demands by the white leadership. Churches, at the heart of the black community, helped communicate information and were seen as an organizational threat to whites. Rumors heard by leaders of the WLI held that the churches were used as arsenals, ready to equip black men with weapons to return fire at the whites. Therefore, at an early stage, the machine guns targeted all the churches and forced ministers to open their doors to searches by whites. St. Stephen's AME Church on the corner of Fifth and Red Cross streets was one of the largest churches in the city, with a congregation of almost 1,600 members. The crew aimed the rapid-fire gun at the church's main entrance and threatened to open fire. The church leaders opened the building to a thorough search, which produced no weapons. John V. B. Metts later recalled that the WLI and the naval militia scoured the churches for guns, but the only items found were large numbers of election flyers encouraging members to "vote for Dockery."[76]

Even though there was sporadic fighting throughout the southern sections of Wilmington's First Ward, other pockets of fighting erupted in response to specific "threats." One such pocket was at Manhattan Park.[77] Around 2:15 P.M., while the Reverend I. S. Lee of St. Stephen's AME Church was escorting Col. William C. Jones and Sterling P. Adams through town to quiet the population, they were shot at by men from inside a building across the street in Manhattan Park.[78] Members of the military were informed that blacks were shooting at whites from Manhattan Park, where there were several businesses, including a "disreputable dance hall run by a negro named Henry Nichols" that was surrounded by a tall fence along Bladen Street. Once a WLI group under the command of Walker Taylor arrived on the scene following a double-quick march, the WLI searched the dance hall and arrested four men inside.[79]

A fifth man fled the building, refusing to stop for the military, and he was summarily shot dead. A witness recalled that the "volley tore off the top" of his head and that he fell to the "pavement on the south side of Bladen near Seventh." Thomas H. Wright, a member of the WLI involved in the incident, recalled that the machine gun squad was situated across from the infantry company's lines and that the men were fearful they would be shot if the gunners had opened fire on the buildings of Manhattan Park. However, Charles H. White of the machine gun squadron recalled that as a black man climbed over a fence, all of the gunners (including Capt. William R. Kenan) followed John Quelch in jumping from the wagon to catch him, leaving White alone with the gun and only a pocketknife for protection.

Wright also recalled that Ben Turlington and the WLI partially tore down the ten-foot-tall fence around the buildings in order to get to the black men inside, arrest them, throw them in a wagon, and take them to jail. The undamaged parts of the fence were destroyed by a barrage of weapons fire, completely eradicating the barrier and opening the Manhattan Park area for the whites to search. The main building was pockmarked with bullet holes, and its windows were shattered by the time the firing stopped.[80] Evidently a large crowd of whites surrounded the Manhattan Park site. John V. B. Metts recalled that a group of citizens had fired first, and "when we [the WLI] fired, the crowd went crazy."[81] Col. Walker Taylor, in his report to the adjutant general of North Carolina, claimed that the shooting of the fifth man to flee the dance hall was the only killing carried out by the military during the conflict. After the man was shot, a member of the group responsible for his death was alleged to have quipped: "When we tu'nd him ovah, Misto Niggah had a look o' 'sprise on his face!"[82]

The WLI, not convinced that the parties responsible for firing at whites had been arrested or were dead—particularly after a shot was aimed at the military company from the direction of Manhattan Park—searched for other shooters. Men speculated that Josh Halsey had fired at the men from the Manhattan Park area; consequently,

Right: This image shows Manhattan Park after the shooting stopped. The fence is demolished, and windows are broken. Image courtesy of the New Hanover County Public Library.

Below: Members of the WLI pose for a photograph following the destruction at Manhattan Park. Image by Henry Cronenberg, courtesy of the New Hanover County Public Library.

a detail was sent to find him. Pvt. J. F. (Frank) Maunder recalled that part of the WLI under Sergeant Harriss was lined up in front of Hill Terry's house at 815 North Fourth Street when they were given orders to find Halsey, whom they found at home near Manhattan Park and subsequently shot dead.[83] Another member of the WLI, Pvt. William Robbins, told Maunder that he was "sick to his stomach" at the prospect of shooting someone. Maunder then told Robbins to "not show the white feather or I will shoot you myself." After the order to fire on Halsey had been executed, Maunder noticed that Robbins had only "snapped" his gun instead of firing it and that his plunger was out and his cartridges were on the ground. Maunder lived in Brooklyn and later indicated that the trying times of living in that section of town had motivated him.[84]

As the day progressed, shots were heard throughout Brooklyn, and contemporary reports point out that groups of emboldened black men encountered groups of white men in armed units. The reports of the day's actions and later accounts by participants read like a list of shootings and deaths.[85] Harry Hayden recounted several killings witnessed by Red Shirts. One claimed he saw six men shot and killed at the Cape Fear Lumber Company plant and buried in a nearby ditch. Another told Hayden that a white man acting as a sniper killed nine men as they fled a building after having shot at whites from inside. He also reported that near Fourth and Nixon streets a "youth" shot a "Negro rabble rouser" as the man stood on a dry goods box denouncing whites. Hayden's account of the shootings also offers the only instance of a body being thrown into the Cape Fear River. "An observer" told Hayden that a black man had been shot on the wharf and his body tossed into the river after he "sassed" two white men there.[86] Many of Hayden's accounts provide geographic markers that place the shootings in town; however, many shooting anecdotes, as well as some found in the local papers, provide only for an individual being shot, particularly black men for failure to stop for patrols well into the evening hours of the tenth and the early morning hours of the eleventh.[87]

Throughout the day, while fighting raged in the northern sections of Wilmington, the rest of

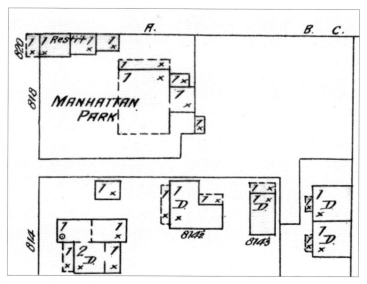

Eyewitness accounts and the map shown above reveal that the area known as Manhattan Park was in a block bounded by Sixth, Seventh, Brunswick, and Bladen streets. Portion adapted from the April 1898 Sanborn Fire Insurance Map for Wilmington. Reproduced with permission, Sanborn Map Library, LCC.

the city was mostly quiet. One observer noted that "The fighting . . . was way over in Brooklyn and except that every spare man in the neighborhood stood on the street corners adjacent [to their homes] with guns everything was quieter than Sunday."[88] Analysis of information on the day's events reveals that only a few reported shootings occurred outside the Brooklyn neighborhood. One, in particular, is disturbing because it suggested premeditation. Hayden stated that a Red Shirt killed a black policeman named Perkins as the officer left his home in the Dry Pond area; the Red Shirt claimed that he had waited four days to accomplish the shooting.[89] Two other reports of shootings, both related to black men who refused to stop for patrols, are the only additional sources of such activity outside Brooklyn. One report cited by Hayden indicated that a black man was shot at Front and Princess streets after being warned not to pass a picket line. The other, which appears in the *Evening Dispatch*, took place at the corner of Tenth and Princess at about eight o'clock at night when a black man refused to stop for a patrol.[90]

As the riot continued, word of the fighting spread throughout the state and nation, with telegrams dispatched back and forth between Wilmington, Raleigh, Charlotte, and President William McKinley in Washington, D.C. Telegrams were sent from Wilmington to the Raleigh *News and Observer*, first at 11:00 A.M., and later regular updates were posted at its offices; and people came by to read and discuss the situation. The governor responded by dispatching several additional State Guard units by train to Wilmington. These troops began to arrive in the evening and into the following day. First to arrive, at 11:00 P.M., were the Maxton Guards, and Col. Walker Taylor assigned them to guard the city hospital. The Clinton Guards arrived at 11:30 P.M. and guarded the city jail. The Kinston Naval Reserves arrived at 2:30 A.M. on the eleventh and were assigned patrol duty before they relieved the Clinton Guards at the jail. President McKinley met with his staff to discuss the riot but did not move to activate troops because Governor Russell made no official request for assistance from him.[91]

Another aspect of the violence, with particular ramifications for black women and children, was the mass exodus of African Americans that began almost as soon as Alfred Moore Waddell's group descended upon the *Daily Record* office. With children in tow, women fled their homes for the outskirts of town. The women were soon followed by those men who were able to escape the shooting and patrols through town. Most often, cemeteries and swamps served as the stopping points or respites for those refugees. The records are replete with reports of the disappearance of blacks from the city and the grim conditions of the wilderness in which they hid.[92]

The weather conditions on those November days and nights were typical of autumn in North Carolina—mild, but, in the space of a few hours, chilly with cold mists.[93] Newspapers reported that the roads were lined with refugees carrying bedding or personal belongings and that it was "pitiable to see the children hurrying in fright after their parents." The refugees then spent the nights of the tenth and eleventh in the woods. The Raleigh *News and Observer* noted that these people were "thoroughly subdued and frightened" as they filled every road leading from the town "loaded with packs . . . fleeing in the darkness to make their home elsewhere." Other black refugees sought protection in the homes of friends and relatives, as well as those of whites. Former slaves of the Newkirk family made their way to the outlying home of their former masters near modern-day Landfall. Family tradition in the Newkirk family holds that families of former slaves hid in the home's basement while the whites fed and protected them for as long as a week.[94]

The Reverend J. Allen Kirk of Wilmington's Central Baptist Church, protesting the atrocities against his fellow citizens, related that "thousands of women, children and men rushed to the swamps and there lay upon the earth in the cold to freeze and starve." Kirk hid his own wife and family in Pine Forest Cemetery, designated for black burials, even as he himself continued to move farther away from the fighting, spending time in Castle Hayne, nine miles from Wilmington. Thomas Rivera, a black undertaker, realized that his life was in danger, and, although he was not slated for banishment by white leaders, departed and spent the night in white Oakdale Cemetery until things quieted down. Another minister, North Carolina native Rev. Charles S. Morris, delivered a speech in January 1899 to the International Association of Colored Clergymen in Boston in which he recounted the horrors of the riot and recalled that thousands of women and children fled into the "darkness of the night, out under a gray and angry sky, from which [fell] a cold and bone-chilling rain," during which, he

claimed, "crouching waist-deep in the icy waters of neighboring swamps . . . , terrified women gave birth" to infants who died of exposure.[95]

Coup d'etat

While the city streets were rampant with bloodshed, local leaders of the Democratic Party moved forward with their plans to retake control of the government. The Democratic Party was in control of the state legislature. Republican governor Russell, threatened with impeachment and death, was effectively silenced politically. On the other hand, control of Wilmington's city government was still in the hands of the Republican Party and would remain that way until the next election, which would not be held until the following year. Thus, Wilmington's political elite chose to mount a coup d'etat to retake control of the city. Citing ineffectual leadership, corrupt officials, and soaring crime, the men justified their actions as necessary for the greater good of Wilmington society. Paving the way for the seizure of power was the perceived ineffectiveness of the city's mayor and board of aldermen, as consistently and conspicuously emphasized in articles and cartoons circulated throughout the city and state prior to the 1898 election.[96]

Assured of success from the time the first shots were fired, attorney George Rountree, a primary facilitator of the coup, began working to ensure that the amendment to the White Declaration of Independence calling for the resignation of the mayor would be fulfilled. If opposition to the incumbent city government were strong enough, Rountree and his associates hoped, other members of the board of aldermen might follow suit and resign, although such an objective was not specifically stated in the version of the declaration passed at the meeting on the previous Wednesday.[97]

Rountree spoke with businessman William H. Chadbourn at the post office during the early stages of the riot. Chadbourn promised to induce the current mayor and board to resign if the businessmen would select a new slate of officials. Afterward, while in Brooklyn witnessing the early rioting near Fourth and Harnett streets, Rountree encountered Iredell Meares and informed him of

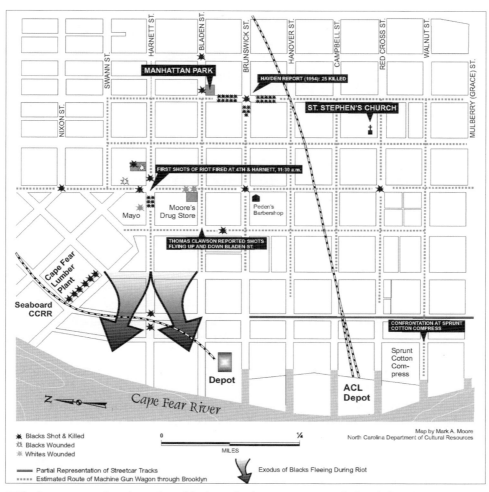

A section of a Wilmington map showing where blacks and whites were wounded or killed during the violence. Map by Mark A. Moore.

the proposal that Chadbourn had put forth. Meares, a member of Waddell's Committee of Twenty-five, agreed with the plan. Rountree again sought out Chadbourn and asked him to request the current members of the city's government to call a meeting. Rountree then went to the Cape Fear Club to mull over his next step. While at the club, Charles W. Worth, another member of the committee, asked Rountree to attend a meeting of Waddell's Committee of Twenty-five at the Seaboard Air Line Building and to present Chadbourn's offer to the committee. At the meeting, Rountree informed the committee that he could promise the resignations of the mayor and board of aldermen if the committee would select replacements.[98]

In addition to the machinations of Chadbourn and Rountree, another man, Daniel L. Gore, a member of the sitting board of aldermen, contacted

newly elected United States representative John D. Bellamy. Gore told Bellamy that he could influence the mayor and aldermen to resign if Bellamy could contact the "gentlemen in charge of matters in Wilmington" and suggest that they select property owners and men of intelligence to serve on the board. Bellamy likewise attended the early after-noon meeting of Waddell's committee at the railroad offices to present this information to that body on Gore's behalf.[99]

Fully intending to act in their "elected" capacity as members of the Committee of Twenty-five to enact the resolutions of the declaration, Waddell's committee had also worked to persuade Mayor Silas P. Wright and his administration to vacate their posts. Frank Stedman and Charles Worth were selected from the committee to contact Mayor Wright, the aldermen, and Chief of Police John R. Melton and encourage them to submit their resignations. Wright, in the face of overpowering intimidation in city hall and armed conflict in the streets, disliked resigning under such pressure but agreed to do so. Melton, too, agreed to resign if he were given the remainder of his salary as police chief.[100]

Waddell's committee considered its options and selected as a new board of aldermen—if the resignations of the sitting board came to fruition—a slate of men representative of their respective wards. As a group, the committee went to city hall about three o'clock to meet with the existing members, whom various representatives of the committee, Gore, or Chadbourn had called to city hall for a special meeting at four o'clock. One by one, each sitting member of the board resigned and voted to approve in his place a new member; thus, the old board was phased into a new body.[101] The last to resign was Mayor Wright, who offered as his reason for stepping down his belief that "the business men had expressed dissatisfaction" with his administration and had requested that he do so. Waddell, unanimously elected by the new board, subsequently replaced Wright as mayor.[102]

One of the black aldermen forced to resign was John G. Norwood, whom the governor had appointed to his position to represent the Second Ward following the restructuring of the city's charter in 1897. The city clerk and treasurer told Norwood to report to the city's offices at four o'clock on the afternoon of the rioting. Upon his arrival at city hall, Norwood was met by other members of the Wright administration. As they began their meeting, two vacancies on the board were filled by C. H. Ganzer for the Fifth Ward and Henry P. West for the Second Ward.[103] Other members of the Wright administration were likewise compelled to resign, among them Chief of Police Melton, whom Rountree in a private conversation advised to do so because he could not guarantee Melton's safety otherwise. Melton recalled that there were one hundred to two hundred armed men in the corridors of city hall at the time. After he resigned, a new chief was immediately sworn in. Melton told Rountree that he could not organize his police force well enough to restore order and that his resignation would enable the group to obtain "force enough to

restore order." Melton returned home, only to be sent out of town the following day.[104]

As bullets were flying through Brooklyn and the city's government fell to armed politicians—men who were privy to the discussions of the Secret Nine—the Wilmington Merchants Association, the Committee of Twenty-five, WGU clubs, and other organizations established a systematic program of banishment for black leaders and white Republicans. The leaders of the white community perceived as a threat many of those targeted for banishment. The first group of black men the whites so identified was the Committee of Colored Citizens (CCC), assembled to hear the demands of the Committee of Twenty-five and the White Declaration of Independence. Some of the men of the CCC were seized and summarily arrested during the riot, while others were arrested or coerced into leaving during the days and weeks that followed.

During the riot, the WLI cooperated with the banishment campaign by detailing squads to arrest men named by the Secret Nine. Others were allowed to remain in Wilmington as long as they "knew their place." While only the primary leaders of the black community were named as targets for banishment, others were arrested for their own safety during the turmoil of November 10 and 11. While white men behind the scenes such as attorneys and businessmen wished only to see the departure of primary obstacles to white rule, others added their own choices for banishment, carrying the arrest and confinement processes into the days following the riot. Much to the despair of the coup's leaders, this secondary banishment campaign was out of their control and threatened to prolong hostilities and cripple the city.[105]

By the end of the day on November 10, the white leaders of Wilmington had successfully manipulated the masses into open warfare. The beneficiaries of the violence were those leaders themselves, who essentially regained control of city affairs through a coup d'etat. In a multitude of ways, the foremost victims of the tragedy were the city's African Americans, who suffered banishment, the fear of further murders, deaths of loved ones, destruction of property, exile into cold swampland, or injury from gunfire.

Chapter 6

Resounding Change

In this manner wanes the slow night amid threat, uncertainty and bloodshed. On every block the steady trump of guards is heard. As the yellow lamplight pales in the gray morning, the negroes failed to re-appear on the streets.

—*News and Observer* (Raleigh),
November 13, 1898

By nightfall on November 10, thousands of men, women, and children in Wilmington knew their lives had been forever changed by the Democrats in their quest for victory in the election of 1898. The violence that erupted as a result of Democratic Party machinations fractured the relatively peaceful and progressive city. Many in Wilmington's African American community feared for their lives. Bipartisan politics was dead, and the city soon returned to post-Reconstruction status quo, with wealthy Democrats in firm control of county and municipal government. As the end of November and the Thanksgiving holiday approached, families in Wilmington either rejoiced or recuperated. A hostile environment, unfriendly to non-Democrats of either race, persisted. African Americans fared much worse than did their white Fusionist counterparts. They faced the coming winter with little prospect of improvement, reductions in pay and job availability, and increased blatant racism on a daily basis.[1]

In the immediate aftermath of the violence of November 10, the paramilitary system of action and communication established by Col. Roger Moore, Col. Walker Taylor, and other leaders held sway. Plans for establishing headquarters, safe houses for family members, and access to wagons and trains, among other details, had been worked out and thoroughly understood well before the election. Once violence broke out on the tenth, the plan fell smoothly into place—the riot alarm being sounded at the first shots, the guard details on every block who "interviewed" all blacks who tried to pass, and, finally, the transfer of control

"Officers of Battalion in service during race conflict or revolution at Wilmington, November 10th, 1898." Seated, third from left, George Morton; fourth, Walker Taylor; and fifth, Thomas C. James. The rest of the men are officers and staff of the Maxton Guards, the Kinston Naval Reserves, and the Sampson Light Infantry, which provided "prompt and efficient services" during and after the shooting ceased. Image courtesy of the Cape Fear Museum.

over the city to military forces.[2] Colonel Taylor, given charge of the city by the governor and state adjutant general, instituted martial law at about 2:30 in the afternoon and demanded that all blacks be off the streets before nightfall. Taylor ordered his second-in-command, Col. George Morton of the North Carolina Naval Militia, to enforce the curfew. Morton made his home at 720 North Fourth Street, his base of operations. As many as 400 special policemen were deputized to assist the military units already in place in the city.[3]

The day after the riot, rumors ran rampant that trouble was brewing in other townships in New Hanover County, where blacks allegedly were attempting to extract revenge. As a result, armed patrols kept up their vigils, assisted by the influx of State Guard troops. On the evening of the eleventh, new mayor Alfred Moore Waddell personally met with armed citizens in the streets and encouraged them to go home. Waddell then had the military establish a picket line along Wilmington's northern perimeter. The following day, November 12, out-of-town military units were withdrawn, leaving the city under full control of municipal leaders backed by the local troops of the Wilmington Light Infantry (WLI), who terminated their service on the fourteenth.[4]

The transfer of control of the city's affairs into the hands of the new mayor and board of alderman effectively took place on the afternoon of the tenth, but it was clear that the men who planned the Democratic campaign and coup d'etat still directed affairs in the city. A newspaper article published five days after the riot declared that "it was all planned in advance" and that the "citizens committee is all-powerful still, and while outwardly it is taking little part in affairs, in reality it is standing squarely behind Mayor Waddell and will continue to do so." The writer even hinted that the violence attributed to the Red Shirts and Rough Riders was part of the larger plan: "As long as they were sober the 'rough riders' could be controlled easily enough, but had they had access to an unlimited amount of liquor there would have been many more bodies for the coroner's jury." The article related that leaders of the Democratic Party had informed the reporter in confidence that "they never intended to resort to

force save as a last expedient" and that resorting to violence during the voting process would have "given the negroes strong grounds upon which to have contested [Democratic Congressman John D.] Bellamy's election." The article concluded with the reporter's opinion that although the machinations of the white leaders may have sounded very "cold-blooded," they were in fact "grounded in mighty good horse sense," given the state of affairs in the city.[5]

The Banishment Campaign

The banishment campaign began on the afternoon of the riot as African American and white leaders were arrested according to the dictates of the Secret Nine. The men selected for banishment fell into several different categories. First were the African American leaders who were vocal supporters of full participation in government by blacks and open opponents of the white-supremacy campaign. Second were African American businessmen and entrepreneurs whose financial successes were galling to the white upper and working classes. Third were white Republicans who benefited from African American voting support. The initial targets were logically *Daily Record* editor Alexander Manly and his staff. According to family tradition and other accounts, Manly escaped from the city well before the march on the press and perhaps even before the issuance of the White Declaration of Independence. Thomas Clawson, editor of the *Messenger*, who had sold a printing press to Manly, recalled that he asked Col. Walker Taylor if he could approach Manly on the ninth and tell him to leave town as soon as possible. Manly's family recalled that Clawson had given Manly a certain code to enable him to pass through Red Shirt picket lines on the outskirts of the city, as well as twenty-five dollars to assist in his escape. According to that tradition, Alexander Manly and his brother Frank left the city in a buggy and used the pass code several times as they passed for whites. According to other accounts, Frank Manly and *Daily Record* staff member John N. Goins were in Wilmington when Waddell began his march to the press. Hearing gunshots, the two fled the city before pickets ordered out by Col. Roger Moore were in place. With Manly and his staff out of the picture, the white leaders gravitated toward removing other men who could forestall or expose their reclamation of the city.[6]

Guided by a list provided by the Secret Nine, Colonel Taylor dispatched units of the WLI to find and arrest men slated for banishment.[7] Those who could be located on the tenth were placed in jail overnight, and the search continued into the following days for other men who evaded capture. Some of the men, such as African Americans Robert Reardon and James Redmon, were never captured.[8] Six men were taken into custody on the tenth as they met at Peden's Barber Shop near Fourth and Brunswick. According to white rumors, the men were meeting at the shop to decide how best to retaliate against white aggression. When arrested, the men were "tossed into Burkheimer's wagon like cordwood."[9] Another group of three or four men were arrested and "jailed for safekeeping" during the action around Manhattan Park—even as a fifth man fled the dance hall and was shot dead.[10]

The men taken into custody were transported to the city jail and detained for their safety. A crowd composed principally of Red Shirts surrounded the jail about 10:30 on the night of the riot and called for the men to be lynched. The armed guards stationed at points around the jail, posted by Col. Roger Moore and manned by military units under Colonel Taylor's command, refused to give in to the mob. Moore's wife recalled that he personally stood guard at the door from ten o'clock at night on the tenth until sunrise on the eleventh. Walter MacRae, newly appointed acting sheriff, declared that he would not surrender the prisoners and that his authority was backed by many of Wilmington's leading white citizens, including Waddell and Moore.[11]

Two white clergymen were involved in the riot at several stages. Father Christopher Dennen of St. Thomas Church stationed himself between the mob and the jail entrance. Rev. Robert Strange of St. James Episcopal Church was informed that a mob was going to the jail and was asked to stop them because lynching men in jail would be a "lasting disgrace" to the town. Strange helped

107

Peden's Barber Shop, located at the southwest corner of Fourth and Brunswick streets, was the site where six black men, accused of plotting to burn the town, were arrested on November 10, 1898. Image courtesy of the New Hanover County Public Library.

place men from Fayetteville around the jail and then talked the matter over with Waddell, who was also on hand. Strange, Waddell, Moore, and other leaders remained at the jail until daybreak because the mob repeatedly attempted to lure the guards away from the jail just long enough to break in and seize those inside. The three men obviously felt that their presence at the jail would be the only deterrent to such activity. Strange later offered this comment on the riot and the events at the jail: "[W]e saw what was needed and what could have happened and when we think of what did happen, we all know that it was the best managed thing that ever did happen."[12] Early the following morning, Col. George Morton's naval militia, acting as guards, marched to the train station the black men who had spent the night in jail. A newspaper reported that the men were given tickets to Richmond and told never to return to North Carolina.[13]

As for the men sent from the city, it is a useful exercise to understand the background of those taken into custody and targeted for banishment, as opposed to those allowed to remain in the city unmolested. The leading targets were Salem J. Bell, Ari Bryant, Thomas C. Miller, and Robert B. Pickens, who were arrested for "using language calculated to incite the negroes."[14] Those men were also leading businessmen, with Bell and Pickens operating a fish and oyster business, Bryant owning a butcher shop, and Miller engaged as a money lender and real estate developer.

Conversely, other leaders, including many other businessmen identified as part of the Committee of Colored Citizens, were not slated for removal.

The capture of Thomas C. Miller is documented by several accounts. Harry Hayden's history of the Wilmington Light Infantry explained that Miller was arrested according to dictates of the Secret Nine because during the campaign he had threatened to "wash his black hands in the red blood of some whites." Miller, a wealthy man by Wilmington standards, had worked himself up from slavery to become a financial power who regularly bought and sold land, loaned money, and entered into mortgages both with blacks and whites. In Hayden's account, Miller first resisted efforts by police captain John Furlong to jail him but was nonetheless escorted to jail in a wagon. Hayden recounted that Miller's daughter followed the wagon to the jail. Miller supposedly declared while en route that "he would rather be dead than to have to undergo such humiliation." Hayden further recounted that Furlong replied to Miller that if he wanted to die, all he needed to do was to jump off the wagon. Thomas H. Wright of the WLI reported that when his squad arrived at Miller's home, his daughter was on the porch and said he was not at home. Miller was found to be at home, and, after he was arrested, Wright observed that Miller was "one negro we could not make keep quiet and he talked and talked until Ed McKoy's gun went 'click click' and when we told him to shut up, he kept a little quieter."[15]

Another black leader, Carter Peamon, presents an interesting case of banishment. Peamon, a politically active barber, escorted white leaders through Brooklyn to encourage black residents to stay in their homes and not cause trouble. Furthermore, Peamon saved the lives of two white men, M. F. Heiskel Gouverneur and Capt. James I. Metts, when they were surrounded

The Wilmington Light Infantry and the Naval Reserve troops escorting captured blacks out of town. From *Collier's Weekly*, November 26, 1898. Image courtesy of the State Archives.

by blacks. Peamon was then "sent out of the city" by way of the Wilmington, Columbia, and Augusta Railroad. It was reported that Peamon tried to jump from the train as it reached the outskirts of town and was shot by men on board the train. Peamon's jail time was short, and he apparently was put aboard the train on the tenth, earlier than the other banished men. The *Evening Dispatch* reported that Peamon was put on the southbound Atlantic Coast Line train and that his life was saved by Metts, who protected him from whites who "would have taken summary vengeance" on Peamon for his attempts to "incite the negroes." Armed men were on the train with Peamon, and by the time it reached Hilton Park at the northern edge of town, he was dead—"lying in the woods." A passenger on the train telephoned in the report from Hilton of Peamon's death. Details of Peamon's actions on the day are also recorded in a letter from John V. B. Metts, who said that Peamon was the "leader of the crowd in that section."[16]

Several white men were likewise slated for banishment for their activities on behalf of the Republican Party—Deputy Sheriff George Z. French, Mayor Silas Wright, Robert Bunting, police chief John R. Melton, Charles McAlister, and Charles H. Gilbert. Some of the white men were even jailed and found themselves "in danger of severe treatment by red shirts." A Wilmington newspaper reported that the military provided protection to Melton, Bunting, and Gilbert at the armory because of "grave threats of violence" against them. The paper noted that the "necessity" of sending the three men out of the city "is very much regretted by the more conservative of our people, especially because one of them, R. H. Bunting, is a United States Commissioner, and respect for his office, they say, should have been a protection." The paper concluded that, despite Bunting's position, his "political record in cooperating with the negro element . . . had so embittered many people . . . that it was feared that they could not be restrained from violence."[17]

The white men were put on trains on the eleventh and sent to New Bern, where they were ushered further north, toward Virginia.[18] Justice Robert Bunting was particularly distasteful to white men in that he had married a black woman, and they believed "his police courts . . . held the scales of justice so as to favor the negroes and severely punish the whites."[19] White men "visited" his dwelling and ransacked it; they also hung portraits of Bunting and his wife in the street at Seventh and Market to further incite white-supremacy-fueled hatred of miscegenation. The day after the riot, Bunting appealed to white leaders for protection and was escorted to the city limits for that purpose.[20]

Like Peamon, George French was treated differently from the others. Before a squad "found" French at the Orton Hotel and escorted him to the train, Col. George Morton had located him earlier during the day of the riot and "asked" him to pen support for deployment of the naval militia. Morton reported to the adjutant general that he "found the Sheriff at the Orton Hotel, in his room, and notified him of the state of affairs and demanded as a citizen that he go out and preserve the peace." French, as acting sheriff in Elijah Hewlett's stead, "declined" to leave his room but instead wrote an order for Colonel Morton and Col. Walker Taylor of the Wilmington Light Infantry to "use all force at your disposal to quell the existing violation of the peace in this city."[21] Previous threats had circulated that French was to be hanged on "Church Street, between Front and Surry, directly in front of the old James J. Darby home." In response to the threats, Orton clerk James J. Allen hid French and later declared that he had done so not "out of any friendship for the 'carpetbagger' but simply to assist in keeping down violence." While at the station, French was attacked by a group of men who placed a noose around his neck and started to hang him from a light pole on North Front Street. French was struggling for breath and "uttered the Masonic cry of distress." French's life was spared by the intervention of Frank Stedman, a member of the Committee of Twenty-five, who told French that he saved him because of their mutual membership in the fraternal order. French was so detested because the Democrats saw him as "a white politician of influence with the negroes."

While boarding the northbound train, French was told to "leave North Carolina and never return again upon peril of his life."[22]

Newspapers and members of the Democratic Party proclaimed the arrest and banishment of Chief of Police John Melton, Populist and leading public figure identified as a member of the Big Six in the campaign. The *News and Observer* reported that Melton was captured amid "sensation" by a "crowd of rough riders who would have committed violence had not the military interfered."[23] John V. B. Metts recalled in 1905 that he would "never forget how Melton looked as he sat under a tree at the Armory, he could not eat and when one of the boys went upstairs and took a rope with a noose in it and threw it at his feet, he turned just as white as a sheet."[24] Melton knew that his life was endangered as a result of the campaign propaganda about the Big Six—white men identified as ringleaders of black voters—and the general attitude of white Democrats toward his activities as chief of police. Nevertheless, he continued to live and work in the city despite the danger.

On November 10 Melton had observed the march on Manly's press, and by the time the first shots were fired, he was stationed at city hall, where he received reports that squads of from fifteen to thirty armed white men were spread out all over the city. An officer then informed him that "there had been a riot over the railroad and a lot of men killed." The officer could not tell Melton how many had been killed at that point. Melton then received word at city hall that "they were coming over [to] demand the offices, and take them by force if we didn't resign." Melton later recalled that after he had resigned his office, he went home and was not bothered that night. He did not leave home again until the next morning, when he went back to city hall to help with the transition to the new police force led by Edgar G. Parmele. On that day, November 11, C. H. Gilbert and L. H. Bryant met Melton just before a mob of about 300 armed whites surrounded the three men to take Melton and Gilbert into custody. Melton asked them why and by whose authority they were acting. In response, he was escorted to justice of the peace John Fowler, who

Edgar G. Parmele was appointed the new police chief of Wilmington on November 10, 1898. Image from deRosset, *Pictorial and Historical New Hanover County and Wilmington*, [92].

instructed Melton to do whatever the mob told him to do.[25]

Melton and Gilbert were then marched up Market Street to the armory, where some soldiers joined Melton's escort. They were then accompanied to "near Seventh and Market" and left there for ten minutes before being marched to the national cemetery, where they, along with Robert Bunting, were kept under guard until about one o'clock in the afternoon. The three men were then moved back to the armory and fed. Melton indicated that he repeatedly asked what was to be done with them but received no answers. At two o'clock they were marched down Market Street and up Front Street amid yells and shouts from mobs to the Wilmington and Weldon Railroad depot. Melton recalled that near the intersection of Princess and Front streets, a man rushed out of the crowd wearing a "special police badge" and punched him in the temple with a rifle. A. P. Adrian of the WLI intervened and stopped the attacker with his sword. At the depot, the men were forced aboard the train bound for New Bern.[26]

The whites in New Bern had received advance warning that the train was on its way, and leaders there did not allow the men to stop in town.

Although Melton knew the New Bern chief of police, he could not obtain protection inasmuch as the New Bern police "hourly expected a similar trouble to that we had in Wilmington." From New Bern, Melton and the others were sent by boat to Elizabeth City and from there by train to Norfolk, where they met "some little abuse." From Norfolk, the exiles headed to Washington, D.C. Melton had not returned to Wilmington since his exile and was instead living in limbo, calling the town of Magnolia his home. Melton closed his account of his treatment at the hands of the mob by recalling that his captors took "the pleasure of marching me right in front of my wife and children."[27]

Mayor Silas P. Wright was likewise targeted. He was advised to leave the city on the eleventh, and he requested an extension of a day to collect his effects. Wright was able to make arrangements for his departure quickly and slipped out of town by nightfall on the eleventh in order to avoid treatment similar to that received by Melton, Bunting, Gilbert, and French. Before his departure, Wright was seen riding through town accompanied by James Sprunt as the two men attempted to "abate the excitement and prevent needless bloodshed."[28] The Democratic leaders disliked Wright because he personified the specter of relocated northerner who courted black votes. Moreover, many Democrats claimed he was unqualified for the job of mayor.[29]

The harassment of the banished men at the hands of Wilmington leaders and other advocates of white supremacy did not end at the city limits or as time progressed. Melton, Bunting, Manly, Miller, and Bryant, among others, were tracked as various modes of transport moved them further northward. Short articles in Wilmington and Raleigh newspapers provided daily updates on the progress of the men, with headlines such as "Arrived in Washington," "Keep 'Em Moving," and "Wicked Find No Consolation."[30] During the exiles' progress northward, white residents of Wilmington dispatched telegrams warning of the impending arrivals and requesting recipients of the telegrams to continue to urge the men along. The men were pushed further north from Manchester, Virginia, on the fifteenth.[31]

Although Democratic leaders sought to end the banishment campaign once the few readily identified "troublemakers" had been expelled from the city, at least one newspaper noted that many "are still leaving of their own accord."[32] Many of both races who had been low-level political appointees from city and county government were not forcibly ejected from the city but were encouraged to leave. W. J. Harris, a fifty-year-old white Republican, reported in 1899 that he had no home because he had been "run away from it." Prior to the election, one newspaper had characterized Harris as a man who was "white of skin but black of heart," and leading Democrats viewed his departure from the city as necessary.[33] One newspaper reported that Caleb B. Lockey, Fusion attorney for the city, had departed in the aftermath of the coup.[34]

Additionally, men such as attorneys William E. Henderson and Armond Scott were informed that they should leave for their own safety. Scott fled the city hurriedly on the morning of the riot with the protection and assistance of his brother-in-law Dr. Thomas R. Mask, white Democratic Party leader Frank Stedman, and a white train conductor.[35] On the night of the riot a mob of whites notified Henderson that he should leave the city, but he was allowed to remain for a brief time to put his affairs in order. He and his family were then escorted to a train bound for Richmond. White leaders viewed Henderson as a liability, since he had attempted to challenge Waddell at the meeting between the Committee of Twenty-five and the Committee of Colored Citizens.[36] Young attorney Armond Scott had been given the responsibility of delivering the CCC's response to Waddell. After the riot, whites cited the missed delivery time, caused in part by Scott's actions, as one reason for the march to the *Daily Record* and its destruction. Scott was also "waited upon by a committee of citizens," who told him to leave the city. Five men put him on a southbound train and escorted him out of town.[37]

The experiences of two other men, John C. Dancy and J. Allen Kirk, illuminate the dilemma facing black leaders. Dancy was the federally appointed collector of customs for Wilmington, the highest-paying federal position in the state.

He served as port collector from 1891 to 1893, when President Grover Cleveland replaced him; but President William McKinley reinstated him to the position in 1897. In 1898 Dancy had just arrived in Wilmington to enter upon his second term as port collector. Many Democrats regarded Dancy's reappointment as another example of "negro domination." Dancy, like other black leaders, fled the city for his safety but was not identified as a leader to be harassed, in part because of his federally appointed position and because he had political connections in Washington, D.C., as well as the president's favor. Dancy escaped the violence of 1898 because the white leaders of the coup knew that interference with Dancy's official duties would certainly result in federal intervention. In the immediate aftermath of the riot, Dancy attempted to ameliorate black-white relations by publishing a letter in the *Morning Star*. He appealed to fellow blacks to "do nothing that will in the slightest degree inflame new passions or revive old ones." He further made a plea to "be quiet, orderly, submissive to authority and refrain from any utterance or conduct that will excite passion in others" so that city officials could "keep the peace at all hazards."[38] Dancy returned to Wilmington after peace prevailed. He resumed his duties as port collector and served in that capacity until 1901, when President Theodore Roosevelt appointed him recorder of deeds for Washington, D.C.; Dancy remained in that position until 1910.[39]

The Reverend J. Allen Kirk, recently arrived in Wilmington to serve as pastor of the city's black Central Baptist Church, was another African American leader singled out by whites as someone who should leave. As a minister and member of the city's ministerial union, Kirk realized that he was a target. He was aware that the *Evening Dispatch* had referred to him before the election as "the negro who came from Boston here to lead the Negroes in their depredations" and had further declared that he "had better take his departure and shake the dust of the city from his feet." On the

day of the riot, knowing that his life was in danger, Kirk evacuated his family to Pine Forest Cemetery. Kirk described his wife as a heroine in the face of danger as she sent her husband farther away from the violence. Kirk left her in the swamp near the cemetery, boarded a boat, and "sailed down the creek . . . waded the swamp and went through the wood and by-paths nine miles from the city." At that point Kirk stopped at Castle Hayne, where he remained until Sunday, at which time his family joined him. Kirk then left his family "in a country hut in the swamps of North Carolina" and boarded a northbound train. Aboard the train, he was met by Red Shirts, who threatened him. Kirk met attorney William A. Moore, another black evacuee from Wilmington. Moore had planned to get off the train at Wilson but was forced back on it. (Kirk claimed that he distracted the Red Shirts outside of Wilson and that Moore was able to jump from the train and escape unharmed.) Although Kirk had planned to depart the train at Weldon, he evaded the Red Shirts at the Rocky Mount stop, secured a horse, and rode all night to Whitakers, where he boarded a "freight" to Petersburg.[40]

Rev. J. Allen Kirk evacuated his family to Pine Forest Cemetery. This ca. 1896 view of the cemetery shows how it looked before the riot. Documentation of burials there has been difficult because of damaged or missing tombstones. Image from Julian Ralph, *Dixie; or, Southern Scenes and Sketches* (New York: Harper & Brothers, 1896), n.p., reprinted in Reaves, *"Strength through Struggle,"* 178.

Kirk later wrote that many of the city's ministers had been "exiled and scattered over the country from our pulpits and our people, without having time to get our property or our money or any other means of protection for our families." He also commented on the power of the network the Democrats had developed to control every facet of life in North Carolina. He explained that his ordeal in leaving the state revealed the "complete organic strength of this most regretful and dreadful movement going on in North Carolina. The telegraph, the telephone and even it seems the very railroad train knows how to move against the Negro."[41]

Kirk and Dancy exemplified the mass exodus from Wilmington that followed the riot. During the riot, untold numbers of African American men, women, and children fled the city to hide in swamps and cemeteries for their immediate safety. Once the gunfire stopped, many black residents of the city were hesitant to return to their homes. Despite promises of safety proffered by white and black leaders, many did not return, choosing instead to move to other towns and cities. As early as two days after the riot, however, the newspapers noted that "negroes who fled to the woods in droves Thursday and have since been in hiding are coming back into town, many of them in a famished condition," while others were leaving the city "loaded with packs and bundles, fleeing in the darkness to make their home elsewhere." It is not known how many people fled the city, and, of that number, how many returned permanently.[42]

The banishment campaign effectively removed political leaders and others in position to counter Democratic claims regarding municipal mismanagement or dire circumstances facing the city's whites. Moreover, black men "obnoxious" to white Democrats because of their economic or political success were expelled, as was Robert Bunting's African American wife and other black women "who have been talking too much."[43] For whites, too, the banishment campaign had its costs. The new city leaders were obliged to address the financial burden of the banishment process and then had to press for an end to the practice. In wrapping up the final "official" costs of the banishment campaign, the board of aldermen paid $61.70

to the Atlantic Coast Line Railroad for transporting seven blacks and other whites out of the city on the day after the riot.[44] Further, with black leaders removed from the city, a new set of men had to be found to serve as liaisons between whites and blacks.[45]

Blacks and whites continued to leave Wilmington over the next few days, and the Democrats, satisfied that the "worst and most objectionable leaders in the city" were banished, "allowed" them to depart.[46] One newspaper acknowledged that a citizens' committee was handling the banishment campaign and reported that "the committee which has been attending to this war of purification tonight promised to desist" and "lay down their arms."[47] Members of the Secret Nine and other Democrats differed in their opinions on how long the banishment campaign should persist. Harry Hayden credited Hugh MacRae with persuading J. Allan Taylor to stop Red Shirt Mike Dowling from continuing the campaign.[48]

In retrospect, only a small number of prominent white and black leaders were made to leave Wilmington by force. Nonetheless, a large number, perhaps in the thousands, departed during the days and weeks following the riot to make their homes elsewhere. The banishment campaign enabled the white leaders to extend their influence into the core of the African American community and to remove those men deemed too dangerous to tolerate in the city because of the political or economic challenges they posed for whites. The ordeal labeled for life those men banished by force. As for those who sought to move beyond banishment, North Carolina Democrats with far-reaching resources continued to plague their lives.[49]

Dead and Wounded

Even as Waddell and Moore sought to prevent the deaths of the men imprisoned at the jail, skirmishes between blacks and whites continued into the night. The *Messenger* reported that at about 8:35 on the evening of the eleventh, blacks and whites exchanged gunfire along Belcher's Row in Brooklyn. About an hour later, more

113

Men Banished from Wilmington during and after the November 10 Violence

Name	Identification	Post-riot Destination/Fate
Bell, Salem J. (black)	Partner in fish/oyster business h) 512 Walnut (1897 C.D.) (CCC)	Banished N&O (Raleigh), 11/12/1898: marched to train station by George Morton en route to Richmond
Bryant, Ari (black)	Butcher h) 1010 N. Fifth (1897 C.D.)	Banished N&O, 11/12/1898: marched to train station by George Morton en route to Richmond
Bunting, Robert H. (white)	U.S. commissioner h) 1307 Market (1897 C.D.)	Banished N&O, 11/12/1898: on train to New Bern
French, George Z. (white)	Deputy sheriff; boarder at Orton Hotel (1897 C.D.)	Banished
Gilbert, C. H. (white)	Policeman h) 213 N. Seventh (1897 C.D.)	Banished N&O, 11/12/1898: on train to New Bern
Green, Henry B. (black)	Police sergeant (CCC)	Banished but allowed to return when near death
Henderson, William E. (black)	Attorney (CCC)	Banished
Kirk, Rev. J. Allen (black)	Central Baptist Church	Banished
Loften, Isaac (black)		Banished N&O, 11/12/1898: on train to New Bern
Loughlin, James (white)	Clerk at Front St. Market h) 614 S. Front (1897 C.D.)	Banished N&O, 11/12/1898: banished because sold weapons to blacks
Manly, Alex L. (black)	h) 514 McRae (1897 C.D.)	Banished
Manly, Frank P. (black)	h) 514 McRae (1897 C.D.)	Banished
McAllister, Charles (white)	Salesman, A. David & Co. h) 412 N. Front (1897 C.D.)	Banished N&O, 11/12/1898: on train to New Bern
Melton, John R. (white)	Chief of police h) 1215 Market (1897 C.D.)	Banished N&O, 11/12/1898: on train to New Bern
Miller, Thomas C. (black)	Real estate/pawnbroker (CCC)	Banished N&O, 11/12/1898: marched to train station by George Morton en route to Richmond
Moore, William A. (Bill) (black)	Lawyer Wilmington Livery Stable Co. h) 413 S. Seventh (1897 C.D.) (CCC)	Banished but may have been allowed to return
Pickens, Robert B. (black)	Partner in fish/oyster business h) 317 S. Seventh (1897 C.D.) (CCC)	Banished N&O, 11/12/1898: marched to train station by George Morton en route to Richmond
Reardon, Robert (black)	Barber h) 29 Market (1897 C.D.) (CCC)	Banished
Scott, Armond (black)	Attorney (CCC)	Banished
Toomer, F. P.(black)	Policeman h) 916 Love Ave. (1897 C.D.)	Banished Morning Star (Wilmington), 11/19/1898: fled to New Bern and asked to return, told no by Mayor Alfred M. Waddell Not in 1900 C.D.
Wright, Silas P. (white)	Mayor h) boarder at Orton Hotel (1897 C.D.)	Banished

Key:
CCC-Committee of Colored Citizens
N&O-Raleigh News and Observer

C.D.-1897 or 1900 Wilmington City Directory
h-home address
o-office/business location

Wilmington's City-County Hospital treated African Americans in the aftermath of the violence. Image courtesy of the New Hanover County Public Library.

shots were fired along Fourth Street, near Harnett. Sporadic fighting had raged through the day on the tenth and into the night, and the bodies of the dead were "allowed to remain stretched on their backs with their eyes open as a warning to other blacks."[50] White doctors asked authorities to explain to all concerned that blacks would be treated at the hospital, and, as a result, a number of black patients were brought into the facility on the eleventh.[51]

On the afternoon of the riot, African American coroner David Jacobs had driven through town and moved some of the dead to the D. C. Evans Funeral Home on Second Street, near Princess, for the purpose of conducting inquests.

Most likely those Jacobs picked up for inquest and interment had family in the city with the means to provide for proper burial. Other, less fortunate, men were interred under the cover of darkness by family members who were unable to pay for burial and grave markers. Among the men upon whom Jacobs conducted an inquest were John Gregory, Josh Halsey, Charles Lindsay, William Mouzon, John Townsend, and Dan Wright, each of whom was buried on the eleventh.[52]

Jacobs's investigation was disrupted and delayed. The coroner initially attempted to conduct an inquest at the funeral home on the eleventh at ten o'clock in the morning. The putative hearing was put off until three o'clock that afternoon, then not only postponed until nine o'clock on the morning of the twelfth but also moved to the courthouse. When the inquest occurred on the twelfth, the coroner's jury consisted of four white men—Col. John W. Atkinson, E. P. Bailey, J. B. Huggins, William M. Cumming—and two black men, Elijah Lane and J. W. Yarborough.[53] The jury called ten people to testify regarding the violent events of the tenth and the causes of death for the subjects of the inquest. Among those called were Mildred Clinton, Josh Halsey's sister, who had identified him for the authorities when they viewed his body the previous day. The official records of the coroner's office for 1898 have not survived, but the newspapers reported that after taking testimony the jury and coroner concluded that "the said deceased came to their deaths by gunshot wounds inflicted by some person or persons to this jury unknown." An outside correspondent noted that the testimony was "couched in profoundly vague terms" and that the resulting jury verdict was "justified by the evidence" presented.[54]

A correspondent of the Raleigh *News and Observer* who was in Wilmington observed that he had "seen no more grewsome [sic] sight than was that presented the morning after the fight." He explained that he watched as men in an undertaker's office on Second Street made wooden coffins for six men. He described the scene as the corpses of the dead men, clad in their working clothes, lay on the floor near the carpenters and "around them stood negro women with sad faces." Two days after the riot, a Charleston newspaper noted that "several unpretentious funeral processions in the negro quarters were reminders of the deadly work of the Winchesters."[55]

In response to a call by doctors, representatives of the Red Cross and others traveled through the city late on the tenth and into the eleventh to tend to the needs of the wounded and transport them to the hospital.[56] Several black men taken to the hospital were identified. Dan Wright, riddled by at least thirteen bullets and left lying in the street, was taken to the hospital late in the afternoon of the riot and died from his wounds the following day. Taken there on the eleventh were George Henry Davis (shot 6 times), George Miller (shot twice), John Dow (shot twice), Alfred White, William Lindsay, Sam McFarland (shot 4 times and died on November 12), and John R. Davis (shot in the kidneys and back). On the twelfth, a John Brown (or J. William Bryan) was admitted with three bullet wounds in his left leg and one in his right.[57]

Dr. Robert Zachary, a resident at Wilmington's City-County Hospital at the time of the riot, later described to his colleagues how he had treated gunshot wounds received by two white and twelve black men admitted to the facility on November 10. Zachary recalled that "all except the two white men were shot in the back" and that one of the white men had been shot in the foot. All of the men admitted that day recovered, except for two black men who died soon after arriving at the facility. Zachary prided himself on the fact that "twelve of the fourteen will perhaps live to tell their grandchildren of their experience in the famous Wilmington race riot, how bravely they stood up and faced the enemy."[58]

As to the actual number of dead, contemporary sources and subsequent enumerations vary greatly. "There has always been a tendency to minimize or magnify the casualties," said Harry Hayden, explaining that many victims were "removed from time to time from places of hiding under buildings, houses and shanties and in the woods" after dying from their wounds.[59] One Wilmington newspaper predicted that an accurate count of the dead would never be compiled. Thomas Clawson, editor of the *Wilmington Messenger*, stated that 10 to 12 blacks died and 2 whites were seriously wounded. George Rountree believed that 6 or 7 blacks were killed. Fayetteville businessman Peter Mallett recorded in his daybook that 8 blacks and several whites were reported dead as a result of the riot.

Willie Parsley believed that 12 to 15 were killed. "I felt sure that in the event of a collision there would be several hundred [killed]," he later wrote, "but I overestimated their courage or foolhardiness." James Worth wrote his wife that "there couldn't have been less than 18 or 20 blacks killed and scores wounded." African American restaurant owner John D. Franklin recalled that he worked with coroner Jacobs and saw 4 dead men at the funeral home, plus 1 man dead at his home on Sixth Street between Brunswick and Bladen. Franklin also recalled that 2 black men died at the hospital.[60]

Rev. J. Allen Kirk wrote that the streets were "dotted" with dead, and a white man informed him that he saw 10 men at the undertaker's office. Kirk also noted that some dead were found later as a result of the "stench and miasma that came forth from their decaying bodies under their houses." Kirk claimed that an eyewitness told him she believed that more than 100 people were killed. In Raleigh, reports on the twelfth had it that 10 were dead outright and that at least 25 were seriously wounded.[61] The following day it was reported that "before the firing had ceased, half a dozen negroes were biting the dust in death, three white men were wounded and three times as many negroes." These varying accounts from local and statewide sources, many by eyewitnesses, suggest that the actual number of dead will never be known.[62]

The following lists provide, in as much detail as possible, the names of dead and wounded men and the location in which they were murdered. The names of some dead will remain unknown, whereas others have been identified. Again, because of the paucity of definitive sources for the names of the dead, the locations at which murders took place, and conflicting information provided by existing sources, no accurate tally can be made. It is unclear whether or not Wilmington's whites sought to conceal many of the deaths or if they were boastful of the numbers of dead. Another impediment to making calculations is the scarcity of tombstones to mark the graves of men who died immediately, as well as those who died from their wounds after languishing in the hospital and homes of Brooklyn. Also, many newspaper accounts did not provide specifics.

African Americans Killed or Wounded

The following lists were compiled from various sources and contain the names of men who were wounded or killed as a result of the violence on November 10. Also included are several unknown deceased men whose place of death has been recorded. Not found are the names of others, or the locations of shootings, that have only vague references. Many such references are listed in newspaper accounts or in Hayden's account.

Name	Sources	Notes
[Gray] Bizzell	*Star*, 11/11/1898: shot and died at home on 411 Harnett (where George Henry Davis was found)	Killed
John H. Brown	*Messenger*, 11/13/1898: taken to hospital on twelfth	Wounded, fate unknown. Several listed in C.D. and tax list
George Henry Davis	*Messenger*, 11/11/1898: to hospital on tenth; *Dispatch*, 11/11/1898: in hospital, expected to die; *Messenger*, 11/12/1898: in hospital; Hayden's *History of the WLI*, p. 89	Wounded, fate unknown. Several listed in C.D. and tax list
J. R. Davis	*Messenger*, 11/11/1898: taken to hospital on tenth; *Messenger*, 11/12/1898: at hospital, wounded in kidneys	Wounded, fate unknown
John Dow/Daw	*Messenger*, 11/11/1898: to hospital on tenth; *Dispatch*, 11/11/1898: in hospital, expected to die; *Messenger*, 11/12/1898: in hospital	Wounded, fate unknown
George Gregory	*Star*, 11/11/1898: given a coroner's inquest—probably same as John L. Gregory, who received an inquest	Wounded, fate unknown
John L. Gregory	*Messenger*, 11/11/1898: died on Third between Harnett and Swann; *Star*, 11/12/1898: given inquest on twelfth; *Messenger*, 11/13/1898: given inquest on twelfth	Killed h) 1301 N. Fifth Street, laborer
Sam Gregory	*Dispatch*, 11/11/1898: died at Fourth and Harnett; *Messenger*, 11/11/1898 and 11/14/1898: died between Harnett and Swann	Killed
Josh Halsey	*Messenger*, 11/12/1898: killed, Bladen near Seventh; *Star*, 11/12/1898: inquest given; *Messenger*, 11/13/1898: sister Mildred Clinton testified at inquest on twelfth that body she saw in street was her brother; *Association of the WLI* mentions his shooting in a couple of places; Hayden's *History of the WLI*, p. 92 (Seventh and Bladen)	Killed
Charles Lindsay	*Dispatch*, 11/11/1898: listed as "unknown" and first to die at Fourth and Harnett; *Messenger*, 11/12/1898: among first killed at Fourth and Harnett, buried 11/11; *Messenger*, 11/13/1898: given inquest on twelfth; *Star*, 11/13/98: inquest on twelfth; Hayden's *History of the WLI*, p. 92	Killed Age: 25 (1897 tax list)
William Lindsay	*Dispatch*, 11/11/1898: wounded and taken to hospital on eleventh; *Messenger*, 11/12/1898: same info	Wounded, fate unknown
Sam McFallon	*Dispatch*, 11/11/1898: an unknown man found dead under the house; *Star*, 11/12/1898: wounded and taken to hospital—had crawled under house on Fourth between Harnett and Swann—was discovered on eleventh and taken to hospital, expected to die	Killed 1897 tax list: Two Simon McFallons: one an elderly father that owned property and another, possibly a son, age 32. Neither listed in 1900 records.

Name	Sources	Notes
Sam McFarland	*Dispatch*, 11/11/1898: in hospital; *Messenger*, 11/12/1898: wounded and taken to hospital; *Messenger*, 11/13/1898: died 11/12/1898, shot and thought dead on Harnett at SAL tracks; *Messenger*, 11/13/1898: gives details of his life, job, work, etc.; The 1897 C.D. also listed a Sam McFarlan, a laborer who lived at 1014 N. Second Street	Killed 1897 C.D.: h) 512 Taylor, laborer 1897 tax list: age, 47
George Miller	*Messenger*, 11/11/1898: to hospital on tenth; *Dispatch*, 11/11/1898: in hospital, expected to die; *Messenger*, 11/12/1898: in hospital	Killed
William Mouzon	*Dispatch*, 11/11/1898: listed as "unknown" and first to die at Fourth and Harnett; *Messenger*, 11/12/1898: among first killed at Fourth and Harnett; buried 11/11; *Messenger*, 11/13/1898: given inquest on twelfth; *Star*, 11/13/98: inquest on twelfth; Hayden's *History of the WLI*, p. 92	Killed
Carter Peamon	*Messenger*, 11/11/1898: shot as he jumped off train; *Dispatch*, 11/11/1898: body still lying in woods near tracks	Killed
Tom Rowan	June Nash, "Cost of Violence," *Journal of Black Studies* 4 (1973): 168—was a bar owner killed on wharf	Killed
John Townsend	*Dispatch*, 11/11/1898: listed as "unknown" and first to die at Fourth and Harnett; *Messenger*, 11/12/1898: among first killed at Fourth and Harnett, buried 11/11; *Messenger*, 11/13/1898: given inquest on twelfth; *Star*, 11/13/98: inquest on twelfth; Hayden's *History of the WLI*, p. 92	Killed
Alfred White	*Dispatch*, 11/11/1898: in hospital; *Messenger*, 11/12/1898: wounded and taken to hospital on eleventh	Wounded, fate unknown Several listed in C.D. and tax list
Daniel Wright	*Messenger*, 11/11/1898 and 11/12/1898 on his death; *Dispatch*, 11/11/1898: Mayo's assailant, died at hospital on eleventh; *Messenger*, 11/13/1898: given inquest on twelfth; *Star*, 11/13/98: inquest on twelfth; *Association of the WLI* mentions his shooting; Hayden's *History of the WLI*, p. 90	Killed 1897 tax list: age, 40 1897 C.D.: h) 810 N. Third, laborer
Unknown	*Messenger*, 11/11/1898 and 11/14/1898: killed at Carolina Central Tracks west of Second on Harnett	Killed
Unknown	*Messenger*, 11/11/1898: killed as he shot at whites east of railroad repair shop near Third at 4:00 P.M. on tenth; *Messenger*, 11/14/1898: left where he was shot and body still on tracks at nightfall	Killed
Unknown	*Messenger*, 11/14/1898: killed at Manhattan Park [Halsey?]; Hayden's *History of the WLI*, p. 92	Killed
Unknown	*Morning Star*, 11/11/1898: shot dead by guard at 4:30 P.M. on the tenth at Fourth Street Bridge after he snapped a musket at the guard. *Dispatch*, 11/11/1898: killed on ACL tracks near Fourth Street Bridge	Killed
Unknown	*Evening Dispatch*, 11/11/1898: killed at Seventh and Bladen [Halsey?]; Hayden's *History of the WLI*, p. 92	Killed
Unknown	*Dispatch*, 11/11/1898: shot on Fourth near Red Cross, supposed dead	Killed
Unknown	*Dispatch*, 11/11/1898: killed at Tenth and Princess at 8:00 P.M. on tenth for refusing to stop for a patrol	Killed

Name	Sources	Notes
Unknown	*N&O*, 11/12/1898: killed at railroad tracks early in the morning of the eleventh by a soldier	Killed
Unknown	*N&O*, 11/12/1898: killed at Tenth and Mulberry (Grace) for failure to stop for a patrol	Killed
Unknown	*Messenger*, 11/11/1898 and 11/14/1898: wounded and treated at home on Davis Street by a doctor	Wounded, fate unknown
Unknown	*Star*, 11/11/1898: wounded at Front and Castle for refusing to stop for patrol, attended by a doctor, not fatal	Wounded, fate unknown

General Newspaper Accounts:

Wilmington Messenger, 11/11/1898: some bodies moved to D. C. Evans Funeral Home by Jacobs shortly after shooting, but others still lay in street at nightfall.

Evening Dispatch, 11/11/1898: "In addition to this list there are a number killed not accounted for and who will never be accounted for."

Harry Hayden's history of the Wilmington Light Infantry proved a valuable source for oral traditions within the white community regarding the deaths of black men. Hayden's work, written decades after the riot, was based on oral interviews and printed accounts in newspapers and other contemporary sources. Hayden's list has been compared with other sources, and some of the deaths reported in his work are found in the list above. Other deaths could not be substantiated. Hayden also wrote that Walker Taylor reported 11 deaths but later estimated the number at 20, that others contended that more than 100 were killed because bodies were tossed into the river or buried in secret, and that additional claims ranged as high as 250 deaths. Harry Hayden, "The Wilmington Light Infantry," a typed, unpublished memoir housed at the New Hanover County Public Library.

Hayden's List:

1) Two died at Fourth and Harnett
2) Shooting after Mayo wounding => 5-6 laborers in coveralls killed
3) 1 killed at Sixth and Brunswick by machine gunners
4) 6 shot to death at Fourth and Harnett (partial duplicate of #1), including John Townsend, Charles Lindsay, William Mouzon
5) 25 killed by rifle fire after machine gunners shot at near Sixth and Brunswick
6) Red Shirt claimed 6 shot near Cape Fear Lumber Co. plant and buried in nearby ditch
7) 9 killed by white marksman
8) A youth shot "rabble rouser" as he spoke to a crowd near Fourth & Nixon
9) Red Shirt reported that a deaf negro killed because he did not hear command to stop
10) 1 killed near Front and Princess for refusing to obey command not to advance
11) 1 killed on wharf and tossed into river after he "sassed" two whites
12) Red Shirt killed policeman in Dry Pond
13) Witness account to Hayden of a black man killed on N. Fourth by Fayetteville Light Infantry immediately after it arrived in city
14) Witness account to Hayden of 20 bodies on Cowan Livery Stable wagon driven by his house and later saw 20 bodies at a mortuary near Second and Princess
15) A number of other dead negroes were later removed from time to time from places of hiding

Other Targets

Although the violence was centered in Wilmington, men throughout the state were threatened with bodily harm both before and after the election. A gradual shift in both the racial and political makeup of the state was reflected in the political rhetoric of the white-supremacy campaign. Whereas many residents of Wilmington were either killed or banished as a result of the election campaign or the violence on November 10, a few white men such as Wilmington Populist Benjamin Keith, U.S. senator Marion Butler, and Gov. Daniel Russell, assured by leading Democrat and Red Shirt leaders that they were no longer targeted to be killed, were relieved to have escaped with their lives. All experienced physical threats, with Keith living in constant fear in Wilmington, Russell barricaded in the Executive Mansion in Raleigh, and Butler moving between North Carolina and Washington, D.C. Keith maintained throughout the rest of his life that men such as Furnifold Simmons worked to ruin him financially and politically, even threatening his family well into the twentieth century. Keith managed to keep his prospects open; in 1903 President Theodore Roosevelt appointed him collector of customs for the port of Wilmington, a position he retained for more than twelve years. In the period before the riot and in the ensuing decades, Keith constantly remained on the defensive in business and politics in order to forestall efforts by Democrats to deprive him of either income or political station.[63]

Soon after the election and the frenzy surrounding the riot, Governor Russell went to Asheville with his wife on November 14 for reasons connected with her health. Russell wrote Butler on the twelfth that "Mrs. Russell has been through such a terrible ordeal that I am getting uneasy about her." He was afraid that she was on the verge of a breakdown, and as a result, he was taking her on the trip "for a day or so." One of the stress factors weighing upon the Russells was the realization that his "friends in Wilmington" had tried to assassinate him. While they were there, Russell met with leading Republicans to discuss the party's defeat.[64] Upon his return to Raleigh, Russell found himself isolated from the Republican

Party and obliged to face an aggressive Democratic legislature in 1899. Russell feared that if he resigned or were impeached, he would not be able to return to Wilmington because "the devils [there] are breaking up our business and it looks like we will be driven from our home." Uncertain about his future, Russell even asked his friend Benjamin Duke if he could secure a job with Duke's tobacco firm in New York. Russell confided to Duke that "being a Republican and living in the South are getting to be too rank to be borne."[65]

When the General Assembly convened in 1899, Russell's biennial message, although cautious, addressed the issue of race and politics. Russell denied Democratic Party accusations of "negro domination" under Fusion and offered proof by citing actual statistics of black office-holding both in Wilmington and around the state. Throughout the remaining sessions of the legislature, Russell remained relatively quiet and was unable to forestall actions by the Democrats as they set about to dismantle most of the Fusionist reforms. The Democrats eliminated local self-government in favor of centralized control of local officials, rewrote election laws, and placed a suffrage amendment on the calendar.[66] Russell did return to Wilmington in 1901 and successfully engaged in several court battles, one of which forced North Carolina's state government, controlled by Democrats, to pay some of its previously repudiated Reconstruction debts.[67]

As a senator, Marion Butler was in Washington for the beginning phases of the 1898 campaign, but by November he was involved in attempts to organize and hold together the Populist Party at both the local and national levels. Butler had used his newspaper, the *Caucasian*, to deride Democrats to no avail. Following the 1898 election, his paper claimed that intimidation, bloodshed, and unlimited financial assets were used effectively to prevent about 30,000 men from casting their votes.[68] Once the Democrats regained control of state government, Butler's very life was in danger, as articles in newspapers and letters from associates made clear the Democratic hatred toward him.[69] During the summer of 1899, Butler studied law and was admitted to the bar, aware that his political career, as well as the life of the Populist Party's influence, was coming to an end. Butler lost his Senate seat in 1900 and, although he remained true to the principles of the Populist Party, joined the Republican Party in 1904.[70]

Waddell and His Cabinet

In order to justify their political coup and maintain a measure of public support, Waddell and other white leaders knew that they must restore order to Wilmington, entice blacks to return to their homes and workplaces, and push for validation of the election.[71] Failure to accomplish those tasks would surely invite outside investigation or the introduction of federal troops to the city. Consequently, Waddell and his board of aldermen met daily to achieve an end to the bloodshed and effect peace in the city.[72] The minutes of the board of aldermen reflect the turmoil only marginally and hint at confusion.[73]

Waddell and the board of aldermen met officially for the first time on Friday, November 11. Eight aldermen—C. H. Ganzer, Rev. J. W. Kramer, Preston L. Bridgers, W. H. Sprunt, A. B. Skelding, B. Frank King, Charles W. Worth, and Henry P. West—were present. Waddell's purpose for the special meeting was to "reorganize the police force and take action in keeping peace." New chief of police Edgar Parmele reported that, in addition to the 200 special policemen he had sworn in the night before, only 9 policemen had been on duty the previous night, and only 4 were on duty the morning of the board meeting. On the motion of Alderman Worth, the board, offering assurance that the city would be fully policed by nightfall, voted to authorize Waddell to "confer with the military as to police in the city" and instructed him to issue "a proclamation for all good citizens to stay at their homes." Waddell's cabinet accepted the resignations of Alderman Charles D. Morrell and Superintendent of Streets L. H. Bryant. By the end of the meeting, "the officers of the military were present and the Mayor stated the object of Alderman Worth's motion and explained at some length as to what he wished done." In response, Col. Walker Taylor spoke to the board and "offered the assistance of the military."[74]

The following day, Waddell's board of aldermen again met and selected thirty-seven men to serve as "temporary policemen" for thirty days. The board also voted to extend until November 16 the ordinance that closed saloons. Alderman Benjamin Keith's resignation was accepted before the group adjourned. Waddell's board did not officially meet again until November 14, when J. Allan Taylor and Hugh MacRae were elected aldermen from the Third Ward. The group then adjourned until the fifteenth, at which time Waddell and the aldermen decided on committee appointments and city patronage positions.[75] The next day the board met to discuss reorganization of the city's fire companies and the purchase of equipment necessary to establish a mounted police patrol; additionally, it declared that all city officers who had not tendered their resignations were discharged from their posts.[76]

Waddell's board of aldermen took another break until November 22, when it met to discuss the timing of the resignation of city clerk and treasurer William Struthers. Struthers had dutifully recorded the minutes of the Wright administration, as well as the transfer of power to Waddell. He took the minutes of the November 22 meeting, then added the notation that he would resign his office on January 1, 1899; Josh James was elected to replace Struthers on the latter date. The board also declared the position of city attorney vacant unless the incumbent, Caleb B. Lockey, resigned before December 1. Thomas Strange was elected to replace Lockey on that date. Alderman J. W. Kramer offered a motion to return the wages of street hands to $1.00 per day. The motion failed, and the street hands continued receiving their current pay of 8 cents per hour. Three days later the board met again to address the matter of unpaid bills from railroad companies that had transported soldiers into Wilmington and a number of banished citizens away from town. The aldermen agreed to pay a bill for the transportation of seven men to Richmond and two to New Bern, as well as a number of hotel bills for soldiers. The matter of pay for street hands was brought up again, possibly in response to pressure from the employees, and the board raised it to $1.00 per day, as requested earlier.[77]

CHAS. SCHNIBBEN,
CHIEF OF FIRE DEPARTMENT

Fire Chief Charles Schnibben (1867–1933) was probably the only city employee to keep his job after the coup. Image by Henry Cronenberg, ca. 1905, courtesy of the New Hanover County Public Library.

A full changeover to a purely Democratic regime slowly evolved by the end of 1898. By December the resignation of Caleb Lockey as city attorney was in hand, and three aldermen put in office after the coup resigned and were replaced.[78] Fire Chief Charles Schnibben was possibly the only city employee who managed to retain his job. Schnibben had been appointed chief under Wright's administration in 1897, and in December the aldermen decided that he should remain in place. At the first meeting that month, the board received a report that 83 people had been arrested following the riot—42 whites and 41 blacks. The majority of arrests were for drunk and disorderly behavior. Four whites were placed under arrrest for firing pistols in the city, 3 people were incarcerated for throwing rocks, and 6 whites were arrested for larceny.[79]

A Democratic majority dominated the proceedings of the New Hanover County commissioners, but Fusionists hampered its efforts at every turn. The Democrats had regained control of the county after a series of court battles in mid-1898, but they were obliged to rely upon Fusionists in the sheriff's office and courts to accomplish any tasks. Since Fusionists and Democrats could not cooperate in bipartisan spirit, the board, led by Col. Roger Moore, achieved very little. Once the municipal government was under Waddell's command, the county government worked to recognize the validity of the coup and to eliminate any political opposition to Democratic policy changes by ridding itself of

black and Fusionist officeholders. Just as resignations of Wilmington's black and Republican leaders and employees had been coerced, so too were resignations at the county level. By mid-December, most of the Fusionists resigned, and their replacements were chosen. One county department, the board of education, was thoroughly restructured after the coup. The new board, selected by the county commissioners, met on December 13 and decided that school committees would be comprised "exclusively of white citizens"—even for black school districts. All blacks who were members of such committees in the county were expected to resign, as was M. C. S. Noble, white superintendent of Wilmington's city schools.[80]

Straddling city and county affairs was the board of audit and finance. The board held the purse strings for the city and reported to the county. John H. Webber, the only black member of the body, resigned under duress on November 15. During the meeting at which his resignation was accepted, the board, which consisted of Henry C. McQueen, C. W. Yates, and S. P. McNair, approved an expenditure by the Wilmington Board of Aldermen to hire one hundred policemen for a period of thirty days. The board of audit and finance deferred replacement of Webber until a suitable person from the First Ward could be found to replace him. The board also received formal notice of the resignation of Wright's administration and the election of the new municipal regime led by Waddell.[81]

Wilmington, N.C.   November 18, 1898

Dear Sir; –
    Please tell your Block Captain to see each man under their control before bed time to night and urge them to use their influence to see that no threats of any kind are made against negroes in their neighborhood.
    The City Government is willing and desirous to investigate any special cases reported to it.
By order of the Mayor.   ROGER MOORE
                                                              J. E. Mathews.

By order of the mayor, Roger Moore instructed all block captains to make sure "that no threats of any kind are made against negroes in their neighborhood." These instructions were typed on a small piece of paper found in the Alice Borden Moore Sisson Collection, New Hanover County Public Library.

Peace Restored

Continuing to employ the newspapers to their advantage, the Democrats, through the auspices of the mayor and board of aldermen, sought to end blatant violations of the law in the name of white supremacy. Waddell moved to halt the unauthorized use of weapons by vigilantes. To stop those men and to provide official condemnation of violence by outsiders, Waddell issued a proclamation that was published in the papers: "The comparatively few persons in this city who seem disposed to abuse the opportunity of carrying arms which recent events afforded and who are doing some very foolish talking and acting are notified that no further turbulence or disorderly conduct will be tolerated." Waddell's threat carried the backing of the police, and he stated that "no armed patrol will be allowed to appear on the streets except those authorized by the chief of police." One newspaper, echoing the Democrats' desire to end the banishment campaign, noted that "the boys are going too far with this and it is hoped we will all now get back in the ways of peace and good order."[82] To demonstrate his administration's commitment to peace, Waddell on November 14 held the first session of a special mayoral court (of which he served as judge), during which several whites were tried, found guilty, and fined for

disorderly conduct. One African American, Primus Bowen, had been arrested for "having too much oil in his possession for an ordinary peaceable negro" but was released when it was discovered that he was employed as a lamplighter.[83]

Some black citizens, desiring normal conditions in their daily lives, attempted to return to work amid armed patrols that searched every black man who crossed their lines.[84] Black workers were fearful of leaving their factories, so Mayor Waddell made available special police units to escort them safely home. Again, following the lead of prominent Democrats, one newspaper declared that the new "administration will guarantee protection to all—white and black—who are worthy of citizenship."[85] One black man, Henry Macon, chose to leave town for a short time and secured a note from leading Democrat William Cumming to ensure his safe passage through the city. The document, dated the day after the riot, explained that Macon was "frightened on account of the recent riot" and that he wished to leave town. Cumming vouched for Macon's character as a "peaceably disposed and quiet man, and neither took part in the recent riot nor voted in the last election." He described Macon as a plumber who had done a "good deal of work for me in the last three or four years and I have found his charges reasonable, and his work good."[86] Conversely,

123

The cover of *North Carolina's Glorious Victory, 1898*, by C. Beauregard Poland. This booklet was published to celebrate the victory of white supremacy. It was dedicated to "Hon. F. M. Simmons, State Chairman, and the Grand Old Democratic party." Image from the State Library of North Carolina.

another black employee, known only by his first name, George, worked for James Worth and returned to work by the sixteenth. Worth wrote that George was "back at work again and is happy as can be[,] whistling at his work—I am quite satisfied that he as well as all the best darkies are glad the change has been made."[87]

Democrats Celebrate

Letters circulating among prominent Democratic North Carolinians rejoiced in the election victory, but some also expressed regret at the violence that had been unleashed on November 10.[88] The state's Democratic Party leaders planned for an immense celebration in Raleigh on November 15. The "jollification" was held at night, with the city illuminated by more than 2 000 torches and 500 barrels of tar. Thousands of fireworks were set off along a parade route that wound through downtown. To mark the occasion, the Democrats compiled and published a booklet titled *North Carolina's Glorious Victory, 1898*, which provided details of the campaign and biographical sketches of the men who facilitated the triumph across the state.[89]

As soon as the fighting stopped, some Wilmington whites began to celebrate both the election victory and the victory over the blacks. On the very day after the riot, the military, mirroring Red Shirt gatherings during the campaign, staged a parade in which five companies of troops marched throughout the city along with two Colt rapid-fire guns and the naval militia's Hotchkiss gun. Many of Wilmington's white citizens cheered the march and the parade, which a newspaper described as a "formidable demonstration of the resources for the maintenance of order now at hand."[90]

In their sermons on Sunday, November 13, Wilmington's white clergy justified the campaign and violence. Prior to the riot, ministers had employed their pulpits to aid and abet the leaders of the white-supremacy campaign and the resulting political coup. Just before the riot, for example, Rev. Christopher Dennen of St. Thomas Catholic Church had attempted to calm Red Shirt leader and election officer Mike Dowling and also urged him not to upset the schemes of the insurgents. Capt. Thomas C. James, commander of the State Guard militia unit of the Wilmington Light Infantry, later claimed that ministers of every denomination had supported efforts to effect the coup.[91]

Excerpts of sermons by prominent Wilmington ministers appeared in the newspapers the following week. The main themes were the redemption of the city, victory, and duty. The papers devoted the most attention to Rev. Peyton H. Hoge of the First Presbyterian Church, who offered Biblical justification for the coup in a passage from Proverbs: "He that ruleth his spirit is better than he that taketh a city." Hoge explained

that "since we last met in these walls we have taken a city." The whites, he said, now had a responsibility to rule with deliberate, cool-headed self-control buttressed by legislation to limit black suffrage and to do their duty to the black race through educational and spiritual uplift. Rev. A. D. McClure told his congregation that they "must now join heart and hand to secure by lawful means order out of confusion." Rev. J. W. Kramer of the Brooklyn Baptist Church claimed that "whites were doing God's service," and Rev. Blackwell of the First Baptist Church drew comparisons between the victory of whites over blacks in battle and the victories of angels over the devil and his "black robed angels." Additional special services for the soldiers were held on Sunday afternoon at the armory.[92]

Likewise joining in the post-riot jubilation were Wilmington's white women, who had supported their husbands as they marched on nightly patrols and attended white-supremacy meetings. The women, dressed in white gowns, had also participated in the pre-election parades and had generally engaged in such supportive activities as preparing coffee for white block guards on patrol. After troops began to arrive in the city, Wilmington's women served as hostesses to out-of-town guard units and reporters. The most visible support the women provided was the effort to feed the soldiers in town for the riot. Mrs. Thomas C. James, wife of the WLI's commanding officer, oversaw the accommodations and provisions for the visiting military companies. Mrs. Edward Wootten wrote her son that she had been at the armory washing dishes while the military was in town and that the men ate in the armory yard at long tables as the ladies waited on them. She served food for three days and later declared: "you never saw so many dishes to be washed and then they were needed for more men before we could get them washed."[93]

Harry Hayden, writing decades later, praised the women who had remained at home without protection while their men were out in the fray and then stepped into action to feed the men: "[C]offee was prepared in 50-pound lard cans, buckwheat cakes with plenty of butter and stacked high on large platters, and fried ham and eggs and bacon and sausage were served the guardsmen in bountiful supply by the housewives."[94] On the day of the riot, as the WLI marched on patrols around town, Pvt. James D. Nutt went by wagon to Frank Maunder's home at 624 North Fourth Street, where Mrs. Maunder "gave us something good to eat."[95] In response to the activities of the city's women to feed the troops, the Maxton Guards posted a letter in a Wilmington newspaper thanking the ladies for their "kind and considerate attention" to the needs of the men while in the city.[96] Afterward, one woman wrote to the paper to ask that the names of the men who "volunteered to preserve the peace on Thursday night" be published; the paper responded that the compilation of such a list would be the equivalent of the white city directory.[97]

Repayment for Services Rendered

Following the riot, Mayor Waddell and Wilmington's leaders were overwhelmed by the number of men within the city requesting appointment to the police force, fire-fighting units, or other positions in return for their support of the campaign. "Quite a number of applications for various city offices were handed in to the Board but action was deferred," one newspaper reported.[98] Two days after the fighting ended, one Wilmington newspaper, reminding city leaders of their obligations to followers, expressed the opinion that the "white laboring men in this city have not been treated fairly in the past." The paper objected to hiring black laborers when whites were unemployed and "hoped . . . that [the obligations] will not end in empty declarations but in deeds."[99] The city's leaders sought to make good on an unspoken but implicit understanding that they would favor whites over blacks in the hiring of laborers. They rewarded white men instrumental in the election victory and coup of November 10 with paid positions in the police and fire departments. There were, however, problems related to the exclusion of highly qualified African Americans in favor of less-experienced whites, some of whom did not have the educational background or knowledge necessary to fill public

clerical positions.[100] Red Shirt leader Mike Dowling was a newly appointed fire fighter but was discharged for drunkenness shortly after being hired in March 1899.[101] Other personnel issues surfaced when two white policemen were suspended for intoxication while on duty in February 1899.[102]

The Wilmington Fire Department, originally an all-volunteer organization with both white and black firehouses, had been reorganized in November 1897 and made an official paid department of the city. As part of that changeover, the volunteer firehouses gave to the city for use by the fire department equipment and tools proudly acquired by donation and hard work.[103] The all-black Cape Fear Steam Fire Engine Company No. 3, under Valentine Howe, which boasted some of the best equipment in the state, was one of the first stations to undergo a complete change after Waddell and his board came into power. On November 15, 1898, all black fire fighters were fired, and white men were hired in their place. That subjugation of a source of pride within the black community proved as galling as other aspects of the coup, inasmuch as the men lost not only their valuable equipment, the result of their labors on behalf of the greater community, but also their income as paid fire fighters, as well as a camaraderie that had

Valentine Howe of the Cape Fear Steam Fire Engine Company. Formed in 1871, it was the first all-black steam engine company in the nation. Image from Reaves, *"Strength through Struggle,"* 199.

Members of a Wilmington Volunteer Hose Reel Fire Company, probably the Phoenix Hose Reel Company. Image from Reaves, *"Strength through Struggle,"* 185.

developed between them and the neighborhoods they served. At least one new firehouse, the Phoenix, was closed and not reopened after the coup. The end result was that fire-fighting capabilities in the black sections of town were severely diminished.[104]

Besides municipal and county patronage positions, some repayment of political debts occurred within social circles. For example, Congressman John Bellamy "entertained" with a meal and fellowship the men of the Second Regimental Band as thanks for their support of his "cause" in the election. For many of the men, the evening spent in Bellamy's dining room and parlor was the first time they entered, on an almost equal footing, the social world of Wilmington's elite. Such social elevation could thrust men from anonymity into the limelight and translate into financial boons.[105]

Problems soon cropped up among the city's newly hired white work force, particularly in the lumber mills, factories, and other job sites traditionally populated by black laborers. Employers found a poor work ethic among white employees, particularly those in the mills; others who had observed that black workers were the "least troublesome labor" were proven correct.[106] White workers also expected higher pay. Even before the election, the papers had speculated that white workers taking over traditionally black jobs would be hired at the same pay scale as their predecessors—wages that many whites were likely to feel were less than adequate. After the "boycott" of black labor began, Mayor Waddell remarked to a northern reporter that he thought it would be better if black workers left the South for northern employment; but he also acknowledged that there was "a certain class of black labor that we could not well get along without." Those invaluable workers, in Waddell's opinion, were cooks, laundresses, and stablemen. "I expect the whole south would have dyspepsia in a week," the mayor declared, "if we had to live on northern cooking, we are so used to the southern way of preparing dishes." Waddell concluded that "wages are very low in the south and I doubt if we could get white men to come down here and work for anything like the negroes receive."[107]

African American life in Wilmington was changed irrevocably with the loss of a political voice in city government and the orchestrated effort to downgrade black employment prospects.

Municipal jobs became largely patronage positions awarded by the mayor and aldermen to supporters in the wake of political victories. Because most municipal positions—certainly the most lucrative and best—were restricted to white workers after the coup, many blacks who had traditionally relied upon the city for income were suddenly unemployed. For example, in 1897 the city's fire department hired sixteen African American firemen to staff the two all-black fire stations. In 1898 those positions were converted into white jobs, and one of the fire stations was closed. Moreover, in 1897 at least twelve of the city's regular police officers were African American, and, following the coup, those men were likewise out of a job. Within just those two high-profile municipal job categories, black workers lost a source of moderate income, with no hope of finding an equivalent position. The change in city employment from a mixed-race staff to an all-white one gradually trickled down to clerks and janitorial workers.[108]

By 1898 the main tenets of Jim Crow legislation were already in effect in many regions of the South.[109] The aftermath of the riot and coup brought resounding change to Wilmington's race relations as well, as evolving policies favored whites over blacks at every turn. The city's racial climate was permanently altered; blacks were removed from visible participation in city operations, and many sought work elsewhere, leaving the victors in control for generations to come.

128

Chapter 7

Destiny of a Race

The destiny of a race is not in the keeping of one President or one party or one epoch of history. I have an abiding faith in the future.

—Timothy Thomas Fortune to
Booker T. Washington
December 17, 1898

The news of the riot spread quickly throughout North Carolina. Leading the effort to publicize the events in Wilmington was Josephus Daniels, editor and publisher of the Raleigh *News and Observer*, which trumpeted headlines from Wilmington, Raleigh, and Washington, D.C., to show that state and national interest had focused on Wilmington. Within a week of the violence, John Spencer Bassett, history professor at Trinity College in Durham, wrote to colleague Herbert Baxter Adams that the riot was "justifiable at no point." Monitoring the campaign and violence from his academic tower, Bassett observed that Wilmington's black population was "cowed" and that most whites in the state did not believe the claims of "negro domination" tossed about by Democrats. Bassett saw the irony in the situation, writing that when Alfred Moore Waddell, who had just led a mob to destroy the *Daily Record* press office, was named mayor, his first order of business was to demand an end to the violence: "If he [Waddell] had any sense of humor he must have split his undergarments laughing at his own joke."[1]

State and National Reaction

Gov. Daniel L. Russell first learned of the crisis in Wilmington in a series of telegrams from Col. Walker Taylor, post commander of the Wilmington Light Infantry, and Commander George Morton, in charge of federal troops from a North Carolina Naval Militia unit dispatched to Wilmington. He reacted by sending several state militia companies from nearby towns to the port city. But Russell's hands were tied by political maneuvers by the Democrats, who had threatened impeachment, and by the Red Shirts, who had threatened bodily harm. Two days after the riot, a Wilmington newspaper pointed out that many had "freely predicted that Governor Russell will be on his good behavior henceforth in view of the Democratic Legislature which is elected."[2] Following the election and coup, Russell considered resigning his office, even after Democrats toned down their impeachment rhetoric. He decided not to do so, however, and the Democrats began to move forward with their agenda despite the fact that Russell still had two more years in office.[3]

The Democratic Party's effort to silence and threaten Republicans and Populists was effective. Other state government officeholders followed Russell's example, remaining quiet and uninvolved. As part of his Fusion campaign, the governor had tried to bridge differences in Republican, Democratic, and Populist Party leadership circles by distributing political appointments among the parties. As a consequence, once the Democrats began their campaign, Russell may not have been able to communicate well with some members of his Council of State. Russell regularly called meetings of that body, and on November 10, 1898, it met, but only to discuss a printing contract. None of its official minutes address the problems in Wilmington before or after the violence.[4] One member of Russell's council, Attorney General Zebulon Walser, could have followed the lead of the national attorney general and conducted an investigation into the events of November 10, but it appears that Walser's agency took no such action.[5] Assuming a leading role insofar as state government was concerned was Adjutant General Andrew Cowles, who offered aid to Col. Walker Taylor at the request of the governor after Russell had ordered out state militia companies in the region.[6]

At the national level, men such as U.S. senator Jeter Pritchard and John C. Dancy, whom President William McKinley had appointed collector of customs at Wilmington, had warned the president before the 1898 election that the city was armed and that violence was expected at any time. McKinley received word of the conflict by telegram and held a cabinet meeting to discuss the situation.

McKinley's sources were limited to newspaper reports, inasmuch as no communication went to the president from the governor's office. Apart from

comparable to military occupation during Reconstruction.

Residents of Wilmington on both sides of the issue, as well as others acting on behalf of the black citizens of Wilmington, subsequently corresponded and even visited with McKinley and his staff repeatedly after the violence ended.[7] Over the next few days, a number of Wilmington's African American residents wrote to the president begging for help and pleading with him on behalf of other blacks in the South.[8] The letters clearly reflect the fearfulness of the city's blacks: "[A]re we to die like rats in a trap?" one correspondent asked. Three days after the riot, another correspondent, who said that she could

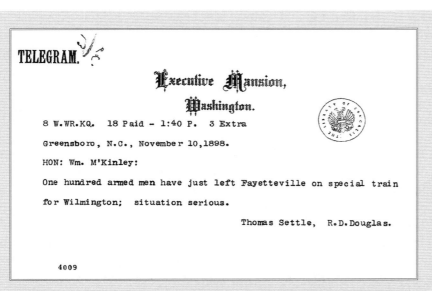

Attorneys Thomas Settle (1865–1919) and R[obert] D. Douglas (1876–1960) sent a telegram to President William McKinley informing him of the riot at Wilmington. Telegram from the William McKinley Papers, (microfilm) 1843–1901, 1847–1902, 98 reels, National Archives, Washington, D.C.

the cabinet meeting, the president and Secretary of War Russell Alger met for two hours to discuss the situation. At a press conference following the meeting, Alger called the affair a "disgrace" to North Carolina. He said that his department had received news of eight dead and declared that he would have dispatched federal troops had Russell requested assistance. North Carolina papers called the threat of sending in troops a "crime" and implied that the use of such a force was an offense

not "sign [her] name and live," wrote a detailed account of the violence and intimidation she had experienced and the banishment campaign she had witnessed. At the top of her letter, she asked the president to "send relief as soon as possible or we perish." In the body of her note, she explained that many in the city would gladly go to Africa because of the violence. "[T]oday," she wrote, "we are mourners in a strange land with no protection near. God help us." Still another correspondent who was "afraid to own [his] name" wrote to McKinley that blacks had been overpowered "with the rapid fire of the guns, and they [the whites] had cannons, in wagons, and they set fire to almost half of the City."[9]

Harry Hayden of the WLI, writing well after 1898, recorded that McKinley met with Mrs. A. B. Skelding, wife of one of the members of Group Six, who was privy to the plans for the coup. According to Hayden, Mrs. Skelding was a native of Ohio and a neighbor to the president when they were young. She visited with him in Washington after the violence to explain her views of the situation and counseled that the "Wilmington Rebellion" was necessary to return the city to white rule. Hayden quoted the president as saying that he understood the issues at hand and had "neither the wish nor intention of interfering."[10]

The newspapers and leaders of the Democratic Party kept abreast of the events in Washington out of concern about the possibility of federal inter-vention. Two days after the riot, it was reported that the president had consulted with his attorney general and cabinet on the matter but that "it was too late to interfere" since, so far as the federal officials knew, all was quiet. The president and his advisers made it clear that the troops would be called out only if hostilities in the city or state began anew. Compounding the situation was the fact that violent activity had also broken out in neighboring South Carolina. Some speculated that the two incidents, if considered together, could in time warrant federal intervention.[11]

Federal troops were, in fact, moved from nearby Fort Caswell into Wilmington, but by the time they arrived relative calm had been reestablished through martial law, and the new city leaders were working to encourage peace.[12] Some speculation has arisen that the president failed to step in because the recent victorious conclusion of the Spanish-American War had engendered national unity and patriotic fervor, north and south, that many did not want to upset.[13] Some southerners contended that the introduction of federal troops into the state would be an insult similar to that of Reconstruction and would act as another divide between northern and southern interests.[14]

Legal Strategies to Address Violence

In response to increased correspondence and calls for action from throughout the nation by leading blacks and some whites, U.S. Attorney General John Griggs and other Washington officials determined that an investigation of the troubles in the two Carolinas was necessary. Wilmington papers reported that Republican senator Jeter Prichard planned to propose a congressional investigation of the violence when the session reconvened in January 1899. North Carolina's Democratic press asserted that such an investigation by Congress would threaten an emerging North-South unity as extolled by President McKinley and "intensify race feelings in the south and . . . make the negro problem still more difficult."[15]

On December 3, 1898, Attorney General Griggs instructed Claude Bernard, U.S. attorney for the Eastern District of North Carolina, to investigate the reports of murder, as well as accusations by federal commissioner Robert Bunting of mistreatment and forced removal at the hands of Wilmington's white leaders.[16] Griggs informed Bernard that "complaint is made that organized and armed bodies of persons, by violence, intimidation, and threats, deprived certain citizens . . . of rights and privileges guaranteed to them under the Constitution and laws of the United States." Griggs wanted Bernard to determine whether or not Commissioner Bunting had been ejected from the city by force and threatened with death if he returned. If so, Griggs regarded the matter as "a most flagrant and high handed violation of the criminal law of the United States" that required "immediate and energetic prosecution."[17]

Bernard replied to Griggs that he had no credible information save newspaper accounts; nor had he received complaints from Wilmington citizens. He did, however, request the assistance of Griggs's office in bringing to justice those who violated the law using "high handed revolutionary methods." In response, Attorney General Griggs and Assistant Attorney General James E. Boyd traveled to Raleigh to provide additional support for Bernard's investigation. By December 12, however, Griggs and Boyd had returned to Washington without calling for a grand jury to be convened.[18] Wilmington whites were relieved to learn that Griggs had entrusted the case to his assistant Boyd, a man who thirty years earlier had been arrested for support of the Ku Klux Klan.[19] Possibly bolstered by support from Washington and despite his lack of witnesses, Bernard soon subpoenaed several men and assembled a grand jury.[20] Men such as George Z. French, Flavel Foster, and Robert Bunting were reportedly asked to give testimony. Despite Bernard's efforts to secure testimony, which almost certainly would have implicated many men of Wilmington, the grand jury was discharged on December 17 without hearing from those witnesses.[21]

Griggs apparently encouraged Bernard well into 1899 to persist. As a result, Bernard requested the assistance of undercover agents to infiltrate Wilmington's white community and to find the "rough and toughs" who were "incited and led and directed by other men of high official and social standing." Bernard informed Griggs that the city was "the storm center from which emanated most of the election crime and intimidation, for one entire Congressional District as well as other parts of this state."[22] The investigation languished until August 1900, when a new acting attorney general told Bernard to halt the investigation because it was "inexpedient" to send undercover agents to the city. Bernard was instructed to justify continuation of the investigation. With the loss of federal support, Bernard terminated his efforts.[23]

Concurrently with Claude Bernard's efforts to conduct an investigation, Oliver Dockery, the Republican candidate who had lost the 1898 election to represent North Carolina's Sixth Congressional District in the U.S. House of Representatives to Wilmington Democrat John D. Bellamy, began working to overturn the election. As early as December 6, 1898, one Wilmington paper reported that Dockery had employed attorneys to contest Bellamy's election in the House of Representatives and through the court system.[24]

Dockery notified Bellamy that he would challenge the election because, he claimed, it had

Oliver H. Dockery (1830–1906), Republican candidate for Congress, lost the 1898 election to Democrat John D. Bellamy. He contested the election to no avail. Engraving from J. G. de Roulhac Hamilton, *North Carolina since 1860* (Chicago and New York: Lewis Publishing Company, 1919), facing 81.

been conducted fraudulently in some sections of the district. Dockery then began to seek testimony from voters and election officials throughout the district. His attorneys sought to demonstrate intimidation by Red Shirts before the election and at the polls. (Bellamy's attorneys chose not to focus on the riot, however, inasmuch as it had occurred after the election.) In instances where there were clear violations of election law, Bellamy's attorneys sought to discredit witnesses. Dockery's attorneys were often frustrated by difficult witnesses who would not fully answer questions or whose testimony clearly favored the Democratic Party. Several Republican witnesses acknowledged that they could not speak about their knowledge of pre-election intimidation because they feared consequences for themselves or their families.[25] Newspapers across the state carried news of the proceedings and often reprinted portions of testimony, adding further to the public nature of the inquiry.[26] Despite setbacks, Dockery managed to file testimony in the House of Representatives. Both he and Bellamy filed briefs on the case according to House rules, but the body took no action on the matter, and Bellamy took his seat in Congress.[27]

African American Reaction

In the weeks following the riot, Wilmington's black churches looked for answers, while white congregations rejoiced. African American minister J. Allen Kirk noted that while a funeral was being performed at Central Baptist Church, the building was surrounded by whites, who thought Kirk was in attendance. Kirk explained that the whites had visited ministers and other church leaders on the Saturday following the riot to determine what sermons would be preached on Sunday. Kirk, from a distance, and others in Wilmington sought

Central Baptist Church, located at the corner of Seventh and Red Cross streets. The building was surrounded by whites while a funeral was going on. They were looking for Rev. J. Allen Kirk, an African American minister who was involved in political activities and warned to leave the city. Sketch of the church from the *Wilmington Messenger*, May 9, 1897, reprinted in Reaves, *"Strength through Struggle,"* 82.

to persuade blacks to "try by all means to keep the peace . . . ever trusting God." Kirk realized that the black ministers were leaders in the community and that whites planned to remove them from the city to ensure that the blacks who remained would be "better and obedient servants."[28] African American church leaders approached white leaders, who assured them that their services would not be interrupted.

The sermons delivered on the Sunday following the riot contained elements of acquiescence and acceptance of their congregants' new situation as endangered second-class citizens. One correspondent who begged the president to interfere on her behalf informed him that "to day (Sunday) we dare not go to our places of worship."[29] At Central Baptist Church, pastor A. S. Dunston urged his congregation to "let the past bury the past" because "what is done cannot be undone." He wished for his followers to "be still, be quiet," and "all will be well." Rev. J. T. Lee, pastor at St. Stephen's AME Church, home to one of the city's largest congregations, had fled the city, and in his place the sermon was delivered by deacon L. B. Kennedy. Kennedy's sermon warned his flock to "watch and pray that ye enter not into temptation" as they did their duty to "obey God's laws" and to "do as the authorities direct." Following a similar line of thought, pastor E. R. Bennett of St. Mark's Episcopal Church reminded members to obey the law and Jesus's instruction to "[R]ender unto Caesar the things that are Caesar's and unto God the things that are God's." Bennett contended that they should "obey first and argue afterwards" because "God will protect His own."

Other congregations heard similar appeals. At Mt. Zion AME Church, pastor James W. Telfair preached a funeral sermon for Sam McFarland, a casualty of the riot. Telfair described the events of November 10 as a catastrophe wrought by God

Ministers like James Alexander Bonner (1864–post 1921) preached submission to the will of God and white authority. He preached at Chestnut Street Presbyterian Church. Image from Arthur Bunyan Caldwell, ed., *History of the American Negro and His Institutions*, vol. 4 (Atlanta, Ga.: A. B. Caldwell Publishing Co., 1921), 127.

133

and declared that the congregation should "obey the law and keep the peace." The pastor at Chestnut Street Presbyterian Church, J. A. Bonner, likewise preached submission to the will of God and white authority. At Christ Colored Congregational Church, F. C. Ragland's sermon encouraged members to "love your enemies, bless them that curse you, do good to them that hate you and pray for them that abuse you." Ragland reminded his congregants of the abiding words spoken by their enslaved forefathers when he said that "God will avenge us" because "in His hands shall it rest" and that "He will act in His own good time." The minister at Ebenezer Baptist Church preached on following the letter of the law. At St. Luke's AME Church, next door to the burned-out remains of Alexander Manly's newspaper office, minister M. L. Blalock discussed the fiery trials of Biblical figures and claimed that "if the negro trusted in God and minded his own business . . . all would be well."[30]

In line with the ministers' pleas, blacks tempered their reactions in ways designed to restore peace, prevent further deaths, and encourage others to strive for calm. A Wilmington newspaper published a letter from S. B. Hunter, a black resident of Wilmington and church leader, who endorsed appeasement. Hunter explained that he had voted without incident and that he believed the city's black women were as responsible as any other group for the violence. He claimed that the women's threats against black men, challenging the men to violence, helped to fuel the conflict.[31] John C. Dancy, black Republican leader in local and state politics, explained that he had attempted to work with Manly to appease whites before the riot. He was quoted as saying that whites had not forced him out of the city but that he had left after calm had returned. He urged that "people exercise good judgment" to relieve the "perturbed situation in the state" because he felt that "calm reason may appease."[32]

On the national level, following the rioting in the two Carolinas, conferences were held throughout the nation to protest against the Democrats' actions in the South.[33] One of the main organizing forces behind such meetings was Timothy Thomas Fortune, a pioneering black

Timothy Thomas Fortune (1856–1928), a leading black orator and editor, led an unsuccessful national grass-roots offensive against white supremacy. Image from D. W. Culp, ed., *Twentieth Century Negro Literature* (Atlanta, Ga.: J. L. Nichols & Co., 1902), facing 226.

journalist, editor, and activist in New York. Fortune was well known in African American circles and corresponded regularly with Booker T. Washington. He called for changes to national laws to address failures of whites to protect the lives of black citizens in southern states. Further, in response to calls for black disfranchisement, Fortune argued that if southern states were to prohibit blacks from voting, then their representation in the House of Representatives should be reapportioned to reflect their diminished voting populations.[34]

The largest of the meetings was held on November 17, 1898, at the Cooper Union in New York City. At the meeting, which Fortune arranged to coincide with similar gatherings in other states, more than six thousand people heard Fortune and other African American leaders speak about the violence. Accounts of the "indignation meeting," as the Democratic press called it, circulated to a multitude of outlets, including North Carolina newspapers. The meeting adopted a series of resolutions that protested the violence, derided state governors of North and South Carolina for their inaction, and pressured politicians for justice. One of the leading proposals to come out of the meeting was a proffered amendment to the U.S. Constitution to enable the president to step in and protect citizens from

134

mob rule without requests for assistance from governors.[35]

One of the speakers at the Cooper Union gathering who gained national and local attention was white activist Elizabeth Grannis. Grannis's speech challenging the color line was, like Manly's editorial, misquoted throughout the South, and she was ridiculed in the press. Hatred of Grannis grew to the point that secret meetings were held in Virginia and North Carolina to formulate speeches expressing white male disgust at her remarks. News of the meetings reached Grannis, who in a response published in a Wilmington newspaper defended her position even as she explained the misquoted speech. The editor appended to Grannis's letter his own paternalistic observations that she had simply chosen to be in the wrong place and in the wrong company.[36]

Other speakers, while just as controversial, failed to attract equal attention. The Reverend W. H. Brooks believed that the trouble was rooted in the white upper classes and that when a few blacks "of the worst sort committed outrages," the whole of the black population suffered. Referring to Wilmington, Brooks said that whites were "too strong" by virtue of the use of guns, telephones, and telegraphs. He urged blacks to remain vigilant and strong—"out of his trials and difficulties shall yet be developed an honest manhood"—and to bide their time but not to "die alone" in the last resort.[37]

Timothy Fortune's grass-roots offensive against white supremacy faltered. Other black leaders, seeking to ease tensions, began to push for a halt to the meetings Fortune had helped to organize because, as one editor phrased it, "over zealous indignation meetings do the race irreparable harm."[38] William Henry Baldwin Jr., railroad magnate and trustee of Alabama's Tuskegee Institute, wrote Booker T. Washington that he thought "Fortune and his kind are wrong . . . and, if they are allowed to go on as they have been, [they] will cause a bad setback to their people." Although Baldwin clearly believed that Fortune was going about his business the wrong way, he shared the view that something should be done to address the violence. He expressed sympathy for Washington's position as a peacemaker and

lamented that Washington had not been invited to speak on the issue in any major forum. Baldwin also pointed out that in Virginia black railroad employees were being forced out of their jobs, and he offered the opinion that "it never would have occurred but for the Wilmington troubles."[39]

The Wilmington violence held far-reaching implications for blacks nationwide. The response of national black leaders such as Fortune and Washington was split between radical and conservative elements. The division was largely one of personal philosophy among black intellectuals, but it proved a boon to whites who sought to divide black opinion. A good example can be found in a *Washington Post* interview that misquotes Fortune and casts him as an anti-Booker T. Washington radical. Fortune, troubled by the errant *Post* interview and realizing that white newspapermen were sometimes less than honorable in their intentions, subsequently apologized to Washington, with whom he had a close relationship.[40] The divide between black activists and intellectuals continued for years and limited cohesion among black leaders.[41] Still, black leaders across the country united in advocating better treatment of blacks in the South. In the words of a proclamation issued by one African American church organization in 1899, "we deplore the sad and barbarous incident at Wilmington, N.C., which has blacked the fair name of the Old North State."[42]

When local and national efforts failed to relieve pressures exerted by Democrats, some Wilmington blacks voted with their feet and departed Wilmington. The exodus continued into December, with newspapers reporting that over one thousand blacks had left since November 10. Many bought railroad tickets to points north of Richmond or south to South Carolina and Georgia, while others moved to rural New Hanover or surrounding counties. White property owners who depended upon rental income from black tenants saw an immediate drop in revenue, particularly in the Brooklyn neighborhood. One newspaper sought to put a positive spin on the turn of events by observing that many whites were making their way into the city to supplant the lost black population. The editor surmised that as

135

many as 250 to 300 whites had arrived recently in the city from other counties and that those new arrivals were filling vacant rental houses and searching for jobs "of all classes" previously held by blacks.[43]

Democrats Practice Damage Control

Wilmington Democrats sought in every way possible to counter the claims made by blacks nationwide. Alfred Moore Waddell's narrative in *Collier's Weekly*, published on November 26, 1898, became the common theme: whites engaged in an act of revolution to wrench the city from the brink of lawlessness and chaos.[44] Others, such as William H. Chadbourn, the white Wilmington Republican and businessman who had converted to the Democratic Party under immense pressure, traveled to Chicago to dispute claims of harassment published by Wilmington exile William E. Henderson in the *Chicago Daily Blade*. Henderson, an African American attorney, had recounted his experiences in the riot for the *Freeman*, an Indianapolis newspaper. He challenged the Democratic claims of Negro domination of municipal offices and suggested that the reason for the violence was a Democratic lust for absolute power. He described the violence, as well as his family's flight from the city. (Henderson had not been banished from the city by force but was told to leave within hours of the first shots during the riot.)[45] In response, Chadbourn maintained that the unrest in Wilmington was attributable to the inefficient Fusion government and the Manly editorial. He said that he knew of no reason for Henderson to leave, countering Henderson's claims of threats against his life. Chadbourn contended that the solution to the problem was to establish limits on black suffrage. He closed by suggesting that Wilmington was one of the most progressive cities in the South.[46]

Even while refuting claims that they had engaged in organized violence on November 10, white Democrats worked to ensure that their banishment and intimidation campaign would succeed in preventing the return of men who could effect change. On December 20, one Wilmington newspaper warned banished men that to return

would be to "tread on dangerous ground" (the paper singled out Republican George Z. French). Another article justified the banishment process as perfectly legal: "[P]ublic sentiment is primary law; primary law banished certain corrupt and offensive men from this community." The paper also warned blacks who might have "failed to comprehend or have forgotten the 10th of November" that "white men are determined to govern this city and county" and that "the 10th of November will prove to have been child's play to what the consequences will be to the negroes" if "insolent lawlessness" or "midnight deviltry" should arise. The paper urged "decent" black residents to rid the community of troublemakers.[47] When one banished man, African American butcher Ari Bryant, returned home in June 1899, he discovered that whites were still willing to kill black men who challenged their authority. Armed white men surrounded Bryant's home with the intent to whip him and, had he not escaped in time, possibly kill him.[48]

Legislation to Affirm the Coup

As protests against the actions of November 10 spread throughout the nation and local whites marshaled arguments to justify their actions, the newly elected North Carolina General Assembly convened in January 1899. One of the new legislature's principal goals was to reverse Fusion reform at every level. Wilmington's leaders played a pivotal role in some of the changes, foremost of which was a complete overhaul of the city's charter to eliminate the possibility that Governor Russell, acting under the existing charter, might again nominate Republicans to posts on the board of aldermen.

Anticipating changes to the charter, the Wilmington Chamber of Commerce met on December 1, 1898, to discuss proposals for the upcoming legislative session. During the meeting the chamber appointed a committee to draft a new city charter and to "confer and advise with the representatives to the North Carolina General Assembly."[49] As soon as the new legislature convened, George Rountree, a newly elected representative from the New Hanover County House district, introduced the proposed changes to the charter, which were enacted into law on March 4, 1899. The new measures represented a complete repeal of the Fusionist alterations to the charter in 1895 and 1897.

The 1899 charter solidified Democrats' control over the city. Aldermen were to be popularly elected from each ward, primaries were to be held in response to public demand, voter eligibility could be more easily challenged, and safeguards against voter fraud were strengthened. The new charter increased the mayor's salary and empowered him to force unemployed "vagrants" to leave the city or work on the city's streets for thirty days if they failed to find a job.[50] In accordance with the legislature's changes to the city charter, municipal elections were held in March 1899 to choose new aldermen to serve two-year terms. Few blacks registered to vote in the election, and not a single Republican candidate was nominated in the two predominantly black wards, essentially assuring that the Democratic ticket faced no opposition. Therefore, in light of the changes to the charter made by the legislature at the recommendation of the city's leaders, the coup was affirmed, and those men brought to power as a result were legitimized in their positions for two years.[51]

To solidify Democratic control over county governments statewide, the North Carolina General Assembly on March 6, 1898, ratified "An Act to Restore Good Government to the Counties of North Carolina." The legislation affected New Hanover and twelve other counties, primarily those with black majorities or near-majorities. The law removed the election of county commissioners from the popular vote and instead made it the responsibility of justices of the peace appointed by the General Assembly. In one bold stroke the Democrats eliminated from thirteen North Carolina counties local self-rule by popular vote as put in place by Fusionists and replaced it with county government controlled by the legislature. As a direct result, Democrats were able to ensure the success of their agenda and their candidates in future elections.[52]

The legislature of 1899, dominated by Democrats, moved quickly to revise statewide election laws to assist them in capturing the 1900 elections. At the head of the Democrats' agenda was a plan to place control over elections both in a seven-member State Board of Elections and in local county boards of elections. The new bodies would be empowered to appoint registrars and other election officials and redraw precinct lines as they saw fit. Even more control over the voting process came as the Democrats redefined registration procedures to make voter qualification and registration more difficult while at the same time making challenges to voter eligibility easier for their own party.[53]

Fulfilling campaign promises, the Democratic legislature passed its first measures to codify racial segregation. The 1899 General Assembly enacted the first of the new Jim Crow laws, which provided for segregation of train compartments. The action ushered in a body of legislation that established in law the concept of "separate but equal" public facilities and legally codified virtually all aspects of interaction between African Americans and whites.[54] In Wilmington, Jim Crow legislation was immediately applied to the trains and trolleys and was later applied to other aspects of life, including the courts. In 1903 a local court judge ruled that blacks and whites must use separate Bibles when being sworn in to give testimony.[55]

137

A white actor in New York put on blackface to create the highly stereotypical black character "Jim Crow." The term was used as a racial slur, and by the end of the nineteenth century it was employed to describe laws and customs designated to oppress African Americans. Image from Reaves, *"Strength through Struggle,"* 267.

Disfranchisement

After the euphoria of election victory subsided and the state returned to relative calm, calls for disfranchisement of blacks began to be heard. The Raleigh *News and Observer* cautioned that "the lessons of the recent past teach that it is neither prudent nor wise to delay a permanent solution of the suffrage problem." As the voice of the Democratic Party, the paper interpreted the election results to suggest that "the people have voted to put an end" to black suffrage and its complement of "problems" for white voters. Moreover, the journal saw the overwhelming Democratic victory as a mandate for the new legislature to "settle once and [for] all time the question of regulating suffrage."[56]

The 1899 General Assembly quickly responded to such proposals by enacting legislation at the hands of state representatives George Rountree, Francis Winston, and others to solve the perceived "problem" of black voting.[57] The suffrage amendment went through several mutations before the General Assembly approved it on February 21, 1899. It was based on similar legislation passed in other states and relied upon recent court decisions that supported the rights of states to disfranchise citizens through literacy tests.[58] The final version of the amendment required voters to pass a literacy test and pay a poll tax. Opposition to the bill came from Populists, who claimed that the scheme's restrictions might possibly ensnare some white men and limit their ability to vote. Democrats conceded that some whites would have to sacrifice their vote for the greater good of the white population. To reassure skeptics that illiterate whites would not be disfranchised, the amendment included a "grandfather clause": "[N]o male person who was on January 1, 1867, or at any time prior thereto, entitled to vote under the laws of the state in the United States wherein he then resided, and no lineal descendent of such person, shall be denied the right to register to vote at any election in this State by reason of his failure to pass the education qualification." A codicil to the clause specified that it was effective only through December 1, 1908. After that date, all men who were not already registered would have to pass a literacy test. The amendment as constructed in the legislature went to the voters for approval during the November general elections.[59]

Blacks reacted to the suffrage amendment in various ways, reflecting the ideological split among various national factions. Men such as Wilmington's John C. Dancy, who counseled peaceful accommodation of the more strident white demands for limited suffrage, voiced their concerns cautiously. More than eighty of those men, including Dancy, met in Raleigh and appealed to legislators not to "blunt our aspirations, ruin our manhood and lessen our usefulness as citizens, but guarantee us an equal chance with other men to work out our destiny." The request represented a compromise of sorts within the black community, because a more vocal leadership element—men such as George H. White—preferred to encourage black emigration from the state should the Democrats make their lives there "intolerable."[60]

Despite such accommodative efforts by black leaders, North Carolina's voters in a 1900 referendum approved the suffrage amendment. Because the Democratic-dominated General Assembly of 1899 had made such a multitude of changes to Fusion legislation—all intended to reverse gains made for average voters—blacks were unable to use their collective voice at the polls in 1900. And because few were willing to brave Red Shirt intimidation and register to vote, the overall outcome strongly benefited the Democrats.[61]

The 1900 Election

The 1900 election season and subsequent Democratic victory closed the door on Republicans and their involvement in state politics. At the top of the agenda was ratification of the suffrage amendment to limit black voting. New Bern attorney and state Democratic Party chairman Furnifold M. Simmons led the Democratic campaign, which again manifested itself in print, speechmaking, and intimidation. Among newspapers, the Raleigh *News and Observer* led the way; popular speaker and gubernatorial candidate Charles B. Aycock traveled throughout the state with other speakers to preach the Democratic Party mantra of white supremacy; and Red Shirts were again on the ride, using intimidation and fear to maintain solidarity among whites and repression of blacks.

As a result of the violent and well-organized Democratic campaign of 1898 and the ensuing changes to state government, Populists and Republicans were in disarray. Leaders of both parties, privately acknowledging that the issue of race was problematic, minimized the topic in their campaigns. As early as October 1898 Populists had realized that its practice of courting black voters, once a necessity, had been rendered "inadequate and unadvisable" by the successful white-supremacy platform put forth by the Democrats.[62] In Wilmington, wealthy businessman and Populist Benjamin F. Keith attempted unsuccessfully to revive that party for the 1900 elections by seeking to unite men opposed to the activities of the Red Shirts Populists saw much danger in the Red Shirt campaign and feared that further Democratic encouragement of such activities would lead to voter intimidation, as well as "riot, slander, abuse, physical violence and general anarchy" throughout the state. The Populists attempted to counter the crux of the Democratic Party's campaign—white supremacy and fear of "negro domination"—by removing it from the stage. Fusionist Jeter C. Pritchard acknowledged that "candidacy of colored people at this time for local offices would do more to assist the Democrats in their unjust and unwarranted assertions, than all other causes combined."[63]

Gov. Daniel Russell and the Republicans likewise responded to Democratic fear-mongering on the subject of Negro rule. In early 1900 Russell said that if southerners had accepted more readily the early terms of Reconstruction, Congress would not have been forced to employ the Fifteenth Amendment to press black suffrage on them. He argued that the state suffrage amendment proposed in North Carolina sought to negate the federal amendment and challenged northern Republicans to become more involved in assuring the rights of blacks, as they had done

after the Civil War. Many whites in North Carolina misinterpreted Russell's arguments and chose to believe that, at heart, he supported the suffrage amendment. A resulting squabble that played out in the state's newspapers drove a wedge between Russell and many of his fellow Republicans. Because of such misunderstandings, the disjointed party could not mount an offensive against the more powerful and emboldened Simmons.[64]

Simmons and his Democratic Party workers followed the 1898 blueprint, adding the suffrage amendment into the mix. Red Shirts, the White Government Union (WGU), and print campaigns followed much of the same pattern, although the tone was more aggressive and focused on maintaining the upper hand gained by victories two years earlier. At one July 1900 rally, Democratic speakers proposed to remove the black vote from politics through "peaceful methods" but reserved the option of force "if a conflict comes."[65]

Throughout the 1900 campaign, Wilmington was relatively quiet, largely because Republican, Populist, and black opposition had already been crushed. The Democratic ticket in New Hanover County went unopposed, and only a few eligible black voters who remained in the city registered to vote. Among all the counties in North Carolina, New Hanover had the fewest votes against the suffrage amendment, with only two cast against it and 2,967 for it.[66] Democrats likewise triumphed in the gubernatorial election: with only one exception, New Hanover had returned a Republican majority in every governor's race from 1868 until 1896, but in 1900 the county voted overwhelmingly Democratic for Aycock. The implicit threat of violence, changes to Wilmington's city charter, revised election laws, and new methods of electing county commissioners had all combined to eliminate the black voice in political matters. Not one of the heavily black counties of eastern North Carolina voted against the suffrage amendment, demonstrating the far-reaching effects of the birth of white supremacy in 1898. The result—one-party rule—took root in the state, and Republicans did not elect another candidate to statewide office for seventy years.

Historical Voting Statistics for New Hanover County

Governor

Year	Total Vote	% of Vote Democrat	% of Vote Republican	% of Vote Other	Plurality Dem/Rep
1868	5,799	38.5	61.5		1,337 (R)
1872	5,875	38.5	61.5		1,353 (R)
1876	4,610	35.2	64.8		1,366 (R)
1880	3,708	36.7	63.3		990 (R)
1884	4,629	37.8	62.2		1,127 (R)
1888	4,740	39.7	60.2	0.1	976 (R)
1892	3,960	61.8	33.5	4.7	1,121 (D)
1896	5,438	40.8	57.8	1.4	927 (R)
1900	2,966	99.9	0.1		2,960 (D)

President

Year	Total Vote	% of Vote Democrat	% of Vote Republican	% of Vote Other	Plurality Dem/Rep
1868	6,258	36.6	63.4		1,678 (R)
1872	5,322	35.3	64.7		1,568 (R)
1876	4,628	35.3	64.7		1,117 (R)
1880	3,638	39.5	60.5		762 (R)
1884	4,639	37.6	62.4		1,149 (R)
1888	4,726	39.6	60.4		986 (R)
1892	3,946	61.0	38.0	1.0	908 (D)
1896	5,283	39.8	60.2		1,083 (R)
1900	2,307	97.4	2.6		2,187 (D)

These tables are based on information found in Donald R. Matthews, ed., *North Carolina Votes: General Election Returns, by County, for President of the United States, 1868–1960, Governor of North Carolina, 1868–1960, United States Senator from North Carolina, 1914-1960* (Chapel Hill: University of North Carolina Press, 1962), 71, 176.

Moving Forward

For residents of Wilmington who were not members of the WGU, the Red Shirt brigade, or the Democratic Party, recovery from the 1898 election campaign and violence was difficult. Most of those citizens, primarily African Americans, maintained a tenuous existence as wage earners in white households or as laborers on the docks of white employers. Upper-class African American families maintained their property ownership, but their sons and daughters began to move away from the city.[67]

Former Democrats who had supported the Fusion ticket tried to salvage their political and social standing. Frank Dempsey, a white man who had been forced to resign his position on the New Hanover County Board of Education, later

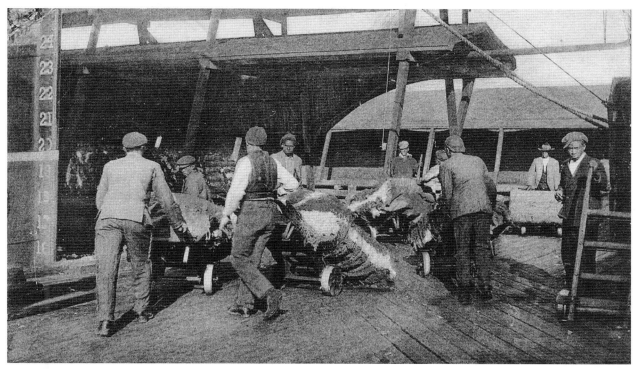

Many African Americans earned a living as laborers on the docks of white employers. This image, from a ca. 1910 postcard, shows cotton being unloaded from a steamer. Image courtesy of Stephen E. Massengill of Cary.

141

declared that he would not "be led off as [he] was before by designing men and intend not to serve in any office in which a negro [was] with [him] in said office." Wilmington grew increasingly hostile to white non-Democrats, and some men sought either to make peace with the new Democratic power brokers or to simply leave the city.[68] For its part, the Democratic Party tried to keep non-Democrats under its thumb. When a rumor circulated that President McKinley planned to reinstate prominent northern Republican George Z. French to the city as postmaster, local businessmen sent a petition to McKinley. "Mr. French has rendered himself peculiarly obnoxious to the citizens here," the petition declared, "and his presence . . . would roughly jar the peace . . . that now possesses the community." The businessmen also threatened French, who, they contended, was "sufficiently aware of the temper of the white people of Wilmington to know that it would not do for him to return to this city even with a United States commission in his pocket."[69]

The "negro problem" persisted, even after the state suffrage amendment had been ratified. Many felt the answer to the "question" was twofold—disfranchisement and proper education. Some white educators such as Charles L. Coon attempted to make available to blacks what they deemed a proper education—the training to be good workers. Reflecting that sentiment in newspapers and intellectual discussions both in black and white circles, John J. Blair, white superintendent of New Hanover County schools in 1905, asserted that the "solution of the race problem" lay in the proper education of African American boys and girls. Black education, Blair thought, should teach a student "how to live and how to labor . . . to sustain himself and aid others, to gain from his books a reasonable amount of learning and receive lasting lessons in morals and manners."[70] Conversely, men such as Alfred Moore Waddell held that whites should stop trying to educate blacks, because it would not solve "social and political evils." Such men, who became known as exclusionists, pointed out the "failure" of black education—that it made blacks more assertive. They believed that new generations of blacks were "indifferent, unreliable, untrained, and indolent" as a result of an educational system that promoted equal education for both races.[71]

Changes in Education for African Americans

Regardless of the differing opinions expressed about education for African Americans, Wilmington boasted some of the best educational options for blacks in North Carolina. The city was home to a series of well-established public and private institutions for both primary and secondary learning, and many of the city's graduates moved on to universities and colleges elsewhere in the state and nation.[72]

As previously mentioned, progressive educator and New Hanover County school superintendent M. C. S. Noble left Wilmington in 1898 to become a professor at the University of North Carolina in Chapel Hill, his alma mater. His departure was a setback for the city's educational system. While in Wilmington, Noble had proven himself to be a man of considerable insight and an advocate of equality in education. He understood that the education of whites and blacks should parallel each other. He believed that if whites were shown that blacks could be well educated and could use their education for the benefit of society, relationships between the races would improve over time. He argued that Orange County should fund a black educational institute "in the shadow" of UNC because "a good, practical, successful school right before their [white students at UNC] eyes from day to day [would] be a compelling argument for negro education which [would] bear fruit when these students [took] their place as men in the public affairs of the state."[73] Noble envisioned a school that would combine education in practical skills, such as carpentry and trades, with literary studies. His ideal school was loosely tied to the model proposed by many educators who applauded the success of Tuskegee Institute. As a result of Noble's influence, schools for African Americans began to focus on trades and the goal of producing better workers.[74]

The North Carolina General Assembly, led by Democrats, had legitimized financial disparity between white and black schools in 1883 and 1885 by authorizing local school districts to distribute tax revenue along racial lines. Such a method of financing virtually ensured inequality for black institutions.[75] In 1901, after regaining full control of state government in the wake of the previous year's election, Democrats sought the enactment into law of two bills designed to limit funding for black schools. Gov. Charles B. Aycock, who felt that black education was the answer to the "negro question," employed his influence to quash the legislation. He insisted that whites could not continue to rule through "force and repression" and instead had a vested interest in black education.[76] Despite attempts by men such as Aycock to advocate for black educational standards, the trend of reduced school funding persisted. The only way Wilmington's black schools were able to provide any degree of higher education to their students was through northern benevolence and the determination of local African American leaders to press for the best options for their children.[77]

In Wilmington there were two school districts for whites and two for blacks.[78] Although black school-age children outnumbered their white counterparts both before and after November 10, 1898, the city's schools for black students regularly received less funding for maintenance, books, and salaries than did the white schools.[79] The gap in funding between white and black schools grew even wider after 1898.[80] White educators, administrators, and politicians justified the disparity by referring to the amount of taxes paid by whites and blacks.[81] Because whites traditionally paid more taxes for property and businesses, their taxes were considerably more than those of blacks, who owned relatively little taxable property.

Statistics reflect inequity in funding for the black schools. In November 1898 white schools were given $858.02 to operate, whereas black schools received only $523.16. Operating costs included maintenance, textbooks, wood for heat, janitorial services, and other standard necessities. A year later, white schools received an average of $909.08 each, while black schools received $416.50 each. By January 1903, the figures grew still more disproportionate, with white schools receiving $1,617.26 and black schools receiving $383.65 per school in the city district. Statewide, black teachers were paid significantly less than white teachers, and school buildings for blacks

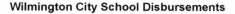

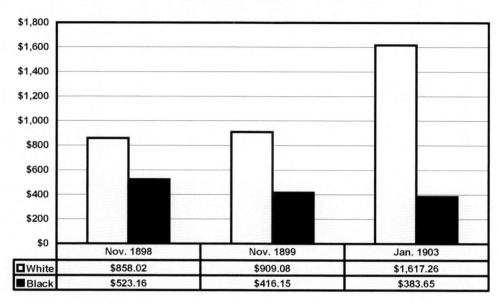

Wilmington City School Disbursements

	Nov. 1898	Nov. 1899	Jan. 1903
White	$858.02	$909.08	$1,617.26
Black	$523.16	$416.15	$383.65

SOURCE: Minutes, New Hanover County Board of County Commissioners, 1887–1918, State Archives.

143

received much less funding for construction and repair. The graph above shows funding provided to Wilmington schools for all expenses except teacher salaries. White schools consistently received more funding, even though black schools served more students. The difference grew dramatically from a gap of just over $300 per school in 1898 to more than $1,200 per school in 1903.[82] Although Wilmington is at the center of this study, the lingering effects of the white-supremacy campaign did not adversely affect the city's black schools disproportionately when compared to other such schools throughout the state.[83]

Low teacher pay exacerbated the difficulties faced by African American schools. In November 1898 Wilmington's white teachers were paid $36.84 per month, while their black counterparts received $35.64—a difference of $1.20 per month. A year later, white teachers in the city received $7.08 more than their black colleagues. By 1900 the disparity was even greater, with municipal white teachers earning almost $16 per month more than blacks.[84] Men were routinely paid more than women, and administrators, who also served as teachers, received higher pay. Race skewed the

formula, however. For example, Mary E. Cook, white principal at Union School, was the teacher with the highest pay—$60 for her work in November 1898; John A. Holt, black principal at Williston, was paid but $40 for that same month's work.[85]

Wilmington's African American leaders pressed the city's board of education for improvements to the school system. In 1920 a group of leaders appealed to the board to improve education across the board for the city's blacks: "The negro citizens respectfully appeal to your body for a larger, more adequate, more intensive personal interest in the education of our people by your people."[86] Such requests reflected a growing effort across North Carolina to improve traditionally African American school districts through better funding, better organization of African American teachers, and improved curriculum.[87]

Employment

The "white labor movement," characterized by organized groups of white workers who sought employment in fields traditionally dominated by

Average Monthly Salaries of New Hanover County Teachers by Race								
	1897	1898	1899	1900	1901	1902	1903	1904	1905
White	36.23	38.40	53.39	52.50	38.00	44.00	48.38	48.38	42.70
Black	35.23	35.38	38.55	36.58	29.00	30.00	32.60	30.10	35.00

Average Monthly Salaries of North Carolina Teachers by Race								
	1897	1898	1899	1900	1901	1902	1903	1904	1905
White	22.01	23.81	25.24	24.80	25.40	26.79	28.37	29.05	31.40
Black	19.90	20.75	21.12	20.48	22.07	22.19	22.64	22.27	23.00

SOURCE: Department of Public Instruction, Superintendents' Annual Reports, 1880–1920, State Archives.

black laborers, received much attention following the coup.[88] Not only did the Wilmington Chamber of Commerce work to ensure the hiring of whites and the firing of blacks, but others in the state also watched the labor movement in Wilmington closely. Newspapers reported that a White Laborers' Union had secured permanent jobs for more than sixty white men and anticipated placing many more with leading manufacturers in the city. In virtually every job category, blacks saw themselves replaced by white workers, many of whom agreed to do "disagreeable and arduous work." White laborers streamed into the city from the countryside, motivated in part by sinking prices for farm products. To promote white employment, the newspapers pledged to print the names of white workers and their qualifications as a means of assisting employers who needed mechanics, draymen, masons, carpenters, and other skilled workers.[89]

James Sprunt continued to employ African American stevedores at his cotton compress, even though the white labor movement promoted the hiring of white men over black. "Weighing Cotton on Compress Docks," ca. 1900. Image courtesy of the New Hanover County Public Library.

By the 1920s, African Americans were still being hired as stevedores. Image courtesy of the Louis T. Moore Photograph Collection, New Hanover County Public Library.

Among the jobs dominated by African American labor before November 1898 were stevedores—dock workers who loaded and off-loaded goods between ships and warehouses along the shore. Beginning in 1891, stevedores were required to register and post a bond to operate. Typically, there was a "boss" stevedore, who organized several other men under his supervision. One of the requirements placed upon the bosses was the obligation, under bond, to handle contracts promptly and to pay employees accordingly. Between 1891 and 1898, of the stevedore bonds issued, seven were for white bosses and three for black bosses. The black firm with the most staying power was Lee, Starnes, and Company, operated by Joseph Starnes, Major Lee, Fred Williams, and John Turner. In 1898 two of its principals partnered with two whites to establish the Wilmington Stevedore Company. That firm soon became the city's major source for stevedore labor. By 1900, however, it was a completely white operation.[90]

Not all employers abandoned their black laborers in the face of pressure from the white labor movement. James Sprunt continued his practice of hiring black workers at his cotton compress. Within three days of the riot, his businesses were again operating, and ships were coming into port. Newspapers hastened to report that the city and its businesses were recuperating from the riot. Nevertheless, all was not well in the shipping businesses, since many African American draymen still had not returned to work. That state of affairs was particularly troublesome for Sprunt in that he faced immediate financial loss if his crews could not off-load cotton aboard ships waiting at anchor. On November 13, 1898, only two-thirds of Sprunt's work force was on hand, and shipping was being "greatly retarded" because nine ships were waiting to be cleared. He anticipated that the contract for off-loading seven of those vessels would expire before the ships could be docked. To encourage a return to normal working conditions for laborers, Sprunt offered to the newspapers a rare interview in which he expressed his belief that quiet and peaceful blacks willing to return to work would not be harmed. He expressed the hope that black workers could be convinced of their safe passage to and from the docks so they could return to their duties and resolve the current labor shortages. Sprunt openly expressed those sentiments even while the white labor movement was fiercely promoting the hiring of white men over black.[91]

Complete Change

As the Wilmington community attempted to adjust to the changes wrought by the events of November 10, one newspaper editor waxed philosophical: "The eyes of the world are upon us and we must keep up the record we are making as the only city on record that has overthrown corruption and established good government in the short space of eight hours."[92] Other papers in the state acknowledged that the turmoil in Wilmington marked the beginning of a larger phenomenon: "Negro rule is at an end in North Carolina forever," a Raleigh journal asserted. "The events of the past week in Wilmington and elsewhere place that fact beyond all question."[93] Both editorial comments proved prophetic. Whites and blacks across the state, and arguably across the nation, watched as the white-supremacy campaign grew unchecked, men were robbed of their civil liberties at the polls, violence and murders took place in broad daylight, and municipal government was overthrown by force—all without consequence for the perpetrators or solace for the victims. In Wilmington, through violence, intimidation, and murder, the Democratic Party had teminated "Negro rule"—black Republican voting power. Throughout North Carolina, Democrats hastened to take pride in the Wilmington violence and repeatedly employed it to stifle political ambitions of blacks; indeed, reciting the tale of what happened on that November day in Wilmington became a staple of future campaigns.[94]

An indicator of the heightened sense of potential violence in Wilmington can be found in the 1903 city directory—one of the first in which the publication included a section that identified locations of fire alarm call boxes throughout the city. Such call boxes included mechanisms whereby a user, by executing a certain number of "taps," might request special assistance (such as an extra

hose wagon) in case of fire or might summon the police to respond to, for example, a riot call (such a signal required ten taps). Of 34 such call boxes in Wilmington, 15 were situated in the north side of town, 7 were located in the south side, and the rest could be found in the downtown business district or in the outlying industrial areas. The location pattern suggests that Wilmington's officials anticipated that trouble would occur more often in the traditionally black sections of town and stationed enough call boxes in those sections to ensure that if violence or danger erupted, a call box was nearby.[95]

Prospects for equal civil rights for African Americans were darkened as a result of the events of 1898. As the newly elected Democratically controlled General Assembly enacted the state's first Jim Crow legislation in 1899, North Carolina joined the rest of the South in undermining the efforts of Republicans, both before and after Reconstruction, to equalize the races in the realms of education, employment, and political involvement. Future generations of Democratic Party politicians built upon the foundations of discrimination and economic disadvantage established in 1898. The Democratic press heralded the twentieth century and the election of Democrats throughout the state as the beginning of a great dynasty for the state and an era of growth. Indeed, the state did prosper as Democratic businessmen, satisfied that their party was now in control of government, turned their minds from political intrigue to financial matters. The resulting prosperity, limited largely to upper- and middle-class whites, was short-lived, however, and scarcely benefited African Americans or poor whites.

Chapter 8

Rebuilding

To build may have to be the slow and laborious task of years. To destroy can be the thoughtless act of a single day.

—Winston S. Churchill
BBC radio broadcast, February 9, 1941

The long-term results of the events that occurred in Wilmington on November 10, 1898, are difficult to measure. How did the violence of that day, preceded by months of white-supremacy rhetoric voiced by the Democratic Party and followed by years of Jim Crow oppression, veiled threats, and further violence, affect the city's African American residents? Consequences for that sector of the community were wide-ranging and touched all aspects of life—political, economic, and cultural.

Political Consequences

The political ramifications of the coup were clearly visible by the spring of 1899, when the newly elected General Assembly, controlled by the Democrats, convened and Wilmington held municipal elections. In November 1900 the Democratic Party, having campaigned successfully on behalf of its disfranchisement agenda, solidified its control of North Carolina with the election of Charles B. Aycock as governor and even larger majorities in the General Assembly. Ratification by the voters of the suffrage amendment had removed from the electorate the majority of African American voters—the broad political base of the Republican Party. In the wake of the ratification and the resounding defeat at the polls, leaders of the Republican Party concluded that the party must sever its connection to its black voter base and make itself "lily-white." Without the large black voter base, Republicans lost their ability to elect officials statewide, and, as part of their efforts to reinvent the party, chose to discontinue their previous practice of awarding patronage positions to African Americans. Such patronage had long been a vital method by which African Americans

Dramatic changes swept through Wilmington as a result of the white-supremacy campaign and violence of November 1898. These white-supremacy banners hung along the wharf as a physical reminder of white unity against "negro domination." Image courtesy of the Lower Cape Fear Historical Society.

made advances in Wilmington and other parts of the state, but after the 1900 elections the practice was effectively ended.[1] It has been argued that once African Americans lost their political voice, they refocused their energies on economic and educational progress.[2]

Economic Consequences

To address the economic impact of the race riot in Wilmington, the North Carolina Office of Archives and History collaborated with the Institute of African American Research at the University of North Carolina at Chapel Hill to study Wilmington's city directories and census data.[3] Representatives of the two agencies analyzed city directory data, census data, tax records, and deed records to provide insight into the economic consequences of the campaign and riot. New in-depth, computer-aided analysis of data derived from Wilmington's 1897 and 1900 city directories provided revealing information about the economic environment for the city's black community. Entries for both races in the residential section of the directory, including all related information such as occupation and addresses for businesses and residences, were entered into a database.[4] To address concerns that the directories may contain data skewed along racial or gender lines, researchers conducted a thorough evaluation of the data before applying statistical analysis. The evaluation suggested that the directories are relatively reflective of the city's racial diversity both before and after the violence of 1898.[5] Because of that conclusion, and because the directories are the only known data sets containing information about black employment so soon before and after November 1898, they were employed to formulate some conclusions about the impact of the violence and the white-supremacy campaign on the economic condition of the city's African Americans.[6]

Consolidation of the data into fifteen occupational categories reflective of the peculiar business climate associated with Wilmington's port status demonstrates that the city offered a diverse working environment for its African American citizens.[7] The 1897 city directory records a total of 3,462 African Americans and their respective occupations. Of those, the two largest categories were general laborers (1,325) and washerwomen, butlers, or other domestic houseworkers (1,063) employed by white households.[8] It is unknown what types of work were most performed by men who reported their occupation as laborer, but such workers generally received low pay, had minimal degrees of job security, and were typically classified as unskilled. Those two categories—laborers and domestics—together represented 68 percent of the city's African American employment in 1897.

The remaining 32 percent of the city's black workers in 1897 were employed in skilled, retail, service, government, and professional occupations. Within those categories, the greatest number were associated with railroads, building trades, skilled trades, and with work associated with the port as stevedores, draymen, or drivers.[9] Two of those categories—skilled artisans and building trades—were areas that traditionally offered prosperity to African Americans in the city. Some of the city's oldest and wealthiest African American families, such as the Howes, Norwoods, Howards, and Sadgwars, had their roots in the city's building trades well before the Civil War, and fathers passed the trade to sons for many generations. Similarly, the Hargrave family had long been in the city as blacksmiths and prospered for many generations before their trade became obsolete.[10] Unlike the Hargraves, however, skilled artisans and tradesmen whose professions included plumbers and tailors persisted in the city as it evolved into the modern age.

Another group of workers, those who labored in retail, service, and restaurant occupations, led the African American community into the twentieth century. They were most often self-employed and entrepreneurial, working as barbers, grocers, and butchers, as well as boot makers and shoemakers, hostlers, provisions dealers, and sales clerks. The food or restaurant business was an integral part of the industrial city, providing meals for workers through a variety of facilities known as cook-shops, eating houses, or restaurants, some located in close proximity to the business district to cater to the lunch trade.[11]

148

1897 and 1900 Employment Data for Wilmington

	1897			1900		
	Total	*Black*	*White*	*Total*	*Black*	*White*
Population	7,673	3,760	3,913	8,124	3,575	4,549
Number Employed	6,486	3,462	2,990	5,943	2,546	3,375

Occupations listed in the city directory accounted for a slightly smaller number than the total population. If no occupation was given, it is assumed that an individual was unemployed. Data taken from the 1897 and 1900 editions of *J. L. Hill Printing Co.'s Directory of Wilmington, N.C.* (Richmond, Va.: J. L. Hill Printing Company).

The number of government workers (58) was relatively small in 1897, and the number changed over time because the campaign of 1898 specifically targeted that category of employee. Such jobs included postal workers, who were appointed through the patronage system, and city and county employees, who worked in the police, health, and fire departments. As a result of the power wielded by the state's African American congressman George H. White, North Carolina had more black postmasters than any other state. While Wilmington's postmaster, William H. Chadbourn, was white, he was a Republican and had made it a policy to reward local blacks with well-paying jobs as clerks and carriers. Black postmasters, letter carriers, and clerks became targets of the white-supremacy campaign of 1898, and in the wake of Democratic victories in 1898

and 1900, the number of black postal workers steadily declined.[12] There were 9 postal workers in the city in 1897, but by 1900 the number had dropped to 4.

The occupational category with the highest level of status and economic impact was the professional sector. Professional positions required a higher level of educational training, and men and women in such positions were well known throughout Wilmington. In 1897 there were 67 black professionals in the city. Of that number, the largest groups were educators (33) and ministers (21). Most of the educators were female teachers, but there were also 3 principals, including at least 1 woman, and 1 "professor." There were 5 black physicians in the city in 1897, but only 1 African American attorney was listed in the city directory for that year.

The 1897 city directory for Wilmington records washerwomen and other domestic houseworkers as one of the largest categories of occupations for African Americans. This 1920s image is courtesy of the Louis T. Moore Photograph Collection, New Hanover County Public Library.

1897 and 1900 Occupation Comparisons by Race for Wilmington

Occupation Category	1897 Blacks	1897 Whites	1900 Blacks	1900 Whites
Laborer	1,325	188	1,532	242
Domestic	1,063	30	144	17
Railroad Worker	21	74	39	90
Cargo/Transport Trades	352	51	280	64
Skilled Artisan/Trades	99	203	83	214
Building Trades	139	173	142	247
Service	155	80	102	107
Retail	63	361	52	448
Professional	67	179	64	175
Food service	57	55	52	73
Government	58	62	6	127
Industrial	28	282	19	270
Clerical	21	795	16	778
Maritime	7	65	13	62
Cotton Industry	7	20	2	90
Total	**3,462**	**2,618**	**2,546**	**3,004**

SOURCE: *J. L. Hill Printing Co.'s Directory of Wilmington*, (1897 and 1900).

Changes Revealed by the 1900 City Directory

By 1900 Wilmingon's city directory reflected the dramatic changes that had swept through the city as a result of the white-supremacy campaign and violence of November 1898. The publication contains the names of 2,546 African American workers—nearly 1,000 fewer than appear in the 1897 directory—and lists their respective occupations. A comparison of the two directories reveals changes that took place in the city as a result of the white-supremacy campaign, violence, a mass exodus, and efforts by whites to alter hiring practices in order to favor white employees over black. At first glance, it is obvious that there is a general downward shift in terms of relative status and economic factors: there are fewer skilled tradesmen, domestics, stevedores, clerical workers, retail and service workers, and professionals—but there are more laborers, carpenters, and maritime workers.

The largest category of workers (1,532) by far was that of laborer. One significant change can be seen in the dramatic reduction in the number of domestic employees—down from more than 1,000 to 144. In the 1897 directory the domestic-worker category rivaled that of laborer, but the number of workers in that category is distinctly lower in the 1900 directory. It is unclear why this number is so much lower. Most of the jobs classified as domestic in the directory were those as cooks, a role traditionally reserved for women. In the 1900 directory, however, more of the domestic jobs listed were considered as being typically filled by males (butler, waiter, bellman, for example) than were so regarded in the 1897 directory. The disparity in the latter category is even more apparent when traditionally female jobs are viewed across categories. The numbers of cooks, nurses, teachers, laundresses, and maids declined significantly, while the percentage of men working in domestic jobs increased slightly.[13]

Although most categories of workers dropped in numbers, some categories lost fewer workers than others, possibly a reflection of Wilmington's evolving nature as an industrial city that required skilled workers, regardless of race. Employment in a broad range of maritime trades such as boatmen and fishermen increased. In 1897 most maritime workers were deck hands and boatmen; by 1900 some workers had achieved the higher-paying, more rewarding status of captain or pilot.

The 1900 directory reveals a noteworthy shift that occurred within the professional category. The overall number of professionals decreased

188 African American businesses, most with second addresses provided for establishments such as grocery stores, barbershops, restaurants, butcher shops, shoe shops, and other endeavors that required a storefront. By 1900, however, the number of African American businesses had dropped to 166, and many of them had been moved into homes, indicating a significant decline in the number of black-owned enterprises with secondary locations within a business district.[15]

Several businesses that existed in 1897, mostly grocers, eating houses, and barbershops, were able to weather economic downfalls and survived until

An interesting sidelight is that in 1897 there were only 7 women running businesses, primarily eating houses. By 1900 the number had increased to 22, also mostly eating houses; this statistic suggests that women had to enter the work force in order to make up for the lost wages of their husbands.

151

slightly, reflecting a loss of educators—from 33 in 1897 to 14 in 1900. (The city lost only 1 African American principal, and the aforementioned "professor" remained.) Offsetting the overall decrease in the number of education professionals was an influx of ministers; the city saw an increase from 21 in 1897 to 33 in 1900. It is not known why additional clergymen came to the city following the violence, particularly since the number of churches remained constant.[14]

African American Entrepreneurship after 1898

A number of the city's African American entrepreneurs, men and women who owned and operated their own businesses or worked independently experienced a decline in occupational status in the years immediately following the riot. A few other entrepreneurial-minded individuals managed to overcome challenges and improved their lot by opening new businesses during the year following the violence. Both directories include a considerable number of entries for men and women who provided a second address for their businesses. In 1897 there were approximately

1900.[16] Several new enterprises came to the city as well. By 1900 there were 36 new businesses, mostly barbers, grocers, and restaurateurs. By contrast, 54 businesses closed, with many of their owners leaving town for less hostile locations. By 1946 Wilmington's African American community had succeeded in reviving its black businesses and boasted 196 of them, ranging from 63 grocers and 22 barbershops to 6 physicians and 50 beauty parlors.[17]

Until November 1898, the dominant professional positions in Wilmington had been filled by attorneys, physicians, teachers, and ministers. Of the leaders banished from the city, most were from those categories. As a result of the banishment and intimidation campaign, 4 lawyers departed the city, and no African American attorney practiced law in the city until 1902. By that year teachers and ministers accounted for the predominant number of professional blacks in Wilmington—although 3 physicians practiced there during that year. Mid-level professional jobs, mainly those of postal clerks, were likewise affected. In 1897 9 blacks were affiliated with the postal system in various positions, but by 1902 only 2 remained.[18]

Most of the city's black workers, however, remained laborers employed by whites. Those workers were the ones most affected by the white-supremacy campaign's promises of jobs for white workers. Skilled African American workers sustained the most dramatic losses in the city over the years following the coup. By the time the 1902 city directory was printed, black skilled, semi-skilled, and transportation workers had been displaced, and the number of black unskilled and unemployed workers had grown.[19]

Out-migration after 1898

Out-migration from the city posed problems both for white employers and the local black community. A continued exodus of black workers plagued the city into the turn of the twentieth century. Author and former Wilmington resident Charles Waddell Chesnutt told a Boston newspaper in March 1901 that his sources in Wilmington told him that since the "massacre" (as blacks called it; whites called it the "Revolution"), more than 1,500 of the "best blacks" had left the city.[20] Chesnutt's "best blacks" were most likely entrepreneurs who closed their businesses and moved because they saw better opportunities in other parts of the state or nation.

The 1900 census reflected the out-migration of African Americans from Wilmington. The city's black population dropped by more than 900 people in the ten years between 1890 and 1900, and, for the first time since the Civil War, whites outnumbered blacks in the city. While the black population was decreasing during those years, the white population was increasing. The black out-migration from Wilmington and New Hanover County preceded the nationwide Great Migration by almost a decade, but as some historians have noted, racial violence such as that experienced in Wilmington may have been a contributing factor as important to the impetus to leave as was an economic downturn.[21]

Comparisons of the 1880 and 1900 censuses for states other than North Carolina reveal that the number of blacks born in North Carolina but residing elsewhere increased substantially in Pennsylvania and New Jersey. States such as New

Charles Waddell Chesnutt (1858–1932), an author, told a Boston newspaper that the "best blacks" had fled Wilmington. Photograph (ca. early 1880s) courtesy of the Charles Waddell Chesnutt Collection, Special Collections, Franklin Library, Fisk University, Nashville, Tenn.

York, Virginia, Delaware, and Maryland likewise saw an increase in their black populations native to North Carolina. The influx of African Americans from Wilmington into Brooklyn, New York, made headlines in a local paper, which noted that there was an increasing number of blacks from Wilmington because of "unsettled conditions" there.[22]

As previously noted, most of the African American workers who left Wilmington had been employed as laborers, cooks, washerwomen, porters, and nurses, and the void left by their departure was partially filled by other workers moving into the city. One major Wilmington enterprise, the naval-stores and turpentine industry, suffered as a result of the exodus. In 1901 an article in a Wilmington newspaper sought to explain an "Exodus of Turpentine Hands." It declared that two "coach loads of negro turpentine hands" had left the city for Florida's turpentine regions. It also reported that other black workers would soon follow, that "labor [was] already scarce," and that

Number and Percentage of N.C.-born Nonwhite Residents in Other States

State	1880	1900
Connecticut	334 (65%)	876 (67%)
Delaware	17 (23%)	89 (53%)
District of Columbia	497 (63%)	1,891 (62%)
Louisiana	4,708 (77%)	3,867 (79%)
Maryland	484 (39%)	1,622 (49%)
Massachusetts	645 (72%)	2,573 (72%)
New Jersey	306 (52%)	3,586 (77%)
New York	1,270 (56%)	5,866 (68%)
Ohio	2,376 (62%)	1,998 (60%)
Pennsylvania	629 (45%)	4,862 (74%)
Rhode Island	118 (73%)	297 (66%)
South Carolina	7,942 (40%)	6,654 (24%)
Virginia	10,213 (44%)	27,994 (50%)

SOURCE: Population statistics for 1880–1900, "U.S. Census Bureau," http://www.census.gov/prod/www/abs/decennial/index.htm.

the exodus would "make the scarcity all the greater." James Sprunt's cotton compress operations suffered the loss of workers earlier than did the turpentine trade. By August 1899 Sprunt experienced a shortage of employees because more than half of his work force was then in New York City employed as hotel workers. A former black worker from Wilmington told a reporter for a Brooklyn newspaper that he did not think many of Sprunt's former employees would return south because "they can't get over the idea that their lives will be threatened again." The newspaper reported that black women and girls had likewise left Wilmington, that their exodus had resulted in a "lack of domestic servants," and that white women "say they can't get help now." Moreover, the paper declared that many of the refugees then living in New York owned homes in Wilmington that they couldn't sell or rent and that they had lost money in "bank troubles" in the port city.[23]

A concentration of refugees from Wilmington settled in Whitesboro, New Jersey. Congressman George H. White understood that black men and women living in Wilmington could not prosper in the post-1898 environment and encouraged them to migrate northward. White realized his vision of a black town for Wilmington refugees in 1901 when an organization with which he was affiliated, the Afro-American Equitable Association, purchased land in Cape May County, New Jersey, for settlement. The resulting town, Whitesboro, emerged as an example of the success black towns could achieve when their residents worked to develop "group self-reliance and solidarity that enriched local civic pride, purpose, and duty." A review of the census for Whitesboro and Cape May County in 1900 and 1910 reveals the names of many African American natives of North Carolina who had relocated there, and many of them can be tied to Wilmington. Surnames such as Sadgwar, Fales, Yarborough, Green, Scott, Spaulding, Pearsall, and Merrick all have clear ties to Wilmington. One man known to have been banished from Wilmington, McClain Lofton, resided in Cape May County in 1910.[24]

Those Who Remained and Those Who Arrived after 1898

Many of the African Americans who remained in Wilmington after 1898 overcame the initial shock to their economic system and rebuilt an infrastructure that supported the black community into the early years of the twentieth century. More difficult to document, but evident from studies of city directory and census data, is a small influx of African American workers into the city after the turn of the twentieth century.[25] After 1900, with the help of new and old residents, black businesses developed in predominantly black neighborhoods and catered to black customers. The community clusters evolved into self-contained, self-supporting units of interdependence and sustainability for their residents. As one longtime resident of the city recalled, black neighborhood businesses in the era of Jim Crow were places blacks could go to obtain credit in hard times and where they knew they would not be made to feel uncomfortable on the basis of skin color.[26] Through the development of such adaptive networks, the African American business community rebounded in the early twentieth century, compelling one author to conclude that by 1915 Wilmington represented a "relatively attractive business environment."[27]

By the advent of the First World War, the economic downturn Wilmington's African Americans experienced in the late 1890s and early 1900s was being reversed.[28] By 1915, for example, blacks were operating more than 31 percent of the city's businesses (in 1897 that figure was just over 20 percent). A 1915 business directory reveals a particularly robust increase in the number of African American grocers.[29] (That finding supports the theory that neighborhood businesses developed to support localized needs.) Nationwide efforts after 1916 to mobilize for America's entry into World War I and the war effort itself brought prosperity to Wilmington's shipyards and provided employment opportunities for the city's African American workers, particularly within the skilled trades.

One of the groups that tended to remain in Wilmington after 1898 was the small number of African American homeowners. Those black property owners were encouraged to hold their ground. A local newspaper advised: "I counsel not to leave your bought and paid for homes and whatever little is dear and belongs to you. . . . If you possess any property in Wilmington don't sell just now. Keep it till things tone down and you can get a fairer price if you sell at all."[30] As one researcher discovered, black property owners were less likely to leave and were most able to adapt to the changed political and economic landscape of white supremacy. Carrie Taylor Wright, daughter of African American deputy collector of customs John E. Taylor, explained that her father remained in the city after the violence because he "had all his earnings here. My grandfather was here. He owned all the property, so there was no reason for him to leave. This was home."[31]

Property Ownership

By acquiring real estate, African Americans in Wilmington had been able to increase and maintain their wealth prior to the violence of 1898. Throughout North Carolina, about 4,000 blacks owned real property in 1870, and the number

steadily increased as the years progressed. In most cases, however, African Americans did not own the house or property in which they lived. Even so, between 1875 and 1895 urban property ownership among African Americans in North Carolina increased at a faster rate than did black rural property ownership.[32] By 1897, 1,016 African Americans owned real estate in Wilmington.[33]

Some discussions of the riot have touched on claims by Wilmington's displaced African American residents that after November 10, 1898, their

Thomas C. Miller, a wealthy black business leader, owned his own home, built ca. 1896. This image is courtesy of the Historic Wilmington Foundation and is reprinted in Reaves, *"Strength through Struggle,"* 282.

property was seized and given to poor whites. One frequently cited source of those claims is a vivid scene described in *Hanover; or, the Persecution of the Lowly, A Story of the Wilmington Massacre*, a thinly veiled fictional account of the riot published in 1900 by black journalist and fiction writer David Bryant Fulton.[34] Soon after the riot, Alexander Manly speculated that whites conspired to deprive African Americans of their property. Manly's son Milo perpetuated his father's claims as late as 1977 and cited losses sustained by his father and by wealthy Wilmington black business leader Thomas C. Miller.[35]

The accepted method for researching property ownership and transfers is by following deed transactions. However, Milo Manly expressed the concerns of many African Americans when he stated that checking deed records and other legal materials in the New Hanover County Court-house would prove fruitless because records had been "altered or stolen or lost" to the extent that it could never be proven that his father and others ever owned disputed property. Whether Manly's claims are founded in truth is open to debate; what is left in the written records is all that survives from the period to provide an understanding of African American property ownership in the city both before and after the riot.[36] One fact cannot be overlooked: between 1897 and 1900 the number of African Americans owning real estate in Wilmington dropped by only twelve—from 1,016 to 1,004.[37]

In 2000 researcher Sue Ann Cody sought to determine if blacks owned much land in Wilmington before 1898 and if after the violence they were forced to sell their land for a loss.[38] Her initial study led her to conclude that "African Americans owned a significant amount of property both before and after the violence and that there was not a significant spike in the number of sales immediately following the violence." Cody further found both gains and losses in the sales of property by African Americans following the riot for all categories of property holders—banished, voluntary migrants, and those who stayed.[39] The official records do not support a conclusion that Wilmington's black property owners were forced to sell their holdings en masse in the seven years following the riot—nor did they, on average, lose money when they sold property. Moreover, surviving records, primarily deeds, likewise fail to support the claim, originally made in 1898 and perpetuated into the modern era, that whites openly redistributed black property among themselves.[40] A partial explanation for the myths concerning the seizure of property may lie in the fact that after 1898 African American property seized and sold for nonpayment of a debt often would fall into the hands of white purchasers through legal actions. Perhaps such activity evolved into a memory of wide-ranging changes in black ownership of property—that is, a few examples grew to be perceived as the norm instead of the exception.

Census Analysis

Economist Tod Hamilton conducted a study of census statistics for the Wilmington area over all the years for which data is available, and his findings provide insight into the situation facing Wilmington's population as it moved into the twentieth century. Hamilton's conclusions pull together, in statistical format, what can be learned from the census about the city's educational opportunities, economy, working environment, and social framework. The tables below contain summary statistics for the Wilmington area's black and white population, as well as the overall black and white population for the state.[41]

The New Hanover County educational system—although it underwent a significant reduction in funding for black schools—consistently managed to produce a significant number of literate African Americans. Wilmington's African American community always prided itself on its educational heritage and the influence that educators had on the city's students. The statistical data demonstrates that the educators—despite a reduction in the number of teachers, wages, and overall funding for school management following the 1898 campaign—succeeded in providing the basics of education in less-than-ideal situations.[42] In 1880 the literacy rate of the city's African American population ranked above the state average, but by 1900 it had fallen below that average, only to surpass it again in 1910 and 1920. The illiteracy rate of Wilmington's black population numbered near or above the statewide average until 1920, when it dropped below the rest of the state. Wilmington whites consistently remained well above the state average for full literacy and below the state average for illiteracy.

The second data set provides information concerning home ownership. More individuals among Wilmington's African American population than elsewhere in the state owned homes, as can be seen in the 1900 figures. (The data also reinforces the previously discussed conclusion that large numbers of the city's black property owners were not forced into selling their holdings immediately after the violence.) However, a slump in home ownership can be seen by 1910, with the

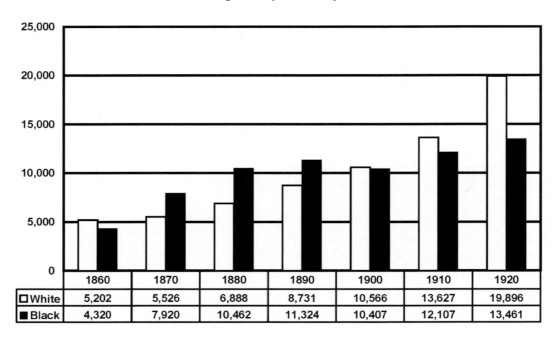

Wilmington Population by Race

	1860	1870	1880	1890	1900	1910	1920
☐ White	5,202	5,526	6,888	8,731	10,566	13,627	19,896
■ Black	4,320	7,920	10,462	11,324	10,407	12,107	13,461

SOURCE: Population statistics for 1860–1920, "U.S. Census Bureau," http://www.census.gov/prod/www/abs/decennial/index.htm.

area's average ownership rate falling below the state average. The slump was overcome by 1920, when, once again, more African Americans in Wilmington than in other portions of the state owned property.

For the city's white population, home ownership remained relatively constant, rising slightly in 1910 but declining slightly in 1920, while white ownership in the rest of the state held steady with only slight variation over the three decades. The increase in white ownership in 1910 was 5 percent, whereas the decrease in black ownership was 8 percent. (Further research in deed books is needed to determine whether there is a correlation between a decline in black property ownership and an increase in white ownership.) The trend was reversed by 1920, with the black losses of 1910 wiped away and gains jumping to well over the 1900 level. White ownership saw a 2 percent decline that year.

The last two data sets are figures assigned by economists based upon occupations and a calculation derived from occupation and other indicators to provide the social/economic index score (SEI). The occupational score is developed based on a ranking system that places a higher score, or number, for higher-paying, higher-status jobs. Therefore, occupations such as attorney, doctor, or teacher have higher scores than those of laborer, maid, or janitor—the higher the score, the higher the pay. Similarly, the SEI scores are reflective of the social and economic status associated with an occupation—the higher the score, the more respected that individual (or group) will be in the community.

The average occupational score and SEI for Wilmington-area African Americans in 1900 and 1910 was lower than that for the rest of the state's black workers. That disparity likely reflects both the stated commitment of the white-supremacy campaign to favor white workers over black in the realm of hiring and the exodus from the city of many skilled workers who sought employment elsewhere. By 1920 the scores had increased to above the state average—probably indicative of the influx of industrial workers and related

Literacy Rates for Wilmington and North Carolina by Race

Blacks	1880		1900		1910		1920	
	Wilm.	N.C.	Wilm.	N.C.	Wilm.	N.C.	Wilm.	N.C.
Fully Literate	20%	17%	35%	37%	58%	57%	73%	67%
Partially Literate	6%	7%	6%	8%	2%	6%	1%	2%
Non-Literate	74%	75%	59%	55%	39%	37%	25%	30%

Whites	1880		1900		1910		1920	
	Wilm.	N.C.	Wilm.	N.C.	Wilm.	N.C.	Wilm.	N.C.
Fully Literate	78%	71%	88%	79%	92%	85%	95%	90%
Partially Literate	3%	7%	3%	5%	2%	4%	.2%	1%
Non-Literate	19%	23%	9%	15%	5%	11%	5%	9%

SOURCE: Population statistics for 1880–1920, "U.S. Census Bureau," http://www.census.gov/prod/www/abs/decennial/index.htm.

occupations during the wartime buildup. The figures suggest that by 1910 the majority of Wilmington's black workers were employed in low-paying jobs with little prestige, whereas by 1920 they had achieved at least some measurable progress. The occupational score for the Wilmington area's white workers was below the state average in 1900 but jumped well above that average following the 1898 campaign. Interestingly, the occupational score and SEI both for Wilmington's black and white residents were in close proximity in 1900; by 1910 the disparity is much larger, with Wilmington's black population languishing at much the same level; by 1920 the occupational scores were slightly closer, with whites still working in more higher-paying jobs than blacks. The difference in SEI scores is great in the latter year, however, with nearly 7 points separating the two races, indicating that whites enjoyed a higher status level and economic return in their jobs.

In order to provide more detailed insight into conditions in Wilmington soon after the violence, Tod Hamilton focused additional study on a 5 percent sampling of the 1900 census. He analyzed data related to residents between the ages of twenty-five and sixty-five, an age range indicative of the working populations in the city. Women outnumbered men in both white and black groups; but African American women represented 65 percent of the black population, whereas white women numbered 53 percent of their race. More black workers (95 percent) were born in North Carolina than were

157

Comparison of Home Ownership for Wilmington and North Carolina

	1900		1910		1920	
	Wilm.	N.C.	Wilm.	N.C.	Wilm.	N.C.
Owned/Mortgaged Home (African American)	35%	27%	27%	34%	43%	35%
Owned/Mortgaged Home (White)	50%	60%	55%	58%	53%	60%

SOURCE: Population statistics for 1900–1920, "U.S. Census Bureau," http://www.census.gov/prod/www/abs/decennial/index.htm.

Social/Economic Indicators Based on Occupation by Race

Blacks	1880		1900		1910		1920	
	Wilm.	N.C.	Wilm.	N.C.	Wilm.	N.C.	Wilm.	N.C.
Occupational Score	9.60	8.67	8.06	9.5	8.97	9.99	10.44	9.75
SEI (social/economic index)	7.20	6.66	7.07	8.1	7.77	9.14	9.72	9.43

Whites	1880		1900		1910		1920	
	Wilm.	N.C.	Wilm.	N.C.	Wilm.	N.C.	Wilm.	N.C.
Occupational Score	9.74	8.51	8.53	9.80	12.01	10.89	12.85	11.37
SEI (social/economic index)	11.29	9.28	7.90	11.40	14.79	12.60	16.20	13.92

SOURCE: Population statistics for 1880–1920, "U.S. Census Bureau," http://www.census.gov/prod/www/abs/decennial/index.htm.

white workers (83 percent). Only about half of the black population was literate, whereas more than 90 percent of whites could read and write. After reviewing occupation scores, Hamilton concluded that the impact of being black in Wilmington negatively affected wage-earning abilities: "[T]he only factor to indicate why a male, age 25, working in Wilmington is paid less than another," Hamilton declared, "is his race."[43]

Case Studies

Demographic studies of some of the key participants in 1898 reveal that a shift took place in the city over the decade following the violence. A primary reason for the shift was that of the thirty-three members of the Committee of Colored Citizens (CCC) summoned by whites, most were over the age of forty, with the largest majority of them older than fifty. Many of the men remained in the city and withstood the changes in society created by the whirlwind of 1898. Some of them, such as Daniel Howard and John G. Norwood, were longtime leaders of the community and died within a few years of the riot, leaving their estates to children or relatives who then moved from the city once their connection to Wilmington's stable past was gone.[44] Within the white community, most participants in the Democratic Party campaign were also over forty years old, although the average age of the men who were part of the Secret Nine was thirty-seven. As previously noted,

many of those leading white men were related to each other either by blood or marriage, further strengthening their mutual interests and standing in the community. The aging black population with an entrenched history in Wilmington was replaced by a younger group with less of a connection to the city's infrastructure, and the younger white population built upon its already tight network of family and business relationships.[45]

The following case studies of six of the major African American targets of the white-supremacy campaign provide insight into many of the changes that faced Wilmington's residents after 1898. Of those seven men, only one, Thomas C. Miller, was physically banished by the white leaders of the coup on November 10. John Goins, an employee of Alexander Manly's *Daily Record*, left the city because of his association with the paper. The rest of the men were affected in various ways, as summarized below.

Daniel Howard

Daniel Howard rose to prominence in Wilmington in the 1870s and 1880s. He led the African American Giblem Lodge, took an active role in Republican politics, led Emancipation Day celebrations, and served on various boards. He joined with local black entrepreneurs in investing in railroad development and life insurance enterprises. He also helped to establish the Metropolitan Trust Company, one of the most successful black enterprises in the city. Howard's occupation changed over time from drayman in 1870 to county jailer in 1880 to house carpenter in 1900. In 1897 Howard owned property valued at almost $2,900 in eight locations in the city; three years later he retained his properties, which had either held their value or increased slightly.

Howard died in 1909 at the age of seventy-four, and in his will he divided his estate among his first and second wives and several children. Howard's will emphasized that his children should "share and share alike" and included a provision for the sale of some property so that the funds could be evenly divided among the siblings. Under the terms of that provision, some of Howard's properties were sold, and others were subdivided as many as four or fives times. Consequently, the wealth and prosperity Daniel Howard had worked so hard to develop after emancipation dissipated soon after his death and did not pass down to his children. By 1910 only two of his sons resided in the city, and neither owned the homes in which they lived. One son lived with his father-in-law while working as a carpenter, and the other was a "scavenger" and lived on the outskirts of town in a rented house. However, one of Howard's sons, Benjamin, did embody the changes brought on by improvements to the city's African American community after World War I. In 1924 he followed his father's example, helping to establish the Wilmington Colored Chamber of Commerce. By that time, he had assumed a position as a letter carrier for the U.S. Post Office Department and was paying a mortgage on his home.[46]

A detailed record of Daniel Howard's estate, provided by his executor for an explanation of income and expenses, is a telling snapshot of black and white business activity in Wilmington. The estate record reports income from Howard's investment in the Virginia Life Insurance Company, the Wilmington Saving Trust Company, and the Atlantic Banking and Trust Company, as well as from members of Giblem Lodge and property rentals and sales. It further indicates that Howard invested both in African

American and white businesses and banks. Disbursements from his estate suggested both a dependence on white professionals and attempts to use African American sources whenever possible. Howard relied upon white and black physicians for his treatment but only upon whites for his groceries, legal services, and a newspaper—presumably because those services were not adequately supplied by the black community. Even though an African American business community had developed to service the needs of black residents, many, such as Howard, were required to patronize white businesses in order to fulfill their needs.[47]

John G. Norwood

John G. Norwood was likewise a leading member of the community, serving as senior warden of St. Mark's Episcopal Church and as a longtime member of the board of directors of Pine Forest Cemetery. Norwood owned a great deal of land in Wilmington, which totaled more than $3,000 in value in 1897. By 1900, however, his property values had dropped to just above $2,700. Norwood was a carpenter throughout his life, and he provided educational opportunities for his seven children, enabling them to become carpenters, politicians, teachers, and musicians. In 1900 Norwood was seventy-two years old, and his son Charles, a carpenter who had been unemployed for the last six months, was living with him. One of his other sons was living in the city, owned his own home, and worked as a mail carrier. Norwood died in 1906, and in his will decreed that his property should be divided among his widow and children. The 1910 census reveals that none of his sons were living in Wilmington but rather four of them resided in northern cities, where they rented their homes instead of owning them outright. Just as Howard's estate was divided among his sons, such was the fate of Norwood's property. However, Norwood's sons and their families were all gone from the city within four years of their father's death and had improved their lives somewhat, working in professional and semi-professional fields in several different northern

159

states. For Wilmington, however, the male branches of the Norwood family tree—potential generations of leadership in the community—were gone.[48]

Isham Quick

Study of Isham Quick and his family provides another avenue by which to understand the impact of 1898. Quick was born in South Carolina and had moved to Wilmington by 1867. It is unclear whether he was a slave or a free man before the Civil War (in 1860 large numbers of men and women of the Quick family were residing as free blacks in South Carolina). By 1870 Quick was working as a drayman and had acquired real estate valued at $300. He remained a drayman for the rest of his working life and was able to support a large family throughout his lifetime, sending his children to school as he continued to acquire more property. Throughout his life, Quick acquired and sold multiple properties throughout the city, though in 1897 and 1900 he owned only two properties. The two parcels were valued at a total of $800 in 1897 but declined in value by 1900 to a total worth of $750. Quick died sometime after 1910, and by 1920 his children were less active than their father in business affairs. Most of his family remained in Wilmington after their father's death, although one son, Isham, may have moved to New York by 1910. Two of his sons were working as draymen, and another was a porter with the Atlantic Coast Line Railroad; two rented their homes. According to the 1915 tax list, Quick's wife and son William were able to maintain ownership of some property until at least that date. One of Quick's daughters, Cornelia, had moved in with William F. Dodd as his "adopted daughter" and was working as a nurse. No copy of Quick's will has survived in the official county records, but, just as with Norwood and Howard, the property he acquired through hard work did not pass on to the next generation. It is unclear how or why those succeeding generations were unable to become property owners like their fathers, particularly when they inherited property by estate division.[49]

Elijah Green

Elijah Green provides a unique portrait of a man who remained in Wilmington and prospered, despite the changes forced by the white-supremacy campaign. Green was employed as a stevedore at the Sprunt-owned cotton compress and was able to keep his job, eventually earning the title of foreman. He was a trusted Sprunt employee. As a result, in August 1899 Sprunt enlisted him to travel to New York and Philadelphia to persuade as many as one hundred of Sprunt's former workers to return to Wilmington in exchange for promises of employment. It is unclear how many workers Green encouraged to return. Green was part of a large extended family that included many well-connected leaders in the African American community. He owned his home and other properties in the city both before and after the riot and was able to overcome personal tragedy (all three of his children preceded him in death by 1900) to help his extended family by opening his home to nieces and nephews. Green died at the age of seventy-five in 1930 and left his estate to his wife Emma. Green was an active member of his church, Price Chapel AME Zion, and before the 1898 campaign was an active member of the Republican Party.[50]

Thomas C. Miller

Two of the men in the case study were removed from Wilmington by the effects of the riot. The first, Thomas C. Miller, was forcefully banished but managed to find a life for himself in Norfolk, Virginia, before his death in 1903. Miller, a native of Wilmington, had accumulated considerable property holdings by the time of his eviction.[51] Although he departed the city on November 11, 1898, his wife, adult son, and minor children remained there. His wife, Annie, likewise a native of the city, worked to manage Miller's property holdings on his behalf after he left. Despite his absence, Miller was able to engage in land transactions in Wilmington after he left, and Annie won a court case as executrix of his estate.

Annie managed the estate for Miller's heirs in both North Carolina and Virginia. At least some of his children remained in the city, and his son Thomas appeared to benefit in a small degree from his father's wealth. Thomas C. Miller Jr. lived in his father's first home on North Sixth Street until his death in 1913, and his heirs sold the property in 1947.[52]

Miller was left distraught by what happened to him in 1898 and undoubtedly felt betrayed by men, black and white, whom he had known since childhood. In a 1902 letter to John D. Taylor, the white clerk of New Hanover County Superior Court, Miller discussed both business matters and his treatment. Miller asked Taylor to "pardon me for the way I write you, but when I think about it all[,] knowing I am not Guilty[,] it all most drives me mad—just to think how my own people could treat me as they have with out a Cause knowingly. Oh my God." Miller further wrote that he had been treated "worse than a dog" but that he was "Well and doing Well," although he was not allowed to come to the city to his mother's funeral. He ended the letter as a "heart broken" man.[53] Miller must have known that he was still an example for other blacks in the city. An article published in a local newspaper in 1899 asserted that "there are two elements . . . among the negroes . . . the kindly, affectionate, faithful, sober, well-meaning class and the low, vicious, unprincipled, saucy, bullying dangerous class . . . there are not many Tom Millers among them, but when revolutions set in the Toms are politely invited to pack and go and keep going."[54] After Miller's death, his body was returned to Wilmington for funeral services and burial at Pine Forest Cemetery.

John N. Goins

Another man forced to leave the city in search of a new life was John N. Goins. Goins was not a native of the city and was one of the youngest men affected by the riot. Goins, only twenty-nine years old at the time of the riot, had worked himself up from a South Carolina farm laborer with little education to working with Manly's newspaper. By 1900 he was living with the Manly brothers and other "exiles" from North Carolina in Washington, D.C., and was working as a commercial printer. He remained in Washington and continued to work as a printer for the next several decades, eventually finding a wife and securing a stable life for himself as a self-employed printer. Goins exemplifies the improved conditions encountered by many young men who fled Wilmington as a result of the 1898 riot.

161

Among the other young men who left Wilmington and found opportunity to prosper elsewhere were attorneys William E. Henderson and Armond Scott. Armond Scott (1873–1960) was targeted for banishment because he was an attorney. He escaped to Washington, D.C., where President Theodore Roosevelt appointed him a judge. Image from Reaves, "Strength through Struggle," 462.

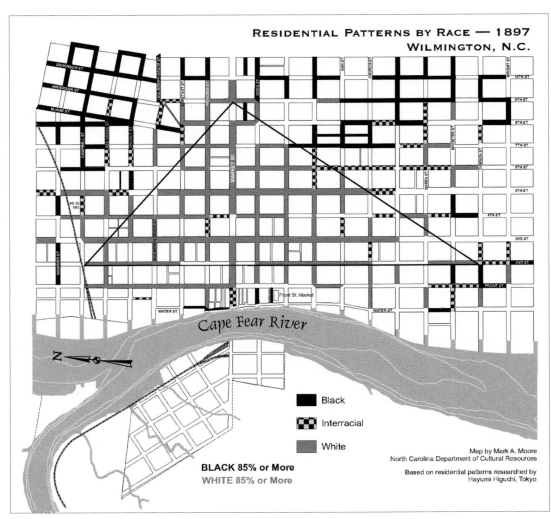

Mapping the City

While a graduate student at UNC-CH in the 1970s, Japanese scholar Hayumi Higuchi employed Wilmington's city directories of 1897, 1902, and 1905 to study changes in the city's residential patterns. Higuchi found that in 1897 the core of the city was dominated by whites in a triangular pattern beginning at Ninth and Market streets and extending outward to Second and Dawson and Second and Campbell. She discovered minor exceptions along two neighboring streets—North Fourth and Princess, near Market Street—where the racial mix was evenly distributed between whites and blacks. At the edges of the triangle were transition streets along which blacks comprised as much as half of the population before the neighborhood became predominantly black. The transitions between predominantly black

neighborhoods and majority white neighborhoods were one to two blocks in length, with higher concentrations of interracial neighborhoods along sections of South Sixth Street between Ann and Castle streets and down Castle Street to Third. One area in which a predominantly white neighborhood encroached on a predominantly black neighborhood was the section of Brooklyn in which the fighting broke out in November 1898. More white families than black lived along North Fourth Street, but most of the cross streets were either predominantly black or transitional neighborhoods with a mixture of white and black residents. The physical proximity of blacks to whites evident in parts of the Brooklyn neighborhood may have played a role in the buildup of tensions that erupted on November 10. Many of the men who claimed that their wives could not safely walk the streets lived in that area.[55]

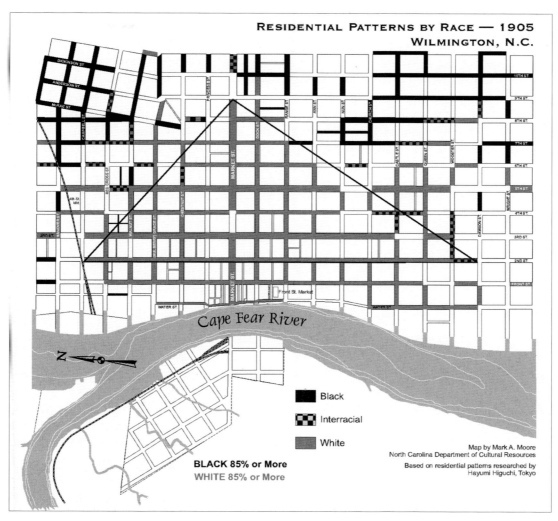

RESIDENTIAL PATTERNS BY RACE — 1905
WILMINGTON, N.C.

Cape Fear River

Black
Interracial
White

BLACK 85% or More
WHITE 85% or More

Map by Mark A. Moore
North Carolina Department of Cultural Resources
Based on residential patterns researched by
Hayumi Higuchi, Tokyo

Higuchi analyzed two twentieth-century city directories in the same manner and noted that the greatest change in residential patterns occurred about 1905 instead of immediately after the violence. By that date, the predominantly white sections of town had spread out, pushing the transition blocks between the black and white sections further toward the perimeters of town. The small grouping of integrated neighborhoods along North Fourth and Princess, near Market, had disappeared. The large number of blocks that contained both black and white residents along Sixth and Castle streets likewise vanished, with the concentration trending more toward a white majority. The area along North Fourth Street in Brooklyn was still a transition zone, with slightly more encroachment by whites into cross streets and onto North Fifth Street.

Overall, Higuchi's findings demonstrate the outflow of the city's African American residents away from the city center and a corresponding increase in white population as reflected in the census. Moreover, Higuchi's work demonstrates the changes in the attitudes of whites toward blacks as neighbors. The city became more and more segregated with the advent of Jim Crow. Prior to the violence of 1898, the core of the city, including the business sector, was dominated by white residents, but a few African Americans were able to maintain a foothold with land and homes acquired in traditionally white neighborhoods. After the violence of 1898 and the development of a more hostile, more predominantly white environment for African American businesses and families, members of the African American community physically stepped back from their white neighbors and moved to the perimeter of the city. Just as the economic climate changed for the city's African Americans as many developed businesses to serve their own race exclusively, their neighborhoods likewise changed, becoming less integrated and more homogeneous. In her research, Hayumi Higuchi was able to offer a new perspective on the 1898 race riot by demonstrating that the whites and blacks of Brooklyn lived in close proximity to each other in 1898 and, perhaps because of that proximity, became mortal enemies as neighbor shot neighbor.

Social Consequences

Many facets of African American life were affected by the events of 1898. After the month of November, one of Wilmington's first public celebrations would have been the Christmas holiday season and the tradition of "Jonkonnu." Jonkonnu was a custom dating to slavery in which blacks would dress in outlandish outfits, parade through white neighborhoods, knock on doors, and usually walk away with sweets or coins. The survival of Jonkonnu in Wilmington after slavery was remarkable, and by the 1880s the celebration had peaked in participation.[56] On December 26, 1898, however, the city's board of aldermen prohibited "the wearing of disguises of any kind by any person or number of persons, whether in the form of masks or otherwise on the streets or other public places of the city." The new law was enforced by police arrest and a ten-dollar fine.[57] By the mid-twentieth century, oral tradition among older African Americans in the Wilmington community attributed the end of the Jonkonnu celebrations to the violence of 1898.[58] Whites took over the celebrations, with young boys following the "Coonering" tradition and enjoying the ritual for themselves as early as 1905.[59]

Another public celebration discontinued as a result of the violence was the annual Emancipation Day observance. The celebration routinely took place on New Year's Day each year, with festivities including a parade, speeches, and music. By 1874 a permanent organization had been created to plan the event, and chairmen were selected to organize each year's celebration. The planning and preparations took place throughout the year, and many who recalled slavery regarded Emancipation Day as a yearly highlight. One of the largest commemorations took place in 1895 with a parade through the center of town and speeches delivered in a packed Thalian Hall. Wilmington's white newspapers routinely reported the event, but coverage became sporadic after November 1898. It is unclear whether or not the January 1899 celebration took place. One paper declared that the parade was not held, although services could have taken place in churches. The local leaders reorganized, and by 1902 the day was once again marked by speeches, parades, and music.[60] Emancipation Day celebrations declined nationwide around 1910, although they persisted in Wilmington with regularity until mid-century. One historian characterized the declining interest in Emancipation Day as a normal shift in cultural focus, one in which the African American community saw a greater purpose in working toward the current issue of regaining access to civil rights that had been taken away.[61]

The effect of the 1898 riot on Wilmington's African American Masonic Order and other black fraternal, social, and benevolent organizations is largely unknown, but it can be surmised that the role of such organizations became more pronounced and important to the development of an independent African American community.[62] African American Masonic lodges in North Carolina opened soon after the Civil War; and the leading members of the lodges were landowners and skilled tradesmen. Indeed, more than half of Giblem Lodge's members were landowners. There was a close connection between membership in a lodge and economic success. Communities such as Wilmington that were supported by a strong and active lodge benefited financially. Nevertheless, Giblem experienced a major shift in membership by the turn of the twentieth century. In 1900 only five of the lodge's officers had been members for more than ten years, and many of its founding members and former leaders were no longer involved in the organization. Because of that decline in membership, and reflective of the fact that many of the lodge's newer members lacked institutional memory and tended to own less land, the overall economic status of lodge

Giblem Lodge, located at the corner of Eighth and Princes streets, experienced a shift in membership after 1900. Despite that, its members aided the black business community. Image from *Wilmington Up-to-Date, The Metropolis of North Carolina Graphically Portrayed* (Wilmington: W. L. De Rosset Jr., Printer, 1902), [26]. This publication was compiled under the auspices of the Chamber of Commerce.

members was lower in 1900 than it had been when the lodge was founded in 1870. Despite changing membership within Giblem Lodge, its members aided the black business community by housing businesses in its large hall at the corner of Eighth and Princess streets and renting portions of its other properties to black businesses.[63] In addition, the lodge continued to participate as a part of the larger statewide and national organization to provide death benefits to members' surviving widows and children.

A bulwark of Wilmington's African American community was the network of religious institutions that developed in the city over the decades following emancipation. Prominent churches such as St. Stephen's AME, St. Mark's Episcopal, and Christ's Congregational (later Gregory Congregational) shepherded their congregations through the aftermath of the riot and provided a core of stability for the city's blacks. Just as Wilmington's African American business community had evolved into sustainable, self-contained units to serve localized markets within their own neighborhoods, the city's black churches developed methods to help many of the city's residents through the difficulties of newfound

unemployment and poverty well into the twentieth century.[64] Despite financial decline among the city's African Americans, parishioners maintained their churches, keeping the buildings and grounds in good repair and providing consistent improvements. The churches financed their activities through various methods, including local fund raisers, as well as sending their ministers to visit northern churches and donors in search of financial aid.[65]

Precisely what path Wilmington's black church leaders traveled in the months following the riot is not known, but the national AME Zion Church, led by men such as North Carolina's Bishop James Walker Hood, sought to bridge a gap between opposing viewpoints within the church as to how African Americans should deal with the "race question." At one extreme, as mentioned earlier, was Booker T. Washington, who counseled temporary surrender of voting and civil rights in favor of educational improvement. Opposing Washington were others such as Timothy T. Fortune who pressed for nothing less than full equality for blacks and justice for those who had been harmed by white mobs. The AME Zion Church chose to encourage a middle-of-the-road

165

Churches remained a bulwark in the African American community after the events of November 1898. St. Mark's Episcopal Church operated several missions in Wilmington to help residents through the difficulties of unemployment and poverty. Image from the *Wilmington Messenger*, May 9, 1897, reprinted in Reaves, "*Strength through Struggle*," 127.

path that focused on education, economic prosperity, and dedication to a long-term goal of equality and unlimited freedoms for blacks.[66]

Although several ministers had been targeted for forced removal from the city as a result of their active participation in Republican Party politics, many others remained. Of those, some likely took a less conspicuous position in political debate or sought to adopt a position considered less militant in the eyes of whites. Wilmington's black ministerial union, which had been dissolved in 1898, was reestablished in 1915. The new body followed the example set by the earlier group and pursued methods to organize the city's churches in order to provide community leadership in all matters religious and civic.[67]

A study of Wilmington's leading churches from 1897 to 1903 reveals that most of the city's African American congregations survived the 1898 upheaval and continued to exist in various sectors of the city.[68] In the years following the riot, some smaller churches such as Mount Calvary (also known as Mount Moriah) moved to various locations within the city before establishing a firm base. One immediate problem facing some of the churches was a steep decline in attendance. The congregations of all churches diminished in size in the immediate weeks and months following the violence because of the mass exodus of blacks from the city. Local oral tradition holds that St. Stephen's AME lost about eight hundred members, about half of its congregation, as a result of the out-migration that occurred following the riot. Only one congregation in the city—St. Thomas Catholic Church—was racially integrated in the years surrounding the violence. (Nonetheless, when the new St. Mary Catholic Church was completed in 1911, the white congregants of St. Thomas turned the church over to its black members.)[69]

Collective Memory

As the men, women, and children who were in Wilmington in 1898 aged, the city's disparate communities developed a collective but varying memory of the violence and coup. Narratives, or explanations, of what happened and why varied according to the age, sex, race, and economic position that narrators occupied in the twentieth century. Most white upper-class families maintained that the events were necessary evils that accomplished what was required to end municipal corruption and dangerous civil conditions. Elder members of some African American families, particularly those that remained in the city during the exodus, informed their children about the riot and warned them to be wary of whites. Still other African Americans moved from the countryside to the city in the wake of the violence to fill vacancies left by those who departed—willingly or under duress. Those newcomers, many of whom arrived fully understanding the ramifications of Jim Crow legislation and racial hatred, learned to adapt and live in the city separated from whites in a way not experienced prior to the cataclysm of November 1898.[70]

The African American story of the riot took shape, in part, as an object lesson on the lengths to which whites would go in order to achieve their agenda. The stories also helped to educate future generations about the difficult relationships between whites and blacks in Wilmington, particularly the challenge of learning which whites were sympathetic to the plight of blacks. For example, Lura Beam, a white northern teacher who moved to the city and taught African American students there between 1908 and 1910, observed that her students "hated the mass of white people but they were proud of learned people, the local cotton king, his home, his family and his horses." She also noted that the students felt "contempt" for the foreigners in town. Despite financial hardships, her native students were proud of their Cape Fear heritage.[71]

Providing further insight into the culture of post-1898 Wilmington, Beam demonstrated that she also learned to be wary of local native whites. As a white woman and outsider who entered the tense world of post-1898 Wilmington, Beam experienced perils as a teacher and was warned by another white teacher from Massachusetts that there was a "policy" that dated to the Civil War regarding black-white interaction in the city. That teacher had been in Wilmington during the riot, and she told Beam where twenty-three murders had occurred and that fires had burned along streets that she walked and that many families still in the city had to run for their lives during the riot. Because of such simmering undercurrents, Beam sensed the "smell of fear" in Wilmington. Blacks related to her horrors of 1898, such as stories of hiding in marshes and swamps, where men pretended to be cypress trees as they hid from bloodhounds that were sent into woods to find them. One family recounted burying their silver and never recovering it. Because Beam was distrustful of local whites, blacks, seeking to protect her and themselves lest someone should conclude that a white woman was endangered or that she fraternized with African American men, would not speak to her in the street.[72] Beam's "education" into black and white roles and relationships was undoubtedly repeated throughout the city among newcomers of all races, ages, and occupations.[73]

As mentioned prevously, the white narrative of the violence and coup suggested that actions by the white citizens of Wilmington were justified as necessary to restore order to the city. In the years that followed, the city attempted to attract new businesses and capital in order to diversify its economy according to the New South model. In a thinly veiled reference to the 1898 riot, the 1900 city directory boasted that the city's population had grown since 1897: "In view of the vicissitudes through which Wilmington has passed since our last publication, this gain is not only gratifying but surprising."[74] In 1902 the Wilmington Chamber of Commerce issued a pamphlet designed to attract outside capital. Realizing the potential hazard of mentioning the riot in such a publication, the organization simply chose to ignore it. The pamphlet proclaimed: "Our business is not with the past, but with the present."[75] Perhaps the most open allusion to the violence came in a discussion of the city's attributes, which favored manufacturing: "The local government is now based upon strict ideas of economy consistent with safe and secure progress." Three years later the local press suggested that the end of rioting marked the beginning of "an era of prosperity which has advanced the city greatly commercially, and this era still holds forth and is bringing

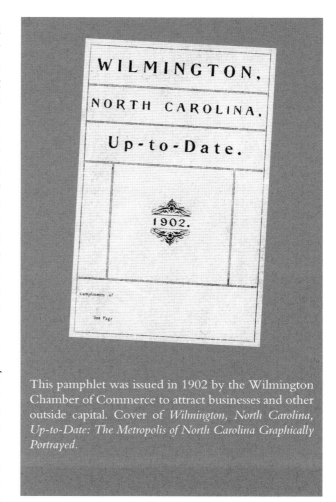

This pamphlet was issued in 1902 by the Wilmington Chamber of Commerce to attract businesses and other outside capital. Cover of *Wilmington, North Carolina, Up-to-Date: The Metropolis of North Carolina Graphically Portrayed.*

increased progressiveness and prosperity to Wilmington."[76] The differentiation between previous and contemporary political conditions suggested that the city had changed hands without referring to the means or the cost of the takeover. The city's businessmen advocated silence on the issue, but the local mentality attributed prosperity to the violence.

The city's leading white businessman and an amateur historian, James Sprunt, employed the following words to chronicle the 1898 race riot in his landmark history of the Cape Fear region, published in 1916—and still used as a standard reference by many historians:

> The year 1898 marked an epoch in the history of North Carolina, and especially the city of Wilmington. Long continued evils, borne by the community with a patience that seems incredible, and which it is no part of my

purpose to describe, culminated, on the 10th day of November, in a radical revolution, accompanied by bloodshed and a thorough reorganization of social and political conditions. . . . It was only under stern necessity that the action of the white people was taken, and while some of the incidents were deplored by the whites generally, yet when we consider the peaceable and amicable relations that have since existed, the good government established and maintained, and the prosperous, happy conditions that have marked the succeeding years, we realize that the results of the Revolution of 1898 have indeed been a blessing to the community.[77]

Sprunt's narrative reflects the traditional story of the violence as developed by participating and leading whites to justify their actions—that the armed overthrow, or "Revolution," was necessary to restore order and prosperity to the city. As the present work has attempted to make clear, however, such a simple explanation cannot suffice—nor was it truly the reason for the violence. The causes and effects of the riot, neatly packaged by Wilmington's elite, became the standard story for inclusion in all statewide historical works by historians such as R. D. W. Connor, J. G. de Roulhac Hamilton, and Samuel A. Ashe. Those men chronicled the history of the state during the first half of the twentieth century, and their prevailing assumptions regarding Wilmington's African American population were clouded by previous authors and close association with some who participated in the coup and violence.

As generations of Wilmington's citizens have shared the stories of 1898, historical fact and fiction have merged, creating alternative narratives that combine hearsay, fact, fictionalized accounts, and episodes from other parts of the city's history. An often repeated story is that the heads of black men who died on November 10, 1898, were placed on pikes along the major entrances to the city, but no historical data has been found to prove that such atrocity ever happened. Such activity did in fact occur in Wilmington in 1831, however, in the wake of hysteria that blossomed in the region in response to the 1831 Nat Turner insurrection in Virginia.[78] Amateur historian Harry Hayden

fueled the confusion when, in one of his works, he declared that blacks and "white agitators" would have done well to delve into Wilmington's history, remarking that rioting in the city was rampant in 1831, with a number of "unruly negroes put to death." He recounted that in that year the heads of men killed because of supposed ties to slave insurrection conspiracies were placed on pikes in conspicuous areas as a warning to others "bent upon stirring up racial tensions."[79]

Wilmington's Riot and Other Racial Clashes in the South

Racial tensions and explosions of violence directed against African Americans were not uncommon in the South at the turn of the twentieth century. The fear and actuality of slave uprisings prior to the Civil War and the growth of spontaneous lynch mobs of the late nineteenth century created a cult of violence. Although clashes between more than one black and more than one white have been called race riots, historian Paul Gilje has sought to clarify the term and the overall phenomenon of rioting in the United States. Gilje defined a "riot" as "any group of twelve or more people attempting to assert their will immediately through the use of force outside the normal bounds of law."[80] He noted further that the first race riots were white invasions of African American communities but that after World War II African Americans used the riot as a tool to vent their frustration with failures in social, political, and economic progress. Gilje and other historians have likewise pointed out that white rioters killed blacks while destroying black property and that such riots were followed by a suppression of the black voice in politics and the media, whereas black rioters usually only destroyed white property, and their actions rarely led to bloodshed.[81] In order to distinguish between the two types of upheavals, historian H. Leon Prather suggested alternative and more appropriate labels for the racial clashes of the late nineteenth and early twentieth century: "massacre," "pogrom," or "race war."[82]

The Wilmington Race Riot followed a model of white invasion into black neighborhoods, loss of black property, and the deaths of black citizens, as well as a virtual silencing of the African American population. It was the first of its kind in the industrial age, although scores of lynchings had taken place throughout the South for many years. Prior to 1898, three noteworthy race riots had taken place in the South. Of those, two occurred in 1866 in response to Reconstruction woes in Memphis and New Orleans; the third, in Danville,

at least six other major race riots occurred throughout the U.S., in which blacks lost their lives and property and experienced ever tightening limitations on their rights. In each instance, the numbers of black dead were never fully tallied, with estimates ranging from as few as seven dead in a Springfield, Illinois, riot to as many as 500 injured in Chicago. Massive property damage and a mass exodus of blacks followed in each case.[84]

Typical of the media at large, newspapers tended to blame Wilmington's blacks for the violence brought against them. Historians generally agree that the scene shown here did not happen. Images like this fueled the flames of racial tension throughout the South. *Collier's Weekly*, November 26, 1898. Image courtesy of the State Archives.

169

Virginia, in 1883, as in the case of Wilmington, erupted during election season in response to attempts by blacks to exercise their full rights as citizens in public spaces.[83]

The year 1898 marked a turning point in violent race relations across the nation. While Wilmington was dealing with its violence, Phoenix, South Carolina, underwent a violent episode in which at least thirteen men, including one white man, were killed by white mobs. After Wilmington's riot, which newspapers throughout the nation followed closely, other states experienced similar unrest. Within a quarter-century of 1898,

With its building tensions, the Atlanta Riot of 1906 closely resembled the outbreak of violence in Wilmington. Atlanta had struggled to recover from the Civil War and reinvent itself as a "New South" city. Attempts to revitalize Atlanta faltered until the turn of the twentieth century, and the violence in 1906 reflected growing tension between whites and blacks regarding segregated public spaces. The white rioters focused their attention on destruction of the upwardly mobile, successful black businessmen of the city. Additional impetus for the violence was linked to reports of black-on-white sexual assault.[85]

Although Georgia and Atlanta had experienced numerous lynchings, the violence in 1906 broke with tradition as white leaders looked to the model established by Wilmington's white leaders in forcing black businessmen from the city and seizing exclusive political control. Indeed, during political rallies gubernatorial candidate Hoke Smith explicitly indicated his willingness to re-create the violence that had overturned Fusion rule in Wilmington.[86] The bravado of the Atlanta campaign suggests that the lack of governmental response to the violence in Wilmington offered southerners implicit license to suppress the black community under the "right" circumstances, as, for example, in response to a perceived black crime wave. Just as Wilmington whites had employed the city's newspapers to assist in their attempts to regain power, Atlanta's leaders used Georgia papers to fuel the flames of the impending riot and, subsequently, to provide a modicum of calm and justification for the violence.[87]

Following the Wilmington and Atlanta riots, southern states experienced relative calm, inasmuch as whites had made huge gains in their ability to control blacks through intimidation and Jim Crow legislation. White lynch mobs still held both blacks and whites in check. The 1921 riot in Tulsa and its 1923 counterpart in Rosewood, Florida, proved that the fear of black-on-white sexual assault remained a potent force in instigating violence; those instances of civil unrest included particularly large numbers of black victims and black property loss. Further, the lack of state and federal response to vigilante violence demonstrated a tolerance of such behavior by white leaders, whose lack of response virtually sanctioned the activity.[88]

Tulsa's riot was likely the most violent racial clash in American history. Following an initial encounter between whites and blacks outside the city's jail on the night of May 31, 1921, whites prepared their invasion. White mobs looted black homes before setting them on fire. The Tulsa police department deputized dozens of whites, who murdered African Americans. Blacks attempted to defend themselves by taking up arms against the white invaders, but the Oklahoma state militia entered an African American enclave

Detail of a burning home in Rosewood, Florida, in 1923, following racial violence there. The image is reminiscent of the burning of the *Daily Record* office and the loss of black property. Image from "Listening between the Lines," http://www.listeningbetweenthelines.org/html/rosewood.html.

known as Greenwood, disarmed blacks, and confined them in the city's parks, leaving their homes and families unprotected. Thirty-five blocks, the heart of the city's black community, were destroyed. Estimates of the death toll vary from 75 to 300. Legal scholar Alfred L. Brophy emphasized the role of the state militia in facilitating the destruction of the black community—an aspect of the riot not unlike the activities witnessed in Wilmington and Atlanta.[89]

Whereas some Wilmington whites had expressed the belief that the 1898 riot marked a positive turning point in the city's history, those in the white communities in Atlanta and Tulsa recognized the need to characterize their riots as aberrations and placate the black community. Such efforts appear to have been directed more toward potential investors than to black victims, particularly given a feeble effort toward compensation. Historian Gregory Mixon contended that Atlanta's commercial-civic elite orchestrated the riot to impose their vision of the city's future. Atlanta and Tulsa presented images of a repentant white leadership that had restored the pre-riot order disrupted by the violence of the lower class of whites. The Civic League and the Colored Co-operative League were established in Atlanta to facilitate communication between the races. Atlanta whites formed a "Committee of Ten" to prove to outsiders that order had been restored and that white elites cared for their black neighbors. The body distributed relief, but its efforts reflected a desire to restore paternalistic relations between whites and blacks. Many blacks expressed their lack of confidence in white paternalism with their feet, fleeing the city for more hospitable northern communities.[90]

A white Tulsa grand jury blamed African Americans for the riot, contending that there was no eminent threat of white violence. Despite receiving such blame, blacks actively pursued restitution, filing five million dollars' worth of claims against the city (only one of which was honored). Within two years, more than one hundred suits arising from riot-related property damage had been filed. Whites attempted to appease blacks on the one hand and steal their property on the other. One hundred thousand dollars was donated to relief rather than reconstruction of the Greenwood neighborhood. Simultaneously, the Tulsa Real Estate Exchange was formed to buy the scorched earth of Greenwood, relocate African Americans farther north and replace black businesses with industrial development. County judges blocked the efforts, and it became clear that African Americans would have to rebuild on their own. In the years that followed the riot, Tulsa became a haven for the Ku Klux Klan, further isolating the city's African American community.[91]

In context, Wilmington's riot can be considered the first of its kind—an all-encompassing event that resulted in the white invasion of African American neighborhoods, an unknown number of black deaths, property destruction, armed overthrow of a legally elected city government, and the marginalization of black political and economic concerns.[92] Future white-on-black race riots grew in scope, affecting many more African Americans and destroying much more property as whites grew bolder in the face of little opposition or retribution. Typical post-riot responses by the cities' white leaders reveal local concerns about race relations but, more significantly, progress. Inaction by state and federal governments effectively validated the riots and demonstrated that white supremacy would triumph. White residents of Wilmington sought to assign to the riot of 1898 a greater good—peace, good government, safe streets, a healthy business climate—whereas the white citizens of Atlanta and Tulsa pursued a policy of compensation that offered outsiders at least the appearance of peace and understanding between the races.[93]

171

Truth, crushed to earth, shall rise again;
The eternal years of God are hers;
But Error, wounded, writhes with pain,
And dies among his worshippers.

Yea, though thou lie upon the dust,
When they who helped thee flee in fear,
Die full of hope and manly trust,
Like those who fell in battle here.

Another hand thy sword shall wield,
Another hand the standard wave,
Till from the trumpet's mouth is pealed
The blast of triumph o'er thy grave.

The last three stanzas of William Cullen Bryant's poem "The Battle-Field" were quoted in a speech given by an African American minister at a protest rally organized by Thomas Fortune on November 17, 1898, in New Jersey, just a week after the violence at Wilmington. The entire poem was originally published in the *United States Democratic Review*, vol. 1 (New York: J. & H. G. Langley, 1837). Indeed, a few blocks in Wilmington served as nothing short of a battlefield on November 10, 1898.

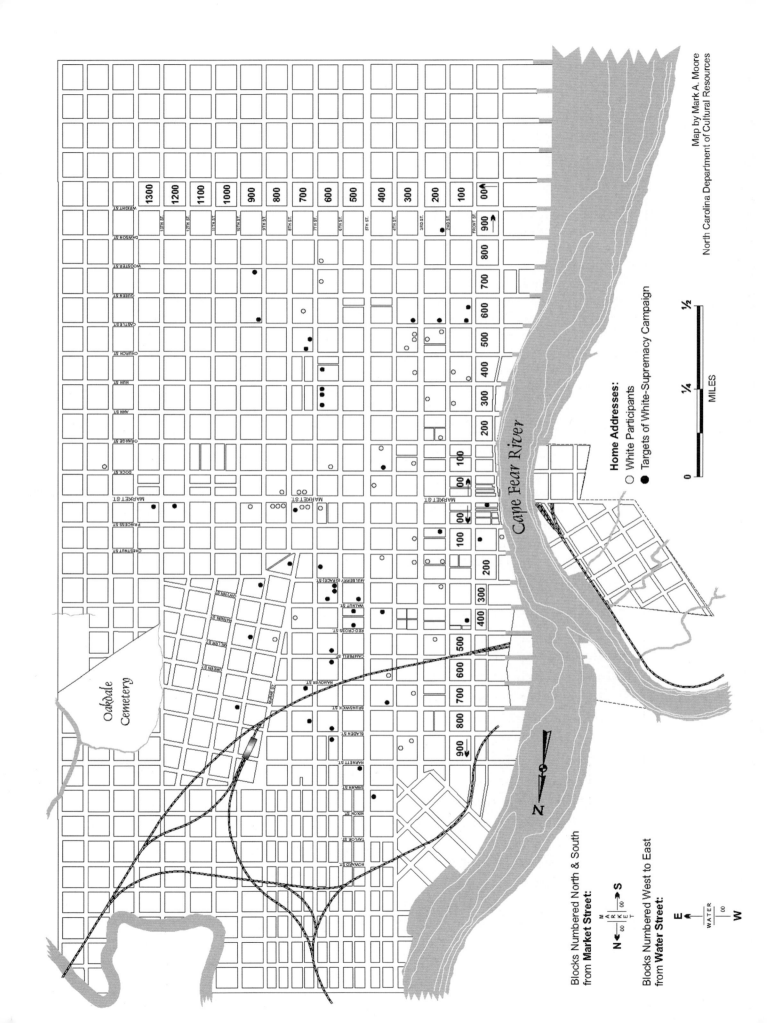

Blocks Numbered North & South
from **Market Street**:

N ← M
A
R
K
E
T
∞ → S

Blocks Numbered West to East
from **Water Street**:

E ←
WATER
∞ → W

Home Addresses:

○ White Participants

● Targets of White-Supremacy Campaign

MILES

0   ¼   ½

Cape Fear River

Oakdale Cemetery

N

Map by Mark A. Moore
North Carolina Department of Cultural Resources

00   100   200   300   400   500   600   700   800   900   1000   1100   1200   1300

Major Participants in Wilmington Race Riot—Map Key

(There were some key participants in both races whose address has not been identified.)

Key Participants – White

Bridgers, Preston L.	114 S 3rd
Clawson, Thomas	116 N 3rd
Crow, John E.	417 Chestnut
Davis, Joseph R.	320 Church
Davis, Junius	207 N 3rd
Dowling, Mike F.	713 S 7th
Ellis, James	
Fechtig, F. H.	220 N 2nd
Fennell, Hardy L.	807 Market
Fishblate, Silas H.	815 Market
Furlong, John J.	219 Red Cross
Galloway, Dr. Walter C.	1 Post Office Alley
Gilchrist, William	714 Market
Harvey, Rev. J. W. S.	801 S 7th
Holmes, Gabriel	218 N 3rd
Johnson, William A.	716 Market
Kenan, William Rand	110 Nun
King, B. Frank, Jr.	521 S 3rd
Kramer, Rev. J. W.	917 N 4th
Lathrop, Edward S.	802 Market
Manning, Pierre B.	714 Market
Maunder, J. F. (Frank)	624 N 4th
Mayo, William	307 Harnett
MacRae, Donald	711 Market
MacRae, Hugh	715 Market
Meares, Iredell	411 Orange
Montgomery, F. A.	203 Castle
Northrop, William H., Sr.	15 S 5th
Parsley, Walter L.	711 Market
Robertson, William F.	202 Orange
Rountree, George	411 N 2nd
Sasser, L. B.	802 Market
Schnibben, Charles	909 Market
Skelding, A. B.	520 S. 3rd
Skipper, Fred B.	708 N. 3rd
Smith, Joseph D.	622 Dock
Spencer, C. L.	
Sprunt, James	400 S Front
Stedman, Frank	311 N 2nd
Taylor, Col. Walker	321 S 3rd
Taylor, J. Allan	14 N 7th
Waddell, Alfred M.	16 N. 5th
Worth, Charles W.	412 S 3rd

Targets of White-Supremacy Campaign

Ashe, Richard	910 Castle
Bell, Salem J.	313 S 7th
Brown, Henry	512 Walnut
Brown, John H.	231 Princess
Bryant, Ari	1010 N 5th
Bunting, Robert H. (w)	1307 Market
Carroll, John	412 Brunswick
French, George Z. (w)	Orton
Gilbert, Charles H. (w)	213 N 7th
Green, Elijah	323 S 7th
Green, Henry	913 Wooster
Green, Henry C.	607 Campbell
Green, James P.	720 Church
Green, Josh	612 Bladen
Holloway, John	810 N 7th
Howard, Daniel	312 N 6th
Howe, John Harris	116 Castle
Howe, John T.	308 Castle
Jacobs, David	914 S 2nd 4
Jones, David R.	210 McRae
Keith, Benjamin F. (w)	407 Walnut
Lee, Rev. W. H.	804 McRae
Loughlin, James (w)	614 S. Front
Mallett, Alex	604 Campbell
Manly, Alexander L.	514 McRae
Manly, Frank	514 McRae
Mask, Dr. Thomas R.	510 S 7th
McAlister, Charles (w)	412 N Front
McMillan, William D.	414 Dock
Melton, John R. (w)	1215 Market
Miller, Thomas C.	216 Castle
Moore, William A.	413 S 7th
Pearson, James	310 N 6th
Pickens, Robert B.	317 S 7th
Quick, Isham	313 N 9th
Reardon, Robert	29 Market
Rivera, Thomas	516 Red Cross
Sadgwar, Frederick, Sr.	15 N 8th
Scott, Armond	519 Walnut
Telfair, Rev. James W.	615 Walnut
Toomer, Frank P.	916 Love Ave.
Walker, Andrew J.	1107 N. 5th
Webber, John H.	719 Hanover
Wright, Silas P. (w)	Orton

Appendix B

Brief Biographical Sketches of Key Figures

Editor's Note: *Although the following sources were employed in creating virtually every one of the biographical sketches in this appendix, in the interest of brevity and simplification they are not cited repetitiously at the conclusion of each sketch. The only sources so cited are those employed only occasionally for specialized information.*

H. Leon Prather, *We Have Taken a City: The Wilmington Racial Massacre and Coup of 1898* (Rutherford, N.J.: Fairleigh Dickinson University Press, 1984).

William M. Reaves, *"Strength through Struggle": The Chronological and Historical Record of the African-American Community in Wilmington, North Carolina, 1865–1950,* ed. Beverly Tetterton (Wilmington: New Hanover County Public Library, 1998).

Eighth Census of the United States, 1860: New Hanover County, North Carolina, Population Schedule, National Archives, Washington, D.C. (microfilm, State Archives, North Carolina Office of Archives and History, Raleigh).

Ninth Census of the United States, 1870: New Hanover County, North Carolina, Population Schedule, National Archives, Washington, D.C. (microfilm, State Archives).

Tenth Census of the United States, 1880: New Hanover County, North Carolina, Population Schedule, National Archives, Washington, D.C. (microfilm, State Archives).

Twelfth Census of the United States, 1900: New Hanover County, North Carolina, Population Schedule, National Archives, Washington, D.C. (microfilm, State Archives).

Thirteenth Census of the United States, 1910: New Hanover County, North Carolina, Population Schedule, National Archives, Washington, D.C. (microfilm, State Archives).

Fourteenth Census of the United States, 1920: New Hanover County, North Carolina, Population Schedule, National Archives, Washington, D.C. (microfilm, State Archives).

Fifteenth Census of the United States, 1930: New Hanover County, North Carolina, Population Schedule, National Archives, Washington, D.C. (microfilm, State Archives).

J. L. Hill Printing Co.'s Directory of Wilmington, N.C. 1897 (Richmond, Va: J. L. Hill Printing Company, 1897).

J. L. Hill Printing Co.'s Directory of Wilmington, N.C. 1900 (Richmond, Va.: J. L. Hill Printing Company, 1900).

Bill Reaves Local and Family History Collection, New Hanover County Public Library, Wilmington.

Jerome McDuffie, "Politics in Wilmington and New Hanover County, North Carolina, 1865–1900: The Genesis of a Race Riot" (Ph.D. diss., Kent State University, 1979).

Sue Ann Cody, "After the Storm: Racial Violence in Wilmington, North Carolina, and Its Consequences for African Americans, 1898–1905" (master's thesis, University of North Carolina at Wilmington, 2000).

New Hanover County Tax Records, 1890, 1897, 1900, State Archives.

J. H. Alston

Alston, aged twenty-seven in 1898 and a member of the Committee of Colored Citizens, could not be identified in the 1860, 1870, or 1880 censuses or in *Hill's 1897 Wilmington City Directory*. He is listed in the 1900 city directory as a physician with an office at 701 N. Fourth Street and a residence at 808 N. Fourth Street. The 1900 census shows his residence at 918 N. Seventh Street and his age as twenty-nine; his wife, Sarah, is shown as age twenty-four. Alston has not been found in censuses after 1900.

Richard Ashe

Ashe, a member of the Committee of Colored Citizens, was thirty-nine years old at the time of the riot. He could not be found in the 1860 or 1870 census, but in 1880 he lived in Wilmington with his father Simon, a woodcutter, and worked as a laborer in a brickyard. Both father and son were born in North Carolina. Ashe is listed in the 1897 and 1900 city directories as a laborer who resided at 910 Castle Street. He was active in community life and served as a director of the People's Perpetual Building and Loan Association. He did not own taxable property in 1890, but the 1897 and 1900 tax lists indicate that he owned property valued at $250. The 1900 census reveals that Ashe was living in Washington, D.C., where he, his wife Mary, and three daughters resided in a rented dwelling and that he worked as a janitor. The family remained in Washington where, by 1910, Ashe was a janitor at a police station. Ashe's father, Simon, remained in Wilmington; in 1900 he was eighty-four years old. The words "home sick" are written on the CCC summons found in Alfred Moore Waddell's papers.

Salem J. Bell (S. J. Salem)

Bell, a member of the Committee of Colored Citizens, was approximately forty-three years old in 1898. He was a partner with Robert B. Pickens in the firm of Bell & Pickens, a fish and oyster business that catered to both individual and wholesale interests and was located on Water Street at the Front Street Market. During the rioting on November 10,

1898, Bell was one of six men "marched" to a train bound for Richmond and forced to leave town. He was probably targeted both because he was an active member of the Republican Party and because his business competed with white fish dealers on Water Street. Bell was a native North Carolinian born to parents likewise born in the state. He could not be found in the 1860 census and most likely was a slave. In the 1870 census, he is shown as fifteen years old, and he then resided in Holden Township, where he worked as a domestic servant in the home of Dr. Elisha Porter (white) and was reported as illiterate. By 1880 Bell was married to Ida E. Bell (age twenty-one) and was working as a turpentine hand. In 1890 he owned four acres of land in Wilmington valued at $200. In 1897 his home was at 313 S. Seventh Street. According to the 1900 city directory and census, his wife still lived at the house they owned on S. Seventh Street, and his son (likewise named Salem Bell) lived at 905 Green Street and worked as a laborer. In the 1900 census, Ida Bell reported that she was widowed. Although she reported that she owned her house, it was mortgaged. By 1918 the house on S. Seventh was occupied by James Walker. Bell has not been clearly identified in the 1900 or 1910 censuses. One possible census entry for Bell was a man listed as a laborer in 1900, an "opener" in an oyster shop in 1910, and a laborer for a club in 1930—all in Fairfield, Connecticut.

175

Henry Brown

Henry Brown, a member of the Committee of Colored Citizens, was forty-two at the time of the riot and was an active political leader. He operated (with James Pearson) Brown & Pearson Barbers at 122 Princess Street and lived at 512 Walnut Street. According to the 1900 city directory, Brown and Pearson still worked as barbers at 122 Princess, and Brown still resided on Walnut Street. Brown has not been conclusively identified in census records prior to 1900, but he may have lived in Harnett Township in 1880. In the 1900 census, Brown is recorded as a North Carolina native who owned his home on Walnut Street. Brown's wife, Sophia, was born in North Carolina to a mother born in Georgia and a German father. The 1900 census also lists a son, Cecil Smith, age twenty-one, in Brown's household.

John H. Brown

John H. Brown was a member of the Committee of Colored Citizens. He was thirty-six years old at the time of the riot and was working as a health officer for the city and as a barber. Brown's workplace was located at 213 Princess Street, and his home was at 519 Brunswick Street. In 1890 Brown owned property valued at $400. By 1900 the taxable value of his property had increased to $475. By 1900 Brown was working as a carpenter and still living on Brunswick Street. Brown could be identified only in the 1880 census. In that year, he lived in Wilmington with his father, Alex, and worked as a laborer. Both father and son were born in North Carolina.

Ari Bryant (Ira R. Arie)

Bryant was one of six black men "marched" to a train and forced to leave town. He was likely targeted because he was an active member of the Republican Party. The *Wilmington Messenger* claimed that he was targeted because he "was looked upon by the negroes as a high and mighty leader. He was of vicious temperament towards the white people and counseled his race to strife . . . inciting the blacks to violence." At the time of the riot, Bryant operated a butcher shop at the Front Street Market. He attempted to challenge his banishment by returning to Wilmington in June 1899. A mob of armed men met at his home to force him to leave again; forewarned, Bryant fled before the mob arrived and hid at the home of a neighbor, Andrew J. Walker. When he left the second time, Bryant boarded a train for Norfolk, possibly to meet with Thomas C. Miller, and then planned to settle in Philadelphia.

In 1879 Bryant lived on N. Fifth Street between Bladen and Harnett but moved to 1010 N. Fifth Street by 1897. In 1900 he was no longer in the city, but his wife, Isadora, still resided at the house on Fifth Street and also operated a cookshop at 1106 N. Fourth Street. By 1918 the Bryant home had become the residence of J. H. Pickett, a white man, and by 1924 S. J. Cherry, another white man, lived there. The 1948 city directory listed the home as the residence of Alex Merrick, black. Bryant could not be located in the 1860 census and was probably a slave. In 1870 Bryant, then seventeen years old, lived

in the household of black laborer LeRoy Hubbard (a native of Kentucky) and his wife Harriet (born in North Carolina) along with David Bryant (age four), Cemante Bryant (age ten), and Amelia Bryant (age fourteen). His application for membership in a Freedmen's Bank, dated July 15, 1873, revealed that he was born in Wilmington, resided on Swann Street between Fifth and Sixth streets, was age twenty-one, had a brown complexion, and that his father's name was Thomas and his mother's name was Harriet. He listed as siblings David, John, Samantha, and Amelia. In the 1880 census Bryant is listed with his wife Agnes and was working as a butcher. SOURCES: William M. Reaves, *North Carolina Freedman's Savings and Trust Company Records*, abstracted by Bill Reaves, ed. Beverly Tetterton (Raleigh: North Carolina Genealogical Society, 1992); *Wilmington Messenger*, June 18, 21, 23, 1899.

L. H. Bryant

L. H. Bryant was superintendent of streets in 1898 and was fired from his job after Alfred Moore Waddell assumed the mayor's office. Bryant has not been identified in the census. A "Louis Bryant" is listed in the 1897 tax list as owning property valued at $900, but the value dropped to $600 in 1900. A will for one "Lewis Bryant" was probated in New Hanover County in 1915. A white "L. Bryant," age forty-nine, working as a carpenter, and married with two children, appears in the 1880 census.

Robert H. Bunting (white)

Bunting was one of the white men marched to the train station and banished from the city. At the time of the riot, he was forty-one years old and was justice of the peace for the U.S. Circuit Court; he resided at 1307 Market Street. He was targeted because of the way he ran his court; moreover, white Democrats claimed that he had married a black woman. According to the 1880 census, Bunting worked as a store clerk and was born in North Carolina to parents likewise born in the state. By 1900 he lived in Washington, D.C., with his wife (who was listed as white in the census) and one-year-old son, who had been born in North Carolina, and was working as a day laborer. The Buntings were not listed in the

1900 city directory. In December 1898, the *Evening Dispatch* (Wilmington) reported that R. H. Bunting and John Melton were living at 318 Pennsylvania Avenue in a "cheap lodging house" in the Bowery section and that they had "kept their tracks well covered and only after persistent efforts was their address discovered." This comment suggests that North Carolina Democrats were consistently following the movements of those who had been banished and that the banished men sought to evade investigation. SOURCES: *News and Observer* (Raleigh), November 12, 1898; *Evening Dispatch*, December 28, 1898.

John Carroll

Carroll, a member of the Committee of Colored Citizens, worked as a janitor for the city. According to the 1897 city directory, he lived at 412 Brunswick Street; he is not listed in the 1900 directory. In 1880, there were at least nine black men by the name of John Carroll in North Carolina, but none lived in New Hanover County. The 1900 census reveals that there were several men by that name in other states who listed their birthplace as North Carolina.

Dr. William M. Carter

The 1897 city directory gives Carter's occupation as "herbal doctor," and he was a boarder at 511 N. Seventh Street. In 1900 two men named William Carter lived in Wilmington; one worked as a day laborer, and the other was a vegetable huckster.

John C. Dancy

Dancy was a conservative black leader and was respected by some whites after the rioting for his attempts at mitigating tensions. On November 23, 1898, the *Evening Dispatch* commended Dancy for his "conservative speeches" during the 1898 campaign and reported that he was "much disturbed over the condition of affairs in the State." The journal quoted Dancy as saying that he was not forced to leave the city and was not "interfered with during the entire disturbance." Dancy is also reported to have said that he left after quiet was restored. Finally, Dancy is credited with attempting to coerce Alex Manly into recanting his article.

John Dancy was born in Tarboro in 1857 as the son of a free black man whose parents had been manumitted. Dancy's father was a well-respected builder and contractor who also served as a county commissioner after the war. Dancy was educated at home and subsequently entered Howard University in 1873. Because of the death of his father, he left school before completing his course of study. He returned home and commenced a career as an educator but soon became involved in politics. He served in various political capacities throughout his lifetime, most notably as a participant in activities of the Republican Party between 1880 and 1890 and as a candidate for office, national convention delegate, and campaign spokesman. Dancy also made significant contributions for many years through his involvement with the African Methodist Episcopal Church and editorship of the church newspaper, the *Star of Zion*. He served in other roles that benefited the black community, including trustee for Livingstone College. Dancy died in 1920, and details of his life can be found in his son's memoir, *Sand Against the Wind*, published in 1966. John C. Dancy Jr. shared his father's vitality and, like his father, was politically active, serving as an integral member of the Detroit Urban League for many years. (The elder Dancy is profiled in chapters 6 and 8 of the present work.) Dancy is listed in the 1900 census as renting a home in Wilmington with his large family at 413 N. Eighth Street. For additional information on Dancy, see the *Dictionary of North Carolina Biography*, s.v. "Dancy, John C."; John C. Dancy, *Sand Against the Wind: The Memoirs of John C. Dancy* (Detroit: Wayne State University Press, 1966); John C. Dancy, ed., *The [AME Zion] Quarterly Almanac* ([Wilmington?]: N.p., [1893?]).

Henry Davis

The Wilmington newspapers name Henry Davis as one of the wounded black men in the violence on November 10. Three different men with the name Henry Davis are enumerated in the 1897 city directory, and all worked as laborers. Their respective addresses were 321 S. Fourth Street, 409 Hane's Alley, and 807 S. Ninth Street. Two men

177

with that name are listed in the 1900 city directory, and one of those was also in the 1897 directory. A search for "Henry Davis" in the 1880 census reveals that there were five men with that name in Wilmington. In 1900 four men with the name Henry Davis are enumerated in the census, which provides the following information on each man: (1) drayman, age 53, of 321 S. Fourth Street, Wilmington; (2) inmate in county jail, age 55; (3) Henry Davis Sr., age 58, and (4) Henry Davis Jr., age 32, both residing in Federal Point Township, New Hanover County. This man could be George Henry Davis.

John Dow

Dow is listed as one of the black men wounded in the violence on November 10. He could not be found in the census or in the 1897 or 1900 city directories. Listed in the 1900 census, however, is a William Dow, born in North Carolina in 1875, who resided with his wife in a rented dwelling at 1106 Love's Alley and worked as a day laborer.

George Z. French (white)

French, a white man important in Wilmington Republican politics, was targeted for banishment by leading Democrats because of his influence with black voters. He was banished from the city on November 11. At the time of the violence, French was sixty-six years old. He was a native of Maine who had relocated to Wilmington from New England after the Civil War. The 1870 census lists him as president of Excelsior Plantation in Holden Township, New Hanover County. In that year his real estate was valued at $50,000, and his personal property was valued at $8,000. There were several families with the last name French in Wilmington and New Hanover County, all of whom immigrated to the city from the North. The 1897 city directory lists French as a deputy sheriff living at the Orton Hotel. After French was banished, he relocated to Rocky Point, Pender County, where he became a farmer and owned his home and farm. He could not be found in the 1910 census.

Henry Gause

The Wilmington newspapers reported that a Henry Gause had been arrested and banished from Wilmington on November 11. Nonetheless, the 1900 census reveals that a Henry Gause (the only one in North Carolina) was living in Wilmington. According to the census, this Henry Gause was unmarried, resided at 413 Nixon Street, worked as a day laborer, and had been born in North Carolina. In 1897 this Henry Gause paid taxes on a property in Wilmington Block 337 valued at $175, and he would have been thirty-five years old at the time of the 1898 violence. In 1880 there were two men named Henry Gause living in New Hanover County. One of them—the one who was living in Wilmington in 1900—lived in Harnett Township in 1880 and worked as a servant; the other, ten years older (he would have been forty-five at the time of the riot), worked as a drayman and was married and had a daughter (his wife, Lucy, was twenty-seven in 1880, and his daughter, Ella, was three in 1880).

Charles H. Gilbert (white)

Gilbert, a white policeman in 1898, was banished from the city, probably because of his ties to the Republican administration of city government. Gilbert and another white man were put on a train to New Bern on November 11 and were pushed further northward, out of the state. The 1897 city directory lists Gilbert as living at 213 N. Seventh Street. SOURCE: *News and Observer*, November 12, 1898.

John N. Goins

Goins was a member of the Committee of Colored Citizens summoned to hear the demands of Waddell's Committee of Twenty-five on November 9, 1898. He was targeted because he worked for Alex Manly at the *Daily Record*. Goins is not listed in the 1897 or 1900 city directories. He was probably born in South Carolina in 1869. By 1900, Goins lived in Washington, D.C., and worked with Alex Manly as a printer. He remained in Washington and continued to work as a printer but was married and self-employed by 1920. (Additional biographical information on Goins can be found in chapter 8 of the present work.)

Elijah Green

Green, like John Goins, was a member of the Committee of Colored Citizens summoned to hear the demands of Waddell's Committee of Twenty-five on November 9, 1898. He was also an alderman from the Fifth Ward and was forced to resign his position on that body the following day. At the time of the violence, Green, a native of South Carolina, was forty-one years old. He was an active member of Price Chapel AME Zion Church. He remained in Wilmington and continued to be a community leader until his death in 1930. He worked at Sprunt's cotton compress and in 1900 was also operating a grocery store at 323 S. Seventh Street. Green both resided in and operated his store in the southern part of Wilmington instead of in Brooklyn, which was situated on the northern side of the city and was the scene of most of the violence on November 10.

On September 15, 1902, Green lost a court case and was ordered to pay $83.75. Documents related to the case reveal that Green then owned three parcels of property in Blocks 23, 80, and 81 of Wilmington, each valued at $300; those properties, combined with the value of Green's residence and furnishings, amounted to $11,651, a considerable sum. Green was part of a large and influential family in Wilmington. Many members of his family were involved in local business interests and prior to 1898 were active in Republican politics. (Green is likewise profiled in chapter 8 of the present work.) SOURCE: Insolvent Debtor and Homestead and Personal Property Exemptions, 1809–1916, New Hanover County Miscellaneous Records, State Archives.

Henry B. Green

Democratic Party leaders targeted African American Henry B. Green in 1898 because he was a sergeant on the city police force. Green, age fifty-seven at the time of the violence, departed Wilmington and moved to Philadelphia. By the following year he had become extremely ill and successfully sought permission to return to his former home in Wilmington, declaring that he would rather "die here than among strangers in Philadelphia"; he subsequently died on May 26, 1899. Green was a native of Raleigh and a veteran of the Civil War. He had enlisted in Company A, 40th Regiment U.S. Colored Troops, in 1866. Following his discharge in 1869, he moved to New Hanover County.

Henry C. Green

Henry C. Green was a member of the Committee of Colored Citizens summoned to hear the demands of Waddell's Committee of Twenty-five on November 9, 1898. Green worked as a butcher at the Fourth Street Market in Brooklyn and was active in Republican politics. He lived at 607 Campbell Street and was an active member of St. Mark's Episcopal Church. Green died in 1907.

James P. Green

Like Henry C. Green, James P. Green was a member of the Committee of Colored Citizens summoned to hear the demands of Waddell and the Committee of Twenty-five. The 1897 city directory lists him as a laborer residing at 720 Church Street. By 1900 he listed his occupation as "driver." According to the 1860 census, Green was a free black living and working in the city as a carpenter. He died in 1913.

Josh Green

Josh Green, too, was a member of the Committee of Colored Citizens summoned to hear the demands of Waddell and the Committee of Twenty-five. The 1897 and 1900 city directories list him as a coal and wood dealer. He was a member of Mt. Nebo Church, a Mason, and a member of the Odd Fellows. Green lived at 612 Bladen Street, and his wood business was located on Orange Street. In 1890 Green owned taxable property valued at $200. His property was valued at $310 in 1897, and it increased in value to $345 by 1900. The 1900 census reveals that Green owned his home on Bladen Street and lived there with his wife and son John, an architect.

Josh Halsey

The Wilmington newspapers identify Halsey as one of the black men killed as a result of the violence on November 10, 1898. He could not be found in the 1880 census. Four Halsey households were listed for Wilmington in 1880, but there is no Josh Halsey. No Josh Halsey is listed in the 1897 city directory.

William E. Henderson

Henderson was a member of the Committee of Colored Citizens summoned to hear the demands of Waddell's Committee of Twenty-five on November 9, 1898. He was a young African American attorney who had arrived in Wilmington the previous year and had established a successful law practice. Earlier in 1898 he had purchased a home. He was targeted for banishment because he allegedly made "incendiary" speeches before the election and had befriended Manly. Henderson was not escorted under armed guard to the train station but was given two days to get his affairs in order before leaving. Following his hasty removal from Wilmington, Henderson spent some time in Salisbury with family but eventually relocated to Indianapolis, where he had relatives. He became an outspoken advocate of black rights and welfare and resumed the practice of law. One of Henderson's descendants has his diary from 1898 and shared portions of it during the centennial celebration. As an attorney, Henderson represented controversial figures in city politics. In June 1898 a Wilmington newspaper reported that he had represented police officer R. H. Benson in a dispute with Chief of Police John R. Melton at a special meeting of the Wilmington Board of Aldermen. SOURCE: *Morning Star* (Wilmington), June 9, 1898.

John Holloway

Holloway, like Henderson, was a member of the Committee of Colored Citizens summoned to hear the demands of Waddell's Committee of Twenty-five on November 9, 1898. Holloway was a post office clerk, a director of the Metropolitan Trust Company, and a railroad entrepreneur, serving as president of the Wilmington, Wrightsville and Onslow Railroad. He was a native of Virginia but grew up in Robeson County. From 1887 to 1889 he was a member of the North Carolina House of Representatives. Holloway was involved in Wilmington politics and was a community leader and a member of the Masonic Order. The 1900 city directory identifies him as a clerk living at 810 N. Seventh Street.

Daniel Howard

Daniel Howard was a member of the Committee of Colored Citizens summoned to hear the demands of Waddell's Committee of Twenty-five on November 9, 1898. He was active in Wilmington politics, serving as a member of the Republican Executive Committee, a director of the Metropolitan Trust Company, and a director of the People's Perpetual Building and Loan Association. His home was located at 312 N. Sixth Street. (Howard is profiled in chapter 8 of the present work.)

John Harriss Howe

John H. Howe was a member of the Committee of Colored Citizens summoned to hear the demands of Waddell's Committee of Twenty-five on November 9, 1898. He was a contractor and builder, and he resided at 116 Castle Street. Howe was an active member of St. Mark's Episcopal Church. He remained in the city after the violence and died in 1902.

John T. Howe

Like so many others profiled here, John T. Howe was a member of the Committee of Colored Citizens summoned to hear the demands of Waddell's Committee of Twenty-five on November 9, 1898. Howe worked in various careers and was a mail carrier and teacher before serving in the North Carolina House of Representatives in 1897. In 1897 Howe was an agent for Alex Manly's *Daily Record*. His home was at 308 Castle Street. Although he was affiliated with Manly, he was not forced to leave Wilmington, probably because of his family's long ties to the city.

Howe Family

The Howe family descended from Anthony Walker Howe and Tenah Howe. According to family tradition, Anthony was the son of an Ibo chieftain in Africa. A white slaveholder whose last name was Walker purchased him as a young slave. After Walker's death, his slaves were sold to Robert Howe, a prominent landowner. Anthony Walker Howe was a carpenter and builder. According to tradition, Tenah was a Tuscarora Indian adopted as a baby by the Howe family. The white Howe family allowed Tenah to marry Anthony Walker, but the couple had to agree that all children born to the couple would have the last name Howe. Robert Howe granted Anthony his freedom. Five of Anthony and Tenah's children—Anthony, Pompey, Alfred, Isabella, and Polly—survived to adulthood. All of the Walker/Howe children were free blacks and were taught carpentry skills; they worked in Wilmington prior to the Civil War. Anthony Walker/Howe died in 1837, and Tenah died in 1852. Their descendants became prominent members of the community and were leaders after the Civil War. SOURCE: Cynthia J. Brown (Howe descendant), interview with author, Wilmington, July 2004

David Jacobs

David Jacobs was a member of the Committee of Colored Citizens summoned to hear the demands of Waddell's Committee of Twenty-five on November 9, 1898. In 1898 he was employed both as a barber and as a county coroner. In 1897 his home was at 914 S. Second Street, and his business was situated at 15 Dock Street. Jacobs was born in 1851 and died in 1905. He was still working as a barber on Dock Street in 1900. He was an active member of Mt. Olive AME Zion Church. The 1870 census reveals that Jacobs was living in the household of African American carpenter Thomas Allen and working as a barber's apprentice. Jacobs lived next door to his future wife, Mary Battle. By 1880 Jacobs and Mary were married; their household included two sons and Mary Jacobs's parents (George and Hester Battle) and sister (Virginia Battle). The census of 1900 reveals that Jacobs rented his home at 916

S. Second Street. Also living with Jacobs at that time were his wife, two adult sons, and a boarder. Jacobs was forty-six years old at the time of the violence in 1898.

William L. Jeffries

Jeffries was born in Pittsburgh and was graduated from Lincoln University. He was a member of the staff at the *Daily Record*. He could not be found in the city directory or census for New Hanover before or after 1898. SOURCE: *Morning Star*, December 10, 1898.

David R. Jones

David Jones was a member of the Committee of Colored Citizens summoned to hear the demands of Waddell's Committee of Twenty-five on November 9, 1898. He was employed as a drayman and was a director of the Metropolitan Trust Company. According to the 1897 city directory, he lived at 210 McRae Street, but by 1900 he had moved to 510 Swann Street. The 1900 census reveals that Jones was working as a drayman and owned his home. Also living with Jones was his adult son, Albert, who worked as a day laborer, and his grandson, Eddie. Jones was fifty-four at the time of the violence in 1898, and his son was twenty-two. In 1897 the elder Jones paid taxes on property located in Wilmington Block 307 and valued in 1900 at $50. Albert Jones paid taxes on property in Blocks 31, 34, 47, and 60 valued at a total of $1,050 in 1897 and 1900.

Benjamin F. Keith (white)

Keith, a Silver Democrat or Populist at various times, was a white member of the Fusionist board of aldermen but was forced to relinquish his position. He was not present at the afternoon changeover of government on November 10 but later resigned. During the 1898 campaign, Keith, a successful businessman, experienced immense pressure and intimidation both from Democrats and Red Shirts to "convert" openly to the Democratic Party. Keith maintained his resolve and withstood the pressures, despite personal and financial ruin as a result of the campaign of intimidation. Keith wrote of his

181

experiences to Sen. Marion Butler and to other political figures. He also penned an autobiographical sketch of his life titled "Memories." Keith lived at 407 Walnut Street. (He is profiled in chapter 3 of the present work.)

Rev. J. Allen Kirk

Kirk arrived in Wilmington in 1897 to serve as minister to the African American congregation at Central Baptist Church. After he had become involved in political activities, the editor of the *Evening Dispatch* warned him to leave the city. Kirk responded to the threat by publishing a strongly worded piece of propaganda titled, *A Statement of Facts Concerning the Bloody Riot in Wilmington, N.C., of Interest to Every Citizen of the United States* ([Wilmington?: the author?, 1898?]) (available online at http://docsouth.unc.edu/nc/kirk/menu.html). Kirk detailed his escape from the city and the conditions that existed there prior to the election. Members of the Sadgwar family claimed that the Reverend Kirk did not live in Wilmington at the time of the riot and that he did not "experience" the riot. Kirk's name does not appear in the 1897 or 1900 Wilmington city directory. (Additional information on Kirk can be found in chapter 6 of the present work.) SOURCES: Kirk, *A Statement of Facts Concerning the Riot*; Felice Sadgwar and Mabel Sadgwar Manly, interview by Beverly Smalls, Wilmington, May 14, 1985, transcript of interview in Oral History Files, Cape Fear Museum, Wilmington.

Thomas Lane

Thomas Lane was arrested during the violence of November 10, 1898, because white rioters identified him as the man who fired a shot at the Wilmington Light Infantry (WLI). He was put on trial before Mayor Waddell, convicted of the shooting, and sent to jail. Although he did not kill anyone, he was blamed for the shooting of Josh Halsey, who was in fact murdered by the WLI near Manhattan Park. (For additional information on the shooting at Manhattan Park, see chapter 5 of the present work.) Lane could not be found in the 1880 census of New Hanover County or the Wilmington city directories.

According to one Wilmington newspaper, a Susan Lane returned in 1915 from New York to 513 S. Twelfth Street in Wilmington but "didn't have claim to property" and was moved out by police because "others had claim to property." It is not known whether or not this Susan Lane was related to Thomas Lane. Neither is it known how long Susan Lane remained in jail or whether or not she was released at a later date. SOURCES: *Morning Star*, November 16, 1898, October 9, 1915.

Rev. John William (I. W.) Lee

Lee, a member of the Committee of Colored Citizens summoned to hear the demands of Waddell's Committee of Twenty-five on November 9, 1898, was targeted because he was chairman of the New Hanover County Republican Party Executive Committee. The 1897 city directory identifies him not only as the minister to the large congregation of St. Stephen's AME Church but also as a laborer. In 1897 Lee lived at 804 McRae Street, but by 1900 he had moved to 101 S. Thirteenth Street and was no longer listed as minister of St. Stephen's.

Isaac Loften/Loftin/Lofton or McLean (McLain) Loftin

An African American man by the last name of Lofton or Loftin was one of the black men arrested on November 10 and banished from Wilmington on the following day. He was targeted because of his activity in support of the Republican Party, and white leaders claimed that as a merchant in the city he tried to purchase weapons for blacks in the community. There may be some confusion in the sources, and Isaac and McLean may be either the same man or two individuals confused in the records over time. Research on the two has not been able to clarify the confusion. According to his application for membership in a Freedmen's Bank, dated April 23, 1873, Isaac Lofton was born in Middle Sound, N.C., and his residence was in the Scotts Hill community in Pender County. Lofton reported that he was a farmer, that he was married (his wife's name was Lecie), and that he had no children. His father was Jessie Hansley, and his mother was named Hannah. Lofton retained ownership of his land on

West Scotts Hill Road as late as 1919 and possibly returned to the outskirts of Wilmington to live on Dock Street near Fifteenth Street by 1901. Lofton was forty-eight years old at the time of the violence.

McLean Lofton was active in city affairs and served the community in various roles, including as a director of the Metropolitan Trust Company. In the 1897 and 1900 tax lists, a "McLain Loftin"—almost certainly the same man—owned property in Wilmington Block 482 valued at $500. In 1910 McLean Lofton was living in Cape May County, New Jersey, along with other émigrés from Wilmington and other parts of North Carolina. SOURCES: *Morning Star*, February 12, 1919; *Wilmington Messenger*, June 6, 1901.

James Loughlin (white)

Loughlin, a white clerk at the Front Street Market, was targeted because of his support of Fusion politics and claims that he tried to sell weapons to blacks. He was probably one of the white men ordered to leave town and escorted to a train on the afternoon of November 11. Loughlin was not found in Wilmington in the 1880 census, although there were 109 other men by that name in the U.S. at the time. Loughlin lived at 614 S. Front Street in 1897. The 1900 city directory includes a man with the same name and lists him as a carpenter living at 514 S. Second Street. The 1900 census reveals that Loughlin then resided at 514 S. Second Street and was working as a carpenter.

Charles McAlister (white)

McAlister was a white man escorted to a train for New Bern on November 11, 1898. A Wilmington newspaper reported that McAlister "burst into tears" while aboard the train as it departed the city and that he left a wife and five children behind. McAlister worked as a salesman for A. David and Company and may have been targeted because he sympathized with blacks in the city and tried to assist in protecting them, especially by selling them weapons. McAlister lived at 412 N. Front Street in 1897 but was not listed in the 1900 city directory.

William D. McMillan

McMillan was the African American superintendent of health for Wilmington and was summarily fired after Waddell's administration took control of the city on November 10. According to the 1897 city directory, McMillan lived at 414 Dock Street. His name does not appear in the 1900 directory. SOURCE: Thomas C. Miller, Norfolk, Virginia, to John D. Taylor, Clerk of Court, Wilmington, July 9, 1902, Correspondence, 1824–1906, New Hanover County Miscellaneous Records, State Archives.

Alex Mallett

Mallett was a member of the Committee of Colored Citizens summoned to hear the demands of Waddell's Committee of Twenty-five on November 9, 1898. He was forty-eight years old at the time of the violence. The 1897 city directory shows him as a "packer" who lived at 604 Campbell Street. By 1900 Mallett had moved to 14 N. Front Street and was employed as a porter. In 1897 he paid taxes on a property in Wilmington Block 237 valued at $1,200. The 1880 census lists Mallett as a store clerk living with his grandmother on Campbell Street. The 1900 census reveals that he rented his home at 212 S. Seventh Street. Mallett was a native of North Carolina.

Alexander L. Manly (Manley)

Manly was born near Raleigh in 1866. Family tradition held that his father was Charles Manly, who served as governor of North Carolina from 1849 to 1851. There is some confusion about Manly's father, and Alexander Manly may have been Governor Manly's grandson or nephew instead. Manly's legal father, Trim, was a slave on the governor's plantation. Family tradition also has it that Alex's mother Corrine was an enslaved maid in the household. Manly and his brothers were well educated and attended Hampton Institute. The 1880 census reveals that Alexander resided in his father's household in Selma. Finally, family tradition has held that Manly resented his heritage and that hatred may have driven him to react so strongly to Rebecca Felton's words.

Manly was the target of the Democratic Party in the political campaign of 1898, and a mob led by Alfred Moore Waddell destroyed his printing office on November 10 of that year. Soon after Manly published his contentious article in August 1898, the owner of the building, M. J. Heyer, evicted Manly's printing business. At the same time, a group of black men surrounded the press to protect it from impending destruction by a group of white men. Manly then retaliated by proposing that blacks boycott white businesses. On the night prior to the riot, a Red Shirt mob searched for him but could not find him. If members of the mob had been able to find Manly on November 10, they almost certainly would have lynched or shot him; but, because he was informed of the threat to his life, Manly and his brother Frank escaped the city. Some accounts claim that he departed Wilmington prior to the violence, but others indicate that he left on the day of the riot. Tradition holds that Thomas Clawson gave Manly the pass code and money to leave town and that he and Frank were light-skinned enough to pass as white through the checkpoints armed by white men. Other, contradicting evidence indicates that Manly may have left the city much earlier. Still another account indicates that Manly's youngest brother, eleven-year-old Thomas, warned him of the approach of the mob. Thomas was reportedly as light-skinned as Alex and because of that fact was able to learn about the impending danger to his brother from Red Shirts as they were marching toward the press. A recent history of Wilmington's St. James Episcopal Church reports that Robert Strange personally escorted Manly out of the city in his carriage.

Manly relocated to Washington, D.C., by 1900 and rented a house at 1607 Eleventh Street. Family tradition holds that he was first given asylum by Congressman George H. White. According to the 1900 census, Manly lived in Washington with his brothers Frank (born in 1869) and Henry (born in 1879) and boarders John P. Meyers (born in South Carolina in 1877) and John Goins (born in South Carolina in 1869). Manly listed his occupation as a journalist. His brother Henry listed his occupation as commercial printer, as did Meyers and Goins. Manly's youngest brother Thomas, previously mentioned, apparently lived in Wilmington. Thomas later married Mabel Sadgwar, daughter of

Frederick Sadgwar and sister to Caroline Sadgwar, Alex Manly's fiancée in 1898. Mabel said that Thomas passed as white most of his life. After they were married, Mabel and Thomas moved to Pennsylvania, where Thomas worked as an electrical engineer. Mabel and Caroline were the daughters of prominent community leader and Wilmington native Frederick Sadgwar Sr. (see entry for him below).

While in Wilmington, Alex Manly lived with his brother Frank at 514 McRae Street. Alex was involved in Wilmington civic life as an active member of Chestnut Street Presbyterian Church and was engaged to Caroline Sadgwar at the time of the violence. Caroline was educated at Gregory Normal School and attended Fisk University in Tennessee. Caroline was a talented vocalist and toured the world with the Fisk Jubilee Singers. She was performing in England at the time of the violence, and as soon as she returned to the United States she married Alex Manly at the residence of Congressman George H. White in Washington, where Manly was then living. The couple later moved to Philadelphia, where they had two sons—Milo and Lewin—and Alex worked as a painter. Manly and his wife were able to return to Wilmington for visits with her family for many years after the violence—although he may have traveled under disguise. Alex Manly undoubtedly returned to the city in 1925 for the funeral of his father-in-law, Frederick Sadgwar Sr. Manly and his son Milo maintained that property he owned in Wilmington was seized for nonpayment of taxes. No confirmation of that claim has been found.

Manly became active in numerous activities after leaving Wilmington. He was a leader in the Afro-American Newspaper Council and most likely knew Timothy T. Fortune, prominent African American editor in New York. Manly also knew Booker T. Washington and W. E. B. DuBois. He helped to establish the Armstrong Association, a forebear of the Urban League. In a 1985 oral history interview, Manly's sister-in-law, Mabel Sadgwar Manly, indicated that David Bryant Fulton worked for Manly at the *Record* for a short time and that he was the son of Levinia Robinson Fulton, one of the founders of the Congregational church in Wilmington. Transcripts of the interview are on file at the Cape Fear Museum. In addition to the biographical profile of Manly that appears in chapter 4 of the present work, historian Robert Wooley has compiled additional information on Manly for a forthcoming book about the controversial printer.

Manly realized the importance of the black vote to Wilmington. In 1895, soon after he and his brother Frank had assumed ownership and management of the *Record*, he wrote: "The air is full of politics, the woods are full of politicians. Some clever traps are being made upon the political board. In North Carolina the Negro holds the balance of power which he can use to the advantage of the race, state, and nation if he has the manhood to stand on principles and contend for the rights of a man." SOURCES: Susan Taylor Block, *Temple of Our Fathers: St. James Church, 1729–2004* (Wilmington: Artspeaks, 2004); Robert Wooley, telephone conversation with author, summer 2004; *Record* (Wilmington), September 28, 1895, original in North Carolina Collection, Wilson Library, University of North Carolina at Chapel Hill; *Evening Dispatch*, August 25, 1898; *Wilmington Messenger*, August 25, 1898; *News and Observer*, November 19, 1898; Sadgwar and Manly interview.

Frank Manly

Alex Manly's younger brother Frank relocated to Wilmington to work at the *Record*. Frank worked as a journalist but also managed the paper's business affairs. By 1920 he had moved to Alabama and was teaching at Tuskegee Institute for Booker T. Washington. While in Wilmington, Frank lived with Alex at 514 McRae Street, and, after they were exiled from the city, he again resided with his brother in Washington, D.C., and listed his occupation as journalist. SOURCES: Block, *Temple of Our Fathers*; Wooley telephone conversation; *Record*, September 28, 1895, original in North Carolina Collection; *Evening Dispatch*, August 25, 1898; *Wilmington Messenger*, August 25, 1898.

Dr. Thomas R. Mask

Thomas Mask was a member of the Committee of Colored Citizens summoned to hear the demands of Waddell and the Committee of Twenty-five on November 9, 1898. Mask was thirty-six years old at the time of the violence and had recently returned to the city after serving briefly with the 3rd Regiment, North Carolina Troops, in the Spanish-American War. Mask, a physician, was educated at Leonard Medical School in Raleigh. The 1897 and 1900 city directories show his address as 510 S. Seventh Street. The 1900 census confirms that address and reveals that he resided there with his wife and two sons. After the violence of 1898, Mask became a local leader and held positions in community and civic organizations until his death in 1911. Thomas C. Miller, likewise a leader in Wilmington's African American community, respected Mask and declared that "he has treated me right." Mask's brother, John H. W. Mask, relocated to Wilmington and likewise became a physician after he graduated from Leonard Medical School in 1898. SOURCES: Thomas C. Miller to John D. Taylor, July 9, 1902, Correspondence, 1824–1906, New Hanover County Miscellaneous Records, State Archives.

John R. Melton (white)

Melton was the white chief of police in 1898 and was forced to resign his position in city government before being arrested and banished from the city. (His capture and banishment are detailed in chapter 6 of the present work.) Melton was a Populist. In 1880 he was living in Wilmington with his wife Augusta and three daughters and worked as a butcher. He is listed in the 1897 city directory as living at 1215 Market Street. Melton tried to return to Wilmington in 1899. The 1900 city directory has him still living on Market Street, but no occupation is shown. By 1910 Melton was living in Wayne County. SOURCE: Thomas C. Miller to John D. Taylor, July 9, 1902, Correspondence, 1824–1906, New Hanover County Miscellaneous Records, State Archives.

George Miller

George Miller was one of the black men reported as wounded as a result of the violence on November 10. He was shot twice and died at City Hospital. The 1880 census lists Miller as residing in Cape Fear Township, New Hanover County. His name could not be found in the 1897 city directory. Miller was twenty-eight years old at the time of his death. SOURCES: *Evening Dispatch*, November 11, 1898; Thomas C. Miller to John D. Taylor, July 9, 1902, Correspondence, 1824–1906, New Hanover County Miscellaneous Records, State Archives.

Thomas C. Miller

Thomas C. Miller was an African American leader targeted for banishment because of his activity in the Republican Party and, as oral tradition has it, because he was one of the most successful businessmen in Wilmington and a substantial creditor to blacks and whites. A newspaper quoted Miller as threatening to wash his hands in white man's blood before nightfall on the day of the riot. Miller relocated to Norfolk following his banishment. (Miller's arrest and banishment are discussed in chapter 6 of the present work.)

In 1880 Miller had been a deputy sheriff and was married to his first wife, Sally Miller, age thirty, and resided at 216 Castle Street. His son, Thomas C. Miller Jr., was then four years old. In 1889 Miller was operating a saloon and restaurant at 15 S. Water Street, the only such business operated by a black person among eighteen such establishments in Wilmington at that time. The 1897 city directory indicates that Miller was a pawnbroker and was also operating a real-estate business at 7-9 Dock Street and that he still resided on Castle Street. Thomas C. Miller Jr. worked for his father during that year. (The 1900 city directory indicates that the younger Miller had no occupation and resided at 309 N. Sixth Street; his name could not be found in the 1900 census.)

Miller was deeply affected by his arrest and banishment and asked to return to Wilmington in 1899. His request was denied. He still maintained business contact with various people in the city, and his second wife, Annie E. Miller, and son had remained there to handle the bulk of his affairs. Miller died in 1903 at age fifty-two of paralysis resulting from a stroke in Norfolk. His remains were brought back to his Wilmington residence on Sixth Street for a funeral and burial at Pine Forest Cemetery. Speculation at the time of Miller's death had it that he left an estate valued at $10,000, although he had been disposing of his real estate in the city before his death. Miller's death certificate listed his occupation as saloon keeper and indicated that he lived at 176 Queen Street in Norfolk. It also indicated that he and his parents had been born in North Carolina. While in Norfolk, Miller operated a barroom and in 1901, with an associate, purchased property. He and his son resided in Norfolk.

Thomas C. Miller and his family were connected to the Sadgwars, Riveras, Howes, Colletts, and other prominent New Hanover County families. Annie E. Miller was married to Fred Sadgwar Jr. by 1910. The 1910 census indicates that she was thirty-six years old and had been born in North Carolina. Thomas C. Miller's daughter Charity, who resided in the household with Annie and Fred Sadgwar, was born in Pennsylvania in 1903. Annie Sadgwar died in 1946. It is likely that Annie, along with her husband, managed Thomas C. Miller's estate holdings for the benefit of Charity and other Miller children. An examination of deeds executed by the Millers and Sadgwars, two of Wilmington's largest black landowning families, would help to clarify the ultimate division of Thomas C. Miller's property. The Miller House on Sixth Street, originally built for him, was inherited by his son and remained in the Miller family until 1947, when Frederick Sadgwar Jr., stepfather to Thomas C. Miller's younger children, acquired it for use as rental property. The Sadgwar family owned the house until 1988. SOURCES: *Wilmington Messenger,* November 30, 1899, March 31, 1903; *Morning Star,* March 27, 1903; Thomas C. Miller to John D. Taylor, July 9, 1902, Correspondence, 1824–1906, New Hanover County Miscellaneous Records, State Archives; *Directory of the City of Wilmington, North Carolina, 1889* (Wilmington: Julius A. Bonitz Publisher, 1889); Administrators' Bonds, New Hanover County Estates Records, State Archives; T. C. Miller House File, New Hanover County Public Library; *Norfolk, Portsmouth, and Berkley, Virginia 1903 Directory* (Norfolk, Richmond, Newport News, Va.: Hill Directory Company, 1903); City of Norfolk Death Records, Library of Virginia, Richmond; *Charlotte Observer,* November 19, 2006.

William A. (Bill) Moore

Moore was a member of the Committee of Colored Citizens summoned to hear the demands of Waddell and the Committee of Twenty-five on November 9, 1898. Moore worked as a lawyer and was targeted for removal from the city because of his political activity and his occupation. He was a controversial figure and one of several leaders, all subsequently banished, who in January 1898 signed a resolution to repeal compulsory vaccination laws. Moore was involved in establishing the Wilmington Livery Stable Company. In 1897 his law office, which he shared with George H. White, was situated at the corner of Market and Second streets, and his residence was at 413 S. Seventh Street. During the 1898 election campaign, the law office was broken into and vandalized. Several men named William Moore were living in Wilmington at about the same time, making full identification difficult. One Wilmington newspaper reported that Moore's father was an escaped slave named Rev. Thomas Jones, from New Bedford, Massachusetts. Moore was living near Masonboro Sound near the time of his death. SOURCES: Thomas C. Miller to John D. Taylor, July 9, 1902, Correspondence, 1824–1906, New Hanover County Miscellaneous Records, State Archives; *Evening Dispatch*, January 26, 1898; *Morning Star*, June 10, 1890, June 8, 1897.

Charles Norwood

Charles Norwood was county treasurer in 1898 and was forced to resign his position as a result of the coup on November 10. Norwood's father was John G. Norwood of Wilmington. Charles departed Wilmington and relocated to New York, where he worked in the customs service at the port. By 1910 he was living in Philadelphia with his family. His brother William likewise relocated to Philadelphia and worked as a building laborer.

John G. Norwood

John G. Norwood, father of Charles and William Norwood, was an alderman under Mayor Silas Wright and was forced to resign. He worked as a carpenter and lived at 202 Walnut Street. He was wealthy and was active in St. Mark's Episcopal Church. (Both Norwoods are profiled in chapter 8 of the present work.)

Carter Peamon (Pearmon, Pearman)

Peamon was a member of the Committee of Colored Citizens summoned to hear demands of Waddell and the Committee of Twenty-five on November 9, 1898. He was active in the Republican Party and operated a barbershop with his brother Moses.

On the day of the violence, Carter Peamon was killed. (Additional information on his death can be found in chapter 5 of the present work.) Carter Peamon is not listed in the 1897 city directory, but his brother and partner Moses is shown as operating a barbershop at 820 N. Fourth Street and residing at 9126 N. Eighth Street. Like his brother, Moses Peamon was forced to leave Wilmington on the day of the violence. Carter Peamon could not be found in any census. A man by the name of Carter Payman appears in the 1870 census. Carter Payman (age forty-five) had been born in South Carolina and was working as a laborer in Mobile, Alabama, at the time. If this is the Carter Peamon who was murdered in Wilmington, he would have been seventy-three at the time of the violence. A George Peamon, probably related to Carter, was in Wilmington by 1880 working as a barber. He lived at 719 N. Fourth Street, was born in North Carolina, and was nineteen years old. George moved to Norfolk by 1900 and continued to work as a barber. The 1897 city directory lists Moses Peamon, Carter's brother, as a barber working at 916 N. Eighth Street and living at 820 N. Fourth Street. A Moses Payman appears in the 1870 Wilmington census as residing with his mother, Susan; both had been born in Virginia. SOURCES: *Morning Star*, November 15, 1893, November 12, 1898.

James Pearson

Pearson was a member of the Committee of Colored Citizens summoned to hear the demands of Waddell and the Committee of Twenty-five on November 9, 1898. He was a barber and politician and operated a barbershop at 312 N. Sixth Street. Pearson was not forced to leave the city and remained in business. His home was at 310 N. Sixth Street.

Robert B. Pickens

Pickens was a member of the Committee of Colored Citizens summoned to hear the demands of Waddell and the Committee of Twenty-five on November 9, 1898. He was forty-four years old at the time. He was targeted because of his activity in the Republican Party. Pickens was forced to leave Wilmington and was placed aboard a train on November 11, 1898. He operated a fish and oyster business with Salem

Bell, who was likewise forced to leave the city. The 1897 city directory reveals that Pickens resided in Wilmington at 317 S. Seventh Street. By 1900 he was working in Newport News, Virginia, as a "coal trimmer" and living in a rented dwelling with his wife Amelia and a large household (including five male boarders from North Carolina, all of whom were coal trimmers).

In 1896 Pickens had entered into a mortgage agreement to purchase for $700 a property in Wilmington Block 119. In 1899, with $96.25 due on the instrument, the mortgagee foreclosed and sold the property at auction to one Godfrey Hart, who thereupon sold it to a black teacher. The Pickens home at 720 Ann Street was the residence of Thomas Knight from 1918 to 1938.

Isham Quick

Quick was a member of the Committee of Colored Citizens summoned to hear the demands of Waddell and the Committee of Twenty-five on November 9, 1898. Quick was a wood dealer/drayman in 1897 and lived at 313 N. Ninth Street. He remained in the city with his family after the violence. (He is profiled in chapter 8 of the present work.)

Robert Reardon

Reardon was a member of the Committee of Colored Citizens summoned to hear the demands of Waddell and the Committee of Twenty-five on November 9, 1898. He was targeted for banishment but escaped the city before he was captured. (Information on his banishment can be found in chapter 6 of the present work.) Reardon operated a barbershop at 29 Market Street in 1897. By 1900 he had moved to Washington, D.C., where he continued to work as a barber. Reardon was born in South Carolina and was thirty-five years old at the time of the violence. The 1900 census reveals that his father was a native of Ireland. In 1895 Reardon was the manager of the black pavilion at Ocean View, an entertainment and recreational facility at Wrightsville Beach. During that same year, he operated the Wilmington Intelligence Bureau and Advertising Agency in the city and had "erected a neat building" for an office on Second Street

between Dock and Orange streets. In 1897 he was referred to as "Professor Reardon," a "tonsorial artist" who was planning to open a barbershop at Carolina Beach.

Thomas Rivera

Thomas Rivera was a member of the Committee of Colored Citizens summoned to hear the demands of Waddell and the Committee of Twenty-five on November 9, 1898. Rivera, a longtime resident of the city, worked as an undertaker. He was active in Republican politics and served on the board of the Wilmington Colored Educational Institute. His home was at 516 Red Cross Street. Rivera was born in Wilmington in 1826 and had once operated a grocery store at 22 N. Front Street. By 1879 he worked as an undertaker at 304 Princess Street. The following year, he helped to develop the Peabody School. He was an active member at St. Stephen's AME Church and died at his home in 1906. Rivera's niece was Annie E. Miller, wife of Thomas C. Miller. (Rivera is profiled in chapter 8 of the present work.)

Frederick Sadgwar Sr.

Sadgwar was one of the black men summoned to hear the demands of Waddell and the Committee of Twenty-five on November 9, 1898. His children, who were young at the time of the riot, did not realize that he was one of the men who attended the meeting. Family tradition holds that Sadgwar worked for Walter L. Parsley, a member of the Secret Nine, at the time of the violence of 1898 and was taken by surprise by the extent of the rioting on November 10. Moreover, the Sadgwar family believed that the "better whites," such as Parsley, even though they were privy to the plans made by the white leaders, had no part in the violence but instead protected the family at their home during the rioting. Indeed, the Sadgwars have maintained that the protection given them by whites extended into the early twentieth century. (Despite the family's favorable opinion of Wilmington's "better whites," Parsley was in fact a member of the "Secret Nine," the group that planned the coup and whose actions led to the violence.) Some of the Sadgwar children were in school when the rioting began and were escorted home, unmolested, by their older brother, Ted, who was in his thirties and worked with their father as a carpenter.

The Sadgwar family was close to the Chesnutt family, and Frederick Sadgwar's children grew up with relatives of the renowned African American author Charles Waddell Chesnutt, author of *The Marrow of Tradition* (1901). Family tradition also has it that the Sadgwar men helped to protect the white missionaries who were in Wilmington teaching at Gregory Congregational Church. Sadgwar was born in Wilmington and worked as a building contractor. He was on the board of directors of the Wilmington Livery Stable Company and United Charities. He resided at 15 North Eighth Street on property purchased by his father. In 1883 he was working as a mail carrier. SOURCES: Sadgwar, Wright, and Kennedy interviews.

Armond Scott

Scott was one of the Committee of Colored Citizens and was charged with delivering that body's reply to Alfred Moore Waddell by 7:30 on the morning of November 10, 1898. Scott, unable to reach Waddell's home because of white patrols, instead placed the letter in the mail. Scott was targeted for banishment because he was an attorney. He was a member of a prominent Wilmington family, and local residents, white and black, reportedly helped him escape from the city. (Discussion of his escape can be found in chapter 6 of the present work.) Scott graduated from Johnson C. Smith University in 1896 with a law degree. At the time of the violence in 1898, he was twenty-five years old. Despite his banishment, Scott returned frequently to Wilmington to visit his family. The 1880 census lists Scott as living with his father, Benjamin, a native of Virginia. Armond Scott's name does not appear in the 1897 directory, but that year his father operated a grocery store at his home at 519 Walnut Street. The 1900 census reveals that Scott, then residing in New York, was working as an elevator operator. By 1910 he had relocated to Washington, D.C., and was working as an attorney and renting a home with his wife and infant son. The 1920 and 1930 censuses reveal that he remained in the nation's capital during those

years. By 1920 he owned his home in that city, and by 1930 his son was employed as a teacher, and Scott's property was valued at $16,000. President Franklin D. Roosevelt later appointed Scott a judge; he continued in that position through the administrations of Harry Truman and Dwight Eisenhower. Scott reportedly titled his memoirs "Up from Hell"; they are in the possession of his descendants.

Frank Shephard

Shephard was listed as one of the black men wounded as a result of the violence on November 10, 1898. He lived with his mother Cornelia at the home of Thomas Stevenson, white, in 1880. Shephard was eighteen years old and worked as a hostler at the time of the riot.

Willis (Drake) Stevens

On May 3, 1897, the New Hanover County Board of Commissioners agreed to pay $8.80 for tools and materials for Willis Stevens so that he would not become a ward of the county. It was "understood that the tools shall at all times be the property of the county and his keeping them will depend on his good behavior." A contemporary article in a Wilmington newspaper noted that Stevens, also known as "Drake," previously had been declared insane and ordered to the asylum, but the county attorney, Marsden Bellamy, had secured his release. Terms of his release specified that Stevens be gainfully employed in his trade as a shoemaker. He "promised the board to go to work with the understanding that if there is any more foolishness his tools will be taken away from him." Precisely what led to Stevens's institutionalization could not be determined, and no court records can be found to provide details. In October 1898 Wilmington newspapers described the scene at a precinct in the First Ward where Stevens had attempted to register to vote. Rev. J. W. Kramer, a Democrat, challenged Stevens's credentials to register, and a riot ensued. Kramer declared that Stevens was insane and ineligible to vote. One newspaper belittled Stevens as a "half-witted negro who imagined a year or so ago that he had a cinch on the mayorality." Before any other African Americans could step in, Stevens continued to defend his eligibility to register and threatened a lawsuit. At that point, Carter Peamon, a barber and community leader, stepped in to advocate on behalf of Stevens in the face of several Red Shirts, including S. Hill Terry. Peamon and Terry got into a scuffle, during which Peamon snatched a knife out of Terry's hands. The scuffle was settled, and Peamon thereupon told Rev. J. W. Kramer that he wished he could "slap the jaws of every white man." It is unclear whether or not Stevens was allowed to register, but the fortitude of the white registrars and Red Shirts probably prevented him from doing so. (Stevens is profiled in chapter 4 of the present work.) SOURCES: Minutes, New Hanover County Board of Commissioners, 1887–1918, State Archives; *Wilmington Messenger,* May 4, 1897, October 2, 1898; *Morning Star,* October 2, 1898.

John E. Taylor

Taylor was born in 1858 and was a graduate of Howard University. He was the deputy customs collector for Wilmington in 1898 and served in that role for a total of twenty-five years. His home was at 122 N. Eighth Street. In 1896 Taylor was made city clerk and treasurer. He owned a great deal of property and was president of the Metropolitan Trust Company. (Taylor is profiled in chapter 8 of the present work.)

Rev. James W. Telfair

Telfair was a member of the Committee of Colored Citizens summoned to hear the demands of Waddell and the Committee of Twenty-five on November 9, 1898. He was a minister at Mt. Zion AME Church and was a Mason. His home was at 615 Walnut Street. Telfair had been a slave of the DeRossett family and later worked as a manager at the Sprunt cotton compress. He remained a minister in the city after the violence and died at his home in 1914. Telfair was sixty years old at the time of the riot and had worked in the city as a ship's carpenter in 1870 and also as a stevedore. In 1897 and 1900 he owned taxable property valued at $750 in Wilmington Blocks 96 and 223.

Frank P. Toomer

Toomer was a policeman in Wilmington under Mayor Silas Wright and was one of the black men banished from the city on November 11, 1898. In late November 1898 Toomer wrote Mayor Waddell from New Bern, requesting permission to return to the city. Waddell responded that Toomer should not return because he had been "obnoxious" to people and it was best for him to stay away. Toomer's name could not be found in the 1880 census, although there were several people with that surname in the county. He resided at 916 Love Avenue in 1897. Toomer married Rose Wilson in 1871 in Wilmington.

Andrew J. Walker

African American community leader Andrew Walker was an alderman from the First Ward while Silas Wright was mayor and was forced to resign on November 10, 1898. Walker owned a considerable amount of property in Wilmington and worked as a stevedore. In 1880 he was twenty-nine years old and lived in the city with his sister Polly. By 1890 Walker owned taxable property worth $1,400. Seven years later the tax value of that property remained constant at $1,450, but by 1900 it, along with some newly acquired property, had increased in value to $2,100. Walker lived at 1107 N. Fifth Street. He had been an officer in the 3rd Regiment, North Carolina Volunteers, during the Spanish-American War but had returned to Wilmington in June 1898. Walker was active at Central Baptist Church and died in 1907.

John H. Webber

Webber, an African American member of the Wilmington Board of Audit and Finance, was forced to resign after the coup led by Waddell on November 10, 1898. Webber was forty-three years old at the time. He owned property in Wilmington Block 267 valued at $350 in 1897 and 1900. The 1897 and 1900 city directories list Webber as a laborer. He resided at 719 Hanover Street. The 1918 and 1924 Wilmington city directories give his occupation as a woodworker. Webber's name could not be found in the 1870 or 1880 census but did appear in the 1900 census, which shows his occupation as day laborer. In 1890 Webber was president of the Young Men's Republican Club. He served as president of the Phoenix Hose Reel Co. No. 1 in 1895–1896. Webber worked for Chadbourn Lumber Company for thirty-eight years.

Daniel Wright

Wright was one of the black men killed on November 10, 1898. (His murder is recounted in chapter 5 of the present work.) Wright had been a member of the New Hanover County Republican Executive Committee, and in 1897 his home was at 810 N. Third Street. The 1880 census lists Wright as a worker in the rice fields near Wilmington. In late November 1898, a local newspaper reported that the remains of a John S. Wright, a black man who had drowned in the Cape Fear River, had been found near the Navassa community of New Hanover County after Wright had been missing for two weeks. It is not known if the two men were related. SOURCE: *Morning Star*, November 28, 1898.

Silas P. Wright (white)

Silas Wright was the white Republican mayor of Wilmington who was forced to resign his office during the coup led by Waddell on November 10, 1898. Wright was then banished from the city. The 1897 city directory reveals that he was a boarder at the Orton Hotel. By 1870 Wright, originally from Massachussets, had relocated with his wife to Wilmington, where he worked as a revenue collector. By 1900 he had moved to Knoxville, Tennessee, and was renting a home while he worked as a physician. (Additional information on Wright can be found in chapters 5 and 6 of the present work.)

Endnotes

Chapter 1: Into Reconstruction and Out Again

1. The chapter title has been borrowed from Andrew Howell, *The Book of Wilmington* (Wilmington: The Author, 1930), 150. James Sprunt, *Chronicles of the Cape Fear River, 1660–1916*, 2nd ed. (Raleigh: Edwards and Broughton Printing Company, 1916), 45–46.

2. The populations of North Carolina's largest towns in 1860 were Wilmington, 6,522; New Bern, 5,432; Fayetteville, 4,790; Raleigh, 4,780; Salisbury, 2,420; and Charlotte, 2,265.

3. When it was completed in 1840, the Wilmington and Weldon Railroad was the longest rail line in the world at 162 miles between the two destinations. For additional information on the importance of Wilmington as a port, see Alan D. Watson, *Wilmington, Port of North Carolina* (Columbia: University of South Carolina Press, 1992). Robert B. Outland III, *Tapping the Pines: The Naval Stores Industry in the American South* (Baton Rouge: Louisiana State University Press, 2004), 52–54; Tony P. Wrenn, *Wilmington, North Carolina: An Architectural and Historical Portrait* (Charlottesville: University of Virginia Press, 1984), 3.

4. William McKee Evans, *Ballots and Fence Rails: Reconstruction on the Lower Cape Fear* (Athens: University of Georgia Press, 1995), 239.

5. After the Federal siege of Charleston began in 1863, Wilmington became the most important port to the Confederacy. Evans, *Ballots and Fence Rails*, 7; Chris Fonvielle Jr., *The Wilmington Campaign: Last Rays of Departing Hope* (Campbell, Calif.: Savas Publishing Company, 1997), 18.

6. Before the war, the city was closely divided between pro-Union and secessionist groups. Those who supported the pro-Union position did so for economic as well as political reasons, inasmuch as merchants did not want to jeopardize their northern shipping contacts. Fonvielle, *The Wilmington Campaign*, 439–441, 459.

7. Noah A. Trudeau, *Like Men of War: Black Troops in the Civil War, 1862-1865* (Boston: Little, Brown and Company, 1998), 363–365.

8. Whitelaw Reid, *After the War: A Southern Tour, May 1, 1865, to May 1, 1866* (Cincinnati and New York: Moore, Wilstach & Baldwin, 1866; reprint, New York: Harper Torchbooks, 1965), quoted in Catherine W. Bishir, *The Bellamy Mansion, Wilmington, North Carolina:*

An Antebellum Architectural Treasure and Its People (Wilmington: Bellamy Mansion Museum; Raleigh: Preservation North Carolina, 2004), 47. Union Leagues were first established in 1862 in Northern states such as Ohio, Pennsylvania, and New York. The organizations sought to increase loyalty to the Union, and members worked to provide physical and mental support to Federal soldiers by providing them with supplies. Additionally, the leagues enlisted African American troops at their own expense, sent teachers southward to educate freed slaves, provided care to blacks both in camps and in the North, and, after the war, lobbied for black suffrage. Union Leagues, also known as Loyal Leagues, were organized in areas with high concentrations of blacks in order to coordinate voting campaigns. Walter L. Fleming, "Union League Documents" in Walter L. Fleming, ed., *Documents Relating to Reconstruction* (Morgantown, W.Va.: N.p., 1904), 3–6.

9. For additional information on the connections between freedmen and slave artisan entrepreneurship before and after the Civil War, see Robert C. Kenzer, *Enterprising Southerners: Black Economic Success in North Carolina, 1865–1915* (Charlottesville: University of Virginia Press, 1997), 43–47.

10. Paul D. Escott, "White Republicanism and Ku Klux Klan Terror: The North Carolina Piedmont during Reconstruction," in *Race, Class, and Politics in Southern History: Essays in Honor of Robert F. Durden*, ed. Jeffrey J. Crow, Paul D. Escott, and Charles L. Flynn Jr. (Baton Rouge: Louisiana State University Press, 1989), 15–17.

11. An overview of the destruction wrought by the Civil War on North Carolina's economy, physical environment, and citizens can be found in John G. Barrett, *The Civil War in North Carolina* (Chapel Hill: University of North Carolina Press, 1963); Barrett, *North Carolina as a Civil War Battleground* (Raleigh: State Department of Archives and History, 1960); Christopher M. Watford, ed., *The Civil War in North Carolina: Soldiers' and Civilians' Letters and Diaries, 1861–1865* (Jefferson, N.C.: McFarland, 2003); and Laura F. Edwards, *Scarlett Doesn't Live Here Anymore: Southern Women in the Civil War Era* (Urbana: University of Illinois Press, 2000).

12. For reading on antebellum upper-class elite mind-sets, see Bertram Wyatt-Brown, *Southern Honor: Ethics and Behavior in the Old South* (New York: Oxford University Press, 1982); Kenneth Greenberg, *Masters and Statesmen: The Political Culture of American Slavery* (Baltimore: Johns Hopkins University Press, 1985); and

John B. Boles, ed., *A Companion to the American South* (Malden, Mass.: Blackwell Publishers, 2002).

13. Jerome McDuffie, "Politics in Wilmington and New Hanover County, North Carolina, 1865–1900: The Genesis of a Race Riot" (Ph.D. diss., Kent State University, 1979), 31–32. Many of the state's political leaders were able to trace their family roots to the Cape Fear region.

14. Evans, *Ballots and Fence Rails*, 9.

15. Slave populations of the ten largest slaveholding counties in North Carolina in 1860 were Granville, 11,086; Wake, 10,733; Warren, 10,401; Halifax, 10,349; Edgecombe, 10,108; Caswell, 9,355; Pitt, 8,473; Bertie, 8,185; Duplin, 7,124; and New Hanover, 7,103. As to New Hanover County's slaveholding patterns in 1860, most slaveholders owned only a few slaves. Historical Census Browser. Retrieved January 5, 2005, from the University of Virginia, Geospatial and Statistical Data Center: http://fisher.lib.virginia.edu/collections/stats/histcensus/index.html.

16. Merchant wealth was tied to assets that could be liquidated, whereas planter wealth was tied to seasonal crop production and to the ownership of land and slaves. Planters and farmers alike were indebted to merchants, who extended them credit for purchases until crops were sold. Roger L. Ransom and Richard Sutch, *One Kind of Freedom: The Economic Consequences of Emancipation* (Cambridge and New York: Cambridge University Press, 1977), 106–109, 117–123; Sprunt, *Chronicles of the Cape Fear River*, 167–168.

17. A survey of the 1860 census reveals that many of the city's merchants had been born in northern states such as Rhode Island, Vermont, New York, Massachusetts, or Pennsylvania. In general, these merchants were financially secure; as a representative example, one merchant originally from New York reported that his real estate was valued at $35,000 and his personal property at $45,000.

18. According to one business directory, approximately thirty major commission merchants existed in Wilmington in 1854. Fonvielle, *The Wilmington Campaign*, 14; John P. Campbell, comp., *The Southern Business Directory and General Commercial Advertiser* (Charleston, S.C.: Walker and James, 1854), 397–399.

19. Evans, *Ballots and Fence Rails*, 122–123.

20. Elizabeth F. McKoy, *Early Wilmington Block by Block: From 1733 On* (Wilmington: The Author, 1967), 134–135.

21. Foremost among social organizations for German immigrants were local churches. Because of the large number arriving in Wilmington in the 1840s and 1850s, the North Carolina Lutheran Synod established a mission in the city in 1858. A significant number of Jewish

residents of German origin likewise settled in Wilmington and helped to organize the state's first synagogue there. Wrenn, *Wilmington, North Carolina*, 117–119, 217–218; Evans, *Ballots and Fence Rails*, 123.

22. Evans, *Ballots and Fence Rails*, 21.

23. One example of racial friction came to the fore during the early phases of Reconstruction when blacks made use of agricultural farmland or timber properties that they did not own. Upper- and lower-class whites, whose traditions were grounded in respect for each other's property rights, disliked what they perceived as disrespect for "white" property. Most blacks, having only recently emerged from slavery, however, were propertyless and did not share such concepts of ownership. Since slaves had no such property-owning traditions, they were simply practicing the same sort of agricultural dependence known to them before slavery's end, and some even harbored the notion that the property they worked on their former masters' farms belonged to them. Furthermore, historian John Hope Franklin has pointed out that free black artisans and skilled workers were often targets of organized action by their white counterparts—even to the point of using the courts to prevent other whites from hiring free black artisans.

Railroads, among the larger slaveholding entities in North Carolina prior to the Civil War, represented another source of racial friction. Most of the workers employed by the North Carolina Railroad were enslaved, removing potentially lucrative and stable jobs from the white workers' market. White railroad laborers were paid low wages, had little job security, and were the first employees to be laid off. Moreover, historian John Haley has concluded that "the contempt whites had for blacks manifested itself in negative attitudes" regarding black "efficiency, character, and intelligence." Evans, *Ballots and Fence Rails*, 53–54, 74; Dylan Penningroth, *The Claims of Kinfolk: African American Property and Community in the Nineteenth-Century South* (Chapel Hill: University of North Carolina Press, 2003), 130–161; John Hope Franklin, *The Free Negro in North Carolina, 1790–1860* (Chapel Hill: University of North Carolina Press, 1943), 136–141; Allen W. Trelease, *The North Carolina Railroad, 1849–1871, and the Modernization of North Carolina* (Chapel Hill: University of North Carolina Press, 1991), 62–69; John Haley, *Charles N. Hunter and Race Relations in North Carolina* (Chapel Hill: University of North Carolina Press, 1987), 4.

24. Haley, *Charles N. Hunter*, 4, 12.

25. John D. Bellamy, *Memoirs of an Octogenarian* (Charlotte: Observer Printing House, 1942), 8. Bellamy's view of white artisans is somewhat skewed; modern research has revealed that many whites in Wilmington were working in the building trades. For information on

the history of architects and builders in Wilmington and North Carolina, see Catherine W. Bishir et al., *Architects and Builders in North Carolina: A History of the Practice of Building* (Chapel Hill: University of North Carolina Press, 1990), and Bishir, *The Bellamy Mansion.*

26. Joel Williamson, *The Crucible of Race: Black-White Relations in the American South since Reconstruction* (New York: Oxford University Press, 1984), 33–34. Williamson posits that in their efforts to succeed, working whites often were more helpless and dependent on the generosity of the white ruling elite than were free blacks.

27. In 1860 New Hanover County's wage earners of all classes received an average of $226.50 per year, whereas the statewide average was $189.17. Historical Census Browser. Retrieved January 5, 2005.

28. Of the 2,624 white males over the age of fourteen working in Wilmington in 1860, only 695 (27%) were employed in manufacturing industries. Very few women worked in manufacturing jobs at that time. Historical Census Browser. Retrieved January 5, 2005.

29. McDuffie, *Politics in Wilmington*, 32–34.

30. Historical Census Browser. Retrieved January 5, 2005. Franklin, *The Free Negro in North Carolina*, 18.

31. Eighth Census of the United States, 1860: New Hanover County, North Carolina, Population Schedule, National Archives, Washington, D.C. (microfilm, State Archives, North Carolina Office of Archives and History, Raleigh); Bellamy, *Memoirs of an Octogenarian*, 8.

32. For additional information on legal pathways to freedom for slaves and the difficulties in maintaining freedom, see chapter 1 of Franklin, *The Free Negro in North Carolina.*

33. William M. Reaves, *"Strength through Struggle:" The Chronological and Historical Record of the African-American Community in Wilmington, North Carolina, 1865–1950*, ed. Beverly Tetterton (Wilmington: New Hanover County Public Library, 1998), 460–461. For additional information on the lives of the Howes and other African American families in Wilmington, see Appendix B.

34. New Hanover was the third largest county in numbers of slaveholders in 1860, following top-ranked Wake and Granville counties. Although it had one of the highest concentrations of slaveholders, New Hanover did not rank among the highest in concentrations of slaves. By a wide margin, the counties in the northeastern section of the state held more slaves than did New Hanover. Historical Census Browser. Retrieved January 5, 2005.

35. For a detailed analysis of the role of urban slaves in the Bellamy family, see Bishir, *The Bellamy Mansion.*

36. In 1860 the Wilmington and Weldon Railroad owned twenty-five slaves outright, and its officers and directors were among the larger slaveholders in New Hanover County. The slaves owned by the railroad were all males ranging in age from twenty-one to forty-five. Most enslaved railroad workers performed unskilled labor, but some worked in higher-status positions such as mechanics, firemen, and brakemen. Other slaves held by businessmen worked in sawmills and turpentine distilleries. Of seventy-four Wilmington slaves whose occupation records as insured property have been revealed by modern insurance companies, most were categorized as laborers. Review both of owner names and slave occupations reveals that the primary employer of insured slaves within that record group was either a sawmill or a turpentine distillery. A small number of bondsmen were enumerated as domestic servants, and others were listed as artisans working as brick masons, carpenters, or boot or shoemakers. Eighth Census, 1860: New Hanover County, Population, Slave Schedules; Trelease, *The North Carolina Railroad*, 62; "California Slavery Era Insurance Registry": http://www.insurance.ca.gov/0100-consumers/0300-public-programs/0200-slavery-era-insur/. Retrieved November 21, 2005. "Illinois Slavery Era Insurance Registries": http://www.ins.state.il.us/Consumer/ Slavery/ Reporting.nsf/. Retrieved November 21, 2005.

37. For informative discussions of the roles of maritime trades in antebellum slave life, see David S. Cecelski, *The Waterman's Song: Slavery and Freedom in Maritime North Carolina* (Chapel Hill: University of North Carolina Press, 2001).

38. Analysis of the lives of several prominent African American families in Wilmington reveals that many of their progenitors were skilled artisans before the Civil War. (See Appendix B for a biography of the Sadgwar family.) Additionally, recent study has indicated that many who were enslaved before the Civil War in maritime or urban environments possessed a better understanding of political and economic issues facing the state and nation than previously thought. Such an example can be seen in enslaved plasterer George W. Price, who helped to construct the Bellamy Mansion and later escaped from Wilmington in 1862 to join the U.S. Navy. Price returned to the city after the war to become a prominent member of the new black upper class that emerged by 1898. Franklin, *The Free Negro in North Carolina*, 142; David S. Cecelski, "Abraham Galloway: Wilmington's Lost Prophet and the Rise of Black Radicalism in the American South," in David S. Cecelski and Timothy B. Tyson, eds., *Democracy Betrayed: The Wilmington Race Riot of 1898 and Its Legacy* (Chapel Hill: University of North Carolina Press, 1998); David S. Cecelski, "The Shores of Freedom," *North Carolina Historical Review* 71 (April 1994): 174, 184–185, 192; Reaves, *"Strength through Struggle,"* 449–451; Bishir, *The Bellamy Mansion*, 27, 39, 55.

39. In their careful study of several southern cities, economists Roger Ransom and Richard Sutch determined that, following emancipation, artisan slaves did not benefit greatly from their skills but instead met with hostility when they migrated to cities and began to compete with white artisans. That broad generalization appears not to apply to Wilmington's free and enslaved populations, however. Within Wilmington, many prewar artisans such as the Howes, Sadgwars, and Sampsons were able to begin participating in government, acquiring property, and competing with whites in business almost immediately. The 1865 Wilmington tax list includes the names of fourteen African Americans who paid property taxes that year, among them Elvin Artis, James Galley, Alfred Howe, and William Kellogg, all carpenters. Ransom and Sutch, *One Kind of Freedom*, 35–39, 147–148, 346; Delmas D. Haskett and Bill Reaves, *New Hanover County 1865 Tax List* (Wilmington: New Hanover County Public Library, 1990); Eighth Census, 1860: Wilmington Township, Population Schedule; Ninth Census of the United States, 1870: New Hanover County, North Carolina, Wilmington Township, Population Schedule, National Archives, Washington, D.C. (microfilm, State Archives).

40. Ransom and Sutch, *One Kind of Freedom*, 80, 87–88.

41. Many members of the following families figure prominently in the conservative element so important to Wilmington's history in the final thirty years of the nineteenth century and into the early twentieth: DeRossett, MacRae, Meares, Moore, Taylor, and Waddell. Evans, *Ballots and Fence Rails*, 36–37, 57–58, 122–125, 213; Bryant Whitlock Ruark, "Some Phases of Reconstruction in Wilmington and the County of New Hanover," in *Historical Papers of the Trinity College Historical Society* (Durham: N.p., 1915), 102–103.

42. To feed the wartime cotton boom, local compresses worked to produce as many bales for export as they could. More than 30,000 bales were shipped in the first nine months of 1863 alone. Wrenn, *Wilmington, North Carolina*, 5; Fonvielle, *The Wilmington Campaign*, 7; Watson, *Wilmington, Port of North Carolina*, 93–94.

43. In addition to the rail lines, the establishment of regular steamship routes between New York, Philadelphia, Baltimore, and other inland destinations further strengthened the city's port trade. Howell, *The Book of Wilmington*, 156.

44. During Wilmington's long history as a primary railroad depot, four major railroad operations and three minor ones served the city. As Wilmington grew, a number of small early railroad operations were consolidated into the larger lines. For additional information on Wilmington's railroad history, see Charles Kernan, *Rails to Weeds* (Wilmington: Wilmington Railroad

Museum, 1988), 3–15, and Evans, *Ballots and Fence Rails*, 185–192.

45. Although naval stores had begun to decline in importance by the 1880s as a result of deforestation of nearby pine forests, waning demand, and increased competition from cotton, they still provided considerable income to merchants, shippers, and distillers. Rice production began to fall as the nineteenth century neared its end. In the New Hanover community of Navassa and at other nearby locations, the commercial manufacture of fertilizer from imported guano helped to offset the decline in naval stores and rice. For additional information on Wilmington's economy before and after the Civil War, see Watson, *Wilmington, Port of North* Carolina; *Directory of the City of Wilmington, North Carolina, 1889* (Wilmington: Julius A. Bonitz Publisher, 1889). For additional information on the naval stores and timber industries, see Outland, *Tapping the Pines*.

46. Ruark, "Some Phases of Reconstruction in Wilmington," 103–104.

47. In 1870 New Hanover County led North Carolina in pay for workers; its wage earners received an average of $445.68 annually, whereas, on average, workers throughout the state earned only $161.19— lower than the prewar level. Of the 5,292 males of all races in New Hanover County over the age of eighteen, only 822 (16 percent) were employed in manufacturing trades. Historical Census Browser. Retrieved January 5, 2005.

48. Longtime Wilmington resident Henry B. McKoy described the location of Dry Pond as unfixed and moving. McKoy's father recalled that in the 1860s the area was situated south of Ann Street and west of Third Street and that during Henry's childhood it extended beyond Castle Street. McKoy's sister Elizabeth wrote that the area known as Dry Pond was a moving target because it was commonly understood to be a marginalized area of development that moved southward as the city grew. Others in Wilmington recalled it as being near Sixth and Castle streets. These descriptions suggest that Dry Pond was more of a socioeconomic label than a specific geographic place. Henry B. McKoy, *Wilmington, Do You Remember When?* (Greenville, S.C.: The Author, 1957), 19–20; McKoy, *Early Wilmington Block by Block*, 127–128.

49. The 1884 Sanborn Fire Insurance Map of Wilmington indicates that the Wilmington Cotton Mill employed 125 at the time the map was drawn. Howell, *The Book of Wilmington*, 158.

50. New Hanover County was divided to create Pender County in 1875, leaving only the southern third of the original county intact. The section from which Pender was created was predominantly rural and agricultural in nature, with additional income provided by the naval

stores industry. Historical Census Browser. Retrieved January 5, 2005; Evans, *Ballots and Fence Rails*, 167.

51. A psychological change took place among many of the former slaves, who sought to redefine themselves as free people. Among Wilmington natives, black and white, this change was subtle and detectable only among themselves. Many visitors from outside Wilmington tended to be oblivious to the emerging white fear of black "insolence"—as the change in attitude came to be called. Evans, *Ballots and Fence Rails*, 78–79.

52. Some native whites and occupying white soldiers intermingled socially and united to ensure that blacks remained submissive, particularly during Presidential Reconstruction. Evans, *Ballots and Fence Rails*, 65.

53. Richard L. Zuber, *North Carolina during Reconstruction* (Raleigh: State Department of Archives and History, 1969), 1–3; J. G. de Roulhac Hamilton, *Reconstruction in North Carolina* (Raleigh: Presses of Edwards and Broughton, 1906), 107–109.

54. Zuber, *North Carolina during Reconstruction*, 4. Once the delegation met in Raleigh, it was expected to repeal the state's secession ordinance of 1861; invalidate laws protecting slavery; repudiate or cancel the state's debts related to the Confederate war effort; and ratify the Thirteenth Amendment, approved by Congress in January 1865 to abolish slavery in states that were still members of the United States. Re-entry into the Union by southern states was contingent, among other stipulations, on ratification of the amendment. Moreover, the convention was expected to plan for regular statewide elections for governor and representatives at the state and national levels. Eric Foner, *Reconstruction: America's Unfinished Revolution, 1863–1877* (New York: Harper and Row, 1988), 66–67, 199; Hamilton, *Reconstruction in North Carolina*, 109, 111.

55. Hamilton, *Reconstruction in North Carolina*, 150; Evans, *Ballots and Fence Rails*, 86–94, 110–112. For the quotation from Rev. James Walker Hood and more on the convention, see Roberta Sue Alexander, *North Carolina Faces the Freedmen: Race Relations during Presidential Reconstruction, 1865–67* (Durham: Duke University Press, 1985), 17–31; Cecelski, "Abraham Galloway," 56.

56. Prior to his election as governor, Jonathan Worth lamented to colleagues the defeat of the Confederacy and the advent of the Republican Party. Worth considered blacks to be inferior and claimed that it was "supreme nonsense" to attempt to make them equal to whites. Jonathan Worth, quoted in Haley, *Charles N. Hunter*, 3.

57. Hamilton, *Reconstruction in North Carolina*, 120–133, 139.

58. The political organization that became formally known as the Democratic Party was commonly referred to as the Conservative Party after the Civil War. It was not until 1876 that the party officially adopted the name "Democrat." Some members of the Conservative Party were referred to as "Bourbon" Democrats because as the state emerged from Reconstruction in the 1880s, they, like the former French monarchs with the same name, committed themselves firmly to the past instead of seeking progressive reforms in government. Zuber, *North Carolina during Reconstruction*, 4–6, 50; Hamilton, *Reconstruction in North Carolina*, 144; William S. Powell, *North Carolina through Four Centuries* (Chapel Hill: University of North Carolina Press, 1989), 422; for additional information on early Reconstruction efforts in North Carolina, see Alexander, *North Carolina Faces the Freedmen.*

59. Congress approved the Thirteenth Amendment and sent it to the states for ratification in January 1865. The amendment did not officially become law until December 1865, when the last of the southern states ratified it. (North Carolina was the next-to-last state to do so.) It prohibited slavery throughout the United States.

60. In 1866 a constitutional convention drafted a new state constitution to accommodate attempts by the state to rejoin the Union, but voters rejected it. Zuber, *North Carolina during Reconstruction*, 6; Powell, *North Carolina through Four Centuries*, 383; Alexander, *North Carolina Faces the Freedmen*, 49–52; Hamilton, *Reconstruction in North Carolina*, 174–176.

61. The Freedmen's Bureau created the Freedman's Savings Bank and opened a branch in Wilmington and elsewhere in North Carolina. Because of mismanagement, political shortcomings, and other problems, the bank failed in the state and returned only a portion of its deposits to members. Hamilton felt that the losses sustained by African Americans who invested in the bank probably made them less eager to make use of other banks in the future. Alexander, *North Carolina Faces the Freedmen*, 99–100; Hamilton, *Reconstruction in North Carolina*, 299, 304–308, 313–314.

62. Hamilton's history of Reconstruction in North Carolina is reflective of the view generally adopted by white historians once white supremacy had become entrenched in the early twentieth century. Hamilton's history, while a useful resource, is nonetheless clouded with a biased view that emphasizes evils perceived to be inherent in Reconstruction. Alexander, *North Carolina Faces the Freedmen*, 99–103, 159; Zuber, *North Carolina during Reconstruction*, 6; Maxine Jones, " 'A Glorious Work': The American Missionary Association and Black North Carolinians, 1863–1880" (Ph.D. diss., Florida State University, 1982), 123; Hamilton, *Reconstruction in North Carolina*, 295–296, 318–325.

63. Hamilton, *Reconstruction in North Carolina*, 216–219; Haley, *Charles N. Hunter*, 17.

197

198

64. Powell, *North Carolina through Four Centuries*, 386–387; Hamilton, *Reconstruction in North Carolina*, 221.

65. Hamilton, *Reconstruction in North Carolina*, 233–240.

66. Most historians agree that carpetbagger Albion W. Tourgée brought the Union League to North Carolina by introducing it in Guilford County in 1866 and serving as the statewide organization's first president. Despite Tourgée's traditional status as league founder, two Union League units were already in place in Wilmington by April 1865, when they participated in a Lincoln memorial procession. Perhaps formed by native escaped slave Abraham Galloway, those league chapters were well organized by July 1865 as they pressed for municipal appointments for Wilmington blacks. Holden succeeded Tourgée as president in 1867, and membership grew to include not only black males but also white carpetbaggers and native Republicans. The rise of the Union League, and the national support it represented, assisted Holden in the development of the Republican Party. By April 1867 the league was so well organized that approximately 90 percent of black voters could be counted on to vote according to its dictates. The Union League, a stringent organization with secret codes and initiation practices, did not tolerate dissension and carried out several of its many threats of violence against both black and white members. Additionally, the league formed, equipped, and drilled militia companies, creating much distress within the white communities where it held public parades. The Union League flourished for awhile in North Carolina but disappeared by 1870 under the immense pressures exerted by the Ku Klux Klan during Holden's governorship. For additional information on Holden and the Union League, see Fleming, "Union League Documents"; Edgar E. Folk and Bynum Shaw, *W. W. Holden: A Political Biography* (Winston-Salem: John F. Blair, Publisher, 1982), 203–204; Horace W. Raper, *William W. Holden: North Carolina's Political Enigma* (Chapel Hill: University of North Carolina Press, 1985), 95; William C. Harris, *William Woods Holden: Firebrand of North Carolina Politics* (Baton Rouge: Louisiana State University Press, 1987), 223; Allen W. Trelease, *White Terror: The Ku Klux Klan Conspiracy and Southern Reconstruction* (New York: Harper and Row, 1971), 225; Hamilton, *Reconstruction in North Carolina*, 158, 244, 328–342; Evans, *Ballots and Fence Rails*, 86; and Cecelski, "Abraham Galloway," 58.

67. On May 1, 1867, before the election, General Canby ordered all municipal offices in Wilmington closed. The military authorities appointed a new set of officers, with Mayor J. H. Neff, a native white Republican, presiding over a board composed of 3 blacks, 2 native white Republicans, and 2 carpetbaggers. The appointed commissioners ruled for less than two months before a new election in July 1868 placed Republicans in office. Ruark, "Some Phases of Reconstruction," 98–99; Hamilton, *Reconstruction in North Carolina*, 252.

68. The Conservative Party repeatedly maligned New Hanover's Republican delegates and 1868 legislative candidates. Most of the derogatory comments were based on observations that the men had never paid taxes in Wilmington, where the minority white population owned the majority of the wealth. Blacks joined the Republican Party because it was seen as their only option—to ally with the party that elected Lincoln and gave them their freedom. Seventy-three percent of Wilmington's black electorate turned out to vote. Blacks comprised 63 percent of the total electorate at the time of the 1868 election. Review of the election returns statewide reveals that New Hanover was one of nineteen counties that had a black voting majority. John L. Cheney Jr., ed., *North Carolina Government, 1585–1979: A Narrative and Statistical History* (Raleigh: North Carolina Department of the Secretary of State, 1981), 845–846; Hamilton, *Reconstruction in North Carolina*, 285; Evans, *Ballots and Fence Rails*, 96; Ruark, "Some Phases of Reconstruction," 109; Haley, *Charles N. Hunter*, 15.

69. Conservative southerners coined the derogatory terms "carpetbagger" to define men who relocated from the North to the South after the war and "scalawag" to refer to native southerners who supported the Republican Party. *Encyclopedia of Southern Culture*, s.v. "Radical Republicans."

70. Powell, *North Carolina through Four Centuries*, 394; Hamilton, *Reconstruction in North Carolina*, 266–269, 273–278.

71. Prior to the appearance of the Klan in Wilmington, another group, called "Regulators," came together in early 1867 to raid and damage the farms and homes of African Americans. The white community did not respond to stop the raids, despite outcries from white Republicans and the Freedmen's Bureau. Zuber, *North Carolina during Reconstruction*, 25; Trelease, *White Terror*, 69; Hamilton, *Reconstruction in North Carolina*, 284–285; Evans, *Ballots and Fence Rails*, 131.

72. New Hanover's population was 58 percent "colored" at election time, and 62 percent of the votes cast in the county were Republican. Evans, *Ballots and Fence Rails*, 102.

73. The General Assembly's implementation of several changes to the state's government, as mandated by Congress, was another important factor in enabling the state to be allowed back into the Union. Hamilton, *Reconstruction in North Carolina*, 288–292.

74. Zuber, *North Carolina during Reconstruction*, 19–23; Powell, *North Carolina through Four Centuries*, 396–397; Hamilton, *Reconstruction in North Carolina*, 292, 412–416.

75. Zuber, *North Carolina during Reconstruction*, 19–23; Powell, *North Carolina through Four Centuries*, 395–396; Hamilton, *Reconstruction in North Carolina*, 287.

76. Evans, *Ballots and Fence Rails*, 98–102; Trelease, *White Terror*, 70.

77. Hamilton, *Reconstruction in North Carolina*, 396, 465; Trelease, *White Terror*, 114; Evans, *Ballots and Fence Rails*, 255.

78. Governor Holden's efforts to halt the actions of the Klan in North Carolina's Piedmont counties, commonly called the Kirk-Holden War, resulted in occupation of Caswell and Alamance counties by forces under the command of Col. George Kirk of Tennessee. The Klan's activities in those areas had become exceedingly violent, and Holden sought to end the violence before the election. Kirk's forces occupied the counties, arresting about one hundred suspected Klan members from a list provided by the governor. The result was that several such members who had favored ending Klan terrorism came forward and renounced their membership in the group. Holden hoped to hold military trials for the arrested men; but legal maneuvers by Democrats kept most of them from such tribunals, and most were eventually released from jail. Evans, *Ballots and Fence Rails*, 146–149; Trelease, *White Terror*, 216–223; Hamilton, *Reconstruction in North Carolina*, 496–533.

79. Evans, *Ballots and Fence Rails*, 158–159.

80. The Republican Party established the practice of using wealthy white Republicans to sponsor popular blacks as politicians, resulting in factionalism among publicly visible Republicans who vied for sponsorships. Such an organizational structure existed in Wilmington, and the leading whites came to be known as the "Ring." Approximately 2,000 black Republicans and between 100 and 150 white Republicans were in Wilmington at the time, and all were managed by 15 to 20 white Republican businessmen. Of those men in the Ring, about six were first- and second-generation New Englanders who had arrived in Wilmington before the Civil War, and others had Union army connections. Native members of the Ring included Edward Cantwell, the Russell family, and black members of the Sampson and Howe families. Evans, *Ballots and Fence Rails*, 153–155, 162–165.

81. Evans, *Ballots and Fence Rails*, 223–225; Zuber, *North Carolina during Reconstruction*, 41–44.

82. Historian J. G. de Roulhac Hamilton wrote that as a result of its actions in securing Democratic victory, the Klan applied "illegal force which overthrew Reconstruction and ultimately restored political power to the white race." He pointed out that Klan action was usually carefully planned, but, as the organization grew, control over camps broke down and discipline of members relaxed. By the end of the Klan's lifetime during Reconstruction, Hamilton asserted, "it had clearly outlived any usefulness it may have had." Hamilton, *Reconstruction in North Carolina*, 453–480, 572–581; Zuber, *North Carolina during Reconstruction*, 44–47; Trelease, *White Terror*, 348.

83. Conservatives sought every means possible to challenge or nullify the demands of Congressional Reconstruction. North Carolina became a model for southern opposition to Reconstruction as it legislated resistance to Washington. Southern politicians felt that North Carolina's lead would compel other states to follow suit and slowly overturn federal Reconstruction policies. Zuber, *North Carolina during Reconstruction*, 48–49; Hamilton, *Reconstruction in North Carolina*, 592, 594, 595–604; Haley, *Charles N. Hunter*, 22.

84. Conservatives felt that if they could separate New Hanover's rural population from Wilmington's influence, their interests could more easily dominate rural black sharecroppers. The result was that New Hanover's representation in the state House of Representatives was reduced from three to two. The creation of Pender backfired on the Conservatives: in the first county election, Republicans won all seats. The effort to assure Conservative control of Wilmington's government was accomplished by gerrymandering the city's voting districts. A new charter created three wards in the city based on equivalents of property values. The result was that the First and Second Wards were located in the city's center, with about 21 percent of the population represented there; the other 79 percent of the population—mostly poor whites and blacks—were lumped into the Third Ward. Republicans boycotted the first municipal election held under the auspices of the new redistricting, and the Conservatives, to no one's surprise, swept the election. The incumbent Republican board of aldermen declared the new charter unconstitutional and the election invalid and refused to turn over control of the city. Conservatives, in the face of a Republican majority in the city, were obliged to sue in court over the issue. After four months of litigation and municipal limbo, the Republican-controlled state supreme court declared the gerry-mandered wards unconstitutional and the election void. Evans, *Ballots and Fence Rails*, 167–171.

85. The *Wilmington Journal* was founded in 1844 and was the first regular daily paper in the city. Hamilton, *Reconstruction in North Carolina*, 605–606; Howell, *The Book of Wilmington*, 151.

86. The "negro question" became an important factor in the 1876 election because Democratic candidates

developed their first cohesive rebuttals to the Republican Party, and their platforms did not attempt to placate black voters. The 1876 election was also one of the first campaigns in which the Democratic Party encouraged its candidates to visit voters throughout their constituencies and "stump" for votes for the duration of the campaign. Haley, *Charles N. Hunter*, 40, 42; Hamilton, *Reconstruction in North Carolina*, 648–649.

87. Historian R. D. W. Connor described the 1876 election as the "greatest political contest in the history of North Carolina." Connor further declared that the election "marked the beginning of a new era" and that the "administration of the state government passed into the hands of the party that best represented the intelligence, the property, and the patriotism of North Carolina." Historian Samuel A. Ashe explained that after the 1876 election the "skies were bright; apparently the storm was over and a rainbow arched the heavens" because "Conservatives under the lead of the patriots in 1861–65 had addressed themselves to the duty of rescuing the people of the state from the domination of the carpetbaggers and Africans." R. D. W. Connor, *North Carolina: Rebuilding an Ancient Commonwealth*, 2 vols. (Chicago: American Historical Society, 1929), 2:351–352; Samuel A. Ashe, *History of North Carolina*, vol. 2 (Raleigh: Edwards and Broughton Company, 1925), 1166–1167.

88. R. D. W. Connor and J. G. de Roulhac Hamilton were principals at Wilmington (formerly Tileston) High School early in their careers and were intimately familiar with the city's history and leaders. Hamilton, *Reconstruction in North Carolina*, 654, 662.

89. To cement their control over Wilmington, Conservatives again amended the city's charter in 1877 with revisions similar to those implemented in 1875. The new provisions of the charter divided the city into five wards, with two aldermen chosen to represent each ward. The First, Second, and Third wards represented the city's center, predominantly Conservative and populated by approximately 1,150 white voters; whereas the Fourth and Fifth wards encompassed Dry Pond, a low-income white area to the south, and Brooklyn, a predominantly black area to the north, both areas heavily Republican and inhabited by about 2,300 voters of both races. Because of this less-than-equitable redistricting by the Conservatives, Republicans were relegated to a four-to-six minority on the board of aldermen. Evans, *Ballots and Fence Rails*, 172–173.

90. Watson, *Wilmington, Port of North Carolina*, 115–117.

91. W. N. Hartshorn and George W. Penniman, eds., *An Era of Progress and Promise, 1863–1910: The Religious, Moral, and Educational Development of the American Negro since His Emancipation* (Boston: Priscilla Publishing Company, 1910), 87–92, 160.

92. Haley, *Charles N. Hunter*, 60–61.

93. Fonvielle, *The Wilmington Campaign*, 445, 452; Howell, *The Book of Wilmington*, 147.

94. General Hawley seized Cape Fear plantations, redistributed properties to former slaves, and rendered assistance to job-seeking blacks and whites. Fonvielle, *The Wilmington Campaign*, 456.

95. Quoted in Fonvielle, *The Wilmington Campaign*, 457.

96. Those critical of the Wilmington resolution maligned the signers of the document by labeling them as foreigners, transplanted Yankees, or Confederate deserters. Nevertheless, the names of eight "highly respectable gentlemen" found among the signatures presented the Confederacy with a conundrum, particularly since some of those men had sons and brothers still fighting. Fonvielle, *The Wilmington Campaign*, 457–458.

97. In a personal account published in a Raleigh newspaper, Rev. L. S. Burkhead of Wilmington's Front Street Methodist Church detailed instances of black soldiers attempting to advocate on behalf of freedmen. Black members of Burkhead's congregation, relying upon claims based on oral tradition and the missionary work of William Meredith among Wilmington's black population in the eighteenth century, sought ownership of the church and its property after the city fell to Union control in 1865. Burkhead and the white congregation were able to maintain control of the property despite efforts of black soldiers and parishioners to petition the Union army for reconciliation. William K. Boyd, ed., "History of the Difficulties of the Pastorate of the Front Street Methodist Church, Wilmington, N.C. for the Year 1865," *Historical Papers of Trinity College* (Durham: Trinity College Historical Society, 1908–1909), 35–118; Hamilton, *Reconstruction in North Carolina*, 159–161.

98. Evans, *Ballots and Fence Rails*, 250.

99. Ibid., 79, 103, 141, 249.

100. In an attempt to guarantee to blacks equal rights in the realm of public accommodations and jury duty, Congress in 1875 enacted a civil rights bill. The white owners of some Wilmington businesses reacted negatively to the bill and, when some blacks demanded equal service, closed their doors in protest. Many of the city's African American leaders resented both the actions of the white business owners and those of their race who sought to "create unnecessary strife." Reaves, *"Strength through Struggle,"* 236–237; Williamson, *The Crucible of Race*, 112.

101. By the end of 1868, Union troops numbered about 53 in the city. Evans, *Ballots and Fence Rails*, 141, 153–161.

102. Evans, *Ballots and Fence Rails*, 255.

103. In addition to the presence of the Union army, Governor Holden had reinforced Republican control by successfully urging passage by the General Assembly of the Militia Act of 1868, which created the 22nd North Carolina Militia in Wilmington. The 22nd was comprised of five companies and included many blacks. Col. George Mabson, a mulatto Union veteran, commanded the units alongside Col. William P. Cannaday, a North Carolina Confederate veteran and a founder of the state's Republican Party. The black militia unit slowly faded from existence after Conservatives regained control and was all but gone by the 1890s. Evans, *Ballots and Fence Rails*, 137–141.

104. Wilmington historian Andrew Howell notes that throughout the political travails of Reconstruction, businessmen "kept quiet" and prospered financially. He describes the 1880s in Wilmington as a "decade of substance" marked by a series of physical improvements to the city's infrastructure, an increase in business activity, and higher profits in the cotton-export, naval stores, and fertilizer industries. Howell, *The Book of Wilmington*, 154, 162–172.

105. In Wilmington the Odd Fellows boasted a high level of participation and by the mid-1880s had constructed at 401 S. Seventh Street a large three-story lodge known as Ruth Hall. The Masons, the oldest black fraternal organization in the nation, had operated a lodge in Wilmington as early as 1866. Construction of a building for the Masons' Giblem Lodge began in 1871 at the corner of Princess and Eighth streets. Reaves, *"Strength through Struggle,"* 20–24.

106. Correspondence and newspaper articles from 1879 and 1880 indicate that African Americans who departed the South in search of greater prosperity in the western United States, and especially in Kansas—known at the time as "exodusters"—instead encountered low wages, substandard housing, and inflated prices for goods and services. Those who remained in the South generally concluded that their situations were much better there than elsewhere. Upper-class blacks such as politicians, ministers, and businessmen generally opposed the black out-migration, whereas the illiterate and semiliterate laboring classes, eager for a chance at a new life, were more receptive to the movement. Reaves, *"Strength through Struggle,"* 274–281; Frenise A. Logan, *The Negro in North Carolina, 1876–1894* (Chapel Hill: University of North Carolina Press, 1964), 132.

107. Wilmington's first formal commemoration of Emancipation Day (January 1) was held in 1868, and well-planned future celebrations followed. Such commemorations moved over time from a central location to predominantly black communities. White speakers had disappeared from podiums by the beginning of the twentieth century. Memorial Day observances followed a similar pattern, with the first Memorial Day parade occurring in 1868. Other observances memorialized the Confederate evacuation of the city in 1865 and celebrated the visit of Frederick Douglass in 1872. Reaves, *"Strength through Struggle,"* 3–6, 7–9.

108. The Colored Literary Society was formed in 1870, the Benjamin Banneker Literary and Library Association was created in 1883, the United Order of Tents (a women's benevolent society) was established in 1875, and the Love and Charity Benevolent Association was organized in 1878. As early as 1869, African American baseball teams were competing in the city, and the tradition survived into the early twentieth century. Reaves, *"Strength through Struggle,"* 10–14, 39–43.

109. Jonkonnu was celebrated in Wilmington well into the twentieth century by both blacks and whites. Participants, known as *kunners*, dressed in bright, outrageous costumes, sang and danced with drums and rattles, and moved from street to street seeking donations for their performances. For a brief period during Reconstruction, laws enacted to restrict the activities of the Ku Klux Klan prohibited parades and the wearing of masks in public, briefly halting the annual Jonkonnu festivities. Reaves, *"Strength through Struggle,"* 34–37. For additional information on Jonkonnu, see Elizabeth A. Fenn, " 'A Perfect Equality Seemed to Reign': Slave Society and Jonkonnu," *North Carolina Historical Review* 65 (April 1988): 127–153. For additional information on the changes to African American celebrations resulting from the 1898 race riot, see chapter 8.

110. Despite attempts by benevolent organizations to improve educational opportunities for African Americans, native whites hindered black education by occasionally burning schools and by electing legislative leaders who largely ignored the needs of black students. Although whites acknowledged that the education of blacks was a necessity, they began to disagree on what sort of education should be provided. Black leaders joined whites in favoring a segregated educational system in which black schools would provide employment for educated blacks. Blacks insisted that fellow black teachers could best teach students of their own race because they possessed similar backgrounds and attitudes. Moreover, black leaders feared that white teachers might emphasize white supremacy and black inadequacy in their lessons instead of providing encouragement and strength. For additional information on the history of African American education in Wilmington, see Reaves, *"Strength through Struggle,"* 144–173; and Haley, *Charles N. Hunter*, 12, 36.

111. The city assumed control of its previously volunteer fire departments in 1897 and began to pay fire

fighters. The agreement between the fire companies and the city specified that the equipment the volunteer companies had acquired would be turned over to the city. In the aftermath of the upheaval of November 1898, all black fire companies were replaced with white fire fighters, and the equipment originally purchased by the blacks remained city property. Reaves, *"Strength through Struggle,"* 185–198.

112. For additional information on the Republican Party in Wilmington and North Carolina in the 1880s and 1890s, see Reaves, *"Strength through Struggle,"* 232–248, and Helen G. Edmonds, *The Negro and Fusion Politics in North Carolina, 1894–1901* (Chapel Hill: University of North Carolina Press, 1951), 14–20.

113. Reaves, *"Strength through Struggle,"* 288–308, 325–327.

Chapter 2: Forces of Change

1. St. Stephen's observed the anniversary in 1887 with a number of prominent national leaders of the AME Church in attendance. J. S. Reilly, *Wilmington. Past, Present & Future, Embracing Historical Sketches of Its Growth and Progress from its Establishment to the Present Time, Together with Outline of North Carolina History* (Wilmington: N.p., 1884), 22; William M. Reaves, *"Strength through Struggle": The Chronological and Historical Record of the African-American Community in Wilmington, North Carolina, 1865–1950*, ed. Beverly Tetterton (Wilmington: New Hanover County Public Library, 1998), 104–105.

2. Daniel Lindsay Russell was born in 1845 near Wilmington on his family's plantation in Brunswick County. The Russells, wealthy planters, did not support secession, although young Daniel joined the Confederacy for a brief period after graduating from the University of North Carolina. After leaving Confederate service because of stormy relationships with Confederate officials, Russell became an ardent Republican. For additional information on Russell's career, see Jeffrey J. Crow and Robert F. Durden, *Maverick Republican in the Old North State: A Political Biography of Daniel L. Russell* (Baton Rouge: Louisiana State University Press, 1977); Reaves, *"Strength through Struggle,"* 104–105, 114.

3. Reaves, *"Strength through Struggle,"* 114–115.

4. Helen G. Edmonds, *The Negro and Fusion Politics in North Carolina, 1894–1901* (Chapel Hill: University of North Carolina Press, 1951), 20–25; Jerome McDuffie, "Politics in Wilmington and New Hanover County, North Carolina, 1865–1900: The Genesis of a Race Riot" (Ph.D. diss., Kent State University, 1979), 387.

5. Crow and Durden, *Maverick Republican,* 46.

6. For additional information on the problems inherent in Fusion politics, see Joseph F. Steelman, "Republican Party Strategists and the Issue of Fusion with Populists in North Carolina, 1893–1894," *North Carolina Historical Review* 47 (July 1970): 244–269; William Mabry, "Negro Suffrage and Fusion Rule in North Carolina," *North Carolina Historical Review* 12 (April 1935): 79–102; Jeffrey J. Crow, "Fusion, Confusion, and Negroism: Schisms among Negro Republicans in North Carolina," *North Carolina Historical Review* 53 (October 1976): 364–384; Allen W. Trelease, "The Fusion Legislatures of 1895 and 1897: A Roll-Call Analysis of the North Carolina House of Representatives," *North Carolina Historical Review* 57 (July 1980): 280–309; James L. Hunt, *Marion Butler and American Populism* (Chapel Hill: University of North Carolina Press, 2003); Edmonds, *The Negro and Fusion Politics,* 25–28; and McDuffie, "Politics in Wilmington," 390–391, 393.

7. Edmonds, *The Negro and Fusion Politics,* 34–37; McDuffie, "Politics in Wilmington," 395.

8. The nomination committee consisted of four whites (Daniel Russell, William H. Chadbourn, Flavel Foster, and George Z. French) and three blacks (Thomas C. Miller, Daniel L. Howard, and J. O. Nixon). McDuffie, "Politics in Wilmington," 396–399.

9. Edmonds, *The Negro and Fusion Politics,* 37–38; McDuffie, "Politics in Wilmington," 411. Statistics for the 1894 elections results table are excerpted from *The Negro and Fusion Politics,* 37–38.

10. Once the fusion legislature convened, its first order of business was to elect Populist Marion Butler to a full six-year term in the United States Senate and to choose Republican Jeter C. Pritchard to serve out the remainder of the senatorial term of Zebulon B. Vance, who had died in office in April 1894. *Wilmington Messenger,* November 7, 9, 1894; Daniel L. Russell to Thomas Settle, December 20, 1890, Thomas Settle Papers, Southern Historical Collection, Wilson Library, University of North Carolina at Chapel Hill, Chapel Hill, quoted in McDuffie, "Politics in Wilmington," 411; McDuffie, "Politics in Wilmington," 398–401, 404–405. Democrats throughout the state challenged the election results. In New Hanover County, Thomas Strange, Democratic Reform candidate for the lower house, challenged the election of George Z. French to that office on the grounds that French had not lived in the county for twelve consecutive months. The Democratic election board ruled in favor of French and declared the election valid. Democratic Reformers thereupon sought to challenge the election of two local Republicans as county sheriff and treasurer. Following two days of debate and hearings, the New Hanover County Board of Commissioners, all Democrats, refused the challenge and validated the Republican victories. As a result of such internal strife, the

county's Democrats were unable to unite to defeat the Republicans. McDuffie, "Politics in Wilmington," 401–404; *Wilmington Messenger*, November 9, 11, 1894.

11. Only three African Americans had been elected to the General Assembly in 1894: William H. Crews of Granville County, Moses Peace of Vance County, and James H. Young of Wake County. Another African American, Abe R. Middleton, received a patronage position as an assistant doorkeeper. Edmonds, *The Negro and Fusion Politics*, 41–45; Jeffrey J. Crow, Paul D. Escott, and Flora J. Hatley, *A History of African Americans in North Carolina* (Raleigh: Office of Archives and History, North Carolina Department of Cultural Resources, rev. ed., 2002), 234.

12. *Private Laws of North Carolina, 1876–77*, 230–237; McDuffie, "Politics in Wilmington," 416–417.

13. Edmonds, *The Negro and Fusion Politics*, 128.

14. McDuffie, "Politics in Wilmington," 419–422.

15. Ibid., 422–425.

16. *Wilmington Messenger*, August 20, 1894, as cited in McDuffie, "Politics in Wilmington," 420.

17. For additional information on Daniels and his role in politics and publishing in North Carolina, see Josephus Daniels, *Editor in Politics* (Chapel Hill: University of North Carolina Press, 1941).

18. Edmonds, *The Negro and Fusion Politics*, 48–54.

19. McDuffie, "Politics in Wilmington," 428–432.

20. Crow and Durden, *Maverick Republican*, 63; McDuffie, "Politics in Wilmington," 433.

21. Edmonds, *The Negro and Fusion Politics*, 54–55; McDuffie, "Politics in Wilmington," 440–444.

22. McDuffie, "Politics in Wilmington," 442–450.

23. In an attempt to counter losses to Fusionists in 1896, Democratic Party leaders in New Hanover County successfully petitioned a Superior Court judge to appoint to the county board of commissioners Democrats W. F. Alexander and Roger Moore. The petitioners expressed their concerns that the "business of the County . . . if left entirely in the hands of the three Commissioners elected at the last election will be improperly managed and that 200 citizens of the said County . . . request the appointment of two honest and discreet citizens . . . of opposite party from the majority of the present Board of Commissioners." Election Records, 1832–1919 [1882–1896], New Hanover County Election Records, State Archives, North Carolina Office of Archives and History; McDuffie, "Politics in Wilmington," 447–448; Edmonds, *The Negro and Fusion Politics*, 56–60, 65–66; Crow, Escott, and Hatley, *African Americans in North Carolina*, 233–235.

24. Crow and Durden, *Maverick Republican*, 81–87.

25. Edmonds, *The Negro and Fusion Politics*, 62–64.

26. In order to limit the Democrats' political power in North Carolina's urban areas, Fusionists attempted to amend the charters of other cities. They targeted three types of municipalities. First were cities with a black voting majority (examples included Edenton, New Bern, Raleigh, Washington, Wilmington, and Winston); second were those characterized by an even split between whites and blacks (Elizabeth City, Fayetteville, Oxford, and Rocky Mount); and third were cities in which whites held voting majorities (Asheville, Concord, Durham, Goldsboro, Greenville, and Kinston). McDuffie, "Politics in Wilmington," 459–461; Edmonds, *The Negro and Fusion Politics*, 124–131.

27. As to banking, the Fusionists lowered interest rates, thereby depriving banks of revenue. They also amended revenue regulations by providing for the taxing of capital stock at its face value and strengthened railroad regulations by enlarging the powers of the state's railroad commission. McDuffie, "Politics in Wilmington," 461.

28. According to the board of aldermen's minute book, the most recent municipal elections had been held in 1893. Minutes of the Wilmington Board of Aldermen, 1884–1906 (microfilm), State Archives; H. Leon Prather Sr., *We Have Taken a City: Wilmington Massacre and Coup of 1898* (Rutherford, N.J.: Fairleigh Dickinson University Press, 1984), 36–39.

29. Prather, *We Have Taken a City*, 36–40; Crow and Durden, *Maverick Republican*, 97.

30. Prather, *We Have Taken a City*, 40–41; Minutes of the Wilmington Board of Aldermen, 1884–1906, State Archives.

31. A similar confusion of multiple municipal officers likewise took place in New Bern. Prather, *We Have Taken a City*, 42–43; Crow and Durden, *Maverick Republican*, 98.

32. Prather, *We Have Taken a City*, 43–45.

33. Prather, *We Have Taken a City*, 44–48; Crow and Durden, *Maverick Republican*, 98; *North Carolina Reports*, Vol. 121: *Cases Argued and Determined in the Supreme Court of North Carolina, September Term 1897*, Reported by Robert T. Gray, Raleigh, N.C. (Goldsboro: Nash Brothers, Book and Job Printers, 1898), 172–183.

34. Analysis of multiple sources provides a glimpse into the city's African American work ethic and business life. Although the city directories of the 1880s and 1890s are incomplete in their listings, the volumes do provide a wealth of information regarding black business ownership, as well as employment and housing trends. Further detail on the financial situation of the city's black population can be gleaned from tax and census records, as well as other records generated by corporations and businesses. The city directories often list only heads of household, whereas

203

censuses, beginning in 1850, recorded the names of all men, women, and children who resided in each household. For example, historian H. Leon Prather points out that the 1897 Wilmington city directory includes the names of 3,759 blacks residing in the city, whereas the 1900 census enumerates the names of 11,324 black residents living in the city that year. Prather, *We Have Taken a City*, 31. For additional analysis of shortcomings in the Wilmington city directories, see Sue Ann Cody, "After the Storm: Racial Violence in Wilmington, North Carolina, and Its Consequences for African Americans, 1898–1905" (master's thesis, University of North Carolina at Wilmington, 2000), 95–99.

35. Correspondence and newspaper articles from 1889 and 1890 indicate that many blacks who left Wilmington in search of greater prosperity in the West instead found low wages, substandard housing, and inflated prices for goods and services. See endnote 106 in chapter 1.

36. Robert C. Kenzer, *Enterprising Southerners: Black Economic Success in North Carolina, 1865–1915* (Charlottesville: University of Virginia Press, 1997), 43–47, 65.

37. Historian Frenise A. Logan studied reference books from the Mercantile Association of the Carolinas over several decades and noted that Wilmington's growth in the numbers of black businesses surpassed that of other cities and approached the leader, New Bern, by 1889. By 1893, Wilmington boasted twenty-four black-owned businesses, whereas the number of such enterprises in New Bern had dropped to nine. Hayumi Higuchi, "White Supremacy on the Cape Fear: The Wilmington Affair of 1898" (master's thesis, University of North Carolina at Chapel Hill, 1980), 105; Logan, *The Negro in North Carolina*, 112; *Reference Book of the Mercantile Association of the Carolinas for the States of North and South Carolina* (Wilmington: Jackson and Bell, 1893), 76–80, 214–225, 317–321.

38. Frenise Logan's study of African American businesses found that clergymen, educators, government officials, and physicians generally represented the "ruling element" of black society. Logan discovered that more than 95 percent of the 2,036 blacks who worked as professionals in North Carolina in 1890 were either clergymen or teachers, two fields of endeavor in which African Americans were free to serve others of their race without competition from whites. Black physicians and attorneys, however, were often obliged to compete with whites for clients. Logan, *The Negro in North Carolina*, 105; Kenzer, *Enterprising Southerners*, 65, 86, 88.

39. Labor organizations still operated in Wilmington during the early years of the 1890s. By 1894, however, the Knights of Labor, a statewide organization, was reported to be defunct. Higuchi, "White Supremacy on the Cape Fear," 106; Logan, *The Negro in North Carolina*, 104.

40. Throughout North Carolina, skilled African American laborers represented almost 10 percent of the state's total skilled work force in trades, transportation, manufacturing, and the mechanical industries in 1890. In 1897 skilled and semi-skilled black laborers, and those employed in the transportation industry, represented 32 percent of Wilmington's total work force. In 1889 a substantial portion of Wilmington's black workers, 57.3 percent, were employed in the service industries—most often as barbers, fire fighters, janitors, laborers, laundresses, nurses, restaurant and saloon keepers, policemen, and domestic servants. By 1897, however, only 24 percent of them were so employed, indicating that during the 1890s Wilmington's black working population was evolving from service-oriented jobs toward other types of employment. Some statistics generated from Cody, "After the Storm," 100; *J. L. Hill Printing Co.'s Directory of Wilmington, N.C. 1897* (Richmond, Va: J. L. Hill Printing Company, 1897; hereafter cited as *Hill's 1897 Wilmington City Directory*); Higuchi, "White Supremacy on the Cape Fear," 144–146; Logan, *The Negro in North Carolina*, 87.

41. *Reference Book of the Mercantile Association of the Carolinas*, 214–225.

42. The Wilmington Livery Stable Company operated for only one year, closing its doors after November 1898. Incorporations, 1879–1906, New Hanover County Miscellaneous Records, State Archives. Reaves; *"Strength through Struggle,"* 296–297.

43. Other stevedores, black and white, working between 1891 and 1898 included John M. Cazaux, George W. Doyle, Charles Foreman, J. W. H. Fuchs, William Goodsman, W. W. Harriss, Alex Heide, W. H. Howe, Hans A. Kure, Major Lee, John McDowell, Joseph McFarland, H. Robinson, Henry Robinson, Joseph Starnes, John Turner, Andrew J. Walker, E. D. Williams, Fred Williams, and C. W. Worth. Beginning in 1898, increased numbers of white boss stevedores and independent stevedores appeared, and after 1900 all of Wilmington's stevedore firms were white. Stevedore Records, Incorporations, 1879–1906, New Hanover County Miscellaneous Records, State Archives.

44. Interest on loans provided by the Peoples Perpetual Building and Loan Association averaged between 6 and 8 percent, and shareholders mortgaged their property as loan collateral. Only a handful of the seventy-five mortgage loans were not canceled. Lending by the association ended in December 1898, with the exception of three deeds of trust serviced between 1899 and 1906. Index to Real Estate Conveyances, Grantee and Grantor, 1729–1954, New Hanover County Land Records (microfilm), State Archives; Incorporations, 1879–1906, New Hanover County Miscellaneous Records, State Archives.

45. Attorney W. E. Henderson, as quoted in the *Freeman* (Indianapolis, Ind.), December 3, 1898, and cited in Cody, "After the Storm," 121.

46. Incorporations, 1879–1906, New Hanover County Miscellaneous Records, State Archives.

47. The AUA acquired block 540 in 1897 and 541 in 1899. The blocks were located in the northeastern section of town and were bounded by Anderson, Miller, Rankin, and Woods streets. Subdivided portions of each block were then redistributed. The association handled the most deeds in 1898 (7) and 1899 (9), with activity ranging from 1 to 4 deeds in subsequent years. Incorporations, 1879–1906, New Hanover County Miscellaneous Records, State Archives.; Index to Real Estate Conveyances, Grantee and Grantor, 1729–1954, New Hanover County Land Records (microfilm), State Archives.

48. Of Wilmington's black population, 8 percent owned taxable real estate in 1890. Wilmington Tax Roll, New Hanover County Records, State Archives. For more on this topic, see Cody, "After the Storm."

49. The Wilmington Colored Educational Institute (WCEI) leased its Peabody school property to the Wilmington School Committee District No. 1 for use as a free public school in 1897, and the WCEI filed new articles of incorporation in 1898. Reaves, *"Strength through Struggle,"* 146–148; Incorporations, 1879–1906, New Hanover County Miscellaneous Records, State Archives.

50. Mary Washington Howe, daughter of respected freedman Alfred Howe, was educated in the North and became principal of Williston School. Teachers Nellie Chesnut, Susie Kennedy, Mabel Sadgwar, and Katie Telfair were all daughters of prominent black Wilmington leaders. Reaves, *"Strength through Struggle,"* 383, 410, 459, 474; Minutes, Board of County Commissioners, 1887–1918, New Hanover County Miscellaneous Records, State Archives.

51. In October and November 1898, black teachers in Wilmington averaged $35.64 per pay period, and an average of $523.16 was spent on black schools. In contrast, during the same pay period white teachers averaged $36.84, and $858.02 was the average amount spent on white schools. For the 1897–1898 school year, 51 percent of the city's black children (2,290 students) attended public schools (figures for private-school attendance are unavailable). Teacher pay, disbursements for schools, and attendance changed radically in the years following 1898. Department of Public Instruction, Superintendents' Annual Reports, State Archives; Minutes, Board of County Commissioners, 1887–1918, New Hanover County Miscellaneous Records, State Archives.

52. Other scholarly works by historians, such as Bart Landry's *The New Black Middle Class* (Berkeley: University of California Press, 1987) and Joel Williamson's *New People, Miscegenation and Mulattoes in the Untied States* (New York: Free Press, 1980), support Beam's findings. Lura Beam, *He Called Them by the Lightning: A Teacher's Odyssey in the Negro South, 1908–1919* (Indianapolis: Bobbs-Merrill Company, 1967), 40–42.

53. In the beginning stages of the white-supremacy campaign of 1898, a Democratic newspaper pointed out that in Wilmington there were 40 black magistrates (justices of the peace), 6 black members of the school board, 4 or 5 black deputy sheriffs, 14 black policemen, a black legislator, a black register of deeds, 3 black aldermen, 4 black health officers, and a black collector of customs. Additionally, blacks held at least 12 federal jobs in the city. *Morning Star* (Wilmington), August 20, 1898.

54. In 1897 President William McKinley reappointed Dancy to the post, where he remained until 1901. Logan, *The Negro in North Carolina*, 46–47, 106; Reaves, *"Strength through Struggle,"* 385.

55. In his self-published 1936 work *The Story of the Wilmington Rebellion*, Hayden, a Wilmington journalist and author, sought to explain the tensions that led to the violence in 1898. Hayden also composed a complete history of the Wilmington Light Infantry (WLI), an important local volunteer military group formed before the Civil War and which continued to exist into the early twentieth century, that further documents the events of November 10, 1898. The typed, unpublished memoir is currently held by the New Hanover County Public Library in Wilmington. Although Hayden's two works are tainted with rhetoric reminiscent of the 1898 and 1900 white-supremacy campaigns, they offer valuable insights into the motivations of the white leaders responsible for the political frenzy that culminated in the violence and coup d'etat. Harry Hayden, *The Story of the Wilmington Rebellion* (Wilmington: The Author, 1936), 2; Hayden, "The Wilmington Light Infantry," 61; Prather, *We Have Taken a City*, 61–62.

56. There is some evidence that this belief on the part of white businessmen in Wilmington was valid. In 1895 Wilmington's leading businessmen issued a prospectus to establish a textile mill in the city but later blamed changes to city government wrought by Fusion reform for their inability to act on it. In the immediate wake of the 1898 election, however, new business ventures emerged in the city. Those instrumental in the election campaign undoubtedly promised investors that once the contest was over, the city would be under their control and that business could resume much as it had been conducted in the fifteen years prior to the Fusion reforms of 1897. Key developments included construction of the Delgado

205

Cotton Mill in Wilmington in 1899 and establishment there of the headquarters for the Atlantic Coast Line Railroad in 1900. Piedmont textile magnate Edwin C. Holt, who had familial ties with Wilmington's elite, constructed the Delgado mill. In February 1900, just after the facility opened, Holt declared that he "would not have invested his money nor advised his friends to do likewise had the political scene in Wilmington stayed under the same administration prior to November of 1898." The mill cost $300,000 to construct, and in its first year it housed 440 looms and 10,300 spindles and could produce 25,000 yards of white cloth daily. By 1902 the mill employed 350 workers, all of them white—a common practice within the industry statewide. Rebecca Sawyer, "The Delgado-Spofford Textile Mill and Its Village: The Fabric of Wilmington's 20th Century Landscape" (master's thesis, University of North Carolina at Wilmington, 2001); Alan D. Watson, *Wilmington, Port of North Carolina* (Columbia: University of South Carolina Press, 1992), 116–117; *Wilmington Messenger*, February 21, 1900; Michael Honey, "Class, Race and Power," in David S. Cecelski and Timothy B. Tyson, eds., *Democracy Betrayed: The Wilmington Race Riot of 1898 and Its Legacy* (Chapel Hill: University of North Carolina Press, 1998), 171.

57. The chamber of commerce and the merchants association met regularly to discuss methods to improve their business options within the city. More important, the two organizations were instrumental in encouraging the growth of white labor unions, which increasingly became important vehicles for asserting the notion of white supremacy within Wilmington's labor market and for inflaming passions and provoking discord during the 1898 election campaign. The chamber of commerce issued numerous statements to the newspapers in support of the Democratic Party, and its increasingly strident appeals to whites culminated on November 2 with a formal declaration "against negro domination." The body offered a resolution declaring that "prosperity, peace and happiness" were not possible in Wilmington under the current regime and that black/Republican rule in the city was "detrimental to every business interest, arrests enterprise, hampers commerce and repels capital which might otherwise find investment in our midst." *Wilmington Messenger*, November 2, 1898.

Chapter 3: Practical Politics

1. During a white supremacy rally and parade in Wilmington, ladies along the parade route waved both U.S. and Cuban flags. *Wilmington Messenger*, November 4, 1898.

2. The act precipitating the war was the February 15 sinking of the U.S. battleship *Maine*, which had been docked in Havana following rioting in the city between Cubans and representatives of the Spanish government. Most members of Company K were mustered into service on May 13, 1898, and mustered out on November 18, 1898. Donald MacRae, brother of Hugh MacRae, was captain of Company K. William Lord deRosset, *Pictorial and Historical New Hanover County and Wilmington, North Carolina, 1723–1938* (Wilmington: The Author, 1938), [89]; Adjutant General's Office, *Roster of North Carolina Volunteers in the Spanish-American War, 1898–1899* (Raleigh: Edwards and Broughton and E. M. Uzzell, State Printers, 1900), 79–81.

3. Wilmington's contribution to the roster of the Third Regiment was 40 privates, 16 officers, 2 wagoners, and 1 musician. The Third Regiment was camped near Fort Macon in the summer and fall of 1898, and its men often visited Wilmington and other coastal towns. When the men visited, they enraged whites by demanding "equal treatment." In September the regiment was transferred from the coast to Tennessee, where it remained throughout the rest of the campaign season. Some have speculated that if, as in the case of the Second Regiment, the men of the Third Regiment had been furloughed and returned to Wilmington by the fall of 1898, the election and ensuing violence might have turned out differently. *Roster of North Carolina Volunteers in the Spanish-American War*, 92–117; Willard B. Gatewood Jr., "North Carolina's Negro Regiment in the Spanish-American War," *North Carolina Historical Review* 48 (October 1971): 370–387.

4. Evidence of that abating federal commitment is suggested by the inability of Congress to enact into law in 1890 the so-called Lodge Force Bill, which would have made intimidation and fraud at polling places federal offenses, and the finding of the Supreme Court of the United States in the *Plessy v. Ferguson* case (1896), which essentially validated the legal doctrine of separate but equal in public accommodations and codified legal segregation of the races over the next sixty years. The Lodge Force Bill passed in the House of Representatives but failed approval in the Senate. The *Plessy* ruling, 161 U.S. 537 (1896), upheld Louisiana law that separated black and white railroad passengers by cars as long as the cars specifically set aside for blacks were equal in accommodation to those for whites. Joel Williamson, *The Crucible of Race: Black-White Relations in the American South since Reconstruction* (New York: Oxford University Press, 1984), 113, 253; Jerome McDuffie, "Politics in Wilmington and New Hanover County, North Carolina, 1865–1900: The Genesis of a Race Riot" (Ph.D. diss., Kent State University, 1979), 464–467.

5. Jeffrey J. Crow and Robert F. Durden, *Maverick Republican in the Old North State: A Political Biography of*

206

Daniel L. Russell (Baton Rouge: Louisiana State University Press, 1977), 117.

6. Not until later in the twentieth century did North Carolina governors have the option to run for a second term. Nevertheless, in the matter of selecting a successor candidate, outgoing governors traditionally wielded a certain amount of influence within their parties. Russell lost control of the Republican Party through a series of conflicts related to Fusion politics and a lack of trust on the part of African Americans. McDuffie, "Politics in Wilmington," 552; Crow and Durden, *Maverick Republican*, 123–125; Josephus Daniels, *Editor in Politics* (Chapel Hill: University of North Carolina Press, 1941), 285.

7. McDuffie, "Politics in Wilmington," 525–533; Daniels, *Editor in Politics*, 285; *Progressive Farmer*, October 25, 1898.

8. McDuffie, "Politics in Wilmington," 537–538; State Democratic Executive Committee of North Carolina, *Democratic Party Handbook*, (Raleigh: Edwards and Broughton, 1898).

9. James Fred Rippy, *F. M. Simmons: Statesman of the New South, Memoirs and Addresses* (Durham: Duke University Press, 1936), 21.

10. In 1898 the State Democratic Party Committee was comprised of Simmons as chairman, John W. Thompson as secretary, Francis Winston, and Heriot Clarkson. P. M. Pearsall was the head of the committee's public-speaking department. He made 410 speaking appointments, most of them on behalf of Charles B. Aycock. Pearsall was a close associate of Simmons and wrote 50 to 150 letters a day on his behalf. C. Beauregard Poland, *North Carolina's Glorious Victory, 1898, Sketches of Able Democratic Leaders and Statesmen* (Raleigh: [Democratic Executive Commitee], 1899), 23.

11. *Democratic Party Handbook*, 35.

12. Ibid., 37–38.

13. Poland, *North Carolina's Glorious Victory*, 4; Rippy, *F. M. Simmons*, 19, 22–23.

14. Crow and Durden, *Maverick Republican*, 125; Daniels, *Editor in Politics*, 284.

15. A large Democratic Party rally that took place in Goldsboro in October 1898 featured a number of prominent speakers, among them Charles B. Aycock and Alfred Moore Waddell. Waddell's speech outlined numerous examples of "negro domination" in Wilmington and what he considered examples of poor Fusion government in the city. Daniels, *Editor in Politics*, 283–312; Harry Hayden, "The Wilmington Light Infantry" (typed, unpublished memoir), New Hanover County Public Library, Wilmington, 68; *Wilmington Messenger*,

October 28, 29, 1898; *Morning Star* (Wilmington), October 28, 1898; McDuffie, "Politics in Wilmington," 583.

16. Daniels, *Editor in Politics*, 295.

17. Just as Carr had assisted in the start-up of the *News and Observer*, he assisted Jennett's efforts as well. Jennett attended art school in New York with funding provided by Carr, and by the time of the 1898 campaign his newfound skills were highly prized by his North Carolina backers. Daniels called Jennett's cartoons "hard-hitting" and claimed that they represented the first example of "cartooning in a North Carolina paper." After the election, Jennett returned to New York to work for the New York *Herald*. Daniels, *Editor in Politics*, 147–150. The North Carolina Collection, Wilson Library, University of North Carolina at Chapel Hill, Chapel Hill, has digitized Jennett's cartoons. Access to the digitized cartoons is part of "The North Carolina Election of 1898," http://www.lib.unc.edu/ncc/1898/1898.html.

18. Historian Helen G. Edmonds claimed that the paper "led in a campaign of prejudice, bitterness, vilification, misrepresentation, and exaggeration to influence the emotions of the whites against the Negro." She added that the "cartoons were no less exciting and calculated to strike terror to unsuspecting whites." Josephus Daniels's impact on the 1898 campaign was so overarching that one writer characterizes him as the "precipitator of the riot." Helen G. Edmonds, *The Negro and Fusion Politics in North Carolina, 1894–1901* (Chapel Hill: University of North Carolina Press, 1951), 141; Alexander Weld Hodges, "Josephus Daniels, Precipitator of the Wilmington Race Riot of 1898" (honors essay, Department of History, University of North Carolina at Chapel Hill, 1990); Daniels, *Editor in Politics*, 284–285, 295–296.

19. There is also evidence that the *News and Observer* worked closely with editors and writers from the *Atlanta Constitution* and the *Washington Post*. Bryant later recalled that Wilmington's chief of police, John R. Melton, had "damned him" and that some in the city blamed his activities for instigating the race riot. "Simmons Hands: Lady-Like Touch Strong as Steel," n.d., H. E. C. Bryant Papers, Private Collections, State Archives, North Carolina Office of Archives and History, Raleigh; *Dictionary of North Carolina Biography*, s.v. "Bryant, Henry Edward Cowan"; "Red Shirts Organized," Isaac Spencer London Papers, Private Collections, State Archives.

20. Poland, *North Carolina's Glorious Victory*, 3–5.

21. Ibid., 4.

22. R. D. W. Connor and Clarence Poe, *The Life and Speeches of Charles Brantley Aycock* (Garden City, N.Y.: Doubleday, Page and Company, 1912), xii.

23. Although he had been a candidate for governor and other political offices in previous elections, Aycock was not a candidate in the 1898 campaign. (He was, however, elected governor by a large majority in 1900 on a platform of white supremacy and educational reform.) Connor wished "to speak to the negroes and let them understand how I feel towards them but, just now I would not be understood." In the 1898 campaign, Connor was elected to the state House of Representatives from Wilson County. Because of his work in that contest, he was rewarded with the post of Speaker of the House in 1899. Connor and Poe, *The Life and Speeches of Aycock*, 61–72; *Dictionary of North Carolina Biography*, s.v. "Aycock, Charles Brantley"; Henry Connor to George Howard, November 11, 1898, and Henry Connor to George Howard, October 20, 1898, Henry G. Connor Papers, Southern Historical Collection, Wilson Library, University of North Carolina at Chapel Hill; Josephus Daniels, "Henry Groves Connor: State Senator, Representative and Speaker of the North Carolina House of Representatives . . . an Address by Josephus Daniels Presenting the Portrait of Judge Connor . . . to the Supreme Court" (1929), pamphlet held by the State Library of North Carolina, 7–9; Poland, *North Carolina's Glorious Victory*, 34.

24. The constitution and bylaws of the White Government Union defined its goals and procedures and included the following words: "Our State is the only community in the world, with a majority of white voters, where the officers selected to administer the Government are the choice of negroes and not of the whites. This condition has been brought about by an unfortunate division among the white people; and it is likely to continue until that division is removed, and unity again prevails among them as it did prior to 1892. The necessity for a closer union of the white people of the State is so apparent that it requires management and that necessity has called for the organization of THE WHITE GOVERNMENT UNION." White Government Union, *Constitution and By-Laws of the White Government Union, 1898* (Raleigh: Edwards and Broughton, 1898), 2, William B. McKoy Collection, Lower Cape Fear Historical Society, Wilmington; Poland, *North Carolina's Glorious Victory*, 4.

25. *Constitution and By-Laws of the White Government Union*, 2–8, McKoy Collection.

26. No definitive differentiation has been drawn between the Red Shirts and the Rough Riders. The expression "Rough Riders" was first applied to the First U.S. Cavalry Regiment, organized during the Spanish-American War under Lt. Col. Theodore Roosevelt. Roosevelt's Rough Riders were instrumental in the American victory at the Battle of San Juan Hill, and their

bravery became widely celebrated. In his history of the Red Shirts in South Carolina, Alfred Williams wrote that the common explanation for the development of the red shirt as a uniform emerged during the 1876 campaign when, in response to the use of bloodied shirts of murdered blacks as banners to rally Republican supporters, South Carolina Democrats countered the "bloody shirt" argument by wearing red shirts of their own in order to mock and belittle the Republican symbolism. Cameron Morrison, a future governor of North Carolina, was a recognized statewide leader of North Carolina's Red Shirts. H. Leon Prather, "The Red Shirt Movement in North Carolina, 1898–1900," *Journal of Negro History* 62 (April 1977): 174–175; "Red Shirts Organized," London Papers; Alfred Williams, *Hampton and His Red Shirts: South Carolina's Deliverance in 1876* (Charleston, S.C.: Walker, Evans and Cogswell Co., 1935), 105. For additional information on Tillman, see Francis Butler Simkins, *Pitchfork Ben Tillman, South Carolinian* (Baton Rouge: Louisiana State University Press, 1944), and Stephen Kantrowitz, *Ben Tillman and the Politics of White Supremacy* (Chapel Hill: University of North Carolina Press, 2000). Roster of Young Men's Democratic Club of Wilmington, Merchant Account Book, n.d., Private Collections, State Archives.

27. Just as the Ku Klux Klan had a short-lived usefulness for the North Carolina Democratic Party, the Red Shirts existed in the state only during the 1898 and 1900 elections. Prather, "The Red Shirt Movement," 175; Daniels, *Editor in Politics*, 293.

28. A notable example of Red Shirt intimidation of whites appears in the autobiography of prominent Wilmington businessman and alderman Benjamin Keith and in Keith's testimony at an 1899 hearing pertaining to a legal challenge in which Republican Oliver Hart Dockery contested the election of Democrat John D. Bellamy to the U.S. House of Representatives. W. J. Harris, a white Republican, testified that Democrats constantly attempted to force him to join their party, and that even women "made efforts to intimidate . . . by remarks and tell me individually to come over and be a white man." Daniels, *Editor in Politics*, 292–295; Prather, "The Red Shirt Movement," 176; *Contested Election Case of Oliver H. Dockery vs. John D. Bellamy from the Sixth Congressional District of the State of North Carolina* (Washington, D.C.: Government Printing Office, 1899), 387 (hereafter cited as *Contested Election Case*).

29. Henry Hewett, a Wilmington printer, testified that he was a member of the WGU and that he rode in a Red Shirt parade and attended the speeches that followed in Wilmington's Hilton Park. For details of the planning and events surrounding Red Shirt rallies in Laurinburg and Wilmington, see articles in the *Wilmington Messenger* and

the *Evening Dispatch* (Wilmington), November 1–10, 1898. Moreover, Wilmington Democratic representative John D Bellamy of Wilmington later testified that he knew "there were men, and they were gentlemen, many of them men of property and character and influence, who wore a red shirt at some of their political meetings as a simple badge of their Democratic club." *Contested Election Case*, 219–220, 252–253.

30. Daniels, *Editor in Politics*, 294.

31. Richard L. Watson Jr., "A Political Leader Bolts— F. M. Simmons in the Presidential Election of 1928," *North Carolina Historical Review* 37 (October 1960): 529, 539; Glenda Elizabeth Gilmore, *Gender and Jim Crow: Women and the Politics of White Supremacy in North Carolina, 1896–1920* (Chapel Hill: University of North Carolina Press, 1996), 98–99.

32. Edmonds, *The Negro and Fusion Politics*, 143; Russell is quoted in Crow and Durden, *Maverick Republican*, 126.

33. *Caucasian* (Clinton and Raleigh), September 22, October 27, 1898, quoted in Crow and Durden, *Maverick Republican*, 127.

34. Young became a target of Daniels and the Democratic Party. Daniels later admitted that he was harsh on Young during the campaign. Crow and Durden, *Maverick Republican*, 124.

35. *Morning Star*, October 25, 1898; McDuffie, "Politics in Wilmington," 637; Crow and Durden, *Maverick Republican*, 124, 127; Daniels, *Editor in Politics*, 302; *Wilmington Messenger*, October 26, 1898.

36. At the stop in Maxton, Red Shirt leader and future governor Cameron Morrison warned Russell that his life was in danger. Morrison and some of his men remained aboard the train, and when other Red Shirts halted the train in Hamlet and searched it, Russell was hidden for his safety. According to the newspapers, approximately one hundred Red Shirts met Russell in Maxton. The *Wilmington Messenger* reported that the Red Shirts "appeared to be in for a good time" and that Russell "took their visit good naturedly." H. Leon Prather Sr., *We Have Taken a City: Wilmington Massacre and Coup of 1898* (Rutherford, N.J.: Fairleigh Dickinson University Press, 1984), 101–102; *Wilmington Messenger*, November 10, 1898; Daniels, *Editor in Politics*, 290, 303–304; Crow and Durden, *Maverick Republican*, 134; Douglas C. Abrams, "A Progressive-Conservative Deal: The 1920 Democratic Gubernatorial Primaries in North Carolina," *North Carolina Historical Review* 55 (October 1978): 426.

37. Wilmington resident George Rountree later recalled that about twenty of the city's best businessmen were organized into a campaign committee to support Strange's activities. Rountree was selected to join E. G.

Parmele, Frank Stedman, and Col. Walker Taylor in managing the campaign. Moreover, the campaign committee raised "a considerable amount of money" for the impending contest. George Rountree, "Memorandum of My Personal Recollection of the Election of 1898," n.d., Connor Papers (hereafter cited as Rountree, "My Personal Recollection of the Election of 1898.")

38. Rountree, born in Kinston and educated at Harvard, was a successful attorney. He lived and worked in New York and Richmond before returning to his native Kinston to operate law offices there. He married Meta Davis of Wilmington in 1881, and the couple moved to the city in 1890. Some speculation has it that Democratic Party leaders may have brought Rountree into the election contest as a strategic move to protect their own interests. Particularly useful for Democrats, Rountree purportedly had firsthand experience with white-supremacy campaigns and disfranchisement movements in Georgia. Rountree, "My Personal Recollection of the Election of 1898"; *Dictionary of North Carolina Biography*, s.v. "Rountree, George."

39. *Wilmington Messenger*, May 1, 1898.

40. A Democratic newspaper circular from about 1900 put the matter this way: "Negro domination does not mean that the government in every part of the entire State is under control of negro influences—few negroes live in the western part of our State. When the great controlling element is the negro vote, and when that vote and its influences name the officials and dictate the policy of a town, city or county, then it is dominant. When it elects negro officials of a town or county, there is negro domination." Edmund Smithwick and Family Papers, Private Collections, State Archives; Hayden, "The Wilmington Light Infantry," 58–59; McDuffie, "Politics in Wilmington," 537.

41. Benjamin Keith was a prominent Wilmington businessman and reluctant politician in the city and, like Waddell, Sprunt, and others, had a long family tradition of prominence in southeastern North Carolina. Keith sought to improve his city and state through third-party politics and as a Russell-appointed member of the board of aldermen. Years after the campaign was over, Keith was respected for his fortitude but still held deep resentment for his treatment at the hands of Democrats. Even as late as 1921, he was still battling with Democrats over his patronage position as collector of customs in the city. In a letter to President Warren G. Harding, Keith related details of the threats and dangers he and his family withstood during the 1898 election campaign. Keith recalled that when the Democrats realized they "could not buy with offices or could not intimidate me to join their red shirt mob," he was notified that unless he joined, he "would be killed and put in the Cape Fear River unless I

left the city at once." Keith, believing that Wilmington businessman James Fore was the author of a widely published article that discredited him, went to Fore's business—where, Keith claimed, forty to fifty Red Shirts were employed—and pummeled Fore. Fore was the partner of Flavel Foster in the Fore and Foster Planing Mill. As a result of the unbased slander, Fore lost favor in the city and departed for the remainder of the campaign. B. F. Keith to Marion Butler, November 2, 1898, Marion Butler Papers, Southern Historical Collection; Benjamin F. Keith to President Warren G. Harding, July 5, 1921, photocopy on file in the Research Branch, North Carolina Office of Archives and History, original in possession of Thomas J. Keith; Benjamin F. Keith, *Memories* (Raleigh: Bynum Printing Company, 1922), 79–111; James Sprunt, *Chronicles of the Cape Fear River, 1660–1916*, 2nd ed. (Raleigh: Edwards and Broughton Printing Company, 1916), 595–597; Crow and Durden, *Maverick Republican*, 131; R. D. W. Connor, William K. Boyd, and J. G. de Roulhac Hamilton, *History of North Carolina: North Carolina Biographies*, vol. 5 (Chicago: Lewis Publishing Company, 1919), 117–121; *Contested Election Case*, 361; Keith, *Memories*, 107–108; *J. L. Hill Printing Co.'s Directory of Wilmington, N.C. 1897* (Richmond, Va: J. L. Hill Printing Company, 1897; hereafter cited as *Hill's 1897 Wilmington City Directory*).

42. *Contested Election Case*, 390.

43. Following his capitulation, Chadbourn left the city to visit relatives in Maine and returned just before the election. In a jovial manner, James Worth of Wilmington wrote his wife that Chadbourn and his family had "gone to Maine for his health." Chadbourn's conversion was so complete that he allowed his Democratic Party employees to use his horses and buggy on voter registration day, presumably to get as many people as possible to the registration sites. *Contested Election Case*, 390; McDuffie, "Politics in Wilmington," 630; James S. Worth to Josephine, November 4, 1898, James Spencer Worth Papers, Southern Historical Collection.

44. McDuffie, "Politics in Wilmington," 605; *Contested Election Case*, 361.

45. Chief of Police John Melton later testified that Foster's statement was published as a letter in a local newspaper on October 21, 1898, but that he didn't believe that Foster authored the piece. The article indicated that an unnamed reporter had interviewed Foster, "ascertaining his views upon the present condition of affairs in our city," and explained that Foster "recognized the fact that the situation here was extremely grave, with imminent danger of trouble between the races," and "believed the city would not recover from the ill effect of such a conflict in years to come." Although the article portrayed Foster as a staunch Republican, it quoted him as

saying that "it would be best at this time for the Republicans not to put a county ticket in the field." The alleged interviewer was hopeful that Foster's standing within the Republican community would influence others and took care to explain Foster's role as "one of our most public spirited citizens and no man here has been more earnestly interest[ed] in the up building and prosperity of our city." *Wilmington Messenger*, October 21, 1898; *Contested Election Case*, 378; Rountree, "My Personal Recollection of the Election of 1898."

46. In order to make peace, Governor Russell and his supporters had made a pledge to the effect that, prior to the election, Republican candidates would voluntarily withdraw from certain races in favor of Democratic candidates. Costin's note also suggests that signatures on any one of the papers bearing the names of "prominent citizens" could have been coerced. Various accounts, some exaggerated, indicate that the coercion was both physical and verbal. James S. Worth to Josephine, November 4, 1898, Worth Papers; Costin to Cronly, Cronly Family Papers, Rare Book, Manuscript, and Special Collections Library, Duke University, Durham.

47. James H. Cowan, "The Wilmington Race Riot" (undated, unpublished memoir), Louis T. Moore Local History Collection, New Hanover County Public Library.

48. Democrat George Rountree penned an explanation of his belief in white Republican control of black votes. He claimed that on election day in 1894 he had watched as a group of black voters changed their votes at the whim of Daniel Russell, who had called for the election of Republican George Z. French over Democrat Thomas Strange. Rountree claimed that a black voter was a mere "automaton" and that what he had witnessed was proof for him of "absolute control by the leaders of the negro vote." Rountree, "Memorandum of My Personal Reasons for the Passage of the Suffrage Amendment to the Constitution (Grandfather Clause)," n.d., Connor Papers, Southern Historical Collection; Daniels, *Editor in Politics*, 311–312.

49. Rountree recalled that once Wilmington Democrats discovered that Fusion leaders had planned a rally in the city, they feared that "if they [Fusionists] spoke and the negroes became inflamed, and had a brass band and a torch light procession, there certainly would be a riot." The Democrats appointed a committee to "have an interview" with Governor Russell and Senators Butler and Pritchard in order to "point out to them the extreme danger of a race riot that would follow an attempt on their part to speak." Rountree later expressed subtle approval of the committee's actions but claimed to have opposed the use of "harsh" language in the warning to the Fusionists. Rountree, "My Personal Recollection of the Election of

1898"; *Contested Election Case*, 360–362; McDuffie, "Politics in Wilmington," 639–640; *Evening Dispatch*, October 25, 1898.

50. James H. Cowan, editor of the *Evening Dispatch*, echoed Clawson's claims that the citizens had planned a coup for up to a year prior to the 1898 election. Thomas W. Clawson, "The Wilmington Race Riot in 1898, Recollections and Memories" (unpublished memoir, Louis T. Moore Collection, Private Collections, State Archives; Cowan, "The Wilmington Race Riot."

51. Historians have followed Hayden's lead. Under close scrutiny, many writers who have discussed the actions of the city's white leaders have described the same men performing many of the same actions, but with different perspectives based on each writer's bias or perspective. Hayden's time lines fall apart when closely examined, particularly in regard to instances of pre-election scheming by the Secret Nine. It must be acknowledged that the men of Hayden's Secret Nine and Group Six were quite visible leaders who very well could have merged their social and political agendas, employing all of the tools at their disposal. There is no doubt that a central group of men managed the Democratic campaign and planned the ensuing coup d'etat. The disciplined regimentation of so many disparate groups could not have taken place without the firm control of a group of close-knit, well-placed individuals. Historian Helen Edmonds acknowledged that "a certain element of preparation stood out in the activities which preceded the riot," suggesting a high degree of conspiracy and preparation. Edmonds, *The Negro and Fusion Politics*, 166.

52. Hayden, "The Wilmington Light Infantry," 66–70; Rountree, "My Personal Recollection of the Election of 1898."

53. *Wilmington Messenger*, November 2, 1898; *Evening Dispatch* October 8, 1898. Several men were members of more than one pro-Democratic group. Members of the Democratic Party's campaign committee included Edgar Parmele, George Rountree, Frank Stedman, and Col. Walker Taylor. James H. Chadbourn Jr. served as president of the Wilmington Chamber of Commerce, and members of the chamber included John L. Cantwell, Thomas Clawson, S. H. Fishblate, Thomas C. James, William R. Kenan, Hugh MacRae, Samuel Northrop, Walter L. Parsley, George Rountree, Frank Stedman, Thomas Strange, J. Allan Taylor, Col. Walker Taylor, and William E. Worth. Hayden, "The Wilmington Light Infantry," 66–67, 72; Harry Hayden, *The Story of the Wilmington Rebellion* (Wilmington: The Author, 1936), 1–8; Prather, *We Have Taken a City*, 49.

54. Sidewalk encounters in which white women were perceived to be in danger from black "insolents," male and female, peppered the papers. For additional information on

the newspaper campaign, see Prather, *We Have Taken a City*, 52–55; McDuffie, "Politics in Wilmington," 574–575, 602–605; Sheila Smith McKoy, *When Whites Riot: Writing Race and Violence in American and South African Cultures* (Madison: University of Wisconsin Press, 2001), 42; Andrea M. Kirshenbaum, "Race, Gender and Riot: The Wilmington, North Carolina, White Supremacy Campaign of 1898" (master's thesis, Duke University, 1996), chapter 3.

55. *Morning Star*, October 25, 1898; *Wilmington Messenger*, October 21, 29, 1898.

56. Henry Litchfield West of the *Washington Post* and P. R. Noel of the *Richmond Times* were escorted through town during a parade and seated among dignitaries at speeches. *Wilmington Messenger*, November 4, 1898.

57. Taylor's prepared statement is perhaps the letter of capitulation penned by William H. Chadbourn while under pressure from the Democratic Party and the Red Shirts. Hayden, "The Wilmington Light Infantry," 68.

58. Rountree, "My Personal Recollection of the Election of 1898."

59. Waddell (1834–1912) was born in Hillsborough to parents who descended from leading Cape Fear families. He graduated from the University of North Carolina and practiced law before the Civil War. He attained the rank of lieutenant colonel in the 41st North Carolina Regiment but resigned his position because of ill health. Waddell, an effective orator, was sought after to provide moving speeches for political campaigns and civic ceremonies. He prided himself on his family lineage and, as a result, penned several works on the history of his family and the Cape Fear region. Waddell's third wife, Gabrielle, noted in her journal that he delivered a "great" speech at the Opera House in Wilmington on October 24, 1898. A relative wrote that there was "such demand for him all over the state since (what they call) his wonderful speech."

Historians have speculated on Waddell's motivation to thrust himself into the spotlight. Leon Prather claimed that although Waddell appeared to be a calm-tempered man, his "speeches contained some of the most violent tirades ever uttered from the rostrum." Moreover, Waddell, unemployed for some time prior to 1898, was likely experiencing difficult financial burdens by that year. Chief of Police John Melton believed that Waddell's motivation was to "get a position and office," since "he had been out of public life for a long time, and that was his opportunity to put himself before the people and pose as a patriot, thereby getting to the feed trough." To support that claim, Melton later testified that Waddell was "hired to attend elections and see that men voted correctly." Waddell's wife provided additional financial support for the household by teaching music daily. According to Jerome McDuffie, who interviewed numerous

211

Wilmington residents, Waddell's law practice was in decline, and he "had been seeking an office" in order to "lighten the burden of his wife." *Dictionary of North Carolina Biography*, s.v. "Waddell, Alfred Moore"; Diary of Gabrielle DeRosset Waddell, October 24, 1898, and letter to R. A. Meares, October 29, 1898, Meares and DeRosset Family Papers, Southern Historical Collection; Daniels, *Editor in Politics*, 301; McDuffie, "Politics in Wilmington," 579, 644; H. Leon Prather, "We Have Taken a City: A Centennial Essay," in David S. Cecelski and Timothy B. Tyson, eds., *Democracy Betrayed: The Wilmington Race Riot of 1898 and Its Legacy* (Chapel Hill: University of North Carolina Press, 1998), 25–26, 87–88; Gilmore, *Gender and Jim Crow*, 109; Benjamin Keith to Marion Butler, November 17, 1898, Butler Papers; *Contested Election Case*, 378–379, 381.

60. Waddell's speech appears in its entirety in the *Wilmington Messenger* for October 25, 1898.

61. *Wilmington Messenger*, October 25, 1898.

62. *Wilmington Messenger*, October 28, 29, 1898; *Morning Star*, October 28, 1898.

63. Cameron to Waddell, October 26, 1898, Alfred M. Waddell Papers, Southern Historical Collection; Gilmore, *Gender and Jim Crow*, 110–111.

64. A. M. Waddell to Bennehan Cameron, November 16, 1898, Bennehan Cameron Papers, Southern Historical Collection.

65. Rountree, "My Personal Recollection of the Election of 1898."

66. Keith, *Memories*, 97.

67. Henry West, "The Race War in North Carolina," *The Forum* 26 (January 1899): 580.

68. Daniels, *Editor in Politics*, 288.

69. James S. Worth to Josephine Worth, November 3, 1898, Worth Papers; Louis Meares to Richard Meares, November 5, 1898, Meares and DeRosset Family Papers.

70. Jane Cronly, "Account of the Race Riot" (unpublished memoir, n.d.), Cronly Family Papers.

71. Mary Parsley to Sallie, November 2, 1898, Mother to Sallie, November 9, 1898, Eccles Family Papers, Southern Historical Collection.

72. Mason was the cashier for the North Carolina Cotton Oil Company. R. Beverly Mason to Bess, November 8, 1898, John S. Henderson Papers, Southern Historical Collection; *Hill's 1897 Wilmington City Directory*.

73. Louis Meares to Richard Meares, November 5, 1898, Meares and DeRosset Family Papers.

74. *Morning Star* (Wilmington), August 11, 18, 19, 25, 26, 27, September 2, 3, 9, 18, 21, 22, 1898; *Evening Dispatch*, August 24, 25, October 8, 24, 1898; *Wilmington Messenger*, November 8, 1898.

75. The information from Dowling regarding his activity in the Red Shirt/Rough Rider brigade, as well as in the WGU, was obtained by Republican Oliver Dockery, Bellamy's opponent in the 1898 election. Dockery challenged the validity of Bellamy's election and subpoenaed Dowling's testimony. Dowling had been rewarded with a city job after the violence but by 1900 had had several run-ins with Wilmington leaders and thus had no reason to protect them. *Union Republican* (Winston), March 15, 1900.

76. L. H. Bryant testified in 1899 that he was a Populist and that armed men, carpenters from the railroad, visited his home and told him not to vote. *Contested Election Case*, 394–395.

77. It is not known how many men participated in the parade. One Wilmington newspaper claimed that one hundred Red Shirts marched in the parade and that more than 1,000 people gathered at Hilton Park. Henry L. Hewett later testified that he rode in the procession but would not estimate the number of participants. Chief of Police John Melton likewise testified that on the day of the Red Shirt parade there was sporadic shooting into homes, particularly that of Dixon Toomer, an African American man, and into a black school on Campbell Square. Melton identified Theodore Swann as the leader of the Rough Riders. G. W. Bornemann was the leader of the "Fifth Ward Rough Riders" during the parade. *Evening Dispatch*, November 3, 1898; *Contested Election Case*, 219, 360–387.

78. James S. Worth wrote to his wife:

We had a little row last night about dark that might have brought on something worse. Some of the Fifth Ward "Rough Riders" on a spree ran foul of some darkies downtown early in the evening and maltreated several. The boys were "run in" by the police a little later and were today fined $25.00 each and the costs. Rather expensive "fun" for that class of boys. Down on Front Street about dark last night they tackled every nigger that came along regardless and ran several across the street and into nearby alleys. Fortunately they had no arms or there might have been serious trouble as a crowd of both colors quickly formed; but very little was done except to make the boys move on.

James S. Worth to Josephine, November 4, 1898, Worth Papers; *Evening Dispatch*, November 5, 1898.

79. *Contested Election Case*, 362.

80. In an interview with Harry Hayden, Capt. Thomas C. James of the Wilmington Light Infantry referred to Dowling as a "hotheaded" Irishman. Nevertheless, research into the life of Dowling and his family indicates that Dowling was not a newly arrived immigrant but was born in North Carolina and that his father served in the Confederacy from the Wilmington

area during the Civil War. Hayden, "The Wilmington Light Infantry," 75.

81. McKoy acknowledged that Wilmington's pre-Civil War population consisted of a large contingent of recent Irish immigrants and that by 1890 many of their descendants were unemployed and lived in substandard housing alongside more recent Irish immigrants. McKoy, *When Whites Riot*, 43.

82. Other scattered speculative explanations for the origin of the Red Shirt are found in the historical record. Historian J. G. de Roulhac Hamilton noted that often the Ku Klux Klan outfits were all in red, indicating that perhaps the Red Shirt movement from South Carolina was an outgrowth of that organization. In *Born Fighting*, James Webb declared that the "warrior aristocracy" of the Scotch-Irish "was still in place in the South of the late 1800s." Webb explained that "a significant percentage" of whites in the South "were living in economic conditions no different than blacks" and that "the diminishment of blacks" was "a device for maintaining social and economic control ordered from above at the threat of losing one's place—or job—in the white community." Webb added that "violence in defense of one's honor had always been the moniker" of the Scotch-Irish culture and that even though whites "believed emphatically in racial separation, the true battle lines . . . were not personal so much as they were political and economic."

Several references to men who were members of the Red Shirts are found throughout the historical record. Theodore Swann was identified as a leader of the Rough Riders. Swann's family had roots in Wilmington, and he was most likely born in the city. The Swanns were carpenters and brick masons, perhaps leading to some competition and tension between the family and prominent African American carpenter families in the city. James Webb, *Born Fighting: How the Scotch-Irish Shaped America* (New York: Broadway Books, 2004), 238–246; J. G. de Roulhac Hamilton, *Reconstruction in North Carolina* (Raleigh: Presses of Edwards and Broughton, 1906), 461; *Wilmington Messenger*, November 4, 1898; Ninth Census of the United States, 1870: New Hanover County, North Carolina, Population Schedule, National Archives, Washington, D.C. (microfilm, State Archives); Twelfth Census of the United States, 1900: New Hanover County, North Carolina, Population Schedule, National Archives, Washington, D.C. (microfilm, State Archives).

83. *Contested Election Case*, 387–394; *Wilmington Messenger*, October 20, 1898.

84. Nada Cotton narrative, McDonald-Howe Family Papers, Special Collections Department, Randall Library, University of North Carolina Wilmington; Cronly, "Account of the Race Riot."

85. James Worth to Josephine, November 7, 1898, Worth Papers.

86. Several news accounts and manuscript records detail blacks claiming hunger and stealing food. James Worth wrote his wife before the election that a black man had approached his house and asked his mother for something to eat, since he had eaten nothing for two days. Another resident of Wilmington, Mrs. Edward Wootten, informed her son that blacks had been "robbing pantries." Perhaps as a result of a hostile environment, with few jobs available, some black men resorted to crime in order to feed themselves and their families. Former chief of police Melton answered a series of questions in 1899 regarding the arson problems faced by the city and replied that the arson cases transpired well before the beginning of the white-supremacy election campaign and that the "firebugs" had been arrested. Melton observed that during the spring and summer months each year, when some residents were out of the city at vacation homes on the beach, crime at those vacated residences increased but was generally the work of young boys breaking and entering to steal minor items. James S. Worth to Josephine, November 3, 1898, Worth Papers; Mother to Edward Wootten, November 8, 1898, Bradley Jewett Wootten Papers, University of North Carolina Wilmington Special Collections; *Contested Election Case*, 369–370.

87. An examination of industrial schedules from the 1890 and 1900 censuses, Wilmington business directories, and port records suggests that after the city returned to Democratic control in 1898, enabling business leaders to focus on business and not on politics, those men were successful in a variety of ventures. The late 1890s was a period of prosperity for businessmen throughout the nation, but it appears that Wilmington's business leaders were unable to capitalize on the wealth being accumulated by railroad and industry magnates until after 1898. *Wilmington Messenger*, November 2, 1898.

88. *Evening Dispatch* (Wilmington), October 8, 1898.

89. *Wilmington Messenger*, October 28, 1898.

90. Ibid.

91. Rountree, "My Personal Recollection of the Election of 1898."

92. It is unclear when the patrols began. James Cowan, editor of the *Evening Dispatch*, claimed that the patrols took place for a year, but most other accounts indicate that they began in the period immediately preceding the election. In August a correspondent of the *News and Observer* visited Wilmington to investigate claims of "negro domination" and discovered "murmurings" of Vigilance Committees at that early stage. Chief of Police Melton later testified that guns were carried on the street during the campaign and that armed men were posted on

every corner in the city all night for a few days before the election. Cowan, "The Wilmington Race Riot"; Hayden, "The Wilmington Light Infantry," 66, 70; Clawson, "The Wilmington Race Riot in 1898"; Minutes of the Organizational Meeting of the Association of Members of the Wilmington Light Infantry, December 14, 1905, North Carolina Collection (hereafter cited as Minutes of the Organizational Meeting of the WLI); West, "The Race War in North Carolina," 579; Daniels, *Editor in Politics*, 285; James S. Worth to Josephine, November 16, 1898, Worth Papers; *Contested Election Case*, 360.

93. Historian Jerome McDuffie observed that because the Vigilance Committee was associated mainly with leading businessmen and property owners, it was less involved in white-supremacy rhetoric. Moreover, he noted that members of that body did not hold rallies or openly intimidate by brandishing weapons and that its discussions were "tempered" with a degree of "moderate paternalism." McDuffie, "Politics in Wilmington," 621; Thomas Strange to Bennehan Cameron, November 16, 1898, Cameron Papers.

94. *Wilmington Messenger*, November 5, 1898.

95. After Moore's death in 1900, his widow defended her late husband's actions. She asserted that Moore had sought to prevent the wholesale slaughter of blacks on the day of the riot, and she praised the "men who spent many sleepless nights watching and guarding the safety and residents of the whole town." But her main purpose was to attach her husband's name to the riot, to assert that his actions saved many lives, and to discredit Alfred Moore Waddell's role in the pre-election and pre-riot planning. Mrs. Moore made a point of explaining that Waddell, despite his speechmaking, did not know of the amount of planning that took place behind closed doors and that only after he was appointed mayor did he learn all the details of the coup. In his history of the county and city, William Lord deRosset corroborates Mrs. Moore's remarks. Mrs. Roger Moore Collection, University of North Carolina Wilmington Special Collections; deRosset, *Pictorial and Historical New Hanover County*, [30–31]; Prather, *We Have Taken a City*, 100–101; Clawson, "The Wilmington Race Riot in 1898"; Cowan, "The Wilmington Race Riot."

96. Tony P. Wrenn, *Wilmington, North Carolina: An Architectural and Historical Portrait* (Charlottesville: University of Virginia Press, 1984), 206–207; Hayden, "The Wilmington Light Infantry," 45; Wilmington Light Infantry, *Constitution and Bylaws* (1904), 15–19, Cape Fear Museum of History and Science, Wilmington (hereafter cited as WLI *Constitution*.)

97. WLI *Constitution*, 15–19; *Wilmington Messenger*, November 26, December 16, 1905; Hayden, "The Wilmington Light Infantry," 45–46.

98. That there were fundamental differences between the WLI and the citizens' patrol is obvious in James Cowan's observation that once the governor mobilized the WLI on the day of the riot, the citizens' patrol ceased to exist because "there was no further need for their services." Cowan, "The Wilmington Race Riot"; John V. B. Metts to an unidentified recipient, November 9, 1898, Hinsdale Family Papers, Duke Special Collections, Duke University.

99. Democratic Party leaders decided that regular U.S. troops should not participate in any activities because their involvement might possibly result in intervention by the federal government. Despite such reservations, many active troops, some at least partially attired in their uniform, participated in rallies and other activities, and even the riot. Rountree, "My Personal Recollection of the Election of 1898"; Minutes of the Organizational Meeting of the WLI.

100. *Wilmington Messenger*, November 5, 1898.

101. Mother to Edward Wootten, November 8, 1898, Wootten Papers. Wilmington newspapers report such quiet female support of the campaign as an undercurrent to parades, attendance at speeches, and WGU events.

102. John Bellamy later testified that Wilmington's merchants purchased the gun for the protection of life and property "separate and apart" from the official sanction of the Democratic-committees and that the purchase was "kept very quiet." *Wilmington Messenger*, November 4, 1898; Iredell Meares, "Wilmington Revolution" (broadside), Edmund Smithwick and Family Papers, Private Collections, State Archives; *Contested Election Case*, 256–257.

103. The rapid-fire gun was fired down the Cape Fear River from near Eagle's Island. The demonstration of the weapon's capabilities proved to the African American leaders present that if it were used against men in the streets, scores would die in a short period of time. *Contested Election Case*, 344–346.

104. *Contested Election Case*, 343–346, 362; *Morning Star*, November 8, 1898; *Evening Dispatch*, November 7, 1898; Meares, "Wilmington Revolution"; Alfred Moore Waddell, quoted in "The North Carolina Race Conflict," *Outlook* 60 (November 19, 1898); *Wilmington Messenger*, November 8, 1898.

105. The fact that the Raleigh *News and Observer* was involved in the matter reflects the important role that Josephus Daniels and the paper played in the 1898 campaign. It was not illegal for blacks to own or purchase guns. McDuffie, "Politics in Wilmington," 625–626; *Wilmington Messenger*, October 9, 1898; *News and Observer*, October 8, 1898; *Evening Dispatch*, October 10, 1898; *Morning Star*, October 9, 1898.

214

106. *Evening Dispatch*, November 2, 1898; Gilmore, *Gender and Jim Crow*, 107–108.

107. After the riot, William Parsley wrote a relative that "every blessed one of them [blacks] had a pistol of some sort and many of them rifles and shotguns loaded with buckshot." William Parsley to Sal [McLaurin], November 12, 1898, Eccles Family Papers.

108. The testimony presented in the challenge to Bellamy's election by his opponent Oliver Dockery has provided much insight into the activities of many of the leading participants in the campaign and riot. *Contested Election Case*, 8–18.

Chapter 4: Eve of Destruction

1. It is unclear when Manly commenced publication of the *Record*, but the earliest extant copy dates from 1895. The *Record*'s archives were apparently destroyed during the riot. H. Leon Prather Sr., *We Have Taken a City: Wilmington Massacre and Coup of 1898* (Rutherford, N.J.: Fairleigh Dickinson University Press, 1984), 68–70; Jerome McDuffie, "Politics in Wilmington and New Hanover County, North Carolina, 1865–1900: The Genesis of a Race Riot" (Ph.D. diss., Kent State University, 1979), 585–586; Andrea M. Kirshenbaum, "Race, Gender and Riot: The Wilmington, North Carolina, White Supremacy Campaign of 1898" (master's thesis, Duke University, 1996), 37–38; Thomas W. Clawson, "The Wilmington Race Riot in 1898, Recollections and Memories" (unpublished memoir), Louis T. Moore Collection, Private Collections, State Archives, North Carolina Office of Archives and History, Raleigh.

2. Some contemporary debate arose among Republicans and Populists not only as to whether or not Manly wrote the editorial but also whether or not the Democrats paid him to publish it. It was speculated that Manly had spoken out against such claims and defended his paper as he claimed responsibility for the work. In later testimony, Chief of Police John R. Melton expressed the belief that the Democrats had indeed prompted Manly to publish the article. Melton claimed to have heard many people state that they thought Manly was paid for the article and that Raleigh newspapers had printed such conjecture. Melton went on to speculate on the pecuniary value of the article: "[I]f Manly did not get a good round price for that editorial," he mused, "he ought to be put in the asylum for crazy." He also observed that if the Democrats had not supported Manly in some way, they would not have allowed him to continue publishing all the way up to the election. Melton claimed to have been told that the paper had not been suppressed because it was an effective campaign tool for the Democrats. After the riot, William L. Jeffries, one of Manly's assistant editors, claimed authorship of the editorial. Jeffries was quoted as saying that he wrote the piece to "show that there were two sides to the question and that the outrages were not all on one side." He added that if Manly, who had fled Wilmington immediately after the riot, were to return to Wilmington, whites would "burn and kill him" but that they would be getting the "wrong man." *Contested Election Case of Oliver H. Dockery vs. John D. Bellamy from the Sixth Congressional District of the State of North Carolina* (Washington, D.C.: Government Printing Office, 1899), 376 (hereafter cited as *Contested Election Case*).

3. The Wilmington *Morning Star* reprinted Felton's speech in August 1898 because Felton's theme and tone fit perfectly into the tenor of the white-supremacy campaign then under way. After delivering the 1897 speech, Felton traveled widely to speak on the topic of the address, and Manly may not have realized that the speech itself was a year old. LeeAnn Whites, "Love, Hate, Rape, Lynching: Rebecca Latimer Felton and the Gender Politics of Racial Violence," in David S. Cecelski and Timothy B. Tyson, eds., *Democracy Betrayed: The Wilmington Race Riot and Its Legacy* (Chapel Hill: University of North Carolina Press, 1998), 143–163; Glenda Elizabeth Gilmore, *Gender and Jim Crow: Women and the Politics of White Supremacy in North Carolina, 1896–1920* (Chapel Hill: University of North Carolina Press, 1996), 105.

4. *Daily Record* (Wilmington), August 18, 1898.

5. Minutes of the Organizational Meeting of the Association of Members of the Wilmington Light Infantry, December 14, 1905, North Carolina Collection, Wilson Library, University of North Carolina at Chapel Hill, Chapel Hill (hereafter cited as Minutes of the Organizational Meeting of the WLI); *Morning Star*, August 24, 1898.

6. Wilmington's ministerial union adopted the following resolution: "Resolved, That the Ministerial Union is in hearty sympathy with the efforts of the *Daily Record* in defending the rights of the race, and that each minister inform his congregation of the present situation and endeavor to sustain the paper by swelling its subscription list and urging prompt payment." Another African American religious group, the Wilmington District Conference and Sunday School Convention of Methodists, resolved to support Manly and his paper "as long as she stands forth in the protection of the ladies of our race" and promised to "stand by you" even in the event of "hazarding our lives." *Wilmington Messenger*, September 13, 16, 1898.

7. *Morning Star*, August 25, 26, 1898; *Contested Election Case*, 377; *Wilmington Messenger*, October 21, 1898.

8. When Republicans rejected the accusation by Democrats that Manly was affiliated with the Republican Party, Democrats responded by pointing out that Manly had once been nominated deputy register of deeds under Republican rule of New Hanover County and that his employees were all Republicans. (One of Manly's employees, John T. Howe, had served as a Republican representative in the General Assembly in 1897.) *Morning Star*, August 25, 26, 31, 1898; Gilmore, *Gender and Jim Crow*, 106–107; Prather, *We Have Taken a City*, 73; *Wilmington Messenger*, September 4, 16, 1898.

9. Reporters from the *Washington Post*, the *New York Herald*, the *New York Times*, the *Baltimore Sun*, the *Atlanta Constitution*, the *Charlotte Daily Observer*, and the *Richmond Times* all visited Wilmington during the height of the campaign against Manly. *Morning Star*, August 1898; *Wilmington Messenger*, August 1898.

10. Tillman is quoted in McDuffie, "Politics in Wilmington," 593; *Wilmington Messenger*, October 22, 1898; *News and Observer* (Raleigh), November 5, 1898.

11. Minutes of the Wilmington Board of Aldermen, 1884–1906 (microfilm), State Archives; McDuffie, "Politics in Wilmington," 627–628; *Wilmington Messenger*, October 13, 1898.

12. Black leaders John H. Brown, J. W. Lee, William A. Moore, Carter Peamon, and John E. Taylor requested the dismissals. Six black men were subsequently dismissed and replaced by whites. *Wilmington Messenger*, September 21, 1898; McDuffie, "Politics in Wilmington," 614; *Morning Star*, October 20, 1898.

13. Also mentioned in the article is a black man, Willis Stevens, also known as "Drake," who had been declared insane and had previously attempted to run for mayor. In May 1897 the county board of commissioners agreed to release Drake from the county's custody on appeal from his attorney. At the attorney's suggestion, the board also purchased shoemaker's tools for Drake, enabling him to make his own living. Soon afterward, a letter to the editor of a Wilmington newspaper asked, "Why should the county commissioners make an appropriation to a 'crazy negro' to get him up in business, when there are numbers of honest white men who are seeking employment without success?" In 1898 white men at the registration site apparently mistreated Drake, leading to Peamon's outburst. During the scuffle a crowd of blacks gathered, and the outnumbered white men left the precinct. McDuffie, "Politics in Wilmington," 616; *Morning Star*, October 2, 1898; *Wilmington Messenger*, October 2, 1898; Minutes, Board of County Commissioners, 1887–1918, New Hanover County Miscellaneous Records, State Archives.

14. As such incidents increased, Fusionist leaders claimed that Democrats paid blacks to incite violence so that the white-supremacy campaign would continue to have newsworthy examples of black "insolence." McDuffie, "Politics in Wilmington," 613; *Morning Star*, November 6, 8, 1898; *Evening Dispatch* (Wilmington), November 7, 1898; *Wilmington Messenger*, November 6, 1898.

15. Josephus Daniels, *Editor in Politics* (Chapel Hill: University of North Carolina Press, 1941), 292, quoting the *Searchlight* (Kinston), an African American newspaper.

16. Jane Cronly, "Account of the Race Riot" (unpublished memoir, n.d.), Cronly Family Papers, Duke Special Collections.

17. African American Hamilton Hargrave later testified that he was employed by Samuel and William Northrop's sawmill and was informed that if he and other black employees registered to vote, they would be fired. Despite the threat, Hargrave voted in the election. *Contested Election Case*, 349; Robert Mason to Bess, November 8, 1898, John S. Henderson Papers, Southern Historical Collection, Wilson Library, University of North Carolina at Chapel Hill; *J. L. Hill Printing Co.'s Directory of Wilmington, N.C. 1897* (Richmond, Va: J. L. Hill Printing Company, 1897).

18. McDuffie, "Politics in Wilmington," 663.

19. Gilmore, *Gender and Jim Crow*, 107.

20. *Wilmington Messenger*, October 21, 1898.

21. Fusionists throughout the state removed the names of opposition candidates, particularly black ones, from the ballot in hopes of peace. The *Messenger* acknowledged the Republican sacrifice on November 5 with a short sentence: "The decision of the Republican managers to place no ticket in the field, making a Democratic county out of a county having a Republican majority of 750[,] was the last move they could make to prevent extreme measures." *Wilmington Messenger*, November 5, 1898; McDuffie, "Politics in Wilmington," 632; John Haley, *Charles N. Hunter and Race Relations in North Carolina* (Chapel Hill: University of North Carolina Press, 1987), 110; Helen G. Edmonds, *The Negro and Fusion Politics in North Carolina, 1894–1901* (Chapel Hill: University of North Carolina Press, 1951), 145; James L. Hunt, *Marion Butler and American Populism* (Chapel Hill: University of North Carolina Press, 2003), 153.

22. Sprunt wrote:

We have been deeply concerned during the past week by the very excited state of our inhabitants in view of the approaching election which threatens to provoke a war between the white and black races. We have frequently observed during political campaigns in the past, a degree of hostility which, at times, appeared to threaten the public peace but which passed off when wiser counsel prevailed; but the present state of excitement is apparently and really beyond bounds and we declare to you our conviction that we are on the brink of a revolution which can only be averted by the suppression of a republican ticket. The white people, and tax payers generally, protest that they have been driven to desperation, and we have no hesitation in saying that, even the unusual indiscretion of political partisans on the next election day, will precipitate a conflict which may cost hundreds, and perhaps thousands of lives and the partial or entire destruction of the city. We therefore on behalf of the conservative business firms of Wilmington deeply interested in the peace and welfare of our community, entreat you as the representative of the republican party here, to meet the emergency and avert a calamity by the means which we have indicated or by some other personal or political sacrifice which would be gratefully recognized and approved by our conservative and patriotic people who look to you in this extremity.

Sprunt to Russell, October 24, 1898, Alexander Sprunt and Son, Inc., Papers, Duke Special Collections (hereafter cited as Sprunt and Son Papers). This letter is also reprinted in the October 28, 1898, issue of the *Wilmington Messenger*.

23. Some of the white businessmen named as potential Republican candidates, particularly Benjamin Keith and D. L. Gore, were openly against running for office during the election. McDuffie, "Politics in Wilmington," 641–643; *Morning Star*, October 28, 1898; *Charlotte Daily Observer*, November 2, 1898.

24. An unsigned note in James Sprunt's papers at Duke University provides insight:

> For the Republican Party of New Hanover County to make no nominations for County Commissioners, Sheriff, Register of Deeds, Treasurer, Coroner, Clerk of Superior Court or Members of the House of Representatives, provided the Dem Party shall support for the house of Representatives any two of the following named gentlemen as representatives of the business interests of the City and County: E. S. Martin, D. L. Fore, Martin Willard, George Rountree, Henry McQueen, William Gilchrist, Roger Moore, R. W. Hicks, Frank McNeil, Junius Davis, J. C. Stevenson, Oscar Pearsall, Sam. Bear, Jr., S. P. McNair, C. W. Yates, J. W. Atkinson. These concessions to be upon the basis that such action will bring about a better state of feeling and result in a peaceable and orderly election for County State Senatorial and Congressional offices, without interference with the rights of lawful voters.

Russell's bargaining likewise removed from the contest the names of several Democrats, including candidates for the General Assembly Joseph Carr and George Peschau, who would have sought his impeachment had they been elected to the legislature. Sprunt and Son Papers; *Contested Election Case*, 255; McDuffie, "Politics in Wilmington," 642.

25. Despite last-minute maneuvering by white Republicans, resistant black leaders urged others to go to the polls "prepared to fight" for their right to vote. McDuffie, "Politics in Wilmington," 623.

26. *Wilmington Messenger*, November 4, 1898.

27. Local Democrats, on the other hand, were encouraged by the compromise and took note of the capitulation in their letters and diaries. Peter Mallett noted in his daily journal that the "Republicans accede to demands of the Citizens." Despite Russell's compromise in order to maintain peace, about a week before the election Democrats in the city became more "emboldened and violent." *Contested Election Case*, 36–37; George Rountree, "Memorandum of My Personal Recollection of the Election of 1898," n.d., Henry G. Connor Papers, Southern Historical Collection (hereafter cited as Rountree, "My Personal Recollection of the Election of 1898"); Peter Mallett Papers, Southern Historical Collection; McDuffie, "Politics in Wilmington," 615.

28. Foster to Sprunt, October 30, 1898, Sprunt and Son Papers.

29. Some of those groups were possibly Populists and independent Republicans. Although no county ticket was mounted, Fusionists still lobbied Wilmington voters on behalf of their candidates for statewide and congressional seats. They also distributed throughout the city printed circulars that encouraged "every man who is opposed to the Democratic machine" to vote for men such as Oliver Dockery, Fusionist congressional candidate. *Wilmington Messenger*, November 3, 4, 5, 1898; *Morning Star*, November 3, 4, 5, 1898; McDuffie, "Politics in Wilmington," 651; telegrams, Russell to Sprunt and Sprunt to Russell, November 4, 1898, Sprunt et al. to Russell, November 5, 1898, Sprunt and Son Papers.

30. *Wilmington Messenger*, October 26, 1898.

31. When the Democratic Party leadership requested Wilmington ministers to build their sermons around specific chapters in the Bible that reinforced the argument for white supremacy, Hoge and other ministers willingly complied. The ministers also participated in rallies and even the riot, joining their parishioners in carrying firearms. The "recommended" Bible chapters were Isa. 17:14 and Jer. 25:35. J. Allen Kirk, *A Statement of Facts Concerning the Bloody Riot in Wilmington, N.C., of Interest to Every Citizen of the United States* ([Wilmington?: The Author? 1898?]), 2–3; online edition available at http://docsouth.unc.edu/nc/kirk/menu.html.

32. For additional information on this meeting, see the *Washington Post*, November 8, 1898, and the *Atlanta Constitution*, November 8, 1898.

33. Kirk, *A Statement of Facts Concerning the Riot*, 8.

34. *Morning Post* (Raleigh), November 9, 1898.

35. McDuffie, "Politics in Wilmington," 633.

217

36. The Raleigh *News and Observer* (November 8, 1898) noted that the city was tense yet ready for whatever happened.

37. *Morning Star*, November 9, 1898.

38. W. N. Harriss, interview by Harry Hayden, in McDuffie, "Politics in Wilmington," 664.

39. Dowling later revealed that Democratic Party leaders had instructed him and others to take weapons to the polls, that the campaign committee had distributed whiskey at the polls in attempts to get Republican election officers drunk, and that specific plans had been made to storm a precinct with a Republican majority in order to overwhelm election officials and replace Republican tickets with Democratic ones. *Union Republican* (Winston), March 15, 1900.

40. The First and Fifth wards were predominantly black and usually supplied a Republican majority. *Morning Star*, November 8, 1898.

41. Jeffrey J. Crow and Robert F. Durden, *Maverick Republican in the Old North State: A Political Biography of Daniel L. Russell* (Baton Rouge: Louisiana State University Press, 1977), 134; *Wilmington Messenger*, November 9, 1898.

42. Metts to an unidentified recipient, November 9, 1898, Hinsdale Family Papers, Duke Special Collections.

43. Each of the city's five wards was divided into smaller voting precincts or divisions.

44. Col. Walker Taylor and Col. Roger Moore had appointed Fulton registrar. Fulton did not sign the election returns until the Monday following the election, when he went to collect his pay for serving as registrar. *Contested Election Case*, 332–337.

45. Bates testified that "the anxiety, fear and terror among the colored people, largely the Republican voters of the city of Wilmington[,] was very great, exceeding that of any occasion." *Contested Election Case*, 338.

46. In a later interview with Harry Hayden, Democratic Party leader William N. Harris, who was present at the precinct on election day 1898, recalled that the building was an old stable and that he led the rush of whites into the building as the votes were being cast. He claimed to have pushed a policeman into a barrel of water as other men knocked oil lamps over. He then said that he stuffed "several hundred" ballots into the Democratic senate candidate's box. Hayden shared his notes from the interview with Jerome McDuffie, who incorporated them into his dissertation. McDuffie, "Politics in Wilmington," 667.

47. Two other election workers—Charles Keen of the fourth division of the First Ward and C. F. Craig, registrar of the second precinct of the First Ward—testified that

their precincts did not experience trouble. *Contested Election Case*, 336–341.

48. *Contested Election Case*, 363.

49. McDuffie, "Politics in Wilmington," 688–670. (McDuffie cited a November 12, 1898, letter from P. B. Manning to E. S. Tennet, in the Louis T. Moore Local History Collection, New Hanover County Public Library, Wilmington. The Manning letter has since disappeared from the library holdings, so McDuffie's interpretation of its content must stand.)

50. Robert Mason to Bess, November 8, 1898, Henderson Papers; John V. B. Metts to an unidentified recipient, November 9, 1898, Hinsdale Family Papers; "Mother" to Sallie, November 9, 1898, Eliza Hall Parsley Papers, Southern Historical Collection; Kirk, *A Statement of Facts Concerning the Riot*, 5.

51. Conversely, African American pastor J. Allen Kirk noted that about five hundred Democrats participated in "a great Jubilee march" through the city. Because the march wound through all of the city's black neighborhoods and past black businesses, churches, and halls, Kirk viewed the celebration as an effort to "intimidate and demoralize" blacks. Kirk, *A Statement of Facts Concerning the Riot*, 8–9; *Contested Election Case*, 364.

52. Cronly, "Account of the Race Riot."

53. Harry Hayden and others claimed that Hugh MacRae of the Secret Nine called the mass meeting, presumably to address the issue of Alexander Manly and to pacify hotheaded Red Shirts who had been prepared to burn the *Daily Record*'s press office on the evening of the election. Several sources indicate that the mass meeting was scheduled somewhat ahead of time by someone not a member of the official Democratic Party campaign committee. Hayden stated that on the afternoon of the election, Mike Dowling and the Red Shirts were making preparations to burn the *Daily Record*'s office and lynch Manly. While on the way to Manly's office, Dowling met MacRae, who persuaded him to stop his men so as not to jeopardize the election. MacRae and Dowling met at L. B. Sasser's drugstore. Sasser, himself a member of the Secret Nine, helped MacRae convince the Red Shirts to desist and in return revealed to Dowling one of the machinations of the Secret Nine—a document the group had drawn up that has come to be known as the "White Declaration of Independence." The Declaration was to have been read in public the following day at a meeting McRae called to pacify Dowling. The *Morning Star* included a notice that summoned "every good white citizen" to the meeting, which the paper claimed to have been called in response to another meeting held the previous night by a group of "representative businessmen of the city." *Wilmington Messenger*, November 9, 1898;

Harry Hayden, *The Story of the Wilmington Rebellion* (Wilmington: The Author, 1936), 6–9; Prather, *We Have Taken a City*, 107; *Morning Star*, November 9, 1898.

54. Rountree recalled that he had stayed up almost all night on election day and that on the morning of the ninth he was at home "sleeping the sleep of the just when my wife came in about nine o'clock and showed me an advertisement in the paper that stated that there would be a public meeting" that he had not known was planned. Rountree, "My Personal Recollection of the Election of 1898."

55. *Contested Election Case*, 257.

56. Bellamy later claimed that in his remarks at the courthouse, he "approved of the desire to rid the community of such a venomous reptile" but urged that they "act with moderation and proceed lawfully and in order." *Contested Election Case*, 257.

57. Roger Moore's widow confirmed that Waddell knew nothing of the scheme hatched by the business leaders. Mrs. Roger Moore Collection, Special Collections Department, Randall Library, University of North Carolina Wilmington.

58. Reporters representing the Chicago *Record*, the Washington *Star*, the Charleston (S.C.) *News and Courier*, the *Wilmington Messenger*, and the Wilmington *Morning Star* acted as secretaries. *Morning Star*, November 10, 1898.

59. *Wilmington Messenger*, November 10, 1898; *Morning Star*, November 10, 1898.

60. Manning's statement suggests that he and others were confident that the new Democratically controlled legislature would reverse Fusionist changes to the city's charter. *Wilmington Messenger*, November 10, 1898; *Morning Star*, November 10, 1898.

61. *Wilmington Messenger*, November 10, 1898; *Morning Star*, November 10, 1898; Rountree, "My Personal Recollection of the Election of 1898."

62. Members of the Committee of Twenty-five were: Preston L. Bridgers, John E. Crow, Joseph R. Davis, Junius Davis, James Ellis, F. H. Fechtig, Dr. W. C. Galloway, Rev. J. W. S. Harvey, Gabe Holmes, B. Frank King, Rev. J. W. Kramer, E. S. Lathrop, Hugh MacRae, Frank Maunder, Iredell Meares, F. A. Montgomery, W. H. Northrop Sr., W. F. Robertson, A. B. Skelding, Fred Skipper, Joseph D. Smith, C. L. Spencer, Frank Stedman, J. Allan Taylor, and C. W. Worth. Rountree was taken aback that Waddell purposefully left him off the list. Three members of the committee also held membership in the Secret Nine. *Wilmington Messenger*, November 10, 1898; *Morning Star*, November 10, 1898; Rountree, "My Personal Recollection of the Election of 1898."

63. John V. B. Metts to an unidentified recipient, November 9, 1898, Hinsdale Family Papers.

64. James Worth to Josephine, November 9, 1898, James Spencer Worth Papers, Southern Historical Collection.

65. Members of the Committee of Colored Citizens (CCC) were Dr. J. H. Alston, Richard Ashe, Salem J. Bell, Henry Brown, John H. Brown, John Carroll, John Goins, Elijah Green, Henry Green, Henry C. Green, James P. Green, Josh Green, William Everett Henderson, John Holloway, Daniel Howard, John Harriss Howe, John T. Howe, David Jacobs, David R. Jones, Rev. I. S. Lee (of St. Stephen's AME Church), J. W. Lee, Alex Mallett, Dr. Thomas R. Mask, Thomas C. Miller, William A. Moore, Carter Peamon, James Pearson, Robert B. Pickens, Isham Quick, Robert Reardon, Thomas Rivera, Frederick Sadgwar, Armond Scott, and Rev. James W. Telfair. A handwritten copy of the list of men identified as the CCC, including check marks to denote those who had been contacted, and some with an "x" by their name, is in the Alfred M. Waddell Papers at the Southern Historical Collection. Because of the fear of federal intervention, high-ranking federal appointees such as John C. Dancy and John E. Taylor, although prominent leaders of the African American community, were not among those named as members of the CCC. *Wilmington Messenger*, November 10, 1898; *Morning Star*, November 10, 1898; Alfred M. Waddell Papers, Southern Historical Collection.

66. *Wilmington Messenger*, November 10, 1898; *Morning Star*, November 10, 1898; Waddell Papers.

67. Hayden's *Story of the Wilmington Rebellion* (p. 13) indicates that the two committees met at the Cape Fear Club on Front Street at 6:00 P.M. on November 9. (Hayden's booklet has the date wrong.)

68. Confusion as to whether Manly had already departed the city was evident both in the white and black communities.

69. In a pre-approved plan, Waddell arranged to meet with the Committee of Twenty-five at the armory at eight o'clock on the morning of November 10 to provide them with the details of the CCC response. McDuffie, "Politics in Wilmington," 684; Hayden, *The Story of the Wilmington Rebellion*, 13.

70. In his doctoral dissertation, McDuffie relied upon a sketch by Armond Scott titled "Up From Hell" (which was in the possession of Scott's widow in Washington, D.C.) for information on Scott's role in delivering the CCC letter, as well as details relating to the CCC. McDuffie, "Politics in Wilmington," 686; Rountree, "My Personal Recollection of the Election of 1898."

219

71. McDuffie, "Politics in Wilmington," 686; Rountree, "My Personal Recollection of the Election of 1898."

72. *Wilmington Messenger*, November 10, 1898.

73. The new pastor of the First Baptist Church, a Reverend Blackwell, was a hearty supporter of the white supremacy campaign. In the wake of the violence of November 10, the Raleigh *News and Observer* quoted his views on the subject. Additional information on the clandestine meeting was apparently found in P. B. Manning's letter to E. S. Tennet, originally included in the Louis T. Moore Local History Collection at the New Hanover County Public Library. As mentioned previously, the letter has disappeared, and references to the meeting and its plans as detailed in the missive can be found in McDuffie, "Politics in Wilmington," 687. *News and Observer*, November 15, 1898.

74. Harry Hayden, "The Wilmington Light Infantry" (typed, unpublished memoir), New Hanover County Public Library, Wilmington, 70–120; Hayden, *The Story of the Wilmington Rebellion*, 1–36.

75. James Worth to Josephine, November 9, 1898, Worth Papers.

Chapter 5: November 10: "Hell Jolted Loose"

1. E. Y. Wootten to "Edward," November 8, 1898, Bradley Jewett Wootten Papers, Special Collections Department, Randall Library, University of North Carolina Wilmington.

2. *Wilmington Messenger*, November 15, 1898.

3. According to one theory of group aggression, a series of triggering factors is necessary to facilitate a riot. In his book *The Psychology of Group Aggression* (Sussex, England: John Wiley and Sons, 2002), psychologist Arnold Goldstein explains theories developed by other experts and brings together examples of group aggression from throughout history. The post-election mass meeting in Wilmington on November 9 clearly fits the model Goldstein formulated and was a precipitating event that led to the riot on the following day. While Goldstein did not specifically study the Wilmington riot, many of the theories he advances are directly applicable to the development in the port city of an environment that facilitated the rise of violence on November 10, 1898.

4. Jerome McDuffie, "Politics in Wilmington and New Hanover County, North Carolina, 1865–1900: The Genesis of a Race Riot" (Ph.D. diss., Kent State University, 1979), 693; George Rountree, "Memorandum of My Personal Recollection of the Election of 1898," n.d., Henry G. Connor Papers, Southern Historical Collection, Wilson Library, University of North Carolina at Chapel Hill, Chapel Hill (hereafter cited as Rountree, "My Personal Recollection of the Election of 1898.")

5. The armory building, originally the home of John Allan Taylor, was constructed about 1847. The volunteer military organization acquired it for use as its headquarters and armory in 1892. Tony P. Wrenn, *Wilmington, North Carolina: An Architectural and Historical Portrait* (Charlottesville: University of Virginia Press, 1984), 223; *Wilmington Messenger*, November 11, 1898; McDuffie, "Politics in Wilmington," 694; Harry Hayden, *The Story of the Wilmington Rebellion* (Wilmington: The Author, 1936), 21.

6. Earlier in 1898 Gov. Daniel Russell had called up some members of the Wilmington Light Infantry (WLI) to serve on active duty in the Spanish-American War as part of Company K, 2nd North Carolina Volunteer Infantry. Those men had just returned home on furlough in late September after seeing no action on the battlefield. Capt. Donald MacRae fretted over the return of his troops to Wilmington in the midst of heated speeches and marches in support of white supremacy during the upcoming election. In a letter written from Raleigh on September 18, 1898, Captain MacRae warned Douglas Cronly, former captain of the WLI and member of Company K, that he had suggested to Capt. Thomas C. James of the WLI "in as delicate as way as possible that it would be advisable to 'water' any stimulants which may be provided for the boys" during the festivities to mark their return home. MacRae's worries were well founded: many North Carolina soldiers who returned to Raleigh at the war's end had found themselves in drunken brawls and shoot-outs with black citizens of the capital city. Josephus Daniels and the Democratic Party had circulated copies of the Raleigh *News and Observer* among the troops while they were stationed in Florida, so the returning men were aware of the white-supremacy campaign.

Members of Commander George Morton's naval militia likewise returned to Wilmington in the fall of 1898. The naval militia crew represented a wider spectrum of Wilmington's population than did the roster of the WLI. The men came from both the upper classes of society and the lower, laboring classes, including a small number of African Americans. Members of the naval militia experienced an even more limited participation in the war than did the WLI forces. Their ship, the *Nantucket*, limped into Port Royal, South Carolina, and did not depart for the duration of the war, serving instead as a defense and training vessel in that port. Once the *Nantucket*'s flag was lowered in August, the crew disbanded, returned to Wilmington without their ship, and mustered out of service in September. Adjutant General's Office, *Roster of North Carolina Volunteers in the Spanish-American War*,

1898–1899 (Raleigh: Edwards and Broughton and E. M. Uzzell, State Printers, 1900), 45–48; MacRae to Cronly, September 18, 1898, Cronly Family Papers, Rare Book, Manuscript, and Special Collections Library, Duke University, Durham; Josephus Daniels, *Editor in Politics* (Chapel Hill: University of North Carolina Press, 1941), 277, 280 281; William Lord deRosset, *Pictorial and Historical New Hanover County and Wilmington, North Carolina, 1723–1938* (Wilmington: The Author, 1938), [88–89] Catherine McLaurin to Sallie McLaurin, November 9, 1898, Eccles Family Papers, Southern Historical Collection.

7. Harry Hayden recalled that after the first shots were fired, the "Red Shirts began to ride and the Negroes began to run!" Harry Hayden, "The Wilmington Light Infantry" (typed, unpublished memoir), New Hanover County Public Library, Wilmington, 92; James H. Cowan, "The Wilmington Race Riot" (undated, unpublished memoir), Louis T. Moore Local History Collection, New Hanover County Public Library; Mrs. Roger Moore, letter to the editor of the *Wilmington Messenger*, n.d., Accession No. 130, Mrs. Roger Moore Collection, University of North Carolina Wilmington Special Collections; J. R. Kennedy, "Colonel Moore Recalled," *Morning Star* (Wilmington), November 24, 1936.

8. Hayden, *The Story of the Wilmington Rebellion*, 21; McDuffie, "Politics in Wilmington," 693–694; Cowan, "The Wilmington Race Riot." Accounts of Moore's position vary; McDuffie claims he was at the corner of Fifth and Chestnut streets; F. A. Lord, a white participant, recalled that Moore was stationed at the jail. F. A. Lord to Louis T. Moore, 1936, Louis T. Moore Local History Collection, New Hanover County Public Library.

9. Taylor, at a meeting of riot "veterans" in 1905, recalled that "I got a telephone message that a crowd was at the Armory and wanted the military to lead them up to the Record Office and as I was Post Commander at that time and my duty would have been to disband them, I did not go down until Capt. James telephoned me that they had all gone and then I went down and Capt. James and I went over the situation" and then sent a telegram to the governor. Minutes of the Organizational Meeting of the Association of Members of the Wilmington Light Infantry, December 14, 1905, North Carolina Collection, Wilson Library, University of North Carolina at Chapel Hill (hereafter cited as Minutes of the Organizational Meeting of the WLI).

10. The men reportedly formed themselves into columns in accordance with military drills, and by the time their formation was complete they presented a formidable front, twelve men across for two blocks. There are contradictions regarding Bellamy's participation. An unsigned letter to President William McKinley from an African American resident of Wilmington claimed that Bellamy was at the head of the march, but Bellamy's testimony in court contradicts that statement: "Question: Mr. Bellamy, were you present at any time during the destruction, or any part of the destruction, of the Manly printing office and printing press? Answer: I was not present; I was not even in the crowd that went there; I don't know who went there, except upon information, and had nothing to do with it, and have never seen the building, as I recall, either prior to or since the destruction." Further, Bellamy contended on another occasion that he was out of town at the time. *Contested Election Case of Oliver H. Dockery vs. John D. Bellamy from the Sixth Congressional District of the State of North Carolina* (Washington, D.C.: Government Printing Office, 1899), 249 (hereafter cited as *Contested Election Case*); unsigned letter to President William McKinley, November 13, 1898, General Records of the Department of Justice, Record Group 60, National Archives, Washington, D.C.; John D. Bellamy, *Memoirs of an Octogenarian* (Charlotte: Observer Printing House, 1942), 133–134; Hayden, "The Wilmington Light Infantry," 85; *Wilmington Messenger*, November 11, 1898; Hayden, *The Story of the Wilmington Rebellion*, 22.

11. Taylor to Russell, November 10, 1898, Daniel L. Russell, Governors' Papers, State Archives, North Carolina Office of Archives and History, Raleigh.

12. John V. B. Metts to "Miss Elizabeth," November 12, 1898, Hinsdale Family Papers, Duke Special Collections.

13. Minutes of the Organizational Meeting of the WLI.

14. William Parsley to Sal [McLaurin], n.d., Eccles Family Papers.

15. The hall, which Harry Hayden also called "Free Love Lodge," was operated by the Grand United Order of Love and Charity, an association formed in 1878 to provide help for the poor, sick, and indigent through its association with St. Luke's AME Church. It had been constructed in 1897. After Manly had been evicted in August 1898 from the rented downtown property occupied by the *Daily Record*, he moved the paper's office and printing press to Love and Charity Hall. After the hall was destroyed during the November rioting, contributions from the white community reimbursed the Grand United Order for its losses; construction commenced on a new hall in April 1899. Hayumi Higuchi, unpublished map of Wilmington in 1897; *Contested Election Case*, 364; William M. Reaves, *"Strength through Struggle": The Chronological and Historical Record of the African-American Community in Wilmington, North*

221

Carolina, 1865–1950, ed. Beverly Tetterton (Wilmington: New Hanover County Public Library, 1998), 17–18.

16. *Evening Dispatch* (Wilmington), August 25, 1898; F. A. Lord to Louis T. Moore, August 8, 1936, Louis T. Moore Local History Collection, New Hanover County Public Library.

17. Thomas W. Clawson, "The Wilmington Race Riot in 1898, Recollections and Memories" (unpublished memoir), Louis T. Moore Collection, Private Collections, State Archives. One report had it that a black man near the door failed to move out of the way fast enough and was shot in the neck. This is the only recorded instance of this man's being shot. McDuffie, "Politics in Wilmington," 695–696.

18. H. Leon Prather Sr., *We Have Taken a City: Wilmington Massacre and Coup of 1898* (Rutherford, N.J.: Fairleigh Dickinson University Press, 1984), 113.

19. Hayden, "The Wilmington Light Infantry," 85; *Evening Dispatch*, November 10, 1898.

20. Harry Hayden later recalled that "a mob, no matter how well disciplined, is no stronger than its weakest link." Hayden, *The Story of the Wilmington Rebellion*, 15.

21. Henry West, "The Race War in North Carolina," *The Forum* 26 (January 1899): 583–584.

22. Hayden, "The Wilmington Light Infantry," 86; Prather, *We Have Taken a City*, 113. These men were part of the Cape Fear Steam Fire Engine Company No. 3, an all-black fire station. The company was organized in 1871 and was the first all-black steam fire engine company in the United States. Both Schnibben and Savage were possibly members of the Red Shirts and the White Government Union. Reaves, *"Strength through Struggle,"* 186–192.

23. *Evening Dispatch*, November 10, 1898.

24. Hayden, *The Story of the Wilmington Rebellion*, 15.

25. West, "The Race War in North Carolina," 585.

26. Several witnesses in the *Contested Election Case* recalled seeing smoke and hearing the fire bells. Wilmington resident Jane Cronly remembered hearing the shouts and fire bells. *Evening Dispatch*, November 10, 1898; Jane Cronly, "Account of the Race Riot" (unpublished memoir, n.d.), Cronly Family Papers, Duke Special Collections.

27. McDuffie, "Politics in Wilmington," 697; Hayden, "The Wilmington Light Infantry," 86.

28. In 1879 Wilmington and Raleigh were the first two cities in North Carolina to establish telephone exchanges. Initially, access to telephones was limited to businesses and leading businessmen. The 1897 Wilmington city directory provides the telephone numbers of fifty-three patrons of the Southern Bell Telephone and Telegraph Company and twenty-seven customers of the Interstate Telephone and Telegraph Company. Patrons included many men central to the riot: Hardy Fennell, Iredell Meares, Col. Roger Moore, Robert Orrell, Charles Schnibben, Walker Taylor, and James Woolvin. Andrew Howell, *The Book of Wilmington* (Wilmington: The Author, 1930), 162; *J. L. Hill Printing Co.'s Directory of Wilmington, N.C. 1897* (Richmond, Va: J. L. Hill Printing Company, 1897; hereafter cited as *Hill's 1897 Wilmington City Directory*); Cronly, "Account of the Race Riot."

29. Many of the letters and accounts cited in this report include references to exhaustion on the part of the participants, who were frequently awakened for patrol duty and to assemble to counter threats by armed blacks that never materialized. Collections containing such letters include the Cronly Family Papers and the Hinsdale Family Papers, Duke Special Collections; the James Spencer Worth Papers and the Eccles Family Papers, Southern Historical Collection; the Bradley Jewett Wootten Papers, University of North Carolina Wilmington Special Collections; and the Louis T. Moore Local History Collection, New Hanover County Public Library. E. Y. Wootten to "Edward," November 8, 1898, Wootten Papers.

30. Brooklyn has historically been considered the African American section of Wilmington. Documents relating to the violence of November 10 indicate that Brooklyn "began" at the Fourth Street Bridge. Research using the city directory and maps generated by graduate student Hayumi Higuchi reveals that the area around Fourth and Harnett streets was a mixed-race neighborhood with a nearly 50-50 mix of whites and blacks. The white men identified as the first to exchange gunfire with blacks in the Brooklyn neighborhood were actually residents of the area.

31. Rountree, "My Personal Recollection of the Election of 1898"; "Story of the Wilmington Riot, A Pure Bred Negro Relates It," *Charlotte Daily Observer*, May 24, 1905.

32. Cowan, "The Wilmington Race Riot."

33. McDuffie, "Politics in Wilmington," 709.

34. "Story of the Wilmington Riot."

35. Cowan, "The Wilmington Race Riot."

36. Minutes of the Organizational Meeting of the WLI.

37. Ibid.

38. Chadbourn had previously supported the Republican Party wholeheartedly, being appointed to the police board under the Republican administration of

Silas P Wright and postmaster for the city. However, under immense pressure from local Democrats in Wilmington, Chadbourn publicly recanted his support of the Republican Party and pledged himself to "white rule." Prather, *We Have Taken a City*, 62–65; Rountree, "My Personal Recollection of the Election of 1898."

39. Thomas Rivera, an African American citizen of Wilmington at the time of the riot, related to historian Helen G. Edmonds that Sprunt, in an attempt to protect his workers, had his private yacht brought around so that the vessel's guns could be aimed at the armed whites while the compress doors were barricaded to keep his workers safely inside. Sprunt could very well have had guns aboard his yacht: in April 1898, just after war was declared on Spain, the U.S. Navy compiled a list of Cape Fear steamers and drew up instructions for equipping those steamers with one- and six-pound cannons. McDuffie, "Politics in Wilmington," 709; Rountree, "My Personal Recollection of the Election of 1898"; Helen G. Edmonds, *The Negro and Fusion Politics in North Carolina, 1894–1901* (Chapel Hill: University of North Carolina Press, 1951), 169; "Story of the Wilmington Riot"; Alan D. Watson, *Wilmington, Port of North Carolina* (Columbia: University of South Carolina Press, 1992), 128.

40. *Wilmington Messenger*, November 11, 1898.

41. Prather, *We Have Taken a City*, 122.

42. Among the men on the streetcar was Sam Matthews, armed with a navy rifle, even though he was not an active member of the naval militia. Hayden, "The Wilmington Light Infantry," 91. A roster of the crew of the *Nantucket* appears in deRosset, *Pictorial and Historical New Hanover County*, [89].

43. Hayden, "The Wilmington Light Infantry," 88.

44. Just before the election, the Wilmington Board of Aldermen had instituted a ban on the sale of alcoholic beverages to last until 6:00 A.M. on November 10. After the riot began, the board met again at 12:50 P.M. at Alderman Charles D. Morrell's home at 210 North Sixth Street to extend the ban. Aaron Lockamy's post was probably at Boesch's grocery at 319 Brunswick Street, some two blocks away from the site of the first shots. White men who shot at the blacks near the intersection were Theodore Curtis, Sam Matthews, George Piner, and S. Hill Terry. *Contested Election Case*, 341–343; Prather, *We Have Taken a City*, 119; *Evening Dispatch*, November 10, 1898; *Morning Star*, November 11, 1898; *Wilmington Messenger*, November 11, 1898; Minutes of the Wilmington Board of Aldermen, 1884–1906 (microfilm), State Archives; *Hill's 1897 Wilmington City Directory*; Hayden, *The Story of the Wilmington Rebellion*, 24–26.

45. *Wilmington Messenger*, November 11, 1898; *Contested Election Case*, 341–342. See endnote 58 for the text of the affidavit taken by Rountree.

46. Clawson, "The Wilmington Race Riot in 1898."

47. *Wilmington Messenger*, November 11, 1898; *Morning Star*, November 11, 1898; Hayden, "The Wilmington Light Infantry," 88–89, 91; McDuffie "Politics in Wilmington," 741; H. Leon Prather, "We Have Taken a City: A Centennial Essay," in David S. Cecelski and Timothy B. Tyson, eds., *Democracy Betrayed: The Wilmington Race Riot of 1898 and Its Legacy* (Chapel Hill: University of North Carolina Press, 1998), 32.

48. Prather, *We Have Taken a City*, 118–119; Minutes of the Organizational Meeting of the WLI.

49. McDuffie, "Politics in Wilmington," 719.

50. Telegram, Russell to Taylor, November 10, 1898, Daniel L. Russell, Governors' Papers, State Archives.

51. *Annual Report of the Adjutant-General of the State of North Carolina for the Year 1899*, North Carolina Public Documents, Document 9, State Archives.

52. The wounding of Mayo became a symbolic rallying point for the white men. A .44 caliber Winchester bullet hit Mayo and went through his left side and both lungs before exiting his body. Numerous accounts of the riot by white people declared that Mayo had been standing on his porch at the time of the shooting and that he was shot as his assailant ran down the street. It is unclear whether or not Mayo was part of the crowd that had just returned from burning the *Daily Record* office, was a member of the Citizens' Patrol, or was armed at the time he was shot. It is likewise unclear exactly who shot him. There is even some speculation that perhaps Mayo was shot in an incidence of "friendly fire" that may have occurred while whites were shooting at blacks running in his general direction. William F. Jones, a streetcar driver, conveyed Mayo to Moore's Drug Store, where Dr. Schonwald stopped the bleeding; a group of young boys and their ambulances stationed at Cowan's Livery Stable then transported Mayo to the hospital. Rev. Christopher C. Dennen of St. Thomas the Apostle Catholic Church administered last rites to Mayo while on the way to the hospital just in case he did not survive his wound. *Wilmington Messenger*, November 11, 1898; Hayden, "The Wilmington Light Infantry," 88, 90–91.

53. Chadwick was wounded with a .44 caliber bullet that passed though the muscle in his left arm without breaking the arm, and Piner was shot with a .44 caliber bullet that entered his abdomen on the left side and exited on the right. Another interpretation of the Mayo shooting had Wright near the intersection of Fourth and Harnett as he shot Mayo, who was actually a block away at Third and Harnett instead of on his porch. This account also has it

that, after shooting Mayo, Wright "wheeled around" and shot George Piner, who was standing at the intersection of Bladen and Fourth streets. Hayden, "The Wilmington Light Infantry," 91; *Wilmington Messenger*, November 11, 1898; *Evening Dispatch*, November 10, 1898; Hayden, *The Story of the Wilmington Rebellion*, 26.

54. Hayden, "The Wilmington Light Infantry," 90.

55. Minutes of the Organizational Meeting of the WLI.

56. H. Leon Prather Sr., relying upon Helen G. Edmonds's interview with Thomas Rivera, stated that Terry and Bland were killed. However, the 1900 census has Hill Terry, a member of the WLI, serving as deputy sheriff and residing at 815 North Fourth Street. George Bland, age twenty-five, according to the 1900 census, was Terry's son-in-law, lived with Terry, and worked as a liveryman. The 1880 census lists Hill Terry as having a son, Will, age twelve, but Will is not found in the 1900 census. It is unknown whether Will Terry was involved and possibly killed by Wright. A later account of the fighting noted that S. Hill Terry hanged himself while in jail awaiting trial for murdering his son-in-law. In a letter dated November 12, 1898, John V. B. Metts recounted his version of the event: "The negro who shot our white man very nearly killing him was sought and got on his knees begging for mercy, saying he had five little children home—but the crowd of citizens who had him said go and he hadn't gone ten feet before the top of his head was cut off by bullets. It was a horrible sight." This account includes elements related to Wright as Mayo's assailant, as well as to another man, Josh Halsey, who was killed in action around Manhattan Park. Metts to "Miss Elizabeth," November 12, 1898, Hinsdale Family Papers; Hayden, *The Story of the Wilmington Rebellion*, 24–26.

57. Minutes of the Organizational Meeting of the WLI; *Wilmington Messenger*, November 11, 12, 1898; Edmonds, *The Negro and Fusion Politics*, 169; Prather, *We Have Taken a City*, 125, 129.

58. The text of William McAllister's affidavit reads:

I, William McAllister, being duly sworn, make the following affidavit: 1. That I am yard master for the Atlantic Coast Line. My duty is to make up trains on the yard of the said company in the city of Wilmington. 2. That at about 11 o'clock this morning I started to go to bed, and my wife called me to the window. I live on North Fourth Street, next to St. Mark's Lutheran church. My wife said: "Billy, there is going to be trouble." I jumped up and went to the window and saw a white man remonstrating with a negro with gesticulations. I heard the white man say, "Go on, go on." The negro went about ten paces, and then I saw the negro shoot. He pointed a pistol towards the white man and then fired. Immediately I saw blood flow from the said white man's right arm. Then there was another shot

fired from the negro assemblage, and then there was firing from the white assemblage, with the result that three negroes fell. The negroes then dispersed. Then the white men proceeded towards Moore's drug store to telephone for assistance. Sworn to before me, this 10th day of November, AD 1898 William McAllister. Notarized by J. H. Boatwright.

News and Observer (Raleigh), November 11, 1898.

59. Rountree, "My Personal Recollection of the Election of 1898."

60. Minutes of the Organizational Meeting of the WLI. The WLI must have stopped in front of James Woolvin's funeral parlor at 105 North Third. James D. Nutt recalled that Woolvin "turned white as a ghost, except for his hair which was still red" when the WLI stopped in front of his establishment.

61. Minutes of the Organizational Meeting of the WLI.

62. John V. B. Metts to "Miss Elizabeth," November 12, 1898, Hinsdale Family Papers.

63. James H. Cowan, in his typed, unpublished memoir of the riot, wrote that Col. Roger Moore was in control of the armed men of Wilmington until Col. Walker Taylor and the military were activated. Moore turned "control" of his men over to Taylor at that time. Cowan, "The Wilmington Race Riot"; Prather, "We Have Taken a City: A Centennial Essay," 33.

64. *Wilmington Messenger*, November 11, 1898.

65. Speculation has arisen that the man found under Mrs. Strauss's house at 1012 North Fourth Street was either Sam McFarland, Sam Gregory, or John L. Gregory. The *Morning Star* reported that "Sam McFallon" was found under the house and taken to the hospital on November 11 but was expected to die. No McFallon can be found in *Hill's 1897 Wilmington City Directory*, although two black laborers—Samuel McFarlan of 1014 North Second and Samuel McFarland of 512 Taylor Street—are listed in that source (but not in its 1900 counterpart). John L. Gregory, a black laborer who lived at 1301 North Fifth Street, can be found in the 1897 but not the 1900 directory. Perhaps the man who died was one of those men.

Sam McFarland's death was well documented in the newspapers. He was shot on the Seaboard Air Line tracks where they crossed Harnett Street and was taken to the hospital. The *Messenger* devoted extensive coverage to McFarland's wounding, detailing his transport to the hospital, his death, his employer, his address, and that he left a widow. Sam Gregory's death is widely described as the first one to result from the shooting at Fourth and Harnett, with the *Messenger* and the *Dispatch* agreeing on his name and location of death. John Gregory's death is reported in the *Messenger*, and he and other men were subjects of a November 12 inquest; the *Messenger* gives the location of his death as Third Street between Harnett and Swann. *Wilmington Messenger*, November 12-14, 1898; *Morning Star*, November 12, 1898; *Evening Dispatch*, November 11, 1898.

66. *Wilmington Messenger*, November 13, 1898.

67. Clawson, "The Wilmington Race Riot in 1898."

68. On November 1—a week before the election—the machine gun purchased by the businessmen was taken out on the Cape Fear River and demonstrated for black leaders as an intimidating measure. Testimony from retired Confederate artillery colonel John W. Atkinson conflicts with that of Charles H. White, a member of the machine gun squadron, as to the type of rapid-fire gun used by the WLI. Atkinson said he thought the gun was a Gatling that was a "very rapid firing gun," whereas White recalled the weapon was a Colt that could fire 420 shots per minute. *Contested Election Case*, 267, 344; Clawson, "The Wilmington Race Riot in 1898."

69. Several of the men on the machine gun squad were members of Company K. Hayden, "The Wilmington Light Infantry," 90; Clawson, "The Wilmington Race Riot in 1898."

70. In his history of the WLI, Hayden twice recounted the shooting of twenty-five men at the intersection, marking through his words once and replacing them at a different location in the text. Hayden also stated that the machine gunners shot and killed only one man at Sixth and Brunswick streets. From various accounts of the activities of the machine gun squad and the Red Shirts, it is possible that the gunners did kill only one man at that intersection and that the Red Shirts, rather than the gun squad, killed or possibly wounded the other twenty-four in the vicinity of the intersection. It is noteworthy, though, that Hayden twice felt the need to write that the machine gunners killed twenty-five men at that spot. Hayden, "The Wilmington Light Infantry," 89-92.

71. *Freeman* (Indianapolis, Ind.), December 3, 1898.

72. Hayden, "The Wilmington Light Infantry," 89-92; Clawson, "The Wilmington Race Riot in 1898."

73. Still another high-profile weapon, a Gatling gun purchased by the Secret Nine, was put under the control of Capt. Harry McIlhenny. *Wilmington Messenger*, November 8, 1898; Hayden, *The Story of the Wilmington Rebellion*, 30.

74. Most of the men involved at the time the first shots were fired were those who lived in the transitional neighborhoods that divided the white and black citizenry in Brooklyn; the others who made their way there soon afterward were outsiders from other parts of town or members of the WLI or other paramilitary organizations. S. Hill Terry resided at 815 North Fourth Street,

Theodore Curtis boarded at 712 North Fourth Street, and Sam Matthews lived at 917 North Fourth Street. *Hill's 1897 Wilmington City Directory*; Higuchi, unpublished map of Wilmington in 1897.

75. Clawson, "The Wilmington Race Riot in 1898."

76. Minutes of the Organizational Meeting of the WLI; J. Allen Kirk, *A Statement of Facts Concerning the Bloody Riot in Wilmington, N.C., of Interest to Every Citizen of the United States* ([Wilmington?: The Author?, 1898?]), 11; online edition available at http://docsouth.unc.edu/nc/kirk/menu.html.

77. There is confusion among contemporary accounts, as well as those given by participants years afterward, but it appears that at least one man, Josh Halsey, lost his life as a result of fighting at Manhattan Park, although some accounts indicate that an unnamed man *and* Halsey died at the scene. For additional information on the events at Manhattan Park, see Clawson, "The Wilmington Race Riot in 1898"; *Wilmington Messenger*, November 11-14, 1898; Minutes of the Organizational Meeting of the WLI; Hayden, "The Wilmington Light Infantry," 92, 94; Cronly, "Account of the Race Riot"; *Evening Dispatch*, November 11, 1898; *Morning Star*, November 12, 13, 16, 1898; Prather, *We Have Taken a City*, 124-125; McDuffie, "Politics in Wilmington," 716. Thalia Howe, a member of Wilmington's black elite, witnessed a similar event from her home when a black man was shot in the street, his head ripped apart by the gunfire. Ms. Howe's recollections were passed to subsequent generations and provided to the author by Howe descendant Cynthia J. Brown in July 2004. See also endnote 56, which quotes a letter from Metts regarding the shooting of either Wright or Halsey.

78. Adams, Jones, and Lee, members of the civilian organization under Hugh MacRae and J. Allan Taylor, were on the northeast corner of Sixth and Bladen streets when shots were fired in their direction from Manhattan Park. In response, they forced black ministers to accompany them throughout Brooklyn as they ordered black citizens to remain in their homes or in the woods before nightfall. Col. William C. Jones was a former captain of the WLI, and Sterling P. Adams was an assistant engineer for the Atlantic Coast Line Railroad. *Wilmington Messenger*, November 11, 1898; McDuffie, "Politics in Wilmington," 719.

79. There is some confusion in the sources as to the number and names of the men arrested at the dance hall. Taylor's report to the state adjutant general indicated that four men were arrested. The *Wilmington Messenger* reported that six men—Wisconsin Edwards, James Hill, S. T. Knight, Tom Lane, Henry Nichols, and William Tate—were arrested at the scene. They were later released on the sixteenth inasmuch as there was no evidence

against them. *Annual Report of the Adjutant-General of the State of North Carolina for the Year 1899*; *Wilmington Messenger*, November 11, 1898; *Morning Star*, November 16, 1898.

80. Minutes of the Organizational Meeting of the WLI; *Contested Election Case*, 344; image of Manhattan Park in Hayden, "The Wilmington Light Infantry"; Prather, *We Have Taken a City*, 124.

81. Minutes of the Organizational Meeting of the WLI.

82. Prather, *We Have Taken a City*, 124; *Annual Report of the Adjutant-General of the State of North Carolina for the Year 1899*; Alfred Moore Waddell, "The Story of the Wilmington, N.C. Race Riot," *Collier's Weekly* 22 (November 26, 1898): 4–5.

83. Jane Cronly's account of Halsey's shooting indicates that Halsey ran home in fright and then fled from his home via the back door because his daughter begged him to run for his life from the approaching soldiers, who then shot him "down like a dog" as he ran. Maunder's account, in the WLI Association minutes, indicates that Halsey was given the opportunity to "run the gauntlet" and was shot at by the squad. He was killed immediately. Cronly, "Account of the Race Riot"; Minutes of the Organizational Meeting of the WLI; Prather, *We Have Taken a City*, 124–125.

84. Another man, Thomas Lane, was arrested and, following a trial on November 16, found guilty of shooting at the WLI during the activity at Manhattan Park. The *Morning Star* observed that if Lane had not "fired into the military it would not have been necessary for them to have shot Josh Halsey, the negro inmate of the place who was killed as a sequel to Lane's fiendish effort to kill one of the members of the Light Infantry." Maunder, a clerk with M. W. Divine Company, a sash, blind, and paint dealer, lived at 624 North Fourth Street, a predominantly white neighborhood in Brooklyn near the transition between majority white and black sections. Minutes of the Organizational Meeting of the WLI; *Morning Star*, November 16, 1898; Higuchi, unpublished map of Wilmington in 1897; *Hill's 1897 Wilmington City Directory*.

85. Harry Hayden provided accounts of shootings that have not been corroborated by other sources. Perhaps that is because he sought interviews with participants whose recollections went unreported in newspaper accounts or in the recollections by members of the WLI's association.

86. Hayden, "The Wilmington Light Infantry," 92.

87. Hayden indicated that a deaf man was shot for failure to stop because he did not hear the command to halt. Hayden, "The Wilmington Light Infantry," 92; see also *Wilmington Messenger*, November 11–15, 1898.

88. William Parsley to "Sal," November 12, 1898, Eccles Family Papers.

89. The reference is the only record of this incident. The only Perkins listed in *Hill's 1897 City Directory* is Dennis Perkins, a black shoemaker who lived at 617 South Second Street. Perkins can be found in the 1900 census as residing at the same location and still working as a shoemaker. If this is the same man, he could have been appointed a special policeman during the pre-election Red Shirt parades but somehow managed to survive the riot and continued to live in a predominantly white neighborhood in the dwelling he owned. Perhaps the Red Shirt so angry at Perkins had been arrested and later fined for his rowdy behavior in the days preceding the riot and wished to take his anger out on the policeman. This case presents a problem since the Red Shirt Hayden interviewed clearly believed he shot and killed Perkins. Nonetheless, the only Perkins that can be identified in the same area at the same time is clearly alive a year and a half after the riot, still living in a predominantly white neighborhood. Perhaps this is a caveat against accepting all of Hayden's writings without substantiation; and of course it is possible that the Perkins in question was not listed in the city directory. Hayden, "The Wilmington Light Infantry," 93; *Hill's 1897 Wilmington City Directory*; Twelfth Census of the United States, 1900: New Hanover County, North Carolina, Population Schedule, National Archives, Washington, D.C. (microfilm, State Archives); *Evening Dispatch*, November 3, 1898; Higuchi, unpublished map of Wilmington in 1897.

90. Hayden, "The Wilmington Light Infantry," 92; *Evening Dispatch*, November 11, 1898.

91. Prather, *We Have Taken a City*, 120; Hayden, "The Wilmington Light Infantry," 98–99; *Annual Report of the Adjutant-General of the State of North Carolina for the Year 1899*; *News and Observer*, November 11, 1898.

92. James Cowan wrote that "many negroes were frightened to the point of distraction with the turn of events [and] went to the woods near the city. They thought their lives were in jeopardy." John V. B. Metts declared that "the negroes are frightened out of their wits. Most of them have left town." Edward Wootten's mother wrote on November 21, 1898, that a friend's black laborer named Stephen had been fired for registering to vote, and then, after he was told of the dangers to his life, "left for parts unknown and is still there, nobody has seen him since." Cowan, "The Wilmington Race Riot"; John V. B. Metts to "Miss Elizabeth," November 12, 1898, Hinsdale Family Papers; E. Y. Wootten to "Edward," November 21, 1898, Wootten Papers.

93. Benjamin Keith wrote to Sen. Marion Butler on November 17 that "the poor negroes have been in the woods like so many cattle during all this bad weather."

Peter Mallett, a white Fayetteville merchant with close ties to Wilmington, recorded in his daybook on November 10, 1898, that there was "rain and some hail," along with his entry that "war commenced at Wilmington today . . . negroes suffer" and that it was "cloudy and cold" on the eleventh. The *Messenger* reported that it was "sufficiently cool . . . to cause suffering" and that the "approaching darkness and a threatening storm added to the dread and horror of the situation." Keith to Butler, November 17, 1898, Marion Butler Papers, Southern Historical Collection; daybook, Peter Mallett Papers, Southern Historical Collection; *Wilmington Messenger*, November 13, 14, 1898.

94. *News and Observer*, November 13, 1898; Haywood Newkirk, telephone conversation with author, March 31, 2006. A handful of black and white Newkirks are listed in the 1897 and 1900 Wilmington city directories and the 1900 census. Bryan Newkirk's will, dated April 2, 1863, lists his slaves by name. Some of the black Newkirks in the city directories and census bear those names. More research is needed to clarify the relationships between the white and black Newkirk residents of Wilmington, New Hanover County, and Pender County. Will of Bryan Newkirk April 2, 1863, Book D, pp. 128–130 (microfilm), New Hanover County Record of Wills, State Archives.

95. Historian Helen G. Edmonds interviewed longtime Wilmington African American resident Thomas Rivera on July 20, 1944, and Rivera's recollections can be found in her work. Rev. Charles S. Morris was a southerner by birth and experienced the terror of white-supremacy racism, but he probably was not living in Wilmington during the riot. The 1900 census reveals that Morris (who had been born in Kentucky), then age twenty-three, was residing in Middlesex, Massachusetts; his wife was born in South Carolina and their eleven-month-old son was born in Massachusetts. Preaching to the Boston audience, the Reverend Morris was expressing for northern African Americans the horrors of white supremacy in order to mobilize their political clout to push for federal intervention in the South. Kirk, *A Statement of Facts Concerning the Riot*, 10; Edmonds, *The Negro and Fusion Politics*, 168–169; Charles S. Morris, "The Wilmington Massacre," in *The Voice of Black America: Major Speeches by Negroes in the United States, 1797–1971*, ed. Philip S. Foner (New York: Simon and Schuster, 1972), 604–607.

96. In 1997, at the request of Chancellor James R. Leutze of University of North Carolina at Wilmington, the staff of the Office of Archives and History's Research Branch looked into several questions relating to the violence of 1898. The staff investigated the following topics: Was Wilmington in financial distress at the time of the riot, and, if so, was that problem unique to Wilmington? Was the local government corrupt? Was there a rise in Wilmington's crime rate prior to the riot? How many buildings or businesses were destroyed during the riot?

The staff found no conclusive evidence that the town's finances were in danger of default; indeed, local businesses were flourishing—although inland towns such as Raleigh, Charlotte, and Durham were then on the verge of prospering and surpassing Wilmington as the state's largest city and primary industrial giant. No conclusive evidence was found to prove corruption in the local government; on the contrary, the Fusion municipal government had developed a "meticulous and fair tax code." Review of criminal and court dockets suggested that there was a slight increase in larcenies, whereas other types of crime occurred at similar or lower frequencies than during the previous year; overall, the judicial system was in full operation, trying and jailing blacks and whites alike. As for the destruction of buildings, only Love and Charity Hall was documented as destroyed, although scores of homes, churches, and businesses belonging to African Americans and white Republicans were ransacked. 1898 Wilmington Race Riot Commission and LeRae Umfleet, *1898 Wilmington Race Riot Report* (online document) (Raleigh: Research Branch, Office of Archives and History, North Carolina Department of Cultural Resources, 2006; available online at http://www.history.ncdcr.gov/ 1898-wrrc/report/report.htm.

97. During the discussions regarding the amendment to the White Declaration of Independence, former mayor Fishblate had employed more direct language in calling for the entire city leadership to resign. However, attorneys such as Rountree and Hugh MacRae sought to soften the language and call only for resignations from the mayor and chief of police. At the meeting, Rountree had assured businessman Nathaniel Jacobi that the issue of the resignations of the other members of the board of aldermen "would be attended to." Rountree, "My Personal Recollection of the Election of 1898"; *Wilmington Messenger*, November 10, 1898.

98. Rountree, "My Personal Recollection of the Election of 1898"; *Evening Dispatch*, November 10, 1898.

99. *Contested Election Case*, 249.

100. McDuffie, "Politics in Wilmington," 698–699; *Wilmington Messenger*, November 17, 1898.

101. Bellamy later testified that the transition was "done decently and in order without any friction and under the advice of the most learned lawyers of the city." A few resignations were secured from aldermen after the meeting, and their replacements were similarly elected and sworn in. *Contested Election Case*, 20–21, 249; Benjamin F. Keith, *Memories* (Raleigh: Bynum Printing

Company, 1922), 112; Minutes of the Wilmington Board of Aldermen, 1884–1906, State Archives.

102. The new board consisted of C. H. Ganzer and Rev. J. W. Kramer from the First Ward, H. P. West and William H. Sprunt from the Second Ward, Hugh MacRae and J. Allan Taylor from the Third Ward, Charles W. Worth and Preston L. Bridgers from the Fourth Ward, and B. Frank King and A. B. Skelding from the Fifth Ward. Waddell's new board selected Edgar Parmele to replace Melton as chief of police and named M. F. Heiskel Gouverneur assistant chief of police. John J. Furlong, a member of the machine gun squad, was promoted to police captain. The *Evening Dispatch* of November 10, 1898, went to press while shots were still being fired and the coup was taking place. The paper threw its support behind Waddell for mayor: "In selecting a man for the chief executive of the city, let the committee not forget the services of our most tried and true citizen; the man who led the citizens this morning and avenged their honor; the man who will have good government and peace or blood—Alfred Moore Waddell."

The widow of Roger Moore later wrote that Waddell "was not present at any one of the meetings and knew nothing whatever of the plan of action until the night following his election as mayor, when he asked the leaders for information as it was necessary at that stage of the proceedings for him to be informed as from that time on he would be connected with the movement." She added that Waddell "was also made chairman of the committee of 20 [*sic*] men who were appointed to give the negroes a certain alternative concerning the Record printing press; and also he had charge of the impromptu affair at the armory, a thing not provided for; something unforeseen; and done on the spur of the moment. It was righteous [at] first, at least that part concerning the destruction of the printing press. Firing the building was considered to be a mistake and his being made mayor was something separate and distinct from the organization that was formed for the protection of the town." Hayden, "The Wilmington Light Infantry," 100; Rountree, "My Personal Recollection of the Election of 1898"; Cowan, "The Wilmington Race Riot"; *Wilmington Messenger*, November 10, 11, 1898; Mrs. Roger Moore Collection, University of North Carolina Wilmington Special Collections.

103. *Contested Election Case*, 20–21.

104. Melton later testified that he had heard that armed men were headed to city hall to demand resignations and that as the old board was meeting, an armed crowd of men approached the building. Melton also recounted that Rountree "invited me out into the chamber of the board of finance and said that he would advise me to resign; that he thought he had control over the men, but he had just learned that he could not do

anything with the men, meaning the Democrats; that he had no control over them, and they would not listen to him, and he would not be responsible for the consequence, and he advised me to resign, and I did so." *Contested Election Case*, 364–365.

105. J. Allan Taylor led the banishment campaign for the Secret Nine. McDuffie, "Politics in Wilmington," 719–720; *Wilmington Messenger*, November 12, 1898.

Chapter 6: Resounding Change

1. For example, John S. Cunningham of Person County invited Alfred Moore Waddell's kinswoman, Rebecca Cameron (Mrs. Bennehan Cameron), and her husband to Thanksgiving dinner at his home so that they could "thank our Father, who has blessed us individually in so many ways, [and] we can thank him for the great victory on the 8th day of November." Cunningham to Col. and Mrs. Bennehan Cameron, November 11, 1898, Bennehan Cameron Papers, Southern Historical Collection, Wilson Library, University of North Carolina at Chapel Hill, Chapel Hill.

2. Patrols established in advance of the riot took on a new responsibility as all blacks passing through the city encountered at every street corner a checkpoint at which guards "hold up and search all negroes going and coming from work." Wilmington store clerk J. F. Maunder recalled that he searched about twenty-five blacks and found nothing of consequence. Minutes of the Organizational Meeting of the Association of Members of the Wilmington Light Infantry, December 14, 1905, North Carolina Collection, University of North Carolina Library, Chapel Hill (hereafter cited as Minutes of the Organizational Meeting of the WLI).

3. For additional information on Moore's activities and the network of guards and patrols, see previous chapters. About 60 Maxton Guards arrived about 11:00 P.M., 40 Clinton Guards arrived a half-hour later, and 30 men with the Kinston Naval Reserves arrived at 2:30 A.M. The Fayetteville Light Infantry, the first military unit to arrive on the afternoon of the riot, brought 86 men to the city. Harry Hayden, "The Wilmington Light Infantry" (typed, unpublished memoir), New Hanover County Public Library, Wilmington, 95–97; *Wilmington Messenger*, November 11–14, 1898; *Morning Star* (Wilmington), November 11, 12, 1898; *Evening Dispatch* (Wilmington), November 11, 12, 1898.

4. On behalf of the citizens of Wilmington, Waddell penned thanks to the military for its "prompt and efficient services." Col. Walker Taylor then responded with a message of thanks to the city's residents who had assisted in providing for the needs of the military. Gov. Daniel

Russell had informed Taylor that he could keep the troops on active duty in the city as long as necessary, but Wilmington leaders sought to return to normal conditions as soon as possible. *Evening Dispatch*, November 12, 1898; *Morning Star*, November 13, 14, 1898.

5. Despite attempts by Democrats to safeguard the polls, Bellamy's opponent, Oliver H. Dockery, resorted to legal measures to contest the validity of Bellamy's election. The resulting court proceedings, which took place in 1899, will be discussed in detail in chapter 7. *Wilmington Messenger*, November 15, 1898.

6. Clawson's account is confusing, but he evidently had worked to save Manly's life the day before the riot. He recalled that after the White Declaration of Independence had been written, a group of men sought to lynch Manly, and that he had informed the men that Manly was gone. He boasted that his "trip beyond the dead-line that night caused the negro editors to flee, which made it so the pre-arranged 'lynching' and burning party did not go to Seventh and Nun streets to fall into the ambush set about the Record shop." According to Clawson, that ambush consisted of about "two or three hundred armed negroes" who were hiding in the neighborhood to protect the shop and the *Daily Record* staff. Clawson decided that because of his actions, "the 'lynching party' set for that night of November 9 did not take place, but the very next morning hundreds of enraged and affronted white men smashed the negro newspaper shop." It is not clear whether such activity occurred on the night of the ninth or if Clawson's memories of the events had become jumbled. Clawson's memoir is undated and could have been written years after the event. Jerome McDuffie, "Politics in Wilmington and New Hanover County, North Carolina, 1865–1900: The Genesis of a Race Riot" (Ph.D. diss., Kent State University, 1979)," 687–688; Thomas W. Clawson, "The Wilmington Race Riot in 1898, Recollections and Memories" (unpublished memoir, Louis T. Moore Collection, Private Collections, State Archives, North Carolina Office of Archives and History, Raleigh; Sue Ann Cody, "After the Storm: Racial Violence in Wilmington, North Carolina, and Its Consequences for African Americans" (master's thesis, University of North Carolina at Wilmington, 2000), 21; *Washington Times*, November 22, 1898.

7. J. Allan Taylor, Walker Taylor's brother and a member both of the Secret Nine and the Committee of Twenty-five, was in charge of the banishment campaign. There are discrepancies in the accounts of witnesses as to the men imprisoned in the jail overnight. Thomas Clawson recalled that black and white leaders were jailed together overnight. Waddell said that seven black leaders were arrested and jailed overnight and were the same men that were marched under protection of the military to the

train. Waddell further stated that others, including three whites, had been sent out but were protected from lynching elsewhere and that those men were taken under guard to another train. Thomas Cowan, editor of the *Dispatch*, wrote that several whites were interred in jail overnight and that Waddell and Moore worked together to prevent the lynch mob from taking action. John D. Bellamy said that the men participating in the banishment campaign were not affiliated with the Committee of Twenty-five, headed by Waddell. He further explained that the banishments were carried out by "some self-assumed authority by some young men." Bellamy also observed that "a good number of us" disliked the fact that some of the men were sent out of town. Minutes of the Organizational Meeting of the WLI; Clawson, "The Wilmington Race Riot in 1898"; Alfred Moore Waddell, "The Story of the Wilmington, N.C. Race Riot," *Collier's Weekly* 22 (November 26, 1898): 4–5; James H. Cowan, "The Wilmington Race Riot" (undated, unpublished memoir, n.d.), Louis T. Moore Local History Collection, New Hanover County Public Library; *Contested Election Case of Oliver H. Dockery vs. John D. Bellamy from the Sixth Congressional District of the State of North Carolina* (Washington, D.C.: Government Printing Office, 1899), 258 (hereafter cited as *Contested Election Case*).

8. In 1905 George Boylan recalled the WLI's search for Redmon: "I think the swiftest thing I remember was the negro Redmon's coat tails. A squad had been sent out to find his house and when we got there, there were two houses just alike and there was some dispute as to which was his house and I jumped out of the wagon just about between the two houses. All we saw was a flirt of his coat tail as he went over the fence. We ran around the square and some through the square and although he had no longer to go than we did, we never did see him and he has never been seen from that day to this. I believe his dog was seen a few days after that down the street but that was one badly frightened negro." A "James Redman" is listed in the 1897 Wilmington city directory as a stock clerk working at 519 Campbell Street, and his dwelling was located at 817 Harnett Street. A "James Redmond" is found in the 1900 Wilmington city directory residing at 614 Dickinson Street and working as a laborer. Robert Reardon was considered an "objectionable negro barber." Reardon knew that he was being sought and reportedly fled "down the sound." In the 1897 city directory, Reardon is listed as a barber at 29 Market Street, but his name does not appear in the 1900 directory. *J. L. Hill Printing Co.'s Directory of Wilmington, N.C. 1897* (Richmond, Va: J. L. Hill Printing Company, 1897; hereafter cited as *Hill's 1897 Wilmington City Directory*); *J. L. Hill Printing Co.'s Directory of Wilmington, N.C. 1900*

229

(Richmond, Va.: J. L. Hill Printing Company, 1900); Minutes of the Organizational Meeting of the WLI.

9. It is unclear which Burkheimer lent his wagon for the arrests. *Hill's 1897 Wilmington City Directory* lists several Burkheimers, including a large household of men and women residing at 208 North Fourth Street. Hayden, "The Wilmington Light Infantry," 89.

10. The activity around Manhattan Park on November 10 is covered in the previous chapter. Just as there is much confusion in the record concerning that topic, there are multiple references to the arrest and banishment campaign. After the fighting subsided, African American Henry Gause was arrested for stealing a gun from a young white boy. Gause reportedly took the weapon home and hid it in a mattress. It was subsequently found, and he was arrested. It is unclear whether or not he was put on a train to leave town. Another black man, Beverly Scott, was arrested on the tenth for parading with a gun in the streets before the election. A newspaper article enumerated the names of other men arrested and jailed: Henry Nichols, Wisconsin Edwards, James Hill, S. T. Knight, William Tate, and Tom Love or Lane. The six were named as men arrested for shooting at the naval militia troops from a house in Brooklyn on the tenth. *Morning Star*, November 11, 1898; Zeb Vance Walser, *Biennial Report of the Attorney General of the State of North Carolina, 1897–1898*, North Carolina Public Documents, Document Number 9, State Archives, 29–32.

11. Roger Moore's widow recounted Moore's role in the scenario at the jail: "At night, when a wild surging mob congregated in front of the jail for the purpose of lynching the wretches who were placed there for safe keeping, it was Col. Moore who saved their lives and the city from a stain that would have sullied her fair name for all time. Every effort was made by the mob to get rid of him, even subterfuge was resorted to but without avail. Finally he said 'Men we may as well understand each other; you are here to lynch these men and I am here to prevent it; you can only carry out your purpose over my dead body' and mounting the steps of the jail and placing his back to the door he stood there from 10 o'clock at night until sunrise." Mrs. Roger Moore, letter to the editor of the *Wilmington Messenger*, n.d., Accession No. 130, Mrs. Roger Moore Collection, University of North Carolina Wilmington Special Collections.

12. Hayden, "The Wilmington Light Infantry," 101; *Wilmington Messenger*, November 14, 1898; Clawson, "The Wilmington Race Riot in 1898"; Minutes of the Organizational Meeting of the WLI.

13. Wilmington resident James S. Worth participated in the march to protect at least one banished African American man and escorted others to their homes from the outskirts of the city. A letter he wrote to his wife after the event explains his actions and provides insight into his conflicted attitudes toward the city's blacks:

> You misunderstood me if you thought I meant the negro, as a race, any harm and you would have known I had no ill feelings against them, as a race, if you had seen me taking them home that day—it is a long walk from Hilton river bridge to 8th & Dawson—but I started from the bridge with about 25 & delivered the last one at 8th & Dawson of course I searched them under cover of my gun & had to take them through the picket lines on the battlefield. I had to escort one of the meanest niggers of all out of town on the train & would not have hesitated to kill him if he had attempted to escape—and yet his life had been promised him & I simply requested to go for his protection—By the way that was the reason I happened to be at the RR bridge at Hilton—the train was stopped there for me to get off. I don't hesitate to say I think it would have been better that some of those allowed to leave should have been killed instead & yet I hardly now think you could imagine I mean to do them any harm. They have not been treated as brutes—of course some have suffered on account of their fears but they have been generally well treated. Of course I didn't shoot at any of them—but would not have hesitated a moment to do so if I had been fired on or if any of those I saw fired on had been outnumbered. I could not bring myself to the point of firing at any of those I saw shot down even though I knew they <u>had been</u> doing all they could to kill white people. I am however sorry that some of those sent out of town were not killed at the time captured. One goes through peculiar changes of feeling at such times—one minute ready to shoot a negro & the next seeing one home safely to keep him from being shot. No—I personally did very little guard duty—as I was in charge of my block & simply detailed the others on the block each night & went off scouting on my own hook & helping out whenever I could. The whole town was so well organized that the military were free to go to the seat of war and the boys behaved like veterans and not anyone flinched under fire or failed in his duty.

James S. Worth to "Josephine," November 16, 1898, James Spencer Worth Papers, Southern Historical Collection; *News and Observer* (Raleigh), November 12, 1898.

14. *Wilmington Messenger*, November 14, 1898.

15. Miller's treatment and arrest traumatized him, as did his exile. In 1902 Miller wrote a letter to John D. Taylor, clerk of superior court, regarding a land transaction. Part of the letter read:

> I have been treated not like [a] human but worse than a dog and someday the Lord will punish them that punished me without a Cause. I am Well and doing Well the only thing that worries me is just to think that I were not allowed to come to my Mothers funeral she being 95 years of age and the oldest Citizen on Wrightsville sound just to think of it will last me to my

grave if I were guilty of any Crime or was a Criminal it would not worri [sic] me in the least but oh my god just to think it is enough to run a sane man insane. Col I hope you will pardon me for the way I write you but when I think about it all knowing I am not Guilty it all most drives me mad—just to think how my own people could treat me as they have with out a Cause knowingly. Oh my god.

Miller died the following year in Norfolk, and his remains were brought to Wilmington for burial. Thomas C. Miller, Norfolk, Virginia, to John D. Taylor, Clerk of Superior Court, Wilmington, July 9, 1902, Correspondence, 1824–1906, New Hanover County Miscellaneous Records, State Archives; Minutes of the Organizational Meeting of the WLI; Hayden, "The Wilmington Light Infantry," 102.

16. It is unclear why Peamon was placed aboard a southbound train, while the others were placed on northbound trains. John V. B. Metts to "Miss Elizabeth," November 12, 1898, Hinsdale Family Papers, Rare Book, Manuscript, and Special Collections Library, Duke University, Durham; Evening Dispatch, November 11, 1898; Wilmington Messenger, November 11, 1898.

17. Bunting was a deputy marshal of the U.S. District Court in Wilmington and was a magistrate in the city. Morning Star, November 12, 1898; Branson's North Carolina Business Directory, 1897 (Raleigh: Levi Branson, 1897), 448–449.

18. The Wilmington Messenger reflected the sentiments of the campaign when it noted that the root of the "evil" of race relations were "mean white men"—northerners who came to the South and courted black voters. On the other hand, some of the white men targeted were Wilmington natives or longtime residents of the city. Melton was a Wilmington native. New Bern newspapers reported to the News and Observer that the Atlantic Coast Line train that was to convey the white Republicans from Wilmington had arrived and that the men were escorted from the train to the steamer Neuse, which departed for Elizabeth City. News and Observer, November 12, 1898; Morning Star, November 12, 1898; Contested Election Case, 360; Wilmington Messenger, November 15, 1898.

19. News and Observer, November 12, 1898.

20. Although it was reported that Bunting was escorted to the city limits for his own protection, Chief of Police Melton explained that Bunting was held at the national cemetery until joined by Melton and others. Melton, Bunting, and the other men under guard were marched through Wilmington to the railroad depot, where they were sent out of town. Melton observed that Bunting was the target of verbal abuse while aboard the train. Contested Election Case, 364–366; Evening Dispatch, November 11, 1898; H. Leon Prather Sr., We Have Taken a City: Wilmington Massacre and Coup of 1898 (Rutherford,

N.J.: Fairleigh Dickinson University Press, 1984), 140–141.

21. Walser, Biennial Report of the Attorney General of the State of North Carolina, 1897–1898, 31.

22. Other white leaders who assisted in French's rescue were William H. Bernard, F. H. Fechtig, Henry Bauman, Henry Peschau, Henry G. Fennell, H. M. Chase, George L. Morton, Horace Emerson Sr., and M. F. Heiskel Gouverneur. According to Hayden, Fechtig, Bauman, Peschau, and Fennell were in the process of escorting Armond Scott to the train station to board the same train as French when they happened upon the attempted lynching. It is unclear when French was placed on a train; Hayden recounts that French's train ride began on the afternoon of November 11. Contrary to that account, the Evening Dispatch reported that French departed the city on November 10 aboard the 7:15 P.M. northbound train. Hayden, "The Wilmington Light Infantry," 102–103; News and Observer, November 12, 1898; Evening Dispatch, November 11, 1898.

23. News and Observer, November 12, 1898.

24. Minutes of the Organizational Meeting of the WLI.

25. During the court challenge brought by Republican Oliver H. Dockery against Democrat John D. Bellamy over the congressional election of 1898, Melton testified in Raleigh about his experiences during the riot. Contested Election Case, 360–366, 382, 386.

26. Later reports of the march of Melton, Bunting, and Gilbert indicated that one of the epithets shouted at the men was "white nigger." Morning Star, November 15, 1898.

27. Melton refused to provide all the details of the campaign and riot that he knew because his family still lived in Wilmington, and they had "trouble enough" without his testimony adding "personal controversy." Contested Election Case, 360–366, 382, 386.

28. Wilmington Messenger, November 15, 1898; Morning Star, November 13, 1898.

29. As they were shoved onto outbound trains, the men were "told in forcible language that if ever again they set foot in Wilmington they would be shot on sight." Morning Star, November 15, 1898; Prather, We Have Taken a City, 34, 50.

30. Evening Dispatch, November 16, 17, 1898; Morning Star, November 15, 1898.

31. The papers reported that refugee whites Melton, Bunting, and French, as well as blacks George Brown, T. C. Miller, and another man with the last name Branch, were in Norfolk on November 14. Brown was severely beaten at the post office, although he claimed that he had

231

merely been visiting Wilmington from Canada and working in a confectionary while there. It was reported that the men who attacked Brown thought he was Manly, but it was later discovered that Manly was in New Jersey at the time of the attack. From Norfolk the blacks went to Baltimore, and the whites were not found in Norfolk. Some members of both groups ended up in Washington, D.C., where they sought assistance from the Department of Justice and the president. The *Dispatch* reported that one of the exiles thought it would be safe for them to return to Wilmington but that the others knew that "it would be unwise to return." No additional information can be found regarding the actions of these men while in Washington or the response they received from federal officials. *Morning Star*, November 13, 15, 1898; *Evening Dispatch*, November 14, 16, 17, 1898; *Morning Post* (Raleigh), November 15, 1898.

32. *News and Observer*, November 13, 1898.

33. Harris learned about the treatment received by Melton and Gilbert and that he was to be visited by a group planning to run him out of Wilmington. In response, Harris kissed his wife and left his home. He then had trouble leaving the city because he had to dodge roving bands of Red Shirts who were looking for him. Once he finally escaped, Harris spent the ensuing months moving from place to place in Rocky Point, Goldsboro, Raleigh, Greensboro, and Randolph County. Although Harris had not returned to Wilmington by the time of testimony in April 1899, his wife remained in the city. *Contested Election Case*, 387–391; *Wilmington Messenger*, October 20, 1898.

34. The *Morning Star* of November 12, 1898, noted that Lockey was in Fayetteville "waiting for the clouds to roll by."

35. An oral tradition in Wilmington has it that Scott escaped by being placed in a specially made coffin equipped with air holes and shipped to Washington, D.C. Shirley Webb Smith, telephone conversation with author, June 17, 2005; Helen G. Edmonds, *The Negro and Fusion Politics in North Carolina, 1894–1901* (Chapel Hill: University of North Carolina Press, 1951), 169.

36. On the morning of the riot, Henderson apparently attempted to ameliorate tensions when, according to the *Evening Dispatch*, he presented several leaders with a letter explaining the actions of the Committee of Colored Citizens:

I feel it my duty to set at rest the public minds as to the action of the colored citizens that was intended to meet the white citizens last evening. The object of that meeting too well known to repeat. We discharged the duties entrusted to us by informing the Chairman, Hon. A. M. Waddell, that we would use our individual influence to carry out the wishes of your committee.

The same was mailed to Colonel Waddell. We appointed a committee to search for F. G. Manly and inform him of the facts and to urge him to act at once. We were informed and we believed that Editor A. L. Manly is now and has been out of the city for more than a month. Our committee could not find either of the associate editors, but hoped to find them today. Respectfully, W. E. Henderson.

Henderson kept a diary of his experiences. That volume is owned by his descendants, who attended the 1998 centennial observance of the riot in Wilmington. At that event, one of the descendants, Lisa Adams, shared selections from his diary. *Evening Dispatch*, November 11, 1898; "The 1898 Wilmington Racial Violence and its Legacy: A Symposium" (video recording made by the University of North Carolina at Wilmington Media Services), November 1998, Foundation Collection, University of North Carolina Wilmington.

37. While questioning a railroad employee on the stand, Scott noted that the railroad had a policy of helping only white women disembark, thereby forcing black women to manage by themselves in the absence of such "courtesies." He was described as insolent for making that remark. Local Wilmington papers reported that Scott was in Washington, D.C., by November 13 to plead his case with the president. Scott replied to the report by stating that although he was in Washington, he did not plan to act in any "official capacity" to advocate for federal intervention and that he had "no intention of saying anything to the President." *Morning Star*, November 11, 15, 1898; *Evening Dispatch*, November 11, 14, 1898; *News and Observer*, November 12, 1898.

38. *Morning Star*, November 12, 1898.

39. *Colored American* (Washington, D.C.), December 28, 1901. In his speeches, Dancy emphasized the need for African Americans to focus on improving the race as a whole, even as he lauded the efforts of a wide spectrum of other leading blacks, from Booker T. Washington to Frederick Douglass. Like Washington, Dancy was an accommodationist whose acceptance of white supremacy rhetoric nevertheless had its limits.

40. J. Allen Kirk, *A Statement of Facts Concerning the Bloody Riot in Wilmington, N.C., of Interest to Every Citizen of the United States* ([Wilmington?: The Author?, 1898?]), 9–16; online edition available at http://docsouth.unc.edu/nc/kirk/menu.html.

41. William A. Moore is listed in *Hill's 1897 Wilmington City Directory* as an attorney with offices at the corner of Market and Second streets. His home is given as 413 South Seventh Street. Moore's name does not appear in the 1900 directory. In the summer of 1898 he addressed the city's African American recruits for the Spanish-American War. Kirk, *A Statement of Facts Concerning the*

Riot, 9–16; William M. Reaves, *"Strength through Struggle": The Chronological and Historical Record of the African-American Community in Wilmington, North Carolina, 1865–1950*, ed. Beverly Tetterton (Wilmington: New Hanover County Public Library, 1998), 341.

42. A study of city directories and the census between 1880 and 1920 might illustrate a change in Wilmington's population over time. Such a comprehensive study might offer proof that a goodly number of the African Americans who resided in the city before November 10, 1898, subsequently moved away and that many of those who called Wilmington home in 1910 came to the city *after* the riot. *Morning Star*, November 13, 15, 1898; *Wilmington Messenger*, November 13, 1898; *Evening Dispatch*, November 12, 1898; *News and Observer*, November 13, 1898.

43. Frank P. Toomer, a black policeman who fled to New Bern during the violence, wrote Waddell to ask if he could safely return to Wilmington. Waddell replied that he thought Toomer should not return because he had "made himself very obnoxious to many people." Toomer's request and Waddell's reply were printed in the papers. *News and Observer*, November 12, 1898; *Morning Star*, November 19, 1898.

44. Later reports revealed that the adjutant general of North Carolina was obliged to pay as much as $1,300 in costs for the services and transportation of the State Guard units brought into Wilmington from other areas of the state. Of that money, $180.87 went to the Maxton contingent, $112.13 to a Franklinton unit, and $259.00 to the Atlantic Coast Line Railroad. *Morning Star*, November 26, December 9, 1898; *Evening Dispatch*, December 8, 1898; Minutes of the Wilmington Board of Aldermen, 1884–1906 (microfilm), State Archives.

45. Dancy fit readily into the role of an accommodationist and straddled white and black issues. New ministers had to be found as well. The 1900 city directory included numerous new names of men who worked as ministers—many more than could be found in the 1897 city directory.

46. L. H. Bryant, a white Populist sixty-eight years of age, had lived in Wilmington almost half of his life by the time of the riot. He was coerced into resigning his job as superintendent of streets and moved to Magnolia around the first day of January 1899. Bryant, like others, chose not to depart immediately but rather during the months following the riot. *Contested Election Case*, 394–395.

47. *News and Observer*, November 12, 1898.

48. Hayden, "The Wilmington Light Infantry," 75.

49. For many years the Wilmington *Morning Star* kept up with some of the men, among them former mayor Silas Wright. In September 1948 the paper informed its readers that a local man had received word from an acquaintance in Detroit that Wright, then ninety years old, was living in that city. The last part of the article reminded readers that Wright and others on the board of aldermen had been forced to resign their offices in 1898 in response to pressures from citizens. *Morning Star*, September 24, 1948.

50. Harry Hayden claimed that five or six black men wearing their work coveralls were shot and killed after William Mayo, a white man, was wounded. The *Messenger* reported that although coroner David Jacobs had moved several bodies to a funeral home, some still "lay last night where the men were shot down." Hayden, "The Wilmington Light Infantry," 89; *Wilmington Messenger*, November 11, 1898.

51. The medical facility, known as City-County Hospital, was later replaced by James Walker Hospital. Both facilities were located in the same general vicinity—the area bounded by Rankin, Gwynn, Woods, and Dickinson streets.

52. Only two grave markers in Pine Forest Cemetery bear death dates related to the riot. Cemetery records reveal that John Halsey was born about 1846 and died November 10, 1898, of a gunshot wound and was buried in section C of the Halsey family plot. The record for Sam McFarland indicates that he was born in South Carolina around 1850, "died of a gunshot in his body" on November 12, 1898, and was buried in lot M or N, section 2. A review of the cemetery log proves inconclusive, inasmuch as those two men are the only ones listed. Another person, Samuel Hall, age twelve, died of gunshot wounds and was buried December 22, 1898. No information has been found to suggest whether Hall received his fatal wound as a result of the riot or from some other cause. Parts of the cemetery have disappeared over time, and many burials may have gone unrecorded. Moreover, some private and church cemeteries have likewise disappeared. Pine Forest Cemetery (Wilmington) Records (microfilm), State Archives.

53. *Wilmington Messenger*, November 11–13, 1898; *Wilmington Messenger*, November 15, 1898, quoting *News and Courier* (Charleston, S.C.); *Morning Star*, November 11–13, 1898.

54. As published by the newspapers, the testimony of the various men and women before the coroner's jury mirrored the details of the riot as described in the previous chapter. *Morning Star*, November 13, 1898; *Wilmington Messenger*, November 15, 1898, quoting *News and Courier.*

55. Wilmington newspapers widely circulated the identities of several of the dead, although one Wilmington paper mentioned a rumor that "not one of the negroes who were killed was a native of the state" but came to the city from South Carolina before the election. *News and*

Observer, November 13, 1898; *Wilmington Messenger*, November 15, 1898, quoting *News and Courier*; *Evening Dispatch*, November 12, 1898.

56. *Wilmington Messenger*, November 14, 1898.

57. The records disagree as to the name of the latter man. *Wilmington Messenger*, November 14, 1898.

58. Dr. Zachary overlooked the obvious—that the men shot in the back did not bravely face the enemy. They were, instead, likely running for their lives from the fighting and were possibly unarmed targets. An article in the *Washington Post* noted that "many of the victims of the election race riots in [Wilmington] were taken to the city hospital to have their wounds dressed or their dying moments made easy." The article pointed out that the hospital was on the outskirts of Wilmington and that during the riot the "female white assistants, nurses and others took fright and left the hospital in a body." Therefore, not only was the hospital overrun with emergency patients but many of its staff members also were not on hand to assist. Dr. R. E. Zachary, "Gun-Shot Wounds—With Report of a Case of Gun-Shot Wound of Stomach," *Transactions of the Medical Society of the State of North Carolina, Forty-Sixth Annual Meeting* (Charlotte: Observer Printing and Publishing House, 1899), 134; *Washington Post*, November 14, 1898.

59. At this point in his narrative, Hayden provided reports from other eyewitnesses as to the dead. He pointed out that the coroner held fourteen inquests, although a lack of records has prevented many from being documented. He also recorded the memory of a young man who claimed to have seen a Cowan Livery Stable wagon drive by his house with twenty dead blacks piled on like "cordwood" and later saw twenty bodies at a black mortuary. As an example of officially unreported murders, Hayden recounted that a Red Shirt claimed to have witnessed the shooting deaths of six men near the Cape Fear Lumber Company plant and their remains buried in a nearby ditch. Hayden, "The Wilmington Light Infantry," 92–94.

60. *Evening Dispatch*, November 11, 1898; Clawson, "The Wilmington Race Riot in 1898"; George Rountree, "Memorandum of My Personal Recollection of the Election of 1898," n.d., Henry G. Connor Papers, Southern Historical Collection. On the day of the violence Mallett wrote in his daybook: "War commenced/Race at Wilmington today—8 negroes reported killed and several whites—Col. Waddell and best citizens in[.] More trouble feared tonight/ Russell[,] French and other scum did keep out of the way—negroes suffer." Daybook, November 10, 1898, Peter Mallett Papers, Willie to Sallie [November 12, 1898], Eccles Family Papers, James S. Worth to "Josephine," November 16, 1898, Worth Papers, all housed at the

Southern Historical Collection; *Contested Election Case*, 19–20.

61. Kirk and Hayden both acknowledged that mortally wounded men fled the fighting and were later found dead in a variety of settings. Because North Carolina did not require the completion of death certificates or regulate burials until later in the twentieth century, an accurate accounting of the people who died as a result of the violence is even more difficult to ascertain. (As an example, Scipio Condring, a Civil War veteran who served in the 128th U.S. Colored Troops, is buried in Wilmington's National Cemetery; but no information can be found on the cause of Condring's death, which occurred on November 13, 1898, according to the inscription on his headstone. Research into the soldier's life proved inconclusive, although there is some speculation that his last name was not actually Condring but was instead some derivative of "Connelly." Kirk, *A Statement of Facts Concerning the Riot*, 10–15.)

62. The *Progressive Farmer* enumerated 11 blacks killed and 3 whites wounded. The report of Wilmington's superintendent of health as published in a newspaper accounted for a total of eight killed during the riot. Only one white man, William Mayo, was seriously wounded. Mayo's recovery was well documented in local papers in November and December. Another white man, B. F. King Jr., died about four days after the riot from influenza contracted while patrolling the city. It is not known whether others of either race suffered the same fate. *Progressive Farmer* (Raleigh), November 15, 1898; *Morning Star*, November 15, December 1, 1898; *Evening Dispatch*, December 7, 1898; Kirk, *A Statement of Facts Concerning the Riot*, 10–15.

63. Benjamin F. Keith, *Memories* (Raleigh: Bynum Printing Company, 1922), 112–121; Samuel A. Ashe, Stephen B. Weeks, and Charles L. Van Noppen, eds., *Biographical History of North Carolina from Colonial Times to the Present*, 8 vols. (Greensboro: Charles L. Van Noppen, 1905–1917), 5:116–117. Although Keith retained the respect of some of Wilmington's businessmen after the 1898 coup, he had just as many enemies. In 1921, in an attempt to secure reappointment as the collector of customs for the port, Keith penned a long letter to President Warren G. Harding in which he detailed his personal and political trials: "[A]fter destroying my business, they for years tried to ostracize me and my family." Keith to Harding, July 5, 1921, original owned by Thomas J. Keith. Photocopy on file in the Research Branch, North Carolina Office of Archives and History.

64. A discussion of the attempted assassination of Russell can be found in chapter 4. *Morning Post*, November 15, 1898; Gov. Daniel L. Russell to Marion Butler, November 12, 1898, Marion Butler Papers, Southern Historical Collection.

65. Russell to Duke, November 19, December 2, 1898, 3. N. Duke Papers, Duke Special Collections, as cited in Jeffrey J. Crow and Robert F. Durden, *Maverick Republican in the Old North State: A Political Biography of Daniel L. Russell* (Baton Rouge: Louisiana State University Press, 1977), 136.

66. The suffrage amendment was proposed as a means of limiting the ability of African Americans to vote. Further discussion of the disfranchisement amendment will be found in chapter 7. Address of Governor Daniel Russell, *North Carolina Public Documents*, 1899, Document No. 1, State Archives, 3–26; Crow and Durden, *Maverick Republican*, 140–141.

67. Russell died at his plantation in 1908 and received lukewarm eulogies in the state's newspapers. Crow and Durden, *Maverick Republican*, 160–185, 187–188.

68. James L. Hunt, *Marion Butler and American Populism* (Chapel Hill: University of North Carolina Press, 2003), 154.

69. James B. Lloyd wrote Butler that he was afraid someone would try to kill him, particularly after a threatening article about Butler was published in the *Charlotte Daily Observer*. Lloyd urged Butler to get back to Washington as quickly as possible for his own safety. Governor Russell wrote Butler to reassure him that it was not likely that "they will try to assassinate you." Russell did not think Butler was in jeopardy but told him to "be a little careful." Lloyd to Butler, November 13, 1898, Russell to Butler, November 12, 1898, Butler Papers.

70. Hunt, *Marion Butler*, 161.

71. The returns from the election held on November 8, 1898, had to be validated by state officials as a true account of the votes cast. One requirement was that the returns from each precinct had to be signed by the registrars and others appointed to jobs at the precincts. In the Fifth Precinct of the First Ward, where the ballot counting was interrupted, at least two of the officials were African American and had left the precinct before all of the votes were counted. As a result, they did not sign the final tally sheets of the night. Abram Fulton was called to the courthouse on the Monday following the riot to sign the returns and to receive his pay. Verifying the signatures on the returns was one step in proving the validity of the vote tally in case of a contested election. The *Morning Star* of November 10, 1898, reported that the official vote would be recorded in the clerk of Superior Court's office that day, and the official returns were published the following day. Because the riot took precedence on the front page, the returns were published only for the congressional election of Bellamy, in which he received 289 more votes than Dockery in New Hanover County and an overall majority of almost 6,000 votes in the whole of the Sixth District. *Morning Star*, November 10, 11, 1898; *Contested Election Case*, 332–336.

72. One of the first actions of Waddell and the board was to assure Wilmington residents and outside observers that the new administration would create a peaceful city: "To the good white people of Wilmington: The undersigned, upon whom has been placed a great responsibility by the action of his fellow citizens, takes the method of assuring the good people of this city that all the power with which he is invested will be exerted to preserve order and peace in this community, and that power is amply sufficient for the purpose. All well disposed persons are earnestly requested to co-operate with the municipal authorities in every way possible to secure the permanent establishment of good government. The law will be rigidly enforced and impartially administered to white and black people alike. A. M. Waddell, Mayor." *Evening Dispatch*, November 11, 1898.

73. For example, page 15 records the meeting of the board of aldermen convened by Mayor Wright at 12:50 A.M. on November 10 at the home of Alderman Charles D. Morrell. Clerk William Struthers recorded the actions of Wright's administration in extending the ban on the sale of alcoholic beverages, even as the riot was under way. On page 16 are the signatures of Democrats who claimed to be sworn in as aldermen and the oath of Waddell as mayor. The next page has another sworn statement and the signature of Waddell as mayor. The signatures on pages 16 and 17 are out of order in that the next page, 18, includes the formal minutes of the resignations and the election of successors, which took place at 4 o'clock on the tenth. William Struthers likewise recorded the information pertaining to the actual transition. Minutes of the Wilmington Board of Aldermen, 1884–1906, State Archives.

74. Minutes of the Wilmington Board of Aldermen.

75. Appointments were as follows: captain of police, John J. Furlong; police lieutenant, Fred Skipper; first sergeant, J. L. Stallings; second sergeant, Joseph R. Davis; third sergeant, J. D. Orrell; day janitor for City Hall, R. A. Benson; night janitor for City Hall, J. A. Lane; health officers, G. W. Cameron and M. Kirchbaum; superintendent of streets, J. A. Perry. Minutes of the Wilmington Board of Aldermen.

76. The meeting held on November 16 was a special session designed to make "selections of whites to fill places of Negro firemen." New fire department leaders were J. J. Bell, engineer of Engine Co. No. 2; L. Freemuth, foreman of Engine Co. No. 2; and M. F. Dowling, foreman of Hose Reel Co. No. 3. Firemen hired included Theodore Swann, as well as sixteen other white men. George Irving was elected cattle weigher. A Raleigh paper ran a headline titled "Elimination of Negroes Complete—All

of Departments in Wilmington in White Hands" to assure outsiders that Waddell and the city were following through with their pre-election promises. *Morning Star*, November 17, 18, 1898; *Morning Post*, November 17, 1898; Minutes of the Wilmington Board of Aldermen.

77. Minutes of the Wilmington Board of Aldermen.

78. Party infighting resulted in the resignations and a substantial delay in the selection of replacements. Bridgers and King claimed that personal business pressures required them to dedicate themselves to their businesses; Kramer resigned to accept a pastorate in another city. McDuffie, "Politics in Wilmington," 770; *Wilmington Messenger*, November 24–December 10, 1898; *Morning Star*, November 24–December 10, 1898.

79. One of Waddell's attempts to control municipal crime through a special mayoral court involved a hearing for Thomas Lane, the black man accused of firing at the Wilmington Light Infantry. The WLI and white leaders contended that if Lane had not shot at the military, it would have not been necessary for troops to kill John Halsey. Lane was convicted and sentenced to jail time. For additional information on Halsey's murder, see chapter 5. Minutes of the Wilmington Board of Aldermen.

80. It is unclear whether or not the New Hanover County Board of Education demanded Noble's resignation. Marcus Cicero Stephens Noble (1855–1942), the son of a Confederate officer, arrived in Wilmington in 1882 to serve as superintendent of the city's schools. He earned statewide acclaim for excellence in managing Wilmington's schools and for progressive educational methods. By November 1898 the University of North Carolina had invited him to return to Chapel Hill to serve as a professor of pedagogy. The political climate notwithstanding, it is uncertain whether Noble would have continued to serve as city schools superintendent or voluntarily resigned. Regardless of circumstances, with Noble's departure Wilmington's schools lost a strong education advocate both for blacks and whites. Minutes, Board of County Commissioners, 1887–1918, New Hanover County Miscellaneous Records, State Archives; *Morning Star*, December 4, 7, 14, 1898; *Evening Dispatch*, December 6, 1898; *Dictionary of North Carolina Biography* s.v. "Noble, Marcus Cicero Stephens."

81. *Morning Star*, November 16, 1898; Minutes of the New Hanover County Board of Commissioners.

82. *Wilmington Messenger*, November 12, 1898; *Morning Star*, November 12, 1898. Harry Hayden referred to another proclamation issued by Waddell, in which he claimed the new mayor employed the following words: "Self-Appointed vigilantes are responsible for much of this misery because of the indiscriminate way they have gone about banishing objectionable persons; and in some instances unscrupulous whites have gratified their personal spite in dealing with the negroes." Hayden, "The Wilmington Light Infantry," 107.

83. *Morning Star*, November 15, 1898.

84. Many accounts point out that blacks were routinely searched at every street corner, regardless of age or sex. Some of the searches were conducted by young men and boys, who were considered too youthful to be carrying guns in the armed guard units. Although such searches were intended to find weapons, only a few small items, such as knives or brass knuckles, were found. Hayden, "The Wilmington Light Infantry," 93, 105; Minutes of the Organizational Meeting of the WLI.

85. *Wilmington Messenger*, November 14, 1898.

86. According to the city directories, Macon was a plumber who lived at 508 South Sixth Street both in 1897 and 1900. By 1903 his occupation was listed as laborer. A review of the census indicates that Macon was born about 1870 and was married in 1890. He had three sons and one daughter. He rented his home on Sixth Street, but the 1910 census does not show him as a resident of New Hanover County. By that year, all three of his sons had moved to Rocky Mount and were living with their aunt and uncle, Ruffin and Anna Harris, and attending school. *Wilmington Messenger*, November 11, 1898; William Cumming, pass for Henry Macon, November 11, 1898, Cape Fear Museum, Wilmington.

87. Worth added that he thought the rest of the "best darkies" were "glad that 'dark town' has been taught a lesson, as one bad nigger will harm the rest." James S. Worth to "Josephine," November 16, 1898, Worth Papers.

88. Peter Mallett, a Fayetteville merchant with ties to Wilmington, recorded in a daybook on the eleventh that he had received a telegram from James Sprunt indicating that Wilmington was quiet but excited and that there was "great rejoicing over Democratic victory in N.C." Charles B. Aycock wrote Henry G. Connor on the eleventh that he was happy about the election victory: "it is a glorious victory that we have won and the very extent of it frightened me. We shall need wisdom to prove ourselves worthy of it." He then said that he regretted "the Wilmington affair of yesterday greatly." Bennehan Cameron of Durham received a note from a creditor in Virginia: "Now that we have white supremacy in North Carolina I hope you will sell your crops and send me a check." Cameron also received from Thomas W. Strange of Wilmington correspondence that thanked him for his offers of assistance during the riot. (Strange expected Cameron to pay for the telegram because he was saving every cent and hoped that Cameron would understand his financial "plight.") Still another letter to Cameron arrived

in late December from Julian S. Carr, chairman of the Durham County Democratic Executive Committee. In the letter, Carr spoke of the election victory, hoping that "the results of our November victory long abide with us and our children," and provided Cameron with a "souvenir badge of that grand and glorious event." Mallett Papers, Cameron Papers, and Connor Papers, Southern Historical Collection.

89. Part of the city's decorations was a series of "transparencies" that reflected as headlines the sentiments of many Democrats: "It is a hard pill, Governor, but shut your eyes and swallow it"; "There is retribution in politics"; "Hurrah for Wilmington"; "White Supremacy means work for all"; and "There's a hot time coming, Mr. Russell." *News and Observer*, November 10, 11, 12, 15, 16, 1898; C. Beauregard Poland, *North Carolina's Glorious Victory, 1898, Sketches of Able Democratic Leaders and Statesmen* (Raleigh: [Democratic Executive Committee], 1899).

90. *Morning Star*, November 12, 1898.

91. Hayden, "The Wilmington Light Infantry," 75.

92. The Reverend Hoge was also quoted as saying that the "process" of the preceding week was an "act of stern necessity." The prominence given to Hoge's sermon in the newspapers prompted historian Leon Prather to use Hoge's Biblical quote—"we have taken a city"—as the title for his in-depth book on the coup and violence. Black ministers and lay people "consulted" with white authorities to ensure that their services would not be interrupted, and they were encouraged to counsel moderation to their congregations. It is unclear whether or not sermons delivered in the black churches were monitored or scripted by whites, but all contain similar strains of language, mainly that of accommodation and submission to white domination. *Evening Dispatch*, November 15, 1898; *Wilmington Messenger*, November 15, 1898.

93. E. Y. Wootten to "Edward," November 21, 1898, Bradley Jewett Wootten Papers, University of North Carolina Wilmington Special Collections.

94. Hayden, "The Wilmington Light Infantry," 105.

95. Minutes of the Organizational Meeting of the WLI.

96. *Morning Star*, November 16, 1898.

97. *Morning Star*, November 15, 1898.

98. Ibid.

99. *Wilmington Messenger*, November 12, 1898.

100. Prather, *We Have Taken a City*, 144.

101. Dowling was also elected president of the newly formed White Laborers' Union when that body assembled on November 24 with more than one hundred members

in attendance. At the meeting, the union adopted a constitution and bylaws and passed a resolution to counter attempts by Waddell's administration to curb spending. The resolution took issue with proposals to lower salaries for some city employees: "We . . . uncompromising laboring men," the resolution read, "who worked and voted to place the Democrats in power . . . have been shocked and surprised" by the pay cuts. The union further challenged city leaders to maintain the wages paid by the previous Fusion administration. Following on the heels of the resolution, Waddell's administration halted attempts to reduce municipal worker wages. News of this conflict soon reached Raleigh, and later in November a Raleigh newspaper remarked that the city of Wilmington should maintain its adherence to all of the pledges of the White Declaration of Independence: "[I]t remains to be seen," the paper mused, "whether the community will stand on the declarations it has made" regarding white workers. The paper concluded that if the city wanted to be "progressive," it should hire only whites, since it considered black labor stagnant and without merit.

On March 6, 1899, Dowling was suspended until the mayor's office was able to hold a formal inquiry, through which Dowling could attend a meeting of the board of aldermen and plead his case. In response, Dowling sent a reply to the board informing it that they "go to Hell." The aldermen thereupon dismissed him for "incompetency, drunkenness, and insubordination." *Morning Star*, November 24, 1898; *Morning Post*, November 30, 1898; Minutes of the Wilmington Board of Aldermen.

102. Another Red Shirt leader, Theodore Swann, was rewarded with a job in the Waddell administration. On February 6, 1899, officers C. L. Frost and J. D. Hargrave were discharged for being drunk while on police duty. Minutes of the Wilmington Board of Aldermen; *Contested Election Case*, 383.

103. Prior to the changeover, the Cape Fear Steam Fire Engine Company No. 3, the best-equipped crew in Wilmington, had donated its engine, horses, and other equipment to the city. The Phoenix Hose Reel Company in Brooklyn had just moved into a new firehouse in 1894 and had purchased a new hose wagon in February 1898. Following the riot, the Phoenix company was disbanded, and the firehouse was torn down in 1900. Reaves, *"Strength through Struggle,"* 191–198.

104. Melton testimony, *Contested Election Case*, 370; *Morning Star*, November 12, 1898; Reaves, *"Strength through Struggle,"* 191–198.

105. *Morning Star*, November 16, 1898.

106. Prather, *We Have Taken a City*, 146; R. Beverly Mason to "Bess," November 8, 1898, John S. Henderson Papers, Southern Historical Collection.

237

107. *Asbury Park* (N.J.) *Evening News*, November 21, 1898; *Morning Star*, October 28, November 2, 4, 1898.

108. Minutes of the Wilmington Board of Aldermen.

109. By 1898 Louisiana and other southern states had already legalized racial segregation and had restricted voting rights for African Americans.

Chapter 7: Destiny of a Race

1. Bassett to Adams, November 15, 1898, Herbert Baxter Adams Papers, Johns Hopkins University, Baltimore, quoted in Jerome McDuffie, "Politics in Wilmington and New Hanover County, North Carolina, 1865–1900: The Genesis of a Race Riot" (Ph.D. diss., Kent State University, 1979), 749.

2. *Morning Star* (Wilmington), November 12, 1898.

3. Murmur of impeachment made it to the newspapers as soon as the dust settled from the election and violence. On November 12, 1898, the *Wilmington Messenger* asked its readers if it was possible that the newly elected Democratic legislature would impeach Russell in 1899. For additional information on the impact of the 1898 election on Russell's administration, see Jeffrey J. Crow and Robert F. Durden, *Maverick Republican in the Old North State: A Political Biography of Daniel L. Russell* (Baton Rouge: Louisiana State University Press, 1977), 134–188.

4. Council of State Minutes, 1898–1899, Daniel L. Russell, Governors' Papers, State Archives, North Carolina Office of Archives and History, Raleigh.

5. A review of the attorney general's records does, however, reveal a significant statewide increase in litigation over contested elections and the refusal of some incumbent appointed and elected officials to surrender their offices to newly elected Democrats following the November 1898 elections. State Attorney General's Office, Central Files, Correspondence, Letter Books, and Closed Case Files, 1898–1900, State Archives.

6. *Annual Report of the Adjutant-General of the State of North Carolina for the Year 1899*, North Carolina Public Documents, Document 9, State Archives; Daniel L. Russell, Governors' Papers, State Archives.

7. The *Washington Post* reported that a dozen men from Wilmington were in Washington attempting to meet with the president concerning the rioting. Some of the men had arrived there the day after the riot, and others—"refugees"—were scattered throughout the city, staying with friends and discussing the events in North Carolina. Julian S. Carr, chairman of the Durham County Democratic Executive Committee and a wealthy and influential businessman, penned a note to President McKinley that later appeared in the newspapers. Carr's letter explained, according to the papers, that white men "are leading the victorious column this morning and will rule North Carolina . . . no need of troops now." The actual letter was much less flowery. Carr told the president not to send troops to the state and made "no apologies for being a Southern Democrat." He offered to help McKinley "in solving the question" and promised to be in Washington as soon as needed to discuss the issues. Carr staked his claim as an important businessman by informing McKinley that he employed 1,000 men, "largely colored and they would die for me." He closed by declaring to the president that he was "in position to answer for the South and especially North Carolina." A brief postscript informed McKinley that Carr paid large sums of money in taxes and, as a result, felt that "no one is more interested in good stable government." *Evening Dispatch* (Wilmington), November 14, 1898; *Wilmington Messenger*, November 12, 1898; Carr to McKinley, November 12, 1898, McKinley Papers, Record Group 60, General Records of the Department of Justice, Box 1117A "Year Files," National Archives, Washington, D.C.

8. The Department of Justice files for 1898 include a collection of letters written to McKinley. One of them was written by S. E. Huffman of the United States Anti-Mob and Lynch Law Association to Marcus Hanna, Republican U.S. senator from Ohio and McKinley confidant. Huffman asked Hanna to use his influence with the president to facilitate an investigation of events in Wilmington. Huffman to Hanna, November 29, 1898, General Records of the Department of Justice, Box 1117A "Year Files," National Archives.

9. Letters to President McKinley, General Records of the Department of Justice, Box 1117A "Year Files," National Archives.

10. Harry Hayden, "The Wilmington Light Infantry" (typed, unpublished memoir), New Hanover County Public Library, Wilmington, 98.

11. The Democratic campaign was successful in stirring aggressive racist sentiment throughout the state and beyond. In cities such as New Bern and Wilson, people expected violence at any moment and expressed anxiety similar to the fears that gripped the citizens of Wilmington. In late October 1898 the Lumberton area had experienced an outbreak of violence. (One newspaper referred to the incident as the "Ashpole Riot.") On the night of November 9 a disturbance in Wilson nearly resulted in a riot. Only after a biracial meeting on the tenth and the coincidental disturbance in Wilmington was violence averted. Violence broke out just before election day in the town of Phoenix in Greenwood County, South Carolina. On November 6 about one hundred white men lynched four black men who had been implicated in killing a white man the previous day. The violence in

South Carolina brought the death of about ten black men and one white, and many of both races were wounded on election day. A number of whites fled the area and made their way to Washington, D.C., to plead their case with the president. Regarding the unrest, the *New York Journal* commented that the "race problem in the South has cast a shadow over the entire land by the recent bloodshed in the Carolinas." As advocates for federal intervention in Wilmington sought to thrust the city's violence into the national spotlight, the murders in South Carolina were added to the discussions. But because the two incidents came to be seen as examples of a larger, endemic problem of racial friction, the federal response to each matter was more subdued. *Farmer and Mechanic* (Raleigh), November 29, 1898, quoting *New York Journal*; *Farmer and Mechanic*, November 15, 1898; *News and Observer* (Raleigh), November 11, 12, 1898; *Evening Dispatch*, November 12, 1898; *Morning Star*, November 10, 11, 18, 1898; *Morning Post* (Raleigh), November 13, 1898; *Daily Free Press* (Kinston), October 24, 1898.

12. Those same federal troops saw more trouble later in the month when about thirty black laborers who were working at Fort Caswell became involved in a "row" with several soldiers stationed there. The resulting fight ended with the stabbing of one soldier. Other soldiers tried to retaliate against the workers, and a guard detail had to be established to protect the black men. Hayden, "The Wilmington Light Infantry," 98; *Morning Star*, November 28, 1898.

13. An example of the new bond between the North and South was a speech delivered by President McKinley in Atlanta as part of a "peace jubilee." McKinley said that "sectional lines no longer mar the map of the United States" and that "the cordial feeling now happily existing between the North and the South" would be helpful if the two sections faced "new problems now pressing upon us" together. Some African Americans took exception to the speech, particularly since McKinley exhibited an "incomprehensible silence" on the issue when he failed to acknowledge the "race problem" in the South and the recent violence. Former North Carolina Republican politician Albion Tourgée wrote McKinley that he feared the recent violence heralded the opening of a new chapter in race relations, in which blacks were "again placed under the heel of race prejudice in the United States." Tourgée astutely recognized that a newly emerging sectional harmony and nationalism connected with America's recent victory in the Spanish-American War would divert the attention of national leaders and enable them to ignore the plight of southern blacks and instead leave them to the devices of southern whites. An example of African American reaction in the North to McKinley's speech was a meeting of the Afro-American Council in Washington,

D.C., during which the council cautioned blacks that "the time has come for the colored men to act; to act with firmness, calmness and after due deliberation." *News and Observer*, December 15, 1898; Timothy Thomas Fortune to Booker T. Washington, December 17, 1898, quoted in Louis R. Harlan, ed., *The Booker T. Washington Papers*, 13 vols. (Urbana: University of Illinois Press, 1972–1989), 4:535; *Morning Star*, December 30, 1898.

14. Harry Hayden recounted that a "hotheaded Wilmingtonian" had telegraphed federal officials that if troops were sent into the city, "caskets should be included in their equipment" because fellow citizens "would not brook any outside interference." Hayden, "The Wilmington Light Infantry," 98.

15. The so-called "negro problem" had multiple facets. The renowned African American writer and social reformer W. E. B. DuBois observed in 1897 that although he and other contemporaries "ordinarily speak of the Negro problem as though it were one unchanged question . . . it is not one problem, but rather a plexus of social problems, some new, some old, some simple, some complex." DuBois attributed most of the obstacles faced by blacks in economics, politics, and education to their collective history as slaves and then, following emancipation, as second-class citizens without equal rights. He also claimed that the nation had witnessed a rebirth of the caste system for blacks similar to that which had existed under slavery. DuBois summarized three arguments by which whites justified the new caste system in which blacks were second-class citizens without equal rights: enfranchisement of blacks was a mistake, African Americans are inherently inferior to whites, and a final resolution of the race problem will be "open and legal recognition" of black inferiority. Intellectuals on both sides of the color line began to use the phrases "negro problem" or "negro question" in discussions of topics ranging from education and disfranchisement to strains on north-south relations.

The biographer of Gov. Daniel Russell defines the "negro question" as a "shibboleth for disfranchisement" by whites. Owen Aldis, a wealthy real-estate developer of Chicago, wrote Virginia writer Thomas Nelson Page that "this North Carolina affair shows that neither this generation nor the next will ever be through with the dangers arising from the negro." Aldis also observed that he did not believe "that the education of the intellect of the negro will alone solve the problem." Another prominent Virginian, Thomas H. Carter of Charlottesville, concluded that "the idea of the north that the [Civil] war solved the negro problem" was wrong and that the "problem" still persisted with no answer. North Carolina's Democratic press asserted that investigation by Congress would threaten the newly recognized north-south unity as extolled by President McKinley and "intensify race feelings in the south and . . . make the negro problem still more difficult." Discussions of the "negro problem" persisted long after the Carolina riots faded from the papers. *Wilmington Messenger*, December 6, 1898; *Morning Star*, December 9, 1898; speech by W. E. B. DuBois titled "The Study of Negro Problems" (delivered in Atlanta, 1898), in *Annals of the American Academy of Political and Social Science*, 1898, reprinted in Philip S. Foner, ed., *W. E. B. DuBois Speaks: Speeches and Addresses, 1890–1919*, 2 vols. (New York: Pathfinder Press, 1970), 1:104–108; speech by W. E. B. DuBois titled "The Evolution of the Race Problem" (delivered in New York, 1909), in *Proceedings of the National Negro Conference in New York, 1909*, reprinted in Foner, *W. E. B. DuBois Speaks*, 1:196–199; Aldis to Page, November 10, 1898; Carter to Page, December 1, 1898, Thomas Nelson Page Papers, Rare Book, Manuscript, and Special Collections Library, Duke University, Durham; Crow and Durden, *Maverick Republican*, 138.

16. Griggs apparently took the matter seriously and in 1899 and 1900 assisted black congressman George H. White in proposing legislation to make lynching and murder by mob rule treasonable offenses punishable by execution. The major impetus for Griggs's investigation was the experience of federal commissioner Robert Bunting concerning his treatment and banishment by Wilmington leaders. Benjamin R. Justesen, *George Henry White: An Even Chance in the Race of Life* (Baton Rouge: Louisiana State University Press, 2001), 278–279.

17. Griggs to Bernard, quoted in McDuffie, "Politics in Wilmington," 556–557, and found in the papers of the Attorney General's Office, General Records of the Department of Justice, National Archives. Just after the 1898 election, B. F. McLean, attorney and U.S. commissioner of justice for the Eastern District of North Carolina, had likewise written to Attorney General Griggs and others in Washington to describe intimidation by the Red Shirts and to ask if those men would be liable for prosecution. Bernard to Griggs, quoted in McDuffie, "Politics in Wilmington," 757–758, and found in the papers of the Attorney General's Office, General Records of the Department of Justice, Record Group 60, National Archives; McLean to Griggs, November 9, 1898, General Records of the Department of Justice, National Archives, quoted in H. Leon Prather Sr., *We Have Taken a City: Wilmington Massacre and Coup of 1898* (Rutherford, N.J.: Fairleigh Dickinson University Press, 1984), 153.

18. *Wilmington Messenger*, December 16, 1898.

19. Ibid., December 9, 1898.

20. No records from the office of the U.S. attorney for the Eastern District of North Carolina have survived to document Bernard's activities. A survey of documents held by the National Archives' Regional Records Center in Atlanta reveals that correspondence, grand jury records, and dockets from Raleigh have not been preserved. Details of Bernard's grand jury investigation can be found only in newspaper sources.

21. *Wilmington Messenger*, December 20, 23, 1898.

22. Bernard to Griggs, April 22, 1899, General Records of the Department of Justice, National Archives, quoted in McDuffie, "Politics in Wilmington," 759.

23. Acting Attorney General to Bernard, August 30, 1900, Instructions to United States Attorneys and Marshals, General Records of the Department of Justice, National Archives, quoted in McDuffie, "Politics in Wilmington," 760.

24. *Wilmington Messenger*, December 6, 1898.

25. For additional information on Dockery's lawsuit, see *Contested Election Case of Oliver H. Dockery vs. John D. Bellamy from the Sixth Congressional District of the State of North Carolina* (Washington, D.C.: Government Printing Office, 1899) (hereafter cited as *Contested Election Case*). Testimony in the contested election case, particularly that of former chief of police John R. Melton and several African American election officials, provides useful details of the events leading up to the violence of November 10, as well as those of that day.

26. Most of the information concerning the contested election and testimony about it was found either in newspaper accounts or in *Contested Election Case*. Some contradictory testimony, unflattering to Bellamy and found neither in Democratic newspapers nor in the *Contested Election Case*, appears in the *Union Republican* (Winston) of March 15, 1900.

27. A list of contested elections filed in the House Documents file of the Fifty-sixth Congress includes a calendar of filings for the Dockery-Bellamy case. However, another House document does not list the case as being heard by a Committee on Elections in the Fifty-sixth Congress. Furthermore, in his autobiography, John D. Bellamy admitted that Dockery requested that Congress prohibit him from taking his seat in the House; but because of fraternal ties with many influential Washington insiders, among them Attorney General Griggs, he was able to escape investigation. An article published in the Wilmington *Morning Star* in July 1899 indicated that Dockery's representative was in Washington filing papers concerning the case. The article also stated that Republicans were focusing their attention on contesting the Bellamy election. "Letter from the Clerk of the House transmitting a List of the Contested Election Cases in the Fifty-Sixth Congress," U.S. House of Representatives, *House Documents*, Document No. 23, 56th Congress, 1st Session, December 5, 1899; Chester H.

Rowell, *A Historical and Legal Digest of All the Contested Election Cases in the House of Representatives of the United States from the First to the Fifty-Sixth Congress, 1789–1901,* House Document No. 510, 56th Congress, 2nd Session, 1901, 581–582; John D. Bellamy, *Memoirs of an Octogenarian* (Charlotte: Observer Printing House, 1942), 139–141.

28. J. Allen Kirk, *A Statement of Facts Concerning the Bloody Riot in Wilmington, N.C., of Interest to Every Citizen of the United States* ([Wilmington?: The Author?, 1898?]), 11, 15–16; online edition available at http://docsouth.unc.edu/nc/kirk/menu.html.

29. Unidentified author to President William McKinley, November 13, 1898, General Records of the Department of Justice, National Archives.

30. It is unclear how the newspapers were able to access such detailed snippets of the sermons given at such a wide variety of African American churches, but in printing the passages from the various ministers, the papers reinforced to non-churchgoing blacks the necessity of submission to whites and at the same time demonstrated to whites that black leaders who remained in the city were encouraging others not to retaliate. A correspondent for the *Baltimore Sun* composed the article containing the sermon extracts, and the piece appeared in newspapers published in Wilmington, Raleigh, and Baltimore. The article could have been another Democratic propaganda tool. *Wilmington Messenger,* November 15, 1898; *Evening Dispatch,* November 15, 1898; *News and Observer,* November 15, 1898.

31. *Morning Star,* November 15, 1898.

32. Throughout the post-violence period, Dancy walked a fine line between the interests of the black community and his attempts to retain the respect of white leaders as he sought to bridge the gap between the two and prevent further violence and hatred. Dancy's son recalled that his father had been out of town on the day of the riot and that his stepmother had frantically gathered her children to evacuate the city. *Evening Dispatch,* November 23, 1898; John C. Dancy, *Sand Against the Wind: The Memoir of John C. Dancy* (Detroit: Wayne State University Press, 1966), 69–70.

33. A Raleigh newspaper noted that there were concerted efforts in many major cities to coordinate meetings throughout the northern states. At a gathering in New York, the city's ministers met to condemn the riots, and some argued that new Wilmington mayor Alfred M. Waddell, South Carolina politician Ben Tillman, and Wilmington's new police chief Edgar Parmele should be lynched. The New York ministers also took up collections to help Wilmington blacks. A similar meeting was held in Buffalo New York, to press the president to "interfere in behalf of oppressed negroes in North and South

Carolina." Asbury Park, New Jersey, was the scene of yet another such conclave, at which Alexander Manly figured prominently. Manly spoke at the meeting and discussed his infamous editorial. Those in attendance offered a resolution to be sent to the president asking for assistance and took up a collection to aid Manly. A Wilmington newspaper reported that Manly was asked not to speak at some meetings because of the belief in some quarters that "his ideas are of a somewhat radical nature and . . . that he had better not deliver an address as his feelings might get the better of his prudence."

Many northern reformers viewed the election-day violence in Phoenix, South Carolina, and the riot in Wilmington two days later as evidence of the troubled nature of southern black-white relations. Attracting additional attention from northern observers were laws on the books of some southern states, among them Louisiana and Georgia, that limited African American suffrage. In late November 1898 the *The Literary Digest,* published in New York, devoted a lengthy article to the violence that had occurred in the two states. *Morning Post,* November 15, 1898; *Morning Star,* November 17, 24, 25, 1898; "Race Troubles in the Carolinas," *The Literary Digest* 17 (November 26, 1898): 623–627.

34. *Morning Star,* November 13, 1898; *Chicago Daily Tribune,* November 18, 1898; *New York Times,* November 14, 1898; McDuffie, "Politics in Wilmington," 751; *Wilmington Messenger,* December 2, 1898.

35. Both the Constitution and historical precedent limited the powers of the president to intervene in state matters. The right of states to manage their own affairs was still a hotly debated topic decades after the Civil War. Some analysts have attributed President Theodore Roosevelt's failure to intervene in the Atlanta Riot in 1906 to precedent set by William McKinley. Unlike President Grover Cleveland, who in 1894 dispatched federal troops to intervene in a railroad labor dispute, citing as his rationale for that intrusion into a state matter the fact that the strike was disrupting the U.S. mail service, McKinley lacked a specific pretext for intervening in the Wilmington race riot other than the alleged participation of a mob in the forced removal of federal officer Robert Bunting. *Chicago Daily Tribune,* November 18, 1898; *New York Times,* November 14, 1898; Charles Crowe, "Racial Massacre in Atlanta, September 22, 1906," *Journal of Negro History* 54 (April 1969): 167.

36. *Wilmington Messenger,* December 2, 1898; *Chicago Daily Tribune,* November 21, 1898. Peter Mallett of Fayetteville noted in his daybook that he had read in the papers of an "excited meeting of negroes last night at Cooper Union." He added that the blacks were "enflamed to wild excitement by a speech of Mrs. Grannis an old abolition hussy—should be lynched." Daybook, entry for November 18, 1898, Peter Mallett Papers,

241

Southern Historical Collection, Wilson Library, University of North Carolina at Chapel Hill.

37. *New York Times*, November 14, 1898.

38. Letter to the editor, *Washington Post*, December 4, 1898.

39. Baldwin to Washington, December 4, 1898, quoted in Harlan, *The Booker T. Washington Papers*, 4:525–526.

40. Fortune to Washington, November 30, 1898, quoted in Harlan, *The Booker T. Washington Papers*, 4:523–524.

41. In December 1898 the pro-Democratic *Wilmington Messenger* reported to its readers that the editor of a black newspaper in Charlotte "rakes" Booker T. Washington and "the able men of the black race who are in sympathy with that wise man." Moreover, the *Messenger* remarked that the black editor wrote "pacifically in places but the general tone leaves the impression of sore-headedness and growling," That the *Messenger* even took notice of the writings of an obscure black newspaper editor—much less commented on the editor's writing style—suggests that whites were paying close attention to the black press and the tone of its product.

In January 1899 Booker T. Washington received word from Edward Clement, one of his white supporters in Massachusetts, that opposition to Washington's methods was growing among blacks. Clement admitted to Washington that he was "impressed with the protests of such men as Dubois and [the poet Paul Laurence] Dunbar against the new outburst of intolerance in the South." Fortune's organized meetings, plus the networks established by men such as Washington and DuBois, provided the groundwork for what would eventually lead to the formation of modern organizations such as the Urban League and the National Association for the Advancement of Colored People in the twentieth century. Edward Clement to Booker T. Washington, January 2, 1899, quoted in Harlan, *The Booker T. Washington Papers*, 5:5.

42. The Afro-American Council and several conferences of the AME Zion Church met in the spring of 1899 and issued proclamations and memorials denouncing the violence. *Wilmington Messenger*, May 16, 1899; *Morning Star*, May 5, 1899.

43. *Wilmington Messenger*, December 6, 1898.

44. Waddell offered *Collier's Weekly* a firsthand account of the Wilmington Race Riot. His version of the events of November 10, 1898, provided the structure and substance for the collective memory of events for nearly a century. Waddell's story whitewashed the bloodshed and disorder that historians have since associated with the riot. Waddell attributed the disturbance to the leading white Fusionists, among them Gov. Daniel L. Russell, "the engineer of all the deviltry and meanness." (The "deviltry" to which Waddell referred was the political and economic advancement of African Americans in Wilmington; he declared that whites should restore proper white government in the city.) Waddell argued that he had preserved order on November 10 and prevented the brutal lynchings that had been associated with the South in the 1890s. He described the fire at Alexander Manly's offices as "purely accidental." Pointing out that the fire "was unintentional on our part," Waddell asserted that white leaders did not intend to destroy private property. He implied that the poor classes of whites who served in Mike Dowling's Red Shirt brigade had set the fire. He recalled the speech he delivered in the aftermath of the destruction of the *Daily Record* offices, in which he pleaded for order: "[L]et us go quietly to our homes, and about our business, and obey the law, unless we are forced, in self-defense, to do otherwise."

In another incident, Waddell recounted a mob's futile attempt to remove seven blacks from the jail and "destroy them." As the newly "elected" mayor, Waddell claimed that he stood for law and order, "stay[ing] up the whole night myself, and the forces stayed up all night, and we saved those wretched creatures' lives." Waddell knew that the image of the South had been tarnished by accounts of lynchings across the region; his essay deflected any comparisons between mob violence and the riot by simply overlooking the bloodshed. Instead, he emphasized the ways in which white leaders protected the interests of African Americans. He assured readers that the disorder had subsided and that black citizens of Wilmington embraced the new order. Alfred Moore Waddell, "The Story of the Wilmington, N.C., Race Riot," *Collier's Weekly* 22 (November 26, 1898): 4–5.

45. Henderson recorded his life experiences in a diary that is currently in possession of family members. The diary was not available for research in the course of this project, but, according to excerpts read by a descendant during the 1998 centennial commemorations in Wilmington, it contains valuable information relative to the riot, Henderson's escape from Wilmington, and his life thereafter.

46. *Freeman* (Indianapolis, Ind.), December 3, 1898; *Morning Star*, December 25, 30, 1898; *Wilmington Messenger*, December 27, 1898. A. G. Ricaud, a former mayor of Wilmington and law partner of Gov. Daniel Russell, gave a similar interview to the *Baltimore Sun*. Ricaud had relocated to the North and was a respected businessman but was enlisted to throw his support behind Waddell's administration. He expressed his support for white supremacy but denounced bloodshed even as he favored a suffrage amendment to limit black voting rights.

Evening Dispatch, November 16, 1898. The latter article states that Ricaud had served as mayor from 1891 to 1893.

47. *Wilmington Messenger*, December 20, 1898.

48. Bryant felt that instead of merely administering a whipping, the mob intended to "pepper him with bullets from Winchesters." Another report from earlier in 1899 warned former chief of police John Melton not to return to Wilmington because another exile had tried to do so and had been frightened into leaving again because "one night voices were heard and forms were seen ominously circumambulating around his house. . . . [It was] never learned whether it were Rough Riders or ghosts that made the manifestations." White businessman A. J. Taylor may have forewarned Bryant; Taylor later defended his action to Democrats by declaring that he had merely encouraged Bryant to depart the city. *Wilmington Messenger*, March 31, June 18, 21, 23, 1899.

49. *Wilmington Messenger*, December 6, 1898.

50. The 1866 charter set the mayor's salary at $2,000 per year, but changes enacted in 1895 and 1897 lowered it to $1,000; the 1899 charter raised it back up to between $1,200 and $2,000 per year. *Public Laws of North Carolina, 1866*, c 2, s. 7; *Public Laws of North Carolina, 1895*, c. 121, s. 3; *Public Laws of North Carolina, 1897*, c. 150, s. 6; *Private Laws of the State of North Carolina Passed by the General Assembly at its Session of 1899* (Raleigh: Edwards and Broughton and E. M. Uzzell, 1899), 591–596. The 1901, 1903, and 1905 General Assemblies subsequently made additional changes to the city's charter.

51. Members of the new board of aldermen were John Harriss, J. F. Littleton, Hugh MacRae, F. A. Montgomery, C. C. Parker, C. L. Spencer, William E. Springer, J. Allan Taylor, Henry P. West, J. M. Woolard, and Charles W. Worth; Alfred Moore Waddell was unanimously elected mayor. Minutes of the Wilmington Board of Aldermen, 1884–1906 (microfilm), State Archives; *Morning Star*, March 14–24, 1899.

52. McDuffie, "Politics in Wilmington," 775–776; *Journal of the House of Representatives of North Carolina, 1899*, p. 51; *Morning Star*, March 1–6, 1899.

53. *Public Laws of North Carolina, 1899*, c. 487; McDuffie, "Politics in Wilmington," 784–785.

54. Legislation concerned with racial segregation eventually applied to virtually all aspects of everyday life. Politicians sought to segregate textbooks for public schools, cadavers sent to white and black medical schools, and all public facilities; eventually they sought to force blacks into separate housing and communities. Helen G. Edmonds, *The Negro and Fusion Politics in North Carolina, 1894–1901* (Chapel Hill: University of North Carolina Press, 1951), 189–190; James L. Leloudis, *Schooling the New South: Pedagogy, Self, and Society in North Carolina,*

1880–1920 (Chapel Hill: University of North Carolina Press, 1996), 137; C. Vann Woodward, *The Strange Career of Jim Crow* (New York: Oxford University Press, 1955), 100–102; Joel Williamson, *The Crucible of Race: Black-White Relations in the American South since Reconstruction* (New York: Oxford University Press, 1984), 253–254; Edward L. Ayers, *The Promise of the New South: Life after Reconstruction* (New York: Oxford University Press, 1992), 429.

55. Wilmington's white leaders consistently reworked the rules to provide for segregation of the city's streetcars. In 1907, following passage of a new streetcar law, blacks boycotted the system, reducing patronage by 50 to 75 percent. The transportation companies were concerned about the economic impact the boycott might have but were reassured that it would not last because similar boycotts in other cities had been only temporary. William M. Reaves, *"Strength through Struggle": The Chronological and Historical Record of the African-American Community in Wilmington, North Carolina, 1865–1950*, ed. Beverly Tetterton (Wilmington: New Hanover County Public Library, 1998), 268–269.

56. *News and Observer*, November 23, 1898.

57. In this context, the focus of the "negro problem" was the right of blacks to vote, and the argument was made that the former bondsmen should not have been given that right as soon as they had been granted freedom after the Civil War but instead should have been required to earn it through dutiful employment and proper education. For an argument posited by whites concerning black suffrage, see Rountree's "Memorandum of My Personal Reasons for the Passage of the Suffrage Amendment to the Constitution (Grandfather Clause)" in the Henry G. Connor Papers, Southern Historical Collection.

58. In *Williams v. Mississippi*, 170 U.S. 213 (1898), the Supreme Court of the United States sanctioned the right of a state to disfranchise its citizens by means of a literacy test. The primary purpose of the test was to eliminate the black vote, but the court declared it legal because the law never mentioned race. Ayers, *The Promise of the New South*, 304.

59. *Wilmington Messenger*, December 2, 1898; McDuffie, "Politics in Wilmington," 780–789.

60. White eventually relocated to the North and founded Whitesboro, New Jersey, as a resettlement destination for Wilmington refugees. McDuffie, "Politics in Wilmington," 782.

61. Jeffrey J. Crow and Flora J. Hatley, eds., *Black Americans in North Carolina and the South* (Chapel Hill: University of North Carolina Press, 1984), 149.

62. Joseph M. King to Marion Butler, October 25, 1898, Marion Butler Papers, Southern Historical Collection.

63. Hal Ayer to Marion Butler, December 30, 1899, Butler Papers; Jeter Pritchard to Charles N. Hunter, January 26, 1900, Charles N. Hunter Papers, Duke Special Collections.

64. Crow and Durden, *Maverick Republican*, 145–148.

65. *Washington Post*, July 27, 1900.

66. The overall state totals were 182,217 votes for the amendment and 128,285 against it. In some of North Carolina's western counties with relatively small black populations, such as Anson, Henderson, Rutherford and Wilkes, the amendment was defeated. *Wilmington Messenger*, August 5, 1900; *North Carolina Manual, 1913*, 1016–1018.

67. For a useful overview of the condition of Wilmington's African American community at the beginning of the twentieth century, see Reaves, *"Strength through Struggle."*

68. *Contested Election Case*, 387, 394. For articles demonstrating how Wilmington's climate had changed for non-Democrats, see the *Morning Star*, November 16, 17, 1898, and the *Wilmington Messenger*, November 16–December 7, 1898.

69. *Wilmington Messenger*, August 1, 1899; *Morning Star*, August 3, 1899; McDuffie, "Politics in Wilmington," 790.

70. Reaves, *"Strength through Struggle,"* 154, quoting *Wilmington Messenger*, June 7, 1905.

71. Waddell is quoted in Leloudis, *Schooling the New South*, 177–178.

72. Prior to 1898 Wilmington's African American community had benefited from a progressive educational system. Not only were there publicly supported schools available to blacks in various sections of the city, but there were also several highly respected privately funded schools. The first concerted efforts to establish schools for blacks were those initiated at the end of the Civil War by the Freedmen's Bureau. Following on the heels of the Freedmen's Bureau schools were those established by other northern benevolent interests, such as the American Missionary Association. About 1870 the Freedmen's Bureau turned the operation of its schools over to local interests, and philanthropists provided funding to maintain them. Such schools became the core of the city's public school system. Although African American schools had always experienced low financial support from the city and county both before and after the 1898 violence and coup, the period extending from those events well into the twentieth century witnessed consistently diminishing public financial support for the city's African American schools.

73. Noble is quoted in Leloudis, *Schooling the New South*, 200. It is interesting to note that Noble, in writing the history of public education in North Carolina, failed to mention Wilmington's schools in discussing the progressive nature of public education in the state during the last quarter of the nineteenth century, even though his career benefited from that very aspect of his work in the city. Despite the progressive steps Noble implemented while in Wilmington, the city's black students still suffered financial setbacks and mirrored a larger problem for black education statewide. M. C. S. Noble, *A History of the Public Schools of North Carolina* (Chapel Hill: University of North Carolina Press, 1930).

74. Historian James L. Leloudis explained that the vocational curricula of Booker T. Washington's highly successful Tuskegee Institute offered white educators an option for improving black educational programs. Training blacks to be good workers in trades and agriculture became a major focus designed to address what whites perceived as the needs and desires of blacks. Moreover, Leloudis noted, "Industrial education promised to cultivate a new sense of self and social place among African American school children, convincing them to accept their subordination as a normal and inevitable fact of life." Aiding in the development of vocational training was the arrival of "Jeannes teachers" in the first decades of the twentieth century. Jeannes teachers, funded by a northern philanthropist, traveled throughout the rural South and instructed students and teachers in a variety of subjects. Leloudis, *Schooling the New South*, 148, 182, 184–185.

75. Many African American leaders denounced the 1883 legislation, known as the Dortch Act (named for state senator William Dortch of Goldsboro, who introduced the bill), and the North Carolina Supreme Court eventually declared it unconstitutional. Subsequent legislation in 1885 reworked the Dortch law and granted leniency to local districts to distribute their tax revenues as they saw fit. Leloudis, *Schooling the New South*, 121–122.

76. Aycock realized that distributing school funding along racial lines might well invite federal intervention. He proposed that black students be properly educated through curriculum and oversight tightly controlled by North Carolina whites. Aycock also chose to promote fully the separation of the races in education, expressing the belief that the end result of the practice would be beneficial to blacks by helping to fit them into their subordinate role. Leloudis, *Schooling the New South*, 177–180; R. D. W. Connor and Clarence Poe, *The Life and Speeches of Charles Brantley Aycock* (Garden City, N.Y.: Doubleday, Page and Company, 1912), 111–139.

77. Donations for salaries, supplies, and buildings for schools in Wilmington and elsewhere in North Carolina

came from northern benefactors such as George Peabody, James Gregory, the American Missionary Association, and, later, the philanthropy of Julius Rosenwald, whose generosity contributed significantly to the construction of school buildings during the 1920s. Reaves, *"Strength through Struggle,"* 144–173.

78. The two white districts were Hemenway and Union School; the two black districts were Peabody and Williston.

79. In July 1898 there were 1,763 white students (55 percent of all white school-age children in New Hanover County) and 2,290 black students (51 percent of black school-age children in the county) enrolled in Wilmington's public schools. The property values of the white schools in the county totaled $37,250, and those of the black schools totaled $12,850. Report of Superintendent M. C. S. Noble to State Department of Public Instruction, July 1898, Superintendents' Annual Reports, Department of Public Instruction, State Archives.

80. In July 1899 the total number of students of both races declined to only 1,188 white students (57 percent of all white school-age children in the county) and 2,110 black students (47 percent of all black school-age children in the county), whereas property values increased to $76,690 for white schools and $17,500 for black schools. The numbers gap widened again in 1900 and 1901. By 1901, 63 percent (2,087) of the white school-age children in the county attended school, but only 40 percent (1,175) of African American school-age children did so. That year, white school properties were valued at $82,600 and black school properties at $18,050. Leloudis noted that the low funding for black schools resulted in "overcrowded, ramshackle classrooms." Report of Superintendent of New Hanover County Schools to State Department of Public Instruction, July 1899, July 1900, July 1901, Superintendents' Annual Reports; Leloudis, *Schooling the New South*, 211.

81. References to disparate amounts of taxes paid by the two races as the rationale for differences in school funding can be seen in contemporary literature generated by reports of the Department of Public Instruction, as well as in newspapers, letters, and legislative actions. Tables in the *Biennial Report of the Superintendent of Public Instruction of North Carolina for the Scholastic Years 1898–99 and 1899–1900* (Raleigh: Edwards and Broughton, 1900) show the amounts apportioned to white and black schools according to taxation and property valuations for the county. Data in the biennial reports was culled from reports filed by the county superintendents.

82. Minutes. Board of County Commissioners, 1887–1918, New Hanover County Miscellaneous Records, State Archives.

83. In 1927 an article that appeared in *The Crisis*, published by W. E. B. DuBois for the NAACP, showed that African American schools in North Carolina were still funded at rates significantly lower than their white counterparts. Leloudis, *Schooling the New South*, 226.

84. *Morning Star*, June 11, 1920.

85. Minutes. Board of County Commissioners, 1887–1918, New Hanover County Miscellaneous Records.

86. Beginning in 1915, another white philanthropist, Julius Rosenwald, helped to fund the construction of about 767 schools in North Carolina, including seven in Wilmington. The North Carolina Teachers Association, founded by Wilmington educator Charles Moore in 1880, did not gain in membership and collective strength until 1900. Thomas W. Hanchett, "The Rosenwald Schools and Black Education in North Carolina," *North Carolina Historical Review* 65 (October 1988): 387–444; Percy Murray, *History of the North Carolina Teachers Association* ([Washington, D.C.]: National Education Association, [1984]), 15–19, 33.

87. In November 1899 the average monthly pay for white teachers was $39.83, and the average monthly pay for black teachers was $32.75. In 1900 the average salary of white teachers was $52.50, as oppposed to $36.58 for African Americans. Minutes. Board of County Commissioners, 1887–1918, New Hanover County Miscellaneous Records; Report of Superintendent of New Hanover County Schools to State Department of Public Instruction, July 1900, Superintendents' Annual Reports.

88. The White Laborers' Union held a meeting on November 21, 1898, and persisted as an organized force into the following year. Union members sported lapel pins and adopted their goal "to aid and assist white men in obtaining situations and work which previously had largely been occupied by negroes." The body accomplished its objective by forming committees to visit businessmen and encourage the hiring of whites. The organization also pressured the county into opening a night school at which to educate white children who were working during the day. Democratic Party leaders, drawing a connection between union involvement in politics and the failure of the Farmers' Alliance, sought to control the union and warned it not to get involved in politics. *Evening Dispatch*, November 21, 1898; *Wilmington Messenger*, February 7, March 5, 7, 1899.

89. "If Wilmington shall find that white labor can be successfully substituted for colored," the Raleigh *News and Observer* declared, "other towns will not be slow to follow her lead." The paper also pointed out that the topic was of statewide interest to blacks and whites alike. The *Wilmington Messenger* published a brief complaint that arose

245

over the discovery that an all-black crew led by a black foreman had secured a contract to tear down an old building on Front Street even though white workers were available. Further analysis of the changes in the labor market for Wilmington's African Americans can be found in chapter 8. *News and Observer*, December 15, 1898; *Morning Star*, February 3, 1898; *Wilmington Messenger*, February 21, March 18, 1899.

90. Officials' Bonds and Records, 1766–1908 [1891–1908], New Hanover County Bonds, State Archives.

91. Further study of Sprunt's voluminous corporate records, held by the Rare Book, Manuscript, and Special Collections Library at Duke University, might shed light on his company's labor force, which apparently continued to include African American stevedores into the twentieth century. The ledgers for Sprunt's compress include records for accounts and receivables, as well as references to cotton brought in and shipped out on most of the days in November 1898. No entries are shown for November 10, apparently because no work was done that day. As indicated by other sources, work was stopped the day of the riot. Entries pick up again on the following day with business as usual. Lura Beam, a northern teacher who moved to Wilmington in 1908, noted that local African Americans highly respected Sprunt, the "local cotton king." A Sprunt employee recalled that his boss would "provide things for the black people," particularly at Christmastime, when he would fill barrels with food and give each employee a full barrel for the holiday. Reaves, *"Strength through Struggle,"* 325; *Morning Star*, November 13, 1898; Account Ledgers, November 1898, Alexander Sprunt and Son, Inc. Papers, Duke Special Collections; Lura Beam, *He Called Them by the Lightning: A Teacher's Odyssey in the Negro South, 1908–1919* (Indianapolis: Bobbs-Merrill, 1967), 15–36; Susan Taylor Block, *Wilmington through the Lens of Louis T. Moore* (Wilmington: Lower Cape Fear Historical Society and New Hanover County Public Library, 2001), 251.

92. *Evening Dispatch*, November 12, 1898.

93. *Farmer and Mechanic*, November 15, 1898.

94. Leslie H. Hossfeld, *Narrative, Political Unconscious, and Racial Violence in Wilmington, North Carolina* (New York: Routledge, 2005), 6.

95. *Wilmington, N.C. Directory, 1903* (Richmond, Va.: Hill Directory Company, 1903).

Chapter 8: Rebuilding

1. Robert C. Kenzer, *Enterprising Southerners: Black Economic Success in North Carolina, 1865–1915* (Charlottesville: University of Virginia Press, 1997), 105–106. Kenzer also posits that because no blacks held seats in the state legislature or retained the power to vote objectionable politicians out of office, legislation favorable to their interests was rarely introduced, and resistance to legislation inimical to their interests was virtually nonexistent. Although African Americans had no votes in the legislature, black leaders managed to influence sympathetic politicians in a variety of ways. The ability of blacks to adapt to the political framework imposed upon them by whites became key to ensuring that they received a modicum of benefit from representative government.

2. Hayumi Higuchi, "White Supremacy on the Cape Fear: The Wilmington Affair of 1898" (master's thesis, University of North Carolina at Chapel Hill, 1980), 140; Kenzer, *Enterprising Southerners*, 125. Kenzer observed that blacks of all socioeconomic backgrounds were able to attain college educations and, as a result, pursued careers in business and private enterprise rather than in trades. He concluded that achieving higher education for all blacks, regardless of pre-emancipation status, was a unifying goal for the community rather than an issue that divided upper and lower classes of African Americans.

3. Hayumi Higuchi, a graduate student at the University of North Carolina (UNC-CH) at Chapel Hill, in 1980 conducted the first comprehensive study of occupations using Wilmington city directories. Sue Ann Cody, a graduate student at the University of North Carolina at Wilmington, in 2000 completed another study of Wilmington city directory data, and Dennis Daniels, a researcher with the North Carolina Office of Archives and History, engaged in still another study of such data for this project in 2002, prior to the joint project with UNC-CH. Cody cited a number of noteworthy drawbacks inherent in employing the directory data. She surmised that the directories were incomplete lists of city residents and were, at best, only a sample of citizens, skewed by race, gender, geography, and age. Since the 1898 Wilmington Race Riot Commission published its official report in 2005, additional study of refined city directory and census data has produced slightly different findings, which will be presented in chapter 8 of this publication.

4. This portion of the study did not take into account gender or age, since the directories provided no information about those two variables. However, some occupations traditionally held by women have been identified, and some marginal conclusions about their work experiences can be drawn from the directory data.

5. Because both directories were compiled by the same company, it can be assumed that the data-collection methods affecting whether or not particular names were or were not included were similar for both directory years. It is therefore safe to assume that people from any given occupation or neighborhood would be equally as likely to be included or excluded from both directories,

making them mutually comparable. Moreover, researcher Tod Hamilton compared the 1900 city directory to the 1900 census, and only minor discrepancies in racial populations appeared. He did discover, however, that the directory was slightly deficient in representing the number of workers in the black community, in that it failed to list as many low-wage African American workers as can be found in the census.

6. The only other available information on occupation would be from the census, but the 1890 census was destroyed by fire in 1921.

7. When working toward a classification scheme for grading occupations, most economists have relied upon standards developed by the U.S. Bureau of Labor Statistics; those standards do not easily apply to Wilmington, however. One example can be seen in the category of unskilled labor, which included stevedores, draymen, and laborers. In Wilmington many stevedores received higher pay than did day laborers and occupied a higher social status because of their jobs at Sprunt's cotton compress. Furthermore, draymen were self-employed and often owned their wagons and horses, placing their working status above laborers and some stevedores. For this study, stevedores, carpenters, and those in maritime and railroad trades were singled out to reflect the specific roles those occupations played in the overall life of Wilmington. Food-service workers were singled out for study because they represented an up-and-coming occupation in the city and reflected some of the first post-1898 entrepreneurial stirrings among blacks.

8. Of the domestic workers, most were employed in jobs such as washerwoman, housemaid, maid, or cook—jobs traditionally reserved for African American women who worked for white employers in white residences. There were 512 cooks and 422 washerwomen or laundresses enumerated in *J. L. Hill Printing Co.'s Directory of Wilmington, N.C. 1897* (Richmond, Va: J. L. Hill Printing Company, 1897; hereafter cited as *Hill's 1897 Wilmington City Directory*). Oral histories of many African American families are peppered with memories of at least one family member who worked for a white family. The pay was low but afforded a guaranteed income, which helped families when male incomes were either nonexistent or were unstable because of seasonal employment. Other people, interviewed for the "Behind the Veil" oral history project conducted by Duke University, indicated that it was an important status symbol to work for a prominent, wealthy white family and recalled such employment with pride.

The category also includes nurses. It is unknown whether or not the modern interpretation of the occupation of nurse as a trained health service provider is appropriate for all individuals so listed. An alternative interpretation of the term could be that these women provided child- or elder-care services in white homes, implying less educational training and pay. Wilmington did have a hospital at the time, but the composition and number of its staff are unknown. A newspaper account from the day of the violence indicated that the hospital staff was predominantly white. For oral histories by Wilmington African Americans, see "Behind the Veil: Documenting African American Life in the Jim Crow South," in the John Hope Franklin Collection of African and African American Documentation, Rare Book, Manuscript, and Special Collections Library, Duke University, Durham, or the oral history files of the Cape Fear Museum, Wilmington.

9. *Hill's 1897 Wilmington City Directory* reported a total of 3,496 black workers in the city in 1897. Of that number, 2,388 were domestic workers or laborers. The remaining work force, 1,108 workers, was dominated by the skilled category of railroad workers, building tradesmen, skilled artisans and tradesmen, and port drivers. Stevedores and draymen were a unique category of workers in Wilmington. Stevedores were generally understood to be the workers who loaded and off-loaded ship cargoes; draymen and teamsters transported cargo between the docks and homes, railroad depots, or warehouses throughout the city. Draymen commanded one horse or mule, and teamsters used a team of animals to pull larger loads. Those laborers, traditionally considered unskilled, were held in high esteem in Wilmington because of their importance to the port. For the import-export trade, the faster those men could load or off-load a ship, the more money the brokerage and manufacturing firms in the city and elsewhere in the world could make. The skills the men exhibited were prized, and, as noted in the previous chapter, because of the importance of the trade, bonds were required of stevedores to ensure that their work would be done in a timely manner and that their employees would be promptly paid.

10. For a history of some of the major African American builders in the city, see the following three works by Catherine W. Bishir: "Black Builders in Antebellum North Carolina," *North Carolina Historical Review* 61 (October 1984): 423–461; *The Bellamy Mansion, Wilmington North Carolina: An Antebellum Architectural Treasure and its People* (Wilmington: Bellamy Mansion Museum; Raleigh: Historic Preservation North Carolina, 2004); "Landmarks of Power: Building a Southern Past in Raleigh and Wilmington, North Carolina, 1885–1915," in Catherine W. Bishir, *Southern Built: American Architecture, Regional Practice* (Charlottesville: University of Virginia Press, 2006), 254–293, as well as relevant sections of William M. Reaves, *"Strength through Struggle": The Chronological and Historical Record of the*

247

African-American Community in Wilmington, North Carolina, 1865–1950, ed. Beverly Tetterton (Wilmington: New Hanover County Public Library, 1998). For a useful history of the Hargrave family's business, see *"Strength through Struggle,"* and Kenzer, *Enterprising Southerners.*

11. African American Charles Fisher, in his oral history of Wilmington, recalled that before he was born in 1919 his mother would make sandwiches and pies to take by wagon to sell to the workers at the cotton compress. The workers would then pay his mother for their lunches on the weekends. The money his mother earned by making lunches supplemented the income of his father, who worked as a wood dealer, most likely a seasonal job. Charles Fisher Oral History File, Cape Fear Museum.

12. One historian observed that the white-supremacy campaign targeted black postal workers because they were the "most widely visible of all federal appointees outside Washington" and that they had "received their jobs because of their political connections." Benjamin R. Justesen, "Black Postmasters and the Rise of White Supremacy in North Carolina," *North Carolina Historical Review* 82 (April 2005): 193–227.

13. It is unclear why the numbers of women working in domestic jobs declined at such a high rate. Speculation has arisen that perhaps the white employers sought to hire white female workers in their stead. (A study of white domestic laboring workers listed in the city directory does not support that conclusion.) It has also been surmised that perhaps women of all occupations are underrepresented in the 1900 city directory. However, it must also be noted that a rise in commercial steam laundries coincided with the drop in the numbers of black washerwomen. There were a few small Chinese laundry operations as well. The Wilmington Steam Laundry was operating in 1897 and grew in prominence. Such competition surely affected the client base for many laundresses. For information on the changing lives and work of laundresses, see Tera W. Hunter, *To 'Joy My Freedom: Southern Black Women's Lives and Labors after the Civil War* (Cambridge, Mass.: Harvard University Press, 1997), 53–57, 208.

14. Additional study of the ministers, on an individual level, both before and after the riot, is needed to determine whether new clergymen arrived in the city from elsewhere after 1897 or current residents became ministers.

15. In 1897 black-owned businesses were located in the primary business district along South Front, North Second, Market, and Princess streets. By 1900 that orientation had changed. Not only were the businesses different but many also had relocated. The greatest number were in the traditionally African American neighborhood of Brooklyn along North Fourth Street. Some businesses remained in areas popular in 1897, but the overall numbers were significantly lower. For example, in 1897 there were 76 black businesses located along streets in the city's central business district; by 1900 the number was down to 33. A slight increase was seen in the numbers of businesses located in the Fourth Street business district.

16. There were 89 businesses found in both the 1897 and 1900 city directories.

17. Rev. J. Irving Boone of Central Baptist Church led an effort to publicize the long-term successes of Wilmington's black entrepreneurs. In 1945 and 1946 he published directories of black businesses in the city. Boone's directories reveal that many of the black businesses established for black consumption managed to prosper and survive over decades following the violence. Black-owned and -operated Shaw's Funeral Home, for example, was still operating in Wilmington, having been in business for fifty years, and had branched into operating funeral parlors in ten other cities. J. Irving Boone, ed., *Directory of Negro Businesses in Wilmington and Southeastern North Carolina* (Wilmington: The Author, 1945); J. Irving Boone, ed., *Negro Business and Professional Men and Women: A Survey of Negro Progress in Varied Sections of North Carolina*, vol. 2 (Wilmington: The Author, 1946).

18. The white-supremacy campaign had targeted black postal workers as especially dangerous, in that those workers came in daily contact with white women in public situations. The documented black postal workers of 1902 were employed in behind-the-scenes jobs and did not deal directly with the public. Sue Ann Cody, "After the Storm: Racial Violence in Wilmington, North Carolina, and Its Consequences for African Americans, 1898–1905" (master's thesis, University of North Carolina at Wilmington, 2000), 106–108.

19. One researcher has surmised that black workers who remained in Wilmington after 1897 were either forced from higher-status (i.e., higher-paying) jobs to those with lower pay or "those in higher-status occupations left and other blacks migrating into the city took unskilled jobs." Cody, "After the Storm," 99–100. (Cody also acknowledged that it was possible that methods of data collection for the city directory changed over time and comparison across directories is not a dependable practice.)

20. *Evening Transcript* (Boston, Mass.), March 20, 1901. Historian Carter G. Woodson's study of the Great Migration, which began in 1916 and lasted until about 1930, has pointed out that the African Americans who departed the South beginning in 1916 were most often the better-educated and skilled workers. Chesnutt's observation about Wilmington's early out-migration forecasted that trend. Statistical study of migrant groups during the Great Migration supports Woodson's theory:

one out of every six literate blacks left the South between 1890 and 1920. Carter G. Woodson, *A Century of Negro Migration* (Washington, D.C.: Association for the Study of Negro Life and History, 1918), 147; Alferdteen Harrison, ed., *Black Exodus: The Great Migration from the American South* (Jackson: University Press of Mississippi, 1991), 46; E. Marvin Goodwin, *Black Migration in America from 1915 to 1960: An Uneasy Exodus* (Lewiston, N.Y.: Edwin Mellen Press, 1990), 10.

21. During the Great Migration, thousands of African Americans left southern states for northern cities. Most historians and government studies point to economic factors as the main reason for the migration—wartime industry needed laborers. However, additional study has revealed that many of the migrants sought to find less-hostile environments in which to live, work, and raise families. For a useful overview of the Great Migration, see Harrison, *Black Exodus*. In an essay included in that work (p. 31), Stewart Tolnay and E. M. Beck contended that blacks exposed to "high levels of lethal violence" chose to leave. The U.S. Department of Labor attributed the migration to "general dissatisfaction with conditions, ravages of boll weevil, floods, change of crop system, low wages, poor houses on plantations, poor school facilities, unsatisfactory crop settlements, rough treatment, cruelty of the law officers, unfairness in courts, lynching, desire for travel, labor agents, the Negro press, letters from friends in the North and finally advice of white friends in the South where crops had failed." U.S. Department of Labor, *Negro Migration in 1916–1917* (Washington: Government Printing Office, 1919), 11–12. Many of the causes cited for the Great Migration could apply to the out-migration from Wilmington that occurred in the years immediately after 1898.

22. *Brooklyn* (N.Y.) *Daily Eagle*, January 30, 1899. The article discussed growth in the AME church in Brooklyn as a result of the influx of African Americans who had been members of a large church of the same denomination in Wilmington that had a building worth $40,000. The church referenced in the article was probably St. Stephen's AME Church.

23. *Wilmington Messenger*, January 5, 1901; *Brooklyn Daily Eagle*, August 25, 1899.

24. Clement Alexander Price, "Home and Hearth: The Black Town and Settlement Movement of Southern New Jersey," in Wendel A. White, *Small Towns, Black Lives: African American Communities in Southern New Jersey* (Oceanville, N.J.: Noyes Museum of Art, 2003), 172–173; Twelfth Census of the United States, 1900: Cape May County, New Jersey, Population Schedule, National Archives, Washington, D.C. (microfilm, State Library); Thirteenth Census, 1910: Cape May County, New Jersey, Population Schedule, National Archives, Washington,

D.C. (microfilm, State Library); Fourteenth Census, 1920: Cape May County, New Jersey, Population Schedule, National Archives, Washington, D.C. (microfilm, State Library).

25. According to the census, the African American population of the city increased after 1910 but at a slower rate than that of the white population. John L. Godwin, *Black Wilmington and the North Carolina Way: A Portrait of a Community in the Era of Civil Rights Protest* (Lanham, Md.: University Press of America, 2000), 19.

26. Countless oral history interviews with lifelong residents of the city elicited fond memories of community support, with neighbors helping neighbors with child rearing, through economic support in difficult times, in church activities, and in a broad spectrum of other social and cultural activities. Among the oral history interviews are those compiled by the "Behind the Veil" project at Duke University.

27. Kenzer, *Enterprising Southerners*, 65.

28. Godwin, *Black Wilmington*, 14.

29. Kenzer, *Enterprising Southerners*, 65.

30. *Morning Star* (Wilmington), November 15, 1898.

31. Cody, "After the Storm," 156; Felice Sadgwar, Carrie Taylor Wright, and Laura Clemmons Kennedy, interview by Beverly Smalls, Wilmington, February 8, 1981; transcript of interview in Oral History Files, Cape Fear Museum, Wilmington.

32. Historian Robert Kenzer has noted that "every ten years from 1865 to 1915 black landowners as a whole would gain ownership of about 1 percent of the value of real estate in North Carolina, even though the black percentage of the state population would actually decline." He observed, however, that "adverse social, economic, and political circumstances prevented most blacks from becoming landowners by 1915." Another study has shown that in North Carolina the number of African Americans owning homes increased to 26 percent by 1910. In the latter year, Wilmington ranked sixth in the state in black home ownership rates, behind Elizabeth City, Fayetteville, Kinston, New Bern, and Washington but well ahead of Charlotte and Durham. Kenzer, *Enterprising Southerners*, 10, 20, 34; Loren Schweninger, *Black Property Owners in the South, 1790–1915* (Urbana: University of Illinois, 1990), 180–181; United States, John Cummings, and Joseph A. Hill, *Negro Population, 1790–1915* (Washington: Government Printing Office, 1918), 473.

33. Cody, "After the Storm," 124. Tracing ownership and transfer of real property by African Americans is extremely problematic since property could be transferred in a number of ways that were not documented in deed books. As an example, Robert Kenzer noted that of the

293 black men who owned land in Halifax County in 1870, none was mentioned in the county's recorded deeds for the entire period between emancipation and the 1870 census. Other methods of transferring property included gifts, court transactions, bequests, and quitclaims, as well as a host of more obscure means. Kenzer, *Enterprising Southerners*, 11.

34. An excerpt from *Hanover*: "She had reached the gate of her cottage, from which she had fled on the night of November 10th to escape insult and murder. A white woman sat upon the steps knitting, her children playing about the yard. The colored woman stood and momentarily gazed in amazement at the intruder upon her premises. 'Well, whart du you wannt?' said the white one, looking up from her work and then down again. 'What do I want?' returned the colored one. 'That's the question for me to ask. What are you doing in my house?' . . . 'Niggers don't own houses in dis here town no mo''; white uns air rulin' now.' . . . 'You poor white trash; I worked hard for this house, and hold the deed for it, so you get out!'" David Bryant Fulton, *Hanover; or, The Persecution of the Lowly, A Story of the Wilmington Massacre* (N.p.: M. C. L. Hill, [1901]), 110.

35. Milo Manly, when asked about his father's property, said that it was sold for failure to pay property taxes, although Alexander Manly tried to prove he paid the taxes. Sue Ann Cody researched the New Hanover County deed records and found one property in the senior Manly's name prior to the riot. Manly held it jointly with Frank Manly and John Goins. The men purchased a tract bounded by Dawson, Wright, Ninth, and Tenth streets in 1897 for one hundred dollars but in 1907 sold it to Manly's father-in-law. Alexander Manly and his wife Carrie acquired another property in Wilmington in 1907 but transferred it to other family members in four transactions between 1909 and 1915. Miller's holdings were much more extensive and cannot be easily summarized. Cody, "After the Storm," 118, 135; H. Leon Prather Sr., *We Have Taken a City: Wilmington Massacre and Coup of 1898* (Rutherford, N.J.: Fairleigh Dickinson University Press, 1984), 159–161; Index to Real Estate Conveyances, Grantee and Grantor, 1729–1954, New Hanover County Land Records (microfilm), State Archives; A. L. Manly et al. to George Lutterloh, February 4, 1899, Book 34, p. 628, New Hanover County Record of Deeds (microfilm), State Archives.

36. A series of duplicate deeds to land in Wilmington, arranged by block, can be found in the William B. McKoy Collection held by the Lower Cape Fear Historical Society in Wilmington. The deeds are not indexed, and some are in fragile condition. McKoy, an attorney for the city, mortgage companies, and insurance firms, was an integral part of the development of the White Govern-

ment Union in the city during the 1898 campaign. Since the discovery of the collection, some have speculated that McKoy contrived plans to duplicate mortgages on property owned by African Americans and slowly dupe the owners out of their properties by a variety of methods. It is unclear how many of the mortgages were for whites or blacks, or whether, as some have suggested, the names on the mortgages are of imaginary people. The collection is voluminous and unindexed, and a thorough study of its contents would be a valuable contribution to an understanding of the development of early-twentieth-century Wilmington.

37. Cody, "After the Storm," 124; New Hanover County Tax Records, 1897, 1900, State Archives.

38. Cody chose to focus her research on deed transactions by African Americans who, according to the 1897 tax records, owned real estate; she further limited her study to purchases and sales made in the seven years prior to the riot and the seven years after the riot by persons whose names began with the letters A through J. She also expressed the opinion that forgery of the complete set of New Hanover County deed books would be daunting, difficult, and impracticable. Cody, "After the Storm," 141–142.

39. Cody also studied three specific groups of people within the city: men who belonged to the Committee of Colored Citizens (CCC), those in the "A-J" deed list who were out of town at the time their property was sold, and those who made property transfers after having been banished. She concluded that most men of the CCC were not affected by property loss after the violence and did not suffer losses as a result of devaluation or sale and that those who left the city following the violence and sold their property from a distance sustained both gains and losses. Cody, "After the Storm," 119–120, 127, 133.

40. Nevertheless, other, more subtle methods of divesting property from black members of the community should be investigated. One example involved businesses, both African American and white, that accepted payments from members of the African American community in the form of mortgages. If someone defaulted on repayment of the mortgage, the businesses or money lenders could then confiscate the property, sell it, and deduct from the proceeds the amount owed for their services, with the residue going to the unfortunate borrower. Typical examples of such businesses were funeral establishments such as Wilmington's Shaw's Funeral Home.

41. Hamilton assembled the information using data from the Integrated Public Use Microdata Series (IPUMS) compiled by the Minnesota Population Center at the University of Minnesota. The sample used for this study is a 1-in-200 national random sample of the population.

250

Consequently, the sample size—173 individuals in Wilmington and the surrounding area in 1900—is small.

42. For additional information on reductions in school funding and the city's educational system, see chapter 7.

43. Tod Hamilton, "An Interpretation of the Economic Impact of the Wilmington Riot of 1898" (unpublished 1898 Wilmington Race Riot Commission report, May 31, 2006), 460–462.

44. Daniel Howard died in 1909 and left the bulk of his substantial estate to be divided equally among his living children. The 1910 census reveals that two of his sons were living in the city, and both were renting their homes instead of living in property they owned as a result of their father's generosity. John Norwood's children were scattered after 1898, with only two of his sons residing in the city in 1900; by 1910 all of his sons were living in northern states. Rivera's adopted son, Thomas, moved his father's undertaking business to Durham in 1906, the year his father died.

45. The men's ages are approximate and were derived from the 1880 and 1900 censuses. Men such as John L. Crow, Junius Davis, Hardy and Henry Fennell, William R. Kenan, William B. McKoy, Donald and Hugh MacRae, Iredell and Thomas Meares, Col. Roger Moore, George L. Morton, Walter Parsley, George Rountree, James Sprunt, J. Allan Taylor, Col. Walker Taylor, Alfred M. Waddell, and Charles Worth were all interrelated through intermarriage or blood kinships.

46. Reaves, "Strength through Struggle," 4, 23, 239, 294, 301–302, 319, 491; Ninth Census, 1870: New Hanover County, North Carolina; Tenth Census, 1880: New Hanover County; Twelfth Census, 1900: New Hanover County; Thirteenth Census, 1910: New Hanover County; Fourteenth Census, 1920: New Hanover County, Population Schedules for each, National Archives (microfilm, State Archives); Will of Daniel Howard, November 11, 1909, Book I, p. 582 (microfilm), New Hanover County Record of Wills, State Archives; New Hanover County Tax Records, 1897, 1900, State Archives.

47. Estate of Daniel Howard, 1909–1913, New Hanover County Estates Records, State Archives.

48. Reaves, "Strength through Struggle," 446–447; Ninth Census, 1870: New Hanover County, North Carolina; Tenth Census, 1880: New Hanover County; Twelfth Census, 1900: New Hanover County; Thirteenth Census, 1910: New Hanover County; Fourteenth Census, 1920: New Hanover County, Population Schedules for each, National Archives (microfilm); Will of John G. Norwood, June 12, 1906, Book I, p. 184, New Hanover County Record of Wills,

(microfilm), State Archives; New Hanover County Tax Records, 1897, 1900, State Archives.

49. In-depth studies of all of the deeds associated with the fathers and their offspring might provide insight into how the sons were divested of the properties over time. Ninth Census, 1870: New Hanover County, North Carolina; Tenth Census, 1880: New Hanover County; Twelfth Census, 1900: New Hanover County; Thirteenth Census, 1910: New Hanover County; Fourteenth Census, 1920: New Hanover County; Fifteenth Census, 1930: New Hanover County, Population Schedules for each, National Archives (microfilm, State Archives); New Hanover County Tax Lists, 1897, 1900, 1915 (microfilm), State Archives.

50. Reaves, "Strength through Struggle," 399; Eighth Census, 1860: New Hanover County, North Carolina; Ninth Census, 1870: New Hanover County; Tenth Census, 1880: New Hanover County; Twelfth Census, 1900: New Hanover County; Thirteenth Census, 1910: New Hanover County; Fourteenth Census, 1920: New Hanover County, Population Schedules for each, National Archives (microfilm, State Archives); New York Times, August 26, 1899.

51. According to the 1897 and 1900 tax lists, Miller owned property valued at more than $3,000 in 1897; by 1900 his property was valued at just over $5,500. He continued to buy and sell land after his banishment, although at a slower pace and in smaller amounts as compared to his pre-November 1898 activity. New Hanover County Tax Lists, 1897, 1900, (microfilm) State Archives; Cody, "After the Storm," 136–140.

52. T. C. Miller House File, New Hanover County Public Library, Wilmington; Administrators' Bonds, 1844–1918 [1894–1918], New Hanover County Estates Records, State Archives; Estate of Thomas Miller, 1902–1903, New Hanover County Estates Records, State Archives; New Hanover County Tax Lists, 1897, 1900, State Archives; Index to Real Estate Conveyances, Grantee and Grantor, 1729–1954, New Hanover County Land Records (microfilm), State Archives; death certificate for Thomas Miller, City of Norfolk Death Records, Library of Virginia, Richmond; Annie E. Miller, administratrix of T. C. Miller estate and guardian of Charity Miller, City of Norfolk Corporation Court Record of Fiduciary Bonds, vol. 3, 1903–1904, Library of Virginia.

53. Thomas C. Miller, Norfolk, Virginia, to John D. Taylor, Clerk of Superior Court, Wilmington, July 9, 1902, Correspondence, New Hanover County Miscellaneous Records, 1824–1906, State Archives.

54. The article discussed how independent thinkers in the black community should be prevented from prospering

251

economically. *Wilmington Messenger*, November 30, 1899; *Morning Star*, March 27, 1903.

55. In order to understand the racial makeup of the city, Higuchi plotted every residence in the directory by race and then determined each street's racial makeup. Streets with fewer than 15 percent black occupancy were considered white streets; those that were 85 percent or more black were considered black streets. (Higuchi established additional increments in the percentage of black residents on a street: 75-84 percent, 60-74 percent, 40-59 percent, 25-39 percent, 15-24 percent, and 0-14 percent. In her original thesis, Higuchi did not include maps showing these percentage categories, but she kindly shared them for use in this work. New maps based on her work are included in this publication.)

56. For a detailed description of Jonkonnu in North Carolina, see Elizabeth A. Fenn, "'A Perfect Equality Seemed to Reign': Slave Society and Jonkonnu," *North Carolina Historical Review* 65 (April 1988): 127–153.

57. At the height of the Ku Klux Klan movement in the 1870s, laws with similar wording had been enacted to discourage the use of masks to conceal the identities of men who threatened or attacked blacks. The 1898 ordinance was clearly designed to affect the Jonkonnu celebrations, however. Minutes of the Wilmington Board of Aldermen, 1884–1906 (microfilm), State Archives.

58. Fenn, "'A Perfect Equality Seemed to Reign.'" 127–153.

59. Henry B. McKoy, *Wilmington, N.C.: Do You Remember When?* (Greenville, S.C.: The Author, 1957), 141–145.

60. Most commemorations of Emancipation Day were held in local churches instead of public spaces such as Thalian Hall. Historian Fitzhugh Brundage described early Emancipation Day celebrations as occasions for blacks to "celebrate their history and participate in civic life in ways that had been impossible during slavery." He contended that the commemorations were "an unmistakable challenge to white understandings of the past." Historian Mitch Kachun suggested that, despite racial violence throughout the South, Emancipation Day celebrations persisted "to a greater extent than one might expect." Kachun explained, however, that instead of public spectacles lauding the merits of African American citizenship and pressing participants to push forward in every way, speakers urged "racial harmony" and uttered statements meant to appease whites. Reaves, *"Strength through Struggle,"* 3–6; *Wilmington Messenger*, January 3, 1899, January 2, 1903; *Morning Star*, January 2, 1898; W. Fitzhugh Brundage, *The Southern Past: A Clash of Race and Memory* (Cambridge, Mass.: Belknap Press, 2005), 10; Mitch Kachun, *Festivals of Freedom: Memory and Meaning in*

African American Emancipation Celebrations, 1808–1915 (Boston: University of Massachusetts Press, 2003), 178–181.

61. Kachun, *Festivals of Freedom*, 260.

62. In addition to the Masons, a number of fraternal organizations for both men and women existed in Wilmington. The second largest male organization was the Odd Fellows. Women created fraternal clubs of their own, most of which were benevolent or charitable in nature. For a detailed description of many of the clubs and societies that prospered in Wilmington, see Reaves, *"Strength through Struggle."*

63. Membership in the lodge was contingent on prompt payment of monthly fees. Failure to pay the fees resulted in revocation of membership. Historian Robert Kenzer found that only about one-third of the new members of Giblem Lodge owned real estate, whereas almost half of the lodge's founders had owned property in the city. Kenzer, *Enterprising Southerners*, 69–72, 73.

64. St. Mark's Episcopal Church operated several missions in the city, including a school on Harnett Street and a supervised summer playground facility on North Eighth. Reaves, *"Strength through Struggle,"* 135–136.

65. In 1899 Mt. Olive AME Church was undergoing remodeling. In 1901 St. Mark's Episcopal raised funds for its programs and for repairs to its chancel and rectory by presenting a melodrama at the Opera House and by sponsoring a trip by its pastor to Washington, Baltimore, Philadelphia, and New Jersey in search of financial assistance. Reaves, *"Strength through Struggle,"* 112, 134.

66. William J. Walls, *The African Methodist Episcopal Zion Church: Reality of the Black Church* (Charlotte: A.M.E. Zion Publishing House, 1974), 507–511.

67. The ministerial union was dissolved after the coup and violence of 1898 because white leaders perceived that the ministers who belonged to the body worked to develop Republican Party backing within their congregations and to organize a united, and potentially armed, resistance to the white-supremacy campaign. As evidence, white leaders pointed to the organization's public support of Alexander Manly, as well as the fact that several ministers were also leading members of the county's Republican Party. For additional information on the ministerial union's involvement in pre-election matters, see chapter 4. Reaves, *"Strength through Struggle,"* 143.

68. Andrew Kraft included an examination of Wilmington's churches in his geographic study of the city. Two of his maps relied upon the 1897 and 1903 city directories in mapping the city's white and black churches. A comparison of the two maps reveals that some African American churches that existed in 1897 had either moved

252

or were displaced by white churches by 1903. (Kraft incorrectly identified two churches—St. Paul's Protestant Episcopal Church and the Fifth Street Methodist Episcopal Church—as African American houses of worship when in fact they were white congregations.) A new comparison of the city's churches before and after the violence of 1898, employing the city directories, Sanborn fire insurance maps, and Reaves, *"Strength through Struggle,"* demonstrates that although some churches underwent reorganization and name changes after 1898, most church locations, as well as the basic religious framework established before 1898, remained in place in the wake of the violence. Andrew C. Kraft, "Wilmington's Political-Racial Revolution of 1898: A Geographical and Cartographic Analysis of the Wilmington, North Carolina, Race Riot" (unpublished report, University of North Carolina at Wilmington, 1993). Only one congregation—St. Thomas Catholic Church—was racially integrated during the years surrounding the violence. Nevertheless, when the new St. Mary Catholic Church was completed in 1911, the white members of St. Thomas turned the church over to its black members. Reaves, *"Strength through Struggle,"* 121–122; Tony P. Wrenn, *Wilmington, North Carolina: An Architectural and Historical Portrait* (Charlottesville: University of Virginia Press, 1984), 224–227.

69. Attempts were made to study the records of some of the city's African Methodist Episcopal churches for this project. The early records of St. Stephen's are scant and in poor condition—the earliest ledger dated to 1898 and recorded mainly Sunday school information. Other records for the church date to the twentieth century. Overall, the records of St. Stephen's do not provide much detail about the church's congregation before or after the riot. The records of St. Luke's cannot be located. The church experienced a catastrophic fire during the mid-twentieth century, and its records could have been destroyed at that time. A search of the records at the Heritage Hall at Livingstone College failed to provide any additional information. Rev. John Burton of St. Stephen's, interview with author, Wilmington, April 30, 2004.

70. Recent scholarship on collective memory has concluded that southerners have selectively remembered and selectively forgotten aspects of their past by constructing a narrative of events to suit the needs of the present. After the Wilmington Race Riot, victorious state Democrats crafted their own narrative about the election and the results that ensued. The popular memory of the event legitimized the rule of the Democratic Party and effectively denied African Americans access to economic and political opportunities. The genre of historical fiction proved to be the most popular means of confronting the public memory of the riot. In the years that followed the riot, two African American writers—David Bryant Fulton and Charles Waddell Chesnutt—challenged the popular narrative of events, but they ultimately failed to capture a wide audience. The dominant memory of the event left little room for a black viewpoint. The popularity of Thomas Dixon's *The Leopard's Spots: A Romance of the White Man's Burden, 1865–1900* (New York: Doubleday, Page & Co., 1902) reflected the nation's willingness to accept the southern white version of history and positioned the Wilmington Race Riot within the larger narrative of sectional reunion and American imperialism. That version of the riot, bolstered by Dixon's novel, remained unchallenged until the 1980s, when historians began analyzing the event in greater detail. When Philip Gerard published *Cape Fear Rising* (Winston-Salem: John F. Blair, 1994), he found an audience more willing to discuss the race riot. Yet, in many ways Wilmington's political and cultural landscape remained under the influence of the narrative constructed by the Democrats in 1898.

For a general survey of southern memories, see W. Fitzhugh Brundage, "Introduction: No Deed but Memory," in *Where These Memories Grow: History, Memory, and Southern Identity*, ed. W. Fitzhugh Brundage (Chapel Hill: University of North Carolina Press, 2000), 1–28. Several authors have utilized the study of collective memory to examine the Wilmington Race Riot. Catherine W. Bishir has noted the impact that the 1898 Democratic victories had upon the cultural landscapes of Raleigh and Wilmington. See Bishir's "Landmarks of Power: Building a Southern Past in Raleigh and Wilmington, 1885–1915," in Catherine W. Bishir, *Southern Built: American Architecture, Regional Practice* (Charlottesville: University of Virginia Press, 2006). In *Whiteness in the Novels of Charles W. Chesnutt* (Jackson: University Press of Mississippi, 2004), Matthew Wilson examined the counter-narrative presented by Charles W. Chesnutt in *The Marrow of Tradition* (Boston: Houghton, Mifflin, 1901). Leslie H. Hossfeld analyzed the political uses of memories of the riot, paying particular attention to silences and changes in the discourse on race relations and memory during the century after the riot. See *Narrative, Political Unconscious, and Racial Violence in Wilmington, North Carolina* (New York: Routledge, 2005).

71. Lura Beam, *He Called Them by the Lightning: A Teacher's Odyssey in the Negro South, 1908–1919* (Indianapolis: Bobbs-Merrill Company, 1967, 15, 18, 27, 36.

72. Beam, *He Called Them by the Lightning*, 28.

73. Another story of how the violence of 1898 affected Wilmington's black community has come from the family history of Gwendolyn Cottman, an African American

253

genealogist and descendant of some of the port city's black families. Cottman's family genealogy, *Just Us*, details her family's lives over several generations. Dispersed within the pages is an underlying story of how her family's collective memory of 1898 affected how children were reared, how family history was told, and how children viewed elderly members of the community who recalled the horrors of that year. An interesting topic appears in Cottman's work—the existence of vacant homes in Brooklyn. Cottman never knew why the dwellings were vacant, but her genealogical work includes insightful research into several homes in the neighborhood around North Tenth/McRae/North Ninth/North Eighth streets. A study of the block book, census, Sanborn fire insurance maps, and tax lists for blocks 327, 310, and 297—blocks Cottman references in *Just Us*—reveals that in the 1920s several properties owned by blacks were considered "vacant and open." It is unclear why some people owned homes in the city but left them fully furnished, unlocked, and open for years. Cottman notes tht the city later tore down the dwellings. Additional research is needed to understand how or why some African American property owners such as Timon Council maintained ownership of property in the city but lived in other parts of the state. Council owned property at 1107 North Ninth Street in the 1920s but lived in Cumberland County. Gwendolyn Cottman, *Just Us* (Baltimore: Gateway Press, 2002), 62–64, 75–76, 81–87, 222; Sanborn Fire Insurance Map of Wilmington, 1925; Fourteenth Census, 1920: New Hanover County; Fifteenth Census, 1930: New Hanover County, Population Schedules for each, National Archives (microfilm, State Archives).

74. *J. L. Hill Printing Co.'s Directory of Wilmington, N.C. 1900* (Richmond, Va.: J. L. Hill Printing Company, 1900), 2.

75. *Wilmington Up-to-Date: The Metropolis of North Carolina Graphically Portrayed* (Wilmington: W. L. De Rossett, Jr., Printer, 1902), [3].

76. "The 'Riot' Seven Years Old" (pamphlet) [7], Bill Reaves Local and Family History Collection, New Hanover County Public Library.

77. James Sprunt, *Chronicles of the Cape Fear River, 1660–1916*, 2nd. ed. (Raleigh: Edwards and Broughton Printing Company, 1916), 554–555.

78. Charles Edward Morris, "Panic and Reprisal: Reaction in North Carolina to the Nat Turner Insurrection, 1831," *North Carolina Historical Review* 62 (January 1985): 29–52.

79. Another interesting oral tradition is that firearms were found in the basement of St. Stephen's AME Church. The tradition holds that the weapons were stored in a concealed entrance to an underground tunnel or crawl space created beneath the church by members who

constructed the building. Harry Hayden, *The Story of the Wilmington Rebellion* (Wilmington: The Author, 1936), 35–36.

80. Paul Gilje, *Rioting in America* (Bloomington: Indiana University Press, 1996), 4.

81. Charles Crowe, "Racial Massacre in Atlanta, September 22, 1906," *Journal of Negro History* 54 (April 1969): 150; Gilje, *Rioting in America*, 155.

82. In discussing the events of November 10, 1898, in Wilmington, Prather also added the term "coup d'etat" to the lexicon of civil unrest. In *We Have Taken a City*, his groundbreaking study of the riot, Prather argues that the violence and forced resignations of the existing board of aldermen under duress constituted nothing less than an armed takeover of the city's government. *Encyclopedia of Southern Culture*, s.v., "Race Riots."

83. Gilje, *Rioting in America*, 96–97; James G. Hollandsworth Jr., *An Absolute Massacre: The New Orleans Race Riot of July 30, 1866* (Baton Rouge: Louisiana State University Press, 2001); Jane Dailey, "Deference and Violence in the Postbellum Urban South: Manners and Massacres in Danville, Virginia," *Journal of Southern History* 63 (August 1997): 553–590.

84. The six riots, in chronological order: Atlanta, Georgia (1906), Springfield, Illinois (1908), East St. Louis, Illinois (1917), Chicago, Illinois (1919), Tulsa, Oklahoma (1921), Rosewood, Florida (1923). Ray Stannard Baker, *Following the Colour Line: An Account of Negro Citizenship in the American Democracy* (New York: Doubleday, Page, and Company, 1908); Charles Crowe, "Racial Violence and Social Reform: Origins of the Atlanta Riot of 1906," *Journal of Negro History* 53 (July 1968): 234–256; Crowe, "Racial Massacre in Atlanta," 150–173; Hunter, *To 'Joy My Freedom*; Allison Dorsey, *To Build Our Lives Together: Community Formation in Black Atlanta, 1875–1906* (Athens: University of Georgia Press, 2004); Gregory Mixon, *The Atlanta Riot: Race, Class, and Violence in a New South City* (Gainesville: University Press of Florida, 2005); Scott Ellsworth, *Death in a Promised Land: The Tulsa Race Riot of 1921* (Baton Rouge: Louisiana State University Press, 1982); Alfred L. Brophy, *Reconstructing a Dreamland: The Tulsa Riot of 1921: Race Reparations, and Reconciliation* (New York: Oxford University Press, 2002); R. Thomas Dye, "The Rosewood Massacre: History and the Making of Public Policy," *Public Historian* 19 (summer 1997): 25–39; Maxine D. Jones, "The Rosewood Massacre and the Women Who Survived It," *Florida Historical Quarterly* 76 (Fall 1997): 193–208; Philip S. Foner, *Organized Labor and the Black Worker, 1619–1973* (New York: Praeger Publishers, 1974), 136–137, 144.

85. Don Doyle, *New Men, New Cities, New South: Atlanta, Nashville, Charleston, Mobile, 1860–1910* (Chapel Hill: University of North Carolina Press, 1990), 13, 34–

37, 318; Mixon, *The Atlanta Riot*, 86; Charles Crowe, "Racial Violence and Social Reform," 158, 236; Hunter, *To 'Joy My Freedom*, 124–126, 178–179; Dorsey, *To Build Our Lives Together*, 159.

86. Mixon, *The Atlanta Riot*, 69–70; Crowe, "Racial Violence and Social Reform," 243; Hunter, *To 'Joy My Freedom*, 124.

87. Baker, *Following the Colour Line*, 5.

88. "A Documented History of the Incident Which Occurred at Rosewood, Florida, in January 1923" (legislative document produced by a team of researchers from Florida A&M University, Florida State University, and the University of Florida and submitted to the Florida Board of Regents on December 22, 1993).

89. Ellsworth, *Death in a Promised Land*, chapter 3.

90. Mixon, *The Atlanta Riot*, 117–119; Baker, *Following the Colour Line*, 14.

91. Brophy, *Reconstructing a Dreamland*, 95–97.

92. Other attempts to overthrow local governments have come to light in the course of this research. Many examples are reflective of the upheavals in municipal affairs that were commonplace throughout the South during Reconstruction, particularly during military occupation. Even after the end of Reconstruction and well into the twentieth century, however, instances of local mob rule abound. Historians have researched and written about events in San Francisco (1966), Athens, Tennessee (1946), Plaquemines Parish, Louisiana (1919), New Orleans (1874), and the Brooks–Baxter War in Arkansas (1874). The 1898 Wilmington coup, unlike many others, was completely successful and at no point was subsequently overturned by federal or state forces.

93. An unapologetic white business community in Wilmington quietly collected funds to "compensate the several negro lodges which owned the *Record* building that was accidentally burned." Because the white mobs had intended only to destroy Alexander Manly's newspaper press and office property and not the building his press occupied, the businessmen raised $690 and presented the funds to a black representative of the lodges. One white Wilmington newspaper lauded the efforts of another black man who had acquired Manly's destroyed press and offered to melt it down to create souvenirs for sale. The same paper remarked upon a wonderful new gavel that had been carved from a wooden table in the destroyed *Daily Record* office and presented to the White Laborers Union by workers at the Wilmington Iron Works. *Morning Star*, February 3, March 17, 1899.

255

Bibliography

Monographs

Alexander, Roberta Sue. *North Carolina Faces the Freedmen: Race Relations during Presidential Reconstruction, 1865–67*. Durham: Duke University Press, 1985.

Ashe, Samuel A. *History of North Carolina*, vol. 2. Raleigh: Edwards and Broughton Company, 1925.

Ayers, Edward L. *The Promise of the New South: Life after Reconstruction*. New York: Oxford University Press, 1992.

Baker, Ray Stannard Baker. *Following the Colour Line: An Account of Negro Citizenship in the American Democracy*. New York: Doubleday, Page, and Company, 1908.

Barrett, John G. *The Civil War in North Carolina*. Chapel Hill: University of North Carolina Press, 1963.

_____. *North Carolina as a Civil War Battleground*. Raleigh: State Department of Archives and History, 1960.

Beam, Lura. *He Called Them by the Lightning: A Teacher's Odyssey in the Negro South, 1908–1919*. Indianapolis: Bobbs-Merrill Company, 1967.

Bellamy, John D. *Memoirs of an Octogenarian*. Charlotte: Observer Printing House, 1942.

Bishir, Catherine W. *The Bellamy Mansion, Wilmington, North Carolina: An Antebellum Architectural Treasure and Its People*. Wilmington: Bellamy Mansion Museum; Raleigh: Preservation North Carolina, 2004.

_____. *Southern Built: American Architecture Regional Practice*. Charlottesville: University of Virginia Press, 2006.

_____, et al. *Architects and Builders in North Carolina: A History of the Practice of Building*. Chapel Hill: University of North Carolina Press, 1990.

Block, Susan Taylor. *Temple of Our Fathers: St. James Church, 1729–2004*. Wilmington: Artspeaks, 2004.

_____. *Wilmington through the Lens of Louis T. Moore*. Wilmington: Lower Cape Fear Historical Society and New Hanover County Public Library, 2001.

Boles, John B., ed. *A Companion to the American South*. Malden, Mass: Blackwell Publishers, 2002

Brophy, Alfred L. *Reconstructing a Dreamland: The Tulsa Riot of 1921: Race Reparations, and Reconciliation*. New York: Oxford University Press, 2002.

Brundage, W. Fitzhugh. *The Southern Past: A Clash of Race and Memory*. Cambridge, Mass.: Belknap Press, 2005.

_____, ed. *Where These Memories Grow: History, Memory, and Southern Identity*. Chapel Hill: University of North Carolina Press, 2000.

Caldwell, Arthur Bunyan, ed. *History of the American Negro and His Institutions*, vol. 4. Atlanta: A. B. Caldwell Publishing Co., 1921.

Cecelski, David S. *The Waterman's Song: Slavery and Freedom in Maritime North Carolina*. Chapel Hill: University of North Carolina Press, 2001.

_____, and Timothy B. Tyson, eds. *Democracy Betrayed: The Wilmington Race Riot of 1898 and Its Legacy*. Chapel Hill: University of North Carolina Press, 1998.

Cheney, John L., Jr., ed. *North Carolina Government, 1585–1979: A Narrative and Statistical History*. Raleigh: North Carolina Department of the Secretary of State, 1981.

Chesnutt, Charles W. *The Marrow of Tradition*. Boston: Houghton, Mifflin, 1901.

Connor, R. D. W. *North Carolina: Rebuilding an Ancient Commonwealth*, 2 vols. Chicago: American Historical Society, 1929.

_____, and Clarence Poe. *The Life and Speeches of Charles Brantley Aycock*. Garden City, N.Y.: Doubleday, Page and Company, 1912.

Cottman, Gwendolyn. *Just Us*. Baltimore: Gateway Press, 2002.

Crow, Jeffrey J., and Robert F. Durden. *Maverick Republican in the Old North State: A Political*

Biography of Daniel L. Russell. Baton Rouge: Louisiana State University Press, 1977.

_____, Paul D. Escott, and Charles L. Flynn Jr., eds. *Race, Class, and Politics in Southern History: Essays in Honor of Robert F. Durden*. Baton Rouge: Louisiana State University Press, 1989.

_____, Paul D. Escott, and Flora J. Hatley. *A History of African Americans in North Carolina*. Raleigh: Office of Archives and History, North Carolina Department of Cultural Resources, rev. ed., 2002.

_____, and Flora J. Hatley, eds. *Black Americans in North Carolina and the South*. Chapel Hill: University of North Carolina Press, 1984.

Culp, D. W., ed. *Twentieth Century Negro Literature*. Atlanta, Ga.: J. L. Nichols & co., 1902.

Dancy, John C. *Sand Against the Wind: The Memoirs of John C. Dancy*. Detroit: Wayne State University Press, 1966.

Daniels, Josephus. *Editor in Politics*. Chapel Hill: University of North Carolina Press, 1941.

deRosset, William Lord. *Pictorial and Historical New Hanover County and Wilmington, North Carolina, 1723–1938*. Wilmington: The Author, 1938.

Dixon, Thomas. *The Leopard's Spots: A Romance of the White Man's Burden, 1865–1900*. New York: Doubleday, Page & Co., 1902.

Dorsey, Allison. *To Build Our Lives Together: Community Formation in Black Atlanta, 1875–1906*. Athens: University of Georgia Press, 2004.

Doyle, Don. *New Men, New Cities, New South: Atlanta, Nashville, Charleston, Mobile, 1860–1910*. Chapel Hill: University of North Carolina Press, 1990.

Edmonds, Helen G. *The Negro and Fusion Politics in North Carolina, 1894–1901*. Chapel Hill: University of North Carolina Press, 1951.

Edwards, Laura F. *Scarlett Doesn't Live Here Anymore: Southern Women in the Civil War Era*. Urbana: University of Illinois Press, 2000.

Ellsworth, Scott. *Death in a Promised Land: The Tulsa Race Riot of 1921*. Baton Rouge: Louisiana State University Press, 1982.

Evans, William McKee. *Ballots and Fence Rails: Reconstruction on the Lower Cape Fear*. Athens: University of Georgia Press, 1995.

Fleming, Walter L., ed. *Documents Relating to Reconstruction*. Morgantown, W.Va.: N.p., 1904.

Folk, Edgar E., and Bynum Shaw. *W. W. Holden: A Political Biography*. Winston-Salem: John F. Blair, Publisher, 1982.

Foner, Eric. *Reconstruction: America's Unfinished Revolution, 1863–1877*. New York: Harper and Row, 1988.

Foner, Philip S. *Organized Labor and the Black Worker, 1619–1973*. New York: Praeger Publishers, 1974.

_____, ed. *The Voice of Black America: Major Speeches by Negroes in the United States, 1797–1971*. New York: Simon and Schuster, 1972.

_____, ed. *W. E. B. DuBois Speaks: Speeches and Addresses, 1890–1919*. 2 vols. New York: Pathfinder Press, 1970.

Fonvielle, Chris, Jr. *The Wilmington Campaign: Last Rays of Departing Hope*. Campbell, Calif.: Savas Publishing Company, 1997.

Franklin, John Hope. *The Free Negro in North Carolina, 1790–1860*. Chapel Hill: University of North Carolina Press, 1943.

Fulton, David Bryant. *Hanover; or, The Persecution of the Lowly, A Story of the Wilmington Massacre*. N.p.: M. C. L. Hill, [1901].

Gerard, Philip. *Cape Fear Rising*. Winston-Salem: John F. Blair, 1994.

Gilje, Paul. *Rioting in America*. Bloomington: Indiana University Press, 1996.

Gilmore, Glenda Elizabeth. *Gender and Jim Crow: Women and the Politics of White Supremacy in North Carolina, 1896–1920*. Chapel Hill: University of North Carolina Press, 1996.

Godwin, John L. *Black Wilmington and the North Carolina Way: A Portrait of a Community in the Era of Civil Rights Protest*. Lanham, Md.: University Press of America, 2000.

Goldstein, Arnold. *The Psychology of Group Aggression*. Sussex, England: John Wiley and Sons, 2002.

Goodwin, E. Marvin. *Black Migration in America from 1915 to 1960: An Uneasy Exodus*. Lewiston, N.Y.: Edwin Mellen Press, 1990.

258

Greenberg, Kenneth. *Masters and Statesmen: The Political Culture of American Slavery*. Baltimore: Johns Hopkins University Press, 1985.

Haley, John. *Charles N. Hunter and Race Relations in North Carolina*. Chapel Hill: University of North Carolina Press, 1987.

Hamilton, J. G. de Roulhac. *North Carolina since 1860*. Chicago and New York: Lewis Publishing Company, 1919.

_____. *Reconstruction in North Carolina*. Raleigh: Presses of Edwards and Broughton, 1906.

Harlan, Louis R., ed., *The Booker T. Washington Papers*, 13 vols. Urbana: University of Illinois Press, 1972–1989. Vol. 4.

Harris, William C. *William Woods Holden: Firebrand of North Carolina Politics*. Baton Rouge: Louisiana State University Press, 1987.

Harrison, Alferdteen, ed., *Black Exodus: The Great Migration from the American South*. Jackson: University Press of Mississippi, 1991.

Hartshorn, W. N., and George W. Penniman, eds. *An Era of Progress and Promise, 1863–1910: The Religious, Moral, and Educational Development of the American Negro since His Emancipation*. Boston: Priscilla Publishing Company, 1910.

Haskett, Delmas D., and Bill Reaves. *New Hanover County 1865 Tax List*. Wilmington: New Hanover County Public Library. 1990.

Hayden, Harry. *The Story of the Wilmington Rebellion*. Wilmington: The Author, 1936.

Hollandsworth, James G., Jr. *An Absolute Massacre: The New Orleans Race Riot of July 30, 1866*. Baton Rouge: Louisiana State University Press, 2001.

Hossfeld, Leslie H. *Narrative, Political Unconscious, and Racial Violence in Wilmington, North Carolina*. New York: Routledge, 2005.

Howell, Andrew. *The Book of Wilmington*. Wilmington: The Author, 1930.

Hunt, James L. *Marion Butler and American Populism*. Chapel Hill: University of North Carolina Press, 2003

Hunter, Tera W. *To 'Joy My Freedom: Southern Black Women's Lives and Labors after the Civil War*. Cambridge, Mass.: Harvard University Press, 1997

Justesen, Benjamin R.. *George Henry White: An Even Chance in the Race of Life*. Baton Rouge: Louisiana State University Press, 2001.

Kachun, Mitch. *Festivals of Freedom: Memory and Meaning in African American Emancipation Celebrations, 1808–1915*. Boston: University of Massachusetts Press, 2003.

Kantrowitz, Stephen. *Ben Tillman and the Politics of White Supremacy*. Chapel Hill: University of North Carolina Press, 2000.

Keith, Benjamin F. *Memories*. Raleigh: Bynum Printing Company, 1922.

Kenzer, Robert C. *Enterprising Southerners: Black Economic Success in North Carolina, 1865–1915*. Charlottesville: University of Virginia Press, 1997.

Kernan, Charles. *Rails to Weeds*. Wilmington: Wilmington Railroad Museum, 1988.

Kirk, J. Allen. *A Statement of Facts Concerning the Bloody Riot in Wilmington, N.C., of Interest to Every Citizen of the United States*. Wilmington?: The Author?, 1898?; online edition available at http://docsouth.unc.edu/nc/kirk/menu.html.

Landry, Bart. *The New Black Middle Class*. Berkeley: University of California Press, 1987.

Leloudis, James L. *Schooling the New South: Pedagogy, Self, and Society in North Carolina, 1880–1920*. Chapel Hill: University of North Carolina Press, 1996.

Logan, Frenise A. *The Negro in North Carolina, 1876–1894*. Chapel Hill: University of North Carolina Press, 1964.

Matthews, Donald R., ed. *North Carolina Votes: General Election Returns, by County, for President of the United States, 1868–1960, Governor of North Carolina, 1868–1960, United States Senator from North Carolina, 1914–1960*. Chapel Hill: University of North Carolina Press, 1962.

McKoy, Elizabeth F. *Early Wilmington Block by Block: From 1733 On*. Wilmington: The Author, 1967.

McKoy, Henry B. *Wilmington, N.C.: Do You Remember When?* Greenville, S.C.: The Author, 1957.

McKoy, Sheila Smith. *When Whites Riot: Writing Race and Violence in American and South African Cultures*. Madison: University of Wisconsin Press, 2001.

259

Mixon, Gregory. *The Atlanta Riot: Race, Class, and Violence in a New South City*. Gainesville: University Press of Florida, 2005.

Murray, Percy. *History of the North Carolina Teachers Association*. [Washington, D.C.]: National Education Association, [1984].

Noble, M. C. S. *A History of the Public Schools of North Carolina*. Chapel Hill: University of North Carolina Press, 1930.

Outland, Robert B., III. *Tapping the Pines: The Naval Stores Industry in the American South*. Baton Rouge: Louisiana State University Press, 2004.

Penn, I. Garland. *The Afro-American Press and Its Editors*. Springfield, Mass.: Wiley & Co., Publishers, 1891.

Penningroth, Dylan. *The Claims of Kinfolk: African American Property and Community in the Nineteenth-Century South*. Chapel Hill: University of North Carolina Press, 2003.

Poland, C. Beauregard. *North Carolina's Glorious Victory, 1898. Sketches of Able Democratic Leaders and Statesmen*. Raleigh: [Democratic Executive Committee, 1899].

Powell, William S. *North Carolina through Four Centuries*. Chapel Hill: University of North Carolina Press, 1989.

Prather, H. Leon, Sr. *We Have Taken a City: Wilmington Massacre and Coup of 1898*. Rutherford, N.J.: Fairleigh Dickinson University Press, 1984.

Quick, W. H. *Negro Stars in All Ages of the World*. Richmond: S. B. Adkins and Co., Printers, second edition, 1898.

Ralph, Julian. *Dixie; or, Southern Scenes and Sketches*. New York: Harper & Brothers, 1896.

Ransom, Roger L., and Richard Sutch. *One Kind of Freedom: The Economic Consequences of Emancipation*. Cambridge and New York: Cambridge University Press, 1977.

Raper, Horace W. *William W. Holden: North Carolina's Political Enigma*. Chapel Hill: University of North Carolina Press, 1985.

[Reaves, William M.] *North Carolina Freedman's Savings and Trust Company Records*. Abstracted by Bill Reaves. Ed. Beverly Tetterton. Raleigh: North Carolina Genealogical Society, 1992.

_____. *"Strength through Struggle": The Chronological and Historical Record of the African-American Community in Wilmington, North Carolina, 1865–1950*, ed. Beverly Tetterton. Wilmington: New Hanover County Public Library, 1998.

Reid, Whitelaw. *After the War: A Southern Tour, May 1, 1865, to May 1, 1866*. Cincinnati and New York: Moore, Wilstach & Baldwin, 1866; reprint, New York: Harper Torchbooks, 1965.

Reilly, J. S. *Wilmington. Past, Present & Future, Embracing Historical Sketches of Its Growth and Progress from its Establishment to the Present Time, Together with Outline of North Carolina History*. Wilmington: N.p., 1884.

Rippy, James Fred. *F. M. Simmons: Statesman of the New South, Memoirs and Addresses*. Durham: Duke University Press, 1936.

Schweninger, Loren. *Black Property Owners in the South, 1790–1915*. Urbana: University of Illinois, 1990.

Simkins, Francis Butler. *Pitchfork Ben Tillman, South Carolinian*. Baton Rouge: Louisiana State University Press, 1944.

Sprunt, James. *Chronicles of the Cape Fear River, 1660–1916*. 2nd ed. Raleigh: Edwards and Broughton Printing Company, 1916.

State Democratic Executive Committee of North Carolina. *Democratic Party Handbook*. Raleigh: Edwards and Broughton, 1898.

Still, William. *The Underground Rail Road*. Philadelphia, Pa.: Porter and Coates, 1872.

Trelease, Allen W. *The North Carolina Railroad, 1849–1871, and the Modernization of North Carolina*. Chapel Hill: University of North Carolina Press, 1991.

_____. *White Terror: The Ku Klux Klan Conspiracy and Southern Reconstruction*. New York: Harper and Row, 1971.

Trudeau, Noah A. *Like Men of War: Black Troops in the Civil War, 1862–1865*. Boston: Little, Brown and Company, 1998.

Walls, William J. *The African Methodist Episcopal Zion Church: Reality of the Black Church*. Charlotte: A.M.E. Zion Publishing House, 1974.

Watford, Christopher M., ed. *The Civil War in North Carolina: Soldiers' and Civilians' Letters and Diaries, 1861–1865.* Jefferson, N.C.: McFarland, 2003.

Watson, Alan D. *Wilmington, Port of North Carolina.* Columbia: University of South Carolina Press, 1992.

Webb, James. *Born Fighting: How the Scotch-Irish Shaped America.* New York: Broadway Books, 2004.

White, Wendel A. *Small Towns, Black Lives: African American Communities in Southern New Jersey.* Oceanville, N.J.: Noyes Museum of Art, 2003.

White Government Union. *Constitution and By-Laws of the White Government Union, 1898.* Raleigh: Edwards and Broughton, 1898.

Williams, Alfred. *Hampton and His Red Shirts: South Carolina's Deliverance in 1876.* Charleston, S.C.: Walker, Evans and Cogswell Co., 1935.

Williamson, Joel. *The Crucible of Race: Black-White Relations in the American South since Reconstruction.* New York: Oxford University Press, 1984.

_____. *New People, Miscegenation and Mulattoes in the United States.* New York: Free Press, 1980.

Wilmington Up-to-Date: The Metropolis of North Carolina Graphically Portrayed. Wilmington: W. L. De Rosset Jr., Printer, 1902.

Wilson, Charles Reagan and William Ferris, eds. *Encyclopedia of Southern Culture.* Chapel Hill: University of North Carolina Press, 1989.

Wilson, Matthew. *Whiteness in the Novels of Charles W. Chesnutt.* Jackson: University Press of Mississippi, 2004.

Woodson, Carter G. *A Century of Negro Migration.* Washington, D.C.: Association for the Study of Negro Life and History, 1918.

Woodward, C. Vann. *The Strange Career of Jim Crow.* New York: Oxford University Press, 1955.

Wrenn, Tony P. *Wilmington, North Carolina: An Architectural and Historical Portrait.* Charlottesville: University of Virginia Press, 1984.

Wyatt-Brown, Bertram. *Southern Honor: Ethics and Behavior in the Old South.* New York: Oxford University Press, 1982.

Zuber, Richard L. *North Carolina during Reconstruction.* Raleigh: State Department of Archives and History, 1969.

Articles and Parts of Books

Abrams, Douglas C. "A Progressive-Conservative Deal: The 1920 Democratic Gubernatorial Primaries in North Carolina." *North Carolina Historical Review* 55 (October 1978): 421–443.

Bishir, Catherine W. "Black Builders in Antebellum North Carolina." *North Carolina Historical Review* 61 (October 1984): 423–461.

_____. "Landmarks of Power: Building a Southern Past in Raleigh and Wilmington, 1885–1915." In Catherine W. Bishir, *Southern Built: American Architecture, Regional Practice.* Charlottesville: University of Virginia Press, 2006. Pp. 254–293.

Boyd, William K. Boyd, ed. "History of the Difficulties of the Pastorate of the Front Street Methodist Church, Wilmington, N.C. for the Year 1865." *Historical Papers of Trinity College.* Durham: Trinity College Historical Society, 1908–1909, 35–118.

Brundage, W. Fitzhugh. "Introduction: No Deed but Memory." In *Where These Memories Grow: History, Memory, and Southern Identity*, ed. W. Fitzhugh Brundage. Chapel Hill: University of North Carolina Press, 2000. Pp. 1–28.

Cecelski, David S. "Abraham Galloway: Wilmington's Lost Prophet and the Rise of Black Radicalism in the American South." In David S. Cecelski and Timothy B. Tyson, eds., *Democracy Betrayed: The Wilmington Race Riot of 1898 and Its Legacy.* Chapel Hill: University of North Carolina Press, 1998. Pp. 43–72.

_____. "The Shores of Freedom." *North Carolina Historical Review* 71 (April 1994): 174–206.

Crow, Jeffrey J. "Fusion, Confusion, and Negroism: Schisms among Negro Republicans in North Carolina." *North Carolina Historical Review* 53 (October 1976): 364–384.

Crowe, Charles. "Racial Massacre in Atlanta, September 22, 1906." *Journal of Negro History* 54 (April 1969): 150–173.

_____. "Racial Violence and Social Reform: Origins of the Atlanta Riot of 1906." *Journal of Negro History* 53 (July 1968): 234–256.

Dailey, Jane. "Deference and Violence in the Postbellum Urban South: Manners and Massacres in Danville, Virginia." *Journal of Southern History* 63 (August 1997): 553–590.

DuBois, W. E. B. Speech by, titled "The Evolution of the Race Problem" (delivered in New York, 1909). In *Proceedings of the National Negro Conference in New York, 1909.* Reprinted in Philip S. Foner, *W. E. B. DuBois Speaks: Speeches and Addresses, 1890–1919*, 2 vols. New York: Pathfinder Press, 1970, 1:196–199.

———. Speech by, titled "The Study of Negro Problems" (delivered in Atlanta, 1898). In *Annals of the American Academy of Political and Social Science*, 1898. Reprinted in Philip S. Foner, ed. *W. E. B. DuBois Speaks: Speeches and Addresses, 1890–1919*, 2 vols. New York: Pathfinder Press, 1970, 1:104–108.

Dye, R. Thomas. "The Rosewood Massacre: History and the Making of Public Policy." *Public Historian* 19 (Summer 1997): 25–39.

Escott, Paul D. "White Republicanism and Ku Klux Klan Terror: The North Carolina Piedmont during Reconstruction." In *Race, Class, and Politics in Southern History: Essays in Honor of Robert F. Durden*, ed. Jeffrey J. Crow, Paul D. Escott, and Charles L. Flynn Jr. Baton Rouge: Louisiana State University Press, 1989. Pp. 3–34.

Fenn, Elizabeth A. " 'A Perfect Equality Seemed to Reign': Slave Society and Jonkonnu." *North Carolina Historical Review* 65 (April 1988): 127–153.

Fleming, Walter L. "Union League Documents." In Walter L. Fleming, ed. *Documents Relating to Reconstruction*. Morgantown, W.Va.: N.p., 1904. Pp. 3–36.

Gatewood, Willard B., Jr. "North Carolina's Negro Regiment in the Spanish-American War." *North Carolina Historical Review* 48 (October 1971): 370–387.

Hanchett, Thomas W. "The Rosenwald Schools and Black Education in North Carolina." *North Carolina Historical Review* 65 (October 1988): 387–444.

Honey, Michael. "Class, Race and Power." In David S. Cecelski and Timothy B. Tyson, eds., *Democracy Betrayed: The Wilmington Race Riot of 1898 and Its Legacy*. Chapel Hill: University of North Carolina Press, 1998. Pp. 163–184.

Jones, Maxine D. "The Rosewood Massacre and the Women Who Survived It." *Florida Historical Quarterly* 76 (Fall 1997): 193–208.

Justesen, Benjamin R. "Black Postmasters and the Rise of White Supremacy in North Carolina." *North Carolina Historical Review* 82 (April 2005): 193–227.

Kennedy, J. R. "Colonel Moore Recalled." *Morning Star* (Wilmington), November 24, 1936.

Mabry, William. "Negro Suffrage and Fusion Rule in North Carolina." *North Carolina Historical Review* 12 (April 1935): 79–102.

Morris, Charles Edward. "Panic and Reprisal: Reaction in North Carolina to the Nat Turner Insurrection, 1831." *North Carolina Historical Review* 62 (January 1985): 29–52.

Morris, Charles S. "The Wilmington Massacre." In *The Voice of Black America: Major Speeches by Negroes in the United States, 1797–1971*, ed. Philip S. Foner. New York: Simon and Schuster, 1972. Pp. 604–607.

Nash, June. "The Cost of Violence." *Journal of Black Studies* 4 (1973): 153–184.

"Negro Views of Race Troubles." *The Literary Digest* 17 (December 3, 1898): 651–653.

"North Carolina Race Conflict, The," *Outlook*, 60 (November 19, 1898): 707–709.

Prather, H. Leon. "The Red Shirt Movement in North Carolina, 1898–1900." *Journal of Negro History* 62 (April 1977): 174–184.

———. "We Have Taken a City: A Centennial Essay." In David S. Cecelski and Timothy B. Tyson, eds., *Democracy Betrayed: The Wilmington Race Riot of 1898 and Its Legacy*. Chapel Hill: University of North Carolina Press, 1998, 15–42.

Price, Clement Alexander. "Home and Hearth: The Black Town and Settlement Movement of Southern New Jersey." In Wendel A. White, *Small Towns, Black Lives: African American Communities in Southern New Jersey*. Oceanville, N.J.: Noyes Museum of Art, 2003. Pp. 168–175.

"Race Troubles in the Carolinas," *The Literary Digest* 17 (November 26, 1898): 623–627.

Ruark, Bryant Whitlock. "Some Phases of Reconstruction in Wilmington and the County of New Hanover." In *Historical Papers of the Trinity College Historical Society*. Durham: N.p., 1915. Pp. 79–112.

Steelman, Joseph F. "Republican Party Strategists and the Issue of Fusion with Populists in North Carolina, 1893–1894." *North Carolina Historical Review* 47 (July 1970): 244–269.

"Story of the Wilmington Riot, A Pure Bred Negro Relates It." *Charlotte Daily Observer*, May 24, 1905

Trelease, Allen W. "The Fusion Legislatures of 1895 and 1897: A Roll-Call Analysis of the North Carolina House of Representatives." *North Carolina Historical Review* 57 (July 1980): 280–309.

Waddell, Alfred Moore. "The Story of the Wilmington, N.C., Race Riot." *Collier's Weekly* 22 (November 26, 1898): 4–5.

Watson, Richard L., Jr. "A Political Leader Bolts— F. M. Simmons in the Presidential Election of 1928." *North Carolina Historical Review* 37 (October 1960): 516–543.

West, Henry Litchfield. "The Race War in North Carolina." *The Forum* 26 (January 1899): 578–591.

Whites, LeeAnn. "Love, Hate, Rape, Lynching: Rebecca Latimer Felton and the Gender Politics of Racial Violence." In David S. Cecelski and Timothy B. Tyson, eds. *Democracy Betrayed: The Wilmington Race Riot and Its Legacy*. Chapel Hill: University of North Carolina Press, 1998. Pp. 143–163.

Zachary, Dr. R. E. "Gun-Shot Wounds—With Report of a Case of Gun-Shot Wound of Stomach." *Transactions of the Medical Society of the State of North Carolina, Forty-Sixth Annual Meeting*. Charlotte: Observer Printing and Publishing House, 1899, 134.

Theses and Dissertations

Cody, Sue Ann. "After the Storm: Racial Violence in Wilmington, North Carolina, and Its Consequences for African Americans, 1898–1905." Master's thesis, University of North Carolina at Wilmington, 2000.

Higuchi, Hayumi. "White Supremacy on the Cape Fear: The Wilmington Affair of 1898." Master's thesis, University of North Carolina at Chapel Hill, 1980.

Jones, Maxine. " 'A Glorious Work': The American Missionary Association and Black North Carolinians, 1863–1880." Ph.D. diss., Florida State University, 1982.

Kirshenbaum, Andrea M. "Race, Gender and Riot: The Wilmington, North Carolina, White Supremacy Campaign of 1898." Master's thesis, Duke University, 1996.

McDuffie, Jerome. "Politics in Wilmington and New Hanover County, North Carolina, 1865–1900: The Genesis of a Race Riot." Ph.D. diss., Kent State University, 1979.

Sawyer, Rebecca. "The Delgado-Spofford Textile Mill and Its Village: The Fabric of Wilmington's 20th Century Landscape." Master's thesis, University of North Carolina at Wilmington, 2001.

Newspapers and Periodicals

Asbury Park (N.J.) *Evening News*. November 21, 1898.

Atlanta Constitution. November 8, 1898.

Baltimore Sun. November 12, 1898.

Brooklyn (N.Y.) *Daily Eagle*. January 30, August 25, 1899.

Caucasian (Clinton and Raleigh). September 22, October 27, 1898.

Charlotte Daily Observer. November 2, 1898; May 24, 1905.

Charlotte Observer. November 19, 2006.

Chicago Daily Tribune. November 18, 21, 1898.

Collier's Weekly (New York). November 26, 1898.

Colored American (Washington, D.C.). December 28, 1901.

Daily Free Press (Kinston). October 24, 1898

Daily Record (Wilmington). August 18, 1898.

Evening Dispatch (Wilmington). January 28, August 24, 25, October 8, 10, 24, 25, November 1–10, 11, 12, 14, 15, 16, 17, 21, 23, December 6, 7, 8, 28, 1898.

Evening Transcript (Boston, Mass.). March 20, 1901.

Farmer and Mechanic (Raleigh). November 15, November 29, 1898, quoting *New York Journal*.

Freeman (Indianapolis, Ind.). December 3, 1898.

Leslie's Weekly Illustrated, [1896].

Morning Post (Raleigh). November 9, 13, 15, 17, 30, 1898.

Morning Star (Wilmington). June 10, 1890; November 15, 1893; June 8, 1897; January 2, February 3, June 9, August (entire month), September 2, 3, 9, 18, 21, 22, October 2, 9, 20, 25, 28, November 2–6, 8–19, 24–December 10, 14, 25, 30, 1898; February 3, March 1–6, 14–24, May 5, August 3, 1899; March 27, 1903; October 9, 1915; February 12, 1919; June 11, 1920; September 24, 1948.

New York Times. November 14, 1898; August 26, 1899.

News and Observer (Raleigh). October 8, November 5, 8, 10, 11, 12, 13, 15, 16, 23, December 15, 1898.

Progressive Farmer (Raleigh). October 25, November 15, 1898.

Record (Wilmington). September 28, 1895. Original in North Carolina Collection, University of North Carolina Library, Chapel Hill.

Union Republican (Winston). March 15, 1900.

Washington Post. November 8, 14, December 4, 1898; July 27, 1900.

Washington Times. November 22, 1898.

Wilmington Messenger. August 20, November 9, 11, 1894; May 4, 1897; May 1, August (entire month), September 4, 13, 16, 21, October 2, 9, 13, 20, 21, 22, 25, 26, 28, 29, November 1–10, 11–15, 16–December 7, 10, 16, 20, 23, 27, 1898; January 3, February 7, 21, March 5, 7, 18, 31, May 16, June 18, 21, 23, August 1, November 30, 1899; February 21, August 5, 1900; January 5, June 6, 1901; January 2, March 31, 1903; June 7, November 26, December 16, 1905.

Interviews and Conversations

Brown, Cynthia J. Interview with author, Wilmington, July 2004.

Burton, Rev. John. Interview with author, Wilmington, April 30, 2004.

Newkirk, Haywood. Telephone conversation with author, March 31, 2006.

Sadgwar Felice, and Mabel Sadgwar Manly. Interview by Beverly Smalls, Wilmington, May 14, 1985. Transcript of interview in Oral History Files, Cape Fear Museum of History and Science, Wilmington.

Sadgwar, Felice, Carrie Taylor Wright, and Laura Clemmons Kennedy. Interview by Beverly Smalls, Wilmington, February 8, 1981. Transcript of interview in Oral History Files, Cape Fear Museum.

Smith, Shirley Webb. Telephone conversation with author, June 17, 2005.

Wooley, Robert. Telephone conversation with author, summer 2004.

Business and City Directories

Boone, J. Irving, ed. *Directory of Negro Businesses in Wilmington and Southeastern North Carolina*. Wilmington: The Author, 1945.

_____. *Negro Business and Professional Men and Women: A Survey of Negro Progress in Varied Sections of North Carolina*, vol. 2. Wilmington: The Author, 1946.

Branson's North Carolina Business Directory, 1897. Raleigh: Levi Branson, 1897.

Campbell, John P., comp. *The Southern Business Directory and General Commercial Advertiser*. Charleston, S.C.: Walker and James, 1854.

Directory of the City of Wilmington, North Carolina, 1889. Wilmington: Julius A. Bonitz Publisher, 1889.

J. L. Hill Printing Co.'s Directory of Wilmington, N.C. 1897. Richmond, Va.: J. L. Hill Printing Company, 1897.

J. L. Hill Printing Co.'s Directory of Wilmington, N.C. 1900. Richmond, Va.: J. L. Hill Printing Company, 1900.

Norfolk, Portsmouth, and Berkley, Virginia 1903 Directory. Norfolk, Richmond, Newport News, Va.: Hill Directory Company, 1903.

Reference Book of the Mercantile Association of the Carolinas for the States of North and South Carolina. Wilmington: Jackson and Bell, 1893.

Wilmington, N.C. Directory, 1903. Richmond, Va.: Hill Directory Company, 1903.

Standard Biographical Works

Ashe, Samuel A., Stephen B. Weeks, and Charles L. Van Noppen, eds. *Biographical History of North Carolina from Colonial Times to the Present,* 8 vols. Greensboro: Charles L. Van Noppen, 1905–1917.

Connor R. D. W., William K. Boyd, and J. G. de Roulhac Hamilton. *History of North Carolina: North Carolina Biographies,* vol. 5. Chicago: Lewis Publishing Company, 1919.

Dictionary of North Carolina Biography. s.v. "Aycock, Charles Brantly," "Bryant, Henry Edward Cowan," "Dancy, John C.," "Noble, Marcus Cicero Stephens," "Rountree, George," "Waddell, Alfred Moore."

Census Data

Eighth Census of the United States, 1860: New Hanover County, North Carolina. Population Schedule. National Archives, Washington, D.C. (microfilm, State Archives, North Carolina Office of Archives and History, Raleigh).

Eighth Census of the United States, 1860: New Hanover County, North Carolina. Slave Schedule. National Archives, Washington, D.C. (microfilm, State Archives).

Ninth Census of the United States, 1870: New Hanover County, North Carolina. Population Schedule. National Archives (microfilm, State Archives).

Tenth Census of the United States, 1880: New Hanover County, North Carolina. Population Schedule. National Archives, Washington, D.C. (microfilm, State Archives).

Twelfth Census of the United States, 1900: Cape May County, New Jersey. Population Schedule. National Archives, Washington, D.C. (microfilm, State Library of North Carolina).

Twelfth Census of the United States, 1900: New Hanover County, North Carolina. Population Schedule. National Archives, Washington, D.C. (microfilm, State Archives).

Thirteenth Census of the United States, 1910: Cape May County, New Jersey. Population Schedule. National Archives, Washington, D.C. (microfilm, State Library).

Thirteenth Census of the United States, 1910: New Hanover County, North Carolina. Population Schedule, National Archives, Washington, D.C. (microfilm, State Archives).

Fourteenth Census of the United States, 1920: Cape May County, New Jersey Population Schedule National Archives, Washington, D.C. (microfilm, State Library).

Fourteenth Census of the United States, 1920: New Hanover County, North Carolina. Population Schedule, National Archives (microfilm, State Archives).

Fifteenth Census of the United States, 1930: New Hanover County, North Carolina. Population Schedule, National Archives (microfilm, State Archives).

City of Wilmington Records

Minutes of the Wilmington Board of Aldermen, 1884–1906 (microfilm). State Archives, North Carolina Office of Archives and History, Raleigh.

Wilmington Tax Roll, New Hanover County Records. State Archives.

New Hanover County Records

(All are located in the State Archives.)
Bonds
  Officials' Bonds and Records, 1766–1908 [1891–1908].
Election Records
  Election Records, 1832–1919 [1882–1896].
Estates Records
  Administrators' Bonds, 1844–1918.
  Estates Records, 1741–1939.
    Daniel Howard, 1909–1913.
    Thomas Miller, 1902–1903.

Land Records
    Index to Real Estate Conveyances, Grantee, 1729–1954. (microfilm)
    Index to Real Estate Conveyances, Grantor, 1729–1954. (microfilm)
    Record of Deeds, 1734–1941. (microfilm)
        A. L. Manly et al. to George Lutterloh, February 4, 1899. Book 34, p. 628.
Miscellaneous Records
    Incorporations, 1879–1906.
    Insolvent Debtor and Homestead and Personal Property Exemptions, 1809–1916.
    Minutes, Board of County Commissioners, 1887–1918.
    Miscellaneous Records, 1756–1945.
        Correspondence, 1824–1906.
            Thomas C. Miller, Norfolk, Virginia, to John D. Taylor, Clerk of Superior Court, Wilmington, July 9, 1902.
Tax and Fiscal Records
    Tax Lists, 1897, 1900, 1915 (microfilm).
    Tax Records, 1779–1909 [1897, 1900].
Wills
    Cross Index to Wills, 1735–1961. (microfilm)
    Record of Wills, 1747–1961. (microfilm)
        Daniel Howard, November 11, 1909. Book I, p. 582
        Bryan Newkirk, April 2, 1863. Book D, pp. 128–130.
        John G. Norwood, June 12, 1906. Book I, p. 184.

State Government Publications and Records

Adjutant General's Office. *Roster of North Carolina Volunteers in the Spanish-American War, 1898–1899.* Raleigh: Edwards and Broughton and E. M. Uzzell, State Printers, 1900.

Annual Report of the Adjutant-General of the State of North Carolina for the Year 1899. North Carolina Public Documents. Document 9, State Archives, North Carolina Office of Archives and History, Raleigh.

Biennial Report of the Superintendent of Public Instruction of North Carolina for the Scholastic Years 1898–99 and 1899–1900. Raleigh: Edwards and Broughton, 1900.

Department of Public Instruction, Superintendents' Annual Reports, 1880–1920. State Archives.
    Report of Superintendent M. C. S. Noble to State Department of Public Instruction, July 1898.
    Report of Superintendent of New Hanover County Schools to State Department of Public Instruction, July 1899, July 1900, July 1901.

Journal of the House of Representatives of North Carolina, 1899.

North Carolina Manual, 1913.

North Carolina Reports, Vol. 121: *Cases Argued and Determined in the Supreme Court of North Carolina, September Term 1897.* Reported by Robert T. Gray, Raleigh, N.C. Goldsboro: Nash Brothers, Book and Job Printers, 1898.

Russell, Daniel L., Governors' Papers. State Archives.
    Council of State Minutes, 1898–1899.

Russell, Daniel, Governor, Address of. *North Carolina Public Documents*, 1899. Document No. 1, State Archives.

State Attorney General's Office. Central Files, Correspondence, Letter Books, and Closed Case Files, 1898–1900. State Archives.

Walser, Zeb Vance. *Biennial Report of the Attorney General of the State of North Carolina, 1897–1898,* North Carolina Public Documents. Document Number 9, State Archives.

Federal Government Documents, Publications, and Records

Contested Election Case of Oliver H. Dockery vs. John D. Bellamy from the Sixth Congressional District of the State of North Carolina. Washington, D.C.: Government Printing Office, 1899.

"Letter from the Clerk of the House transmitting a List of the Contested Election Cases in the Fifty-Sixth Congress." U.S. House of Representatives, *House Documents.* Document No. 23, 56th Congress, 1st Session, December 5, 1899.

Photographs and Graphic Works in the National Archives. College Park, Md.

Prints and Photographs Division, Library of Congress. Washington, D.C.

Record Group 60, General Records of the Department of Justice, National Archives. Washington, D.C.
  Attorney General's Office Records
  William McKinley Papers
  "Year Files," Box 1117A.

Rowell, Chester H. *A Historical and Legal Digest of All the Contested Election Cases in the House of Representatives of the United States from the First to the Fifty-Sixth Congress, 1789–1901.* House Document No. 510, 56th Congress, 2nd Session, 1901.

United States, John Cummings, and Joseph A. Hill. *Negro Population, 1790–1915.* Washington, D.C.: Government Printing Office, 1918.

U.S. Department of Labor. *Negro Migration in 1916–1917.* Washington, D.C.: Government Printing Office, 1919.

Williams v. Mississippi, 170 U.S. 213 (1898).

Laws

Private Laws of North Carolina, 1876–77, 230–237.

Private Laws of the State of North Carolina Passed by the General Assembly at its Session of 1899. Raleigh: Edwards and Broughton and E. M. Uzzell, 1899, 591–596.

Public Laws of North Carolina, 1866, c. 2, s. 7.

Public Laws of North Carolina, 1895, c. 121, s. 3.

Public Laws of North Carolina, 1897, c. 150, s. 6.

Public Laws of North Carolina, 1899, c. 487.

Private Collections

Bryant, H. E. C., Papers. Private Collections, State Archives, North Carolina Office of Archives and History, Raleigh.

Butler, Marion, Papers. Southern Historical Collection, Wilson Library, University of North Carolina at Chapel Hill, Chapel Hill.

Cameron, Bennehan, Papers. Southern Historical Collection.

Chesnutt, Charles Waddell, Collection. John Hope and Aurelia E. Franklin Library, Special Collections. Fisk University, Nashville, Tenn.

Connor, Henry G., Papers. Southern Historical Collection.

Cronenberg, Henry, Photographic Collection. New Hanover County Public Library, Wilmington.

Cronly Family Papers. Rare Book, Manuscript, and Special Collections Library, Duke University, Durham.

Duke, B. N., Papers. Duke Special Collections.

Eccles Family Papers. Southern Historical Collection.

Fisher, Charles, Oral History File. Cape Fear Museum of History and Science, Wilmington.

Funderberg Family Collection. New Hanover County Public Library.

Henderson, John S., Papers. Southern Historical Collection.

Hinsdale Family Papers. Duke Special Collections.

Hunter, Charles N., Papers. Duke Special Collections.

London, Isaac Spencer, Papers. State Archives.

McDonald-Howe Family Papers. Special Collections Department, Randall Library, University of North Carolina Wilmington, Wilmington.

McKoy, William B., Collection. Lower Cape Fear Historical Society, Wilmington.

Mallett, Peter, Papers. Southern Historical Collection.

Massengill, Stephen E. Postcard. Private Collection. Cary, N.C.

Meares and DeRosset Family Papers. Southern Historical Collection.

Moore, Louis T., Collection. State Archives.

Moore, Louis T., Local History Collection. New Hanover County Public Library.

Moore, Louis T., Photograph Collection. New Hanover County Public Library.

Moore, Mrs. Roger, Collection. University of North Carolina Wilmington Special Collections.

Page, Thomas Nelson, Papers. Duke Special Collections.

Parsley, Eliza Hall, Papers. Southern Historical Collection.

267

Reaves, Bill, Local and Family History Collection. New Hanover County Public Library.

Settle, Thomas, Papers. Southern Historical Collection.

Sisson, Alice Borden Moore, Collection. New Hanover County Public Library.

Smithwick, Edmund, and Family, Papers. State Archives.

Sprunt, Alexander, and Son, Inc., Papers. Duke Special Collections.

Waddell, Alfred Moore, Papers. Southern Historical Collection.

Wootten, Bradley Jewett, Papers. University of North Carolina Wilmington.

Worth, James Spencer, Papers. Southern Historical Collection.

Unpublished Essays, Memoirs, Narratives

Clawson, Thomas W. "The Wilmington Race Riot in 1898, Recollections and Memories." Unpublished memoir. Louis T. Moore Collection. Private Collections, State Archives.

Cotton, Nada, narrative. McDonald-Howe Family Papers. Special Collections Department, Randall Library, University of North Carolina Wilmington.

Cowan, James H. "The Wilmington Race Riot." Undated, unpublished memoir. Louis T. Moore Collection, New Hanover County Public Library, Wilmington.

Cronly, Jane. "Account of the Race Riot." Unpublished memoir, n.d., Cronly Family Papers. Rare Book, Manuscript, and Special Collections Library, Duke University, Durham.

Hamilton, Tod. "An Interpretation of the Economic Impact of the Wilmington Riot of 1898." Unpublished 1898 Wilmington Race Riot Commission report, May 31, 2006.

Hayden, Harry. "The Wilmington Light Infantry." Typed, unpublished memoir, New Hanover County Public Library, Wilmington.

Hodges, Alexander Weld. "Josephus Daniels, Precipitator of the Wilmington Race Riot of 1898." Honors essay, Department of History,

University of North Carolina at Chapel Hill, 1990.

Kraft, Andrew C. "Wilmington's Political-Racial Revolution of 1898: A Geographical and Cartographic Analysis of the Wilmington, North Carolina, Race Riot." Unpublished report, University of North Carolina at Wilmington, 1993.

Rountree, George. "Memorandum of My Personal Reasons for the Passage of the Suffrage Amendment to the Constitution (Grandfather Clause)," n.d. Henry G. Connor Papers, Southern Historical Collection, Wilson Library, University of North Carolina at Chapel Hill, Chapel Hill.

_____. "Memorandum of My Personal Recollection of the Election of 1898," n.d. Connor Papers, Southern Historical Collection.

Online Resources

Ancestry.com. http://ancestry.com. Retrieved August 31, 2009.

"California Slavery Era Insurance Registry": http://www.insurance.ca.gov/0100-consumers/0300-public-programs/0200-slavery-era-insur/. Retrieved November 21, 2005.

Historical Census Browser. Geospatial and Statistical Data Center, University of Virginia, Charlottesville. http://fisher.lib.virginia.edu/collections/stats/histcensus/index.html. Retrieved January 5, 2005.

"Illinois Slavery Era Insurance Registries": http://www.ins.state.il.us/Consumer/Slavery/Reporting.nsf/. Retrieved November 21, 2005.

"Listening between the Lines." http://www.listeningbetweenthelines.org/html/rosewood.html. Retrieved August 31, 2009.

"North Carolina Election of 1898, The." http://www.lib.unc.edu/ncc/1898/1898.html. North Carolina Collection, Wilson Library, University of North Carolina at Chapel Hill, Chapel Hill.

"Slavery Era Insurance Policies Registry": http://genealogytrails.com/main/slaveinsurance2.html#nc. Retrieved August 31, 2009.

"U.S. Census Bureau." http://www.census.gov/ proc/www/abs/decennial/index.htm. Retrieved January 5, 2005.

Miscellaneous Sources

"Behind the Veil: Documenting African American Life in the Jim Crow South." In the John Hope Franklin Collection of African and African American Documentation, Rare Book, Manuscript, and Special Collections Library, Duke University, Durham.

City of Norfolk
Corporation Court Record of Fiduciary Bonds, vol. 3, 1903–1904. Library of Virginia, Richmond.
Death Records. Library of Virginia.

Cumming, William. Pass for Henry Macon, November 11, 1898. Cape Fear Museum of History and Science, Wilmington.

Dancy John C., ed. *The [AME Zion] Quarterly Almanac.* [Wilmington?]: N.p., [1893?].

Daniels, Josephus. "Henry Groves Connor: State Senator, Representative and Speaker of the North Carolina House of Representatives . . . an Address by Josephus Daniels Presenting the Portrait of Judge Connor . . . to the Supreme Court." Pamphlet (1929) held by the State Library of North Carolina.

"Documented History of the Incident Which Occurred at Rosewood, Florida, in January 1923, A." Legislative document produced by a team of researchers from Florida A&M University, Florida State University, and the University of Florida and submitted to the Florida Board of Regents on December 22, 1993.

"1898 Wilmington Racial Violence and its Legacy: A Symposium, The." Video recording made by the University of North Carolina at Wilmington Media Services, November 1998. Foundation Collection, University of North Carolina Wilmington.

Higuchi, Hayumi. Unpublished map of Wilmington in 1897.

Keith, Benjamin F., to President Warren G. Harding, July 5, 1921. Photocopy on file in the Research Branch, North Carolina Office of Archives and History, original in possession of Thomas J. Keith.

Maps prepared by Mark A. Moore, Research Branch, North Carolina Office of Archives and History.

Meares, Iredell. "Wilmington Revolution" (broadside). Edmund Smithwick and Family Papers. Private Collections. North Carolina State Archives, Office of Archives and History, Raleigh.

Miller, T. C., House File. New Hanover County Public Library.

Miller, Thomas. Death certificate for. City of Norfolk Death Records. Library of Virginia, Richmond.

Minutes of the Organizational Meeting of the Association of Members of the Wilmington Light Infantry, December 14, 1905. North Carolina Collection, Wilson Library, University of North Carolina at Chapel Hill, Chapel Hill.

Pine Forest Cemetery (Wilmington) Records (microfilm). State Archives.

"Red Shirts Organized." Isaac Spencer London Papers, Private Collections, State Archives.

"'Riot' Seven Years Old, The" (pamphlet). Bill Reaves Local and Family History Collection, New Hanover County Public Library.

Roster of Young Men's Democratic Club of Wilmington. Merchant Account Book, n.d. Private Collections, State Archives.

Sanborn Fire Insurance Maps of Wilmington, 1898, 1925.

"Simmons Hands: Lady-Like Touch Strong as Steel," n.d. H. E. C. Bryant Papers. Private Collections, State Archives.

Wilmington Light Infantry. *Constitution and Bylaws* (1904). Cape Fear Museum of History and Science, Wilmington.

Index

272

C

273

E

277

L

M

281

O

P

283

1868, 12; work to gain political equality for blacks during Congressional Reconstruction, 17

Research Branch, Office of Archives and History, 227n96

Reserve Corps (Wilmington Light Infantry), 57

Respites (for those fleeing violence in Wilmington), 101, 102, 112, 113

Ricaud, A. G., 242n46

Rice, Frederick, 24, 46

Rice culture, 1, 2, 5, 196n45

"Ring" (wealthy white Republicans), 199n80

Riot. See Race riot

Rivera, Thomas, 31, 93, 102, 173, 188, 219n65, 227n95; cited, 223n39

Rivera, Thomas, Jr., 251n44

Rivera family (black), 186

Robbins, William: quoted, 100

Robertson, William F., 47, 173, 219n62

Robinson H., 204n43

Robinson, Henry, 204n43

Roosevelt, Franklin D., 189

Roosevelt, Theodore, 112, 120, 208n26, 241n35

Rosenwald, Julius, 245n77, 245n86

Rosewood, Fla.: undergoes violent racial episode (1933), 170

"Rough Riders" (white-supremacy organization active in 1898 campaign), 41, 42, 54, 82, 95, 106; origin of term, 208n26; and White Government Union, 53

Rountree, George, 36, 46, 48, 68, 74, 75, 78, 81, 87, 88, 90, 102, 103, 136, 138, 173, 209n37, 211n53, 217n24, 219n62, 227n97, 228n104, 251n45; brief biographical sketch of, 209n38; cited, 116; pictured, 75; quoted, 45, 56, 73, 94, 210n48, 210n49, 219n54

Rountree, Meta Davis (Mrs. George Rountree), 209n38

Rowan, Dan, 84

Rowan, Tom: reported as killed, 118

Russell, Daniel L., 21, 22, 35, 36, 44, 46, 65, 67, 69, 70, 101, 102, 136, 210n46, 210n48, 228n4; and aftermath of violence, 120, 129; announces goals of his governorship, 28; blamed by A. M. Waddell for alleged racial crisis in Wilmington, 50; brief biographical sketch of, 202n2; campaigns for governor (1896), 26; compromises with Democrats represented by James Sprunt, 68; demonstrates ability to manage successful political campaigns, 23; elected governor, 27; fills positions on board of aldermen, 29; intimidated by Red Shirts, 71, 129, 209n36; loses control of Republican Party, 207n6; pictured, 21; proclamation against lawlessness issued by, quoted, 69, 70, 120; quoted, 43, 69, 235n69; and suffrage amendment, 139; telegram from, quoted,

93; warns Fusionists of defeat by Democrats in 1896, 25

Russell family, 199n80

Ruth Hall. See Love and Charity Hall

S

Sadgwar, Annie E. Miller (Mrs. Fred Sadgwar Jr.), 186

Sadgwar, Caroline, 184

Sadgwar, Frederick, Jr., 186

Sadgwar, Frederick, Sr., 31, 173, 184, 188–189, 219n65; pictured, 31

Sadgwar, Lewin, 184

Sadgwar, Mabel, 184, 205n50

Sadgwar, Milo, 184

Sadgwar, Ted, 189

Sadgwar family (black), 148, 182, 186, 196n39

Sampson, James D., 3

Sampson, John P., 7; pictured, 7

Sampson family (black), 196n39, 199n80

Sampson Light Infantry (N.C. State Guard unit): members of, pictured, 105

Sand Against the Wind (memoir by John C. Dancy Jr.): cited, 177

Sasser, L. B., 47, 173, 218n53

Saunders, William L., 12, 13

Savage, W. T., 86

Sawyer, E. W., 70

"Scalawags" (southern loyalists), 9t

Schnibben, Charles, 86, 122, 173, 222n28; pictured, 122

Schofield, John, 1, 6, 15

Schonwald, John T., 93

Scott, Armond, 78, 81, 173, 189, 219n65, 220n70, 231n22; pictured, 161; quoted, 26, 26–27; reported as banished, 114; target of banishment campaign, 111

Scott, Benjamin, 189

Scott, Beverly, 230n10

Seaboard Air Line railway, 5, 224n65

Second Regimental Band, 127

Second Ward (Wilmington), 199n84, 200n89

"Secret Nine" (shadowy group of white Wilmington leaders), 47, 55, 70, 73, 79, 81, 104, 107, 108, 113, 158, 211n51, 220n53, 228n105

Settle, Thomas: telegram from, pictured, 130

Sharecropping, 14

Shaw University (Raleigh), 15

Shaw's Funeral Home, 248n17, 250n40

Shephard, Cornelia, 189

Shephard, Frank, 189

Sherman, William T., 6

T

285

287